SOURCES OF

EUROPEAN HISTORY SINCE 1900

SECOND EDITION

■

SOURCES OF EUROPEAN HISTORY SINCE 1900

Second Edition

Marvin Perry
Baruch College, City University of New York

Matthew Berg
John Carroll University

James Krukones
John Carroll University

Australia • Brazil • Japan • Korea • Mexico • Singapore • Spain • United Kingdom • United States

Sources of European History Since 1900, Second Edition
Marvin Perry, Matthew Berg, and James Krukones

Senior Publisher: Suzanne Jeans

Senior Sponsoring Editor: Nancy Blaine

Assistant Editor: Lauren Floyd

Editorial Assistant: Emma Goehring

Senior Marketing Manager: Diane Wenckebach

Marketing Coordinator: Lorreen Pelletier

Marketing Communications Manager: Christine Dobberpuhl

Senior Content Project Manager: Shelley Dickerson

Senior Art Director: Cate Rickard Barr

Manufacturing Buyer: Linda Hsu

Senior Rights Acquisitions Manager, Text: Katie Huha

Senior Photo Editor, Images: Jennifer Meyer Dare

Content Project Manager: Karunakaran Gunasekaran

Cover Designer: Lori Leahy

Cover Image: Modern and contemporary architecture at dusk, Warsaw, Poland. © Gregory Wrona / Alamy

Compositor: Pre-Press PMG

Library of Congress Control Number: 2009929480

ISBN-13: 978-1-4240-6967-5

ISBN-10: 1-4240-6967-X

Wadsworth
20 Channel Center Street
Boston, MA 02210
USA

Cengage Learning is a leading provider of customized learning solutions with office locations around the globe, including Singapore, the United Kingdom, Australia, Mexico, Brazil, and Japan. Locate your local office at **www.cengage.com/global.**

Cengage Learning products are represented in Canada by Nelson Education, Ltd.

To learn more about Wadsworth, visit **www.cengage.com/wadsworth**

Purchase any of our products at your local college store or at our preferred online store **www.ichapters.com.**

Printed in the United States of America
4 5 6 7 8 23 22 21 20 19

CONTENTS

PREFACE

At the beginning of the twentieth century, confidence in Europe's future progress was the dominant mood among Europeans, despite some disquieting signs, such as an increasingly belligerent nationalism. The spread of parliamentary government, the extension of education, improvements in the standard of living, the many advances in science and technology, and the relative absence of conflicts among the Great Powers seemed to justify this optimism. Two decades later, however, after a disastrous world war, many people thought that Western civilization had lost its vitality and was caught in a cycle of breakdown and disintegration. The rise of totalitarian communism and nazism and a second world war, which took the lives of some 50 million people (including 6 million Jews, victims of a policy of extermination) and which left Europe in ruins, cast further doubt on the basic assumptions of Enlightenment humanism, including the efficacy of reason, science, and education and the essential goodness of human nature. Nevertheless, the rapid material recovery of Western Europe, the decline of extreme nationalism (the primary cause of the two world wars), a renewed commitment to liberal democratic government, and the growing cooperation and integration of formerly feuding states began to restore confidence in the core values of European civilization after World War II. On the dark side, however, were Communist Russia's subjugation of Eastern Europe and the cold war between the Soviet Union and the United States, which threatened to trigger a nuclear conflict capable of destroying the planet.

The new Europe that was taking shape in the decades after World War II had to grapple with a new world order in which the former Great Powers were dwarfed by the emergence of two superpowers, the United States and the Soviet Union, and in which formerly subjugated lands beyond Europe had become a force in international affairs. In the last decade of the twentieth century, Europe had to adjust to extraordinary developments—the collapse of the Soviet Union, the liberation of its Eastern European satellites, the demise of Soviet-style communism, and the end of the Cold War. The major problems that confronted Europe in the opening decade of the twenty-first century included a resurgence of Russian power, relations with the United States, integrating the millions of Islamic immigrants into a Western society, and the threat of terrorism by Islamic extremists.

Sources of European History Since 1900 (formerly *Sources of Twentieth-Century Europe*) covers these and other key developments through source readings, which are the raw materials of history. Containing more than 180 selections, most of them primary sources, *Sources of European History Since 1900*, Second Edition, enables students to examine with greater insight the events, personalities, and ideas that have shaped the past century.

We have tried to select documents that bring to life the key events and illustrate the major ideas and relationships that are central to the history of these years. In deciding which selections should be included, we were guided by two overriding concerns: Does the document throw light on a theme crucial to an understanding of this era? Will instructors find the document a helpful supplement to lectures and the assigned text?

An important feature of the reader is the grouping of documents that illuminate a single theme; such constellations of related readings reinforce understanding of important themes and invite comparison, analysis, and interpretation of the readings within each group. For example, in Chapter 2, World War I, the eighth section is titled "The War and European Consciousness" and contains the following four interrelated selections: "Disillusionment," by Paul Valéry; "The Lost Generation," by Erich Maria Remarque; "Brutalization of the Individual," by Ernst von Salomon; and "A Legacy of Embitterment," by Sigmund Freud. In Chapter 8, Western Europe Since the 1960s, the fourth section, "Ethnic Minorities," contains four thematically related selections: "Bringing the Immigration Issue to the Center of Politics," by Enoch Powell; "Muslim-Turkish Children in Germany: Sociocultural Problems," by Zehra Onder; "The Grapes of Neglect—Violence and Xenophobia in Germany," by Joachim Krautz; and a concluding document, "African Immigrants in France: The Controversy over Female Circumcision," by the Commission for the Abolishment of Sexual Mutilations.

A principal concern of the editors in preparing this compilation was to make the documents accessible—to enable students to comprehend and interpret historical documents on their own. We have provided several pedagogical features to facilitate this aim. Introductions of three types explain the historical setting, the authors' intent, and the meaning and significance of the readings. First, introductions to each of the ten chapters provide comprehensive overviews to periods. Second, introductions to each numbered thematic section treat the historical background for the readings that follow. Third, each reading has a brief head note that provides specific details about that reading. Within some readings, interlinear notes, clearly set off from the text of the document, serve as transitions and suggest the main themes of the passages that follow.

To aid students' comprehension, we have occasionally inserted brief, bracketed editorial definitions or notes that explain unfamiliar or foreign terms into the running text. When terms or concepts in the documents require fuller explanations, these appear at the bottom of pages as numbered editors' footnotes. Where helpful, we have retained the notes of authors, translators, or editors from whose works the documents were acquired. The latter have asterisks, daggers, and other symbols to distinguish them from our numbered explanatory notes.

For the second edition we have reworked virtually every chapter, dropping some documents and adding others. All new documents have been carefully edited: extraneous passages deleted, notes inserted to explain historical events, names identified, and technical terms defined. Wherever possible we have extended the constellation format that groups related documents into one section. For this edition, we have added a concluding chapter, Europe Today.

The second edition contains more than thirty new selections. In Chapter 1, a statement from the Pan-German League has been inserted into the constellation "Racial Nationalism." Chapter 2 includes a new section, "The Turkish Assault on Armenians," that contains the testimony of two survivors. A new section, "The Russian Civil War," has been added to Chapter 3; two documents deal with the Red terror, a third with the Whites' hostility to the Bolsheviks. Added to the constellation "The Nazification of Culture and Society" in Chapter 4 is an insightful analysis of the meaning of Nazi book burning by a distinguished German journalist living in exile. In the same chapter, inserted into the constellation "Nazi Persecution of the Jews" is an American official's account of Kristallnacht. Added to Chapter 5 is a new section, "Remilitarization of the Rhineland," that contains William L. Shirer's description of the reaction of the Nazi-controlled parliament upon hearing the news that German troops had marched into the Rhineland. A Russian veteran's account of his experiences has been added to the section "Stalingrad." The constellation "Resistance" now includes a survivor's description of the Warsaw Ghetto Uprising. "The End of the Third Reich," the concluding section in Chapter 5, has been broadened; it now treats the fire-bombing of Dresden; the Nazi defense of Berlin in the last days of the war; the rape of German women committed by vengeful Russians; and Joseph Goebbels' diary entries as Germany was being invaded from east and west. In Chapter 6, Theodore H. White's description of Germany in ruins has been added to the constellation "The Aftermath: Devastation and Hope." Another selection by White has been placed in the section "The New West Germany: Democratic Government, the Nazi Past, and the Economic Miracle." Inserted in the section "The Cold War" is the Communist government's explanation for the construction of the Berlin Wall. In Chapter 7, one new selection, written by Heda Margolius Kovály, has been added to the section "Repression in the Soviet Union and Its Satellites," which describes oppression in Czechoslovakia. In Chapter 8, we have substituted a clearer statement by Margaret Thatcher supporting the free market. The section "The Trauma of Transition from Communism" has been completely redone in Chapter 9. The new selections deal with the atrocities committed in Bosnia, crime and corruption in post-Communist Russia, and the war in Chechnya. Chapter 10, Europe Today, is entirely new. It contains ten selections grouped into six sections: "European Union: Growing Interdependence"; "Anti-Americanism in Contemporary Europe"; "Russia: Creeping Autocracy and Burgeoning Nationalism"; "Islam in Europe: Failure of Assimilation and the Threat of Terrorism"; "The New Anti-Semitism: Old Hatreds Revived"; and "In Defense of European Values."

We are grateful to the staff of Wadsworth/Cengage Learning who lent their talents to the project. A special thanks to Nancy Blaine, senior sponsoring editor, who recognized the need for a second edition, and to Lauren Floyd, assistant editor, who efficiently prepared the revision for production. We thank too Ashley McDonald, copy editor, who read the manuscript with a trained eye, and Shelley Dickerson, senior content project manager, who, assisted by freelancer Karunakaran Gunasekaran, skillfully guided the book through production. Also deserving our gratitude are Katie Huha, senior rights acquisition account manager, and Mary Dalton-Hoffman, a freelance permissions researcher, who managed the difficult task of obtaining permissions smoothly. We appreciate the efforts of Jennifer Meyer Dare, senior photo editor, and freelancer Lisa Jelly Smith, who researched the chapter-opening photos. We also want to thank Cate Rickard Barr, senior art director, who oversaw the design of the cover.

Matthew Berg and James Krukones wish to thank the staff of Grasselli Library at John Carroll University for their expertise and efficiency in securing documentary materials. As always, Marvin Perry is grateful to his wife, Phyllis G. Perry, for her encouragement and computer skills.

M. P.
M. B.
J. K.

CHAPTER ONE

THE NINETEENTH-CENTURY INHERITANCE

IN THEIR STRUGGLE FOR THE VOTE, British feminists engaged in frequent demonstrations. In this 1906 picture, Emmeline Pankhurst, a leading British suffragist, is being restrained by the police. *(The Art Archive/Culver Pictures)*

In the last half of the nineteenth century, the people of Europe, more numerous than ever and concentrated in ever-growing cities, interacted with each other in a busy exchange of goods, ideas, and services, which led to remarkable creativity in industry, science, and the arts. The physical sciences flourished; medical science advanced; the psychoanalytic method developed under Sigmund Freud. New technologies speeded communication and transportation, which intensified human contact and competition. Industrialization, promoted by capitalist enterprise, spread throughout Europe and the United States, raising the standard of living and advancing expectations among the poor for a better life. The new mobility and social interdependence provided greater opportunity for individual advancement, but they also increased social and political tensions.

One source of tension arose from the growing demands among the lower classes for social justice and a share of political power; the misery of the poor and disenfranchised masses became a hot political issue. At the same time, the agitation for women's rights mounted; women wanted to have rights equal to men in education and politics. Although women faced strenuous resistance with regard to suffrage, they continued to fight toward that goal. A third troublesome factor in European politics and society was nationalism.

In the first half of the nineteenth century, nationalism and liberalism had gone hand in hand. Liberals had sought both the rights of the individual and national independence and unification. Liberal nationalists believed that a unified state free of foreign subjugation was in harmony with the principle of natural rights, and they insisted that love of country led to love of humanity. "With all my ardent love of my nation," said Francis Palacky, a Czech patriot, "I always esteem more highly the good of mankind and of learning than the good of the nation." Addressing the Slavs, the Italian statesman Mazzini declared: "We who have ourselves arisen in the name of our national right, believe in your right, and offer to help you to win it. But the purpose of our mission is the permanent and peaceful organization of Europe."

As nationalism grew more extreme, however, its profound difference from liberalism became more apparent. The extreme nationalism of the late nineteenth and early twentieth centuries contributed to World War I and to the rise of fascism after the war. It was the seedbed of totalitarian nationalism.

Concerned exclusively with the greatness of the nation, extreme nationalists rejected the liberal emphasis on political liberty. They attacked parliamentary government as a barrier to national unity and greatness, and maintained that authoritarian leadership was needed to meet national emergencies. The needs of the nation, they said, transcended the rights of the individual. Extreme nationalists also rejected the liberal ideal of equality. Placing the nation above everything, nationalists accused national minorities of corrupting the nation's spirit; and they glorified war as a symbol of the nation's resolve and will. In the name of national power and unity, they persecuted minorities at home and stirred up hatred against other nations. They also increasingly embraced militaristic, imperialistic, and racist doctrines. At the founding of the Nationalist Association in Italy in 1910, one leader declared:

> Just as socialism teaches the proletariat the value of class struggle, so we must teach Italy the value of international struggle. But international struggle is war? Well, then, let there be war! And nationalism will arouse the will for a victorious war, . . . the only way to national redemption.

Interpreting politics with the logic of emotions, extreme nationalists insisted that they had a sacred mission to regain lands once held in the Middle Ages, to unite with their kinsfolk in other lands, or to rule over peoples considered inferior. They organized patriotic societies, denounced national minorities, particularly Jews, and created a cult of ancestors and a mystique of blood, soil, and a sacred national past. In these ancestral traditions and attachments, the nationalist found a higher reality akin to religious truth. Loyalty to the nation-state was elevated above all other allegiances. The ethnic state became an object of religious reverence; the spiritual energies that formerly had been dedicated to Christianity were now channeled into the worship of the nation-state. In 1902, Friedrich Paulsen, a German philosopher, warned of nationalism's threat to reason and morality:

> A supersensitive nationalism has become a very serious danger for all the peoples of Europe; because of it, they are in danger of losing the feeling for human values. Nationalism, pushed to an extreme, just like sectarianism, destroys moral and even logical consciousness. Just and unjust, good and bad, true and false, lose their meaning; what men condemn as disgraceful and inhuman when done by others, they recommend in the same breath to their own people as something to be done to a foreign country.

In the late nineteenth century, industrial growth and worldwide trade created among Europeans a new global competition for empire. The search for vital raw materials, markets, and investments intensified economic outreach, leading to ruthless exploitation and domination. The expenses of imperialism, usually greater than its economic benefits, were justified by rising nationalism, which fueled the quest for overseas possessions. What counted by the end of the century, as the traditional European rivalries expanded around the world, was global power; overseas possessions enhanced national prestige. Britain, thanks to its seapower, emerged as the colonial giant, provoking imitation by other ambitious European countries. Envious of the British Empire, other states did not want to be left behind.

Despite the impressive achievements of European civilization and the domination of the globe by European states, the continent was becoming more and more deeply divided by the early 1900s. The competition for wealth and power heightened international rivalries. Nationalist ambitions, backed in most countries by popular support, and an arms race further worsened international relations. Although few people at the time recognized it, Europe's period of peace and security was ending. World War I, which broke out in 1914, was on the horizon.

The closing decades of the nineteenth century and the opening of the twentieth witnessed a crisis in Western thought. Rejecting the Enlightenment belief in the essential rationality of human beings, some thinkers—such as Fyodor Dostoyevsky, Friedrich Nietzsche, Sigmund Freud, and Georges Sorel—stressed the immense power of the nonrational in individual and social life. They held that subconscious drives, impulses, and instincts lay at the core of human nature, that people were moved more by religious-mythic images and symbols than by logical thought, that feelings determine human conduct more than reason does. This new image of the individual led to unsettling conclusions. If human beings are not fundamentally rational, then what are the prospects of resolving the immense problems of an industrial civilization? Although most thinkers shared the Enlightenment's vision of humanity's future progress, doubters were also heard.

The crisis of thought also found expression in art and literature. Artists like Pablo Picasso and writers like James Joyce and Franz Kafka exhibited a growing fascination with the nonrational—with dreams, fantasies, sexual conflicts, and guilt, with tortured, fragmented, and dislocated inner lives. In the process, they rejected traditional esthetic standards established during the Renaissance and the Enlightenment and experimented with new forms of artistic and literary representation.

These developments in thought and culture produced insights into human nature and society and opened up new possibilities in art and literature. But such changes also contributed to the disorientation and insecurity that characterized the twentieth century.

1 The Evolution of Liberalism

The principal concern of early nineteenth-century liberalism was protecting the rights of the individual against the demands of the state. For this reason, liberals advocated a constitution that limited the state's authority and a bill of rights that stipulated the citizen's basic freedoms. Believing that state interference in the economy endangered individual liberty and private property, liberals were strong advocates of laissez faire—leaving the market to its own devices.

And convinced that the unpropertied and uneducated masses were not deeply committed to individual freedom, liberals approved property requirements for voting and office holding.

In the last part of the nineteenth century, however, liberalism changed substantially as many liberals came to support government reforms to deal with the problems created by unregulated industrialization. By the early twentieth century, proponents of liberalism found themselves confronted by conservatives on the one hand, and a recently established social democratic labor movement on the other. While the former championed traditional elites and those who shared their values, the latter challenged the fundamental assumptions of a capitalist order and called for a government representative of the interests of working people in urban and rural settings.

L. T. Hobhouse JUSTIFICATION FOR STATE INTERVENTION

Arguing that laissez faire enabled the powerful to exploit the weak, Thomas Hill Green (1836–1882), a British political theorist, urged legislation to promote better conditions of labor, education, and health. In a truly liberal society, said Green, individuals have the opportunity to develop their moral and intellectual abilities. But poor education, inadequate housing, and unhealthy living and working environments deprive people of the opportunity for self-enhancement. For these people, freedom is an empty word. Green insisted that the liberal state must concern itself not just with individual rights but with the common good. L. T. Hobhouse (1864–1929), an academic who also wrote for the *Manchester Guardian,* concurred with Green's views in *Liberalism* (1911).

[It was conceived by an earlier liberalism] that, however deplorable the condition of the working classes might be, the right way of raising them was to trust to individual enterprise and possibly, according to some thinkers, to voluntary combination. By these means the efficiency of labour might be enhanced and its regular remuneration raised. By sternly withholding all external supports we should teach the working classes to stand alone, and if there were pain in the disciplinary process there was yet hope in the future. They would come by degrees to a position of economic independence in which they would be able to face the risks of life, not in reliance upon the State, but by the force of their own brains and the strength of their own right arms.

These views no longer command the same measure of assent. On all sides we find the State making active provision for the poorer classes and not by any means for the destitute alone. We find it educating the children, providing medical inspection, authorizing the feeding of the necessitous at the expense of the ratepayers, helping them to obtain employment through free Labour Exchanges, seeking to organize the labour market with a view to the mitigation of unemployment, and providing old age pensions for all whose incomes fall below thirteen shillings a week, without exacting any contribution. Now, in all this, we may well ask, is the State going forward blindly on the paths of broad and generous but unconsidered charity? Is it and can it remain indifferent to the effect on individual initiative and personal or parental responsibility? Or may we suppose that the wiser heads are well aware of what they are about, have looked at the matter on all sides, and are guided by a reasonable conception of the duty of the State and the responsibilities of the individual? Are we, in fact—for this is really the question—seeking charity or justice?

We said above that it was the function of the State to secure the conditions upon which mind and character may develop themselves. Similarly we may say now that the function of the State is to secure conditions upon which its citizens are able to win by their own efforts all that is necessary to a full civic efficiency. It is not for the State to feed, house, or clothe them. It is for the State to take care that the economic conditions are such that the normal man who is not defective in mind or body or will can by useful labour feed, house, and clothe himself and his family. The "right to work" and the right to a "living wage" are just as valid as the rights of person or property. That is to say, they are integral conditions of a good social order. A society in which a single honest man of normal capacity is definitely unable to find the means of maintaining himself by useful work is to that extent suffering from malorganization. There is somewhere a defect in the social system, a hitch in the economic machine. Now, the individual workman cannot put the machine straight. He is the last person to have any say in the control of the market. It is not his fault if there is over-production in his industry, or if a new and cheaper process has been introduced which makes his particular skill, perhaps the product of years of application, a drug in the market. He does not direct or regulate industry. He is not responsible for its ups and downs, but he has to pay for them. That is why it is not charity but justice for which he is asking. . . .

If this view of the duty of the State and the right of the workman is coming to prevail, it is owing partly to an enhanced sense of common responsibility, and partly to the teaching of experience. . . .

Herbert Spencer
THE MAN VERSUS THE STATE

Committed to a traditional laissez-faire policy, however, some liberals attacked state intervention as a threat to personal freedom and a betrayal of central liberal principles. In *The Man Versus the State* (1884), British philosopher Herbert Spencer (1820–1903) warned that increased government regulation would lead to socialism and slavery.

The extension of this policy . . . [of government legislation] fosters everywhere the tacit assumption that Government should step in whenever anything is not going right. "Surely you would not have this misery continue!" exclaims some one, if you hint . . . [an objection] to much that is now being said and done. Observe what is implied by this exclamation. It takes for granted . . . that every evil can be removed: the truth being that with the existing defects of human nature, many evils can only be thrust out of one place or form into another place or form—often being increased by the change. The exclamation also implies the unhesitating belief, here especially concerning us, that evils of all kinds should be dealt with by the State. . . . Obviously, the more numerous governmental interventions become, the more confirmed does this habit of thought grow, and the more loud and perpetual the demands for intervention.

Every extension of the regulative policy involves an addition to the regulative agents—a further growth of officialism and an increasing power of the organization formed of officials. . . .

. . . Moreover, every additional State interference strengthens the tacit assumption that it is the duty of the State to deal with all evils and secure all benefits. Increasing power of a growing administrative organization is accompanied by decreasing power of the rest of the society to resist its further growth and control. . . .

"But why is this change described as 'the coming-slavery'?" is a question which many will still ask. The reply is simple. All socialism involves slavery. . . .

Evidently then, the changes made, the changes in progress, and the changes urged, will carry us not only towards State-ownership of land and dwellings and means of communication, all to be administered and worked by State-agents, but towards State-usurpation of all industries: the private forms of which, disadvantaged more and more in competition with the State, which can arrange everything for its own convenience, will more and more die away, just as many voluntary schools have in presence of Board-schools. And so will be brought about the desired ideal of the socialists. . . .

. . . It is a matter of common remark, often made when a marriage is impending, that those possessed by strong hopes habitually dwell on the promised pleasures and think nothing of the accompanying pains. A further exemplification of this truth is supplied by these political enthusiasts and fanatical revolutionists. Impressed with the miseries existing under our present social arrangements, and not regarding these miseries as caused by the ill-working of a human nature but partially adapted to the social state, they imagine them to be forthwith curable by this or that rearrangement. Yet, even did their plans succeed it could only be by substituting one kind of evil for another. A little deliberate thought would show that under their proposed arrangements, their liberties must be surrendered in proportion as their material welfares were cared for.

For no form of co-operation, small or great, can be carried on without regulation, and an implied submission to the regulating agencies. . . .

. . . So that each [individual] would stand toward the governing agency in the relation of slave to master.

"But the governing agency would be a master which he and others made and kept constantly in check; and one which therefore would not control him or others more than was needful for the benefit of each and all."

To which reply the first rejoinder is that, even if so, each member of the community as an individual would be a slave to the community as a whole. Such a relation has habitually existed in militant communities, even under quasi-popular forms of government. In ancient Greece the accepted principle was that the citizen belonged neither to himself nor to his family, but belonged to his city—the city being with the Greek equivalent to the community. And this doctrine, proper to a state of constant warfare, is a doctrine which socialism unawares re-introduces into a state intended to be purely industrial. The services of each will belong to the aggregate of all; and for these services, such returns will be given as the authorities think proper. So that even if the administration is of the beneficent kind intended to be secured, slavery, however mild, must be the outcome of the arrangement. . . .

The function of Liberalism in the past was that of putting a limit to the powers of kings. The function of true Liberalism in the future will be that of putting a limit to the powers of Parliaments.

2 Feminism and Antifeminism

Inspired by the ideals of equality voiced in the Enlightenment and the French Revolution, women in nineteenth-century Europe and the United States began to demand equal rights, foremost the right to vote. In the United States, the women's suffrage movement held its first convention in 1848 in Seneca Falls, New York. The women adopted a Declaration of Principles that said in part: "We hold these truths to be self-evident: that all men and women are created equal." The struggle for equal rights and voting privileges continued, and by the end of the century, women were voting in a few state elections. Finally, in 1920, the Nineteenth Amendment gave women voting privileges throughout the United States.

In England, having failed to persuade Parliament in the mid-1860s to give them the vote, women organized reform societies, drew up petitions, and protested unfair treatment. The Women's Social and Political Union (WSPU), organized by Emmeline Pankhurst, employed militant tactics, which increased the hostility of their opponents.

During World War I, women worked in offices, factories, and service industries at jobs formerly held by men. Their wartime service made it clear that women played an essential role in the economic life of nations, and many political leaders argued for the extension of the vote to them. In 1918, British women over the age of thirty gained the vote, and, in 1928, Parliament lowered the voting age for British women to twenty-one, the same as for men.

The first countries to permit women to vote were New Zealand in 1893 and Australia in 1902. In Europe, women were granted voting rights by stages, first for municipal elections, later for national ones. Finland extended voting rights to women in 1906; the other Scandinavian countries followed suit, but the majority of European countries did not allow women to vote until after World War I.

In their struggle for equal rights, women faced strong opposition. Opponents argued that feminist demands would threaten society by undermining marriage and the family. Thus in 1870, a member of the British House of Commons wondered "what would become, not merely of women's influence, but of her duties at home, her care of the household, her supervision of all those duties and surroundings which make a happy home . . . if we are to see women coming forward and taking part in the government of the country." This concern for the family was combined with a traditional biased view of woman's nature, as one writer for the *Saturday Review,* an English periodical, revealed:

> The power of reasoning is so small in women that they need adventitious help, and if they have not the guidance and check of a religious conscience, it is useless to expect from them self-control on abstract principles. They do not calculate consequences, and they are reckless when they once give way, hence they are to be kept straight only through their affections, the religious sentiment and a well educated moral sense.

John Stuart Mill
THE SUBJECTION OF WOMEN

John Stuart Mill (1806–1873), a British philosopher and a liberal, championed women's rights. His interest in the subject was awakened by Harriet Taylor, a longtime friend and an ardent feminist, whom he married in 1851. Mill and Taylor had an intense intellectual companionship both before and after their marriage, and Taylor helped shape his ideas on the position of women in society and the urgent need for reform. In 1867, Mill, as a member of Parliament, proposed that the suffrage be extended to women (the proposal was rejected by a vote of 194 to 74). In *The Subjection of Women* (1869), Mill argued that male dominance of women constituted a flagrant abuse of power. He maintained that female inequality, "a single relic of an old world of thought and practice exploded in everything else," violated the principle of individual rights and hindered the progress of humanity. Excerpts from Mill's classic in the history of feminism follow.

The object of this Essay is to explain, as clearly as I am able, the grounds of an opinion which I have held from the very earliest period when I had formed any opinions at all on social or political matters, and which, instead of being weakened or modified, has been constantly growing stronger by the progress of reflection and the experience of life: That the principle which regulates the existing social relations between the two sexes—the legal subordination of one sex to the other—is wrong in itself, and now one of the chief hindrances to human improvement; and that it ought to be replaced by a principle of perfect equality, admitting no power or privilege on the one side, nor disability on the other. . . .

. . . The adoption of this system of inequality never was the result of deliberation, or forethought, or any social ideas, or any notion whatever of what conduced to the benefit of humanity or the good order of society. It arose simply from the fact that from the very earliest twilight of human society, every woman (owing to the value attached to her by men, combined with her inferiority in muscular strength) was found in a state of bondage to some man. . . .

But, it will be said, the rule of men over women differs from all these others in not being a rule of force: it is accepted voluntarily; women make no complaint, and are consenting parties to it. In the first place, a great number of women do not accept it. Ever since there have been women able to make their sentiments known by their writings (the only mode of publicity which society permits to them), an increasing number of them have recorded protests against their present social condition: and recently many thousands of them, headed by the most eminent women known to the public, have petitioned Parliament for their admission to the parliamentary suffrage. The claim of women to be educated as solidly, and in the same branches of knowledge, as men, is urged with growing intensity, and with a great prospect of success; while the demand for their admission into professions and occupations hitherto closed against them becomes every year more urgent. Though there are not in this country, as there are in the United States, periodical Conventions and an organized party to agitate for the Rights of Women, there is a numerous and active Society organized and managed by women, for the more limited object of obtaining the political franchise. Nor is it only in our own country and in America that women are beginning to protest, more or less collectively, against the disabilities under which they labour. France, and Italy, and Switzerland, and Russia now afford examples of the same thing. How many more women there are who silently cherish similar aspirations, no one can possibly know; but there are abundant tokens how many *would* cherish them, were they not so strenuously taught to repress them as contrary to the proprieties of their sex. . . .

Men do not want solely the obedience of women, they want their sentiments. All men, except the most brutish, desire to have, in the woman most nearly connected with them, not a forced slave but a willing one; not a slave merely, but a favourite. They have therefore put everything in practice to enslave their minds. The masters of all other slaves rely, for maintaining obedience, on fear; either fear of themselves, or religious fears. The masters of women wanted more than simple obedience, and they turned the whole force of education to effect their purpose. All women are brought up from the very earliest years in the belief that their ideal of character is the very opposite to that of men; not self-will, and government by self-control, but submission, and yielding to the control of others. All the moralities tell them that it is the duty of women, and all the current sentimentalities that it is their nature, to live for others; to make complete abnegation of themselves, and to have no life but in their affections. And by their affections are meant the only ones they are allowed to have—those to the men with whom they are connected, or to the children who constitute an additional and indefeasible tie between them and a man. When we put together three things—first, the natural attraction between opposite sexes; secondly, the wife's entire dependence on the husband, every privilege or pleasure she has being either his gift, or depending entirely on his will; and lastly, that the principal object of human pursuit, consideration, and all objects of social ambition, can in general be sought or obtained by her only through him—it would be a miracle if the object of being attractive to men had not become the polar star of feminine education and formation of character. And, this great means of influence over the minds of women having been acquired, an instinct of selfishness made men avail themselves of it to the utmost as a means of holding women in subjection, by representing to them meekness, submissiveness, and resignation of all individual will into the hands of a man, as an essential part of sexual attractiveness. Can it be doubted that any of the other yokes which mankind have succeeded in breaking would have subsisted till now if the same means had existed, and had been as sedulously [diligently] used to bow down their minds to it?

Mill argues that women should be able to participate in political life and should not be barred from entering the professions.

On the other point which is involved in the just equality of women, their admissibility to all the functions and occupations hitherto retained as the monopoly of the stronger sex. . . . I believe that their disabilities [in occupation and civil life] elsewhere are only clung to in order to maintain their subordination in domestic life; because the generality of the male sex cannot yet tolerate the idea of living with an equal. Were it not for that, I think that almost every one, in the existing state of opinion in politics and political economy, would admit the injustice of excluding half the human race from the greater number of lucrative occupations, and from almost all high social functions; ordaining from their birth either that they are not, and cannot by any possibility become, fit for employments which are legally open to the stupidest and basest of the other sex, or else that however fit they may be, those employments shall be interdicted to them, in order to be preserved for the exclusive benefit of males. . . .

It will perhaps be sufficient if I confine myself, in the details of my argument, to functions of a public nature: since, if I am successful as to those, it probably will be readily granted that women should be admissible to all other occupations. . . . And here let me begin . . . [with] the suffrage, both parliamentary and municipal. . . .

. . . To have a voice in choosing those by whom one is to be governed, is a means of self-protection due to every one, though he were to remain for ever excluded from the function of governing. . . . Under whatever conditions, and within whatever limits, men are admitted to the suffrage, there is not a shadow of justification for not admitting women under the same. The majority of the women of any class are not likely to differ in political opinion from the majority of the men of the same class, unless the question be one in which the interests of women, as such, are in some way involved; and if they are so, women require the suffrage, as their guarantee of just and equal consideration. . . .

With regard to the fitness of women, not only to participate in elections, but themselves to hold offices or practise professions involving important public responsibilities; I have already observed that this consideration is not essential to the practical question in dispute: since any woman, who succeeds in an open profession, proves by that very fact that she is qualified for it. And in the case of public offices, if the political system of the country is such as to exclude unfit men, it will equally exclude unfit women: while if it is not, there is no additional evil in the fact that the unfit persons whom it admits may be either women or men. . . .

. . . There is no country of Europe in which the ablest men have not frequently experienced, and keenly appreciated, the value of the advice and help of clever and experienced women of the world, in the attainment both of private and of public objects; and there are important matters of public administration to which few men are equally competent with such women; among others, the detailed control of expenditure. But what we are now discussing is not the need which society has of the services of women in public business, but the dull and hopeless life to which it so often condemns them, by forbidding them to exercise the practical abilities which many of them are conscious of, in any wider field than one which to some of them never was, and to others is no longer, open. If there is anything vitally important to the happiness of human beings, it is that they should relish their habitual pursuit [that is, they should be happy in their work]. This requisite of an enjoyable life is very imperfectly granted, or altogether denied, to a large part of mankind; and by its absence many a life is a failure, which is provided, in appearance, with every requisite of success.

Emmeline Pankhurst
"WHY WE ARE MILITANT"

Agitation in Great Britain for woman suffrage reached a peak during the turbulent years of parliamentary reform, 1909–1911. Under the leadership of Emmeline Pankhurst (1858–1928) and her daughter Christabel, women engaged in demonstrations, disrupted political meetings, and, when dragged off to jail, resorted to passive resistance and hunger strikes. Some hunger strikers were subjected to the cruelty of force-feeding. In 1913, Emmeline Pankhurst carried her appeal to the United States, where she delivered the speech printed below.

I know that in your minds there are questions like these; you are saying, "Woman Suffrage is sure to come; the emancipation of humanity is an evolutionary process, and how is it that some women, instead of trusting to that evolution, instead of educating the masses of people of their country, instead of educating their own sex to prepare them for citizenship, how is it that these militant women are using violence and upsetting the business arrangements of the country in their undue impatience to attain their end?"

Let me try to explain to you the situation. . . .

The extensions of the franchise to the men of my country have been preceded by very great violence, by something like a revolution, by something like civil war. In 1832, you know we were on the edge of a civil war and on the edge of revolution, and it was at the point of the sword—no, not at the point of the sword—it was after the practice of arson on so large a scale that half the city of Bristol was burned down in a single night, it was because more and greater violence and arson were feared that the Reform Bill of 1832 [which gave the vote to the middle class] was allowed to pass into law. In 1867, . . . rioting went on all over the country, and as the result of that rioting, as the result of that unrest, . . . as a result of the fear of more rioting and violence the Reform Act of 1867 [which gave workers the vote] was put upon the statute books.

In 1884 . . . rioting was threatened and feared, and so the agricultural labourers got the vote.

Meanwhile, during the '80's, women, like men, were asking for the franchise. Appeals, larger and more numerous than for any other reform, were presented in support of Woman's Suffrage. Meetings of the great corporations [groups of principal officials in a town or city government], great town councils, and city councils, passed resolutions asking that women should have the vote. More meetings were held, and larger, for Woman Suffrage than were held for votes for men, and yet the women did not get it. Men got the vote because they were and would be violent. The women did not get it because they were constitutional and law-abiding. . . .

I believed, as many women still in England believe, that women could get their way in some mysterious manner, by purely peaceful methods. We have been so accustomed, we women, to accept one standard for men and another standard for women, that we have even applied that variation of standard to the injury of our political welfare.

Having had better opportunities of education, and having had some training in politics, having in political life come so near to the "superior" being as to see that he was not altogether such a fount of wisdom as they had supposed, that he had his human weaknesses as we had, the twentieth century women began to say to themselves, "Is it not time, since our methods have failed and the men's have succeeded, that we should take a leaf out of their political book?" . . .

Well, we in Great Britain, on the eve of the General Election of 1905, a mere handful of us—why, you could almost count us on the fingers of both hands—set out on the wonderful adventure of forcing the strongest Government of modern times to give the women the vote. . . .

The Suffrage movement was almost dead. The women had lost heart. You could not get a Suffrage meeting that was attended by members of the general public. . . .

Two women changed that in a twinkling of an eye at a great Liberal demonstration in Manchester, where a Liberal leader, Sir Edward Grey, was explaining the programme to be carried out during the Liberals' next turn of office. The two women put the fateful question, "When are you going to give votes to women?" and refused to sit down until they had been answered. These two women were sent to gaol, and from that day to this the women's movement, both militant and constitutional, has never looked back. We had little more than one moribund society for Woman Suffrage in those days. Now we have nearly 50 societies for Woman Suffrage, and they are large in membership, they are rich in money, and their ranks are swelling every day that passes. That is how militancy has put back the clock of Woman Suffrage in Great Britain. . . .

I want to say here and now that the only justification for violence, the only justification for damage to property, the only justification for risk to the comfort of other human beings is the fact that you have tried all other available means and have failed to secure justice, and as a law-abiding person—and I am by nature a law-abiding person, as one hating violence, hating disorder—I want to say that from the moment we began our militant agitation to this day I have felt absolutely guiltless in this matter.

I tell you that in Great Britain there is no other way. . . .

Well, I say the time is long past when it became necessary for women to revolt in order to maintain their self-respect in Great Britain. The women who are waging this war are women who would fight, if it were only for the idea of liberty—if it were only that they might be free citizens of a free country—I myself would fight for that idea alone. But we have, in addition to this love of freedom, intolerable grievances to redress. . . .

Those grievances are so pressing that, so far from it being a duty to be patient and to wait for evolution, in thinking of those grievances the idea of patience is intolerable. We feel that patience is something akin to crime when our patience involves continued suffering on the part of the oppressed.

We are fighting to get the power to alter bad laws; but some people say to us, "Go to the representatives in the House of Commons, point out to them that these laws are bad, and you will find them quite ready to alter them."

Ladies and gentlemen, there are women in my country who have spent long and useful lives trying to get reforms, and because of their voteless condition, they are unable even to get the ear of Members of Parliament, much less are they able to secure those reforms.

Our marriage and divorce laws are a disgrace to civilisation. I sometimes wonder, looking back from the serenity of past middle age, at the courage of women. I wonder that women have the courage to take upon themselves the responsibilities of marriage and motherhood when I see how little protection the law of my country affords them. I wonder that a woman will face the ordeal of childbirth with the knowledge that after she has risked her life to bring a child into the world she has absolutely no parental rights over the future of that child. Think what trust women have in men when a woman will marry a man, knowing, if she has knowledge of the law, that if that man is not all she in her love for him thinks him, he may even bring a strange woman into the house, bring his mistress into the house to live with her, and she cannot get legal relief from such a marriage as that. . . .

. . . [W]e realise how political power, how political influence, which would enable us to get better laws, would make it possible for thousands upon thousands of unhappy women to live happier lives. . . .

Take the industrial side of the question: have men's wages for a hard day's work ever been so low and inadequate as are women's wages today? Have men ever had to suffer from the laws, more injustice than women suffer? Is there a single reason which men have had for demanding liberty that does not also apply to women?

Why, if you were talking to the *men* of any other nation you would not hesitate to reply in the affirmative. There is not a man in this meeting who has not felt sympathy with the uprising of the men of other lands when suffering from intolerable tyranny, when deprived of all representative rights. You are full of sympathy with men in Russia. You are full of sympathy with nations that rise against the domination of the Turk. You are full of sympathy with all struggling people striving for independence. How is it, then, that some of you have nothing but ridicule and contempt and [condemnation] for women who are fighting for exactly the same thing?

All my life I have tried to understand why it is that men who value their citizenship as their dearest possession seem to think citizenship ridiculous when it is to be applied to the women of their race. And I find an explanation, and it is the only one I can think of. It came to me when I was in a prison cell, remembering how I had seen men laugh at the idea of women going to prison. Why they would confess they could not bear a cell door to be shut upon themselves for a single hour without asking to be let out. A thought came to me in my prison cell, and it was this: that to men women are not human beings like themselves. Some men think we are superhuman; they put us on pedestals; they revere us; they think we are too fine and too delicate to come down into the hurly-burly of life. Other men think us sub-human; they think we are a strange species unfortunately having to exist for the perpetuation of the race. They think that we are fit for drudgery, but that in some strange way our minds are not like theirs, our love for great things is not like theirs, and so we are a sort of sub-human species.

We are neither superhuman nor are we sub-human. We are just human beings like yourselves.

Our hearts burn within us when we read the great mottoes which celebrate the liberty of your country; when we go to France and we read the words, liberty, fraternity and equality, don't you think that we appreciate the meaning of those words? And then when we wake to the knowledge that these things are not for us, they are only for our brothers, then there comes a sense of bitterness into the hearts of some women, and they say to themselves, "Will men never understand?" But so far as we in England are concerned, we have come to the conclusion that we are not going to leave men any illusions upon the question.

When we were patient, when we believed in argument and persuasion, they said, "You don't really want it because, if you did, you would do something unmistakable to show you were determined to have it." And then when we did something unmistakable they said, "You are behaving so badly that you show you are not fit for it."

Now, gentlemen, in your heart of hearts you do not believe that. You know perfectly well that there never was a thing worth having that was not worth fighting for. You know perfectly well that if the situation were reversed, if you had no constitutional rights and we had all of them, if you had the duty of paying and obeying and trying to look as pleasant, and we were the proud citizens who could decide our fate and yours, because we knew what was good for you better than you knew yourselves, you know perfectly well that you wouldn't stand it for a single day, and you would be perfectly justified in rebelling against such intolerable conditions.

The Goncourt Brothers ON FEMALE INFERIORITY

The brothers Edmund (1822–1896) and Jules (1830–1870) Goncourt were French writers who produced in partnership novels, plays, and art and literary criticism. Starting in December 1851, they kept a journal in which they recorded, often insightfully, the climate of Parisian cultural and social life. In the following entries the Goncourts reveal an extreme bias against women. Even if these sentiments were not shared by all intellectuals, they do show the traditional prejudices confronting French feminists.

13 October. 1855

A conversation about woman, after a couple of tankards of beer at Binding's. Woman is an evil, stupid animal unless she is educated and civilized to a high degree. She is incapable of dreaming, thinking, or loving. Poetry in a woman is never natural but always a product of education. Only the woman of the world is a woman; the rest are females.

Inferiority of the feminine mind to the masculine mind. All the physical beauty, all the strength, and all the development of a woman is concentrated in and as it were directed towards the central and lower parts of the body: the pelvis, the buttocks, the thighs; the beauty of a man is to be found in the upper, nobler parts, the pectoral muscles, the broad shoulders, the high forehead. Venus has a narrow forehead. Dürer's *Three Graces* have flat heads at the back and little shoulders; only their hips are big and beautiful. As regards the inferiority of the feminine mind, consider the self-assurance of a woman, even when she is only a girl, which allows her to be extremely witty with nothing but a little vivacity and a touch of spontaneity. Only man is endowed with the modesty and timidity which woman lacks and which she uses only as weapons.

Woman: the most beautiful and most admirable of laying machines.

21 May. 1857

Men like ourselves need a woman of little breeding and education who is nothing but gaiety and natural wit, because a woman of that sort can charm and please us like an agreeable animal to which we may become quite attached. But if a mistress has acquired a veneer of breeding, art, or literature, and tries to talk to us on an equal footing about our thoughts and our feeling for beauty; if she wants to be a companion and partner in the cultivation of our tastes or the writing of our books, then she becomes for us as unbearable as a piano out of tune—and very soon an object of dislike.

Almroth E. Wright
THE UNEXPURGATED CASE AGAINST WOMAN SUFFRAGE

Sir Almroth Wright (1861–1947) was an eminent physician and one of the founders of modern immunology. He was also a thinker who attempted to construct "a system of Logic which searches for Truth," as he put it.

Wright's opposition to giving women the vote was expressed in letters to *The Times* of London and in a slender book, *The Unexpurgated Case Against Woman Suffrage* (1913). In the extracts below, he described the disabilities of women which make female suffrage impossible, at one point dismissing the suffrage movement as the product of "sex-hostility" caused by the excess population of women without hope of marrying. All told, he found that women's suffrage would be a recipe for social disaster, resulting in unacceptable demands for economic and intellectual equality.

The primordial argument against giving woman the vote is that that vote would not represent physical force.

Now it is by physical force alone and by prestige—which represents physical force in the background—that a nation protects itself against foreign interference, upholds its rule over subject populations, and enforces its own laws. And nothing could in the end more certainly lead to war and revolt than the decline of the military spirit and loss of prestige which would inevitably follow if man admitted woman into political co-partnership. . . .

[A] virile and imperial race will not brook any attempt at forcible control by women. Again, no military foreign nation or native race would ever believe in the stamina and firmness of purpose of any nation that submitted even to the semblance of such control. . . .

The woman voter would be pernicious to the State not only because she could not back her vote by physical force, but also by reason of her intellectual defects.

Woman's mind . . . arrives at conclusions on incomplete evidence; has a very imperfect sense of proportion; accepts the congenial as true, and rejects the uncongenial as false; takes the imaginary which is desired for reality, and treats the undesired reality which is out of sight as nonexistent—building up for itself in this way, when biased by predilections and aversions, a very unreal picture of the external world.

The explanation of this is to be found in all the physiological attachments of woman's mind: in the fact that mental images are in her over-intimately linked up with emotional reflex responses; that yielding to such reflex responses gives gratification; that intellectual analysis and suspense of judgment involve an inhibition of reflex responses which is felt as neural distress; that precipitate judgment brings relief from this physiological strain; and that woman looks upon her mind not as an implement for the pursuit of truth, but as an instrument for providing her with creature comforts in the form of agreeable mental images. . . .

In further illustration of what has been said above, it may be pointed out that woman, even intelligent woman, nurses all sorts of misconceptions about herself. She, for instance, is constantly picturing to herself that she can as a worker lay claim to the same all-round efficiency as a man—forgetting that woman is notoriously unadapted to tasks in which severe physical hardships have to be confronted; and that hardly any one would, if other alternative offered, employ a woman in any work which imposed upon her a combined physical and mental strain, or in any work where emergencies might have to be faced. . . .

Yet a third point has to come into consideration in connexion with the woman voter. This is, that she would be pernicious to the State also by virtue of her defective moral equipment. . . .

It is only a very exceptional woman who would, when put to her election between the claims of a narrow and domestic and a wider or public morality, subordinate the former to the latter.

In ordinary life, at any rate, one finds her following in such a case the suggestions of domestic—I had almost called it animal—morality.

It would be difficult to find any one who would trust a woman to be just to the rights of others in the case where the material interests of her children, or of a devoted husband, were involved. And even to consider the question of being in such a case intellectually just to any one who came into competition with personal belongings like husband and child would, of course, lie quite beyond the moral horizon of ordinary woman. . . . In this matter one would not be very far from the truth if one alleged that there are no good women, but only women who have lived under the influence of good men. . . .

In countries, such as England, where an excess female population [of three million] has made economic difficulties for woman, and where the severe sexual restrictions, which here obtain, have bred in her sex-hostility, the suffrage movement has as its avowed ulterior object the abrogation of all distinctions which depend upon sex; and the achievement of the economic independence of woman.

To secure this economic independence every post, occupation, and Government service is to be thrown open to woman; she is to receive everywhere the same wages as man; male and female are to work side by side; and they are indiscriminately to be put in command the one over the other. Furthermore, legal rights are to be secured to the wife over her husband's property and earnings. The programme is, in fact, to give to woman an economic independence out of the earnings and taxes of man.

Nor does feminist ambition stop short here. It demands that women shall be included in every advisory committee, every governing board, every jury, every judicial bench, every electorate, every parliament, and every ministerial cabinet; further, that every masculine foundation, university, school of learning, academy, trade union, professional corporation, and scientific society shall be converted into an epicene institution [including both male and female]—until we shall have everywhere one vast cock-and-hen show.

The proposal to bring man and woman together everywhere into extremely intimate relationships raises very grave questions. It brings up, first, the question of sexual complications; secondly, the question as to whether the tradition of modesty and reticence between the sexes is to be definitely sacrificed; and, most important of all, the question as to whether [bringing men and women together] would place obstacles in the way of intellectual work. . . .

The matter cannot so lightly be disposed of. It will be necessary for us to find out whether really intimate association with woman on the purely intellectual plane is realisable. And if it is, in fact, unrealisable, it will be necessary to consider whether it is the exclusion of women from masculine corporations; or the perpetual attempt of women to force their way into these, which would deserve to be characterised as *selfish*. . . .

What we have to ask is whether—even if we leave out of regard the whole system of attractions or, as the case may be, repulsions which comes into operation when the sexes are thrown together—purely intellectual intercourse between man and the typical unselected woman is not barred by the intellectual immoralities and limitations which appear to be secondary sexual characters of woman. . . .

Wherever we look we find aversion to compulsory intellectual co-operation with woman. We see it in the sullen attitude which the ordinary male student takes up towards the presence of women students in his classes. We see it in the fact that the older English universities, which have conceded everything else to women, have made a strong stand against making them actual members of the university; for this would impose them on men as intellectual associates. Again we see the aversion in the opposition to the admission of women to the bar.

But we need not look so far afield. Practically every man feels that there is in woman—patent, or hidden away—an element of unreason which, when you come upon it, summarily puts an end to purely intellectual intercourse. One may reflect, for example, upon the way the woman's suffrage controversy has been conducted.

But the feminist will want to argue. She will—taking it as always for granted that woman has a right to all that men's hands or brains have fashioned—argue that it is very important for the intellectual development of woman that she should have exactly the same opportunities as man. And she will, scouting the idea of any differences between the intelligences of man and woman, discourse to you of their intimate affinity. . . .

From these general questions, which affect only the woman with intellectual aspirations, we pass to consider what would be the effect of feminism upon the rank and file of women if it made of these co-partners with man in work. They would suffer, not only because woman's physiological disabilities and the restrictions which arise out of her sex place her at a great disadvantage when she has to enter into competition with man, but also because under feminism man would be less and less disposed to take off woman's shoulders a part of her burden.

And there can be no dispute that the most valuable financial asset of the ordinary woman is the possibility that a man may be willing—and may, if only woman is disposed to fulfil her part of the bargain, be not only willing but anxious—to support her, and to secure for her, if he can, a measure of that freedom which comes from the possession of money.

In view of this every one who has a real fellow-feeling for woman, and who is concerned for her material welfare, as a father is concerned for his daughter's, will above everything else desire to nurture and encourage in man the sentiment of chivalry, and in woman that disposition of mind that makes chivalry possible.

And the woman workers who have to fight the battle of life for themselves would indirectly profit from this fostering of chivalry; for those women who are supported by men do not compete in the limited labour market which is open to the woman worker.

From every point of view, therefore, except perhaps that of the exceptional woman who would be able to hold her own against masculine competition—and men always issue informal letters of [admission] to such an exceptional woman—the woman suffrage which leads up to feminism would be a social disaster.

3 Racial Nationalism

German and British nationalists were especially attracted to racist doctrines. Racist thinkers held that race was the key to history, and that not only physical features, but also moral, esthetic, and intellectual qualities distinguished one race from another. In their view, a race retained its vigor and achieved greatness when it preserved its purity; intermarriage between races was contamination that would result in genetic, cultural, and military decline. Unlike liberals, who held that anyone who accepted German law was a member of the German nation, German racist thinkers argued that a person's nationality was a function of his or her "racial soul" or "blood." On the basis of this new conception of nationality, racists argued that Jews, no matter how many centuries their ancestors had dwelt in Germany, could never think and feel like Germans and should be deprived of citizenship.

Like their Nazi successors, nineteenth-century German racists claimed that the German race was purer than, and therefore superior to, all other races; its superiority was revealed in such physical characteristics as blond hair, blue eyes, and fair skin—all signs of inner qualities lacking in other races. German racists claimed that the Germans were descendants of ancient Aryans. (The Aryans emerged some four thousand years ago, probably between the Caspian Sea and the Hindu Kush Mountains. Intermingling with others, the Aryans lost whatever identity as a people they might have had.) After discovering similarities between core European languages—Latin, Greek, and German—and ancient Persian and Sanskrit (the language of the fair-skinned conquerors of India), nineteenth-century scholars believed that these languages all stemmed from a common tongue spoken by the Aryans. From there, some leaped to the unwarranted conclusion that the Aryans constituted a distinct race endowed with superior racial qualities.

Houston Stewart Chamberlain
THE IMPORTANCE OF RACE

German racist thinkers embraced the ideas of Houston Stewart Chamberlain (1855–1927), an Englishman whose devotion to Germanism led him to adopt German citizenship. In *Foundations of the Nineteenth Century* (1899), Chamberlain attempted to assert in scientific fashion that races differed not only physically but also morally, spiritually, and intellectually and that the struggle between races was the driving force of history. He held that the Germans, allegedly descendants of the ancient Aryans, were physically superior and bearers of a higher culture. He attributed Rome's decline to the dilution of its "racial qualities" through miscegenation. The blond, blue-eyed, long-skulled Germans, possessing the strongest strain of Aryan blood, he argued, and distinguished by an inner spiritual depth, were the true ennoblers of humanity.

Chamberlain's book was enormously popular in Germany. Nationalist organizations frequently cited it. Kaiser Wilhelm II called *Foundations* a "hymn to Germanism" and read it to his children. "Next to the national liberal historians like Heinrich von Treitschke and Heinrich von Sybel," concludes German historian Fritz Fischer, "Houston Stewart Chamberlain had the greatest influence upon the spiritual life of Wilhelmine Germany."

Chamberlain's racist and anti-Semitic views make him a spiritual forerunner of Nazism, and he was praised as such by Alfred Rosenberg, the leading Nazi racial theorist in the early days of Hitler's movement. Josef Goebbels, the Nazi propagandist, hailed Chamberlain as a "pathbreaker" and "pioneer" after meeting him in 1926. Excerpts from Chamberlain's work follow.

Nothing is so convincing as the consciousness of the possession of Race. The man who belongs to a distinct, pure race, never loses the sense of it. . . . Race lifts a man above himself: it endows him with extraordinary—I might almost say supernatural—powers, so entirely does it distinguish him from the individual who springs from the chaotic jumble of peoples drawn from all parts of the world: and should this man of pure origin be perchance gifted above his fellows, then the fact of Race strengthens and elevates him on every hand, and he becomes a genius towering over the rest of mankind, not because he has been thrown upon the earth like a flaming meteor by a freak of nature, but because he soars heavenward like some strong and stately tree, nourished by thousands and thousands of roots—no solitary individual, but the living sum of untold souls striving for the same goal. . . .

. . . As far back as our glance can reach, we see human beings, we see that they differ essentially in their gifts and that some show more vigorous powers of growth than others. Only one thing can be asserted without leaving the basis of historical observation: a high state of excellence is only attained gradually and under particular circumstances, it is only forced activity that can bring it about; under other circumstances it may completely degenerate. The struggle which means destruction for the fundamentally weak race steels the strong; the same struggle, moreover, by eliminating the weaker elements, tends still further to strengthen the strong. Around the childhood of great races, as we observe, even in the case of the metaphysical Indians, the storm of war always rages. . . .

. . . Only quite definite, limited mixtures of blood contribute towards the ennoblement of a race, or, it may be, the origin of a new one. Here again the clearest and least ambiguous examples are furnished by animal breeding. The mixture of blood must be strictly limited as regards time, and it must, in addition, be appropriate; not all and any crossings, but only definite ones can form the basis of ennoblement. By time-limitation I mean that the influx of new blood must take place as quickly as possible and then cease; continual crossing ruins the strongest race. To take an extreme example, the most famous pack of greyhounds in England was crossed once only with bulldogs, whereby it gained in courage and endurance, but further experiments prove that when such a crossing is continued, the characters of both races disappear and quite characterless mongrels remain behind. . . .

. . . Marius and Sulla had, by murdering the flower of the genuine Roman youth, dammed the source of noble blood and at the same time, by the freeing of slaves, brought into the nation perfect floods of African and Asiatic blood, thus transforming Rome into the *cloaca gentium*, the trysting-place of all the mongrels of the world. . . .

Let us attempt a glance into the depths of the soul. What are the specific intellectual and moral characteristics of this Germanic race? Certain anthropologists would fain teach us that all races are equally gifted; we point to history and answer: that is a lie! The races of mankind are markedly different in the nature and also in the extent of their gifts, and the Germanic races belong to the most highly gifted group, the group usually termed Aryan. . . .

The civilisation and culture, which radiating from Northern Europe, to-day dominate (though in very varying degrees) a considerable part of the world, are the work of Teutonism; what is not Teutonic consists either of alien elements not yet exorcised, which were formerly forcibly introduced and still, like baneful germs, circulate in the blood, or of alien wares sailing, to the disadvantage of our work and further development, under the Teutonic flag, under Teutonic protection and privilege, and they will continue to sail thus, until we send these pirate ships to the bottom. This work of Teutonism is beyond question the greatest that has hitherto been accomplished by man. . . . As the youngest of races, we Teutons could profit by the achievements of former ones; but this is no proof of a universal progress of humanity, but solely of the pre-eminent capabilities of a definite human species, capabilities which have been proved to be gradually weakened by influx of non-Teutonic blood.

Pan-German League
"THERE ARE DOMINANT RACES AND SUBORDINATE RACES"

Organized in 1894, the ultranationalist and imperialist Pan-German League called for German expansion both in Europe and overseas. It often expressed blatantly Social Darwinist and racist views as illustrated in the following article, which appeared in 1913 in the league's principal publication.

"The historical view as to the biological evolution of races tells us that there are dominant races and subordinate races. Political history is nothing more than the history of the struggles between the dominant races. Conquest in particular is always a function of the dominant races . . . .

"Where now in all the world does it stand written that conquering races are under obligations to grant after an interval political rights to the conquered? Is not the practice of political rights an advantage which biologically belongs to the dominant races? . . . In my opinion, the rights of men are, first, personal freedom; secondly, the right of free expression of opinion—as well as freedom of the press; . . . and, finally, the right to work, in case one is without means. . . .

"In like manner there is the school question. The man with political rights sets up schools, and the speech used in the instruction is his speech. . . . The purpose must be to crush the [individuality of the] conquered people and its political and lingual existence. . . .

"The conquerors are acting only according to biological principles if they suppress alien languages and undertake to destroy strange popular customs. . . . Only the conquering race must be populous, so that it can overrun the territory it has won. Nations that are populous are, moreover, the only nations which have a moral claim to conquest, for it is wrong that in one country there should be overpopulation while close at hand—and at the same time on better soil—a less numerous population stretches its limbs at ease.

[As to the inferior races:] "From political life they are to be excluded. They are eligible only to positions of a non-political character, to commercial commissions, chambers of commerce, etc. . . . The principal thing for the conqueror is the outspoken will to rule and the will to destroy the political and national life of the conquered. . . ."

Cecil Rhodes
THE SUPERIOR ANGLO-SAXON RACE

Several British advocates of imperial expansion used racist arguments to justify their position. Often, these arguments were based on Social Darwinist assumptions (see page 24). Cecil Rhodes (1853–1902), who built a diamond and gold-mining empire in southern Africa, was a staunch supporter of spreading Anglo-Saxon power throughout the world. In 1877, when he was twenty-four years old, he wrote, for his own desk drawer, a "Confession of Faith," which offered a vision of racist expansionism popular before World War I. It was not published during his lifetime. Following are excerpts from Rhodes' "Confession of Faith."

. . . I contend that we are the finest race in the world and that the more of the world we inhabit the better it is for the human race. Just fancy those parts that are at present inhabited by the most despicable specimens of human beings what an alteration there would be if they were brought under Anglo-Saxon influence, look again at the extra employment a new country added to our dominions gives. I contend that every acre added to our territory means in the future birth to some more of the English race who otherwise would not be brought into existence. Added to this the absorption of the greater portion of the world under our rule simply means the end of all wars. . . .

The idea gleaming and dancing before one's eyes like a will-of-the-wisp at last frames itself into a plan. Why should we not form a secret society with but one object the furtherance of the British Empire and the bringing of the whole uncivilised world under British rule for the recovery of the United States for the making the Anglo-Saxon race but one Empire. . . .

. . . We know the size of the world we know the total extent. Africa is still lying ready for us it is our duty to take it. It is our duty to seize every opportunity of acquiring more territory and we should keep this one idea steadily before our eyes that more territory simply means more of the Anglo-Saxon race more of the best the most human, most honourable race the world possesses.

To forward such a scheme what a splendid help a secret society would be a society not openly acknowledged but who would work in secret for such an object.

I contend that there are at the present moment numbers of the ablest men in the world who would devote their whole lives to it.

4 Imperialism

In 1872, the British statesman Benjamin Disraeli (1804–1881) delivered a famous speech at the Crystal Palace in London that posed a crucial choice for his country: it was either insignificance in world affairs or imperial power with prosperity and global prestige. His speech was soon followed by an outburst of speeches, lectures, and books in which imperialists made claims for British worldwide superiority buttressed by arguments drawn from racist and Darwinian convictions popular at the time.

Joseph Chamberlain
THE BRITISH EMPIRE: COLONIAL COMMERCE AND "THE WHITE MAN'S BURDEN"

British imperialists like Joseph Chamberlain (1836–1914) argued that the welfare of Britain depended upon the preservation and extension of the empire, for colonies fostered trade and served as a source of raw materials. In addition, Chamberlain asserted that the British Empire had a sacred duty to carry civilization, Christianity, and British law to the "backward" peoples of Africa and Asia. As a leading statesman, Chamberlain made many speeches, both in Parliament and before local political groups, that endorsed imperialist ventures. Excerpts from these speeches, later collected and published under the title *Foreign and Colonial Speeches,* follow.

June 10, 1896

. . . The Empire, to parody a celebrated expression, is commerce. It was created by commerce, it is founded on commerce, and it could not exist a day without commerce. (Cheers.) . . . The fact is history teaches us that no nation has ever achieved real greatness without the aid of commerce, and the greatness of no nation has survived the decay of its trade. Well, then, gentlemen, we have reason to be proud of our commerce and to be resolved to guard it from attack. (Cheers.) . . .

March 31, 1897

. . . We have suffered much in this country from depression of trade. We know how many of our fellow-subjects are at this moment unemployed. Is there any man in his senses who believes that the crowded population of these islands could exist for a single day if we were to cut adrift from us the great dependencies which now look to us for protection and assistance, and which are the natural markets for our trade? (Cheers.) The area of the United Kingdom is only 120,000 miles; the area of the British Empire is over 9,000,000 square miles, of which nearly 500,000 are to be found in the portion of Africa with which we have been dealing. If tomorrow it were possible, as some people apparently desire, to reduce by a stroke of the pen the British Empire to the dimensions of the United Kingdom, half at least of our population would be starved (Cheers.) . . .

January 22, 1894

We must look this matter in the face, and must recognise that in order that we may have more employment to give we must create more demand. (Hear, hear.) Give me the demand for more goods and then I will undertake to give plenty of employment in making the goods; and the only thing, in my opinion, that the Government can do in order to meet this great difficulty that we are considering, is so to arrange its policy that every inducement shall be given to the demand; that new markets shall be created, and that old markets shall be effectually developed. (Cheers.) . . . I am convinced that it is a necessity as well as a duty for us to uphold the dominion and empire which we now possess. (Loud cheers.) . . . I would never lose the hold which we now have over our great Indian dependency—(hear, hear)—by far the greatest and most valuable of all the customers we have or ever shall have in this country. For the same reasons I approve of the continued occupation of Egypt; and for the same reasons I have urged upon this Government, and upon previous Governments, the necessity for using every legitimate opportunity to extend our influence and control in that great African continent which is now being opened up to civilisation and to commerce; and, lastly, it is for the same reasons that I hold that our navy should be strengthened—(loud cheers)—until its supremacy is so assured that we cannot be shaken in any of the possessions which we hold or may hold hereafter.

Believe me, if in any one of the places to which I have referred any change took place which deprived us of that control and influence of which I have been speaking, the first to suffer would be the working-men of this country. Then, indeed, we should see a distress which would not be temporary, but which would be chronic, and we should find that England was entirely unable to support the enormous population which is now maintained by the aid of her foreign trade. If the working-men of this country understand, as I believe they do—I am one of those who have had good reason through my life to rely upon their intelligence and shrewdness—if they understand their own interests, they will never lend any countenance to the doctrines of those politicians who never lose an opportunity of pouring contempt and abuse upon the brave Englishmen, who, even at this moment, in all parts of the world are carving out new dominions for Britain, and are opening up fresh markets for British commerce, and laying out fresh fields for British labour. (Applause.) . . .

March 31, 1897

. . . We feel now that our rule over these territories can only be justified if we can show that it adds to the happiness and prosperity of the people—(cheers)—and I maintain that our rule does, and has, brought security and peace and comparative prosperity to countries that never knew these blessings before. (Cheers.)

In carrying out this work of civilisation we are fulfilling what I believe to be our national mission, and we are finding scope for the exercise of those faculties and qualities which have made of us a great governing race. (Cheers.) I do not say that our success has been perfect in every case. I do not say that all our methods have been beyond reproach; but I do say that in almost every instance in which the rule of the Queen has been established and the great *Pax Britannica*[1] has been enforced, there has come with it greater security to life and property, and a material improvement in the condition of the bulk of the population. (Cheers.) No doubt, in the first instance, when these conquests have been made, there has been bloodshed, there has been loss of life among the native populations, loss of still more precious lives among those who have been sent out to bring these countries into some kind of disciplined order, but it must be remembered that this is the condition of the mission we have to fulfil. . . .

---

[1]*Pax Britannica* means "British Peace" in the tradition of the *Pax Romana*—the peace, stability, and prosperity that characterized the Roman Empire at its height in the first two centuries A.D.

. . . You cannot have omelettes without breaking eggs; you cannot destroy the practices of barbarism, of slavery, of superstition, which for centuries have desolated the interior of Africa, without the use of force; but if you will fairly contrast the gain to humanity with the price we are bound to pay for it, I think you may well rejoice in the result of such expeditions as those which have recently been conducted with such signal success—(cheers)—in Nyassaland, Ashanti, Benin, and Nupé [regions in Africa]—expeditions which may have, and indeed have, cost valuable lives, but as to which we may rest assured that for one life lost a hundred will be gained, and the cause of civilisation and the prosperity of the people will in the long run be eminently advanced. (Cheers.) But no doubt such a state of things, such a mission as I have described, involve heavy responsibility. . . . and it is a gigantic task that we have undertaken when we have determined to wield the sceptre of empire. Great is the task, great is the responsibility, but great is the honour—(cheers); and I am convinced that the conscience and the spirit of the country will rise to the height of its obligations, and that we shall have the strength to fulfil the mission which our history and our national character have imposed upon us. (Cheers.)

Karl Pearson
SOCIAL DARWINISM: IMPERIALISM JUSTIFIED BY NATURE

In the last part of the nineteenth century, the spirit of expansionism was buttressed by application of Darwin's theory of evolution to human society. Theorists called Social Darwinists argued that nations and races, like the species of animals, were locked in a struggle for existence in which only the fittest survived and deserved to survive. British and American imperialists employed the language of Social Darwinism to promote and justify Anglo-Saxon expansion and domination of other peoples. Social Darwinist ideas spread to Germany, which was inspired by the examples of British and American expansion. In a lecture given in 1900 and titled "National Life from the Standpoint of Science," Karl Pearson (1857–1936), a British professor of mathematics, expressed the beliefs of Social Darwinists.

What I have said about bad stock seems to me to hold for the lower races of man. How many centuries, how many thousands of years, have the Kaffir [a tribe in southern Africa] or the negro held large districts in Africa undisturbed by the white man? Yet their intertribal struggles have not yet produced a civilization in the least comparable with the Aryan.[1] Educate and nurture them as you will, I do not believe that you will succeed in modifying the stock. History shows me one way, and one way only, in which a high state of civilization has been produced, namely, the struggle of race with race, and the survival of the physically and mentally fitter race. . . .

. . . Let us suppose we could prevent the white man, if we liked, from going to lands of which the agricultural and mineral resources are not worked to the full; then I should say a thousand times better for him that he should not go than that he should settle down and live alongside the inferior race. The only healthy alternative is that he should go and

---

[1]Most European languages derive from the Aryan language spoken by people who lived thousands of years ago in the region from the Caspian Sea to the Hindu Kush Mountains. Around 2000 B.C., some Aryan-speaking people migrated to Europe and India. Nineteenth-century racialist thinkers held that Europeans, descendants of the ancient Aryans, were racially superior to other peoples.

completely drive out the inferior race. That is practically what the white man has done in North America. . . . But I venture to say that no man calmly judging will wish either that the whites had never gone to America, or would desire that whites and Red Indians were to-day living alongside each other as negro and white in the Southern States, as Kaffir and European in South Africa, still less that they had mixed their blood as Spaniard and Indian in South America. . . . I venture to assert, then, that the struggle for existence between white and red man, painful and even terrible as it was in its details, has given us a good far out-balancing its immediate evil. In place of the red man, contributing practically nothing to the work and thought of the world, we have a great nation, mistress of many arts, and able, with its youthful imagination and fresh, un-trammelled impulses, to contribute much to the common stock of civilized man. . . .

But America is but one case in which we have to mark a masterful human progress following an inter-racial struggle. The Australian nation is another case of great civilization sup-planting a lower race unable to work to the full the land and its resources. . . . The struggle means suffering, intense suffering, while it is in progress; but that struggle and that suffering have been the stages by which the white man has reached his present stage of development, and they account for the fact that he no longer lives in caves and feeds on roots and nuts. This dependence of progress on the survival of the fitter race, terribly black as it may seem to some of you, gives the struggle for existence its redeeming features; it is the fiery crucible out of which comes the finer metal. You may hope for a time when the sword shall be turned into the ploughshare, when American and German and English traders shall no longer compete in the markets of the world for their raw material and for their food supply, when the white man and the dark shall share the soil between them, and each till it as he lists [pleases]. But, believe me, when that day comes mankind will no longer progress; there will be nothing to check the fertility of inferior stock; the relentless law of heredity will not be controlled and guided by natural selection. Man will stagnate. . . .

The . . . great function of science in national life . . . is to show us what national life means, and how the nation is a vast organism subject . . . to the great forces of evolution. . . . There is a struggle of race against race and of nation against nation. In the early days of that struggle it was a blind, unconscious struggle of barbaric tribes. At the present day, in the case of the civilized white man, it has become more and more the conscious, carefully directed attempt of the nation to fit itself to a continuously changing environment. The nation has to foresee how and where the struggle will be carried on; the maintenance of national position is becoming more and more a conscious preparation for changing conditions, an insight into the needs of coming environments. . . .

. . . If a nation is to maintain its position in this struggle, it must be fully provided with trained brains in every department of national activity, from the government to the factory, and have, if possible, a *reserve of brain and physique* to fall back upon in times of national crisis. . . .

You will see that my view—and I think it may be called the scientific view of a nation—is that of an organized whole, kept up to a high pitch of internal efficiency by insuring that its numbers are substantially recruited from the better stocks, and kept up to a high pitch of external efficiency by contest, chiefly by way of war with inferior races, and with equal races by the struggle for trade-routes and for the sources of raw material and of food supply. This is the natural history view of mankind, and I do not think you can in its main features subvert it. . . .

. . . Is it not a fact that the daily bread of our millions of workers depends on their having somebody to work for? that if we give up the contest for trade-routes and for free markets and for waste lands, we indirectly give up our food-supply? Is it not a fact that our strength depends on these and upon our colonies, and that our colonies have been won by the ejection of inferior races, and are maintained against equal races only by respect for the present power of our empire? . . .

. . . We find that the law of the survival of the fitter is true of mankind, but that the struggle is that of the gregarious animal. A community not knit together by strong social instincts, by sympathy between man and man, and class and class, cannot face the external contest, the competition with other nations, by peace or by war, for the raw material of production and for its food supply. This struggle of tribe with tribe, and nation with nation, may have its mournful side; but we see as a result of it the gradual progress of mankind to higher intellectual and physical efficiency. It is idle to condemn it; we can only see that it exists and recognise what we have gained by it—civilization and social sympathy. But while the statesman has to watch this external struggle, . . . he must be very cautious that the nation is not silently rotting at its core. He must insure that the fertility of the inferior stocks is checked, and that of the superior stocks encouraged; he must regard with suspicion anything that tempts the physically and mentally fitter men and women to remain childless. . . .

. . . The path of progress is strewn with the wrecks of nations; traces are everywhere to be seen of the hecatombs [slaughtered remains] of inferior races, and of victims who found not the narrow way to perfection. Yet these dead people are, in very truth, the stepping stones on which mankind has arisen to the higher intellectual and deeper emotional life of today.

5 Anti-Semitism: Regression to Mythical Thinking

Anti-Semitism, a European phenomenon of long standing, rose to new prominence in the late nineteenth century. Formerly segregated by law into ghettoes, Jews, under the aegis of the Enlightenment and the French Revolution, had gained legal equality in most European lands. In the nineteenth century, Jews participated in the economic and cultural progress of the times and often achieved distinction in business, the professions, and the arts and sciences. However, driven by irrational fears and mythical conceptions that had survived from the Middle Ages, many people regarded Jews as a dangerous race of international conspirators and foreign intruders who threatened their nations.

Throughout the nineteenth century, anti-Semitic outrages occurred in many European lands. Russian anti-Semitism assumed a particularly violent form in the infamous pogroms—murderous mob attacks on Jews. Between 1881 and 1921 there were three large-scale waves of pogroms in Russia. The civil and military authorities generally made no attempt to stop the murderous rampages and, at times, provided support. The worst of the pogroms occurred during the civil war that followed the Bolshevik Revolution of 1917; some 60,000 Jews were slaughtered, particularly in Ukraine, long a hotbed of anti-Semitism. Even in France, the center of the Enlightenment, anti-Semitism proved a powerful force. At the time of the Dreyfus affair, Catholic and nationalist zealots demanded that Jews be deprived of their civil rights. In Germany, anti-Semitism became associated with the ideological defense of a distinctive German culture, the volkish

thought popular in the last part of the nineteenth century. After the foundation of the German Empire in 1871, the pace of economic and cultural change quickened, and with it the cultural disorientation that fanned anti-Semitism. Volkish thinkers, who valued traditional Germany—the landscape, the peasant, and the village—associated Jews with the changes brought about by rapid industrialization and modernization. Compounding the problem was the influx into Germany of Jewish immigrants from the Russian Empire, who were searching for a better life and brought with them their own distinctive culture and religion, which many Germans found offensive. Nationalists and conservatives used anti-Semitism in an effort to gain a mass following.

Racial-nationalist considerations were the decisive force behind modern anti-Semitism. Racists said that the Jews were a wicked race of Asiatics, condemned by their genes; they differed physically, intellectually, and spiritually from Europeans who were descendants of ancient Ayrans.

German racists in particular embraced the ideas of Stewart Houston Chamberlain, who pitted Aryans and Jews against each other in a struggle of world historical importance. As agents of a spiritually empty capitalism and divisive liberalism, the Jews, said Chamberlain, were the opposite of the idealistic, heroic, and faithful Germans. Chamberlain denied that Jesus was a Jew, hinting that he was of Aryan stock, and held that the goal of the Jew was "to put his foot upon the neck of all the nations of the world and be lord and possessor of the whole earth." Racial anti-Semitism became a powerful force in European intellectual life, especially in Germany. It was the seedbed of Hitler's movement.

Hermann Ahlwardt
THE SEMITIC VERSUS THE TEUTONIC RACE

In the following reading, Hermann Ahlwardt (1846–1914), an anti-Semitic member of the Reichstag and author of *The Desperate Struggle Between Aryan and Jew,* addresses the chamber on March 6, 1895, with a plea to close Germany's borders to Jewish immigrants. His speech reflects the anti-Semitic rhetoric popular among German conservatives before World War I. The material in parentheses is by Paul W. Massing, translator and editor.

It is certainly true that there are Jews in our country of whom nothing adverse can be said. Nevertheless, the Jews as a whole must be considered harmful, for the racial traits of this people are of a kind that in the long run do not agree with the racial traits of the Teutons.[1] Every Jew who at this very moment has not as yet transgressed is likely to do so at some future time under given circumstances because his racial characteristics drive him on in that direction. . . .

My political friends do not hold the view that we fight the Jews because of their religion. . . . We could not dream of waging a political struggle against anyone because of his

[1]Teutons refers to the quintessential Germans. The name comes from a German tribe that once defeated a Roman army.

religion. . . . We hold the view that the Jews are a different race, a different people with entirely different character traits.

Experience in all fields of nature shows that innate racial characteristics which have been acquired by the race in the course of many thousands of years are the strongest and most enduring factors that exist, and that therefore we can rid ourselves of the characteristics of our race no more than can the Jews. One need not fight the Jew individually, and we are not doing that, by the way. But, when countless specimens prove the existence of certain racial characteristics and when these characters are such as to make impossible a common life, well, then I believe that we who are natives here, who have tilled the soil and defended it against all enemies—that we have a duty to take a stand against the Jews who are of a quite different nature.

We Teutons are rooted in the cultural soil of labor. . . . The Jews do not believe in the culture of labor, they do not want to create values themselves, but want to appropriate, without working, the values which others have created; that is the cardinal difference that guides us in all our considerations. . . .

Herr Deputy Rickert[2] here has just expounded how few Jews we have altogether and that their number is steadily declining. Well, gentlemen, why don't you go to the main business centers and see for yourselves whether the percentages indicated by Herr Rickert prevail there too. Why don't you walk along the Leipzigerstrasse (in Berlin) or the Zeil in Frankfurt and have a look at the shops? Wherever there are opportunities to make money, the Jews have established themselves, but not in order to work—no, they let others work for them and take what the others have produced by their labor.

Deputy Hasse . . . has committed the grave mistake of putting the Jews and other peoples on the same level, and that is the worst mistake that we could possibly make.

The Jews have an attitude toward us which differs totally from that of other peoples. It is one thing when a Pole, a Russian, a Frenchman, a Dane immigrates to our country, and quite another thing when a Jew settles here. . . . Once our (Polish, etc.) guests have lived here for ten, twenty years, they come to resemble us. For they have stood with us on the same cultural soil of labor. . . . After thirty, forty years they have become Germans and their grandchildren would be indistinguishable from us except for the strange-sounding names they still bear. The Jews have lived here for 700, 800 years, but have they become Germans? Have they placed themselves on the cultural soil of labor? They never even dreamed of such a thing; as soon as they arrived, they started to cheat and they have been doing that ever since they have been in Germany. . . .

The Jews should not be admitted, whether or not there is overpopulation, for they do not belong to a productive race, they are exploiters, parasites. . . .

(Answering Rickert's arguments that . . . it would be a shame if fifty million Germans were afraid of a few Jews, Ahlwardt continued:) . . .

Herr Rickert, who is just as tall as I am, is afraid of one single cholera bacillus—well, gentlemen, the Jews are just that, cholera bacilli!

Gentlemen, the crux of the matter is Jewry's capacity for contagion and exploitation. . . . How many thousands of Germans have perished as a result of this Jewish exploitation, how many may have hanged themselves, shot themselves, drowned themselves, how many may have ended by the wayside as tramps in America or drawn their last breath in the gutter, all of them people who had worked industriously on the soil their fathers had acquired, perhaps in hundreds of years of hard work. . . . Don't you feel any pity for those countless Germans? Are they to perish unsung? Ah, why were they foolish enough to let themselves be cheated? But the Germans are by no means so foolish, they are far more intelligent than the Jews. All inventions, all great

[2]Heinrich Rickert, a leader of the Progressives and an outspoken opponent of anti-Semitism, had pointed out that the Jews constituted only 1.29 percent of the population of Prussia. What enraged the German Right was that the Jews accounted for 9.58 percent of the university students in Prussia.

ideas come from the Germans and not from the Jews. No, I shall tell you the national difference. The German is fundamentally trusting, his heart is full of loyalty and confidence. The Jew gains this confidence, only to betray it at the proper moment, ruining and pauperizing the German. This abuse of confidence on the part of the Jews is their main weapon. And these Jewish scoundrels are to be defended here! Is there no one to think of all those hundreds of thousands, nor of those millions of workers whose wages grow smaller and smaller because Jewish competition brings the prices down? One always hears: you must be humane toward the Jews. The humanitarianism of our century . . . is our curse. Why aren't you for once humane toward the oppressed? You'd better exterminate those beasts of prey and you'd better start by not letting any more of them into our country. . . .

(Taking issue with the liberals' argument of Jewish achievements in the arts, Ahlwardt declared:)

Art in my opinion is the capacity for expressing one's innermost feelings in such a way as to arouse the same feelings in the other person. Now the Jewish world of emotions (*Gefühlswelt*) and the Teutonic world of emotions are two quite different things. German art can express only German feelings; Jewish art only Jewish feelings. Because Jewry has been thrusting itself forward everywhere, it has also thrust itself forward in the field of art and therefore the art that is now in the foreground is Jewish art. Nowadays the head of a family must be very careful when he decides to take his family to the theater lest his Teutonic feelings be outraged by the infamous Jewish art that has spread everywhere.

The Jew is no German. If you say, the Jew was born in Germany, he was nursed by a German wetnurse, he abides by German laws, he has to serve as a soldier—and what kind of a soldier at that! let's not talk about it—he fulfills all his obligations, he pays his taxes—then I say that all this is not the crucial factor with regard to his nationality; the crucial factor is the race from which he stems. Permit me to make a rather trite comparison which I have already used elsewhere in my speeches: a horse that is born in a cowshed is far from being a cow.

A Jew who was born in Germany does not thereby become a German; he is still a Jew. Therefore it is imperative that we realize that Jewish racial characteristics differ so greatly from ours that a common life of Jews and Germans under the same laws is quite impossible because the Germans will perish. . . .

. . . I beg you from the bottom of my heart not to take this matter* lightly but as a very serious thing. It is a question of life and death for our people. . . .

We wouldn't think of going as far as have the Austrian anti-Semites in the Federal Council (*Reichsrat*) and to move that a bounty be paid for every Jew shot or to decree that he who kills a Jew shall inherit his property. We have no such intention. We shall not go as far as that. What we want is a clear and reasonable separation of the Jews from the Germans. An immediate prerequisite is that we slam the door and see to it that no more of them get in.†

*Prohibition of Jewish immigration.

†At the end of the debate a vote was taken, with 218 representatives present. Of these, 51 voted for, 167 against the motion.

Édouard Drumont
JEWISH FRANCE

Édouard Drumont (1842–1917), a journalist and rabid conservative, became in the 1880s the mouthpiece of French anti-Semitism. Drumont glorified attachment to the soil, obedience to authority, and the moral discipline of an authoritarian Catholic church, addressing himself to peasants and petty bourgeois folk—to

those layers of the population that preferred the simplicity of the past to the fast-moving, urban complexity of the late nineteenth century. He especially deplored the new materialism with its self-indulgence and moral laxity.

To him the chief source of the contemporary degeneracy was the Jews. In 1886, he published the book that made him famous, called *La France Juive (Jewish France).* Advertised as an essay on contemporary history, it ascribed to Jews repulsive moral attributes, repeated the medieval myth that Jews murdered Christian children for ritual purposes, and propagated the bizarre theory that Jews were in a conspiracy to dominate France and the rest of Europe. The Jews, said Drumont, caused the ruin of Europe. Reprinted many times—his book sold over a million copies—it shaped public opinion for the conviction in 1894 of Captain Alfred Dreyfus, the first Jewish officer to be appointed to the General Staff of the French army, on faked evidence of high treason. In the following passage from *La France Juive,* Drumont contrasts the Semitic Jews with the Aryan French.

Let us examine now the essential traits which differentiate Jews from other people, beginning with ethnographic, physiological, and psychological comparisons of the Semite with the Aryan. These are two distinct races irremediably hostile to each other, whose antagonism has troubled the past and will cause still more trouble in the future.

The generic name Aryan derives from a Sanskrit word signifying "noble," "illustrious," "generous," standing for the superior family of the Indo-European family. . . . All the nations of Europe are descended by a straight line from the Aryan race, from which all great civilizations have sprung. . . . The Aryan or Indo-European race alone possesses the notion of justice, the sentiment of freedom, and the concept of the Beautiful. . . .

From the earliest moment of history we find the Aryan at war with the Semite. The dream of the Semite, indeed its obsession, has always been to reduce the Aryan into servants, to throw them into subjection. . . . Today Semitism feels sure of victory. It has replaced violence by wily tricks. The noisy invasion has been replaced by silent, progressive, slow penetration. Armed hordes no longer announce their arrival by shouts, but separate individuals, gathering in small groups, opportunistically infiltrate the state, taking possession of all important positions, all the functions in the country from the lowest to the highest. Spreading out from the area of Vilna [in Russia] they have occupied Germany, leaped over the Vosges mountains, and conquered France.

There was nothing brutal in this advance; it was a soft takeover accomplished in an insinuating manner of chasing the indigenous people from their homes, their source of income, in a velvety way depriving them of their goods, their tradition, their morals, and eventually their religion. . . . By their qualities as well as their faults, the two races [Jews and Aryans] are condemned to hurt each other.

The Semite is mercantile, greedy, scheming, subtle, crafty. The Aryan is enthusiastic, heroic, chivalrous, disinterested, straight-forward, trusting to the point of naiveté. The Semite is earthbound, seeing nothing beyond the present life. The Aryan is the child of heaven, relentlessly preoccupied with superior aspirations. One lives among realities, the other among ideals.

The Semite operates by instinct; he has the vocation of a trader, a genius for exchange, for every occasion to take advantage of his fellow man. The Aryan is devoted to life on the land, a poet, a monk and above all a soldier. War is his true element; he exposes himself joyfully to danger; he braves death. The Semite lacks any creative faculty. By contrast the Aryan is an inventor. The Jew has not made the least invention. He rather exploits, organizes, and utilizes the inventions of creative Aryans, guarding them as though they were his own. . . . The Aryan organizes voyages of adventure and discovers America. The Semite . . . attends to all that has been explored and developed in order to enrich himself at the expense of others.

Theodor Herzl
THE JEWISH STATE

Theodor Herzl (1860–1904) was raised in a comfortable, Jewish, middle-class home. Moving from Budapest, where he was born, to Vienna, the capital of the Austro-Hungarian Empire, he started to practice law, but soon turned to journalism, writing from Paris for the leading Vienna newspaper. A keen observer of the contemporary scene, he vigorously agitated for the ideal of an independent Jewish state. It was not an original idea, but one that had recently found new advocates. Nationalist ferment was rising everywhere, often combined with virulent anti-Semitism. Under the circumstances, Herzl argued, security for Jews could be guaranteed only by a separate national state for Jews, preferably in Palestine.

In 1896, he published his program in a book, *Der Judenstaat (The Jewish State)*, in which he envisaged a glorious future for an independent Jewish state harmoniously cooperating with the local population. In the following year, he presided over the first Congress of Zionist Organizations held in Basel (Switzerland), attended mostly by Jews from central and eastern Europe. In its program the congress called for "a publicly guaranteed homeland for the Jewish people in the land of Israel." Subsequently, Herzl negotiated with the German emperor, the British government, and the sultan of the Ottoman Empire (of which Palestine was a part) for diplomatic support. In 1901, the Jewish National Fund was created to help settlers purchase land in Palestine. At his death, Herzl firmly expected a Jewish state to arise sometime in the future. The following excerpts from his book express the main points in his plea for a Jewish state.

We are a people—one people.

We have honestly endeavored everywhere to merge ourselves in the social life of surrounding communities and to preserve the faith of our fathers. We are not permitted to do so. In vain are we loyal patriots, our loyalty in some places running to extremes; in vain do we make the same sacrifices of life and property as our fellow-citizens; in vain do we strive to increase the fame of our native land in science and art, or her wealth by trade and commerce. In countries where we have lived for centuries we are still cried down as strangers, and often by those whose ancestors were not yet domiciled in the land where Jews had already had experience of suffering. . . . I think we shall not be left in peace.

Oppression and persecution cannot exterminate us. No nation on earth has survived such struggles and sufferings as we have gone through. Jew-baiting has merely stripped off our weaklings; the strong among us were invariably true to their race when persecution broke out against them. . . .

. . . [O]ld prejudices against us still lie deep in the hearts of the people. He who would have proofs of this need only listen to the people where they speak with frankness and simplicity: proverb and fairy-tale are both Anti-Semitic. . . .

No one can deny the gravity of the situation of the Jews. Wherever they live in perceptible numbers, they are more or less persecuted. Their equality before the law, granted by statute, has become practically a dead letter. They are debarred from filling even moderately high positions, either in the army, or in any public or private capacity. And attempts are made to thrust them out of business also: "Don't buy from Jews!"

Attacks in Parliaments, in assemblies, in the press, in the pulpit, in the street, on journeys—for example, their exclusion from certain hotels—even in places of recreation, become daily more numerous. The forms of persecutions vary according to the countries and social circles in which they occur. In Russia, imposts are levied on Jewish villages; in Rumania, a few persons are put to death; in Germany, they get a good beating occasionally; in Austria, Anti-Semites exercise terrorism over all public life; in Algeria, there are travelling agitators; in Paris, the Jews are shut out of the so-called best social circles and excluded from clubs. Shades of anti-Jewish feeling are innumerable. But this is not to be an attempt to make out a doleful category of Jewish hardships.

I do not intend to arouse sympathetic emotions on our behalf. That would be a foolish, futile, and undignified proceeding. I shall content myself with putting the following questions to the Jews: Is it not true that, in countries where we live in perceptible numbers, the position of Jewish lawyers, doctors, technicians, teachers, and employees of all descriptions becomes daily more intolerable? Is it not true, that the Jewish middle classes are seriously threatened? Is it not true, that the passions of the mob are incited against our wealthy people? Is it not true, that our poor endure greater sufferings than any other proletariat? I think that this external pressure makes itself felt everywhere. In our economically upper classes it causes discomfort, in our middle classes continual and grave anxieties, in our lower classes absolute despair.

Everything tends, in fact, to one and the same conclusion, which is clearly enunciated in that classic Berlin phrase: *"Juden Raus!"* (Out with the Jews!)

I shall now put the Question in the briefest possible form: Are we to "get out" now and where to?

Or, may we yet remain? And, how long?

Let us first settle the point of staying where we are. Can we hope for better days, can we possess our souls in patience, can we wait in pious resignation till the princes and peoples of this earth are more mercifully disposed towards us? I say that we cannot hope for a change in the current of feeling. . . . The nations in whose midst Jews live are all either covertly or openly Anti-Semitic. . . .

. . . We might perhaps be able to merge ourselves entirely into surrounding races, if these were to leave us in peace for a period of two generations. But they will not leave us in peace. For a little period they manage to tolerate us, and then their hostility breaks out again and again. . . .

Thus, whether we like it or not, we are now, and shall henceforth remain, a historic group with unmistakable characteristics common to us all.

We are one people—our enemies have made us one without our consent, as repeatedly happens in history. Distress binds us together, and, thus united, we suddenly discover our strength. Yes, we are strong enough to form a State, and, indeed, a model State. We possess all human and material resources necessary for the purpose. . . .

Let the sovereignty be granted us over a portion of the globe large enough to satisfy the rightful requirements of a nation; the rest we shall manage for ourselves.

The creation of a new State is neither ridiculous nor impossible. We have in our day witnessed the process in connection with nations which were not largely members of the middle class, but poorer, less educated, and consequently weaker than ourselves. . . .

Palestine is our ever-memorable historic home. The very name of Palestine would attract our people with a force of marvellous potency. If His Majesty the Sultan were to give us Palestine, we could in return undertake to regulate the whole finances of Turkey. We should there form a portion of a rampart of Europe against Asia, an outpost of civilization as opposed to barbarism. We should as a neutral State remain in contact with all Europe, which would have to guarantee our existence. The sanctuaries of Christendom would be safeguarded by assigning to them an extra-territorial status such as is well-known to the law of nations. We should form a guard of honor about these sanctuaries, answering for the fulfillment of this duty with our existence. This guard of honor would be the great symbol of the solution of the Jewish Question after eighteen centuries of Jewish suffering.

6 Irrationalism

The outlook of the Enlightenment, which stressed science, political freedom, the rational reform of society, and the certainty of progress, was the dominant intellectual current in the late nineteenth century. However, in the closing decades of the century, several thinkers challenged and rejected the Enlightenment outlook. In particular, they maintained that people are not fundamentally rational, that below surface rationality lie impulses, instincts, and drives that constitute a deeper reality.

The new insights into the irrational side of human nature and the growing assault on reason had immense implications for political life. In succeeding decades, these currents of irrationalism would be ideologized and politicized by unscrupulous demagogues, who sought to mobilize and manipulate the masses. The popularity after World War I of fascist movements, which openly denigrated reason and exalted race, blood, action, and will, demonstrated the naiveté of nineteenth-century liberals, who believed that reason had triumphed in human affairs.

Friedrich Nietzsche *THE WILL TO POWER* AND *THE ANTICHRIST*

A powerful attack on the rational-scientific tradition of the Enlightenment came from German philosopher Friedrich Nietzsche (1844–1900). Although scholars pay tribute to Nietzsche's originality and genius, they are often in sharp disagreement over the meaning and influence of his work. Nietzsche was a relentless critic of modern society. He attacked democracy, universal suffrage, equality, and socialism for suppressing a higher type of human existence. Nietzsche was also critical of the Western rational tradition. The theoretical outlook, the excessive intellectualizing of philosophers, he said, smothers the will, thereby stifling creativity and nobility; reason also falsifies life through the claim that it allows apprehension of universal truth. Nietzsche was not opposed to the critical use of the intellect, but like the romantics, he focused on the immense vitality of the emotions. He also held that life is a senseless flux devoid of any overarching purpose. There are no moral values revealed by God. Indeed, Nietzsche proclaimed that God is dead. Nor are values and certainties woven into the fabric of nature that can be apprehended by reason—the "natural rights of man," for example. All the values taught by Christian and bourgeois thinkers are without foundation, said Nietzsche. There is only naked man living in a godless and absurd world.

Nietzsche called for the emergence of the *overman* (sometimes superman), a higher type of man who asserts his will, gives order to chaotic passions, makes great demands on himself, and lives life with a fierce joy. The overman aspires to self-perfection. Without fear or guilt, he creates his own values and defines his own life. In this way, he overcomes nihilism—the belief that there is nothing of ultimate value. It is such rare individuals, the highest specimens of humanity, that concern Nietzsche, not the herdlike masses.

The overman grasps the central reality of human existence—that people instinctively, uncompromisingly, ceaselessly, strive for power. The will to exert power is the determining factor in domestic politics, personal relations, and international affairs. Life is a contest in which the enhancement of power is the ultimate purpose of our actions; it brings supreme enjoyment: "the love of power is the demon of men. Let them have everything—health, food, a place to live, entertainment—they are and remain unhappy and low-spirited: for the demon waits and waits and will be satisfied. Take everything from them and satisfy this and they are almost happy—as happy as men and demons can be."

First published in 1901, one year after Nietzsche's death, *The Will to Power* consists of the author's notes written in the years 1883 to 1888. The following passages from this work show Nietzsche's contempt for democracy and socialism and proclaim the will to power.

THE WILL TO POWER

720 (1886–1887)

The most fearful and fundamental desire in man, his drive for power—this drive is called "freedom"—must be held in check the longest. This is why ethics . . . has hitherto aimed at holding the desire for power in check: it disparages the tyrannical individual and with its glorification of social welfare and patriotism emphasizes the power-instinct of the herd.

728 (March–June 1888)

. . . A society that definitely and *instinctively* gives up war and conquest is in decline: it is ripe for democracy and the rule of shopkeepers—In most cases, to be sure, assurances of peace are merely narcotics.

751 (March–June 1888)

"The will to power" is so hated in democratic ages that their entire psychology seems directed toward belittling and defaming it. . . .

752 (1884)

. . . Democracy represents the disbelief in great human beings and an elite society: "Everyone is equal to everyone else." "At bottom we are one and all self-seeking cattle and mob."

753 (1885)

I am opposed to 1. socialism, because it dreams quite naively of "the good, true, and beautiful" and of "equal rights" (—anarchism also desires the same ideal, but in a more brutal fashion); 2. parliamentary government and the press, because these are the means by which the herd animal becomes master.

762 (1885)

European democracy represents a release of forces only to a very small degree. It is above all a release of laziness, of weariness, of *weakness*.

765 (Jan.–Fall 1888)

. . . Another Christian concept, no less crazy, has passed even more deeply into the tissue of modernity: the concept of the "equality of souls before God." This concept furnishes the prototype of all theories of equal rights: mankind was first taught to stammer the proposition of equality in a religious context, and only later was it made into morality: no wonder that man ended by taking it seriously, taking it practically!—that is to say, politically, democratically, socialistically, in the spirit of the pessimism of indignation.

854 (1884)

In the age of *suffrage universel,* i.e., when everyone may sit in judgment on everyone and everything, I feel impelled to reestablish *order of rank.*

855 (Spring–Fall 1887)

What determines rank, sets off rank, is only quanta of power, and nothing else.

857 (Jan.–Fall 1888)

I distinguish between a type of ascending life and another type of decay, disintegration, weakness. Is it credible that the question of the relative rank of these two types still needs to be posed?

858 (Nov. 1887–March 1888)

What determines your rank is the quantum of power you are: the rest is cowardice.

861 (1884)

A declaration of war on the masses by *higher men* is needed! Everywhere the mediocre are combining in order to make themselves master! Everything that makes soft and effeminate, that serves the ends of the "people" or the "feminine," works in favor of *suffrage universel*, i.e., the dominion of *inferior* men. But we should take reprisal and bring this whole affair (which in Europe commenced with Christianity) to light and to the bar of judgment.

862 (1884)

A doctrine is needed powerful enough to work as a breeding agent: strengthening the strong, paralyzing and destructive for the world-weary.

The annihilation of the decaying races. Decay of Europe.—The annihilation of slavish evaluations.—Dominion over the earth as a means of producing a higher type.—The annihilation of the tartuffery [hypocrisy] called "morality." . . . The annihilation of *suffrage universel;* i.e., the system through which the lowest natures prescribe themselves as laws for the higher.—The annihilation of mediocrity and its acceptance. (The onesided, individuals—peoples; to strive for fullness of nature through the pairing of opposites: race mixture to this end).—The new courage—no *a priori* [innate and universal] truths (such truths were sought by those accustomed to faith!), but a *free* subordination to a ruling idea that has its time: e.g., time as a property of space, etc.

870 (1884)

The root of all evil: that the slavish morality of meekness, chastity, selflessness, absolute obedience, has triumphed—ruling natures were thus condemned (1) to hypocrisy, (2) to torments of conscience—creative natures felt like rebels against God, uncertain and inhibited by eternal values. . . .

In summa: the best things have been slandered because the weak or the immoderate swine have cast a bad light on them—and the best men have remained hidden—and have often misunderstood themselves.

874 (1884)

The degeneration of the rulers and the ruling classes has been the cause of the greatest mischief in history! Without the Roman Caesars and Roman society, the insanity of Christianity would never have come to power.

When lesser men begin to doubt whether higher men exist, then the danger is great! And one ends by discovering that there is *virtue* also among the lowly and subjugated, the poor in spirit, and that *before God* men are equal—which has so far been the . . . [height] of nonsense on earth! For ultimately, the higher men measured themselves according to the standard of virtue of slaves—found they were "proud," etc., found all their higher qualities reprehensible.

997 (1884)

I teach: that there are higher and lower men, and that a single individual can under certain circumstances justify the existence of whole millennia—that is, a full, rich, great, whole human being in relation to countless incomplete fragmentary men.

998 (1884)

The highest men live beyond the rulers, freed from all bonds; and in the rulers they have their instruments.

999 (1884)

Order of rank: He who *determines* values and directs the will of millennia by giving direction to the highest natures is the *highest* man.

1001 (1884)

Not "mankind" but *overman* is the goal!

1067 (1885)

. . . *This world is the will to power—and nothing besides!* And you yourselves are also this will to power—and nothing besides!

Nietzsche regarded Christianity as a life-denying religion that appeals to the masses. Fearful and resentful of their betters, he said, the masses espouse a faith that preaches equality and compassion. He maintained that Christianity has "waged a war to the death against (the) higher type of man." The following passages are from *The Antichrist,* written in 1888.

THE ANTICHRIST

2. What is good?—All that heightens the feeling of power, the will to power, power itself in man.

What is bad?—All that proceeds from weakness.

What is happiness?—The feeling that power *increases*—that a resistance is overcome.

Not contentment, but more power; *not* peace at all, but war; *not* virtue, but proficiency (virtue in the Renaissance style, *virtù,* virtue free of moralic acid).

The weak and ill-constituted shall perish: first principle of *our* philanthropy. And one shall help them to do so.

What is more harmful than any vice?—Active sympathy for the ill-constituted and weak—Christianity. . . .

3. The problem I raise here is not what ought to succeed mankind in the sequence of species (—the human being is an *end*—): but what type of human being one ought to *breed,* ought to *will,* as more valuable, more worthy of life, more certain of the future.

This more valuable type has existed often enough already: but as a lucky accident, as an exception, never as *willed.* He has rather been the most feared, he has hitherto been virtually *the* thing to be feared—and out of fear the reverse type has been willed, bred, *achieved:* the domestic animal, the herd animal, the sick animal man—the Christian. . . .

5. One should not embellish or dress up Christianity: it has waged *a war to the death* against this *higher* type of man, it has excommunicated all the fundamental instincts of this type, it has distilled evil, the *Evil One,* out of

these instincts—the strong human being as the type of reprehensibility, as the "outcast." Christianity has taken the side of everything weak, base, ill-constituted, it has made an ideal out of *opposition* to the preservative instincts of strong life; it has depraved the reason even of the intellectually strongest natures by teaching men to feel the supreme values of intellectuality as sinful, as misleading, as *temptations.* The most deplorable example: the depraving of Pascal,[1] who believed his reason had been depraved by original sin while it had only been depraved by his Christianity! . . .

7. Christianity is called the religion of *pity.*—Pity stands in antithesis to the tonic emotions which enhance the energy of the feeling of life: it has a depressive effect. One loses force when one pities. . . .

15. In Christianity neither morality nor religion come into contact with reality at any point. Nothing but imaginary *causes* ("God," "soul," "ego," "spirit," "free will"—or "unfree will"): nothing but imaginary *effects* ("sin," "redemption," "grace," "punishment," "forgiveness of sins"). . . .

18. The Christian conception of God—God as God of the sick, God as spider, God as spirit—is one of the most corrupt conceptions of God arrived at on earth: perhaps it even represents the low-water mark in the descending development of the God type. God degenerated to the *contradiction of life,* instead of being its transfiguration and eternal *Yes!* In God a declaration of hostility towards life, nature, the will to life! God the formula for every calumny of "this world," for every lie about 'the next world'! In God, nothingness deified, the will to nothingness sanctified! . . .

21. In Christianity the instincts of the subjugated and oppressed come into the foreground: it is the lowest classes which seek their salvation in it. . . .

43. The poison of the doctrine "*equal* rights for all"—this has been more thoroughly sowed by Christianity than by anything else; from the most secret recesses of base instincts, Christianity has waged a war to the death against every feeling of reverence and distance between man and man, against, that is, the *precondition* of every elevation, every increase in culture—it has forged out of the [resentment] of the masses its *chief weapon* against *us,* against everything noble, joyful, high-spirited on earth, against our happiness on earth. . . . "Immortality" granted to every Peter and Paul has been the greatest and most malicious outrage on *noble* mankind ever committed.—*And* let us not underestimate the fatality that has crept out of Christianity even into politics! No one any longer possesses today the courage to claim special privileges or the right to rule, the courage to feel a sense of reverence towards himself and towards his equals—the courage for a *pathos of distance.* . . . Our politics is *morbid* from this lack of courage!—The aristocratic outlook has been undermined most deeply by the lie of equality of souls; and if the belief in the "prerogative of the majority" makes revolutions and *will continue to make them*—it is Christianity, let there be no doubt about it, *Christian* value judgement which translates every revolution into mere blood and crime! Christianity is a revolt of everything that crawls along the ground directed against that which is *elevated:* the Gospel of the "lowly" *makes* low.

[1]Blaise Pascal (1623–1662) was a French mathematician, philosopher, and eloquent defender of the Christian faith.

Sigmund Freud
CIVILIZATION AND ITS DISCONTENTS

After graduating from medical school in Vienna, Sigmund Freud (1856–1939), the founder of psychoanalysis, specialized in the treatment of nervous disorders. By encouraging his patients to speak to him about their troubles, Freud was able to probe deeper into their minds. These investigations led him to conclude

that childhood fears and experiences, often sexual in nature, accounted for neuroses, for example, hysteria, anxiety, depression, and obsessions. So threatening and painful were these childhood emotions and experiences that his patients banished them from conscious memory to the realm of the unconscious. To understand and treat neurotic behavior, Freud said it is necessary to look behind overt symptoms and bring to the surface emotionally charged experiences and fears—childhood traumas—that lie buried in the unconscious. Freud probed the unconscious by urging his patients to say whatever came to their minds. This procedure, called free association, rests on the premise that spontaneous and uninhibited talk reveals a person's underlying preoccupations, his or her inner world. A second avenue to the unconscious is the analysis of dreams; an individual's dreams, said Freud, reveal his or her secret wishes.

Freud's scientific investigation of psychic development led him to conclude that powerful mental processes hidden from consciousness govern human behavior more than reason does. His exploration of the unconscious produced a new image of the human being that has had a profound impact on twentieth-century thought.

In the tradition of the Enlightenment philosophes, Freud valued reason and science, but he did not share the philosophes' confidence in human goodness and humanity's capacity for future progress. In *Civilization and Its Discontents* (1930), excerpted below, Freud posited the frightening theory that human beings are driven by an inherent aggressiveness that threatens civilized life—that civilization is fighting a losing battle with our aggressive instincts. Although Freud's pessimism was no doubt influenced by the tragedy of World War I, many ideas expressed in *Civilization and Its Discontents* derived from views that he had formulated decades earlier.

The element of truth behind all this, which people are so ready to disavow, is that men are not gentle creatures who want to be loved, and who at most can defend themselves if they are attacked; they are, on the contrary, creatures among whose instinctual endowments is to be reckoned a powerful share of aggressiveness. As a result, their neighbour is for them not only a potential helper or sexual object, but also someone who tempts them to satisfy their aggressiveness on him, to exploit his capacity for work without compensation, to use him sexually without his consent, to seize his possessions, to humiliate him, to cause him pain, to torture and to kill him. *Homo homini lupus.* [Man is wolf to man.] Who, in the face of all his experience of life and of history, will have the courage to dispute this assertion? As a rule this cruel aggressiveness waits for some provocation or puts itself at the service of some other purpose, whose goal might also have been reached by milder measures. In circumstances that are favourable to it, when the mental counter-forces which ordinarily inhibit it are out of action, it also manifests itself spontaneously and reveals man as a savage beast to whom consideration towards his own kind is something alien. Anyone who calls to mind the atrocities committed during the racial migrations or the invasions of the Huns, or by the people known as Mongols under Jenghiz Khan and Tamerlane, or at the capture of Jerusalem by the pious Crusaders, or even, indeed, the horrors of the recent World War—anyone who calls these things to mind will have to bow humbly before the truth of this view.

The existence of this inclination to aggression, which we can detect in ourselves and justly assume to be present in others, is the factor which disturbs our relations with our neighbour and which forces civilization into such a high expenditure [of energy]. In consequence of this primary mutual hostility of human beings, civilized society is perpetually threatened with disintegration. The interest of work in common would not hold it together; instinctual passions are stronger than reasonable interests. Civilization has to use its utmost efforts in order to set limits to man's aggressive instincts and to hold the manifestations of them in check by physical reaction-formations. Hence, therefore, the use of methods intended to incite people into identifications and aim-inhibited relationships of love, hence the restriction upon sexual life, and hence too the ideal's commandment to love one's neighbour as oneself—a commandment which is really justified by the fact that nothing else runs so strongly counter to the original nature of man. In spite of every effort, these endeavours of civilization have not so far achieved very much. It hopes to prevent the crudest excesses of brutal violence by itself assuming the right to use violence against criminals, but the law is not able to lay hold of the more cautious and refined manifestations of human aggressiveness. The time comes when each one of us has to give up as illusions the expectations which, in his youth, he pinned upon his fellowmen, and when he may learn how much difficulty and pain has been added to his life by their ill-will. At the same time, it would be unfair to reproach civilization with trying to eliminate strife and competition from human activity. These things are undoubtedly indispensable. But opposition is not necessarily enmity; it is merely misused and made an *occasion* for enmity.

The communists believe that they have found the path to deliverance from our evils. According to them, man is wholly good and is well-disposed to his neighbour; but the institution of private property has corrupted his nature. The ownership of private wealth gives the individual power, and with it the temptation to ill-treat his neighbour; while the man who is excluded from possession is bound to rebel in hostility against his oppressor. If private property were abolished, all wealth held in common, and everyone allowed to share in the enjoyment of it, ill-will and hostility would disappear among men. Since everyone's needs would be satisfied, no one would have any reason to regard another as his enemy; all would willingly undertake the work that was necessary. I have no concern with any economic criticisms of the communist system. . . . But I am able to recognize that the psychological premises on which the system is based are an untenable illusion. In abolishing private property we deprive the human love of aggression of one of its instruments, certainly a strong one, though certainly not the strongest; but we have in no way altered the differences in power and influence which are misused by aggressiveness, nor have we altered anything in its nature. Aggressiveness was not created by property. It reigned almost without limit in primitive times, when property was still very scanty, and it already shows itself in the nursery almost before property has given up its primal, anal form; it forms the basis of every relation of affection and love among people (with the single exception, perhaps, of the mother's relation to her male child). If we do away with personal rights over material wealth, there still remains prerogative in the field of sexual relationships, which is bound to become the source of the strongest dislike and the most violent hostility among men who in other respects are on an equal footing. If we were to remove this factor, too, by allowing complete freedom of sexual life and thus abolishing the family, the germ-cell of civilization, we cannot, it is true, easily foresee what new paths the development of civilization could take; but one thing we can expect, and that is that this indestructible feature of human nature will follow it there.

It is clearly not easy for men to give up the satisfaction of this inclination to aggression. They do not feel comfortable without it. . . .

If civilization imposes such great sacrifices not only on man's sexuality but on his aggressivity, we can understand better why it is hard for him to be happy in that civilization. . . .

In all that follows I adopt the standpoint, therefore, that the inclination to aggression is an original, self-subsisting instinctual disposition in man, and I return to my view that it constitutes the greatest impediment to civilization.

CHAPTER TWO

WORLD WAR I

In August 1914, many people welcomed the outbreak of war, which they saw as a relief from the boredom and materialism of bourgeois society. During these heady days, women too expressed their enthusiasm for the conflict. *(Interfoto/Alamy)*

To many Europeans, the opening years of the twentieth century seemed full of promise. Advances in science and technology, the rising standard of living, the expansion of education, and the absence of wars between the Great Powers since the Franco-Prussian conflict (1870–1871) all contributed to a general feeling of optimism. Yet these accomplishments hid disruptive forces that were propelling Europe toward a cataclysm. On June 28, 1914, Archduke Francis Ferdinand, heir to the throne of Austria-Hungary, was assassinated by Gavrilo Princip, a young Serbian nationalist (and Hapsburg subject), at Sarajevo in the Austrian province of Bosnia, inhabited largely by South Slavs. The assassination triggered those explosive forces that lay below the surface of European life. Six weeks later, Europe was engulfed in a general war that altered the course of Western civilization.

Belligerent, irrational, and extreme nationalism was a principal cause of World War I. Placing their country above everything, nationalists in various countries fomented hatred of other nationalities and called for the expansion of their own nation's borders—attitudes that fostered belligerence in foreign relations. Wedded to nationalism was a militaristic view that regarded war as heroic and as the highest expression of individual and national life.

Yet Europe might have avoided the world war had the nations not been divided into hostile alliance systems. By 1907, the Triple Alliance of Germany, Austria-Hungary, and Italy confronted the loosely organized Triple Entente of France, Russia, and Great Britain. What German chancellor Otto von Bismarck said in 1879 was just as true in 1914: "The great powers of our time are like travellers, unknown to one another, whom chance has brought together in a carriage. They watch each other, and when one of them puts his hand into his pocket, his neighbor gets ready his own revolver in order to be able to fire the first shot."

A danger inherent in an alliance is that a country, knowing that it has the support of allies, may pursue an aggressive foreign policy and may be less likely to compromise during a crisis; also, a war between two states may well draw in the other allied powers. These dangers materialized in 1914.

In the diplomatic furor of July and early August 1914, following the assassination of Francis Ferdinand, several patterns emerged. Austria-Hungary, a multinational empire dominated by Germans and Hungarians, feared the nationalist aspirations of its Slavic minorities. The nationalist yearnings of neighboring Serbs aggravated Austria-Hungary's problems, for the Serbs, a South Slav people, wanted to create a Greater Serbia by uniting with the South Slavs of Austria-Hungary. If Slavic nationalism gained in intensity, the Austro-Hungarian (or Hapsburg) Empire would be broken into states based on nationality. Intent on foiling any attempts to undermine its territorial integrity by upstart states with irredentist claims, the multinational Austria-Hungary decided to use the assassination as justification for crushing Serbia.

The system of alliances escalated the tensions between Austria-Hungary and Serbia into a general European war. Germany saw itself threatened by the Triple Entente (a conviction based more on paranoia than on objective fact) and regarded Austria-Hungary as its only reliable ally. Holding that at all costs its ally must be kept strong, German officials supported Austria-Hungary's decision to crush Serbia. Fearing that Germany and Austria-Hungary aimed to extend their power into southeastern Europe, Russia would not permit the destruction of Serbia. With the support of France, Russia began to mobilize; when it moved to full mobilization, Germany declared war. As German battle plans, drawn up years before, called for a war with both France and Russia, France was drawn into the conflict; Germany's invasion of neutral Belgium brought Great Britain into the war.

Most European statesmen and military men believed the war would be over in a few months. Virtually no one anticipated that it would last more than four years and claim lives numbering in the millions.

World War I was a turning point in European history. In Russia, it led to the collapse of the tsarist autocracy and the rise of the Soviet state. The war created unsettling conditions that led to the emergence of fascist movements in Italy and Germany, and it initiated the steady decline of Britain and France from their positions of global dominance. Finally, the war shattered, perhaps forever, the Enlightenment belief in the inevitable and perpetual progress of Western civilization.

1 Militarism

Historians regard a surging militarism as an underlying cause of World War I. One sign of militarism was the rapid increase in expenditures for armaments in the years prior to 1914. Between 1910 and 1914, both Austria-Hungary and Germany, for example, doubled their military budgets. The arms race intensified suspicion among the Great Powers. A second danger was the increased power of the military in policymaking, particularly in Austria-Hungary and Germany. In the crisis following the assassination, generals tended to press for a military solution.

Heinrich von Treitschke
THE GREATNESS OF WAR

Coupled with the military's influence on state decisions was a romantic glorification of the nation and war, an attitude shared by both the elite and the masses. Although militarism generally pervaded Europe, it was particularly strong in Germany. In the following reading from *Politics,* the influential German historian Heinrich von Treitschke (1834–1896) glorifies warfare.

. . . One must say with the greatest determination: War is for an afflicted people the only remedy. When the State exclaims: My very existence is at stake! then social self-seeking must disappear and all party hatred be silent. The individual must forget his own *ego* and feel himself a member of the whole, he must recognize how negligible is his life compared with the good of the whole. Therein lies the greatness of war that the little man completely vanishes before the great thought of the State. The sacrifice of nationalities for one another is nowhere invested with such beauty as in war. At such a time the corn is separated from the chaff. All who lived through 1870 will understand the saying of Niebuhr[1] with regard to the year 1813, that he then experienced the "bliss of sharing with all his fellow citizens, with the scholar and the ignorant, the one common feeling—no man who enjoyed this experience will to his dying day forget how loving, friendly and strong he felt."

It is indeed political idealism which fosters war, whereas materialism rejects it. What a perversion of morality to want to banish heroism from human life. The heroes of a people are the personalities who fill the youthful souls with delight and enthusiasm, and amongst authors we as boys and youths admire most those whose words sound like a flourish of trumpets. He who cannot take pleasure therein, is too cowardly to take up arms himself for his fatherland. An appeal to Christianity in this matter is perverted. The Bible states expressly that the man in authority shall wield the sword; it states likewise that: "Greater love hath no man than this that he giveth his life for his friend." Those who preach the nonsense about everlasting peace do not understand the life of the Aryan race, the Aryans are before all brave. They have always been men enough to protect by the sword what they had won by the intellect. . . .

To the historian who lives in the realms of the Will, it is quite clear that the furtherance of an everlasting peace is fundamentally reactionary. He sees that to banish war from history would be to banish all progress and becoming. It is only the periods of exhaustion, weariness and mental stagnation that have dallied with the dream of everlasting peace. . . . The living God will see to it that war returns again and again as a terrible medicine for humanity.

[1]Barthold G. Niebuhr (1776–1831) was a Prussian historian. The passage refers to the German War of Liberation against Napoleon, which German patriots regarded as a glorious episode in their national history.

Friedrich von Bernhardi
GERMANY AND THE NEXT WAR

Friedrich von Bernhardi (1849–1930), a German general and influential military writer, considered war "a biological necessity of the first importance." The following excerpt comes from his work *Germany and the Next War*. Published in 1911, it had already gone into a sixth edition by 1913.

. . . War is a biological necessity of the first importance, a regulative element in the life of mankind which cannot be dispensed with, since without it an unhealthy development will follow, which excludes every advancement of the race, and therefore all real civilization. "War is the father of all things." The sages of antiquity long before Darwin recognized this.

The struggle for existence is, in the life of Nature, the basis of all healthy development. . . . The law of the stronger holds good everywhere. Those forms survive which are able to procure themselves the most favourable conditions of life, and to assert themselves in the universal economy of Nature. The weaker succumb. . . .

Struggle is, therefore, a universal law of Nature, and the instinct of self-preservation which leads to struggle is acknowledged to be a natural condition of existence.

Strong, healthy, and flourishing nations increase in numbers. From a given moment they require a continual expansion of their frontiers, they require new territory for the accommodation of their surplus population. Since almost every part of the globe is inhabited, new territory must, as a rule, be obtained at the cost of its possessors—that is to say, by conquest, which thus becomes a law of necessity.

The right of conquest is universally acknowledged.

. . . Vast territories inhabited by uncivilized masses are occupied by more highly civilized States, and made subject to their rule. Higher civilization and the correspondingly greater power are the foundations of the right to annexation. . . .

Lastly, in all times the right of conquest by war has been admitted. It may be that a growing people cannot win colonies from uncivilized races, and yet the State wishes to retain the surplus population which the mother-country can no longer feed. Then the only course left is to acquire the necessary territory by war. Thus the instinct of self-preservation leads inevitably to war, and the conquest of foreign soil. It is not the possessor, but the victor, who then has the right. . . .

In such cases might gives the right to occupy or to conquer. Might is at once the supreme right, and the dispute as to what is right is decided by the arbitrament of war. War gives a biologically just decision, since its decisions rest on the very nature of things. . . .

The knowledge, therefore, that war depends on biological laws leads to the conclusion that every attempt to exclude it from international relations must be demonstrably untenable.

Henri Massis and Alfred de Tarde
THE YOUNG PEOPLE OF TODAY

War fever was not limited to the Central Powers. A few years prior to the war, two French journalists, Henri Massis and Alfred de Tarde, undertook a survey of Parisian students enrolled at various elite educational institutions. The survey, which first appeared as a newspaper article in 1912 and then as a book in 1913, seemed to demonstrate that many young French males between the ages of eighteen and twenty-five had abandoned the Enlightenment humanitarianism of the older generation for a militant Catholicism, fervent nationalism, and romantic militarism. Excerpts from the survey follow.

The sentiment which underlies all these youthful attitudes, which unanimously accords with the deepest tendencies in their thought, is that of patriotic faith. That they are possessed of this sentiment is unequivocal and undeniable. Optimism, that state of mind which defines the attitude of these young people, manifests itself from the outset in the confidence which they place in the future of France: there they find their first motive for acting, the one which determines and directs all their activity.

The young men of today have read the word of their destiny in this French soul, which dictates to them a clear and imperious duty. . . .

Consider something even more significant. Students of advanced rhetoric in Paris, that is, the most cultivated elite among young people, declare that they find in warfare an aesthetic ideal of energy and strength. They believe that "France needs heroism in order to live." "Such is the faith," comments Monsieur Tourolle, "which consumes modern youth."

How many times in the last two years have we heard this repeated: "Better war than this eternal waiting!" There is no bitterness in this avowal, but rather a secret hope. . . .

War! The word has taken on a sudden glamour. It is a youthful word, wholly new, adorned with that seduction which the eternal bellicose instinct has revived in the hearts of men. These young men impute to it all the beauty with which they are in love and of which they have been deprived by ordinary life. Above all, war, in their eyes, is the occasion for the most noble of human virtues, those which they exalt above all others: energy, mastery, and sacrifice for a cause which transcends ourselves. With William James, they believe that life "would become odious if it offered neither risks nor rewards for the courageous man."

A professor of philosophy at the Lycée Henri IV confided to us: "I once spoke about war to my pupils. I explained to them that there were unjust wars, undertaken out of anger, and that it was necessary to justify the bellicose sentiment. Well, the class obviously did not follow me; they rejected that distinction."

Read this passage from a letter written to us by a young student of rhetoric, Alsatian in origin. "The existence that we lead does not satisfy us completely because, even if we possess all the elements of a good life, we cannot organize them in a practical, immediate deed that would take us, body and soul, and hurl us outside of ourselves. One event only will permit that deed—war; and hence we desire it. It is in the life of the camps, it is around the fire that we will experience the supreme expansion of those French powers that are within us. Our intellect will no longer be troubled in the face of the unknowable, since it will be able to concentrate itself entirely on a present duty from which uncertainty and hesitation are excluded."

Above all, perhaps, how can one ignore the success that accounts of our colonialists have had among the young intellectuals under consideration here? The expeditions of Moll, Lenfant, and Baratier arouse their enthusiasm; they search in their own unperilous existences for a moral equivalent to these bold destinies; they attempt to transpose this intrepid valor into their inner lives.

Some go further: their studies completed, they satisfy their taste for action in colonial adventures. It is not enough for them to learn history: they are making it. A young student from the Normale, Monsieur Klipfell, who received his teaching degree in literature in July of 1912, requested to be assigned to active service in Morocco, as a member of the Expeditionary Corps. We can cite many a similar example. One thinks of Jacques Violet, a twenty-year-old officer, who died so gloriously at Ksar-Teuchan, in Adrar: he was killed at the head of his men, at the moment of victory, in a grove of palm trees; among his belongings, they found a pair of white gloves and a copy of *Servitude and Military Grandeur;*[1] it was thus that he went into combat. . . .

For such young men, fired by patriotic faith and the cult of military virtues, only the occasion for heroism is lacking.

[1]Alfred-Victor de Vigny (1797–1863) wrote *Servitude and Military Grandeur* (1835), a combination of his memoirs and short stories. The work glorified martial values and the supreme good of service to God and country, even unto death.

2 Pan-Serbism: Nationalism, Terrorism, and Assassination

The conspiracy to assassinate Archduke Francis Ferdinand was organized by a secret Serbian society called Union or Death, more popularly known as the Black Hand. Founded in 1911, the Black Hand aspired to create a Greater Serbia by

uniting with their kinsmen, the South Slavs dwelling in Austria-Hungary. Thus, Austrian officials regarded the aspirations of Pan-Serbs as a significant threat to the Hapsburg Empire.

THE BLACK HAND

In 1914, the Black Hand had some 2,500 members, most of them army officers. The society indoctrinated members with a fanatic nationalism and trained them in terrorist methods. The initiation ceremony, designed to strengthen a new member's commitment to the cause and to foster obedience to the society's leaders, had the appearance of a sacred rite. The candidate entered a darkened room in which stood a table covered with a black cloth; resting on the table were a dagger, a revolver, and a crucifix. When the candidate declared his readiness to take the oath of allegiance, a masked member of the society's elite entered the room and stood in silence. After the initiate pronounced the oath, the masked man shook his hand and departed without uttering a word. Excerpts of the Black Hand's by-laws, including the oath of allegiance, follow.

BY-LAWS OF THE ORGANIZATION UNION OR DEATH

Article 1. This organization is created for the purpose of realizing the national ideal: the union of all Serbs. Membership is open to every Serb, without distinction of sex, religion, or place of birth, and to all those who are sincerely devoted to this cause.

Article 2. This organization prefers terrorist action to intellectual propaganda, and for this reason it must remain absolutely secret.

Article 3. The organization bears the name *Ujedinjenje ili Smirt* (Union or Death).

Article 4. To fulfill its purpose, the organization will do the following:

1. Exercise influence on government circles, on the various social classes, and on the entire social life of the kingdom of Serbia, which is considered the Piedmont[1] of the Serbian nation;
2. Organize revolutionary action in all territories inhabited by Serbs;
3. Beyond the frontiers of Serbia, fight with all means the enemies of the Serbian national idea;
4. Maintain amicable relations with all states, peoples, organizations, and individuals who support Serbia and the Serbian element;
5. Assist those nations and organizations that are fighting for their own national liberation and unification. . . .

Article 24. Every member has a duty to recruit new members, but the member shall guarantee with his life those whom he introduces into the organization.

Article 25. Members of the organization are forbidden to know each other personally. Only members of the central committee are known to each other.

Article 26. In the organization itself, the members are designated by numbers. Only the central committee in Belgrade knows their names.

Article 27. Members of the organization must obey absolutely the commands given to them by their superiors.

Article 28. Each member has a duty to communicate to the central committee at Belgrade all information that may be of interest to the organization.

Article 29. The interests of the organization stand above all other interests.

[1]The Piedmont was the Italian state that served as the nucleus for the unification of Italy.

Article 30. On entering the organization, each member must know that he loses his own personality, that he can expect neither personal glory nor personal profit, material or moral. Consequently, any member who endeavors to exploit the organization for personal, social, or party motives, will be punished. If by his acts he harms the organization itself, his punishment will be death.

Article 31. Those who enter the organization may never leave it, and no one has the authority to accept a member's resignation.

Article 32. Each member must aid the organization, with weekly contributions. If need be, the organization may procure funds through coercion. . . .

Article 33. When the central committee of Belgrade pronounces a death sentence the only thing that matters is that the execution is carried out unfailingly. The method of execution is of little importance.

Article 34. The organization's seal is composed as follows. On the center of the seal a powerful arm holds in its hand an unfurled flag. On the flag, as a coat of arms, are a skull and crossed bones; by the side of the flag are a knife, a bomb and poison. Around, in a circle, are inscribed the following words reading from left to right: "Unification or Death," and at the base "The Supreme Central Directorate."

Article 35. On joining the organization, the recruit takes the following oath:

"I (name), in becoming a member of the organization, 'Unification or Death,' do swear by the sun that shines on me, by the earth that nourishes me, by God, by the blood of my ancestors, on my honor and my life that from this moment until my death, I shall be faithful to the regulations of the organization and that I will be prepared to make any sacrifice for it. I swear before God, on my honor and on my life, that I shall carry with me to the grave the organization's secrets. May God condemn me and my comrades judge me if I violate or do not respect, consciously or not, my oath."

Article 36. These regulations come into force immediately.

Article 37. These regulations must not be changed.

Belgrade, 9 May 1911.

Baron von Giesl AUSTRIAN RESPONSE TO THE ASSASSINATION

Austrian officials who wanted to use the assassination as a pretext to crush Serbia feared that Pan-Serbism would lead to revolts among Slavs living in the Hapsburg Empire. This attitude was expressed in a memorandum written on July 21, 1914 (three weeks after the assassination), by Baron von Giesl, the Austrian ambassador to Serbia, to foreign minister Count Leopold von Berchtold.

Belgrade, July 21, 1914.

After the lamentable crime of June 28th, I have now been back at my post for some time, and I am able to give some judgment as to the tone which prevails here.

After the annexation crisis[1] the relations between the Monarchy and Servia [Serbia] were poisoned on the Servian side by national chauvinism, animosity and an effective propaganda

[1]Since 1878, Austria-Hungary had administered the provinces of Bosnia and Herzegovina, which were officially a part of the Ottoman Empire. The population of these lands consisted mainly of South Slavs, ethnic cousins of the Serbs. When Austria-Hungary annexed Bosnia and Herzegovina in 1908, Serbia was enraged.

of Great-Servian aspirations carried on in that part of our territory where there is a Servian population; since the last two Balkan Wars [in 1912 and 1913], the success of Servia has increased this chauvinism to a paroxysm, the expression of which in some cases bears the mark of insanity.

I may be excused from bringing proof and evidence of this; they can be had easily everywhere among all parties, in political circles as well as among the lower classes. I put it forward as a well-known axiom that the policy of Servia is built up on the separation of the territories inhabited by Southern Slavs, and as a corollary to this on the abolition of the [Hapsburg] Monarchy as a Great Power; this is its only object.

No one who has taken the trouble to move and take part in political circles here for a week can be blind to this truth. . . .

The crime at Serajevo [the assassination of Ferdinand] has aroused among the Servians an expectation that in the immediate future the Hapsburg States will fall to pieces; it was this on which they had set their hopes even before; there has been dangled before their eyes the cession of those territories in the Monarchy which are inhabited by the Southern Slavs, a revolution in Bosnia and Herzegovina and the unreliability of the Slav regiments—this is regarded as ascertained fact and had brought system and apparent justification into their nationalist madness.

Austria-Hungary, hated as she is, now appears to the Servians as powerless, and as scarcely worthy of waging war with; contempt is mingled with hatred; she is ripe for destruction, and she is to fall without trouble into the lap of the Great-Servian Empire, which is to be realised in the immediate future.

Newspapers, not among the most extreme, discuss the powerlessness and decrepitude of the neighbouring Monarchy in daily articles, and insult its officials without reserve and without fear of reprimand. They do not even stop short of the exalted person of our ruler. Even the official organ refers to the internal condition of Austria-Hungary as the true cause of this wicked crime. There is no longer any fear of being called to account. For decades the people of Servia has been educated by the press, and the policy at any given time is dependent on the party press; the Great-Servian propaganda and its monstrous offspring the crime of June 28th, are a fruit of this education. . . .

. . . The electoral campaign has united all parties on a platform of hostility against Austria-Hungary. None of the parties which aspire to office will incur the suspicion of being held capable of weak compliance towards the Monarchy. The campaign, therefore, is conducted under the catchword of hostility towards Austria-Hungary.

For both internal and external reasons the Monarchy is held to be powerless and incapable of any energetic action, and it is believed that the serious words which were spoken by leading men among us are only "bluff." . . .

I have allowed myself to trespass too long on the patience of Your Excellency, not because I thought that in what I have said I could tell you anything new, but because I considered this picture led up to the conclusion which forces itself upon me that a reckoning with Servia, a war for the position of the Monarchy as a Great Power, even for its existence as such, cannot be permanently avoided.

If we delay in clearing up our relations with Servia, we shall share the responsibility for the difficulties and the unfavourable situation in any future war which must, however, sooner or later be carried through.

For any observer on the spot, and for the representative of Austro-Hungarian interests in Servia, the question takes the form that we cannot any longer put up with any further injury to our prestige. . . .

Half measures, the presentation of demands, followed by long discussions and ending only in an unsound compromise, would be the hardest blow which could be directed against Austria-Hungary's reputation in Servia and her position in Europe.

3 War as Celebration: The Mood in European Capitals

An outpouring of patriotism greeted the proclamation of war. Huge crowds thronged the avenues and squares of each capital city to express their devotion to their nation and their willingness to bear arms. Many Europeans regarded war as a sacred moment that held the promise of adventure and an escape from a humdrum and purposeless daily existence. Going to war seemed to satisfy a yearning to surrender oneself to a noble cause: the greatness of the nation. The image of the nation united in a spirit of fraternity and self-sacrifice was immensely appealing.

Roland Doregelès
PARIS: "THAT FABULOUS DAY"

In "After Fifty Years," Roland Doregelès (1886–1973), a distinguished French writer, recalled the mood in Paris at the outbreak of the war.

"It's come!* It's posted at the district mayor's office," a passerby shouted to me as he ran.

I reached the Rue Drouot in one leap and shouldered through the mob that already filled the courtyard to approach the fascinating white sheet pasted to the door. I read the message at a glance, then reread it slowly, word for word, to convince myself that it was true:

THE FIRST DAY OF
MOBILIZATION WILL BE
SUNDAY, AUGUST 2

Only three lines, written hastily by a hand that trembled. It was an announcement to a million and a half Frenchmen.

The people who had read it moved away, stunned, while others crowded in, but this silent numbness did not last. Suddenly a heroic wind lifted their heads. What? War, was it? Well, then, let's go! Without any signal, the "Marseillaise" poured from thousands of throats, sheafs of flags appeared at windows, and howling processions rolled out on the boulevards. Each column brandished a placard: ALSACE VOLUNTEERS, JEWISH VOLUNTEERS, POLISH VOLUNTEERS. They hailed one another above the bravos of the crowd, and this human torrent, swelling at every corner, moved on to circle around the Place de la Concorde, before the statue of Strasbourg banked with flowers, then flowed toward the Place de la République, where mobs from Belleville and the Faubourg St. Antoine yelled themselves hoarse on the refrain from the great days, *"Aux armes, citoyens!"* (To arms, citizens!) But this time it was better than a song.

To gather the news for my paper, I ran around the city in every direction. At the Cours la Reine I saw the fabled cuirassiers [cavalry] in their horsetail plumes march by, and at the Rue La Fayette footsoldiers in battle garb with women throwing flowers and kisses to them. In a marshaling yard I saw guns being loaded, their long, thin barrels twined around with branches and laurel leaves, while troops in red breeches piled gaily into delivery vans they were scrawling with challenges and caricatures. Young and old, civilians and military men burned with the same excitement. It was like a Brotherhood Day.

*Translated from the French by Sally Abeles.

Dead tired but still exhilarated, I got back to *L'Homme libre* and burst into the office of Georges Clemenceau, our chief.[†]

"What is Paris saying?" he asked me.

"It's singing, sir!"

"Then everything will be all right. . . ."

His old patriot's heart was not wrong; no cloud marred that fabulous day. . . .

Less than twenty-four hours later, seeing their old dreams of peace crumble [socialist workers] would stream out into the boulevards . . . [but] they would break into the "Marseillaise," not the "Internationale"; they would cry, "To Berlin!," not "Down with war!"

What did they have to defend, these black-nailed patriots? Not even a shack, an acre to till, indeed hardly a patch of ground reserved at the Pantin Cemetery; yet they would depart, like their rivals of yesterday, a heroic song on their lips and a flower in their guns. No more poor or rich, proletarians or bourgeois, right-wingers or militant leftists; there were only Frenchmen.

Beginning the next day, thousands of men eager to fight would jostle one another outside recruiting offices, waiting to join up. Men who could have stayed home, with their wives and children or an imploring mama. But no. The word "duty" had a meaning for them, and the word "country" had regained its splendor.

I close my eyes, and they appear to me, those volunteers on the great day; then I see them again in the old kepi [military cap] or blue helmet, shouting, "Here!" when somebody called for men for a raid, or hurling themselves into an attack with fixed bayonets, and I wonder, and I question their bloody [ghosts].

Tell me, comrades in eternal silence, would you have besieged the enlistment offices with the same enthusiasm, would you have fought such a courageous fight had you known that fifty years later those men in gray knit caps or steel helmets you were ordered to kill would no longer be enemies and that we would have to open our arms to them? Wouldn't the heroic "Let's go!" you shouted as you cleared the parapets have stuck in your throats? Deep in the grave where you dwell, don't you regret your sacrifice? "Why did we fight? Why did we let ourselves get killed?" This is the murmur of a million and a half voices rising from the bowels of the earth, and we, the survivors, do not know what to answer.

[†]*L'Homme libre* (The Free Man) was but one of several periodicals Clemenceau founded and directed during his long political career.—Tr.

Stefan Zweig
VIENNA: "THE RUSHING FEELING OF FRATERNITY"

Some intellectuals viewed the war as a way of regenerating the nation; nobility and fraternity would triumph over life's petty concerns. In the following reading, Stefan Zweig (1881–1942), a prominent Austrian literary figure, recalled the scene in Vienna, the capital of the Austro-Hungarian Empire, at the outbreak of World War I. This passage comes from Zweig's autobiography, written in 1941.

The next morning I was in Austria. In every station placards had been put up announcing general mobilization. The trains were filled with fresh recruits, banners were flying, music sounded, and in Vienna I found the entire city in a tumult. The first shock at the news of war—the war that no one, people or government, had wanted—the war which had slipped, much against their will, out of the clumsy hands of the diplomats who had been bluffing and toying with it, had suddenly been transformed into enthusiasm. There were parades in the street, flags, ribbons, and music burst forth everywhere, young recruits were marching triumphantly, their faces lighting up at the cheering—they, the John Does and Richard Roes who usually go unnoticed and uncelebrated.

And to be truthful, I must acknowledge that there was a majestic, rapturous, and even seductive something in this first outbreak of the people from which one could escape only with difficulty. And in spite of all my hatred and aversion for war, I should not like to have missed the memory of those first days. As never before, thousands and hundreds of thousands felt what they should have felt in peace time, that they belonged together. A city of two million, a country of nearly fifty million, in that hour felt that they were participating in world history, in a moment which would never recur, and that each one was called upon to cast his infinitesimal self into the glowing mass, there to be purified of all selfishness. All differences of class, rank, and language were flooded over at that moment by the rushing feeling of fraternity. Strangers spoke to one another in the streets, people who had avoided each other for years shook hands, everywhere one saw excited faces. Each individual experienced an exaltation of his ego, he was no longer the isolated person of former times, he had been incorporated into the mass, he was part of the people, and his person, his hitherto unnoticed person, had been given meaning. The petty mail clerk, who ordinarily sorted letters early and late, who sorted constantly, who sorted from Monday until Saturday without interruption; the clerk, the cobbler, had suddenly achieved a romantic possibility in life: he could become a hero, and everyone who wore a uniform was already being cheered by the women, and greeted beforehand with this romantic appellation by those who had to remain behind. They acknowledged the unknown power which had lifted them out of their everyday existence. Even mothers with their grief, and women with their fears, were ashamed to manifest their quite natural emotions in the face of this first transformation. But it is quite possible that a deeper, more secret power was at work in this frenzy. So deeply, so quickly did the tide break over humanity that, foaming over the surface, it churned up the depths, the subconscious primitive instincts of the human animal—that which Freud so meaningfully calls "the revulsion from culture," the desire to break out of the conventional bourgeois world of codes and statutes, and to permit the primitive instincts of the blood to rage at will. It is also possible that these powers of darkness had their share in the wild frenzy into which everything was thrown—self-sacrifice and alcohol, the spirit of adventure and the spirit of pure faith, the old magic of flags and patriotic slogans, that mysterious frenzy of the millions which can hardly be described in words, but which, for the moment, gave a wild and almost rapturous impetus to the greatest crime of our time. . . .

. . . What did the great mass know of war in 1914, after nearly half a century of peace? They did not know war, they had hardly given it a thought. It had become legendary, and distance had made it seem romantic and heroic. They still saw it in the perspective of their school readers and of paintings in museums; brilliant cavalry attacks in glittering uniforms, the fatal shot always straight through the heart, the entire campaign a resounding march of victory—"We'll be home at Christmas," the recruits shouted laughingly to their mothers in August of 1914. Who in the villages and the cities of Austria remembered "real" war? A few ancients at best, who in 1866 had fought against Prussia, which was now their ally. But what a quick, bloodless far-off war that had been, a campaign that had ended in three weeks with few victims and before it had well started! A rapid excursion into the romantic, a wild, manly adventure—that is how the war of 1914 was painted in the imagination of the simple man, and the young people were honestly afraid that they might miss this most wonderful and exciting experience of their lives; that is why they hurried and thronged to the colors, and that is why they shouted and sang in the trains that carried them to the slaughter; wildly and feverishly the red wave of blood coursed through the veins of the entire nation.

Philipp Scheidemann
BERLIN: "THE HOUR WE YEARNED FOR"

Philipp Scheidemann (1865–1939), one of the founders of the Weimar Republic, described Berlin's martial mood in his memoirs, published in 1929.

At express speed I had returned to Berlin. Everywhere a word could be heard the conversation was of war and rumours of war. There was only one topic of conversation—war. The supporters of war seemed to be in a great majority. Were these pugnacious fellows, young and old, bereft of their senses? Were they so ignorant of the horrors of war? . . . Vast crowds of demonstrators paraded. . . . Schoolboys and students were there in the thousands; their bearded seniors, with their Iron Crosses of 1870–71 on their breasts, were there too in huge numbers.

Treitschke and Bernhardi[1] (to say nothing of the National Liberal beer-swilling heroes) seemed to have multiplied a thousandfold. Patriotic demonstrations had an intoxicating effect and excited the war-mongers to excess. "A call like the voice of thunder." Cheers! "In triumph we will smite France to the ground." "All hail to thee in victor's crown." Cheers! Hurrah!

The counter-demonstrations immediately organized by the Berlin Social Democrats were imposing, and certainly more disciplined than the Jingo [extremely nationalistic] processions, but could not outdo the shouts of the fire-eaters. "Good luck to him who cares for truth and right. Stand firmly round the flag." "Long live peace!" "Socialists, close up your ranks." The Socialist International cheer. The patriots were sometimes silenced by the Proletarians; then they came out on top again. This choral contest . . . went on for days.

"It is the hour we yearned for—our friends know that," so the Pan-German[2] papers shouted, that had for years been shouting for war. The *Post,* conducted by von Stumm, the Independent Conservative leader and big Industrialist, had thus moaned in all its columns in 1900, at the fortieth celebration of the Franco-German War: "Another forty years of peace would be a national misfortune for Germany." Now these firebrands saw the seeds they had planted ripening. Perhaps in the heads of many who had been called upon to make every effort to keep the peace Bernhardi's words, that "the preservation of peace can and never shall be the aim of politics," had done mischief. These words are infernally like the secret instructions given by Baron von Holstein to the German delegates to the first Peace Conference at The Hague:

"For the State there is no higher aim than the preservation of its own interests; among the Great Powers these will not necessarily coincide with the maintenance of peace, but rather with the hostile policy of enemies and rivals."

---

[1]Both Heinrich von Treitschke and General von Bernhardi glorified war (see pages 42–44).

[2]The Pan-German Association, whose membership included professors, schoolteachers, journalists, lawyers, and aristocrats, spread nationalist and racial theories and glorified war as an expression of national vitality.

Bertrand Russell
LONDON: "AVERAGE MEN AND WOMEN WERE DELIGHTED AT THE PROSPECT OF WAR"

Bertrand Russell (1872–1970), the distinguished mathematician and philosopher, was dismayed by the war fever that gripped English men and women. During the war Russell was fined and imprisoned for his pacifistic activities. The following account is from his autobiography.

During the hot days at the end of July, I was at Cambridge, discussing the situation with all and sundry. I found it impossible to believe that Europe would be so mad as to plunge into war, but I was persuaded that, if there was war, England would be involved. I felt strongly that England ought to remain neutral, and I collected the signatures of a large number of professors and Fellows to a statement which appeared in the *Manchester Guardian* to that effect. The day war was declared, almost all of them changed their minds. . . . I spent the evening walking round the streets, especially in the neighbourhood of Trafalgar Square, noticing cheering crowds, and making myself sensitive to the emotions of passers-by. During this and the following days I discovered to my amazement that average men and women were delighted at the prospect of war. I had fondly imagined what most pacifists contended, that wars were forced upon a reluctant population by despotic and Machiavellian governments. . . .

The first days of the war were to me utterly amazing. My best friends, such as the Whiteheads, were savagely warlike. Men like J. L. Hammond, who had been writing for years against participation in a European war, were swept off their feet by Belgium. . . .

Meanwhile, I was living at the highest possible emotional tension. Although I did not foresee anything like the full disaster of the war, I foresaw a great deal more than most people did. The prospect filled me with horror, but what filled me with even more horror was the fact that the anticipation of carnage was delightful to something like ninety per cent of the population. I had to revise my views on human nature. At that time I was wholly ignorant of psychoanalysis, but I arrived for myself at a view of human passions not unlike that of the psychoanalysts. I arrived at this view in an endeavour to understand popular feeling about the War. I had supposed until that time that it was quite common for parents to love their children, but the War persuaded me that it is a rare exception. I had supposed that most people liked money better than almost anything else, but I discovered that they like destruction even better. I had supposed that intellectuals frequently loved truth, but I found here again that not ten per cent of them prefer truth to popularity. . . .

. . . As a lover of truth, the national propaganda of all the belligerent nations sickened me. As a lover of civilization, the return to barbarism appalled me. As a man of thwarted parental feeling, the massacre of the young wrung my heart. I hardly supposed that much good would come of opposing the War, but I felt that for the honour of human nature those who were not swept off their feet should show that they stood firm. . . .

On August 15, 1914, the London *Nation* published a letter written by Russell, part of which follows.

. . . Those who saw the London crowds, during the nights leading up to the Declaration of War saw a whole population, hitherto peaceable and humane, precipitated in a few days down the steep slope to primitive barbarism, letting loose, in a moment, the instincts of hatred and blood lust against which the whole fabric of society has been raised. "Patriots" in all countries acclaim this brutal orgy as a noble determination to vindicate the right; reason and mercy are swept away in one great flood of hatred; dim abstractions of unimaginable wickedness—Germany to us and the French, Russia to the Germans—conceal the simple fact that the enemy are men, like ourselves, neither better nor worse—men who love their homes and the sunshine, and all the simple pleasures of common lives. . . .

M. V. Rodzianko
ST. PETERSBURG: "THERE IS NEITHER DOUBT NOR HESITATION AMONG US"

Like the other Great Powers, Russia greeted the war with public enthusiasm and political reconciliation. In the following selection, Mikhail Rodzianko, president of the Duma, Russia's semirepresentative legislative body, pledges the loyalty of its often fractious membership for the duration of the conflict.

YOUR IMPERIAL MAJESTY!

All Russia has heard with great pride and deep enthusiasm the words of the Russian Tsar, summoning his people to join him in a perfect union at this difficult hour of sore trials which has come upon our country.

Sire! Russia knows that your thoughts and desires have always been to bring about conditions which would make it possible for the nation to live and work in peace, and that your loving heart strove for a stable peace in order to protect the lives of your subjects that are dear to you.

But the terrible hour has struck. All of us, young and old, have seized the significance and profundity of the historical events which have unfolded themselves. A threat has been made against the prosperity and integrity of the State; national honor has been offended; and national honor is dearer to us than life. It is time to show the world how terrible the Russian people, which surrounds its crowned leader with a firm faith in Divine Providence, like an impenetrable wall, can be to the enemy.

Sire! The time has come for a stubborn fight to protect our national dignity, a fight for the integrity and inviolability of the Russian land. There is neither doubt nor hesitation among us. Summoned to participate in the life of the state, at Your Majesty's will, the people's representatives now stand before you. The State Duma, reflecting the unanimous impulse of every section of Russia, and joined together in the single thought which unifies us all, has charged me to say to you, Sire, that your people is ready to fight for the honor and glory of the fatherland.

Without differences of opinions, views, or convictions, the State Duma, speaking in the name of the Russian peasantry, is calmly and firmly saying to its Tsar: "Dare, Sire! The Russian people is with you and, trusting firmly in Divine mercy, will stop at no sacrifice until the enemy is crushed, and the dignity of our native land secured."

4 Trench Warfare

In 1914, the young men of European nations marched off to war, believing they were embarking on a glorious and chivalrous adventure. They were eager to serve their countries, to demonstrate personal valor, and to experience life at its most intense moments. But in the trenches, where unseen enemies fired machine guns and soldiers faced artillery that killed indiscriminately and relentlessly, for many this romantic illusion about combat disintegrated.

Erich Maria Remarque
ALL QUIET ON THE WESTERN FRONT

The following reading comes from Erich Maria Remarque's novel *All Quiet on the Western Front* (1929), the most famous literary work to emerge from World War I. A veteran of the trenches himself, Remarque (1898–1970) graphically described the slaughter that robbed Europe of its young men. His narrator is a young German soldier.

We wake up in the middle of the night. The earth booms. Heavy fire is falling on us. We crouch into corners. We distinguish shells of every calibre.

Each man lays hold of his things and looks again every minute to reassure himself that they are still there. The dug-out heaves, the night roars and flashes. We look at each other in the momentary flashes of light, and with pale faces and pressed lips shake our heads.

Every man is aware of the heavy shells tearing down the parapet, rooting up the embankment and demolishing the upper layers of concrete. When a shell lands in the trench we note how the hollow, furious blast is like a blow from the paw of a raging beast of prey. Already by morning a few of the recruits are green and vomiting. They are too inexperienced. . . .

The bombardment does not diminish. It is falling in the rear too. As far as one can see spout fountains of mud and iron. A wide belt is being raked.

The attack does not come, but the bombardment continues. We are gradually benumbed. Hardly a man speaks. We cannot make ourselves understood.

Our trench is almost gone. At many places it is only eighteen inches high, it is broken by holes, and craters, and mountains of earth. A shell lands square in front of our post. At once it is dark. We are buried and must dig ourselves out. . . .

Towards morning, while it is still dark, there is some excitement. Through the entrance rushes in a swarm of fleeing rats that try to storm the walls. Torches light up the confusion. Everyone yells and curses and slaughters. The madness and despair of many hours unloads itself in this outburst. Faces are distorted, arms strike out, the beasts scream; we just stop in time to avoid attacking one another. . . .

Suddenly it howls and flashes terrifically, the dug-out cracks in all its joints under a direct hit, fortunately only a light one that the concrete blocks are able to withstand. It rings metallically, the walls reel, rifles, helmets, earth, mud, and dust fly everywhere. Sulphur fumes pour in.

If we were in one of those light dug-outs that they have been building lately instead of this deeper one, none of us would be alive.

But the effect is bad enough even so. The recruit starts to rave again and two others follow suit. One jumps up and rushes out, we have trouble with the other two. I start after the one who escapes and wonder whether to shoot him in the leg—then it shrieks again, I fling myself down and when I stand up the wall of the trench is plastered with smoking splinters, lumps of flesh, and bits of uniform. I scramble back.

The first recruit seems actually to have gone insane. He butts his head against the wall like a goat. We must try to-night to take him to the rear. Meanwhile we bind him, but in such a way that in case of attack he can be released at once. . . .

Suddenly the nearer explosions cease. The shelling continues but it has lifted and falls behind us, our trench is free. We seize the hand-grenades, pitch them out in front of the dug-out and jump after them. The bombardment has stopped and a heavy barrage now falls behind us. The attack has come.

No one would believe that in this howling waste there could still be men; but steel helmets now appear on all sides out of the trench, and fifty yards from us a machine-gun is already in position and barking.

The wire entanglements are torn to pieces. Yet they offer some obstacle. We see the storm-troops coming. Our artillery opens fire. Machine-guns rattle, rifles crack. The charge works its way across. Haie and Kropp begin with the hand-grenades. They throw as fast as they can, others pass them, the handles with the strings already pulled. Haie throws seventy-five yards, Kropp sixty, it has been measured, the distance is important. The enemy as they run cannot do much before they are within forty yards.

We recognize the smooth distorted faces, the helmets: they are French. They have already suffered heavily when they reach the remnants of the barbed wire entanglements. A whole line has gone down before our machine-guns; then we have a lot of stoppages and they come nearer.

I see one of them, his face upturned, fall into a wire cradle. His body collapses, his hands remain suspended as though he were praying. Then his body drops clean away and only his hands with the stumps of his arms, shot off, now hang in the wire.

The moment we are about to retreat three faces rise up from the ground in front of us. Under one of the helmets a dark pointed beard and two eyes that are fastened on me. I raise my hand, but I cannot throw into those strange eyes; for one mad moment the whole slaughter whirls like a circus round me, and these two eyes alone are motionless; then the head rises up, a hand, a movement, and my hand-grenade flies through the air and into him.

We make for the rear, pull wire cradles into the trench and leave bombs behind us with the strings pulled, which ensures us a fiery retreat. The machine-guns are already firing from the next position.

We have become wild beasts. We do not fight, we defend ourselves against annihilation. It is not against men that we fling our bombs, what do we know of men in this moment when Death is hunting us down—now, for the first time in three days we can see his face, now for the first time in three days we can oppose him; we feel a mad anger. No longer do we lie helpless, waiting on the scaffold, we can destroy and kill, to save ourselves, to save ourselves and to be revenged.

We crouch behind every corner, behind every barrier of barbed wire, and hurl heaps of explosives at the feet of the advancing enemy before we run. The blast of the hand-grenades impinges powerfully on our arms and legs; crouching like cats we run on, overwhelmed by this wave that bears us along, that fills us with ferocity, turns us into thugs, into murderers, into God only knows what devils; this wave that multiplies our strength with fear and madness and greed of life, seeking and fighting for nothing but our deliverance. If your own father came over with them you would not hesitate to fling a bomb at him.

The forward trenches have been abandoned. Are they still trenches? They are blown to pieces, annihilated—there are only broken bits of trenches, holes linked by cracks, nests of craters, that is all. But the enemy's casualties increase. They did not count on so much resistance.

It is nearly noon. The sun blazes hotly, the sweat stings in our eyes, we wipe it off on our sleeves and often blood with it. At last we reach a trench that is in a somewhat better condition. It is manned and ready for the counterattack, it receives us. Our guns open in full blast and cut off the enemy attack.

The lines behind us stop. They can advance no farther. The attack is crushed by our artillery. We watch. The fire lifts a hundred yards and we break forward. Beside me a lance-corporal has his head torn off. He runs a few steps more while the blood spouts from his neck like a fountain.

It does not come quite to hand-to-hand fighting; they are driven back. We arrive once again at our shattered trench and pass on beyond it. . . .

We have lost all feeling for one another. We can hardly control ourselves when our glance lights on the form of some other man. We are insensible, dead men, who through some trick, some dreadful magic, are still able to run and to kill.

A young Frenchman lags behind, he is overtaken, he puts up his hands, in one he still holds his revolver—does he mean to shoot or to give himself up!—a blow from a spade cleaves through his face. A second sees it and tries to run farther; a bayonet jabs into his back. He leaps in the air, his arms thrown wide, his mouth wide open, yelling; he staggers, in his back the bayonet quivers. A third throws away his rifle, cowers down with his hands before his eyes. He is left behind with a few other prisoners to carry off the wounded.

Suddenly in the pursuit we reach the enemy line.

We are so close on the heels of our retreating enemies that we reach it almost at the same time as they. In this way we suffer few casualties. A machine-gun barks, but is silenced with a bomb. Nevertheless, the couple of seconds has sufficed to give us five stomach wounds. With the butt of his rifle Kat smashes to pulp the face of one of the unwounded machine-gunners. We bayonet the others before they have time to get out their bombs. Then thirstily we drink the water they have for cooling the gun.

Everywhere wire-cutters are snapping, planks are thrown across the entanglements, we jump through the narrow entrances into the trenches. Haie strikes his spade into the neck of a gigantic Frenchman and throws the first hand-grenade; we duck behind a breast-work for a few seconds, then the straight bit of trench ahead of us is empty. The next throw whizzes obliquely over the corner and clears a passage; as we run past we toss handfuls down into the dug-outs, the earth shudders, it crashes, smokes and groans, we stumble over slippery lumps of flesh, over yielding bodies; I fall into an open belly on which lies a clean, new officer's cap.

The fight ceases. We lose touch with the enemy. We cannot stay here long but must retire under cover of our artillery to our own position. No sooner do we know this than we dive into the nearest dug-outs, and with the utmost haste seize on whatever provisions we can see, especially the tins of corned beef and butter, before we clear out.

We get back pretty well. There is no further attack by the enemy. We lie for an hour panting and resting before anyone speaks. We are so completely played out that in spite of our great hunger we do not think of the provisions. Then gradually we become something like men again.

Siegfried Sassoon
"BASE DETAILS"

Front-line soldiers often looked with contempt on generals who, from a safe distance, ordered massive assaults against enemy lines protected by barbed wire and machine guns. Such attacks could cost the lives of tens of thousands of troops in

just a few days. Siegfried Sassoon (1886–1967), a British poet who served at the front for much of the war and earned a Military Cross for bravery, showed his disdain for cold-hearted officers in "Base Details."

If I were fierce, and bald, and short of breath,
I'd live with scarlet Majors at the Base,
And speed glum heroes up the line to death.
You'd see me with my puffy petulant face,
Guzzling and gulping in the best hotel,
Reading the Roll of Honour. 'Poor young chap,'
I'd say—'I used to know his father well;
Yes, we've lost heavily in this last scrap.'
And when the war is done and youth stone dead,
I'd toddle safely home and die—in bed.

Wilfred Owen "DISABLED"

Wilfred Owen (1893–1918), another British poet, volunteered for duty in 1915. At the Battle of the Somme, he sustained shell shock and was sent to a hospital in Britain. In 1918, he returned to the front and was awarded the Military Cross; he died one week before the Armistice. In the following poem, Owen portrays the enduring misery of war.

He sat in a wheeled chair, waiting for dark,
And shivered in his ghastly suit of gray,
Legless, sewn short at elbow. Through the park
Voices of boys rang saddening like a hymn,
Voices of play and pleasure after day,
Till gathering sleep mothered them from him.

About this time Town used to swing so gay
When glow-lamps budded in the light blue trees,
And girls glanced lovelier as the air grew dim,—
In the old times, before he threw away his knees. . . .

He asked to join. He didn't have to beg;
Smiling they wrote his lie: aged nineteen years.
Germans he scarcely thought of; all their guilt,
And Austria's, did not move him. And no fears
Of Fear came yet. He thought of jeweled hilts
For daggers in plaid socks; of smart salutes;
And care of arms; and leave; and pay arrears;
Esprit de corps; and hints for young recruits.

And soon, he was drafted out with drums and cheers. . . .

Now, he will spend a few sick years in Institutes,
And do what things the rules consider wise,
And take whatever pity they may dole.
Tonight he noticed how the women's eyes
Passed from him to the strong men that were whole.
How cold and late it is! Why don't they come
And put him into bed? Why don't they come?

5 Women at War

In order to release men for military service, women throughout Europe responded to their countries' wartime needs and replaced men in all branches of civilian life. They took jobs in munitions factories, worked on farms, and received training as shop clerks and nurses. They drove ambulances, mail trucks, and buses. They worked as laboratory assistants, plumbers' helpers, and bank clerks. By performing effectively in jobs formerly occupied by men, women demonstrated they had an essential role to play in the economic life of their countries. By the end of the war, little opposition remained to granting women political rights.

Naomi Loughnan
GENTEEL WOMEN IN THE FACTORIES

Naomi Loughnan was one of millions of women who replaced men in civilian occupations in all of the belligerent powers during World War I. She was a young, upper-middle-class woman who lived with her family in London and who had never had to work for a living. In her job in a munitions plant, she had to adjust to close associations with women from the London slums, to hostel life, and to twelve-hour shifts doing heavy and sometimes dangerous work. The chief motivation for British women of her class was their desire to aid the war effort, not the opportunity to earn substantial wages.

We little thought when we first put on our overalls and caps and enlisted in the Munition Army how much more inspiring our life was to be than we had dared to hope. Though we munition workers sacrifice our ease we gain a life worth living. Our long days are filled with interest, and with the zest of doing work for our country in the grand cause of Freedom. As we handle the weapons of war we are learning great lessons of life. In the busy, noisy workshops we come face to face with every kind of class, and each one of these classes has something to learn from the others. Our muscles may be aching, and the brightness fading a little from our eyes, but our minds are expanding, our very souls are growing stronger. And excellent, too, is the discipline for our bodies, though we do not always recognize this. . . .

The day is long, the atmosphere is breathed and rebreathed, and the oil smells. Our hands are black with warm, thick oozings from the machines, which coat the work and, incidentally, the workers. We regard our horrible, begrimed members [limbs] with disgust and secret pride. . . .

. . . The genteel among us wear gloves. We vie with each other in finding the most up-to-date grease-removers, just as we used to vie about hats. Our hands are not alone in suffering from dirt. . . . [D]ust-clouds, filled with unwelcome life, find a resting-place in our lungs and noses.

The work is hard. It may be, perhaps, from sheer lifting and carrying and weighing, or merely because of those long dragging hours that keep us sitting on little stools in front of whirring, clattering machines that are all too easy to work. We wish sometimes they were not quite so "fool-proof," for monotony is painful. Or life may appear hard to us by reason of those same creeping hours spent on our feet, up and down, to and fro, and up and down again, hour after hour, until something altogether queer takes place in the muscles of our legs. But we go on. . . . It is amazing what we can do when there is no way of escape but desertion. . . .

. . . The first thing that strikes the newcomer, as the shop door opens, is the great wall of noise that seems to rise and confront one like a tangible substance. The crashing, tearing, rattling whirr of machinery is deafening. And yet, though this may seem almost impossible, the workers get so accustomed to it after a little time that they do not notice it until it stops. . . .

The twelve-hour shift at night, though taking greater toll of nerve and energy, has distinct charms of its own. . . . The first hours seem to go more quickly than the corresponding ones on day work, until at last two o'clock is reached. Then begins a hand-to-hand struggle with Morpheus [Greek god of dreams]. . . . A stern sense of duty, growing feebler as the moments pass, is our only weapon of defence, whereas the crafty god has a veritable armoury of leaden eyelids, weakening pulses, sleep-weighted heads, and slackening wills. He even leads the foremen away to their offices and softens the hearts of languid overlookers. Some of us succumb, but there are those among us who will not give in. An unbecoming greyness alters our faces, however young and fresh by day, a strange wilting process that steals all youth and beauty from us—until the morning. . . .

Engineering mankind is possessed of the unshakable opinion that no woman can have the mechanical sense. If one of us asks humbly why such and such an alteration is not made to prevent this or that drawback to a machine, she is told, with a superior smile, that a man has worked her machine before her for years, and that therefore if there were any improvement possible it would have been made. As long as we do exactly what we are told and do not attempt to use our brains, we give entire satisfaction, and are treated as nice, good children. Any swerving from the easy path prepared for us by our males arouses the most scathing contempt in their manly bosoms. The exceptions are as delightful to meet as they are rare. Women have, however, proved that their entry into the munition world has increased the output. Employers who forget things personal in their patriotic desire for large results are enthusiastic over the success of women in the shops. But their workmen have to be handled with the utmost tenderness and caution lest they should actually imagine it was being suggested that women could do their work equally well, given equal conditions of training—at least where muscle is not the driving force. This undercurrent of jealousy rises to the surface rather often, but as a general rule the men behave with much kindness, and are ready to help with muscle and advice whenever called upon. If eyes are very bright and hair inclined to curl, the muscle and advice do not even wait for a call.

The coming of the mixed classes of women into the factory is slowly but surely having an educative effect upon the men. "Language" is almost unconsciously becoming subdued. There are fiery exceptions who make our hair stand up on end under our close-fitting caps, but a sharp rebuke or a look of horror will often [straighten out] the most truculent. He will at the moment, perhaps, sneer at the "blooming milksop fools of women," but he will be more careful next time. It is grievous to hear the girls also swearing and using disgusting language. Shoulder to shoulder with the children of the slums, the upper classes are having their eyes prised open at last to the awful conditions among which their sisters have dwelt. Foul language, immorality, and many other evils are but the natural outcome of overcrowding and bitter poverty. If some of us, still blind and ignorant of our responsibilities, shrink horrified and repelled from the rougher set, the compliment is returned with open derision and ribald laughter. There is something, too, about the prim prudery of the "genteel" that tickles the East-Ender's [a lower-class person] sharp wit. On the other hand, attempts at friendliness from the more understanding are treated with the utmost suspicion, though once that suspicion is overcome and friendship is established, it is unshakable. Our working hours are highly flavoured by our neighbours' treatment of ourselves and of each other. Laughter, anger, acute confusion, and laughter again, are constantly changing our immediate outlook on life. Sometimes disgust will overcome us, but we are learning with painful clarity that the fault is not theirs whose actions disgust us, but must be placed to the discredit of those other classes who have allowed the continued existence of conditions which generate the things from which we shrink appalled. . . .

Whatever sacrifice we make of wearied bodies, brains dulled by interminable night-shifts, of roughened hands, and faces robbed of their soft curves, it is, after all, so small a thing. We live in safety, we have shelter, and food whenever necessary, and we are even earning quite a lot of money. What is ours beside the great sacrifice? Men in their prime, on the verge of ambition realized, surrounded by the benefits won by their earlier struggles, are offering up their very lives. And those boys with Life, all glorious and untried, spread before them at their feet, are turning a smiling face to Death.

Magda Trott
OPPOSITION TO FEMALE EMPLOYMENT

In the second year of the war, a German woman described the hostility faced by women in the work force.

With the outbreak of war men were drawn away from the management of numerous organizations and, gradually, the lack of experienced personnel made itself felt. Women working in offices were therefore urged not to waste the opportunities offered them by the war, and to continue their education so that they would be prepared to take on the position once held by a male colleague, should the occasion arise.

Such occasions have indeed arisen much sooner than anticipated. The demand for educated women has risen phenomenally during the six months since the war began. Women have been employed in banks, in large commercial businesses, in urban offices—everywhere, in fact, where up till now only men had been employed. They are to be tested in order to see whether they can perform with equal success.

All those who were certain that women would be completely successful substitutes for men were painfully disappointed to discover that many women who had worked for years in a firm and were invited to step up to a higher level, now that the men were absent, suddenly handed in their resignations. An enquiry revealed that, especially in recent days, these notices were coming with great frequency and, strange as it may seem, applied mostly to women who had been working in the same company from four to seven years and had now been offered a better and even better-paid job. They said "no" and since there was no possibility for them to remain in their old jobs, they resigned.

The enemies of women's employment were delighted. Here was their proof that women are incapable of holding down responsible positions. Female workers were quite successful as clerks, stenographers, and typists, in fact, in all those positions that require no independent activity—but as soon as more serious duties were demanded of them, they failed.

Naturally, we enquired of these women why they had given up so quickly, and then the truth of the matter became plain. All women were quite ready, if with some trepidation, to accept the new positions, particularly since the boss made it clear that one of the gentlemen would carefully explain the new assignments to them. Certainly the work was almost entirely new to the young ladies since till now they had only been concerned with their stenography, their books, and so forth. However, they entered their new duties with enthusiasm.

But even on the first day it was noticeable that not everything would proceed as had been supposed. Male colleagues looked askance at the "intruder" who dared to usurp the position and bread of a colleague now fighting for the Fatherland, and who would, it was fervently hoped, return in good health. Moreover, the lady who came as a substitute received exactly half of the salary of the gentleman colleague who had previously occupied the same position. A dangerous implication, since if the lady made good, the boss might continue to draw on female personnel; the saving on salaries would clearly be substantial. It became essential to use all means to show the boss that female help was no substitute for men's work, and a united male front was organized.

It was hardly surprising that all the lady's questions were answered quite vaguely. If she asked again or even a third time, irritated remarks were passed concerning her inadequacy in comprehension, and very soon the male teacher lost patience. Naturally, most of his colleagues supported him and the lady found it difficult, if not impossible, to receive any instruction and was finally forced to resign.

This is what happened in most known cases. We must, however, also admit that occasionally the fault does lie with the lady, who simply did not have sufficient preparation to fill a difficult position. There may be male colleagues who would gladly share information with women; however, these women are unable to understand, because they have too little business experience. In order to prevent this sort of thing, we would counsel all women who are seeking a position in which they hope to advance, to educate themselves as much as possible. All those women who were forced to leave their jobs of long standing might not have been obliged to do so, had they been more concerned in previous years with understanding the overall nature of the business in which they were employed. Their colleagues would surely and generously have answered their questions and given them valuable advice, which would have offered them an overview and thereby avoided the total ignorance with which they entered these advanced positions when they were offered. At least they would have had an inkling and saved themselves the questions that betrayed their great ignorance to their colleagues. They might even have found their way through all the confusion and succeeded in the new position.

Therefore, once again: all you women who want to advance yourselves and create an independent existence, use this time of war as a learning experience and keep your eyes open.

RUSSIAN WOMEN IN COMBAT

From 1915 onwards, accounts began to appear in American magazines of Russian women disguising themselves as men and joining up with male soldiers, or fighting in all-female units of the Russian army. The first women's unit was called "The Battalion of Death," and its valor on the Russian front inspired a movement for a women's army. By the winter of 1917, five thousand women were in training throughout Russia.

No official statistics of women volunteers in the regular Russian Army were kept, but judging by the frequent reports of women soldiers awarded the St. George's Cross for bravery at the front, their numbers were considerable. They came from all classes of Russian society and assumed male names and attire, as the following account relates. It was originally published in a Russian newspaper and was reprinted in the *New York Times*.

Stories are filtering in from the various belligerent countries telling of actual fighting in the ranks by women. . . . A correspondent of the *Novoe Vremya* tells an interesting story of the experiences of twelve young Russian girls who fought in the ranks as soldiers of the line. The story, as related by one of their number, was also authenticated by the Petrograd correspondent of *The London Times,* who wrote as follows:

"She was called Zoya Smirnov. She came to our staff straight from the advanced positions, where she had spent fourteen months wearing soldier's clothes and fighting with the foe on even terms with the men.

"Zoya Smirnov was only 16 years old. Closely cropped hair gave her the appearance of a boy, and only a thin girlish voice involuntarily betrayed her sex.

"At the beginning Zoya was somewhat shy; she carefully chose her words and replied confusedly to our questions; but later she recovered and told us her entire history, which brought tears to the eyes of many a case-hardened veteran who heard it.

"She and her friends decided to go to the war on the eighth day of mobilization—i.e., at the end of July, 1914; and early in August they succeeded in realizing their dream.

"Exactly twelve of them assembled; and they were all nearly the same age and from the same high school. Almost all were natives of Moscow, belonging to the most diversified classes of society, but firmly united in the camaraderie of school life.

> We decided to run away to the war at all costs, said Zoya. It was impossible to run away from Moscow, because we might have been stopped at the station. It was therefore necessary to hire izvozchiks [carriages] and ride out to one of the suburban stations through which the military echelons were continually passing. We left home early in the morning without saying a word to our parents and departed. It was a bit terrible at first; we were very sorry for our fathers and mothers, but the desire to see the war and ourselves kill the Germans overcame all other sentiments.

"And so they attained the desired object. The soldiers treated the little patriots quite paternally and properly, and having concealed them in the cars took them off to the war. A military uniform was obtained for each; they donned these and unobstructed arrived at the Austrian frontier, where they had to detrain and on foot proceed to Lemberg. Here the regimental authorities found out what had happened, but not being able to persuade the young patriots to return home allowed them to march with the regiment.

"The regiment traversed the whole of Galicia; scaled the Carpathians,[1] incessantly participating in battle, and the girls never fell back from it a step, but shared with the men all the privations and horrors of the march and discharged the duties of ordinary privates, since they were taught to shoot and were given rifles.

"Days and months passed.

"The girls almost forgot their past, they hardly responded to their feminine names, for each of them had received a masculine surname, and completely mingled with the men. The soldiers themselves mutually guarded the girls and observed each other's conduct.

"The battles in which the regiment engaged were fierce and sanguinary, particularly in the Spring, when the Germans brought up their heavy artillery to the Carpathians and began to advance upon us with their celebrated phalanx. Our troops underwent a perfect hell and the young volunteers endured it with them.

> "Was it terrible?" an officer asked Zoya. "Were you afraid?"
>
> "I should say so! Who wouldn't be afraid? When for the first time they began to fire with their heavy guns, several of us couldn't stand it and began to cry out."
>
> "What did you cry out?"
>
> "We began to call 'Mamma.' Shura was the first to cry, then Lida. They were both

---

[1]Galicia was an Austrian province in east central Europe, which is today divided between Poland and Ukraine. Lemberg was the capital of Galicia. The Carpathians are a range of mountains stretching through eastern Europe, where many battles were fought in World War I.

> 14 years old, and they remembered their mothers all the time. Besides, it seems that I also cried out as well. We all cried. Well, it was frightful even for the men."

"During one of the Carpathian engagements, at night, one of the twelve friends, the sixteen-year-old Zina Morozov, was killed outright by a shell. It struck immediately at her feet, and the entire small body of the girl was torn into fragments.

> Nevertheless, we managed to collect her remains [Zoya stated with a tender inflexion in her voice]. At dawn the firing died down and we all—that is, all the remaining high school volunteers—assembled near the spot where Zina had perished, and somehow collected her bones and laid them in a hastily dug grave. In the same grave we laid also all Zina's things, such as she had with her. The grave was then filled up and upon the cross which we erected above it the following inscription was written: "Volunteer of such and such a regiment, Zina Morozov, 16 years old, killed in action on such and such a date in such and such year."
>
> On the following day we were already far away, and exactly where Zina's grave is I don't remember well. I only know that it is in the Carpathians at the foot of a steep rocky incline.

"After the death of Zina other of her friends were frequently wounded in turn—Nadya, Zhena, and the fourteen-year-old Shura. Zoya herself was wounded twice—the first time in the leg, and the second time in the side. Both wounds were so serious that Zoya was left unconscious on the battlefield, and the stretcher-bearers subsequently discovered her only by accident. After the second wound she was obliged to lie at a base hospital for over a month. On being discharged she again proceeded to the positions, endeavoring to find her regiment, but on reaching the familiar trenches she could no longer find a single regimental comrade, nor a single fellow-volunteer; they had all gone to another front, and in the trenches sat absolute strangers. The girl lost her presence of mind, and for the first time during the entire campaign began to weep, thus unexpectedly betraying her age and sex. Her unfamiliar fellow-countrymen gazed with amazement upon the strange young non-commissioned officer with the Cross of St. George and medal on her breast, who resembled a stripling and finally proved to be a girl. But the girl had with her all necessary documents, not excepting a certificate giving her the right to wear the St. George's Cross received for a brave and dashing reconnoissance, and distrustful glances promptly gave place to others full of respect.

"Zoya was finally induced to abandon the trenches, at least for the time being, and to try to engage in nursing at one of the advanced hospitals. She is now working at the divisional hospital of the N—division, in the village of K., ten versts from the Austrian town of Z.

"From her remaining friends whom she left with the regiment which went to another front Zoya has no news whatever.

"What has befallen them? Do these amazing Russian girls continue their disinterested and heroic service to the country, or do graves already hold them, similar to that which was dug for the remnants of poor little Zina, who perished so gloriously in the distant Carpathians?"

6 The Turkish Assault on Armenians

From the eleventh century to the early twentieth century, the western reaches of a long-standing Armenian heartland lay in the eastern portion of what is contemporary Turkey. The fate of this population was linked inextricably to the decay

of the Ottoman Empire. After a series of bitter military defeats in southeastern Europe during the first several years of the twentieth century, a new sense of Turkish nationalism emerged through the "Young Turks" movement. Although they comprised university students, military officers, and other reformers with varying agendas, they found common ground in their rejection of what they regarded as an incompetent and outdated monarchy. To a significant degree, they espoused support for liberalism and constitutional government, and were hostile to the role of traditional Islam in Turkish politics and society. After initiating a revolution that forced constitutional government on the Ottoman emperor, the Young Turks strived to consolidate a new, central authority with intent to modernize the land and rally citizens around a sense of Turkish identity, rather than an Islamic religious identity. Such a modernization, they anticipated, would restore Turkish strength and prevent future defeats at the hands of European or other enemies.

The Armenians in the Ottoman Empire were but one of several minority populations. However, many Armenians had achieved a degree of material prosperity through trade or modest manufacturing enterprises, and this led to growing resentment within the broader Turkish and other Ottoman ethnic communities. Moreover, the Armenian population's strong sense of identity—both as a distinct ethnic group and as a Christian religious community—lent it a sense of confidence that the Ottoman authorities perceived as subversive. As Armenians in Eastern Turkey began more intently to seek a degree of local autonomy within the Ottoman state, Young Turk leaders perceived their goal of centralizing administrative control increasingly threatened. When war broke out in 1914, the Turkish government grew concerned that its Armenian population would be a traitorous element, given that a large Armenian population lived across the border within the enemy Russian Empire.

The measures taken against Armenians beginning in 1915 correspond with what we have come to know as ethnic cleansing, and can be characterized as mass murder at the very least. Armenian intellectuals, religious leaders, and political figures found themselves arrested and deported from population centers into Eastern Anatolia, where they and local Armenian men were murdered. Armenian conscripts in the Turkish army, usually segregated into unarmed labor battalions, were executed en masse. Turkish gendarmes marched women, children, and elderly men into the mountains and deserts and ensured their deaths from lack of water and food. Others suffered robbery, rape, or murder at the hands of hostile Turkish or Kurdish villagers. Armenian children were often taken from their families and raised as Turks—another form of ethnic cleansing designed to eliminate every possible trace of "Armenianness." Precise figures vary for Armenian fatalities. Between the most vicious measures in 1915 and the displacements and murders that subsided in 1923 estimates have ranged between 500,000 to perhaps 750,000 at the lower end, and as high as approximately 1.5 million at the higher end.

The Turkish position has long been that the events took place under conditions of bitter warfare, that there were casualties on both sides, and resulted from the necessity of relocating the Armenian population for strategic reasons (i.e., concern for pro-Russian sympathies among Turkish Armenians and solidarity with their brethren across the hostile border). Both the scale of death and the regime's intentionality have been denied since the 1920s, and the subject has become a taboo in Turkish society. Turkish citizens or resident aliens can be prosecuted for insulting Turkish identity under Article 301 of the penal code, and condemnation of the genocide in the French parliament and U.S. Congress met with bitterness and criticism from governmental officials in Ankara and demonstrators in the streets of Turkish towns and cities. Despite such vehement protestations to the contrary, in the eyes of many scholars, the Armenians' experience qualifies as genocide under the terms of the 1948 UN Convention on the Prevention and Punishment of Genocide. For example, historian Rouben Paul Adalian argues: "Young Turk ideologues in Constantinople conceived and implemented the genocide, a total destruction of Armenian society. Military officers and soldiers regarded the policy as a security measure. Others in Ottoman society saw it as a convenient way of ridding themselves of effective economic competitors, not to mention creditors. Others justified the slaughter of the Armenians as a religious duty called upon by the concept of *jihad* [. . .]." Historian Jay Winter argues that the first genocide of the twentieth century is inseparable from the circumstances of total war, which made possible mass murder on an unprecedented scale. During the First World War, virtually entire societies mobilized for conflict; and in order to manage the population to support the war effort, centralized administrative control extended in an unprecedented fashion. New technologies of warfare dramatically increased the lethality of conflict, the differentiation between the home front and military fronts minimized, and the distinction between enemy soldiers and enemy civilians eroded. Winter's argument is a compelling one, and events in Nazi-occupied Eastern Europe a generation later would appear to reinforce his point.

Takhoui Levonian and Yevnig Adrouni THE SURVIVORS REMEMBER

Takhoui Levonian was fifteen years old when she experienced the violent population transfer of Armenians from her town into southeastern Anatolia. Her account of flight, the violence Armenians experienced, and her abduction at the hands of marauding Turks is consistent with the accounts of many other survivors. She eventually settled in Los Angeles and shared her story in 1981.

Yevnig Adrouni, the author of the second selection below, was born in the same region as Takhoui Levonian, and at age ten witnessed the roundup of Armenian men and was aware of the abuse and imprisonment of Armenian soldiers at the hands of the Turkish army. Her experience of flight, misery, and murder was punctuated by tense interactions with other ethnic groups hostile to the Armenians. She survived by assuming a Muslim identity.

When the war began, I could see and sense the men of our town gathering in groups. They were talking and looking very sad. The women used to sigh. The schools shut down and their grounds, as well as the churches, became filled with soldiers. That's how winter passed.

In April, there was talk that they were going to move us out. I was 15 years old then . . . .

Between April 29 and 30 [of 1915], word came that they were going to transfer us to Kharpert. On May first, that news was confirmed and until the fourth [of May] every household began preparations by making *kete* [Armenian bread], preparing chickens, other meats, and so on. My father told my mother not to bother with any of these preparations. He said to just take our bedding on the mules and not to bother burying anything, like so many others had done who thought that they would return to them. He said that if we ever returned, he would be glad to come back to four walls. He was farsighted.

At the onset of the war he imported large amounts of oil, sugar, matches, and all the things that had to be imported. When we left [on the deportation], we distributed all this to our neighbors. They arrested only a few people from our town. The rest they left unharmed. They did not do anything to my father because he was respected by all, since he was so fair with every one—regardless of nationality. He did good equally to all.

We were the first caravan to leave with much tears and anguish since it meant separation for so many. They assigned a few soldiers to us and thus we began. We used to travel by day, and in the evenings we stopped to eat and rest. In five to six days we reached Palu. There, while we were washing up, I will never, never forget, they took my father away, along with all the men down to 12 years of age. The next day our camp was filled with the Turks and Kurds of Palu, looting, dragging away whatever they could, both possessions and young women. They knocked the mules down to kill them. I was grabbing onto my six-year-old brother; my sister was holding her baby, and my two young sisters were grabbing her skirt; my mother was holding the basket of bread. There was so much confusion, and the noise of bullets shooting by us. Some people were getting shot, and the rest of us were running in the field, not knowing where to go . . . .

Then I saw with my own eyes the Turks beating a fellow name Sahag, who had hid under his wife's dress. They were beating him with hammers, axes right in front of me and his wife. He yelled to her to run away, that we are all going to die a "donkey death." And then I saw the husband of my aunt, who was too old to have been taken previously, and he was being beaten in the head with an ax. They then threw him in the river. It finally calmed down. The Turks left some dead, took some with them, and the rest of us found each other.

At this time it was announced that anyone who would become a Turk could remain here. Otherwise, we must continue on. Many stayed. So we took off again. [We felt] much loss, that was not material loss only, but human loss. We were in tears and anguish as we left.

From Palu to Dikranagerd they tormented us a great deal. We suffered a lot. There was no water or food. Whatever my mom had in her bag, she gave us a little at a time. We walked the whole day, 10 to 15 days. No shoes remained on our feet. We finally reached Dikranagerd. There, by the water, we washed, and whatever little dry bread we had we wetted it and ate it.

Word came that the *vali* [governor] wanted from the Armenians a very pretty 12-year-old girl. . . . So by night, they came with their lamps looking for such a girl. They found one, dragged her from the mother, saying to the weeping mother that they will return her. Later, they returned the child, in horrible condition, almost dead, and left her at her mother's knees.

The mother was weeping so badly, and, of course, the child could not make it and died. The women could not comfort her. Finally, several of the women tried to dig a hole, and with the help of one of the *gendarme's* guns, they buried the girl and covered her. Dikranagerd had a large wall around it, so my mother and a few other women wrote on it, "Shushan buried here."

We remained under the walls [where Shushan was buried] for two to three days. Then they made us leave again. This time they assigned to us an elderly *gendarme*. He had tied to his horse a large container of water and the whole way he kept giving it to children and never himself rode the horse, but allowed old women to take turns on it. We went to Mardin. He also always took us near the villages so we could buy some food, and he would not allow the villagers to sell food at expensive prices. A lot of people either died on the way or stayed behind, because they could not keep up. So by the time we reached Mardin we were a lot less in number although still a lot. They deposited us in a large field. There they gave us food . . . . At this point my mother was not with us.

A Kurd woman came and told my sister that two horsemen were going to kidnap me. She panicked and started looking for my mom, but she was not around. So she thought of giving the baby, who was in her arms, to the Kurd woman, so that she would help me. So she disguised me, but when we turned around, the woman was gone with the baby.

Turks used to pay high prices for babies, probably the woman sold him. My poor sister, Zarouhi, went crazy. I, too, was going crazy, feeling that I was the cause. I cried and cried. We remained in Mardin for five days and never found the baby. My poor sister was lactating, and her milk was full but there was no baby to nurse . . . .

It came time to leave, and we had to leave the baby behind with uncontrollable tears. The journey was dreadful. With no shoes on our feet, it was so painful to walk on the paths they took us on. We used to wrap cloth on them to ease the pain, but it didn't really help much. There was no water. In fact, at one stretch, for three full days, we had no water at all. The children would cry: "Water, water, water." One of the children died.

Then toward morning one day, my sister and another woman crawled out of camp to a far place and brought some water in a tin can. Finally, they dumped us next to a small river. There my mother took me to the river to wash my face which was always covered up, except for my eyes. But one of the *gendarmes*, having spotted my eyes, showed up and grabbed me. My mother fainted, and, acting bravely, I shook his hand loose and ran, mingling among the people. I could hear the women yelling to my mother to wake up, that I got away. As the caravan moved again, I kept watching that man, always trying to stay behind him . . . .

The reminiscence of Yevnig Adrouni appears below.

My uncle, my cousin, the government took them away. Later they gathered the noteworthy people, including my father. They took him to prison, to Kharpert. After this they began to gather the men and to take them to the place called Keghvank. That place was a slaughterhouse. I remember my uncle's wife and others used to go there. My father was still in prison at this time. They used to go there and find that their men were missing. They [the Turks] had taken them and killed them with axes even then.

During the time when my father was in prison, there occurred the thing called *Emeliet Tabure*. They recalled all the Armenian soldiers. They set them to work at road construction. In this way they gathered all of them, including the Armenian soldiers, and filled them in the prisons. Later, when my father was still in prison, they set fire to the prison so that the Armenians would be killed. Already they were torturing them every day.

When he escaped from prison, a Kurd saw my father. He was an acquaintance. My father fled with the Kurd to our village. But his nails were pulled out and his body was black and blue. They had tortured my father continuously. He lived but a few days. He died.

This is in 1915. My mother was deported first. A Turk was going to keep us, but he proposed that we Turkify. My mother did not accept. Therefore, since I was young, they thought that if my mother was not with me, they might be able to convince me to Turkify. My mother was deported three months before the rest of us. This happened in spring. As for me, they would say: "Would the daughter of a tough infidel become a Muslim?"

They deported me also, thirsty and hungry, all the way to Deir el Zor. They did not even allow us to drink water. Along the way they took us by very narrow roads. Many of the old people who were hungry and thirsty could not walk. They used to strike them with stones and roll them down the slope. Pregnant women, I have seen with my own eyes . . . I cried a lot. Whenever I go to church, the whole thing is in front of my eyes, the scene, the deportation. They tore open the bellies of pregnant women so that the child was born. It fell free. They used to do that. I have seen such things.

There were some men. They killed them at that time. All of us, hungry, thirsty, we walked all the way to Deir el Zor. They came, Kurds, Arabs, and carried us away from the caravan. When a piece of bread fell in my hands for the first time, I chewed it but could not swallow it because I was starved.

Along the way they did not allow us to drink water. The river was there. It flowed. They did not let us go and drink. A girl, she was 13, 14 perhaps . . . we suddenly saw that the caravan was stopped there in the field. That girl came, her face scratched, bloodied, all her clothes torn. Her mother had sent her secretly in order to fetch water. There were Kurdish boys . . . all the things they have done to the poor girl. The Turkish guards caught her mother. They asked: "Who is her mother? Let her come forward." The caravan was seated. A woman moved her lips. The guards said: "This is her mother." The child was in her lap. They seized the woman and in front of our eyes, they shot her [daughter] dead, saying: "Because you did not have the right. We had forbidden you to send anyone to the river."

They used to take the little ones and carry them away. The Kurds carried me away as well. For eight years I remained lost among the Kurds, the Turks, and the Arabs. I was among the Kurds. I forgot much of the Armenian language, but I did not forget the Lord's Prayer. Later they used to have me tend sheep. They gave me a dog with the name of Khutto. I used to write in the dirt with my finger my name, my last name, and the name of my birthplace. I used to write the alphabet in the dirt and in this way I did not forget the Armenian letters. I did not forget the Lord's Prayer and I did not forget where I was from.

First I was with an Assyrian. They took me to Merdin. Later I was placed with Muslims to be brought up as their child, but I became ill. They returned me to the Assyrians. The Assyrians helped us a great deal. From the church, the sister of the patriarch of the Assyrians took me to her house. They were poor as well. The Assyrians used to go to the road in order to break stones and make a living, and I went along with them. We used to go there to break stones. When that finished, it seems the war was ended, I said I am going to Aleppo. Instead of going to Aleppo, Kurdish tribesmen carried me away. They took me to their villages as a servant. I knew that I had relatives in Aleppo but how would I find them, how would I get there? I was among Kurds.

They took me to the place called Tersellor. Tersellor was a village of Kurds in the environs of Aleppo at the place called Musulme. I remained there tending sheep, but I had made up my mind that I would go to Aleppo. I did not know any other Armenians. There were no Armenians. There was nobody, but I thought to myself that my cousin might be there. By night I escaped. I went down the road. I hid from the Kurds. I saw a traveler on horseback with young ones around him. They saw me.

Now the languages, Arabic, Kurdish, I spoke fluently already. They asked me: "Where are you going?" I said: "I am going to Aleppo." They looked at each other's faces. They said: "We are going to Aleppo. We will take you along." They took me with them. They were from Aleppo, but Muslims. They have villages. In the summer they go to their villages. In the winter they return to Aleppo. They took me with them, but they did not let me out of their house in Aleppo. Next door to the house I was staying in there was an Armenian girl. She was younger than I. She remembered only her name, Mary. She brought news from the outside. She is also Armenian and I am Armenian, but I acted as if

I was a Kurd since I had presented myself as a Kurd to the others. I was afraid to tell the truth to that Armenian girl. She was younger than I.

One day she had fallen down the stairs and broken her foot. They took her to the hospital. At the hospital they told her: "You are Armenian." "No, my name is Fatma," she had said.

I saw that she had come back. When we were taking out the garbage, I asked her: "Where were you?" She related what had taken place. "I was at the hospital." She said that they told her: "You are Armenian." She said: "At first I denied it." After talking for a while she conceded. "Yes, I only remember that we were under a tent. My father, my mother, all, they killed and they took me. Only that much I remember." They [the hospital personnel] said: "Do not go [back to the house]. Now there are Armenians. We have an Armenia." This is at the end of 1922. After I was freed I discovered what the date was. She said [to the hospital personnel]: "No. I go back because they spent ten red gold pieces for my foot."

Look, God sent her for me. I believe that God sent her for me. "But I will escape," she said. "I will escape." I said: "Alright, we will escape together." We had a shoemaker who was Armenian. We did not know that he was Armenian. He was from Aintab. Now I regret very much that I did not take down his name. Eventually, through his assistance, we managed to escape. . . .

So this is my story. But the things which the Turks did, the massacres, I never forget. In front of our eyes ... Haygaz ... on his mother's knees, they butchered him. These sort of things I have seen. And I always cry. I cannot forget.

7 The Paris Peace Conference

The most terrible war the world had experienced ended in November 1918; in January 1919, representatives of the victorious powers assembled in Paris to draw up a peace settlement. The principal figures at the Paris Peace Conference were Woodrow Wilson (1856–1924), president of the United States; David Lloyd George (1863–1945), prime minister of Great Britain; Georges Clemenceau (1841–1929), premier of France; and Vittorio Orlando (1860–1925), premier of Italy. Disillusioned intellectuals and the war-weary masses turned to Wilson as the prince of peace who would fashion a new and better world.

Woodrow Wilson
THE IDEALISTIC VIEW

Wilson sought a peace of justice and reconciliation, one based on democratic and Christian ideals, as the following excerpts from his speeches illustrate.

(May 26, 1917)

We are fighting for the liberty, the self-government, and the undictated development of all peoples, and every feature of the settlement that concludes this war must be conceived and executed for that purpose. Wrongs must first be righted and then adequate safeguards must be created to prevent their being committed again. . . .

. . . No people must be forced under sovereignty under which it does not wish to live. No territory must change hands except for the purpose of securing those who inhabit it a fair chance of life and liberty. No indemnities must be insisted on except those that constitute payment for manifest wrongs done. No readjustments of power must be made except such as will tend to secure the future peace of the world and the future welfare and happiness of its peoples.

And then the free peoples of the world must draw together in some common covenant, some genuine and practical co-öperation that will in effect combine their force to secure peace and justice in the dealings of nations with one another.

The following are excerpts from the Fourteen Points, the plan for peace that Wilson announced on January 8, 1918.

IV. Adequate guarantees given and taken that national armaments will be reduced to the lowest point consistent with domestic safety.

V. A free, open-minded, and absolutely impartial adjustment of all colonial claims, based upon a strict observance of the principle that in determining all such questions of sovereignty the interests of the populations concerned must have equal weight with the equitable claims of the government whose title is to be determined. . . .

VIII. All French territory should be freed and the invaded portions restored, and the wrong done to France by Prussia in 1871 in the matter of Alsace-Lorraine, which has unsettled the peace of the world for nearly fifty years, should be righted, in order that peace may once more be made secure in the interest of all.

IX. A readjustment of the frontiers of Italy should be effected along clearly recognizable lines of nationality.

X. The peoples of Austria-Hungary, whose place among the nations we wish to see safeguarded and assured, should be accorded the freest opportunity of autonomous development. . . .

XII. The Turkish portions of the present Ottoman Empire should be assured a secure sovereignty, but the other nationalities which are now under Turkish rule should be assured an undoubted security of life and an absolutely unmolested opportunity of autonomous development, and the Dardanelles should be permanently opened as a free passage to the ships and commerce of all nations under international guarantees.

XIII. An independent Polish state should be erected which should include the territories inhabited by indisputably Polish populations, which should be assured a free and secure access to the sea, and whose political and economic independence and territorial integrity should be guaranteed by international covenant.

XIV. A general association of nations must be formed under specific covenants for the purpose of affording mutual guarantees of political independence and territorial integrity to great and small states alike.

(February 11, 1918)

. . . The principles to be applied [in the peace settlement] are these:

First, that each part of the final settlement must be based upon the essential justice of that particular case and upon such adjustments as are most likely to bring a peace that will be permanent;

Second, that peoples and provinces are not to be bartered about from sovereignty to sovereignty as if they were mere chattels and pawns in a game, even the great game, now forever discredited, of the balance of power; but that

Third, every territorial settlement involved in this war must be made in the interest and for the benefit of the populations concerned, and not as a part of any mere adjustment or compromise of claims amongst rival states; and

Fourth, that all well-defined national aspirations shall be accorded the utmost satisfaction that can be accorded them without introducing new or perpetuating old elements of discord and antagonism that would be likely in time to break the peace of Europe and consequently of the world.

(April 6, 1918)

. . . We are ready, whenever the final reckoning is made, to be just to the German people, deal fairly with the German power, as with all others. There can be no difference between peoples in the final judgment, if it is indeed to be a righteous judgment. To propose anything but justice, even-handed and dispassionate justice, to Germany at any time, whatever the outcome of the war, would be to renounce and dishonor our own cause. For we ask nothing that we are not willing to accord.

(December 16, 1918)

. . . The war through which we have just passed has illustrated in a way which never can be forgotten the extraordinary wrongs which can be perpetrated by arbitrary and irresponsible power.

It is not possible to secure the happiness and prosperity of the world, to establish an enduring peace, unless the repetition of such wrongs is rendered impossible. This has indeed been a people's war. It has been waged against absolutism and militarism, and these enemies of liberty must from this time forth be shut out from the possibility of working their cruel will upon mankind.

(January 3, 1919)

. . . Our task at Paris is to organize the friendship of the world, to see to it that all the moral forces that make for right and justice and liberty are united and are given a vital organization to which the peoples of the world will readily and gladly respond. In other words, our task is no less colossal than this, to set up a new international psychology, to have a new atmosphere.

(January 25, 1919)

. . . We are . . . here to see that every people in the world shall choose its own masters and govern its own destinies, not as we wish, but as it wishes. We are here to see, in short, that the very foundations of this war are swept away. Those foundations were the private choice of small coteries of civil rulers and military staffs. Those foundations were the aggression of great powers upon the small. Those foundations were the holding together of empires of unwilling subjects by the duress of arms. Those foundations were the power of small bodies of men to work their will upon mankind and use them as pawns in a game. And nothing less than the emancipation of the world from these things will accomplish peace.

Georges Clemenceau
FRENCH DEMANDS FOR SECURITY AND REVENGE

Wilson's promised new world clashed with French demands for security and revenge. Almost all the fighting on the war's western front had taken place in France; its industries and farmlands lay in ruins, and many of its young men had perished. France had been invaded by Germany in 1870 as well as in 1914, so

the French believed that only by crippling Germany could they guarantee their safety. Premier Clemenceau, who was called "the Tiger," dismissed Wilson's vision of a new world as mere noble sentiment divorced from reality, and he fought tenaciously to gain security for France. Clemenceau's profound hatred and mistrust of Germany are revealed in his book *Grandeur and Misery of Victory* (1930), written a decade after the Paris Peace Conference.

For the catastrophe of 1914 the Germans are responsible. Only a professional liar would deny this. . . .

What after all is this war, prepared, undertaken, and waged by the German people, who flung aside every scruple of conscience to let it loose, hoping for a peace of enslavement under the yoke of a militarism destructive of all human dignity? It is simply the continuance, the recrudescence, of those never-ending acts of violence by which the first savage tribes carried out their depredations with all the resources of barbarism. The means improve with the ages. The ends remain the same. . . .

Germany, in this matter, was unfortunate enough to allow herself (in spite of her skill at dissimulation) to be betrayed into an excess of candour by her characteristic tendency to go to extremes. *Deutschland über alles. Germany above everything!* That, and nothing less, is what she asks, and when once her demand is satisfied she will let you enjoy a peace under the yoke. Not only does she make no secret of her aim, but the intolerable arrogance of the German aristocracy, the servile good nature of the intellectual and the scholar, the gross vanity of the most competent leaders in industry, and the wide-spread influence of a violent popular poetry conspire to shatter throughout the world all the time-honoured traditions of individual, as well as international, dignity. . . .

On November 11, 1918, the fighting ceased.

It is not I who will dispute the German soldier's qualities of endurance. But he had been promised a *fresh and frolicsome war,* and for four years he had been pinned down between the anvil and the hammer. . . . Our defeat would have resulted in a relapse of human civilization into violence and bloodshed. . . .

Outrages against human civilization are in the long run defeated by their own excess, and thus I discern in the peculiar mentality of the German soldier, with his *"Deutschland über alles,"* the cause of the premature exhaustion that brought him to beg for an armistice before the French soldier, who was fighting for his independence. . . .

And what is this "Germanic civilization," this monstrous explosion of the will to power, which threatens openly to do away entirely with the diversities established by many evolutions, to set in their place the implacable mastery of a race whose lordly part would be to substitute itself, by force of arms, for all national developments? We need only read [General Friedrich von] Bernhardi's famous pamphlet *Our Future,* in which it is alleged that Germany sums up within herself, as the historian Treitschke asserts, the greatest manifestation of human supremacy, and finds herself condemned, by her very greatness, either to absorb all nations in herself or to return to nothingness. . . . Ought we not all to feel menaced in our very vitals by this mad doctrine of universal Germanic supremacy over England, France, America, and every other country? . . .

What document more suitable to reveal the direction of "German culture" than the famous manifesto of the ninety-three super-intellectuals of Germany,[1] issued to justify the bloodiest and the least excusable of military aggressions against the great centres of civilization? At the moment . . . violated Belgium lay beneath the heel of the malefactor (October 1914) . . . [and German troops were] razing . . . great historical buildings to the ground [and] burning down

---

[1]Shortly after the ourbreak of war, ninety-three leading German scholars and scientists addressed a letter to the world, defending Germany's actions.

. . . libraries. It would need a whole book to tell of the infamous treatment inflicted upon noncombatants, to reckon up those who were shot down, or put to death, or deported, or condemned to forced labour. . . .

Well, this was the hour chosen by German intellectuals to make themselves heard. Let all the nations give ear! . . .

. . . Their learning made of them merely Germans better than all others qualified to formulate, on their own account, the extravagances of Germanic arrogance. The only difference is that they speak louder than the common people, those docile automatons. The fact is that they really believe themselves to be the representatives of a privileged *"culture"* that sets them above the errors of the human race, and confers on them the prerogative of a superior power. . . .

The whole document is nothing but denials without the support of a single proof. *"It is not true* that Germany wanted the War." [Kaiser] William II had for years been *"mocked at by his adversaries of today on account of his unshakable love of peace."* They neglect to tell us whence they got this lie. They forget that from 1871 till 1914 we received from Germany a series of war threats in the course of which Queen Victoria and also the Czar had to intervene with the *Kaiser* direct for the maintenance of peace.

I have already recalled how our German intellectuals account for the violation of the Belgian frontier:

> *It is not true that we criminally violated Belgian neutrality. It can be proved that France and England had made up their minds to violate it. It can be proved that Belgium was willing. It would have been suicide not to forestall them. . . .*

. . . And when a great chemist such as Ostwald tells us, with his colleagues, that our struggle *"against the so-called German militarism"* is really directed *"against German culture,"* we must remember that *this same savant published a history of chemistry* IN WHICH THE NAME OF [eighteenth-century French chemist Antoine] LAVOISIER WAS NOT MENTIONED.

The "intellectuals" take their place in public opinion as the most ardent propagandists of the thesis which makes Germany the very model of the *"chosen people."* The same Professor Ostwald had already written, *"Germany has reached a higher stage of civilization than the other peoples, and the result of the War will be an organization of Europe under German leadership."* Professor Haeckel had demanded *the conquest of London, the division of Belgium between Germany and Holland, the annexation of North-east France, of Poland, the Baltic Provinces, the Congo, and a great part of the English colonies.* Professor Lasson went further still:

> *We are morally and intellectually superior to all men. We are peerless.* So too are our organizations and our institutions. *Germany is the most perfect creation known in history,* and the Imperial Chancellor, Herr von Bethmann-Hollweg, is *the most eminent of living men.*

Ordinary laymen who talked in this strain would be taken off to some safe asylum. Coming from duly hallmarked professors, such statements explain all German warfare by alleging that Germany's destiny is universal domination, and that for this very reason she is bound either to disappear altogether or to exercise violence on all nations with a view to their own betterment. . . .

May I further recall, since we have to emphasize the point, that on September 17, 1914, Erzberger, the well-known German statesman, an eminent member of the Catholic Party, wrote to the Minister of War, General von Falkenhayn, *"We must not worry about committing an offence against the rights of nations nor about violating the laws of humanity. Such feelings today are of secondary importance"*? A month later, on October 21, 1914, he wrote in *Der Tag, "If a way was found of entirely wiping out the whole of London it would be more humane to employ it* than to allow the blood of a SINGLE GERMAN SOLDIER to be shed on the battlefield!" . . .

. . . General von Bernhardi himself, the best pupil, as I have already said, of the historian Treitschke, whose ideas are law in Germany, has just preached the doctrine of "World power or Downfall" at us. So there is nothing left for other nations, as a way of salvation, but to be conquered by Germany. . . .

I have sometimes penetrated into the sacred cave of the Germanic cult, which is, as every one knows, the *Bierhaus* [beer hall]. A great aisle of massive humanity where there accumulate, amid the fumes of tobacco and beer, the popular rumblings of a nationalism upheld by the sonorous brasses blaring to the heavens the supreme voice of Germany, *"Deutschland über alles!"* Men, women, and children, all petrified in reverence before the divine stoneware pot, brows furrowed with irrepressible power, eyes lost in a dream of infinity, mouths twisted by the intensity of will-power, drink in long draughts the celestial hope of vague expectations. These only remain to be realized presently when the chief marked out by Destiny shall have given the word. There you have the ultimate framework of an old but childish race.

German Delegation to the Paris Peace Conference
A PEACE OF MIGHT

A debate raged over the Versailles Treaty, the peace settlement imposed on Germany by the Paris Peace Conference. The treaty's defenders argued that if Germany had won the war, it would have forced far more ruthless terms on France and other losing countries. These defenders pointed to the Treaty of Brest-Litovsk, which Germany compelled the new and weak revolutionary Russian government to sign in 1918, as an example of German peacemaking. Through this treaty, Germany seized 34 percent of Russia's population, 32 percent of its farmland, 54 percent of its industrial enterprise, and 89 percent of its coal mines.

The Germans denounced the Versailles Treaty, which they regarded both as a violation of Wilson's principles as enunciated in the Fourteen Points and other statements and as an Anglo-French plot to keep Germany economically and militarily weak. Leaders of the new German Weimar Republic, formed after a revolution had forced the emperor to abdicate, protested that in punishing and humiliating the new republic for the sins of the monarchy and the military, the peacemakers weakened the foundations of democracy in Germany, kept alive old hatreds, and planted the seeds of future conflicts. Enraged nationalists swore to erase this blot on German honor.

In the excerpts that follow, the German delegation to the Paris Peace Conference voiced its criticism of the Versailles Treaty.

The peace to be concluded with Germany was to be a peace of right, not a peace of might.

In his address to the Mexican journalists on the 9th of June, 1918, President Wilson promised to maintain the principle that the interests of the weakest and of the strongest should be equally sacred. . . . And in his speech before Congress on the 11th of February 1918, the President described the aim of peace as follows: "What we are striving for is a new international order based upon broad and universal principles of right and justice—no mere peace of shreds and patches." . . .

To begin with the territorial questions:

In the West, a purely German territory on the Saar [river that runs through France and

Germany] with a population of at least 650,000 inhabitants is to be separated from the German Empire for at least fifteen years merely for the reason that claims are asserted to the coal abounding there.

The other cessions in the West, German-Austria and German-Bohemia will be mentioned in connection with the right of self-determination.

In Schleswig, the line of demarcation for voting has been traced through purely German districts and goes farther than Denmark herself wishes.

In the East, Upper Silesia is to be separated from Germany and given to Poland, although it has had no political connexion with Poland for the last 750 years. Contrary to this, the provinces of Posen and almost the whole of West Prussia are to be separated from the German Empire in consideration of the former extent of the old Polish state, although millions of Germans are living there. Again, the district of Memel is separated from Germany quite regardless of its historical past, in the obvious attempt to separate Germany from Russia for economic reasons. For the purpose of securing to Poland free access to the sea, East Prussia is to be completely cut off from the rest of the Empire and thereby condemned to economic and national decay. The purely German city of Danzig is to become a Free State under the suzerainty of Poland. Such terms are not founded on any principle of justice. Quite arbitrarily, here the idea of an imprescribable historical right, there the idea of ethnographical possession, there the standpoint of economic interest shall prevail, in every case the decision being unfavourable to Germany.

The settlement of the colonial question is equally contradictory to a peace of justice. For the essence of activity in colonial work does not consist in capitalistic exploitation of a less developed human race, but in raising backward peoples to a higher civilization. This gives the Powers which are advanced in culture a natural claim to take part in colonial work. Germany, whose colonial accomplishments cannot be denied, has also this natural claim, which is not recognized by a treaty of peace that deprives Germany of all of her colonies.

Not only the settlement of the territorial questions but each and every provision of the treaty of peace is governed by the ill-renowned phrase: "Might above Right!"—Here are a few illustrations: . . .

Although President Wilson . . . has acknowledged that "no single fact caused the war, but that in the last analysis the whole European system is in a deeper sense responsible for the war, with its combination of alliances and understandings, a complicated texture of intrigues and espionage that unfailingly caught the whole family of nations in its meshes," . . . Germany is to acknowledge that Germany and her allies are responsible for all damages which the enemy Governments or their subjects have incurred by her and her allies' aggression. . . . Apart from the consideration that there is no incontestable legal foundation for the obligation for reparation imposed upon Germany, the amount of such compensation is to be determined by a commission nominated solely by Germany's enemies, Germany taking no part in the findings of the commission. The commission is plainly to have power to administer Germany like the estate of a bankrupt. . . .

. . . Germany must promise to pay an indemnity, the amount of which at present is not even stated. . . .

These few instances show that that is not the just peace we were promised, not the peace "the very principle of which," according to a word of President Wilson, "is equality and the common participation in a common benefit. The equality of nations upon which peace must be founded if it is to last must be an equality of rights." . . .

In this war, a new fundamental law has arisen which the statesmen of all belligerent peoples have again and again acknowledged to be their aim: the right of self-determination. To make it possible for all nations to put this privilege into practice was intended to be one achievement of the war. . . . On February 11, 1918, President Wilson said in Congress: "Peoples and provinces are not to be bartered about from sovereignty to sovereignty as if they were mere chattels and pawns in a game." . . .

Neither the treatment described above of the inhabitants of the Saar region . . . of consulting the population in the districts of Eupen, Malmédy, and Prussian Moresnet—which, moreover, shall not take place before they have been put under Belgian sovereignty—comply in the least with such a solemn recognition of the right of self-determination.

The same is also true with regard to Alsace-Lorraine.[1] If Germany has pledged herself "to right the wrong of 1871," this does not mean any renunciation of the right of self-determination of the inhabitants of Alsace-Lorraine. A cession of the country without consulting the population would be a new wrong, if for no other reason, because it would be inconsistent with a recognized principle of peace.

On the other hand, it is incompatible with the idea of national self-determination for two and one-half million Germans to be torn away from their native land against their own will. By the proposed demarcation of the boundary, unmistakably German territories are disposed of in favor of their Polish neighbours. Thus, from the Central Silesian districts of Guhrau and Militsch certain portions are to be wrenched away, in which, besides 44,900 Germans, reside at the utmost 3,700 Poles. The same may be said with reference to the towns of Schneidemühl and Bromberg of which the latter has, at the utmost, eighteen per cent Polish inhabitants, whereas in the rural district of Bromberg the Poles do not form even forty per cent of the population. . . . This disrespect of the right of self-determination is shown most grossly in the fact that Danzig is to be separated from the German Empire and made a free state. Neither historical rights nor the present ethnographical conditions of ownership of the Polish people can have any weight as compared with the German past and the German character of that city. Free access to the sea, satisfying the economic wants of Poland, can be secured by guarantees founded on international law, by the creating of free ports. Likewise the cession of the commercial town of Memel, which is to be exacted from Germany, is in no way consistent with the right of self-determination. The same may be said with reference to the fact that millions of Germans in German-Austria are to be denied the union with Germany which they desire and that, further, millions of Germans dwelling along our frontiers are to be forced to remain part of the newly created Czecho-Slovakian State.

[1] Alsace-Lorraine is a region of mixed French and German speakers, which Germany had taken from France in the Franco-Prussian War (1870–1871); it was restored to France by the Versailles Treaty.

8 The War and European Consciousness

World War I caused many intellectuals to have grave doubts about the Enlightenment tradition and the future of the West. More than ever the belief in human goodness, reason, and progress seemed an illusion. Intellectuals contended that Western civilization, despite its many accomplishments, was flawed and might die.

Paul Valéry
DISILLUSIONMENT

Shortly after World War I, Paul Valéry (1871–1945), a prominent French writer, expressed the mood of disillusionment that gripped many intellectuals.

The following reading was written in 1919; the second reading is from a 1922 speech. Both were published in *Variety,* a collection of some of Valéry's works.

We modern civilizations have learned to recognize that we are mortal like the others.

We had heard tell of whole worlds vanished, of empires foundered with all their men and all their engines, sunk to the inexplorable depths of the centuries with their gods and laws, their academies and their pure and applied sciences, their grammars, dictionaries, classics, romantics, symbolists, their critics and the critics of their critics. We knew that all the apparent earth is made of ashes, and that ashes have a meaning. We perceived, through the misty bulk of history, the phantoms of huge vessels once laden with riches and learning. We could not count them. But these wrecks, after all, were no concern of ours.

Elam, Nineveh, Babylon were vague and splendid names; the total ruin of these worlds, for us, meant as little as did their existence. But *France, England, Russia* . . . these names, too, are splendid. . . . And now we see that the abyss of history is deep enough to bury all the world. We feel that a civilization is fragile as a life. The circumstances which will send the works of [John] Keats [English poet] and the works of [Charles] Baudelaire [French poet] to join those of Menander[1] are not at all inconceivable; they are found in the daily papers.

The following passage is from an address that Valéry delivered at the University of Zurich on November 15, 1922.

The storm has died away, and still we are restless, uneasy, as if the storm were about to break. Almost all the affairs of men remain in a terrible uncertainty. We think of what has disappeared, we are almost destroyed by what has been destroyed; we do not know what will be born, and we fear the future, not without reason. We hope vaguely, we dread precisely; our fears are infinitely more precise than our hopes; we confess that the charm of life is behind us, abundance is behind us, but doubt and disorder are in us and with us. There is no thinking man, however shrewd or learned he may be, who can hope to dominate this anxiety, to escape from this impression of darkness, to measure the probable duration of this period when the vital relations of humanity are disturbed profoundly.

We are a very unfortunate generation, whose lot has been to see the moment of our passage through life coincide with the arrival of great and terrifying events, the echo of which will resound through all our lives.

One can say that all the fundamentals of the world have been affected by the war, or more exactly, by the circumstances of the war; something deeper has been worn away than the renewable parts of the machine. You know how greatly the general economic situation has been disturbed, and the polity of states, and the very life of the individual; you are familiar with the universal discomfort, hesitation, apprehension. *But among all these injured things is the Mind.* The Mind has indeed been cruelly wounded; its complaint is heard in the hearts of intellectual man; it passes a mournful judgment on itself. It doubts itself profoundly.

[1]Menander was an ancient Greek poet whose works were lost until fragments were found in Egypt at the end of the nineteeth century.

Erich Maria Remarque
THE LOST GENERATION

In Erich Maria Remarque's *All Quiet on the Western Front,* a wounded German soldier reflects on the war and his future. He sees himself as part of a lost generation. **(See also page 55.)**

Gradually a few of us are allowed to get up. And I am given crutches to hobble around on. But I do not make much use of them; I cannot bear Albert's gaze as I move about the room. His eyes always follow me with such a strange look. So I sometimes escape to the corridor;—there I can move about more freely.

On the next floor below are the abdominal and spine cases, head wounds and double amputations. On the right side of the wing are the jaw wounds, gas cases, nose, ear, and neck wounds. On the left the blind and the lung wounds, pelvis wounds, wounds in the joints, wounds in the kidneys, wounds in the testicles, wounds in the intestines. Here a man realizes for the first time in how many places a man can get hit.

Two fellows die of tetanus. Their skin turns pale, their limbs stiffen, at last only their eyes live—stubbornly. Many of the wounded have their shattered limbs hanging free in the air from a gallows; underneath the wound a basin is placed into which drips the pus. Every two or three hours the vessel is emptied. Other men lie in stretching bandages with heavy weights hanging from the end of the bed. I see intestine wounds that are constantly full of excreta. The surgeon's clerk shows me X-ray photographs of completely smashed hip-bones, knees, and shoulders.

A man cannot realize that above such shattered bodies there are still human faces in which life goes its daily round. And this is only one hospital, one single station; there are hundreds of thousands in Germany, hundreds of thousands in France, hundreds of thousands in Russia. How senseless is everything that can ever be written, done, or thought, when such things are possible. It must be all lies and of no account when the culture of a thousand years could not prevent this stream of blood being poured out, these torture-chambers in their hundreds of thousands. A hospital alone shows what war is.

I am young, I am twenty years old; yet I know nothing of life but despair, death, fear, and fatuous superficiality cast over an abyss of sorrow. I see how peoples are set against one another, and in silence, unknowingly, foolishly, obediently, innocently slay one another. I see that the keenest brains of the world invent weapons and words to make it yet more refined and enduring. And all men of my age, here and over there, throughout the whole world see these things; all my generation is experiencing these things with me. What would our fathers do if we suddenly stood up and came before them and proffered our account? What do they expect of us if a time ever comes when the war is over? Through the years our business has been killing;—it was our first calling in life. Our knowledge of life is limited to death. What will happen afterwards? And what shall come out of us?

Ernst von Salomon
BRUTALIZATION OF THE INDIVIDUAL

The war also produced a fascination with violence that persisted after peace had been declared. Many returned veterans, their whole being enveloped by the war, continued to yearn for the excitement of battle and the fellowship of the trenches. Brutalized by the war, these men became ideal recruits for fascist parties that relished violence and sought the destruction of the liberal state.

Immediately after the war ended, thousands of soldiers and adventurers joined the Free Corps—volunteer brigades that defended Germany's eastern borders against encroachments by the new states of Poland, Latvia, and Estonia, and fought communist revolutionaries. Many of these freebooters later became

members of Hitler's movement. Ernst von Salomon, a leading spokesman of the Free Corps movement, was a sixteen-year-old student in Berlin when the defeated German army marched home. In the passage that follows, he described the soldiers who "will always carry the trenches in their blood."

The soldiers walked quickly, pressed closely to each other. Suddenly the first four came into sight, looking lifeless. They had stony, rigid faces. . . . Then came the others. Their eyes lay deep in dark, gray, sharp-edged hollows under the shadow of their helmets. They looked neither right nor left, but straight ahead, as if under the power of a terrifying target in front of them; as if they peered from a mud hole or a trench over torn-up earth. In front of them lay emptiness. They spoke not a word. . . .

O God, how these men looked, as they came nearer—those utterly exhausted, immobile faces under their steel helmets, those bony limbs, those ragged dusty uniforms! And around them an infinite void. It was as if they had drawn a magic circle around themselves, in which dangerous forces, invisible to outsiders, worked their secret spell. Did they still carry in their minds the madness of a thousand battles compressed into whirling visions, as they carried in their uniforms the dirt and the dust of shell-torn fields? The sight was unbearable. They marched like envoys of death, of dread, of the most deadly and solitary coldness. And here was their homeland, warmth, and happiness. Why were they so silent? Why did they not smile? . . .

. . . When I saw these deadly determined faces, these faces as hard as if hacked out of wood, these eyes that glanced past the onlookers, unresponsive, hostile—yes, hostile indeed—then I knew—it suddenly came over me in a fright—that everything had been utterly different from what we had thought, all of us who stood here watching. . . . What did we know about these men? About the war in the trenches? About our soldiers? Oh God, it was terrible: What we had been told was all untrue. We had been told lies. These were not our beloved heroes, the protectors of our homes—these were men who did not belong to us, gathered here to meet them. They did not want to belong to us; they came from other worlds with other laws and other friendships. And all of a sudden everything that I had hoped and wished for, that had inspired me, turned shallow and empty. . . . What an abysmal error it had been to believe for four years that these men belonged to us. Now that misunderstanding vanished. . . .

Then I suddenly understood. These were not workers, peasants, students; no, these were not mechanics, white-collar employees, businessmen, officials—these were soldiers. . . . These were men who had responded to the secret call of blood, of spirit, volunteers one way or the other, men who had experienced exacting comradeship and the things behind things—who had found a home in war, a fatherland, a community, and a nation. . . .

The homeland belonged to them; the nation belonged to them. What we had blabbered like marketwomen, they had actually lived. . . . The trenches were their home, their fatherland, their nation. And they had never used these words; they never believed in them; they believed in themselves. The war held them in its grip and dominated them; the war will never discharge them; they will never return home; they will always carry the trenches in their blood, the closeness of death, the dread, the intoxication, the iron. And suddenly they were to become peaceful citizens, set again in solid every-day routines? Never! That would mean a counterfeit that was bound to fail. The war is over; the warriors are still marching, . . . dissatisfied when they are demobilized, explosive when they stay together. The war had not given them answers; it had achieved no decision. The soldiers continue to march. . . .

Appeals were posted on the street corners for volunteer units to defend Germany's eastern borders. The day after the troops marched into our town, I volunteered. I was accepted and outfitted. Now I too was a soldier.

Sigmund Freud
A LEGACY OF EMBITTERMENT

In his 1915 essay, "Thoughts of the Times on War and Death," Sigmund Freud said that World War I's fury would shatter the bonds of a common European civilization and engulf Europeans in hatred for years to come. He reflects in the following passage on the singular destructiveness of World War I and its uniqueness in world history to date.

We cannot but feel that no event has ever destroyed so much that is precious in the common possessions of humanity, confused so many of the clearest intelligences, or so thoroughly debased what is highest. Science herself has lost her passionless impartiality; her deeply embittered servants seek for weapons from her with which to contribute towards the struggle with the enemy. Anthropologists feel driven to declare him [the enemy] inferior and degenerate, psychiatrists issue a diagnosis of his disease of mind or spirit. . . .

We had expected the great world-dominating nations of white race upon whom the leadership of the human species has fallen, who were known to have world-wide interests as their concern, to whose creative powers were due not only our technical advances towards the control of nature but the artistic and scientific standards of civilization—we had expected these peoples to succeed in discovering another way of settling misunderstandings and conflicts of interest. Within each of these nations high norms of moral conduct were laid down for the individual, to which his manner of life was bound to conform if he desired to take part in a civilized community. . . .

Relying on this unity among the civilized peoples, countless men and women have exchanged their native home for a foreign one, and made their existence dependent on the intercommunications between friendly nations. Moreover anyone who was not by stress of circumstance confined to one spot could create for himself out of all the advantages and attractions of these civilized countries a new and wider fatherland, in which he could move about without hindrance or suspicion. In this way he enjoyed the blue sea and the grey; the beauty of snow-covered mountains and of green meadow lands; the magic of northern forests and the splendour of southern vegetation; the mood evoked by landscapes that recall great historical events, and the silence of untouched nature. This new fatherland was a museum for him, too, filled with all the treasures which the artists of civilized humanity had in the successive centuries created and left behind. As he wandered from one gallery to another in this museum, he could recognize with impartial appreciation what varied types of perfection a mixture of blood, the course of history, and the special quality of their mother-earth had produced among his compatriots in this wider sense. Here he would find cool, inflexible energy developed to the highest point; there, the graceful art of beautifying existence; elsewhere the feeling for orderliness and law, or others among the qualities which have made mankind the lords of the earth.

Nor must we forget that each of these citizens of the civilized world had created for himself a "Parnassus" and a "School of Athens" [that is, a center of high culture and learning] of his own. From among the great thinkers, writers and artists of all nations he had chosen those to whom he considered he owed the best of what he had been able to achieve in enjoyment and understanding of life, and he had venerated them along with the immortal ancients as well as with the familiar masters of his own tongue. None of these great men had seemed to him foreign because they spoke another language—neither the incomparable explorer of human passions, nor the intoxicated worshipper of beauty, nor the powerful and menacing prophet, nor the subtle satirist; and he never reproached himself on that account for being a renegade towards his own nation and his beloved mother-tongue.

The enjoyment of this common civilization was disturbed from time to time by warning voices, which declared that old traditional differences made wars inevitable, even among the members of a community such as this. We refused to believe it; but if such a war were to happen, how did we picture it? . . . [W]e pictured it as a chivalrous passage of arms, which would limit itself to establishing the superiority of one side in the struggle, while as far as possible avoiding acute suffering that could contribute nothing to the decision, and granting complete immunity for the wounded who had to withdraw from the contest, as well as for the doctors and nurses who devoted themselves to their recovery. There would, of course, be the utmost consideration for the non-combatant classes of the population—for women who take no part in war-work, and for the children who, when they are grown up, should become on both sides one another's friends and helpers. And again, all the international undertakings and institutions in which the common civilization of peace-time had been embodied would be maintained.

Even a war like this would have produced enough horror and suffering; but it would not have interrupted the development of ethical relations between the collective individuals of mankind—the peoples and states.

Then the war in which we had refused to believe broke out, and it brought—disillusionment. Not only is it more bloody and more destructive than any war of other days, because of the enormously increased perfection of weapons of attack and defence; it is at least as cruel, as embittered, as implacable as any that has preceded it. It disregards all the restrictions known as International Law, which in peace-time the states had bound themselves to observe; it ignores the prerogatives of the wounded and the medical service, the distinction between civil and military sections of the population, the claims of private property. It tramples in blind fury on all that comes in its way, as though there were to be no future and no peace among men after it is over. It cuts all the common bonds between the contending peoples, and threatens to leave a legacy of embitterment that will make any renewal of those bonds impossible for a long time to come.

CHAPTER THREE

THE RUSSIAN REVOLUTION AND THE SOVIET UNION

VLADIMIR LENIN announces the end of the Provisional Government and the advent of Communist power before the Second Congress of Soviets in Petrograd on November 8, 1917 (New Style). *(Sovfoto)*

On the eve of World War I, the Russian Empire faced a profound crisis. Ever-closer contact with the West, industrialization, and socioeconomic mobility resulting from a new railroad network were undermining the traditional foundations of state and society. Peasant unrest was mounting, while the new factories had spawned a rebellious working class. The tsar had never trusted the country's intellectuals—too many of them had turned into revolutionaries. Defeat in the war with Japan had led to the revolution of 1905, nearly toppling the tsarist regime. Less than a decade later, as worldwide war approached, conservatives recognized and dreaded the prospect of military collapse followed by revolutionary anarchy. Liberals, less realistically, hoped for a constitutional regime that would let backward Russia catch up to the West. Radicals of utopian vision, like V. I. Lenin, expected the Russian workers to become the vanguard of a revolutionary advance that would bring freedom and justice to oppressed peoples all over the world.

Toward the end of World War I, the conservatives' fears came true. Nicholas II was overthrown in the March revolution of 1917; in the ensuing civic disorganization, the Russian state faced dissolution. The Germans were ready to partition the country. The liberal coalition that had formed a provisional government after the abdication of Nicholas II broke apart in early November. At that point, Lenin's Bolsheviks seized power, supported by the workers and soldiers in the country's capital of Petrograd (formerly St. Petersburg and once again St. Petersburg today). In the civil war that followed, the Bolsheviks proved to be the only force capable of holding together a country faced with defeat, revolution, civil war, foreign intervention, and economic ruin. The government became a socialist dictatorship with Lenin at its head. Soviet Russia was guided by Marxist ideology adapted by Lenin to Russian conditions, and it was run by the professional revolutionaries of the Communist party in the name of elected councils (called soviets) of workers and peasants. To counter the prevailing anarchy, Lenin preached discipline, the discipline of responsible social cooperation, which in Western countries had become, to a large extent, part of civic routine. Lenin believed that among the raw and violence-prone peoples of Russia discipline had to be enforced by compulsion and even terror. The counterrevolution that threatened the very existence of the Communist regime was for Lenin a pressing reason for employing terror. By the end of the civil war, even the workers and soldiers of Petrograd protested against the Communist dictatorship, and the garrison at the nearby Kronstadt naval base rose in revolt in 1921.

The years after the Kronstadt uprising were relatively calm. Russia regained its prewar standards of productivity, but it did not overcome the weaknesses that had led to catastrophe in World War I. To guard Soviet Russia against a similar fate was the burning ambition of Joseph Stalin, who in 1929, after a prolonged struggle, took over the leadership role left vacant when Lenin died in 1924. The product of violence and revolutionary agitation since youth, Stalin started a second revolution far more brutal than Lenin's.

Rapid industrialization under successive Five-Year Plans led to appalling confusion, waste, and hardship, yet also to an impressive increase in production. The forcible collectivization of agriculture, designed to crush the spirit of ever-rebellious peasants and to bring agricultural production under the planned economy, proved a savage process. All along, Stalin's revolution was accompanied by well-orchestrated methods of disciplining the country's heterogeneous, stubborn, and willful peoples, and molding them into docile citizens ready for the sacrifices of overly rapid industrialization and driven by patriotic dedication. The second revolution created a sense of citizenship among the peoples of Russia that was unique in the country's history.

Stalin burned to achieve the age-old Russian dream of overcoming the country's backwardness and matching the advanced Western countries in global power and prestige. His program was a desperate effort to create deliberately by compulsion and in the shortest time possible a modern Russian state that would hold its own in a ruthlessly competitive modern world. With harsh and cruel methods, so repulsive to Western values, Stalin transformed the Soviet Union into an industrial and world power, respected and feared for the next half century. At the same time, his command economy, riddled with inefficiency and corruption, contained the seeds of its own destruction, and that of the Communist system it supported.

1 Russian Society Before World War I

If Russia was by far the largest of the traditional European "Great Powers," it was also the most backward. In the middle of the nineteenth century, at a time when elected parliaments were becoming the leading political institutions of their countries, the tsars still claimed to rule by divine right, overseeing an autocratic structure that was as ineffective as it was antiquated. Nevertheless, important changes were beginning to take place. In the 1860s, Emperor Alexander II initiated a brief period of significant reform the like of which had not been seen since Peter I (1694–1725). Chief among these "Great Reforms" was the emancipation of the serfs. If, however, the peasants were pleased to secure personal freedom, the inadequate economic settlement accompanying their liberation made "land hunger" an increasing problem in the countryside. In addition, toward the end of the nineteenth century Russia finally joined the Industrial Revolution. The enormous enterprises created at this time, along with the miserable working conditions within them, bred widespread dissatisfaction among factory laborers. While the autocracy remained especially fearful of new uprisings in the countryside, it was inadvertently promoting the growth of a revolutionary proletariat.

Sergei Witte
A REPORT FOR TSAR NICHOLAS II

In 1899, Sergei Witte (1849–1915), Russia's minister of finance, prepared a report for Tsar Nicholas II (1894–1917) on the necessity of industrialization. This report offers unusual insights into the tsarist empire's economic weakness and the problems of trying to overcome that weakness. Witte's emphasis on the need for economic mobilization with the help of a carefully planned system foreshadows the subsequent drive for heavy industrialization under the Communist regime.

The Witte system, as it came to be called, justified the high tariff on imports originally imposed in 1891. The tariff raised the prices of imported manufactured goods (as well as of luxuries), which upset the landed nobility—Russia's chief agricultural producers and exporters and the tsar's major support group. The nobility not only preferred Western manufactured goods and resented having to pay more for them but also feared that European nations would impose a retaliatory tariff on Russian agricultural exports. The spokesmen for Russian agriculture demanded free trade and opposed Witte, who, in promoting industrial development with the help of foreign capital and know-how, also had to combat widespread nationalist hostility toward foreigners.

In his report, Witte left no doubt that rapid economic development would bring much hardship for the Russian people, and he therefore pressed the emperor to be bold in his support of these policies. His "firm and strict economic system" was absolutely necessary if the Russian Empire, virtually a colony of western Europe, were to become as strong economically as the United States, already in 1900 serving as a yardstick for Russia's progress. Witte believed that only through industrialization could Russia maintain itself as a great power. Excerpts from Witte's report follow.

Russia remains even at the present essentially an agricultural country. It pays for all its obligations to foreigners by exporting raw materials, chiefly of an agricultural nature, principally grain. It meets its demand for finished goods by imports from abroad. The economic relations of Russia with western Europe are fully comparable to the relations of colonial countries with their [ruling states]. The latter consider their colonies as advantageous markets in which they can freely sell the products of their labor and of their industry and from which they can draw with a powerful hand the raw materials necessary for them. This is the basis of the economic power of the governments of western Europe, and chiefly for that end do they guard their existing colonies or acquire new ones. Russia was, and to a considerable extent still is, such a hospitable colony for all industrially developed states, generously providing them with the cheap products of her soil and buying dearly the products of their labor. But there is a radical difference between Russia and a colony: Russia is an independent and strong power. She has the right and the strength not to want to be the eternal handmaiden of states which are more developed economically. She should know the price of her raw materials and of the natural riches hidden in the womb of her abundant territories, and she is conscious of the great, not yet fully displayed, capacity for work among her people. She is proud of her great might, by which she jealously guards not only the political but also the economic independence of her empire. She wants to be a metropolis herself. On the basis of the people's labor, liberated from the bonds of serfdom, there began to grow our own national economy, which bids fair to become a reliable counterweight to the domination of foreign industry.

The creation of our own national industry—that is the profound task, both economic and political, from which our protectionist system [that is, tariffs to protect emerging Russian industries from foreign competition] arises. . . . The task of our present commercial and industrial policy is thus still a very difficult one. It is necessary not only to create industries but to force them to work cheaply; it is necessary to develop in our growing industrial community an energetic and active life—in a word, to raise our industries qualitatively and quantitatively to such a high level that they cease to be a drain and become a source of prosperity in our national economy.

What do we need to accomplish that? We need capital, knowledge, and the spirit of enterprise. Only these three factors can speed up the creation of a fully independent national industry. But, unfortunately, not all these forces can be artificially implanted. They are mutually interconnected; their own proper development depends upon the very growth of industry. . . .

We have . . . neither capital, nor knowledge, nor the spirit of enterprise. The extension of popular education through general, technical, and commercial schools can have, of course, a beneficial influence; and Your Majesty's government is working on that. But no matter how significant the promotion of enlightenment, that road is too slow; by itself it cannot realize our goal. The natural school of industry is first of all a lively industry. Institutions of learning serve only as one aid toward that end. The first investment of savings awakens in man the restlessness of enterprise, and with the first investment in industry the powerful stimulus of personal interest calls forth such curiosity and love of learning as to make an illiterate peasant into a railway builder, a bold and progressive organizer of industry, and a versatile financier.

Industry gives birth to capital; capital gives rise to enterprise and love of learning; and knowledge, enterprise, and capital combined create new industries. Such is the eternal cycle of economic life, and by the succession of such turns our national economy moves ahead in the process of its natural growth. In Russia this growth is yet too slow, because there is yet too little industry, capital, and spirit of enterprise. But we cannot be content with the continuation of such slow growth. . . .

We must give the country such industrial perfection as has been reached by the United States of America, which firmly bases its prosperity on two pillars—agriculture and industry. . . . I have now analyzed the chief bases of the economic system which has been followed in Russia since the reign of Alexander III. . . .

To obtain cheaper goods, of which the population stands in such urgent need, by a substantial tariff reduction would be too expensive. It would forever deprive the country of the positive results of the protective system, for which a whole generation has made sacrifices; it would upset the industries which we have created with so much effort just when they were ready to repay the nation for its sacrifices.

It would be very dangerous to rely on the competition of foreign goods for the lowering of our prices. But we can attain the same results with the help of the competition of foreign capital, which, by coming into Russia, will help Russian enterprise to promote native industry and speed up the accumulation of native capital. Any obstructions to the influx of foreign capital will only delay the establishment of a mature and all-powerful industry. The country cannot afford to defer that goal for long. . . .

Your Imperial Highness may see from the foregoing that the economic policy which the Russian government has followed for the last eight years is a carefully planned system, in which all parts are inseparably interconnected.

M. I. Pokzovskaya
WORKING CONDITIONS FOR WOMEN IN THE FACTORIES

While all of Russia's factory laborers toiled in misery, the lot of women workers was especially harrowing. Their helplessness in the face of ruthless exploitation and sexual abuse highlighted Russia's lack of the social traditions and working conditions that had promoted Western standards of humaneness and civility. This report describing how women were treated in Russia's factories was written by a Russian woman doctor and published in an English suffragist magazine in 1914.

The matter of fines which are exacted from factory workers by their employers is a very serious one. Fines are imposed for: late arrival, work which is not found to be up to standard, for laughter, even for indisposition. At a certain well-known calendar factory in St. Petersburg the women workers receive 0.45 rbls. [rubles] a day, and the fines have been known to amount to 0.50 rbls. a day. At a weaving factory, also in St. Petersburg, women operatives may earn as much as 1.25 rbls. a day, but owing to deductions for various fines the earnings often sink to as low as 0.25 rbls. a day. If a worker is feeling unwell and sits down, a fine is incurred. . . . If an article is dropped, the fine is [levied and] . . . if the worker fails to "stand to attention" at the entrance of employer or foreman and until he leaves the room, she is fined. . . . At a well-known chocolate factory in Moscow the fine for laughing is 0.75 rbls. and if a worker is 15 minutes late she is dismissed for one week. At another old established and famous chocolate factory in case of sudden illness a woman employee is instantly discharged. In a certain cartridge factory the workers are searched before leaving, and those who persist in having pockets are fined. . . .

In the majority of factories where women are employed the working day is from 10 to 11½ hours, after deducting the dinner and breakfast intervals. On Saturday, in many factories . . . the work sometimes lasts 16 and 18 hours per day. The workers are forced to work overtime on pain of instant dismissal or of transference to inferior employment, and in the case of children actual physical force is used to make them continue in their places. Dining and lunch rooms are rarely provided, and in many places no definite time is allowed for meals. In one well-known factory one hour is allowed for meals, but there is no place where the workers can eat their food except in the work-rooms or in the lavatories.

The position of women workers on the tobacco plantations is the worst. According to a report published by the Sevastopol branch of the Women's Protective Union, young girls are sometimes kept at work during 22 hours in the day. Owing to the difficulties of carrying on the process of breaking the tobacco leaves in the daytime, the girl-workers are driven into the plantations at 4 A.M. where they work until 9 A.M. After that they are engaged in the processes of weighing and tying the packets of tobacco, which work is continued through practically the whole day, with the exception of short intervals for meals. At the same time the women workers are continually exposed to brutal and degrading treatment and assault. Not infrequently their earnings are not paid to them. . . .

It happens sometimes, as on April 25th, 1913, at a cotton spinning factory in St. Petersburg, that the workers strike as a protest against the dismissal of old workers and their replacement by girls between 14 and 16 years of age. The result of the strike was a wholesale dismissal of all the women, whose places were filled by young girls. Not infrequently the women strike on account of the rude treatment which they receive from the foreman, actual bodily ill-treatment not being unknown. Such strikes rarely accomplish anything.

The worst aspect of woman's factory labour is, however, the moral danger to which women are exposed from those in power over them.

Immoral proposals from foremen and from their assistants are of general occurrence, and women who resist are persecuted in every possible way, and sometimes actually violated.

In a large tobacco factory in St. Petersburg the women workers who were asking for raised pay were cynically informed that they could augment their income by prostitution.

All these hard conditions in connection with factory life have the result of driving a certain number of women workers into tolerated houses of prostitution or into the streets. This is directly encouraged by the management of some factories.

Olga Semyonova Tian-Shanskaia
SKETCHES OF PEASANT LIFE

Olga Semyonova (1863–1906) was the daughter of a famous Russian explorer, geographer, and statistician Pyotr Petrovich Semyonov (on whom the emperor bestowed the title Tian-Shanskii for his explorations of the Tien Shan mountains in Central Asia). In 1898, Semyonova undertook a major ethnographic study of the Russian peasantry. For four years, she observed the inhabitants of villages close to her family's estate in the Riazan province of European Russia. Her goal was a realistic portrait of the typical peasant—warts and all—that would undermine the idealized view propagated by Russian Populists, who extolled peasant society as the basis for socialism. Unfinished at the time of her death in 1906, the work was completed by her friend Varvara Shneider and finally published in 1914 as *The Life of Ivan: Sketches of Peasant Life from One of the Black Earth Provinces.* Occasionally judgmental and condescending toward her subjects, Semyonova nonetheless offered memorable descriptions of a world far removed from that of educated, urbanized Russia.

The following excerpts deal with the causes of peasant poverty, the corrupt state of peasant self-administration, and evidence of class antagonism in the countryside.

I have observed that peasants, either out of habit or perhaps from some genetic predisposition, have a deep affection for the land. At any rate, a majority of peasants (even those who have lived in town) envy landowners more than anything else. Peasants regard "capital" [money] as more precarious than land; it can slip from your hands much faster because of the temptations to which it exposes its owner. One of the most deep-rooted and firm convictions among peasants is that one day all the land will become theirs. It is terribly amusing to observe how clever they can sometimes be in avoiding this issue in their conversations with landlords. As for the landlords, older peasants consider them to be "weaklings" or "softies," who squander their capital because they are unable to do hard work. . . .

The conversations of peasant men do not stray far from their domestic affairs, field work, taxes, the township council, and the like. Sometimes they talk about other things, for example, the special favors they expect on the occasion of a tsarist coronation or the birth of an heir to the throne. They naturally hope for an exemption from tax arrears. When parish schools first opened, the men spoke of its being done on the initiative of the new tsaritsa [Alexandra, wife of Nicholas II], for when she married the tsar, it is said, she poked fun at him because of the backwardness of his people. Rumor has it that the tsaritsa is "kind," and peasants tend to think that she "may have some additional favors in store for them." Any favor from the tsar provokes speculation about the possibility of more benefits to come.

Women, of course, almost never participate in these conversations. They normally engage in gossip about neighbors or about the families of the local landlords and their household staffs.

Tax collection, too, provokes much grumbling on the part of the peasants. "Does the tsar really not have enough money? We have so little land, and yet have to pay high taxes," one peasant will say. . . .

But what about the many other reasons for the peasants' destitution? I already mentioned the price fluctuations on basic necessities. Even a shoemaker's prices vary from seven rubles for a pair of boots in a bad harvest year to ten rubles in a good year. Furthermore, enormous amounts are squandered in taverns. I know a family in which the husband, after selling grain in town for twenty rubles, never comes back home with more than fourteen or fifteen rubles in his pocket. The head of another family is a lazy lout who rents out his land allotment just so he can avoid farming it himself,* and he drinks with the money his daughter sends home from the city, where she works as a servant. This family of four is always on the brink of starvation, even in a good harvest year. Unproductive peasants of this kind make up at least 10 percent of the village population. And then there is the money that somehow gets "lost" or "stolen" in a tavern, plus expensive customs like the parties thrown for conscripts and the wedding celebrations out of all proportion to people's real means. Compared to these large outlays, four or five extra rubles in taxes are a drop in the bucket. I am not saying that we should abandon efforts to achieve more equitable taxation, but the taxes are, I repeat, literally a drop in the bucket. . . .

Peasants tend to think of their village assembly as unjust. "Look how very difficult it is to live in this community. Whoever has the most relatives is right. People will vote for a relative, and then it's hard for those without kin. That is why a peasant without such allies is reluctant to take business to the village assembly. Why bother when they will just vote you down anyhow? And then there's the vodka. With some vodka and money, any judge can be persuaded to declare the guilty party to be in the right."

The person having the greatest sway over the destiny of the village is . . . the township supervisor[1] . . . A supervisor receives a salary of six hundred rubles a year, and therefore is usually able to rent or even own much more land than any other peasant in the village. Naturally, his own interests take priority in any decisions he makes. He also controls the village assembly, taking bribes and locating guzzlers who can be paid off to support him with their votes. These guzzlers can be found in any village. The peasants call them "howlers and gullets." They are "gullets" in the sense that they have large throats for howling and for drinking. These stooges carry even more weight in determining a peasant's fate at the assembly than

*Rental might seem to be a business choice, but the rent received was far less than the peasant could earn if he worked the land himself, assuming, of course, that he possessed the livestock and equipment needed for farming.

[1]Township supervisors and other village bureaucrats of peasant background had originated in the emancipation settlement of the 1860s.

do his relatives. Behind these stooges is hidden the township supervisor, who, in turn, often represents the interests of a large landowner from the merchant class with capital amounting to a hundred thousand rubles. The supervisor is a frequent guest at the merchant's table, and for a monetary consideration sees to his patron's interests. He may, for example, press the peasants harder for taxes so that they will be forced to accept low-paying jobs from the merchant. Not long ago one of the supervisors arranged a really remarkable deal for a merchant; he got a peasant community to turn over to the merchant, in exchange for land elsewhere, nearly one hundred acres next to the Purlovo railway station, a site with marvelous possibilities of development, and the merchant had to throw in a mere two thousand rubles extra.

Because of his ability to pay off his stooges, a township supervisor enjoys a secure tenure, and at the end of this three-year term he is reelected. After the election, the peasants who voted against him are likely to suffer when taxpaying time comes. Tax collection normally begins in September, but since the tax applies to the current year, the supervisor can easily demand payment from a peasant one or two months earlier [just when the farmer is busiest and has the least possibility to pay]. . . .

The township supervisor is not the only one who accepts bribes. Other officials take them as well; you do not have to look far to find examples. The ordinary peasants, who are oppressed and mistreated and under the thumb of these local representatives of authority, respond as you would expect. After all, they find themselves caught in a vicious circle. In these conditions, who can rise above the general level of misery and set an example for other villagers? The township supervisor is often also the head of the township court. [How then can one appeal his arbitrary decisions even if one had a mind to do so?]

A strong hand on the part of the township supervisor, even the use of corporal punishment, earns the respect of the peasants, provided it is applied consistently. "Our supervisor is really fierce," they will say. "Always greets you with: 'What do ya want, you rascal?' Honest to God, he says that to everyone!" Capricious anger, however, is scorned by peasants. For example, our land captain, basically a "good guy," has fits of rage that alternate with utter weakness. He administers justice when he is drunk and sometimes even deals out blows, but peasants show very little respect for him; they scoff at him. . . .

Peasants have not acquired the habit of intensive labor;[2] they are deprived of the light of knowledge, and they suffer an oppressive poverty. The problem seems to be that whatever goal a peasant entertains, be it merely the acquisition of a pint of vodka or a pair of galoshes, it is beyond his reach, no matter how hard he works. Another thought that bothers me is how can we, the targets of the people's hatred, alter their goals, open new horizons to them, implant the notion of intensive labor as a source of well-being? They would not believe us and would simply laugh at us, perhaps justifiably.

What is important is that animosity and hatred are on the rise within the peasant population and already, though still rarely, can produce the likes of Mikhalek,[3] who acted on the convictions he came to through his suffering. All the propaganda disseminated by the radical men and women of the 1870s *(semidesiatniki)*[4] who went out and worked among the people, hardly succeeded in producing a single such arsonist.

---

[2]This refers to a method of cultivation that seeks to increase productivity by stepping up the amount of capital and labor invested in a given piece of land.

[3]A few pages back the author discussed Mikhalek, a poor peasant, who, influenced by revolutionary ideas, engaged in sabotaging of equipment and arson to show his hatred of wealthy landlords and storekeepers.

[4]The term *semidesiatniki* refers to the students and intellectuals who moved to the countryside in the 1870s in a disastrous attempt to revolutionize the peasants. Their failure strengthened the position of those who believed that revolution in Russia could occur only by means of conspiratorial planning and violence.

2 The Revolution of 1905

Students of Russian history customarily regard the Revolution of 1905 as the "dress rehearsal for 1917," a precursor to the better known uprisings that swept away the Romanov dynasty and installed the Bolsheviks under Lenin. By 1905, nearly every major population group in the empire had cause for complaint with the old regime—the peasants, workers, soldiers and sailors, liberal intelligentsia, and non-Russian minorities. To their own grievances was added the country's inept performance in the Russo-Japanese War, followed by the slaughter of peaceful demonstrators in front of the Winter Palace on "Bloody Sunday" (January 9). The result was a full year of upheaval throughout Russian society, manifested in labor strikes, land seizures by peasants, and military mutinies. In the end, the tsarist system was able to save itself only by means of political concessions, which, even though grudgingly conceded and quickly diluted, nevertheless undermined the autocracy. Everything now hinged on whether the tsar and his court would take advantage of this last reprieve to carry out the reforms that would make another revolution unnecessary.

George Gapon and Ivan Vasimov
WORKERS' PETITION TO THE TSAR

Revolutionaries had been actively working against the tsarist regime since late in the nineteenth century. The opening shots in the Revolution of 1905, however, came not from revolutionaries but from soldiers who fired at a peaceful procession of workers led by Father George Gapon (1870–1906), a Russian Orthodox priest known for his loyalty to the throne. The workers intended to petition the tsar to relieve their plight; instead they were fired on by order of officials afraid of mob violence in front of the imperial palace. Several hundred people were killed or injured. The mishandling of this incident, called "Bloody Sunday," further revealed the government's incompetence. Severing at last the traditional bonds of loyalty that tied the Russian masses to their "Little Father the Tsar," "Bloody Sunday" became a rallying cry to revolutionary action throughout the country.

These extracts from the workers' petition to the tsar have a peaceful tone, although the workers called for a freely elected constituent assembly that would limit the tsar's powers. The petition provides insight into the conditions that turned Russian workers into a revolutionary force.

Sovereign!

We, the workers and the inhabitants of various social strata of the city of St. Petersburg, our wives, children, and helpless old parents, have come to you, Sovereign, to seek justice and protection. We are impoverished; our employers oppress us, overburden us with work, insult us, consider us inhuman, and treat us as slaves who must suffer a bitter fate in silence. Though we have suffered, they push us deeper and deeper into a gulf of misery, disfranchisement [inability to participate in the political process], and ignorance. Despotism and arbitrariness strangle us and we are gasping for breath. Sovereign, we have no strength left. We have reached the limit of endurance. We have reached that terrible moment when death is preferable to the continuance of unbearable sufferings.

And so we left our work and informed our employers that we shall not resume work until they meet our demands. We do not demand much; we only want what is indispensable to life and without which life is nothing but hard labor and eternal suffering. Our first request was that our employers discuss our needs jointly with us. But they refused to do this; they even denied us the right to speak about our needs, saying that the law does not give us such a right. Also unlawful were our requests to reduce the working day to eight hours; to set wages jointly with us; to examine our disputes with lower echelons of factory administration; to increase the wages of unskilled workers and women to one ruble [about $1.00] per day; to abolish overtime work; to provide medical care without insult. . . .

Sovereign, there are thousands of us here; outwardly we resemble human beings, but in reality neither we nor the Russian people as a whole enjoy any human right, have any right to speak, to think, to assemble, to discuss our needs, or to take measures to improve our conditions. They have enslaved us and they did it under the protection of your officials, with their aid and with their cooperation. They imprison and [even] send into exile any one of us who has the courage to speak on behalf of the interests of the working class and of the people. They punish us for our good heartedness and sympathy as if for a crime. To pity a downtrodden, disfranchised, and oppressed man is to commit a major crime. All the workers and the peasants are at the mercy of bureaucratic administrators consisting of embezzlers of public funds and thieves who not only disregard the interests of the people but also scorn these interests. The bureaucratic administration has brought the country to complete ruin, has brought upon it a disgraceful war [Russo-Japanese war, 1904–1905], and continues to lead it further and further into destruction. We, the workers and the people, have absolutely nothing to say in the matter of expenditure of huge taxes that are collected from us. In fact, we do not know where or for what the money collected from the impoverished people goes. The people are deprived of the opportunity to express their wishes and their demands and to participate in determining taxes and expenditures. The workers are deprived of the opportunity to organize themselves in unions to protect their interests.

Sovereign! Is all this compatible with God's laws, by the grace of which you reign? And is it possible to live under such laws? Wouldn't it be better for all of us if we, the toiling people of all Russia, died? Let the capitalist-exploiters of the working class, the bureaucratic embezzlers of public funds, and the pillagers of the Russian people live and enjoy themselves. Sovereign, these are the problems that we face and these are the reasons that we have gathered before the walls of your palace. Here we seek our last salvation. Do not refuse to come to the aid of your people; lead them out of the grave of disfranchisement, poverty, and ignorance; grant them an opportunity to determine their own destiny, and remove from them the unbearable yoke of bureaucrats. Tear down the wall that separates you from your people and let them rule the country with you. . . . Russia is too great, her needs too diverse and numerous to be administered by bureaucrats only. It is essential to have a popular representation; it is essential that the people help themselves and that they govern themselves. Only they know their real needs. Do not spurn their help; accept it; decree immediately to summon at once representatives of the Russian land from all classes, from all strata, including workers' representatives. Let there be present a capitalist, a worker, a bureaucrat, a priest, a doctor, and a teacher—let everyone regardless of who they are elect their own representatives. Let everyone be equal and free to elect or be elected, and toward that end decree that the elections to the Constituent Assembly be carried out on the basis of universal, secret, and equal suffrage. . . .

Here, Sovereign, are our principal needs with which we came to you. Only if and when they are fulfilled will it be possible to free our country from slavery and poverty; will it be possible for it to flourish; will it be possible for the workers to organize themselves to protect their interests against the insolent exploitation of the capitalists and the thievish government of bureaucrats who strangle the people. Decree and swear that you will realize these [requests] and you will make Russia happy, famous and will imprint forever your name in our hearts and in the hearts of our descendants. And if you will not decree it, if you will not respond to our plea, we shall die here, in this square, before your palace. We have nowhere else to go and it is useless to go. We have only two roads open to us: one leading to freedom and happiness, the other to the grave. Let our life be a sacrifice for suffering Russia. We do not regret this sacrifice. We offer it willingly.

George Gapon, Priest *Ivan Vasimov, Worker*

THE OCTOBER MANIFESTO

With the revolution at its height, a general strike was called in October, and a workers' council (or Soviet) was formed in St. Petersburg to run the city. Sergei Witte informed Nicholas II that he could choose one of two options: institute a military dictatorship or make concessions to the revolutionaries. The tsar, his army still in the Far East, wisely chose the latter. In late October, he issued the October Manifesto, which allowed limited popular participation in the government. This decree, unprecedented in Russian history, succeeded in placating enough of the population to allow the government to restore order and crush any remaining malcontents by the end of the year. The Revolution of 1905 had come to a close, but the old regime now had to fulfill its promises.

The Manifesto appears below in its entirety.

By the grace of God, We, Nicholas II, Emperor and All-Russian Autocrat, King of Poland, Grand Prince of Finland, etc., proclaim to all Our loyal subjects:

Rioting and disturbances in the capitals and in many localities of Our Empire fill Our heart with great and heavy grief. The well-being of the Russian sovereign is inseparable from the well-being of the people; and the people's sorrow is His sorrow. The current disturbances could cause grave disorder among the people and endanger the integrity and unity of Our state.

We are obligated by Our great vow of royal service to use every resource of wisdom and authority to bring a quick end to this dangerous unrest. We have ordered the responsible authorities to take measures to terminate direct manifestations of disorder, lawlessness, and violence, and to protect peaceful persons quietly seeking to do their duty. To successfully fulfill the general measures designed by Us for the pacification of public life, We believe it necessary to coordinate the operations of the higher government.

Therefore we enjoin the government to execute Our inflexible will:

1. To grant the people the inviolable foundations of civic freedom based on the principles of genuine personal inviolability; freedom of conscience, speech, assembly, and association.
2. Without postponing the scheduled elections to the State Duma, to admit to participation in the State Duma, insofar as possible in the brief time that remains before its scheduled meeting, all those classes of the population that are now completely deprived of electoral rights, and to leave the further development

of the principle of universal suffrage to the future legislative order.

3. To establish as an inviolable rule that no law may go into effect without confirmation by the State Duma, and that the elected representatives of the people shall be guaranteed a genuine part in monitoring the legality of actions taken by the officials We shall appoint.

We summon all loyal sons of Russia to remember their duty to their country, to assist in bringing to an end this unprecedented unrest, and together with Us to make every effort to restore peace and tranquility in Our native land.

Given in Peterhof, October 30 [New Style], the year of Our Lord 1905, and of Our reign the eleventh.

Nicholas

3 The Provisional Government in Disarray

Russia after 1905 continued to witness dramatic change. For the first time in its history, the autocracy shared power with a parliament (duma) elected by limited franchise and made up of representatives from a variety of political parties. At the same time, the dynamic Premier Peter Stolypin initiated the formation of a peasant landholding class who, it was hoped, would become the conservative backbone of Russian society. Nevertheless, the gains of these years amounted to nothing once Russia became embroiled in World War I. The logistical demands of the conflict were too much for an already overtaxed population to bear, and incredibly poor military leadership proved disastrous for the army. In Petrograd (formerly St. Petersburg, renamed at the beginning of the war), popular discontent rose to fever pitch and, in March 1917, led to the end of three centuries of Romanov rule. With the abdication of Emperor Nicholas II, the leaders of the Duma took upon themselves the creation of a governing structure for Russia. The members of this new Provisional Government had been prominent in the Progressive Bloc, a broad-based coalition opposed to the tsarist government's handling of the war.

The eight-month tenure of the Provisional Government was the freest period in Russia's history to that time. The civil liberties that the tsarist regime had promised its subjects in the October Manifesto at last became facts of life, and the array of political parties (including those seeking the destruction of the status quo) was dizzying. Nevertheless, the Provisional Government made the fatal mistake of keeping Russia in World War I, the very policy that had brought the autocracy to its knees and would eventually prove its own undoing. At the same time, the Provisional Government, anticipating the day when a democratically elected constituent assembly would create a permanent legal framework for the new Russia, refrained from constructive solutions to the country's most pressing problems, particularly land reform. Little wonder, then, that genuine political authority steadily passed into the hands of the Petrograd Soviet, a council consisting of elected representatives of the peasants, workers, and soldiers, which replicated a similar body that had first appeared in 1905. By the summer of 1917, the Provisional Government was not only battling Imperial Germany on the Eastern Front but also fighting a multiplying number of opponents at home—in the countryside, factories, universities, and its own armed forces.

Army Intelligence Report
THE BREAKDOWN OF MILITARY DISCIPLINE

World War I was a military disaster for the Russian army from the start. As the war continued, the rank and file (overwhelmingly of peasant origin) became increasingly frustrated, demoralized, and responsive to revolutionary propaganda. Military discipline suffered a particular blow as the result of Order No. 1, which the Petrograd Soviet issued just after the March Revolution; it made the military policies of the Provisional Government subject to the approval of the Soviet and provided for the election of deputies to that body from among the soldiers. Subsequent efforts to restore order by the Provisional Government had only temporary success. Even the brilliant oratory of Alexander Kerensky (1881–1970), a member of the Socialist Revolutionary party who became head of the government in July, fell on deaf ears. Instead, Russian troops were deserting the front in ever larger numbers; in Leon Trotsky's words, "they voted with their feet."

The following excerpts are drawn from an army intelligence report from October 1917.

Northern front.—The situation in the army has not changed and may be described as a complete lack of confidence in the officers and the higher commanding personnel. The belief is growing among the soldiers that they cannot be punished for what they do. . . . The influence of Bolshevik ideas is spreading very rapidly. To this must be added a general weariness, an irritability, and a desire for peace at any price.

Any attempt on the part of the officers to regulate the life of the army . . . is looked upon by the soldiers as counter-revolution. . . .

. . . Considerable numbers of soldiers . . . feigning sickness are leaving the front for the hospital. . . .

12th Army.— . . . The press of the political parties is no longer influencing the soldier masses. Again and again one hears the orders of the Provisional Government severely criticized. The committee of the 95th Regiment . . . declared Kerensky a traitor. . . .

Apart from the Bolshevik not a single [political] movement has any popularity. Those who read moderate newspapers are looked upon as [followers of the] "bourgeoisie" and "counter-revolutionists." An intensive agitation is being conducted in favor of an immediate cessation of military operations on all fronts. Whenever a whole regiment or battalion refuses to carry out a military order, the fact is immediately made known to other parts of the army through special agitators. . . .

Western front.— . . . Because of general war weariness, bad nourishment, mistrust of officers, etc., there has developed an intense defeatist agitation accompanied by refusals to carry out orders, threats to the commanding personnel, and attempts to fraternize with Germans. Everywhere one hears voices calling for immediate peace, because, they say, no one will stay in the trenches during the winter. . . . There is a deep-rooted conviction among the rank and file that fraternization with the enemy is a sure way of attaining peace. . . .

[Bolshevik] newspapers . . . openly advocate the immediate cessation of war, the transfer of political and military power to the proletariat, the immediate socialization of land, and a merciless struggle against capitalists and the bourgeoisie. Their method of argument is quite simple and comprehensible to the masses. It runs as follows: All the ministers of the Provisional Government are subservient to the bourgeoisie and are counter-revolutionists; they continue to wage war to please the Allied and the Russian capitalists; the government introduced the death penalty with the view of exterminating the soldiers, workers, and peasants. . . .

Among the phenomena indicative of tendencies in the life in the rear of the Western front are the recent disturbances at the replacement depot in Gomel. On October 1 over eight thousand soldiers who were to be transferred to the front demanded to be sent home instead. . . . Incited by agitators they stormed the armory, took some fifteen hundred suits of winter equipment, and assaulted the Assistant Commissar and a member of the front committee. Similar events . . . have taken place in Smolensk. . . .

Southwestern front.— . . . Defeatist agitation is increasing and the disintegration of the army is in full swing. The Bolshevik wave is growing steadily, owing to general disintegration in the rear, the absence of strong power, and the lack of supplies and equipment. The dominant theme of conversation is peace at any price and under any condition. Every order, no matter what its source, is met with hostility. . . .

The guard-cavalry corps of the 2d Army passed a resolution of no confidence in the majority of officers. The soldiers are engaging in organized armed invasions of the surrounding country estates, plundering provisions . . . of which there is a scarcity in the army. Not a thing can be done to counteract this restlessness . . . as there is no force which could be relied upon in any attempt to enforce order. The activity of the courts is paralyzed because of the hostile attitude of the soldiers. . . .

The following general conclusions may be drawn from the reports of the commissars: The approaching winter campaign has accelerated the disintegration of the army and increased the longing for peace. It is necessary to leave nothing undone which might supply the soldiers with food, shoes, and winter clothing; to see that the army is reduced in numbers; to improve the discipline in the reserve regiments. Otherwise the ranks will be filled with such material as will lead to the complete demoralization and destruction of the army. . . .

[The rest of the report deals with the Rumanian and Caucasian fronts, describing similar conditions.]

Petrograd Telegraph Agency
AGRARIAN UNREST

The army was not the only part of Russian society experiencing collapse in 1917. Frustrated by the slowness of the Stolypin reforms and the inaction of the Provisional Government on the land question, peasants began taking matters into their own hands, often in response to revolutionary agitation. They seized land, torched noble estates, and sometimes put their owners to death.

The following excerpts come from reports of the Petrograd Telegraph Agency.

Kishinev, September 26. Local reports testify to the growth of agrarian disturbances in all uezds.[1] Fear is expressed that the sowing will not be done in time or properly.

Tambov, September 27. Accurate information about the disorders in Kozlov Uezd has not been received up to the present time. It is definitely known that one estate has been pillaged and twenty-five have been burned. . . .

Saratov, October 8. In Serdobsky Uezd the estates of Baroness Cherkassov and of Azarevich have been destroyed by the peasants. The commander of the Serdobsky garrison has been

[1]Units of territorial administration, each consisting of several *volosts* (townships). The largest territorial subdivision was the *guberniia* (province).

instructed to move a detachment to the uezd to restore order.

Saratov, October 10. The agrarian disturbances in Serdobsky Uezd embrace a large district. Peasants are stealing cattle, dividing the land and forests, and carrying off the grain. The uezd officials appealed for the aid of troops. It is feared that a great store of government liquor will be pillaged. The uezd executive committee proposes to transfer all privately owned land to the land committees. The disorder has spread to Atkarsky Uezd.

Kishinev, October 10. Peasants of Megura village, Beletsky Uezd, influenced by propaganda, began to divide among themselves the land and pastures of the neighboring estates of Borchel and Slobodzei. . . .

Voronezh, October 20. In Zadonsky Uezd in the district of the village of Zhivotinsky, the estates of Chertkov and other landowners have been partially destroyed by the peasants. More than 60,000 puds of wheat and other grain have been burned. Valuable old furniture has been destroyed. . . .

Zhitomir, October 23. After returning from a journey to Volhynia the assistant commissar gave a report on the situation. According to him, Volhynia is in a state of complete anarchy. In many uezds there is general destruction of the forests and seizure of privately owned land. In Staro-Konstantinovsky Uezd the Bolsheviks have seized power.

Nikolaevsk (Samara Gubernia), October 24. The executive committee, fearing that the numerous disorders in the uezd would destroy valuable estates, declared all privately owned estates public property and began their immediate confiscation. . . .

Chernigov, October 26. Disorder in the gubernia continues. In the uezds of Sosnitsk and Surazhsk forests and crops are being destroyed.

Penza, October 26. In Novocherkassk Uezd eight estates have been destroyed. Cavalry has been sent to stop the disorder. In Krasnoslobodsky Uezd the estate of Madame Lebedev and in Insarsky Uezd the estate of Andronov have been pillaged.

Spassk, October 27. A wave of destruction swept over the whole uezd. Felling and stealing of trees is going on. The estate of Shreder has been pillaged and set on fire. The estate of Count Grabbe has been destroyed, including his valuable library.

Nizhni-Novgorod, November 1. According to the latest information the uprising has spread over six uezds, in which many estates have been pillaged and burned. The greatest disorder took place in Lukianovsky Uezd, where, according to the commissar, everything valuable is being ruthlessly destroyed. . . .

4 The Bolshevik Revolution

As the Provisional Government demonstrated in 1917, Russian liberals were not capable of ruling the country in times of supreme crisis. The question then became what political system and ideology could overcome anarchy.

An answer had been in the making since 1898, with the founding of the Russian Marxist movement. Its most dynamic leader was Vladimir Ilyich Ulyanov (1870–1924), known by his pen name Lenin. He believed that, on its own, the working class could never achieve a successful revolution; workers without leadership could not rise above petty trade unionism. Throughout his career, Lenin contrasted ignorant working-class "spontaneity" with revolutionary "consciousness," meaning deliberate action guided by the proper comprehension of the circumstances under which revolutionaries must work.

Lenin's vision of a revolutionary movement tailored to the special conditions of Russia led to a split within Russian Marxism in 1903. Those who shared his belief in the need of a secret, conspiratorial party he dubbed Bolsheviks ("people of the majority"); his opponents, who held to the notion of a broadly based political organization, became Mensheviks ("people of the minority"). For years, Lenin tried to maintain the ideological unity of the Bolsheviks by means of countless publications and periodicals, many of them written from his place of self-imposed exile in Geneva. By 1917, he had begun to doubt the possibility of revolution in his own lifetime. The March Revolution, however, energized Lenin and made him eager to return to his homeland. With the help of Imperial Germany (always on the lookout for a chance to weaken its wartime enemy Russia), Lenin traveled to Petrograd aboard a "sealed train." Almost immediately, he issued the "April Theses," in which he not only denounced the war and the Provisional Government but also announced that the time for revolution had arrived. In effect Lenin had created a political platform that gave the Bolsheviks a distinct advantage over their rivals and secured them increasing popular support. By the fall of 1917, Lenin and the Bolshevik organization were ready to seize power.

V. I. Lenin
WHAT IS TO BE DONE?

A seminal document of Marxism-Leninism was Lenin's pamphlet *What Is to Be Done?* published in 1902, fifteen years before the tsar's overthrow. In this tract, Lenin addressed the big questions facing Russian Marxists (who called themselves Social Democrats after the German Social Democratic party that served as their model). How could they effectively channel the mounting discontent in Russian society and especially in the new industrial working class? How could they prevail against the secret police in the tsarist police state (referred to by Lenin as the autocracy)? How could they find Russia's way among the complexities of the modern world and master them? The answers Lenin offered to these difficult questions—found in the following passages—helped shape the Soviet regime.

Without revolutionary theory there can be no revolutionary movement. This idea cannot be insisted upon too strongly. . . . Yet, for Russian Social-Democrats the importance of theory is enhanced by three other circumstances, which are often forgotten: first, by the fact that our Party is only in process of formation, its features are only just becoming defined, and it has as yet far from settled accounts with the other trends of revolutionary thought that threaten to divert the movement from the correct path. . . .

Secondly, the Social-Democratic movement is in its very essence an international movement. This means, not only that we must combat national chauvinism, but that an incipient movement in a young country can be successful only if it makes use of the experiences of other countries. In order to make use of these experiences it is not enough merely to be acquainted with them, or simply to copy out the latest resolutions. What is required is the ability to treat these experiences critically and to test them independently. He who realises how enormously the modern working-class movement has grown and branched out will understand what a reserve of theoretical forces and political (as well as revolutionary) experience is required to carry out this task.

[T]he national tasks of Russian Social-Democracy are such as have never confronted any other socialist party in the world. We shall have occasion further on to deal with the political and organisational duties which the task of emancipating the whole people from the yoke of autocracy imposes upon us. At this point, we wish to state only that the *role of vanguard fighter can be fulfilled only by a party that is guided by the most advanced theory*. . . .

We have said that there *could not have been* Social-Democratic consciousness among the workers. It would have to be brought to them from without. The history of all countries shows that the working class, exclusively by its own effort, is able to develop only trade-union consciousness, i.e. the conviction that it is necessary to combine in unions, fight the employers, and strive to compel the government to pass necessary labour legislation, etc. The theory of socialism, however, grew out of the philosophic, historical, and economic theories elaborated by educated representatives of the propertied classes, by intellectuals. By their social status, the founders of modern scientific socialism, Marx and Engels, themselves belonged to the bourgeois intelligentsia. In the very same way, in Russia, the theoretical doctrine of Social-Democracy arose altogether independently of the spontaneous growth of the working-class movement; it arose as a natural and inevitable outcome of the development of thought among the revolutionary socialist intelligentsia. . . .

Given the ignorance of the working class, said Lenin, revolutionary leadership had to come from a close-knit vanguard of dedicated and disciplined professional revolutionaries as well trained as the tsarist police and always in close touch with the masses. The revolutionary leaders had to raise working-class awareness to a comprehensive understanding of the coming crisis in Russia and the capitalist world generally.

. . . I assert: (1) that no revolutionary movement can endure without a stable organisation of leaders maintaining continuity; (2) that the broader the popular mass drawn spontaneously into the struggle, which forms the basis of the movement and participates in it, the more urgent the need for such an organisation, and the more solid this organisation must be (for it is much easier for all sorts of demagogues to side-track the more backward sections of the masses); (3) that such an organisation must consist chiefly of people professionally engaged in revolutionary activity; (4) that in an autocratic state, the more we *confine* the membership of such an organisation to people who are professionally engaged in revolutionary activity and who have been professionally trained in the art of combating the political police, the more difficult will it be to unearth the organisation; and (5) the *greater* will be the number of people from the working class and from the other social classes who will be able to join the movement and perform active work in it. . . .

. . . Social-Democracy leads the struggle of the working class, not only for better terms for the sale of labour-power, but for the abolition of the social system that compels the propertyless to sell themselves to the rich. Social-Democracy represents the working class, not in its relation to a given group of employers alone, but in its relation to all classes of modern society and to the state as an organised political force. Hence, it follows that not only must Social-Democrats not confine themselves exclusively to the economic struggle, but that they must not allow [investigating mismanagement of the economy] to become the predominant part of their activities. We must take up actively the political education of the working class and the development of its political consciousness.

Lenin did not think there was a danger that the secret, tightly centralized revolutionary organization would establish a dictatorship over the proletariat. He trusted that close comradeship and a sense of responsibility would lead to a superior revolutionary "democratism." He looked to the Russian revolutionaries as the vanguard of the international revolutionary movement.

. . . We can never give a mass organisation that degree of secrecy without which there can be no question of persistent and continuous struggle against the government. To concentrate all secret functions in the hands of as small a number of professional revolutionaries as possible does not mean that the latter will "do the thinking for all" and that the rank and file will not take an active part in the *movement.* On the contrary, the membership will promote increasing numbers of the professional revolutionaries from its ranks; for it will know that it is not enough for a few students and for a few working men waging the economic struggle to gather in order to form a "committee," but that it takes years to train oneself to be a professional revolutionary. . . . Centralisation of the most secret functions in an organisation of revolutionaries will not diminish, but rather increase the extent and enhance the quality of the activity of a large number of other organisations, that are intended for a broad public and are therefore as loose and as non-secret as possible, such as workers' trade unions; workers' self-education circles and circles for reading illegal literature; and socialist, as well as democratic, circles among *all* other sections of the population; etc., etc. We must have such circles, trade unions, and organisations everywhere in *as large a number as possible* and with the widest variety of functions. . . .

. . . The only serious organisational principle for the active workers of our movement should be the strictest secrecy, the strictest selection of members, and the training of professional revolutionaries. Given these qualities, something even more than "democratism" would be guaranteed to us, namely, complete, comradely, mutual confidence among revolutionaries. . . . They have a lively sense of their *responsibility,* knowing as they do from experience that an organisation of real revolutionaries will stop at nothing to rid itself of an unworthy member. . . .

. . . Our worst sin with regard to organisation consists in the fact that *by our primitiveness we have lowered the prestige of revolutionaries in Russia.* A person who is flabby and shaky on questions of theory, who has a narrow outlook, who pleads the spontaneity of the masses as an excuse for his own sluggishness, who resembles a trade-union secretary more than a spokesman of the people, who is unable to conceive of a broad and bold plan that would command the respect even of opponents, and who is inexperienced and clumsy in his own professional art—the art of combating the political police—such a man is not a revolutionary, but a wretched amateur!

N. N. Sukhanov
TROTSKY AROUSES THE PEOPLE

Playing a crucial role in the Bolshevik seizure of power on November 7, 1917, was Leon Trotsky (1879–1940). Born Lev Davidovich Bronstein, the son of a prosperous Jewish farmer in Ukraine, Trotsky was attracted early to the ranks of the revolutionaries, and he shared their fate. Exiled to Siberia in 1902, he escaped to Switzerland with a faked passport in the name of Leon Trotsky. Back in Russia for the Revolution of 1905, he was again exiled and again escaped. After a period abroad, he returned to Russia after the overthrow of the tsar in March 1917 and soon assumed a leading role among the Bolsheviks. In September 1917, as the moderate regime of Kerensky began to totter, Trotsky was

elected chairman of the Petrograd Soviet; soon afterward, he masterminded the Military-Revolutionary Committee, the Bolshevik strike force.

On the evening of November 4, Trotsky delivered a rousing speech at the Peoples' House, a popular theater much used for working-class meetings. His speech is described by an eyewitness, the Menshevik leader N. N. Sukhanov, in his 1917 book *The Russian Revolution.*

The mood of the people, more than 3,000, who filled the hall was definitely tense; they were all silently waiting for something. The audience was of course primarily workers and soldiers, but more than a few typically lower-middle-class men's and women's figures were visible.

Trotsky's ovation seemed to be cut short prematurely, out of curiosity and impatience: what was he going to say? Trotsky at once began to heat up the atmosphere, with his skill and brilliance. I remember that at length and with extraordinary power he drew a picture of the suffering of the trenches. Thoughts flashed through my mind of the inevitable incongruity of the parts in this oratorical whole. But Trotsky knew what he was doing. The whole point lay in the mood. The political conclusions had long been familiar. They could be condensed, as long as there were enough highlights.

Trotsky did this—with enough highlights. The Soviet regime was not only called upon to put an end to the suffering of the trenches. It would give land and heal the internal disorder. Once again the recipes against hunger were repeated: a soldier, a sailor, and a working girl, who would requisition bread from those who had it and distribute it gratis to the cities and front. But Trotsky went even further on this decisive "Day of the Petersburg Soviet."

"The Soviet Government will give everything the country contains to the poor and the men in the trenches. You, bourgeois, have got two fur caps!—give one of them to the soldier, who's freezing in the trenches. Have you got warm boots? Stay at home. The worker needs your boots. . . ."

These were very good and just ideas. They could not but excite the enthusiasm of a crowd who had been reared on the Tsarist whip. In any case, I certify as a direct witness that this was what was said on this last day.

All round me was a mood bordering on ecstasy. It seemed as though the crowd, spontaneously and of its own accord, would break into some religious hymn. Trotsky formulated a brief and general resolution, or pronounced some general formula like "we will defend the worker-peasant cause to the last drop of our blood."

Who was—for? The crowd of thousands, as one man, raised their hands. I saw the raised hands and burning eyes of men, women, youths, soldiers, peasants, and typically lower-middleclass faces. Were they in spiritual transport? Did they see, through the raised curtain, a corner of the "righteous land" of their longing? Or were they penetrated by a consciousness of the *political occasion,* under the influence of the political agitation of a *Socialist?* Ask no questions! Accept it as it was. . . .

Trotsky went on speaking. The innumerable crowd went on holding their hands up. Trotsky rapped out the words: "Let this vote of yours be your vow—with all your strength and at any sacrifice to support the Soviet that has taken on itself the glorious burden of bringing to a conclusion the victory of the revolution and of giving land, bread, and peace!"

The vast crowd was holding up its hands. It agreed. It vowed. Once again, accept this as it was. With an unusual feeling of oppression I looked on at this really magnificent scene.

Trotsky finished. Someone else went out on to the stage. But there was no point in waiting and looking any more.

Throughout Petersburg more or less the same thing was going on. Everywhere there were final reviews and final vows. Thousands, tens of thousands and hundreds of thousands of people. . . . This, actually, was already an insurrection. Things had started. . . .

V. I. Lenin
THE CALL TO POWER

On November 6 (October 24 by the old-style calendar then in use in Russia), Lenin urged immediate action, as the following document reveals.

. . . The situation is critical in the extreme. In fact it is now absolutely clear that to delay the uprising would be fatal.

With all my might I urge comrades to realise that everything now hangs by a thread; that we are confronted by problems which are not to be solved by conferences or congresses (even congresses of Soviets), but exclusively by peoples, by the masses, by the struggle of the armed people.

The bourgeois onslaught of the Kornilovites [followers of General Kornilov, who tried to establish a military dictatorship] show that we must not wait. We must at all costs, this very evening, this very night, arrest the government, having first disarmed the officer cadets (defeating them, if they resist), and so on.

We must not wait! We may lose everything!

Who must take power?

That is not important at present. Let the Revolutionary Military Committee [Bolshevik organization working within the army and navy] do it, or "some other institution" which will declare that it will relinquish power only to the true representatives of the interests of the people, the interests of the army (the immediate proposal of peace), the interests of the peasants (the land to be taken immediately and private property abolished), the interests of the starving.

All districts, all regiments, all forces must be mobilised at once and must immediately send their delegations to the Revolutionary Military Committee and to the Central Committee of the Bolsheviks [governing organization of the Bolshevik party] with the insistent demand that under no circumstances should power be left in the hands of Kerensky and Co. . . . not under any circumstances; the matter must be decided without fail this very evening, or this very night.

History will not forgive revolutionaries for procrastinating when they could be victorious today (and they certainly will be victorious today), while they risk losing much tomorrow; in fact, they risk losing everything.

If we seize power today, we seize it not in opposition to the Soviets but on their behalf.

The seizure of power is the business of the uprising; its political purpose will become clear after the seizure. . . .

. . . It would be an infinite crime on the part of the revolutionaries were they to let the chance slip, knowing that the *salvation of the revolution,* the offer of peace, the salvation of Petrograd, salvation from famine, the transfer of the land to the peasants depend upon them.

The government is tottering. It must be *given the death-blow* at all costs.

To delay action is fatal.

---

5 The Russian Civil War

The Bolshevik Revolution's call for a new society—one free of exploitation—made a profound impression around the world. Yet it relied increasingly on force and compulsion, limiting individual rights, outlawing political parties, and, in January 1918, disbanding the recently elected Constituent Assembly with its majority of non-Bolshevik delegates. Such policies—along with Lenin's insistence

on signing the costly Brest-Litovsk Treaty with Germany in March 1918 so as to remove Russia from the war—helped to foment a new conflict, this time within the country's borders. The Russian Civil War pitted the Bolsheviks (or "Reds") against a broad spectrum of opponents from moderate socialist to reactionary (the "Whites"). Tsarist officers gathered their forces in the south; other anti-Communist centers arose in Siberia, and still others in the extreme north and along the Baltic coast. The Whites received support from foreign governments, including Britain, France, the United States, and Japan. Originally these powers were interested in recreating the Eastern Front in the war against Imperial Germany. After the armistice in November 1918, the interventionists turned their campaign into an anti-Bolshevik crusade, partly in response to Lenin's creation of the Communist International or Comintern, which was dedicated to the cause of fomenting socialist revolution around the globe.

Beset by enemies at home and from abroad, the Bolsheviks at first appeared headed for defeat. By the autumn of 1920, however, they had prevailed over their opponents. The Whites suffered from ideological divisions and were discredited by their association with the tsarist regime. In addition, Lenin cannily played the nationalist card against the Whites on account of their ties to foreign powers. The Reds also benefited from greater popular support, interior lines of communication, and superior political and propaganda skills. The interventionists, weary of fighting that had begun in 1914, soon ended their attempts to overthrow the Bolsheviks by force.

The Communist victory in the civil war came at a price. A total of 1.2 million combatants perished. The Reds, moreover, killed approximately 250,000 peasants for their resistance to grain requisitions and executed tens of thousands of political opponents. In addition, 100,000 Jews perished, most as victims of pogroms perpetrated by the Whites. Even after the armed struggle had ceased, Russia's suffering continued. The famine of 1921–22 claimed around five million victims.

I. I. Vatsetis and Alexis Babine
THE RED TERROR

Like all conflicts of its kind, the Russian Civil War was incredibly brutal and witnessed countless atrocities on both sides. In July 1918, the Bolsheviks murdered Nicholas II and his entire family just east of the Ural Mountains in Ekaterinburg, to which they had been removed. In August, a Socialist Revolutionary named Fannie Kaplan fired shots at Lenin. To deal with the formidable military obstacles confronting them, the Bolsheviks created the Red Army and filled it with the remnants of the former tsarist army. The Red Army became an effective fighting machine, whipped into shape under the personal command of Leon Trotsky, who reintroduced capital punishment into Russia after its abolition by the Provisional Government. Under threat of death, many tsarist officers served in the Red Army, where they were closely monitored by specially appointed political commissars.

In the first of the two selections below, I. I. Vatsetis (1873–1938), the supreme commander in chief of the Red Army, complains to Lenin about the commissars' abuse of tsarist officers who had pledged their service to the new Soviet government. In addition to finding them remarkably reliable, Vatsetis considered the help of these former monarchists essential to the success of the Bolsheviks, who lacked the technical expertise and practical knowledge necessary to run a large state. (This problem would hamper Soviet society for years to come.) At the beginning of the excerpt, the author describes the mistreatment of a tsarist officer named Teodori by M. S. Kedrov, head of the Special Department of the Cheka, the Bolshevik political police that Lenin founded shortly after the revolution in November 1917.

The second selection is drawn from the diary of Alexis Vasilevich Babine (1866–1930). The American scholar Donald Raleigh, who edited the diary and published it in 1988, described the work as "the only non-Bolshevik book-length account that illuminates events in a provincial Russian town during the entire Civil War." Born in Riazan province southeast of Moscow, Babine in 1890 made his way to Cornell University, where he earned B.A. and M.A. degrees in American history. A gifted linguist, Babine worked in several U.S. university libraries and eventually the Library of Congress before returning to Russia in 1910. On the eve of the Bolshevik Revolution he moved to the Volga provincial capital of Saratov as an English instructor and librarian at the local university. While Babine had no particular liking for the tsarist autocracy and criticized the backwardness and brutality of Russian life, the ravages of the Civil War made him an unalloyed anti-Bolshevik. His diary, which he wrote in English with an American audience in mind, covers the five-year period from March 1917 until November 1922. Although far from an objective account and filled with the rumors circulating during that chaotic era, the diary reveals how the country's provincial middle class coped with the problems of daily existence under a new regime. Babine escaped from Russia in 1922 and returned to America, ending his career as assistant head of the Slavic Section at the Library of Congress. The excerpts from his diary reproduced here come from 1918, the first year of the Russian Civil War.

Recently everyone has been especially upset by the sudden arrest of Teodori of GHQ, whom all knew to be a faithful and conscientious person, working for Soviet power in a highly responsible position. Under Comrade Kedrov's instructions, in spite of the fact that all the charges against him have been proved null and void, Teodori still remains under arrest. That can only be attributed to Comrade Kedrov's arbitrary misuse of his powers . . . Indisputably Teodori has been tremendously helpful to us, especially in the summer of 1918. At that time rebellions were rife in our country, and had to be put down by the Operations Section, of which Teodori was the Military Director. Similarly, when we had to fight against the Czechoslovak Corps . . . Teodori gave invaluable service as Military Director of the Operations Section, which was headed by Comrade Aralov.

The Supreme Military Council, which at that time stood at the head of the military apparatus, turned out to be quite incapable of dealing with the press of practical work, and all the duties belonging to that Council were carried out by the Operations Section, with Teodori on its staff. I can bear witness to Teodori's immense contribution to our success on the Volga at that time. It was only thanks to his thrusting energy and his devotion to our cause that we managed to get our country to provide sufficient reserves . . . and to preserve military discipline in the staff who were forming units locally and despatching them to the Eastern Front. His services at that time should not be forgotten . . . Persistent rumours are circulating that Comrade Kedrov's assistant Eynduk declared there to be no charges against Teodori, and that charges would have to be made up.

In the last few days Comrade Selivachev has also been arrested, whom it was intended to appoint to command the Eastern Front. Selivachev I knew even before the war, and he was never a monarchist; quite the opposite—under the monarchy he was one of those who was persecuted. Taken together both these arrests make it look as though hostages are being taken in advance . . .

I request that an enquiry should be set up into Comrade Kedrov's activity, and that he should be brought to book if he is the only guilty party. Comrade Kedrov I know from his highly unsuccessful command of the 6th Army, during which time, quite illegally, without any right to do so, he ordered the arrest of the Commander of the 2nd Army, Comrade Blokhin, and the whole staff of the 2nd Army—adding in his telegram that if need be they should be shot. The 2nd Army was not under Comrade Kedrov's command, and for this act he was dismissed from command of the 6th Army . . . Kedrov destroyed the command of the 2nd Army, as a result of which it disintegrated . . .

In the headquarters of the Eastern Front they recently arrested Khrulev, who was a member of the General Staff. The Revolutionary Tribunal condemned him to five years in prison, though at the same time the man really guilty of the crime got off with just a reprimand.

In the headquarters of the Ural District the entire HQ staff were arrested without any due cause whatsoever.

On 1 April in the headquarters of the 1st Army, by the individual decision of Comrade Kal, member of RVS of 1st Army, the assistant head of the radio-telegraph [section], Vendebaum, was shot without trial or investigation.

All this emphasises what an arbitrary regime is still practised by political workers on a personal basis, both towards individuals in the headquarters, and in their treatment of specialists in general . . . Nothing but harm arises from such conditions of service, that afford no security against unfounded arrest, and this at a time when work demands such stressful concentration . . .

As a result of our temporary setbacks on the Eastern Front many people are overcome by a state of alarm . . . One can observe this among the commissars and the feeling is undoubtedly transmitted to those working on the Staff . . . We shall have to draw some sort of line beyond which it will be forbidden to show suspicion or to mock members of the headquarters staff. In the name of our final victory over our many enemies, we must guarantee complete immunity and freedom to all members of the General Staff now serving in the Red Army, allowing them to be arrested only when definite evidence is produced, and only when their immediate superiors are kept informed.

Besides this I consider it essential to review the case of Khrulev of the General Staff, who was unjustly accused, and to bring to book comrade Kalinin, who shot Vendebaum without any trial or investigation, since this kind of arbitrary behaviour damages the reputation of Soviet power.

C-in-C of all armed forces of the Republic
GHQ, Vatsetis

18 April 1919, Serpukhov

Never a member of the Communist party but always an independent spirit, Vatsetis resigned his military command in 1919 and spent much of the rest of his career teaching in a military academy. In 1937, as Stalin's purges began to decimate the Soviet officer corps, Vatsetis was arrested on trumped-up charges; in 1938 he was executed.

The excerpt from Alexis Babine's diary begins with his arrival in his home town of Elatma after a trip from Saratov via train and steamer.

June 30, 1918

Arrived in Elatma at 7 P.M. Father and everybody else are well. The town is in the hands of the Bolsheviks, with two ex-convict murderers at their head that had been amnestied by the Bolsheviks after their victory over Kerensky and his crew. Fences are covered with illiterate "decrees," one of which prohibits the circulation of all anti-Bolshevik Moscow papers. The latter, therefore, are not delivered to subscribers, but are collected at the post office. The wildest of rumors arise and find credence in consequence.

Our house, along with many others, was looted last March after an unsuccessful local upheaval against the Bolsheviks, looted by the victorious Bolshevik soldiers and by the rabble from nearby villages. A chest of mine was broken open, a large number of trinkets, valuable tools, and a quantity of miscellaneous ammunition and supplies were stolen. My trunk, too, disappeared from Mme. Popov's brick fireproof vault, and with it all my guns, my American flag, etc., etc. . . .

July 9, 1918

Yesterday the local Bolshevik committee posted a warning to the effect that all attempts to overthrow the Bolshevik regime would be punished by death. This afternoon I called at the Bolshevik headquarters in order to get a permit to purchase a shotgun, but was told that Lepniov, *the* commissar, had gone to Alferievo for the day to disarm the local population that had brought all sorts of firearms from the front. The Alferievo rabble was the fiercest at the plundering of Elatma last March, and it struck me as somewhat curious that the same supporters of the Bolsheviks had to be disarmed now. . . .

July 17, 1918

A Kasimov commissar driving through the village of Dmitrievo was astonished to see the house and the lawn and all the buildings of a local landowner in all their pristine glory as though there had been no Bolshevik revolution at all. "Whose house is it?" the commissar wanted to know. "Our old master's," his peasant guides explained. "What?! Why didn't you turn him out?" "Why should we? He never did us any harm." "Get him out at once," the grand official commanded. But the peasants refused to do anything without a written order. So the commissar went to Kasimov and issued a formal order to dispossess the old proprietor. Before the order reached the village council, the landowner had swept the house of absolutely everything he had, and distributed all his belongings among his peasant neighbors. When the storm passed away, he got his goods back to the last trifle. "Not even a single empty shell got lost," he commented on the event, being an inveterate hunter. . . .

August 20, 1918

Wishing to obtain some alcohol for V. V. Kurchatov, of Unzha, to be used in preparation of a rheumatism ointment, I went this morning to Dr. Levashev for a prescription. He wrote it out, but said that there was no alcohol in town: he himself could not get any two days ago. I went nevertheless to our only drugstore to learn from the druggist's wife that they had not a drop of alcohol, that my prescription was not valid without a stamp of the Bolshevik town soviet on it, and that her husband had gone to that same soviet in quest of alcohol. I found the druggist at 12:15 P.M. at the soviet headquarters, waiting for the almighty chief commissar. The druggist explained to me how the drugstore had been left without alcohol: the liquid was issued without loss of time to noted inebriates on physicians' prescriptions that are usually presented at certain intervals by the same persons. The druggist thus finds himself unable to fill bona fide prescriptions. The alcohol is issued to him by the Bolsheviks, who recently let him have one single gallon (and a short one at that) while the rest of the thirty gallons intended for his drugstore was used up by the soviet commissars and their boon companions, the city physician Tikhomirov being one of the chief drunkards, who abuse their official access to the now scarce and precious liquid.

August 23, 1918

All stores were closed today by the Bolsheviks and sealed. All merchandise is to be confiscated, and in the future will be sold from a national store, one for the whole town.

August 25, 1918

Complaints are heard of difficulties in obtaining necessary articles at the national store, insufficiently manned and managed by a capricious and willful individual. . . .

September 9, 1918

Today I heard a new ditty:

> Nicholas [Tsar Nicholas II] was a simpleton—
> In his time bread cost five kopecks.
> Now that we have a republic
> Bread is three rubles a pound. . . .

October 2, 1918

One hundred thirty-five conservatives are being kept on a Volga barge as hostages. They were arrested after the attempt on Lenin's life, in connection with which some twenty persons have been shot in Saratov without even a semblance of a trial.

Since the beginning of Bolshevik rule, about 350 corpses have been brought to the university morgue. Cases are reported when the would-be lifeless forms revived, asked for water, were reported to the powers, and killed for good by Red Army men.

October 19, 1918

Professor Pavlov's charming daughter was buried yesterday. She was killed in a tram accident when the brakes had refused to work on a steep grade and the car, leaving the track, stood on its head. It is said that after the nationalization of the streetcar company last year, three-quarters of all cars got entirely out of repair and that the running ones are mostly unsafe.

October 21, 1918

In order to save wood we have abandoned the use of our regular kitchen oven and cook our food, almost exclusively potato soup and grits, in our big brick Dutch heating stoves, not at all built for that purpose. Our entire evenings are spent at this task, and we have no time to think about books or to prepare thoroughly for our lectures and lessons. Both our, and everybody else's, pervading problem is to keep alive and to outlast the Bolsheviks.

October 22, 1918

My friend Boris Aleksandrovich Shakhmatov, formerly the head of the National Horse Breeding Department, has fallen victim to our local Bolshevik tsars. He was arrested as a hostage after the attempt on Lenin's life and, as a wealthy landowner, was immediately sentenced to death. A charming man personally who had never done anybody harm, he had many friends to intercede for him in Moscow. The peasantry of his own county and of three neighboring counties sought his immediate liberation. A telegraph order finally came from Moscow to release the prisoner. But the local rabble held back the telegram, had the old gentleman shot at once, and explained the execution by a delay in the transmission of the telegram. . . .

November 7, 1918

Today is the anniversary of the seizure of power by the Bolsheviks. The system of bread, produce, and other lines is firmly established. The nation unproductively wastes an immense amount of time in obtaining the supplies that have been removed from the market merely to please the despotic rulers' socialist fancies. No butter, cheese, bacon, sausage, sugar, honey, meat, eggs, are to be had in the face of a great abundance of these items in the country. People still have to get up at 3 A.M. in order to get near enough to the head of lines for kerosene, meat, linseed oil, and other items, and frequently go home empty-handed.

The utter disregard of the people's right to life, liberty, and property, the ease with which everybody endowed with intelligence and foolhardy enough to show the courage of his convictions is swept out of existence by order of a small but cleverly organized band of degenerates and by the hand of its pervert hirelings and blind tools, and the pitiless, bloody cruelty of the band begin more and more to convince the intelligent surviving unwilling thralls of the regime that all liberal declarations and slogans of the Bolsheviks are a humbug; that they are meant merely to fool the dark, uneducated masses, to deceive them by promises of liberty, equality, fraternity, and Communist material blessings without end, and thus to secure their physical aid in overthrowing a civilized and hence unfriendly regime; that the real object of the Communist party is to sweep out of its way everybody to whom the undeceived and awakened people might turn for guidance in their active protest against oppression, and thus to perpetuate its rule.

Baron Peter Nikolaevich Wrangel
THE WHITES' HATRED OF BOLSHEVISM

While the White forces in the Civil War represented an array of non-Bolshevik political opinion, the predominant viewpoint was that of monarchists who identified with the old imperial regime. Typical of these individuals was Baron Peter Nikolaevich Wrangel (1878–1928). Of Baltic German descent, Wrangel served in the tsarist army in World War I. After the Bolshevik Revolution, Wrangel joined the White Volunteer Army. As head of the Army of the Caucasus in 1919, he captured Tsaritsyn (Volgograd). Later he became commander of the White troops in the Crimea, where he also proved to be an effective administrator. Subsequent military defeats, however, caused Wrangel to organize a mass evacuation of White forces via the Black Sea. He himself left Russia in November 1920, by which time the Russian Civil War had come to an end. In later years he founded the Russian All-Military Union to keep alive the White cause abroad. His memoirs appeared in 1928, the year of his death.

The following selection comes from a speech that Baron Wrangel delivered in Brussels in 1927. In his words the flame of Russian nationalism burns as intensely as hatred for the Bolsheviks.

At the end of the year 1917 the Government of Kerensky could no longer retain the executive power in their feeble hands. It was seized by a set of people who built on the lowest sentiments of the populace, operating as demagogues do, and promising peace and plenty with idleness none of these promises were kept. That did not matter to the Bolshevist ringleaders. Russia in its quality of a national State was no concern of theirs. What they sought was a base whence to diffuse their unholy influence over the whole world.

The moment that the Bolshevists laid hands on the executive power, Russia, as a national entity, ceased to exist. Even the name which served to describe it disappeared. All the interests of the State, as such, were sacrificed to those of the Red International. Everywhere this International waged determined war against every element of the national spirit, aggravated class conflicts, and destroyed all the foundations of morality—religion, the fatherland, the family.

Yet, in spite of all, Russia still exists as a nation. Immediately after the Bolshevists seized the reins of power, a few men, stirred by love for their country and jealous for its greatness and glory, raised the national flag that had fallen in the mud. They started in the south of Russia an implacable struggle against the oppressors of their country.

Their appeal was heard; a crowd of officers, soldiers, students, intellectuals, politicians, workers, and peasants flocked to the Don. All those whose hearts were right and courageous, and who could not admit that Russia was dead, gathered under the national flag. There were men of every class and condition of life, of the most varied ages and political views. Enrolling themselves in the ranks of the National Army, they forgot every item of political or social divergence. They were all united by the same warm love of their country, and the same desire to sacrifice themselves for her.

Such, in November 1917, was the birth of the White Army. It was the incarnation of the national sentiment, of the revolt of Russian patriotism. United under the folds of the tricolour, they fought from that time for the national cause. This Army, loyal to all the obligations taken over by previous national governments, still continues the struggle for the honour of its country's name, for the resurrection of Russia as a Nation. Its way of fighting has altered; the outward forms which properly belong to armies have gone; but the idea which directed its making has remained untouched.

What is this idea? It is life devoted to the fatherland, eagerness to save her at the expense of life itself, a passionate desire to tear the red flag down from the Kremlin and hoist in its place the National flag.

The struggle which began in the south of Russia soon raised echoes elsewhere, in the north, the north-west, and Siberia. I will not pause here to tell you past history; I will only recall the brilliant successes with which the White Armies began. The troops of General Denikin occupied a third of Russia and advanced within a short distance of Moscow. In the north-west General Youdenitch was already in sight of the fires of St. Petersburg. In the west, Admiral Koltchak had almost reached the Volga.

Yet victory was not in reserve for the White Armies. . . .

The failure of the White Armies was due to a number of reasons, and I will not weary the reader by examining them in detail. I will confine myself to mentioning the chief of them. A prominent place is due to the political and strategic errors of the leaders who did not sufficiently regard the state of feeling among the masses of the people. They exaggerated the importance of their early successes. They did not think sufficiently about securing the possession of the territories they occupied, organizing them, raising new levies to fill the gaps in their ranks, and looking after the provision of victuals and munitions.

The political ignorance of the people accounted for a good deal. They had not yet lost their illusions concerning the Bolshevist power; they still went on believing in the lying promises of the [radical] agitators. Lastly, the Bolshevist Armies had at their disposition all the resources of an immense country, its reserves of food, its stocks of arms and munitions.

On the other side, the White Armies were short of everything. During the first months of the struggle the only arms and munitions we could draw on were those taken from the enemy. Support from outside was indispensable. It could only come from those by whose side the Russian Army had fought during the Great War. The White Armies who had refused to recognize the shameful peace of Brest-Litovsk[1] and were loyal to their alliances thought they had the right to count on this support.

But the Western Powers were far from realizing the essence of the Bolshevist idea, the danger it threatened to the world. They did not consider fairly the importance of the struggle the White Army was carrying on. They did not understand that this Army, in fighting for its own country, was also fighting for civilization and the culture of Europe. Not only did the White Armies fail to receive sufficient help in time to be of use, they had even on several occasions to run foul of obstacles raised by the former Allies of Russia.

Three years of determined struggle, of fighting and suffering, of heroism, victory, and defeat, followed by fresh victory, then came to an end. We left the last strip of the land of our fathers. . . .

The number of those evacuated was one hundred thousand officers and soldiers and fifty thousand civilians, including among these thirty thousand women and seven thousand children. Of the one hundred thousand officers and soldiers, fifty thousand belonged to the fighting troops, forty thousand to those who served in the rear. There were three thousand pupils from the military schools, and more than six thousand were ill, invalided, or wounded. The fifty thousand civilians included all ranks of society, amongst them peasants and workers. It was no emigration of privileged classes and professions. It was the exodus of National Russia with all the elements that go to make it, its civil organization and its Army. These exiles cherished in their hearts profound faith in a victorious return to the land of their fathers. Of this crowd of *émigrés* it was the Army that from the national point of view formed the most valuable part. It was the only group organized and consolidated by the blood all had shed, the idea they shared. Its new existence showed that the fight for the honour of the country and the remaking of Russia as a nation was not yet ended. It was evident that the Army ought to become the centre to gather round it the Russian *émigrés* scattered in all countries. It was indispensable to keep this nucleus intact. . . .

Six years have passed since the day when we left our native soil. By painful work the Russian Army gains its bread, enduring affronts and humiliations. But in spite of all its privations and misfortunes it has not lost its faith in the approaching triumph of the sacred cause. Slowly the eyes of Europe are being opened to the real meaning of Bolshevism. The nations of Europe are beginning to understand the danger of the Red madness, of the risk the world of civilization runs in the existence of an international hot-bed which uses the immense resources of our land to keep up its destructive work. The heart of our country has been quickened by the forces of sanity; they will grow and cannot be stopped. We are no longer alone in our struggle.

---

[1]The Treaty of Brest-Litovsk, signed in March 1918, officially ended Russia's participation in World War I and thus fulfilled a principal plank in the platform of the Bolsheviks. A true Carthaginian peace by which Germany stripped Russia of much of its land and resources, Brest-Litovsk was a major cause of the Russian Civil War, as Lenin's enemies were convinced that he had sold out the country to the Kaiser. Lenin himself had to use all of the persuasive power at his command to secure support for the treaty among his fellow Bolsheviks.

6 Disillusionment with Bolshevik Rule

During their struggle with the Whites, the Bolsheviks administered Soviet Russia by means of a set of policies known as War Communism. These drastic measures called for the nationalization of all economic enterprises in the country. At the same time, the Bolsheviks resorted to military-style discipline to keep factory laborers at their jobs and terrorized peasants into surrendering their grain for the worthless currency issued by the regime. The growing discontent of the population climaxed in March 1921, when the sailors at the Kronstadt naval base, in league with the workers of nearby Petrograd, revolted against the government. What made this action particularly striking was the fact that the rebels all had been ardent allies of the Bolsheviks in 1917–1918. Now, however, the high expectations created by the revolution clashed brutally with Lenin's ruthless determination to restore order to a country utterly defeated in World War I and threatened with anarchy and dissolution. In their disillusionment, the Kronstadt sailors and their working-class allies reaffirmed their revolutionary ideals by taking up arms against "the dictatorship of the proletariat."

The Kronstadt rebellion, a profound embarrassment to the Communist regime, was quickly crushed by Red troops; a large number of the rebels were executed. At the same time, the uprising helped convince Lenin, now that the White Army had been defeated in the civil war, to initiate a strategic retreat. He instituted the New Economic Policy and secured acceptance of it among his compatriots. Introduced in March 1921, NEP (as it was known) called for the return of smaller economic establishments to the private sector; it also allowed peasants to sell most of their grain on the private market rather than relinquishing it to the state. To outside observers, it may have appeared as though the Soviet experiment had come to a dead end, supplanted by capitalism. Lenin, however, saw NEP simply as a temporary necessity designed to return Russia to economic health before it could continue down the road to socialism. The New Economic Policy succeeded in revitalizing the economy and remained in effect until the end of the 1920s, when Joseph Stalin changed direction once more.

PROCLAMATION OF THE KRONSTADT REBELS

The following statement expresses the idealism of the rebels who took up arms against an increasingly autocratic state in March 1921. This idealism received recognition years later under Mikhail Gorbachev; and in January 1994, President Boris Yeltsin declared the repression of the Kronstadt sailors "illegal and in violation of basic human rights." He decreed that a monument be erected in honor of the victims.

With the October Revolution the working class had hoped to achieve its emancipation. But there resulted an even greater enslavement of human personality.

The power of the police and gendarme monarchy fell into the hands of usurpers—the Communists—who, instead of giving the people liberty, have instilled in them only the constant fear of the Tcheka [secret police], which by its horrors surpasses even the gendarme regime of Tsarism . . . Worst and most criminal of all is the spiritual cabal of the Communists: they have laid their hand also on the internal world of the laboring masses, compelling everyone to think according to Communist prescription.

. . . Russia of the toilers, the first to raise the red banner of labor's emancipation, is drenched with the blood of those martyred for the greater glory of Communist dominion. In that sea of blood the Communists are drowning all the bright promises and possibilities of the workers' revolution. It has now become clear that the Russian Communist party is not the defender of the laboring masses, as it pretends to be. The interests of the working people are foreign to it. Having gained power it is now fearful only of losing it, and therefore it considers all means permissible: defamation, deceit, violence, murder, and vengeance upon the families of the rebels.

There is an end to long-suffering patience. Here and there the land is lit up by the fires of rebellion in a struggle against oppression and violence. Strikes of workers have multiplied, but the Bolshevik police regime has taken every precaution against the outbreak of the inevitable Third Revolution.

But in spite of it all it has come, and it is made by the hands of the laboring masses. The Generals of Communism see clearly that it is the people who have risen, the people who have become convinced that the Communists have betrayed the ideas of Socialism. Fearing for their safety and knowing that there is no place they can hide in from the wrath of the workers, the Communists still try to terrorise the rebels with prison, shooting, and other barbarities. But life under the Communist dictatorship is more terrible than death. . . .

There is no middle road. To conquer or to die! The example is being set by Kronstadt, the terror of counter-revolution from the right and from the left. Here has taken place the great revolutionary deed. Here is raised the banner of rebellion against the three-year-old tyranny and oppression of Communist autocracy, which has put in the shade the three-hundred-year-old despotism of monarchism. Here, in Kronstadt, has been laid the cornerstone of the Third Revolution which is to break the last chains of the worker and open the new, broad road to Socialist creativeness.

This new Revolution will rouse the masses of the East and the West, and it will serve as an example of new Socialist constructiveness, in contradistinction to the governmental, cut-and-dried Communist "construction." The laboring masses will learn that what has been done till now in the name of the workers and peasants was not Socialism.

Without firing a single shot, without shedding a drop of blood, the first step has been taken. Those who labor need no blood. They will shed it only in self-defense. . . . The workers and peasants march on: they are leaving behind them the *utchredilka* (Constituent Assembly) with its bourgeois regime and the Communist party dictatorship with its Tcheka and State capitalism, which have put the noose around the neck of the workers and threaten to strangle them to death.

The present change offers the laboring masses the opportunity of securing, at last, freely elected Soviets which will function without fear of the Party whip; they can now reorganise the governmentalised labor unions into voluntary associations of workers, peasants, and the working intelligentsia. At last is broken the police club of Communist autocracy.

7 Modernize or Perish

Joseph Stalin (1879–1953) was the Communist leader who transformed the Soviet Union into a superpower. He was born Iosif Vissarionovich Dzhugashvili in Trans-Caucasus Georgia. A rebel from childhood, he was one of Lenin's favored professional revolutionaries, trained in the tough schools of underground agitation, tsarist prisons, and Siberian exile. Unscrupulous, energetic, and endowed with a keen nose for the realities of power within the party and the country as a whole, Stalin surpassed his political rivals in strength of will and organizational astuteness. After he was appointed secretary-general of the Communist party (then considered a minor post) in 1922, he concentrated on building, amid the disorganization caused by war, revolution, and civil war, an effective party organization adapted to the temper of the Russian people. With this structure's help, he established himself as Lenin's successor. Stalin, more powerful and more ruthless than Lenin, was determined to force his country to overcome the economic and political weakness that had led to defeat and ruin in 1917. After Lenin's death, Stalin preached the "Leninist style of work," which combined "Russian revolutionary sweep" with "American efficiency."

Joseph Stalin
THE HARD LINE

Firmly entrenched in power by 1929, Stalin started a second revolution (called the Stalin Revolution), mobilizing at top speed the potential of the country, however limited the human and material resources available, whatever the obstacles, and whatever the human price. The alternative, he was sure, was foreign domination that would totally destroy his country's independence. In this spirit, he addressed a gathering of industrial managers in 1931, talking to them not in Marxist-Leninist jargon, but in terms of hard-line Russian nationalism.

It is sometimes asked whether it is not possible to slow down the tempo a bit, to put a check on the movement. No, comrades, it is not possible! The tempo must not be reduced! On the contrary, we must increase it as much as is within our powers and possibilities. This is dictated to us by our obligations to the workers and peasants of the U.S.S.R. This is dictated to us by our obligations to the working class of the whole world.

To slacken the tempo would mean falling behind. And those who fall behind get beaten. But we do not want to be beaten. No, we refuse to be beaten! One feature of the history of old Russia was the continual beatings she suffered for falling behind, for her backwardness. She was beaten by the Mongol Khans. She was beaten by the Turkish beys. She was beaten by the Swedish feudal lords. She was beaten by the Polish and Lithuanian gentry. She was beaten by the British and French capitalists. She was beaten by the Japanese barons. All beat her—for her backwardness: for military backwardness, for cultural backwardness, for political backwardness, for industrial backwardness, for agricultural backwardness. She was beaten because to do so was profitable and could be done with impunity. Do you remember the words of the pre-revolutionary poet [Nikolai Nekrasov]: "You are poor and abundant, mighty and impotent, Mother Russia." These words of the old poet were well learned by those gentlemen. They beat her, saying: "You are abundant," so one can enrich oneself at your expense. They beat her, saying: "You are poor and impotent," so you can be beaten and plundered with impunity. Such is the law of the exploiters—to beat the backward and the weak. It is the jungle law of capitalism. You are backward, you are weak—therefore you are wrong; hence, you can be beaten and enslaved. You are mighty—therefore you are right; hence, we must be wary of you.

That is why we must no longer lag behind.

In the past we had no fatherland, nor could we have one. But now that we have overthrown capitalism and power is in the hands of the working class, we have a fatherland, and we will defend its independence. Do you want our socialist fatherland to be beaten and to lose its independence? If you do not want this you must put an end to its backwardness in the shortest possible time and develop genuine Bolshevik tempo in building up its socialist system of economy. There is no other way. That is why Lenin said during the October Revolution: "Either perish, or overtake and outstrip the advanced capitalist countries."

We are fifty or a hundred years behind the advanced countries. We must make good this distance in ten years. Either we do it, or they crush us.

This is what our obligations to the workers and peasants of the U.S.S.R. dictate to us.

8 Forced Collectivization

The forced collectivization of agriculture that began in 1929 was an integral part of the Stalin Revolution. His argument in favor of it was simple: an economy divided against itself cannot stand—planned industrial mobilization was incompatible with small-scale private agriculture in the traditional manner. Collectivization meant combining many small peasant holdings into large units (an average of one hundred peasant farmsteads per collective farm). Each *kolkhoz* was run in theory by the peasants (now called collective farmers or *kolkhozniks*), but in practice by the collective farm chairman guided by the government's Five-Year Plan.

Joseph Stalin
LIQUIDATION OF THE KULAKS

Collectivization, not surprisingly, met with fierce resistance, especially from the more successful peasants, called kulaks, who were averse to surrendering their private plots and their freedom in running their households. Their resistance therefore had to be broken, and the Communist party fomented a rural class struggle, seeking help from the poorest peasants. Sometimes, however, even the poorer peasants sided with the local kulaks. Under these conditions, Stalin did not shrink from unleashing violence in the countryside aimed at the "liquidation of the kulaks as a class." For Stalin, the collectivization drive meant an all-out

war on what was for him the citadel of backwardness: the peasant tradition and rebelliousness so prominent under the tsars. The following reading—Stalin's address to the Conference of Marxist Students of the Agrarian Question in December 1929—conveys his intentions. It is a good example of Stalin's rhetoric; he drives home his point by continually restating his argument.

The characteristic feature of our work during the past year is: (a) that we, the party and the Soviet government, have developed an offensive on the whole front against the capitalist elements in the countryside; and (b) that this offensive, as you know, has brought about and is bringing about very palpable, *positive* results.

What does this mean? It means that we have passed from the policy of *restricting* the exploiting proclivities of the kulaks to the policy of *eliminating* the kulaks as a class. This means that we have made, and are still making, one of the most decisive turns in our whole policy.

. . . Could we have undertaken such an offensive against the kulaks five years or three years ago? Could we then have counted on success in such an offensive? No, we could not. That would have been the most dangerous adventurism! That would have been playing a very dangerous game at offensive. We would certainly have come to grief and, once we had come to grief, we would have strengthened the position of the kulaks. Why? Because we did not yet have strongholds in the rural districts in the shape of a wide network of state farms and collective farms upon which to rely in a determined offensive against the kulaks. Because at that time we were not yet able to *substitute* for the capitalist production of the kulaks socialist production in the shape of the collective farms and state farms. . . .

But today? What is the position? Today, we have an adequate material base which enables us to strike at the kulaks, to break their resistance, to eliminate them as a class, and to *substitute* for their output the output of the collective farms and state farms. . . .

Now, as you see, we have the material base which enables us to *substitute* for kulak output the output of the collective farms and state farms. That is why our offensive against the kulaks is now meeting with undeniable success. That is how the offensive against the kulaks must be carried on, if we mean a real offensive and not futile declamations against the kulaks.

That is why we have recently passed from the policy of *restricting* the exploiting *proclivities* of the kulaks to the policy of *eliminating the kulaks as a class*. . . . Now we are able to carry on a determined offensive against the kulaks, to break their resistance, to eliminate them as a class and substitute for their output the output of the collective farms and state farms. Now, the kulaks are being expropriated by the masses of poor and middle peasants themselves, by the masses who are putting solid collectivization into practice. Now the expropriation of the kulaks in the regions of solid collectivization is no longer just an administrative measure. Now, the expropriation of the kulaks is an integral part of the formation and development of the collective farms. . . .

. . . [Should] the kulak . . . be permitted to join the collective farms[?] Of course not, for he is a sworn enemy of the collective farm movement. Clear, one would think.

Lev Kopelev
TERROR IN THE COUNTRYSIDE

The liquidation of the kulaks began in late 1929, extending through the length and breadth of the country during the winter. The confiscation of kulak property, the deportations, and the killing rose to a brutal climax in the following spring and continued for another two years, by which time the bulk of the private farms had been eliminated. By some estimates, almost five million people were liquidated. Some were driven from their huts, deprived of all possessions, and left destitute in the dead of winter; the men were sent to forced labor and their families left abandoned. Others killed themselves or were killed outright, sometimes in pitched battles involving a whole village—men, women, and children.

The upheaval destroyed agricultural production in these years; farm animals died or were killed in huge numbers; fields lay barren. In 1932 and 1933, famine stalked the south and southeast, killing additional millions; it was especially severe in Ukraine. The vast tragedy caused by collectivization did not deter Stalin from pursuing his goals: the establishment of state farms run like factories and the subordination of the rebellious and willful peasantry to state authority.

Here, a militant participant in the collectivization drive, Lev Kopelev, recalls some of his experiences. Kopelev, born in 1912 and raised in a Ukrainian, middle-class Jewish family, evolved from a youthful Stalinist into a tolerant, gentle person in later years; he was chastened after World War II by a term in a labor camp reserved for scientists. Subsequently out of favor because of his literary protests against the inhumanities of the Soviet system, he was exiled from the Soviet Union to West Germany in 1980 and died there in 1997.

The grain front! Stalin said the struggle for grain was the struggle for socialism. I was convinced that we were warriors on an invisible front, fighting against kulak sabotage for the grain which was needed by the country, by the five-year plan. Above all, for the grain, but also for the souls of these peasants who were mired in unconscientiousness, in ignorance, who succumbed to enemy agitation, who did not understand the great truth of communism. . . .

The highest measure of coercion on the hardcore holdouts was "undisputed confiscation."

A team consisting of several young kolkhozniks [collective farmers] and members of the village soviet . . . would search the hut, barn, yard, and take away all the stores of seed, lead away the cow, the horse, the pigs.

In some cases they would be merciful and leave some potatoes, peas, corn for feeding the family. But the stricter ones would make a clean sweep. They would take not only the food and livestock, but also "all valuables and surpluses of clothing," including icons in their frames, samovars, painted carpets and even metal kitchen utensils which might be silver. And any money they found stashed away. Special instructions ordered the removal of gold, silver and currency. . . .

Several times Volodya and I were present at such plundering raids. We even took part: we were entrusted to draw up inventories of the confiscated goods. . . . The women howled hysterically, clinging to the bags.

"Oy, that's the last thing we have! That was for the children's kasha [cereal]! Honest to God, the children will starve!"

They wailed, falling on their trunks:

"Oy, that's a keepsake from my dead mama! People, come to my aid, this is my trousseau, never e'en put on!"

I heard the children echoing them with screams, choking, coughing with screams. And I saw the looks of the men: frightened, pleading, hateful, dully impassive, extinguished with despair or flaring up with half-mad, daring ferocity.

"Take it. Take it away. Take everything away. There's still a pot of borscht on the stove. It's plain, got no meat. But still it's got beets, taters 'n' cabbage. And it's salted! Better take it, comrade citizens! Here, hang on, I'll take off my shoes. They're patched and re-patched, but maybe they'll have some use for the proletariat, for our dear Soviet power."

It was excruciating to see and hear all this. And even worse to take part in it. . . . And I persuaded myself, explained to myself. I mustn't give in to debilitating pity. We were realizing historical necessity. We were performing our revolutionary duty. We were obtaining grain for the socialist fatherland. For the five-year plan. . . .

I have always remembered the winter of the last grain collections, the weeks of the great famine. And I have always told about it. But I did not begin to write it down until many years later. . . .

How could all this have happened?

Who was guilty of the famine which destroyed millions of lives?

How could I have participated in it? . . .

We were raised as the fanatical [believers] of a new creed, the only true *religion* of scientific socialism. The party became our church militant, bequeathing to all mankind eternal salvation, eternal peace and the bliss of an earthly paradise. It victoriously surmounted all other churches, schisms and heresies. The works of Marx, Engels and Lenin were accepted as holy writ, and Stalin was the infallible high priest.

. . . Stalin was the most perspicacious, the most wise (at that time they hadn't yet started calling him "great" and "brilliant"). He said: "The struggle for grain is the struggle for socialism." And we believed him unconditionally. And later we believed that unconditional collectivization was unavoidable if we were to overcome the capriciousness and uncertainty of the market and the backwardness of individual farming, to guarantee a steady supply of grain, milk and meat to the cities. And also if we were to reeducate millions of peasants, those petty landowners and hence potential bourgeoisie, potential kulaks, to transform them into laborers with a social conscience, to liberate them from "the idiocy of country life," from ignorance and prejudice, and to accustom them to culture, to all the boons of socialism. . . .

In the following passage Kopelev reflects, even more searchingly, on his own motivation and state of mind as a participant in Stalin's collectivization drive.

With the rest of my generation I firmly believed that the ends justified the means. Our great goal was the universal triumph of Communism, and for the sake of that goal everything was permissible—to lie, to steal, to destroy hundreds of thousands and even millions of people, all those who were hindering our work or could hinder it, everyone who stood in the way. And to hesitate or doubt about all this was to give in to "intellectual squeamishness" and "stupid liberalism," the attributes of people who "could not see the forest for the trees."

That was how I had reasoned, and everyone like me, even when I did have my doubts, when I saw what "total collectivization" meant—how . . . mercilessly they stripped the peasants in the winter of 1932–33. I took part in this myself, scouring the countryside, searching for hidden grain, testing the earth with an iron rod for loose spots that might lead to buried grain. With the others, I emptied out the old folks' storage chests, stopping my ears to the children's crying and the women's wails. For I was convinced that I was accomplishing the great and necessary transformation of the countryside; that in the days to come the people who lived there would be better off for it; that their distress and suffering were a result of their own ignorance or the machinations of the class enemy; that those who sent me—and I myself—knew better than the peasants how they should live, what they should sow and when they should plow.

In the terrible spring of 1933 I saw people dying from hunger. I saw women and children with distended bellies, turning blue, still breathing but with vacant, lifeless eyes. And corpses—corpses in ragged sheepskin coats and cheap felt boots; corpses in peasant huts, in the melting snow of old Vologda, under the bridges of Kharkov. . . . I saw all this and did not go out of my mind or commit suicide. Nor did I curse those who had sent me to take away the peasants' grain in the winter, and in the spring to persuade the barely walking, skeleton-thin or sickly-swollen people to go into the fields in order to "fulfill the Bolshevik sowing plan in shock-worker style."

Nor did I lose my faith. As before, I believed because I wanted to believe. Thus from time immemorial men have believed when possessed by a desire to serve powers and values above and beyond humanity: gods, emperors, states; ideals of virtue, freedom, nation, race, class, party. . . .

Any single-minded attempt to realize these ideals exacts its toll of human sacrifice. In the name of the noblest visions promising eternal happiness to their descendants, such men bring merciless ruin on their contemporaries. Bestowing paradise on the dead, they maim and destroy the living. They become unprincipled liars and unrelenting executioners, all the while seeing themselves as virtuous and honorable militants—convinced that if they are forced into villainy, it is for the sake of future good, and that if they have to lie, it is in the name of eternal truths.

. . . That was how we thought and acted—we, the fanatical disciples of the all-saving ideals of Communism. When we saw the base and cruel acts that were committed in the name of our exalted notions of good, and when we ourselves took part in those actions, what we feared most was to lose our heads, fall into doubt or heresy and forfeit our unbounded faith. . . . The concepts of conscience, honor, humaneness we dismissed as idealistic prejudices, "intellectual" or "bourgeois," and hence, perverse.

Miron Dolot
FAMINE IN UKRAINE

Ukraine had been the traditional breadbasket of the Russian Empire and later the Soviet Union. Here, Stalin's collectivization drive had several goals: the extraction of maximum agricultural output, the imposition of rigid social control, and the destruction of a nationalist movement that challenged Russian dominance of the U.S.S.R. The combination of these goals helps explain the severity of official measures used to crush popular resistance, including even mass starvation. In the following selection, Miron Dolot describes some of the horrors that he witnessed in Ukraine during the early 1930s. Dolot, a survivor of the state-induced famine, later emigrated to the West and recounted his experiences in the book *Execution by Hunger—The Hidden Holocaust,* which was published in 1985.

The year 1932 witnessed the last battle of collectivization: the battle for bread, or to be more specific, for the crop of 1932. On the one side was the Communist government; on the other, the starving farmers. The government forces resorted to any means in getting as many agricultural products from the countryside as possible, without regard to the consequences. The farmers, already on the verge of starvation, desperately tried to keep what food they had left, and, in spite of government efforts to the contrary, tried to stay alive. . . .

The long and cold winter of 1931–1932 was slowly giving way to spring. . . .

Around this time the plight of the villagers became desperate. This was the memorable spring of 1932 when the famine broke out, and the first deaths from hunger began to occur. I remember the endless procession of beggars on roads and paths, going from house to house. They were in different stages of starvation, dirty and ragged. With outstretched hands, they begged for food, any food: a potato, a beet, or at least a kernel of corn. Those were the first victims of starvation: destitute men and women; poor widows and orphaned children who had no chance of surviving the terrible ordeal.

Some starving farmers still tried to earn their food by doing chores in or outside the village. One could see these sullen, emaciated men walking from house to house with an ax, or a shovel, in search of work. Perhaps someone might hire them to dig up the garden, or chop some firewood. They would do it for a couple of potatoes. But not many of us had a couple of potatoes to spare.

Crowds of starving wretches could be seen scattered all over the potato fields. They were looking for potatoes left over from last year's harvest. No matter what shape the potatoes were in, whether frozen or rotten, they were still edible. Others were roaming the forest in search of food; the riverbanks were crowded too; there was much new greenery around: young shoots of reed or other river plants. One might catch something, anything, in the water to eat.

But the majority of those who looked for help would go to the cities as they used to do before. It was always easier to find some work there, either gardening, cleaning backyards, or sweeping streets. But now, times had changed. It was illegal to hire farmers for any work. The purpose of the prohibition was twofold: it was done not only to stop the flow of labor from the collective farms, but also, and primarily, to prevent the farmers from receiving food rations in the cities. . . .

By this time our village was in economic ruin. Poverty was universal. We had never been rich, it is true, but economically, we had always been completely self-sufficient and had never gone hungry for so long. Now starving, we were facing the spring of 1932 with great anxiety for there was no hope of relief from the outside. Deaths from starvation became daily occurrences. There was always some burial in the village cemetery. One could see strange funeral processions: children pulling homemade handwagons with the bodies of their dead parents in them or the parents carting the bodies of their children. There were no coffins; no burial ceremonies performed by priests. The bodies of the starved were just deposited in a large common grave, one upon the other; that was all there was to it. . . .

Looking back to those events now, it seems to me that I lived in some kind of a wicked fantasy world. All the events which I witnessed and experienced then and which I am now describing, seem unreal to me because of their cruelty and unspeakable horror. It is simply too difficult to associate all those happenings with real life in a normal human society. . . .

The battle for the Ukrainian wheat crop of 1932 started almost two months before the harvest.

At the end of May, some strangers appeared in our village, and little by little, we began finding out who they were. The Party had mobilized 112,000 of its most active and reliable members in order to organize a speedy harvest of the new crop, and to secure its swift and smooth requisitioning and final delivery to the State. Soon these members became known to us as the Hundred Thousanders, or just Thousanders. There were nine of them in our village. . . . In no time at all, these new Thousanders took over our entire village like tyrants, imposing their wills and their demands upon us. . . .

Comrade Thousander's announcement that in 1932 we had to deliver the same quota of grain as in 1931 was a hard blow to us. We simply could not fulfill his demands. The 1932 grain quota was not based on the actual amount of grain sown, cultivated, and harvested; it was based upon an unrealistic government plan. . . .

Faced with starvation, the villagers tried everything possible to save themselves and their families. Some of them started eating dogs and cats. Others went hunting for birds: crows, magpies, swallows, sparrows, storks, and even nightingales. One could see starving villagers searching in the bushes along the river for birds' nests or looking for crabs and other small crustaceans in the water. Even their hard shells, though not edible, were cooked and the broth consumed as nourishment. One could see crowds of famished villagers combing the woods in search of roots or mushrooms and berries. Some tried to catch small forest animals.

Driven by hunger, people ate everything and anything: even food that had already rotted—potatoes, beets, and other root vegetables that pigs normally refused to eat. They even ate weeds, the leaves and bark of trees, insects, frogs, and snails. Nor did they shy away from eating the meat of diseased horses and cattle. Often that meat was already decaying and those who ate it died of food poisoning. . . .

One morning in late January 1933, while it was still dark, Mother and I set out along the main street through the center of the village for the county town. We followed the street to the main road which led straight into the town. . . .

Soon, however, as we slowly made our way through the snow toward the village center, graphic evidence of starvation became visible. We noticed a black object which, from afar, looked like a snow-covered tree stump. As we came near, however, we saw that it was the body of a dead man. Frozen limbs protruding from under the snow gave the body the appearance of some grotesque creature. I bent down and cleared the snow off the face. It was Ulas, our elderly neighbor whom we had last seen about a month ago.

A few steps further, we saw another frozen body. It was the corpse of a woman. As I brushed away the snow, horror made my blood turn cold: under her ragged coat, clutched tightly to her bosom with her stiff hands, was the frozen little body of her baby.

We finally left our village behind and stepped onto the open road which led to the county seat. However, another ghostly panorama now opened in front of us. Everywhere we looked dead and frozen bodies lay by the sides of the road. To our right were bodies of those villagers who apparently had tried to reach the town in search of work and food. Weakened by starvation, they were unable to make it and ended up lying or falling down by the roadside, never to rise again. The gentle snow mercifully covered their bodies with its white blanket.

One could easily imagine the fate of those people whose bodies were lying to our left. They most probably were returning from the county town, without having accomplished anything. They had tramped many kilometers in vain, only to be refused a job and a chance to stay alive. They were returning home empty-handed. Death caught up with them as they trudged homeward, resigned to dying in their village.

The wide open kolhosp[1] fields, stretching for kilometers on both sides of the main road, looked like a battlefield after a great war. Littering the fields were the bodies of the starving farmers who had been combing the potato fields over and over again in the hope of finding at least a fragment of a potato that might have been overlooked or left over from the last harvest. They died where they collapsed in their endless search for food. Some of those frozen corpses must have been lying out there for months. Nobody seemed to be in a hurry to cart them away and bury them. . . .

. . . Dmytro had never returned home after he had been taken to the county center.[2] His young wife Solomia was left alone with their

[1]The Ukrainian term for collective farm.

[2]Dmytro, a neighbor and distant relative of the author, had been jailed after punching a collective farm official who accused him of sabotage.

daughter. She had gone to work in the collective farm, taking her little child with her. As the wife of a banished man, she too was considered an "enemy of the people," and her child was refused admission to the nursery. Later, Solomia was expelled from the collective farm, and thus forced to seek a job in the city. That was impossible, however, because she could not show a certificate of release from the collective farm. She found herself trapped in the circle of the Communist death ring. She had to return to her village.

When winter came, Solomia went from house to house, willing to work for just a piece of bread. She was too proud to beg. People were sympathetic and helped her as much as they could. However, as the famine worsened, and the villagers were no longer able to help her, she was not seen on her rounds any more.

We found the front door of Solomia's house open, but the entrance was blocked with snowdrifts, and it was hard to get inside. When we finally reached the living room, we saw a pitiful sight: Solomia was hanging from the ceiling in the middle of the room. She was dressed in her Ukrainian national costume, and at her breast hung a large cross. It was obvious that she had made preparations before committing suicide. Her hair was combed neatly in two braids hanging over her shoulders.

Frightened, we ran to fetch Mother. We helped her take down Solomia's frozen body, and laid it on a bench, and covered it with a handmade blanket. It was only after we finished doing this that we noticed the dead body of her little daughter. The child was lying in a wooden tub in the corner under the icons, clean and dressed in her best clothes. Her little hands were folded across her chest.

On the table was a note:

> Dear Neighbors:
>
> Please bury our bodies properly. I have to leave you, dear neighbors. I can bear this life no longer. There is no food in the house, and there is no sense in living without my little daughter who starved to death, or my husband. If you ever see Dmytro, tell him about us. He will understand our plight, and he will forgive me. Please tell him that I died peacefully, thinking about him and our dear daughter.
>
> I love you, my dear neighbors, and I wish with all my heart that you somehow recover from this disaster. Forgive me for troubling you. Thank you for everything you have done for me.
>
> Solomia.

After reading the note, we stood there for a while, motionless and forlorn. Our mother tried to suppress the sound of her weeping, pressing the corner of her head scarf to her lips. Mykola gazed at the corpses in disbelief.

In my imagination I was recreating the agony of their dying: the child's hunger cries, and then the death convulsions of its exhausted little body.

How great must have been the sufferings of the mother. She had to listen helplessly to the pleas of her child for food, while she herself was near starvation. She must have felt great relief, I thought, when she saw her little daughter breathing for the last time. Then, in my imagination, I saw the mother attending to her lifeless child: dressing her in the best and cleanest clothing she had, praying on her knees near the body, and finally kissing her for the last time before her own suicide. . . .

Toward the end of March, the famine struck us with full force. Life in the village had sunk to its lowest level, an almost animallike struggle for survival of the fittest.

The village ceased to exist as a coherent community. The inhabitants who still managed to stay alive shut themselves within the walls of their houses. People became too weak even to step outside their doors. Each house became an entity in itself. Visits became a rarity. All doors were bolted and barred against any possible intruders. Even between immediate neighbors, there was little, if any, communication, and people ceased caring about one another. In fact, they avoided each other. Friends and even relatives became strangers. Mothers abandoned their children, and brother turned away from brother. . . .

One must consider the inexorable pressure of hunger under which a person can completely become bereft of his or her senses and sink to an absolute animallike level. That happened to many of our villagers. The more resistant ones who kept on living with minimal or no food at all for some time, felt no more of the initial hunger pangs. They either lapsed into comas, or existed in a semicomatose, lethargic stupor. But some reacted differently. They became like madmen. They lost all traces of compassion, honor, and morality. They suffered from hallucinations of food, of something to bite into and chew, to satisfy the gnawing pains of their empty stomachs. Intolerable cravings assailed them; they were ready to sink their teeth into anything, even into their own hands and arms, or into the flesh of others.

The first rumors of actual cannibalism were related to the mysterious and sudden disappearances of people in the village. . . .

As the cases of missing persons grew in number, an arrest was made which shook us to our souls. A woman was taken into custody, charged with killing her two children.

Another woman was found dead, her neck contorted in a crudely made noose. The neighbors who discovered the tragedy also found the reason for it. The flesh of the woman's three-year old daughter was found in the oven.

9 Soviet Indoctrination

Pressed by the necessity to transform their country into a modern state, the Communist leaders used every opportunity to force the population to adopt the attitudes and motivation necessary to effect such a transformation. Education, from nursery school to university, provided special opportunities to mold attitudes. The Soviet regime made impressive gains in promoting education among its diverse people; it also used education to foster dedication to hard work, discipline in social cooperation, and pride in the nation. For a backward country that, as Lenin had said, must "either perish or overtake and outstrip the advanced capitalist countries," such changes were considered essential.

During the Stalin era, artists and writers were compelled to promote the ideals of the Stalin Revolution. In the style of "socialist realism," their heroes were factory workers and farmers who labored tirelessly and enthusiastically to build a new society. Even romance served a political purpose. Novelists wrote love stories following limited, prosaic themes. For example, a young girl might lose her heart to a co-worker who is a leader in the Communist youth organization and who outproduces his comrades at his job; as the newly married couple is needed at the factory, they choose to forgo a honeymoon.

A. O. Avdienko
THE CULT OF STALIN

Among a people so deeply divided by ethnicity and petty localism, and limited by a pervasive narrowness of perspective, building countrywide unity and consensus was a crucial challenge for the government. In the Russian past, the worship of saints and the veneration of the tsar had served that purpose. The political

mobilization of the masses during the revolution required an intensification of that tradition. It led to the "cult of personality," the deliberate fixation of individual dedication and loyalty on the all-powerful leader, whose personality exemplified the challenge of extraordinary times. The following selection illustrates by what emotional bonds the individual was tied to Stalin, and through Stalin to the prodigious transformation of Russian state and society that he was attempting. It originated as a speech by prose-writer A. O. Avdienko to the Seventh Congress of Soviets, which was held in February 1935. The poem had the distinction of appearing in an August 1936 issue of *Pravda,* the official newspaper of the Soviet Communist party.

Thank you, Stalin. Thank you because I am joyful. Thank you because I am well. No matter how old I become, I shall never forget how we received Stalin two days ago. Centuries will pass, and the generation still to come will regard us as the happiest of mortals, as the most fortunate of men, because we lived in the century of centuries, because we were privileged to see Stalin, our inspired leader. Yes, and we regard ourselves as the happiest of mortals because we are the contemporaries of a man who never had an equal in world history.

The men of all ages will call on thy name, which is strong, beautiful, wise and marvellous. Thy name is engraven on every factory, every machine, every place on the earth, and in the hearts of all men.

Every time I have found myself in his presence I have been subjugated by his strength, his charm, his grandeur. I have experienced a great desire to sing, to cry out, to shout with joy and happiness. And now see me—me!—on the same platform where the Great Stalin stood a year ago. In what country, in what part of the world could such a thing happen.

I write books. I am an author. All thanks to thee, O great educator, Stalin. I love a young woman with a renewed love and shall perpetuate myself in my children—all thanks to thee, great educator, Stalin. I shall be eternally happy and joyous, all thanks to thee, great educator, Stalin. Everything belongs to thee, chief of our great country. And when the woman I love presents me with a child the first word it shall utter will be: Stalin.

O great Stalin, O leader of the peoples,
Thou who broughtest man to birth.
Thou who fructifiest the earth,
Thou who restorest the centuries,
Thou who makest bloom the spring,
Thou who makest vibrate the musical
  chords . . .
Thou, splendour of my spring, O Thou,
Sun reflected by millions of hearts. . . .

Yevgeny Yevtushenko
LITERATURE AS PROPAGANDA

After Stalin's death in 1953, Soviet intellectuals breathed more freely, and they protested against the rigid Stalinist controls. In the following extract from his *Precocious Autobiography,* Russian poet Yevgeny Yevtushenko (b. 1933) looks back to the raw days of intellectual repression under Stalin.

Blankly smiling workers and collective farmers looked out from the covers of books. Almost every novel and short story had a happy ending. Painters more and more often took as their subject state banquets, weddings, solemn public meetings, and parades.

The apotheosis of this trend was a movie which in its grand finale showed thousands of collective farmers having a gargantuan feast against the background of a new power station.

Recently I had a talk with its producer, a gifted and intelligent man.

"How could you produce such a film?" I asked. "It is true that I also once wrote verses in that vein, but I was still wet behind the ears, whereas you were adult and mature."

The producer smiled a sad smile. "You know, the strangest thing to me is that I was absolutely sincere. I thought all this was a necessary part of building communism. And then I believed Stalin."

So when we talk about "the cult of personality," we should not be too hasty in accusing all those who, one way or another, were involved in it, debasing themselves with their flattery. There were of course sycophants [servile flatterers] who used the situation for their own ends. But that many people connected with the arts sang Stalin's praises was often not vice but tragedy.

How was it possible for even gifted and intelligent people to be deceived?

To begin with, Stalin was a strong and vivid personality. When he wanted to, Stalin knew how to charm people. He charmed Gorky and Barbusse. In 1937, the cruelest year of the purges, he managed to charm that tough and experienced observer, Lion Feuchtwanger.[1]

In the second place, in the minds of the Soviet people, Stalin's name was indissolubly linked with Lenin's. Stalin knew how popular Lenin was and saw to it that history was rewritten in such a way as to make his own relations with Lenin seem much more friendly than they had been in fact. The rewriting was so thorough that perhaps Stalin himself believed his own version in the end.

There can be no doubt of Stalin's love for Lenin. His speech on Lenin's death, beginning with the words, "In leaving us, Comrade Lenin has bequeathed . . ." reads like a poem in prose. He wanted to stand as Lenin's heir not only in other people's eyes, but in his own eyes too. He deceived himself as well as the others. Even [Boris] Pasternak put the two names side by side.

> Laughter in the village,
> Voice behind the plow,
> Lenin and Stalin,
> And these verses now . . .

In reality, however, Stalin distorted Lenin's ideas, because to Lenin—and this was the whole meaning of his work—communism was to serve man, whereas under Stalin it appeared that man served communism.

Stalin's theory that people were the little cogwheels of communism was put into practice and with horrifying results. . . . Russian poets, who had produced some fine works during the war, turned dull again. If a good poem did appear now and then, it was likely to be about the war—this was simpler to write about.

Poets visited factories and construction sites but wrote more about machines than about the men who made them work. If machines could read, they might have found such poems interesting. Human beings did not.

The size of a printing was not determined by demand but by the poet's official standing. As a result bookstores were cluttered up with books of poetry which no one wanted. . . . A simple, touching poem by the young poet Vanshenkin, about a boy's first love, caused almost a sensation against this background of industrial-agricultural verse. Vinokurov's first poems, handsomely disheveled among the general sleekness, were avidly seized upon—they had human warmth. But the general situation was unchanged. Poetry remained unpopular. The older poets were silent, and when they

---

[1]Gorky was a prominent Russian writer; Barbusse and Feuchtwanger were well-known Western European writers.

did break their silence, it was even worse. The generation of poets that had been spawned by the war and that had raised so many hopes had petered out. Life in peacetime turned out to be more complicated than life at the front. Two of the greatest Russian poets, Zabolotsky and Smelyakov, were in concentration camps. The young poet Mandel (Korzhavin) had been deported. I don't know if Mandel's name will be remembered in the history of Russian poets but it will certainly be remembered in the history of Russian social thought.

He was the only poet who openly wrote and recited verses against Stalin while Stalin was alive. That he recited them seems to be what saved his life, for the authorities evidently thought him insane. In one poem he wrote of Stalin:

> There in Moscow, in whirling darkness,
> Wrapped in his military coat,
> Not understanding Pasternak,
> A hard and cruel man stared at the snow.

. . . Now that ten years have gone by, I realize that Stalin's greatest crime was not the arrests and the shootings he ordered. His greatest crime was the corruption of the human spirit.

10 Stalin's Terror

The victims of Stalin's terror came from all walks of Soviet life, but institutions of the Communist party and the Soviet government were perhaps hardest hit. By 1939, few of the Old Bolsheviks—comrades of Lenin who had toppled the Provisional Government in 1917—were left alive. Likewise, the purges ridded the armed forces of tens of thousands of officers, although many of them were restored to their posts after Hitler's invasion of the Soviet Union. While exact figures are impossible to come by, at least five million people were arrested during the late 1930s, most of them dispatched to prisons and forced labor camps, where mortality rates were high. Stalin had no qualms about sacrificing multitudes of people to build up the Soviet Union's strength and to make it a powerful factor in world politics. In addition, he felt entitled to settle his own private scores as well as national ones against secessionist Ukrainians. The Soviet government's first acknowledgment of Stalin's terror was made by Khrushchev. The full scope of it began to emerge only under Gorbachev in the late 1980s.

Nikita Khrushchev
KHRUSHCHEV'S SECRET SPEECH

Nikita Khrushchev (1894–1971), first secretary of the Communist party (1953–1964) and premier of the Soviet Union (1958–1964), delivered a famous speech to an unofficial, closed session of the Twentieth Party Congress on February 25, 1956. Although the speech was considered confidential, it was soon leaked to outsiders. While safeguarding the moral authority of Lenin, Khrushchev attacked Stalin, revealing some of the crimes committed by him and his closest associates in the 1930s. The following passages from the speech draw on evidence collected by a special commission of inquiry.

We have to consider seriously and analyze correctly this matter [the crimes of the Stalin era] in order that we may preclude any possibility of a repetition in any form whatever of what took place during the life of Stalin, who absolutely did not tolerate collegiality in leadership and in work, and who practiced brutal violence, not only toward everything which opposed him, but also toward that which seemed to his capricious and despotic character, contrary to his concepts.

Stalin acted not through persuasion, explanation, and patient co-operation with people, but by imposing his concepts and demanding absolute submission to his opinion. Whoever opposed this concept or tried to prove his viewpoint, and the correctness of his position, was doomed to removal from the leading collective and to subsequent moral and physical annihilation. This was especially true during the period following the XVIIth Party Congress [1934], when many prominent Party leaders and rank-and-file Party workers, honest and dedicated to the cause of Communism, fell victim to Stalin's despotism. . . .

Stalin originated the concept "enemy of the people." This term automatically rendered it unnecessary that the ideological errors of a man or men engaged in a controversy be proven; this term made possible the usage of the most cruel repression, violating all norms of revolutionary legality, against anyone who in any way disagreed with Stalin, against those who were only suspected of hostile intent, against those who had bad reputations. This concept, "enemy of the people," actually eliminated the possibility of any kind of ideological fight or the making of one's views known on this or that issue, even those of a practical character. In the main, and in actuality, the only proof of guilt used, against all norms of current legal science, was the "confession" of the accused himself; and, as subsequent probing proved, "confessions" were acquired through physical pressures against the accused.

This led to glaring violations of revolutionary legality, and to the fact that many entirely innocent persons, who in the past had defended the Party line, became victims. . . .

The Commission [of inquiry] has become acquainted with a large quantity of materials in the NKVD [secret police, forerunner to the KGB] archives and with other documents and has established many facts pertaining to the fabrication of cases against Communists, to false accusations, to glaring abuses of socialist legality—which resulted in the death of innocent people. It became apparent that many Party, Soviet and economic activists who were branded in 1937–1938 as "enemies" were actually never enemies, spies, wreckers, etc., but were always honest Communists; they were only so stigmatized, and often, no longer able to bear barbaric tortures, they charged themselves (at the order of the investigative judges—falsifiers) with all kinds of grave and unlikely crimes. . . .

Lenin used severe methods only in the most necessary cases, when the exploiting classes were still in existence and were vigorously opposing the revolution, when the struggle for survival was decidedly assuming the sharpest forms, even including a civil war.

Stalin, on the other hand, used extreme methods and mass repressions at a time when the revolution was already victorious, when the Soviet state was strengthened, when the exploiting classes were already liquidated and Socialist relations were rooted solidly in all phases of national economy, when our Party was politically consolidated and had strengthened itself both numerically and ideologically. It is clear that here Stalin showed in a whole series of cases his intolerance, his brutality and his abuse of power. Instead of proving his political correctness and mobilizing the masses, he often chose the path of repression and physical annihilation, not only against actual enemies, but also against individuals who had not committed any crimes against the Party and the Soviet government. . . .

An example of vile provocation, of odious falsification and of criminal violation of revolutionary legality is the case of the former candidate for the Central Committee Political Bureau, one of the most eminent workers of the

Party and of the Soviet government, Comrade Eikhe, who was a Party member since 1905. *(Commotion in the hall.)*

Comrade Eikhe was arrested on April 29, 1938, on the basis of slanderous materials, without the sanction of the Prosecutor of the USSR, which was finally received 15 months after the arrest.

Investigation of Eikhe's case was made in a manner which most brutally violated Soviet legality and was accompanied by willfulness and falsification.

Eikhe was forced under torture to sign ahead of time a protocol of his confession prepared by the investigative judges, in which he and several other eminent Party workers were accused of anti-Soviet activity.

On October 1, 1939, Eikhe sent his declaration to Stalin in which he categorically denied his guilt and asked for an examination of his case. In the declaration he wrote: "There is no more bitter misery than to sit in the jail of a government for which I have always fought."

A second declaration of Eikhe has been preserved which he sent to Stalin on October 27, 1939; in it he cited facts very convincingly and countered the slanderous accusations made against him, arguing that his provocatory accusation was on the one hand the work of real Trotskyites whose arrests he had sanctioned as First Secretary of the West Siberian Krai [local] Party Committee and who conspired in order to take revenge on him, and, on the other hand, the result of the base falsification of materials by the investigative judges. . . .

It would appear that such an important declaration was worth an examination by the Central Committee. This, however, was not done and the declaration was transmitted to Beria [head of the NKVD] while the terrible maltreatment of the Political Bureau candidate, Comrade Eikhe, continued.

On February 2, 1940, Eikhe was brought before the court. Here he did not confess any guilt and said as follows:

> In all the so-called confessions of mine there is not one letter written by me with the exception of my signatures under the protocols which were forced from me. I have made my confession under pressure from the investigative judge who from the time of my arrest tormented me. After that I began to write all this nonsense. . . . The most important thing for me is to tell the court, the Party and Stalin that I am not guilty. I have never been guilty of any conspiracy. I will die believing in the truth of Party policy as I have believed in it during my whole life.

On February 4 Eikhe was shot. *(Indignation in the hall.)*

Lev Razgon
TRUE STORIES

"Corrective labor" was part of Stalin's efforts to terrorize the peoples of the Soviet Union into compliance with his plan to modernize the country's economy and society. All those accused of disloyalty to the party and not killed outright ended up in one of the *gulags. Gulag* is a Russian acronym denoting the system of Soviet forced-labor camps, scattered, like islands in an archipelago, over the entire country. The inhabitants of that archipelago were the *zeks,* as the political prisoners were called. Their labor served a double purpose. It was designed as punishment for their alleged crimes and as a means of obtaining vital raw materials—including lumber and minerals—from areas too inhospitable for, or

outright hostile to, regular labor. Forced labor also built the canal linking the Leningrad area with the White Sea in the far north.

In 1988, Lev Razgon (1908–1999), a survivor of Stalin's camps, published an account of his experiences which, in 1997, was published in English under the title *True Stories.* Razgon was a journalist who married the daughter of a high-ranking member of the Soviet secret police. Gaining access to the Soviet elite, he attended the Seventeenth Party Congress in 1934. In 1937, his father-in-law was arrested for "counter-revolutionary" activities along with many family friends; the following year the police came for Razgon and his wife, who perished in a transit prison on route to a northern camp. Razgon spent the next seven years in a labor camp. Released in 1945, he was confined to various provincial towns, but in 1949 was rearrested and returned to the camps. Finally, he was released again in 1956 after Stalin's death.

Over the years, Razgon began to write down for his desk drawer his prison experiences with the specific intent of preserving the memory of fellow prisoners who did not survive. As the Soviet Union began to crumble, Razgon was able to publish his stories. The following extracts from *True Stories* reveal the brutality and irrationality of the Soviet prison system under Stalin. In the first selection, Razgon reproduces a discussion he had with a former prison warden, whom he met by chance in a hospital ward in 1977. The warden described to Razgon his role as an executioner of political prisoners.

[THE ROUTINE OF EXECUTION]

"It was like this. In the morning we'd hand everything over to the new shift and go into the guardhouse. We'd collect our weapons, and then and there they'd give us each a shot glass of vodka. After that we'd take the list and go round with the senior warden to pick them up from the cells and take them out to the truck."

"What kind of truck?"

"A closed van. Six of them and four of us in each one."

"How many trucks would leave at the same time?"

"Three or four."

"Did they know where they were going? Did someone read them their death sentence before, or what?"

"No, no sentences were announced. No one even spoke, just, 'Come out,' then straight ahead, into the van—fast!"

"Were they in handcuffs?"

"No, we didn't have any."

"How did they behave, once they were in the van?"

"The men, well, they kept quiet. But the women would start crying, they'd say: 'What are you doing, we're not guilty of anything, comrades, what are you doing?' and things like that."

"They used to take men and women together?"

"No, always separately."

"Were the women young? Were there a lot of them?"

"Not so many, about two vanloads a week. No very young ones but there were some about twenty-five or thirty. Most were older, and some even elderly."

"Did you drive them far?"

"Twelve kilometers or so, to the hill. The Distant Hill, it was called. There were hills all around and that's where we unloaded them."

"So you would unload them, and then tell them their sentence?"

"What was there to tell them?! No, we yelled, 'Out! Stand still!' They scrambled down and there was already a trench dug in front of them. They clambered down, clung together and right away we got to work. . . ."

"They didn't make any noise?"

"Some didn't, others began shouting. 'We're Communists, we are being wrongly executed,' that type of thing. But the women would only cry and cling to each other. So we just got on with it. . . ."

"Did you have a doctor with you?"

"What for? We would shoot them, and those still wriggling got another bullet and then we were off to the van. The work team from the Dalag camps was already nearby, waiting."

"What work team was that?"

"There was a team of criminal inmates from Dalag who lived in a separate compound. They were the trusties[1] at Bikin and they also had to dig and fill in the pits. As soon as we left they would fill in that pit and dig a new one for the next day. When they finished their work, they went back to the compound. They got time off their sentences for it and were well fed. It was easy work, not like felling timber."

"And what about you?"

"We would arrive back at the camp, hand in our weapons at the guardhouse and then we could have as much to drink as we wanted. The others used to lap it up—it didn't cost them a kopeck. I always had my shot, went off to the canteen for a hot meal, and then back to sleep in the barracks."

"And did you sleep well? Didn't you feel bad or anything?"

"Why should I?"

"Well, that you had just killed other people. Didn't you feel sorry for them?"

"No, not at all. I didn't give it a thought. No, I slept well and then I'd go for a walk outside the camp. There's some beautiful places around there. Boring, though, with no women."

"Were any of you married?"

"No, they didn't take married men. Of course, the bosses made out all right. There were some real lookers on the Dalag work team! Your head would spin! Cooks, dishwashers, floor cleaners—the bosses had them all. We went without. It was better not to even think about it. . . ."

"Grigory Ivanovich, did you know that the people you were shooting were not guilty at all, that they hadn't done anything wrong?"

"Well, we didn't think about that then. Later, yes. We were summoned to the procurators [officials] and they asked us questions. They explained that those had been innocent people. There had been mistakes, they said, and—what was the word?—excesses. But they told us that it was nothing to do with us, we were not guilty of anything."

"Well, I understand, then you were under orders and you shot people. But when you learned that you had been killing men and women who were not guilty at all, didn't your conscience begin to bother you?"

"Conscience? No, Naum'ich, it didn't bother me. I never think about all that now, and when I do remember something . . . no, nothing at all, as if nothing had happened. You know, I've become so soft-hearted that one look at an old man suffering today and I feel so much pity that I even cry sometimes. But those ones, no, I'm not sorry for them. Not at all, it's just like they never existed. . . ."

The "special operation" at Bikin existed for almost three years. Well, two and a half, to be more exact. It also probably had its holidays and weekends—perhaps no one was shot on Sundays, May Day, Revolution Day and the Day of the Soviet Constitution. Even so, that means that it functioned for a total of 770 days. Every morning on each of those days four trucks set out from Bikin compound for the Distant Hill. Six people in each truck, a total of 24. It took 25–30 minutes for them to reach the waiting pit. The "special operation" thus disposed of 15,000 to 18,000 people during its existence. Yet it was of a standard design, just like any transit camp. The well-tried, well-planned machinery operated without interruption, functioning regularly and efficiently, filling the ready-made pits with bodies—in the hills of the Far East, in the Siberian forests, and in the glades of the Tambov woods or the Meshchera nature reserve.

---

[1]Trusties were convicts regarded as trustworthy, who were given special duties and privileges.

They existed everywhere, yet nothing remains of them now. There are no terrible museums as there are today at Auschwitz, or at Mauthausen in Austria. There are no solemn and funereal memorials like those that testify to the Nazi atrocities at Khatyn* . . . or Lidice.[2] Thousands of unnamed graves, in which there lie mingled the bones of hundreds of thousands of victims, have now been overgrown by bushes, thick luxuriant grass and young new forest. Not exactly the same as the Germans, it must be admitted. The men and women were buried separately here. Our regime made sure that even at that point no moral laxity might occur.

And the murderers? They are still alive.

. . . There were a great many, of course, who took part in these shootings. There were yet more, however, who never made the regular journey to the Distant Hill or the other killing grounds. Only in bourgeois society are the procurator and others obliged to attend an execution. Under our regime, thank God, that was not necessary. There were many, many more involved in these murders than those who simply pulled the trigger. For them a university degree, often in the "humanities," was more common than the rudimentary education of the Niyazovs [the former guard Razgon questioned]. They drafted the instructions and decisions; they signed beneath the words "agreed," "confirmed," "to be sentenced to . . ." Today they are all retired and most of them receive large individual pensions. They sit in the squares and enjoy watching the children play. They go to concerts and are moved by the music. We meet them when we attend a meeting, visit friends, or find ourselves sitting at the same table, celebrating with our common acquaintances. They are alive, and there are many of them.

[COLLECTIVE GUILT]

In the most general terms, paragraph 17 [of the Soviet criminal code] said that each member of a criminal group (and membership in that group was expressed by knowledge of its existence and failure to report it) was responsible not only for his own individual criminal deeds but also for the deeds of the criminal group as a whole and for each of its individual members, taken separately. It did not matter that the individual in question might not know the other members of the group, might be unaware what they were up to, and might not have any idea at all what the group he belonged to was doing. The purpose of the "doctrine of complicity" was to alleviate the exhausting labors of the interrogators. Undoubtedly, however, it also lightened the burden of those under investigation. The techniques of cross-examination became far simpler. Several dozen people were linked together in a group and then one of them, the weakest, was beaten almost to death in order to obtain confessions of espionage, sabotage, subversion, and, of course, attempts on the life of "one of the leaders of the Party and the government." The others could be more gently treated, only requiring beating until they admitted they knew the individual who had given a "complete and full confession." Then the same crimes, in accordance with paragraph 17, were automatically attributed to them as well. What this sounded like during a court hearing I can describe from the words of a man I came to know in the camps.

Yefim Shatalov was a very high-ranking manager and for years he headed the State Cement Administration. Why they needed to send him to prison, God only knows! He had no political interests or involvements and did not wish to have any, since he was always prepared to serve his immediate superior faithfully and truthfully, and was unquestionably loyal to his ultimate chief, Comrade Stalin. Furthermore, he was incredibly

---

*In 1942 German forces massacred all the inhabitants of the Belorussian village of Khatyn. (Not to be confused with Katyn . . . where in 1940 23,500 Polish officers were murdered by the [Soviet] NKVD.)

[2]After Czech resistance fighters assassinated Richard Heydrich, Chief of the Security Police, the Germans took savage revenge on the little Czech village of Lidice. They massacred all the men and deported the women and children to concentration camps (some children with suitable "Aryan features" were sent to live with German families and to be reared as Germans). The Nazis then burned, dynamited, and levelled the village.

circumspect and every step he took was protected by an entire system of safety measures. When he was baldly accused of sabotage he conducted himself so aggressively in court that the judge, in panic, deferred the hearing of his case. Some time after, Shatalov was presented with a new charge sheet and within an hour he was summoned to appear before a new sitting of the Military Tribunal. The chairman now was Ulrich himself. For the defendant Vasya Ulrich was an old, dear and kind acquaintance. For many years they had always sat at the same table at the Party elite's sanatorium, The Pines; they went for walks together, shared a drink or two, and exchanged men's jokes. Evidently the chairman was observing the old principles that justice must be rapid, fair and clement in his conduct of this hearing. What follows includes almost everything that was said, as recalled by Yefim Shatalov.

ULRICH (in a business-like, quiet, and jaded voice): Defendant! you have read the charge sheet? Do you recognize your guilt?

SHATALOV (with all the force of his love and loyalty to the judge): No! I am not guilty in any respect!

ULRICH: Did you know that there was a counter-revolutionary Right-Trotskyist organization in the People's Commissariat of Heavy Industry?

SHATALOV (throwing up his arms): I had no idea whatsoever. I had no suspicion there was such a hostile gang of saboteurs and terrorists there.

ULRICH (gazing with affectionate attention at his former drinking companion): You were not in prison during the last trial of the Right-Trotskyist center, were you?

SHATALOV: No, I was not.

ULRICH: You were reading the newspapers then?

SHATALOV (slowly, trying to grasp the purpose of such a strange question): I did. . . .

ULRICH: So you read Pyatakov's testimony that there was a counter-revolutionary organization in the People's Commissariat of Heavy Industry?

SHATALOV (uncertainly): Of course, of course.

ULRICH (triumphantly): Well, there we are! So you knew there was a counter-revolutionary organization in the People's Commissariat of Heavy Industry. (Turning to the secretary of the court.) Write down: the defendant acknowledges that he knew about the existence of Pyatakov's organization. . . .

SHATALOV (shouts passionately, stuttering from horror): But it was from the newspapers, the newspapers, that I learnt there was an organization there!

ULRICH (calm and satisfied): But to the court it is not important where you found out. You knew! (Hurriedly, like a priest at a poorly paid funeral.) Any questions! No. You want to say a last word? No need for repetition, we've heard it already! (Nodding right and left at his assessors.) I pronounce sentence. Mmmh . . . 15 years . . .

I shall not insist that this trial strictly met the requirement for fairness. Yet compared to others it was clement, leaving Shatalov among the living. And it was indisputably rapid. Evidently the speed was typical. In the late 1950s I attended a memorial evening at the Museum of the Revolution for Kosarev, the 1930s Komsomol leader executed by Stalin. The head of the Central Committee administrative department told me that Khrushchev had entrusted him to re-examine Kosarev's case: "The hearing began at 11:00 a.m.," read the record of the trial, "and ended at 11:10 a.m."

[THE HEARTLESS BUREAUCRACY]

Auntie Pasha, a kindly middle-aged woman, washed the floors in the camp office. She pitied the office workers because they were so helpless and impractical: and she darned and sewed patches on the trousers and quilt jackets of the "trusties" who were not yet privileged to wear first-hand clothing. The story of her life was simple. Auntie Pasha came from Zlatoust in the Urals. Her husband, a furnace man, died during an accident at work and she was left with two teenage sons. Their life was predictably hard. Someone taught Auntie Pasha to go to Chelyabinsk to buy stockings and then sell them (naturally, at a suitably higher price) in Zlatoust where they were not to be found. The rest was recorded in the charge sheet and the sentence passed by the court. "For the purposes of speculation" she had "obtained 72 pairs of knitted stockings in Chelyabinsk which she then tried to resell at the market in Zlatoust." Auntie Pasha was reported, arrested, tried and sentenced to seven years imprisonment with confiscation of all her property. The children were taken in by acquaintances and, besides, they were almost old enough to take up any profession at the trade school. Five years passed, the war began, and Auntie Pasha's boys had reached the age when they could defend the Motherland. So off they went to fight. First Auntie Pasha was informed that her younger son had been killed. Staying behind in the office at night to wash the floors, she moaned and beat her head against the table.

Then one evening she came up to me with a glassy-eyed expression and handed over a thick package which she had been given in Records and Distribution. This contained several medical reports and the decisions of various commissions. To these was added a letter to Auntie Pasha from the hospital administrator. It concerned her elder son. He had been severely wounded and was in the hospital. The doctors had done all within their power and he was, as they put it in his medical history, "fit, to all intents and purposes"—apart, that is, from having lost both arms and one leg. He could be discharged from the hospital if there was some closer relation to look after him. Evidently the son had explained where she was because the administrator advised the mother of this wounded soldier to send an appeal to the USSR Procurator General's Office, including the enclosed documents, after which they would release her and she could come and fetch him.

"Manuilich, dear heart," Auntie Pasha said, starting to cry, "You write for me."

So I wrote, and very persuasively. I attached all the documents and handed in the letter. Two or three months passed, and each day I reassured Auntie Pasha: they received a great many such appeals, I told her, and it would take time to process her release. I described in detail the lengthy procedures as her application passed from one level to another. Auntie Pasha wept, but believed me and each day I gave her paper on which to write her son a letter.

One day I went into Records and Distribution myself. A great pile of mail lay on the table, already sorted out to be handed over, or its contents communicated, to the prisoners. Auntie Pasha's surname caught my eye. I picked up the flimsy sheet of headed paper from the USSR Procurator General's Office and read it through. A public procurator of a certain rank or class informed Auntie Pasha that her application had been examined and her request for early release turned down because there were "no grounds." I carefully placed the single sheet on the table and went out onto the verandah, terrified that I might suddenly meet Auntie Pasha. . . . Everywhere, in the barracks and in the office, there were people I did not want to see. I ran to the latrines and there, clinging to the stinking walls, started to shake uncontrollably. Only two times in my prison life did this happen. Why was I crying? Then I understood: I felt ashamed, terribly ashamed, before Auntie Pasha.

She had already served five years for 72 pairs of stockings. She had given the state her two sons. Now, there it was, there were "no grounds." . . .

Arthur Koestler
DARKNESS AT NOON

Darkness at Noon **(1941) appeared three years after Arthur Koestler (1905–1982), its author, broke with the Communist party in response to the Soviet blood purge. In the novel, Koestler explored the attitudes of the Old Bolsheviks, who were imprisoned, tortured, and executed by Stalin. These dedicated Communists had served**

the party faithfully—many were heroes of the Revolution—but Stalin, fearing opposition, hating intellectuals, and driven by megalomania, denounced them as enemies of the people. In *Darkness at Noon,* the leading character, the imprisoned Rubashov, is a composite of the Old Bolsheviks. Although innocent, and without being physically tortured, Rubashov publicly confesses to political crimes that he never committed. He is also aware of the suffering the party has brought to the people. The following passage, a conversation between Rubashov and his prison interrogator Ivanov, is Koestler's powerful indictment of the Soviet Union.

"The greatest criminals in history," Ivanov went on "are not of the type Nero and Fouché, but of the type Gandhi and Tolstoy. Gandhi's inner voice has done more to prevent the liberation of India than the British guns. To sell oneself for thirty pieces of silver is an honest transaction; but to sell oneself to one's own conscience is to abandon mankind. History is *a priori* amoral; it has no conscience. To want to conduct history according to the maxims of the Sunday school means to leave everything as it is. You know that as well as I do." . . .

"I don't approve of mixing ideologies," Ivanov continued. "There are only two conceptions of human ethics, and they are at opposite poles. One of them is Christian and humane, declares the individual to be sacrosanct, and asserts that the rules of arithmetic are not to be applied to human units. The other starts from the basic principle that a collective aim justifies all means, and not only allows, but demands, that the individual should in every way be subordinated and sacrificed to the community—which may dispose of it as an experimentation rabbit or a sacrificial lamb. The first conception could be called anti-vivisection morality, the second, vivisection morality. Humbugs and dilettantes have always tried to mix the two conceptions; in practice, it is impossible. Whoever is burdened with power and responsibility finds out on the first occasion that he has to choose; and he is fatally driven to the second alternative. Do you know, since the establishment of Christianity as a state religion, a single example of a state which really followed a Christian policy? You can't point out one. In times of need—and politics are chronically in a time of need—the rules were always able to evoke 'exceptional circumstances', which demanded exceptional measures of defence. Since the existence of nations and classes, they live in a permanent state of mutual self-defence, which forces them to defer to another time the putting into practice of humanism. . . ."

Rubashov looked through the window. The melted snow had again frozen and sparkled, an irregular surface of yellow-white crystals. The sentinel on the wall marched up and down with shouldered rifle. The sky was clear but moonless; above the machine-gun turret shimmered the Milky Way.

Rubashov shrugged his shoulders. "Admit," he said, "that humanism and politics, respect for the individual and social progress, are incompatible. Admit that Gandhi is a catastrophe for India; that chasteness in the choice of means leads to political impotence. In negatives we agree. But look where the other alternative has led us. . . ."

"Well," asked Ivanov. "Where?"

Rubashov rubbed his pince-nez on his sleeve, and looked at him shortsightedly. "What a mess," he said, "what a mess we have made of our golden age."

Ivanov smiled. "Maybe," he said happily. "Look at the Gracchi and Saint-Just and the Commune of Paris. Up to now, all revolutions have been made by moralizing dilettantes. They were always in good faith and perished because of their dilettantism. We for the first time are consequent. . . ."

"Yes," said Rubashov. "So consequent, that in the interests of a just distribution of land we deliberately let die of starvation about five million farmers and their families in one year. So consequent were we in the liberation of human beings from the shackles of industrial exploitation that we sent about ten million people to do forced labour in the Arctic regions and the jungles of the East, under conditions similar to those of antique galley slaves. So consequent that, to settle a difference of opinion, we know only one argument: death, whether it is a matter of submarines, manure, or the Party line to be followed in Indo-China. Our engineers work with the constant knowledge that an error in calculation may take them to prison or the scaffold; the higher officials in our administration ruin and destroy their subordinates, because they know that they will be held responsible for the slightest slip and be destroyed themselves; our poets settle discussions on questions of style by denunciations to the Secret Police, because the expressionists consider the naturalistic style counter-revolutionary, and *vice versa.* Acting consequently in the interests of the coming generations, we have laid such terrible privations on the present one that its average length of life is shortened by a quarter. In order to defend the existence of the country, we have to take exceptional measures and make transition-stage laws, which are in every point contrary to the aims of the Revolution. The people's standard of life is lower than it was before the Revolution; the labour conditions are harder, the discipline is more inhuman, the piece-work drudgery worse than in colonial countries with native coolies; we have lowered the age limit for capital punishment down to twelve years; our sexual laws are more narrow-minded than those of England, our leader-worship more Byzantine than that of the reactionary dictatorships. Our Press and our schools cultivate Chauvinism, militarism, dogmatism, conformism and ignorance. The arbitrary power of the Government is unlimited, and unexampled in history; freedom of the Press, of opinion and of movement are as thoroughly exterminated as though the proclamation of the Rights of Man had never been. We have built up the most gigantic police apparatus, with informers made a national institution, and with the most refined scientific system of physical and mental torture. We whip the groaning masses of the country towards a theoretical future happiness, which only we can see. For the energies of this generation are exhausted; they were spent in the Revolution; for this generation is bled white and there is nothing left of it but a moaning, numbed, apathetic lump of sacrificial flesh. . . . Those are the consequences of our consequentialness. You called it vivisection morality. To me it sometimes seems as though the experimenters had torn the skin off the victim and left it standing with bared tissues, muscles and nerves. . . ."

"For a man with your past," Ivanov went on, "this sudden revulsion against experimenting is rather naïve. Every year several million people are killed quite pointlessly by epidemics and other natural catastrophes. And we should shrink from sacrificing a few hundred thousand for the most promising experiment in history? Not to mention the legions of those who die of under-nourishment and tuberculosis in coal and quick-silver mines, rice-fields and cotton plantations. No one takes any notice of them; nobody asks why or what for; but if here we shoot a few thousand objectively harmful people, the humanitarians all over the world foam at the mouth. Yes, we liquidated the parasitic part of the peasantry and let it die of starvation. It was a surgical operation which had to be done once and for all; but in the good old days before the Revolution just as many died in any dry year—only senselessly and pointlessly. The victims of the Yellow River floods in China amount sometimes to hundreds of thousands. Nature is generous in her senseless experiments on mankind. Why should mankind not have the right to experiment on itself?"

He paused; Rubashov did not answer. He went on:

"Have you ever read brochures of an anti-vivisectionist society? They are shattering and heartbreaking; when one reads how some poor cur which has had its liver cut out, whines and licks his tormentor's hands, one is just as nauseated as you were to-night. But if these people had their say, we would have no serums against cholera, typhoid, or diphtheria. . . ."

He emptied the rest of the bottle, yawned, stretched and stood up. He limped over to Rubashov at the window, and looked out.

CHAPTER FOUR

AN ERA OF FASCISM

Both Mussolini and Hitler detested liberal democracy and communism and glorified war. But Fascist Italy, unlike Nazi Germany, lacked the power to dominate the Continent. *(Bettmann/Corbis)*

World War I cast a long shadow over Europe. The physical and psychological devastation was unprecedented and required an extended period of recovery. The peoples of Europe had to adjust themselves to a new map, for four empires had fallen—the German, Austro-Hungarian, Russian, and Ottoman.

Far from being discredited as a principal cause of the Great War, nationalism lost none of its potency. Nationalism (or, more specifically, national self-determination) was enshrined as one of Woodrow Wilson's Fourteen Points and a guiding principle of the peace settlement. It provided justification for formerly suppressed (or ignored) European peoples to claim the right to political independence and cultural autonomy. National self-determination most clearly manifested itself in the new states of East Central Europe—a recreated Poland, a transformed (and separate) Austria and Hungary, and a freshly minted Czechoslovakia and Yugoslavia, among others. These were the "successor" states, so called because they had appeared on the territory occupied by earlier polities. Yet in all the newly created states except Czechoslovakia, democracy collapsed, and various forms of authoritarian government emerged, betraying the promise that national self-determination had held out to them. Nationalism was evident elsewhere, too, in the reactions of most European states to the Great Depression. Desperate politicians used whatever means promised to alleviate the misery within their own countries (currency revaluation, trade quotas, import duties), with little if any regard for their impact on other states.

Perhaps the clearest examples of nationalism during the interwar era, though, involve the most noteworthy new development of these years—the rise of fascism. Following World War I, fascist movements arose in Italy, Germany, and many other European countries. Although these movements differed—each a product of separate national histories and the outlook of its leader—they shared a hatred of liberalism, democracy, and communism; a glorification of the party leader; and, most significantly, a commitment to aggressive nationalism. Fascist leaders cleverly utilized myths, rituals, and pageantry to mobilize and manipulate the masses.

Several conditions fostered the rise of fascism: the fear of communism among the middle and upper classes; the disillusionment of World War I veterans and the mood of violence bred by the war; and the inability of democratic parliamentary governments to cope with the problems that burdened postwar Europe. Fascism's appeal to nationalist feelings also drew people into the movement. In a sense, fascism expressed the aggressive racial nationalism that had emerged in the late nineteenth century. Fascists saw themselves as dedicated idealists engaged in a heroic struggle to rescue their nations from domestic and foreign enemies; they aspired to regain lands lost by their countries in World War I or to acquire lands denied them by the Paris Peace Conference.

Fascists glorified instinct, will, and blood as the true forces of life; they openly attacked the ideals of reason, liberty, and equality—the legacies of the Enlightenment and the French Revolution. At the center of German fascism (national socialism or nazism) was a bizarre racial mythology that preached the superiority of the German race and the inferiority of others, particularly Jews and Slavs. Also, Hitler in Germany, much more so than Mussolini in Italy, moved to establish a totalitarian state that controlled all phases of political, social, and cultural life. Using modern methods of administration and communication, the Nazi state manipulated the lives and thoughts of its citizens to a far greater extent than had absolutist and tyrannical governments of the past.

The memory of World War I, the rise of fascism, and the economic distress accompanying the Depression profoundly disoriented the European mind. Some intellectuals, having lost faith in the core values of Western Civilization, turned their backs on it or found escape in their art. Others sought a new hope in the Soviet experiment; still others reaffirmed the rational-humanist tradition of the Enlightenment. Christian thinkers, repelled by the secularism, materialism, and rootlessness of the modern age, urged Westerners to find renewed meaning and purpose in their ancestral religion.

1 The Rise of Fascism in Italy

Benito Mussolini (1883–1945) started his political life as a socialist and in 1912 was appointed editor of *Avanti,* the leading socialist newspaper. During World War I, Mussolini was expelled from the Socialist party for advocating Italy's entry into the conflict. Immediately after the war, he organized the Fascist party. Exploiting labor unrest, fear of communism, and thwarted nationalist hopes, Mussolini gained followers among veterans and the middle class. Powerful industrialists and landowners, viewing the Fascists as a bulwark against communism, helped to finance the young movement. An opportunist, Mussolini organized a march on Rome in 1922 to bring down the government. King Victor Emmanuel, fearful of civil war, appointed the Fascist leader prime minister. Had Italian liberals and the king taken a firm stand, the government could have crushed the 20,000 lightly armed marchers.

Benito Mussolini
FASCIST DOCTRINES

Ten years after he seized power, Mussolini, assisted by philosopher Giovanni Gentile (1875–1944), contributed an article to the *Italian Encyclopedia* in which he discussed fascist political and social doctrines. In this piece, Mussolini lauded violence as a positive experience; attacked Marxism for denying idealism by subjecting human beings to economic laws and for dividing the nation into warring classes; and denounced liberal democracy for promoting individual selfishness at the expense of the national community and for being unable to solve the

nation's problems. The fascist state, he said, required unity and power, not individual freedom. The following excerpts are from Mussolini's article.

. . . Above all, Fascism, the more it considers and observes the future and the development of humanity quite apart from political considerations of the moment, believes neither in the possibility nor the utility of perpetual peace. It thus repudiates the doctrine of Pacifism—born of a renunciation of the struggle and an act of cowardice in the face of sacrifice. War alone brings up to its highest tension all human energy and puts the stamp of nobility upon the peoples who have the courage to meet it. All other trials are substitutes, which never really put men into the position where they have to make the great decision—the alternative of life or death. Thus a doctrine which is founded upon this harmful postulate of peace is hostile to Fascism. And thus hostile to the spirit of Fascism, though accepted for what use they can be in dealing with particular political situations, are all the international leagues and societies which, as history will show, can be scattered to the winds when once strong national feeling is aroused by any motive—sentimental, ideal, or practical. This anti-pacifist spirit is carried by Fascism even into the life of the individual; the proud motto of the *Squadrista,* "Me ne frego" [It doesn't matter], written on the bandage of the wound, is an act of philosophy not only stoic, the summary of a doctrine not only political—it is the education to combat, the acceptation of the risks which combat implies, and a new way of life for Italy. Thus the Fascist accepts life and loves it, knowing nothing of and despising suicide: he rather conceives of life as duty and struggle and conquest, life which should be high and full, lived for oneself, but above all for others—those who are at hand and those who are far distant, contemporaries, and those who will come after. . . .

. . . Fascism [is] the complete opposite of . . . Marxian Socialism, the materialist conception of history; according to which the history of human civilization can be explained simply through the conflict of interests among the various social groups and by the change and development in the means and instruments of production. That the changes in the economic field—new discoveries of raw materials, new methods of working them, and the inventions of science—have their importance no one can deny; but that these factors are sufficient to explain the history of humanity excluding all others is an absurd delusion. Fascism, now and always, believes in holiness and in heroism; that is to say, in actions influenced by no economic motive, direct or indirect. And if the economic conception of history be denied, according to which theory men are no more than puppets, carried to and fro by the waves of chance, while the real directing forces are quite out of their control, it follows that the existence of an unchangeable and unchanging class-war is also denied—the natural progeny of the economic conception of history. And above all Fascism denies that class-war can be the preponderant force in the transformation of society. . . .

After Socialism, Fascism combats the whole complex system of democratic ideology, and repudiates it, whether in its theoretical premises or in its practical application. Fascism denies that the majority, by the simple fact that it is a majority, can direct human society; it denies that numbers alone can govern by means of a periodical consultation, and it affirms the immutable, beneficial, and fruitful inequality of mankind, which can never be permanently leveled through the mere operation of a mechanical process such as universal suffrage. . . .

. . . Fascism denies, in democracy, the absurd conventional untruth of political equality dressed out in the garb of collective irresponsibility, and the myth of "happiness" and indefinite progress. . . .

. . . Given that the nineteenth century was the century of Socialism, of Liberalism, and of Democracy, it does not necessarily follow that the twentieth century must also be a century of Socialism, Liberalism, and Democracy: political doctrines pass, but humanity remains; and it may rather be expected that this will be a century of authority, . . . a century of Fascism. For if the nineteenth century was a century of individualism (Liberalism always signifying individualism) it may be expected that this will be the century of collectivism, and hence the century of the State. . . .

The foundation of Fascism is the conception of the State, its character, its duty, and its aim. Fascism conceives of the State as an absolute, in comparison with which all individuals or groups are relative, only to be conceived of in their relation to the State. The conception of the Liberal State is not that of a directing force, guiding the play and development, both material and spiritual, of a collective body, but merely a force limited to the function of recording results: on the other hand, the Fascist State is itself conscious and has itself a will and a personality—thus it may be called the "ethic" State. . . .

. . . The Fascist State organizes the nation, but leaves a sufficient margin of liberty to the individual; the latter is deprived of all useless and possibly harmful freedom, but retains what is essential; the deciding power in this question cannot be the individual, but the State alone. . . .

. . . For Fascism, the growth of empire, that is to say the expansion of the nation, is an essential manifestation of vitality, and its opposite a sign of decadence. Peoples which are rising, or rising again after a period of decadence, are always imperialist; any renunciation is a sign of decay and of death. Fascism is the doctrine best adapted to represent the tendencies and the aspirations of a people, like the people of Italy, who are rising again after many centuries of abasement and foreign servitude. But empire demands discipline, the coordination of all forces and a deeply felt sense of duty and sacrifice: this fact explains many aspects of the practical working of the régime, the character of many forces in the State, and the necessarily severe measures which must be taken against those who would oppose this spontaneous and inevitable movement of Italy in the twentieth century, and would oppose it by recalling the outworn ideology of the nineteenth century—repudiated wheresoever there has been the courage to undertake great experiments of social and political transformation; for never before has the nation stood more in need of authority, of direction, and of order. If every age has its own characteristic doctrine, there are a thousand signs which point to Fascism as the characteristic doctrine of our time. For if a doctrine must be a living thing, this is proved by the fact that Fascism has created a living faith; and that this faith is very powerful in the minds of men is demonstrated by those who have suffered and died for it.

2 The Fledgling Weimar Republic

In the last days of World War I, a revolution brought down the German imperial government and led to the creation of a democratic republic. On November 9, 1918, the leaders of the government announced the end of the monarchy, and Kaiser William II fled to Holland. Two days later, the new German republic, headed by Friedrich Ebert (1871–1925), a Social Democrat, signed an armistice agreement ending the war. Many Germans blamed the new democratic republic for the defeat—a baseless accusation, for the German generals, knowing that the war was lost, had sought an armistice.

In February 1919, the recently elected National Assembly met at Weimar and proceeded to draw up a constitution for the new state. The choice of Weimar

was intentional: as Germany's cultural center, it substituted Goethe and Schiller for the sabers and uniforms of the imperial era. The Weimar Republic—born in revolution, which most Germans detested, and military defeat, which many attributed to the new government—faced an uncertain future.

Klara Zetkin, Rosa Luxemburg, Karl Liebknecht, and Franz Mehring SPARTACIST MANIFESTO

Dominated by moderate socialists, the infant republic faced internal threats from both the radical left and the radical right. In January 1919, the newly established German Communist party, or Spartacists, disregarding the advice of their leaders Rosa Luxemburg (1870–1919) and Karl Liebknecht (1871–1919), took to the streets of Berlin and declared Ebert's government deposed. The Spartacists espoused a revolutionary ideology modeled on Bolshevism that put them at odds with the moderate socialists then in political control. To crush the revolution, Ebert turned to the Free Corps: volunteer brigades of ex-soldiers and adventurers, led by officers loyal to the emperor, who had been fighting to protect the eastern borders from encroachments by the new states of Poland, Estonia, and Latvia. The men of the Free Corps relished action and despised Bolshevism. They suppressed the revolution and murdered Luxemburg and Liebknecht on January 15. In May 1919, the Free Corps also marched into Munich to overthrow the soviet republic set up there by communists a few weeks earlier.

Following is the manifesto that the Spartacists issued at the end of 1918, urging workers around the world to overthrow their governments and replace them with revolutionary regimes.

The imperialism of all countries knows no "understanding," it knows only one right—capital's profits; it knows only one language—the sword; it knows only one method—violence. And if it is now talking in all countries, in yours as well as ours, about the "League of Nations," "disarmament," "rights of small nations," "self-determination of the peoples," it is merely using the customary lying phrases of the rulers for the purpose of lulling to sleep the watchfulness of the proletariat.

Proletarians of all countries! This must be the last war! We owe that to the 12,000,000 murdered victims, we owe that to our children, we owe that to humanity.

Europe has been ruined through the infamous international murder. Twelve million bodies cover the grewsome [*sic*] scenes of the imperialistic crime. The flower of youth and the best man power [*sic*] of the peoples have been mowed down. Uncounted productive forces have been annihilated. Humanity is almost ready to bleed to death from the unexampled blood-letting of history. Victors and vanquished stand at the edge of the abyss. Humanity is threatened with the most dreadful famine, a stoppage of the entire mechanism of production, plagues, and degeneration.

The great criminals of this fearful anarchy, of this chaos let loose—the ruling classes—are not able to control their own creation. The beast of capital that conjured up the hell of the world war is not capable of banishing it again, of restoring real order, of insuring bread and work, peace and civilization, justice and liberty, to tortured humanity.

What is being prepared by the ruling classes as peace and justice is only a new work of brutal force from which the hydra of oppression, hatred and fresh, bloody wars raises its thousand heads. . . .

Proletarians! Men and Women of labor! Comrades!

The revolution has made its entry into Germany. The masses of the soldiers who for four years were driven to the slaughterhouse for the sake of capitalistic profits; the masses of workers, who for four years were exploited, crushed, and starved, have revolted. That fearful tool of oppression—Prussian militarism, that scourge of humanity—lies broken on the ground. Its most noticeable representatives, and therewith the most noticeable of those guilty of this war, the Kaiser and the Crown Prince, have fled from the country. Workers and Soldiers' Councils have been formed everywhere. . . .

. . . [T]he hour has struck for a settlement with capitalist class rule.

But this great task cannot be accomplished by the German proletariat alone: it can only fight and triumph by appealing to the solidarity of the proletarians of the whole world.

Socialism alone is in a position to complete the great work of permanent peace, to heal the thousand wounds from which humanity is bleeding, to transform the plains of Europe, trampled down by the passage of the apocryphal horseman of war, into blooming gardens, to conjure up ten productive forces for every one destroyed, to awaken all the physical and moral energies of humanity, and to replace hatred and dissension with fraternal solidarity, harmony, and respect for every human being.

If representatives of the proletarians of all countries stretch out their hands to each other under the banner of socialism for the purpose of making peace, then peace will be concluded in a few hours. Then there will be no disputed questions about the left bank of the Rhine, Mesopotamia, Egypt, or colonies. Then there will be only one people: the toiling human beings of all races and tongues. Then there will be only one right: the equality of all men. Then there will be only one aim: prosperity and progress for everybody. . . .

Therefore the proletariat of Germany is looking toward you in this hour. Germany is pregnant with the social revolution, but socialism can only be realized by the proletariat of the world.

And therefore we call to you: "Arise for the struggle! Arise for action! The time for empty manifestos, platonic resolutions, and high sounding words has gone by! The hour of action has struck for the International!" We ask you to elect Workers' and Soldiers' Councils everywhere that will seize political power and, together with us, will restore peace.

Not Lloyd George and Poincaré, not Sonnino, Wilson, and Erzberger or Scheidemann* must be allowed to make peace. Peace is to be concluded under the waving banner of the socialist world revolution.

Proletarians of all countries! We call upon you to complete the work of socialist liberation, to give a human aspect to the disfigured world and to make true those words with which we often greeted each other in the old days and which we sang as we parted: "And the Internationale shall be the human race."

Klara Zetkin.
Rosa Luxemburg.
Karl Liebknecht.
Franz Mehring.

---

*David Lloyd George, Raymond Poincaré, Sidney Sonnino, and Woodrow Wilson were all leaders of the victorious powers in World War I. Matthias Erzberger and Philipp Scheidemann were members of the new German republic.

Social Democrats
RESISTING THE KAPP PUTSCH

Most opposed to the Weimar Republic was the army officer corps, many of whom felt that the new government had betrayed national interests by signing the Versailles Peace Treaty and that the Social Democrats, the leading party, were no better than the Communists. These officers favored the overthrow of the republic. A chief plotter against the government was Dr. Wolfgang Kapp of Königsberg (1858–1922), who had helped to found the German Fatherland Party in 1917. The Kapp Putsch, as it became known, took place in March 1920, when several thousand regular troops and Free Corps units occupied Berlin. Asked by President Ebert to quell the uprising, General Hans von Seeckt (1866–1936) replied: "German troops do not fire on German troops." Ebert and his ministers were compelled to flee the capital for Dresden, where they intended to establish a temporary capital for the republican government until order could be restored; the reactionary monarchist Kapp proclaimed himself "imperial chancellor" and prime minister of the federal state of Prussia.

The coup proved short-lived, however, mostly due to opposition from Berlin workers who protested with a general strike. Despite threats of capital punishment against the strike leaders, Berlin workers rallied to support the republic. Public transportation in the city and rail travel stopped, the city's water supply was shut off, and the vast majority of food service workers refused to show up at the restaurants or hotels that employed them. Unable to govern, Kapp and his co-conspirators were forced to give up without a fight after five days. Once again the republic had been saved, but the Kapp Putsch—in itself a minor episode—represented the first of several attempts by right-wing forces to undermine the fledgling German democratic system.

The following is the text of the Social Democratic Party's general strike manifesto issued to Berlin workers on 13 March, the very day that Kapp and his rebel units occupied the city. It appeared in *Current History* shortly after the events as part of an eyewitness account.

Workmen, Comrades: The military revolt has come. Erhardt's naval division is marching on Berlin to enforce the reorganization of the Imperial Government. The mercenary troops who were afraid of the disbandment which had been ordered desire to put the reactionaries into the Ministerial posts.

We refuse to bow to this military constraint. We did not make the revolution in order to recognize again today the bloody Government of mercenaries. We enter into no covenant with the Baltic criminals. Workers, comrades, we should be ashamed to look you in the face if we were capable of acting otherwise.

We say "No!" And again "No!" You must indorse what we have done. We carried out your views. Now use every means to destroy this return of bloody reaction.

Strike. Cease to work. Throttle this military dictatorship. Fight with all your means for the preservation of the republic. Put aside all division. There is only one means against the return of Wilhelm II. Paralyze all economic life. Not a hand must move. No proletariat shall help the military dictatorship.

Let there be a general strike along the entire line. Let the proletariat act as a unit.

Konrad Heiden
THE RUINOUS INFLATION, 1923

Economic developments also weakened Weimar. Inflation plagued Germany throughout the first years of the republic, brought on by financing of the war through bonds instead of direct taxes and round-the-clock printing of paper money by German banks. The situation came to a head early in 1923, when French forces occupied the Ruhr to make Germany comply with the steep reparations demands of the Versailles Treaty. The government declared a state of passive resistance, and the inflation accelerated into hyperinflation. By autumn, the currency was valued at 4.2 billion German marks to the American dollar; workers were being paid twice a day and carting home their wages in wheelbarrows. Finally, in November, Chancellor Gustav Stresemann (1878–1929) called off passive resistance, launching a period of reconciliation with Germany's former enemies and of increasing economic stability and prosperity. The hyperinflation had ended, but those who had seen their savings wiped out would hold Weimar responsible.

The following description of the inflation comes from Konrad Heiden's early biography of Adolf Hitler. Heiden (1901–1966) was an author and journalist affiliated with the liberal *Frankfurter Zeitung.* He fled Germany during the 1930s.

On Friday afternoons in 1923, long lines of manual and white-collar workers waited outside the pay-windows of the big German factories, department stores, banks, offices: dead-tired workingmen in grimy shirts open at the neck; gentlemen in shiny blue suits, saved from before the war, in mended white collars, too big for their shrunken necks; young girls, some of them with the new bobbed heads; young men in puttees and gray jackets, from which the tailor had removed the red seams and regimentals, embittered against the girls who had taken their jobs. They all stood in lines outside the pay-windows, staring impatiently at the electric wall clock, slowly advancing until at last they reached the window and received a bag full of paper notes. According to the figures inscribed on them, the paper notes amounted to seven hundred thousand or five hundred million, or three hundred and eighty billion, or eighteen trillion marks—the figures rose from month to month, then from week to week, finally from day to day. With their bags the people moved quickly to the doors, all in haste, the younger ones running. They dashed to the nearest food store, where a line had already formed. Again they moved slowly, oh, how slowly, forward. When you reached the store, a pound of sugar might have been obtainable for two millions; but, by the time you came to the counter, all you could get for two millions was half a pound, and the saleswoman said the dollar had just gone up again. With the millions or billions you bought sardines, sausages, sugar, perhaps even a little butter, but as a rule the cheaper margarine—always things that would keep for a week, until next pay-day, until the next stage in the fall of the mark.

For money could not keep, the most secure of all values had become the most insecure. The mark wasn't just low, it was slipping steadily downward. Goods were still available, but there was no money; there was still labor and consumption, but no economy; you could provide for the moment, but you couldn't plan for the future. It was the end of money. It was the end of the old shining hope that everyone would be rich. The secular religion of the nineteenth century was crumbling amid the profanation of holy property.

Friedrich Jünger
ANTIDEMOCRATIC THOUGHT IN THE WEIMAR REPUBLIC

The rightist attack on the Weimar Republic was multifaceted. Traditional conservatives—aristocrats, army leaders, and industrialists—were contemptuous of democracy and sought a strong government that would protect the nation from communism and check the power of the working class. In a peculiar twist of logic, radical right-wing nationalists blamed Germany's defeat in World War I and the humiliation of the Versailles Treaty on the republic.

The constitution of the Weimar Republic, premised intellectually and emotionally on the liberal-rational tradition, had strong opposition from German conservatives who valued the authoritarian state promoted by Bismarck and the kaisers. In expressing their hostility to the Weimar Republic, radical rightists attacked liberal democracy and reason, and embraced an ultranationalist philosophy of blood, soil, and action. In the brittle disunity and disorientation of German society, conservative nationalists searched for community and certainty in the special qualities of the German soul. Their antirationalism, hostility to democracy, and ultranationalism undermined the Weimar Republic and contributed to the triumph of Nazism.

The selection below is freely adapted from a small book, *The Rise of the New Nationalism* (1926), written by Friedrich Georg Jünger, the brother of Ernst Jünger, who is well known for his literary glorification of the war experience.

The new nationalism envisages a state elevated by popular enthusiasm and gathering in itself the fullness of power as the sole guarantor of Germany's collective future. It is both armor and sword, preserving indigenous culture and destroying the alien elements that arrogantly push against it.

The new nationalism in its formative state throbs with revolutionary excitement. It lives unrestrained in our gut feeling, seething in our blood, although still full of confusion.

The November revolution was the result of a moral collapse promoted by external pressures. It happened at a time when the frightful struggle of the war should have demanded the concentration of all energies. Rightly it was called a stab in the back, because it was led by Germans against Germans, provocatively and from the rear. The revolution proved the shallowness of its promoters. They could not radiate youth, warmth, energy, or greatness. There were deputies, but no leaders. There was no man among them who stood out by his exceptional qualities. We saw the feeble liberals and heard for the hundredth time the promulgation of human rights. One might say, a dusty storeroom was thrown open from which emerged human rights, freedom, toleration, parliament, suffrage, and popular representation. Finally they wrote a liberalist novel: the Weimar constitution.

But the Weimar regime was a body in which there flowed no blood. You could talk about it only in empty phrases. What an overabundance of phrases and phrasemakers! They had plastered the last available fence, the last walls, with their babble.

The new nationalism wants to awaken a sense of the greatness of the German past. Life must be evaluated according to the will to power, which reveals the warlike character of all life. The value of the individual is assessed according to his military value for the state, and the state is recognized as the most creative and toughest source of power. . . .

It is necessary to look at the conditions that have preceded and created the new nationalism. The recent past has destroyed our inherited collective sense of tender intimacy by trying to subvert and weaken all close bonds of community. It has denied all values that create cohesion in the community. Everything conspired to speed the disintegration of human ties in state, church, marriage, family, and many other institutions. A mad urge for throwing off all restraints, for dissolution, for unbridled liberty, dissolved society into driftwood. This urge shaped the flighty masses, depriving them of all convictions of meaningfulness. These excesses finally aroused disgust and a counter movement arose. A new consolidation of purpose began. From it arises the future success of the new nationalism, its resistance to the atomistic liberty and to the freedom of soulless decadence. Social life is never free. A mighty mysterious bond of blood links the lives of individuals and subsumes them in a fateful wholeness. Blood, as it were, sings the song of destiny.

Life is deeply bonded. And only as it remains true to these bonds and is rooted in them, can it fulfill itself. Life withers if these roots are cut or if it seeks nourishment from alien roots. It is tied to the blood; at its core it is part of a community of blood. The intellect enjoys freedom only to the degree to which it is loyal to the blood. The new nationalism is born of the new awareness of blood-bonded community; it wants to make the promptings of the blood prevail. Escaping from the boundlessness of contemporary life, it is driven forward by the yearning for the bonds of blood.

The new nationalism wants to strengthen the blood bonds and form them into a new state. Those who are part of an alien blood community, or those internationalists who feel joined to a transcendent community, are excluded. They have to be driven out, because they weaken the rich and fertile body of the nation that nourishes everything of significance.

The awareness of these blood bonds demands the fight against all movements weakening the spiritual bonds that affirm the community of blood. It judges all values according to that principle. It wants life to be whole, lived in a new intoxicating abundance, responsibly restricted, and not dissipated or fatigued by the intellect. In every nationalism there is something intoxicating, a wild and lusty pride, a mighty heroic vitality. It has no critical or analytic inclinations, which weaken life. It wants no tolerance, because life does not know tolerance. It is fanatical, because the promptings of the blood are fanatical and unjust. It does not care for scientific justification.

Nationalism must apply its force to the masses and try to set them afire by means peculiar to itself. These means are neither parliaments nor parties, but rather military units mobilized by a fierce loyalty to a leader. These units alone are called to carry out the will of the new nationalism. They will be the more powerful and successful the more they act in an organized and disciplined manner, the more unconditionally they subject themselves to the ideal of the nationalist state. The intensity of their discipline is the decisive factor. Next comes the urgent task to create a mighty organization covering all of Germany and to seize the reins of government. The community of blood is given the highest priority. It is defined race-like by the nationalist sentiment. It recognizes no European community, no common humanity. For us, mingling races and wiping out the difference between masters and slaves among the peoples of the world are an abomination. We want the sharpest separation of races.

The new state, obviously, will be authoritarian. The new nationalism is determined to make that authoritarianism absolute, all surpassing, consolidating the state as the new steel-like instrument of power. It values the state as the highest historic fact and the most important vehicle for attaining the nationalist aims. That state shall be the mold for the nation's blood-bound will to power. For that reason the nationalist movement urges the annihilation of all political forms of liberalism. No more parties, parliaments, elections! No more hailshowers of prattle or the bustle of the senile parliamentary intrigues that burden the country! No more packs of petty politicians and literati poking fun at the state! Tremendous energies are wasted in the labyrinth of parliamentary procedure.

The madhouse of parliamentary activity in which every event is dragged out unconscionably without providing a sense of a great future, without consideration for the nation's dignity, reveals the foul sickness of liberalism. Masculine earnestness is dirtied by empty phrases; everything is befogged by the dense steam of corruption. There are no men of distinction in parliament. Universal suffrage is an ingenious sieve working in favor of bustling agitators and zealous blockheads. The assurance and righteousness with which it repels men of talent betray the hatred at the root of liberalistic thinking. These are the people who, after the November revolution, succeeded in driving wedges between people, inciting them against each other. They have paralyzed the nation's role in international relations and are responsible for the country's boundless misery.

While these people debate, vote, and slander each other in the battle of slogans, the new nationalism prepares for the crucial blow. The nationalist revolution proceeds on course; its thunderstorms loom over the horizon. And we can only wish that the explosion will be terrifying. May the elementary liberation of blood sweep away all the debris that burdens the times. The new nationalism is not given to compromise. Every institution needs to be examined whether it responsibly serves the nation or whether it is ripe to be smashed.

The nationalist state makes no claim to be the freest and most just state—that smacks of liberalism and negates its authoritarian character. The nationalist state aims at creating the most disciplined government devoid of any feeling of justice for its enemies. It wants a state permeated by a leader's personality. The personal element, inherent in all contemporary nationalist striving, belongs among the foundations of the new nationalism and of the state it wants to create. The will of the dictator is essential for the future. The craving for the blood-bond concentration of power raises the hope for an absolute leader even higher.

The adoption of the leader principle signifies the basic activation of the state—a state adapted to the tempo of the times; it shapes the nation's volcanic dynamism. The principle of the leader built into the structure of the state, almost resembling the military command structure, makes the will to resist external pressure more fanatical. The concentration of power in one man gives the state incredible strength and vitality. Decisions gain in strength and correctness; the choice of means becomes more effective; the frictions lessen; and the thrust of policy becomes more unified. The state must be prepared for something extraordinary, ready to jump. That this condition be achieved as soon as possible is the anxious yearning rising from our blood.

The great war has not ended. It has been the prelude to a brutal age of armed conflict. According to the deepest insight of the new nationalism, it is the beginning of a terrible, all-demanding struggle. Everything points to the fact that a new age of great violence is in the offing. Our blood is not deceived by the exhausted masses and the intellectual trends that passionately proclaim the dawn of freedom, human brotherhood, and sweet peace for all mankind. Nobody can prevent the war that arises from fateful depths and perhaps tomorrow will blanket the earth with corpses.

The savagery and corruption in the present world prepare mighty upheavals for the future. Then everything incapable and exhausted will be eliminated, and only he who carries within himself an unbounded fighting spirit and is armed to the teeth will be found worthy for the final decision. Under the surface of contemporary humanitarianism there looms a different attitude, vital, cruel, and merciless like steel. In the age of the machine, all means are legitimate. People and methods have been brutalized. Every restraint is like an opiate that diminishes the nation's will to power. At stake is the question: which people will finish the fight and administer the world and its resources in their own name? The convictions of the new nationalism are by necessity imperialist. The rule is: either domination or submission. Domination means being imperialist, having the will to exercise power and achieve superiority. Top priority, therefore, goes to mobilizing human wills. That is best done by the nationalist state. It guarantees total mobilization down to the last detail. The development of technology parallels the trends of political imperialism. It conveys a sense of the coming conflicts. The state, the economy, science—all are slowly geared to imperialist expansion, proving the fatefulness of the trend. Should we avoid it because it demands great sacrifices and the submission of the individual, or because the awesome aims make life cheap? "Never!" cries the nationalist, because he aims at domination and not submission. He does not want to reject fate. He will not retreat even before the prospect of getting wiped out. He looks forward to the great and mighty Germany of the future, the irresistible strength of a hundred million Germans at the core of Europe!

3 The Great Depression

The Great Depression, which began in October 1929 with the collapse of the New York Stock Exchange, soon reached around the globe. In Europe as elsewhere, its effects transcended the realm of economics. To many Germans, the Depression was final evidence that the Weimar Republic had failed. The traumatic experience of unemployment and the sense of hopelessness led millions to embrace Hitler; between 1928 and 1930 Nazi vote totals skyrocketed from 810,000 to 6,400,000. Even in more stable democracies such as Britain and France, the Depression led to a questioning of the ideological bases on which the state rested. To combat popular misery, governments began intervening in their domestic economies to an unprecedented degree, often by balancing budgets, fixing prices and wages, and determining currency and exchange rates. A few voices were heard calling for more innovative and radical measures, such as increasing welfare payments and funding public works programs, but such policies remained the exception rather than the rule.

Max Cohen
I WAS ONE OF THE UNEMPLOYED

Mounting unemployment reinforced a sense of hopelessness in the British and cast a pall over Great Britain. Despite the economic slump of the 1920s and the Great Depression, the country remained politically stable, a testament to the strength of its parliamentary tradition. Neither the Communists nor the newly

formed British Union of Fascists gained mass support. Not until Britain began to rearm did unemployment decline significantly.

Max Cohen was a twenty-year-old cabinetmaker when he lost his job in 1931 and joined over three million unemployed workers in Great Britain. His first-hand account of privation, hunger, and loss of self-respect was published in 1945. In the following selection he describes the psychological wounds suffered by the unemployed.

Many people cannot understand why so many unemployed become, if not out-and-out nervous wrecks, then at least gloomy shadows of their former selves, walking phantoms of worry and dejection. Some people take it upon themselves to "cheer the unemployed up," "make them look on the bright side of life," and so on.

"Tut, tut, my dear fellow," they say, kindly and well-meaningly, "there is no need for you to get downhearted. Every cloud has a silver lining . . . the darkest hour is before the dawn," and similar amiable platitudes.

These people forget, do not know, cannot know, the multifarious sources of worry that can afflict an out-of-work. Unemployment brings into being many diverse sources of worry which become so intermingled and interlocked that their cumulative effect is well-nigh intolerable.

These worries are not merely financial—though of course financial worries are at the root of the whole problem. When a man has been out-of-work for any length of time, he begins to worry about his past, his present, and above all about his future. He worries about himself and about his wife and his children and his parents; in short, about himself and his dependants.

He worries about the Labour Exchange[1]; about how long it will be before his present parlous financial condition gives way to a worse. He worries because he has too much time on his hands, and he worries because nearly all the more pleasant ways of passing his time are barred to him. He worries about his clothes, because they are shabby; and he worries because soon, willy-nilly, he will have to get new ones for himself and his family, and he does not know where the money for them is coming from.

And above all, more bitter than gall is the fact that day after day, despite search after search, application after application, work is denied to him. In the vast edifice of our civilisation there is no useful work to be given to him—work that will at one and the same time enable him to be an equal with his fellow-men, and provide him with the necessities of life and peace of mind.

It may be thought that unemployed single men or women will not be so affected by worry as those unemployed who are married and have children. What must be kept clear, however, is that it is not the fact of marriage and children that is the basic cause of worry to the unemployed. The basic cause of worry is the fact of unemployment. Single men and women are just as much worried by unemployment as married people, with the additional fact that they are often living on their own and have no one with whom to share their more secret and agonising worries. Moreover, young people need that interchange of experience between the sexes known as "romance." Too often unemployment makes a romantic social life impossible; where it comes into being in spite of unemployment it is starved and stultified and poisoned, owing to the lack of the elementary material basis to keep it alive and healthy.

What is astonishing is not that there are some unemployed men and women who are nervous wrecks and psychopathic cases (the medical statistics on this question would surprise many people), but that there are not many more. It is, however, not the least crime of the present social system that there are today, at this very moment, thousands upon thousands of people who

[1]The Labour Exchange is a government office where unemployment compensation is paid out.

are suffering what can be literally described as excruciating mental tortures. They suffer in this way not because they are congenitally more neurotic than the average, but solely and simply because anarchic social forces have uprooted them, and undermined their social, economic, and therefore psychological stability.

Psychological suffering or instability does not necessarily reveal itself openly to the casual observer. There are far more cases of abnormal psychology signing on at the Labour Exchanges than are apparent on the surface, because relatively few are really noticeable. Nevertheless, those who, by reason of their more unbearable existence on the dole,[2] combined with the lesser stability of the temperament, have become somewhat abnormal, are generally those who talk loudest and most vociferously in the queues. They argue vehemently about things that don't matter, and are often very aggrieved and angry over things that are not of very great importance.

Cases of people who have become abnormal because of the intolerable harshness of their economic existence are more noticeable among "down-and-outs" than among others—though whether it is psychological abnormality that has made them down-and-out, or the fact of being down-and-out that has created a psychological instability, is a moot point. Neither conclusion reflects a very flattering light on the present social system. . . .

I myself could not continue living alone for months under intolerable conditions without being affected not merely physically, but mentally. These mental effects could be divided into two kinds. The first was more or less gradual and cumulative in its results. The second was sudden in its onslaught, though more temporary in character.

The first of these effects has been more or less indicated, in passing, in what has been told previously. It consisted of the slow but sure change in my attitude to the world and to myself. It took the form of a lack of self-confidence and an absence of self-respect; a tacit assumption of inferiority to nearly everyone, and an innate certainty that I was not, and never would be, a useful member of society. These unspoken and unconsidered feelings increased and became part of my intellectual make-up in geometrical proportion to the length of my unemployment.

Distressing though these feelings were, particularly when they reached consciousness and were accompanied by depression and pessimism, they were as nothing compared to that which came later. Privation and frustration gave birth to a distress of mind which went beyond reasoning and control.

I had felt for some time vague moods of uneasiness and depression. Then an incident took place which at one stroke catapulted me into a state in which morbidness began to play an ever-increasing rôle.

One day as I stood waiting in the queue at the Labour Exchange, the thought came to me that it was fantastic to be standing waiting so long in a queue just in order to sign one's name. I agreed with myself that it was fantastic, though I felt too tired to reason why it should be more fantastic than anything else. The thought recurred to me: "It's fantastic!" Again the thought recurred, insistently: "It's fantastic!" Suddenly everything seemed fantastic—the whole complex of civilisation, with its underfed and under-clothed unemployed, its idle, sybaritic [luxury loving] upper strata, its teeming millions of earnest workers by hand and brain, so essentially naïve and innocent in the way they tolerated the drones in their beehive—it was all fantastic.

The feeling became more intense: "It's fantastic!", still more intense. "It's fantastic!" I began to be alarmed ("All right, no need to be excited about it! Calm down.") It was unreal—everything was unreal. I could not shake off a nightmarish sense that it was all unreal; everything was unreal: the Labour Exchange was unreal; the clerks were unreal; the notices were unreal; the crowd was unreal; I was unreal. Terror smote me like a blow. My heart began to

[2]The "dole" was unemployment compensation.

pound. What—what was all this about, anyway? ("Keep a grip on yourself, man! What's up with you?") Unreal . . . unreal . . . unreal. . . .

Sweat stood out on my forehead. Where am I? What's happening? ("Keep a grip on yourself, man!") . . . A grey mist was descending before my eyes. There was a sinister roar in my ears. The walls of the Labour Exchange seemed to crowd around me, threatening to shut me tightly in narrow confines. The crowd clamoured from far away. I was weak, my knees were as water, the blood was perceptibly draining from my face. "Am I going to faint?" The thought boomed in the huge, hollow emptiness of my brain. . . .

After this incident an unwelcome visitor began to insinuate himself gradually but persistently into my being. At first he was unnoticed. When I became aware of his presence I tried to dismiss him with increasing anger. Then perforce I accepted his presence. Then I became his slave, and the thought of banishing him from me became as the thought of some unattainable hope. The name of this visitor?—his name was Fear.

I began to be vaguely afraid of different things for brief periods. Then I became more definitely afraid of more things for longer times. Eventually I lived under a menacing cloud of fear that darkened my whole existence.

I became unreasonably afraid of things innocuous in themselves. I began to be afraid of being afraid. Life and its manifestations became transformed into subject-matter for fear. I began after a time subconsciously to approach things from the standpoint of whether they would make me afraid or not. . . .

Ordinary fear sometimes acts as a stimulant. It has a certain dread excitement which is sometimes a spur to action, even to heroism. But this unreasoning and uncontrollable emotion brought with it no such possibilities. There was no immediately obvious cause for it, no objective happenings or surroundings to which it could be immediately traced. It was a hellish brew, compounded of crushing despair, an abysmal sinking of the heart, and a mental distress so acute as to be well-nigh indistinguishable from physical pain.

I grew to an attitude of life that was entirely morbid. I sank deeper and deeper into a vortex of fear, depression, despair.

Heinrich Hauser
"WITH GERMANY'S UNEMPLOYED"

The following article, excerpted from the periodical *Die Tat,* describes the loss of dignity suffered by the unemployed wandering Germany's roads and taking shelter in municipal lodging houses. The author, a German writer, experienced conditions in a public shelter firsthand. Conditions in 1932 as described in the article radicalized millions of Germans, particularly young people.

An almost unbroken chain of homeless men extends the whole length of the great Hamburg-Berlin highway.

There are so many of them moving in both directions, impelled by the wind or making their way against it, that they could shout a message from Hamburg to Berlin by word of mouth.

It is the same scene for the entire two hundred miles, and the same scene repeats itself between Hamburg and Bremen, between Bremen and Kassel, between Kassel and Würzburg, between Würzburg and Munich. All the highways in Germany over which I traveled this year presented the same aspects. . . .

. . . Most of the hikers paid no attention to me. They walked separately or in small groups, with their eyes on the ground. And they had the queer, stumbling gait of barefooted people, for their shoes were slung over their shoulders. Some of them were guild members,—carpenters with embroidered wallets, knee breeches, and broad felt hats; milkmen with striped red shirts, and bricklayers with tall black hats,—but they were in a minority. Far more numerous were those whom one could assign to no special profession or craft—unskilled young people, for the most part, who had been unable to find a place for themselves in any city or town in Germany, and who had never had a job and never expected to have one. There was something else that had never been seen before—whole families that had piled all their goods into baby carriages and wheelbarrows that they were pushing along as they plodded forward in dumb despair. It was a whole nation on the march.

I saw them—and this was the strongest impression that the year 1932 left with me—I saw them, gathered into groups of fifty or a hundred men, attacking fields of potatoes. I saw them digging up the potatoes and throwing them into sacks while the farmer who owned the field watched them in despair and the local policeman looked on gloomily from the distance. I saw them staggering toward the lights of the city as night fell, with their sacks on their backs. What did it remind me of? Of the War, of the worst periods of starvation in 1917 and 1918, but even then people paid for the potatoes. . . .

I saw that the individual can know what is happening only by personal experience. I know what it is to be a tramp. I know what cold and hunger are. I know what it is to spend the night outdoors or behind the thin walls of a shack through which the wind whistles. I have slept in holes such as hunters hide in, in hayricks, under bridges, against the warm walls of boiler houses, under cattle shelters in pastures, on a heap of fir-tree boughs in the forest. But there are two things that I have only recently experienced—begging and spending the night in a municipal lodging house.

I entered the huge Berlin municipal lodging house in a northern quarter of the city. . . .

. . . There was an entrance arched by a brick vaulting, and a watchman sat in a little wooden sentry box. His white coat made him look like a doctor. We stood waiting in the corridor. Heavy steam rose from the men's clothes. Some of them sat down on the floor, pulled off their shoes, and unwound the rags that were bound around their feet. More people were constantly pouring in the door, and we stood closely packed together. Then another door opened. The crowd pushed forward, and people began forcing their way almost eagerly through this door, for it was warm in there. Without knowing it I had already caught the rhythm of the municipal lodging house. It means waiting, waiting, standing around, and then suddenly jumping up.

We now stand in a long hall, down the length of which runs a bar dividing the hall into a narrow and a wide space. All the light is on the narrow side. There under yellow lamps that hang from the ceiling on long wires sit men in white smocks. We arrange ourselves in long lines, each leading up to one of these men, and the mill begins to grind. . . .

. . . As the line passes in a single file the official does not look up at each new person to appear. He only looks at the paper that is handed to him. These papers are for the most part invalid cards or unemployment certificates. The very fact that the official does not look up robs the homeless applicant of self-respect, although he may look too beaten down to feel any. . . .

. . . Now it is my turn and the questions and answers flow as smoothly as if I were an old hand. But finally I am asked, "Have you ever been here before?"

"No."

"No?" The question reverberates through the whole room. The clerk refuses to believe me and looks through his card catalogue. But no, my name is not there. The clerk thinks this strange, for he cannot have made a mistake, and the terrible thing that one notices in all these clerks is that they expect you to lie. They do not believe what you say. They do not regard you as a human being but as an infection, something foul that one keeps at a distance. He goes on. "How did you come here from Hamburg?"

"By truck."

"Where have you spent the last three nights?"

I lie coolly.

"Have you begged?"

I feel a warm blush spreading over my face. It is welling up from the bourgeois world that I have come from. "No."

A coarse peal of laughter rises from the line, and a loud, piercing voice grips me as if someone had seized me by the throat: "Never mind. The day will come, comrade, when there's nothing else to do." And the line breaks into laughter again, the bitterest laughter I have ever heard, the laughter of damnation and despair. . . .

Again the crowd pushes back in the kind of rhythm that is so typical of a lodging house, and we are all herded into the undressing room. It is like all the other rooms except that it is divided by benches and shelves like a fourth-class railway carriage. I cling to the man who spoke to me. He is a Saxon with a friendly manner and he has noticed that I am a stranger here. A certain sensitiveness, an almost perverse, spiritual alertness makes me like him very much.

Out of a big iron chest each of us takes a coat hanger that would serve admirably to hit somebody over the head with. As we undress the room becomes filled with the heavy breath of poverty. We are so close together that we brush against each other every time we move. Anyone who has been a soldier, anyone who has been to a public bath is perfectly accustomed to the look of naked bodies. But I have never seen anything quite so repulsive as all these hundreds of withered human frames. For in the homeless army the majority are men who have already been defeated in the struggle of life, the crippled, old, and sick. There is no repulsive disease of which traces are not to be seen here. There is no form of mutilation or degeneracy that is not represented, and the naked bodies of the old men are in a disgusting state of decline. . . .

It is superfluous to describe what follows. Towels are handed out by the same methods described above. Then nightgowns—long, sacklike affairs made of plain unbleached cotton but freshly washed. Then slippers. All at once a new sound goes up from the moving mass that has been walking silently on bare feet. The shuffling and rattling of the hard soles of the slippers ring through the corridor.

Distribution of spoons, distribution of enameledware bowls with the words "Property of the City of Berlin" written on their sides. Then the meal itself. A big kettle is carried in. Men with yellow smocks have brought it and men with yellow smocks ladle out the food. These men, too, are homeless and they have been expressly picked by the establishment and given free food and lodging and a little pocket money in exchange for their work about the house.

Where have I seen this kind of food distribution before? In a prison that I once helped to guard in the winter of 1919 during the German civil war. There was the same hunger then, the same trembling, anxious expectation of rations. Now the men are standing in a long row, dressed in their plain nightshirts that reach to the ground, and the noise of their shuffling feet is like the noise of big wild animals walking up and down the stone floor of their cages before feeding time. The men lean far over the kettle so that the warm steam from the food envelops them and they hold out their bowls as if begging and whisper to the attendant, "Give me a real helping. Give me a little more." A piece of bread is handed out with every bowl.

My next recollection is sitting at table in another room on a crowded bench that is like a seat in a fourth-class railway carriage. Hundreds of hungry mouths make an enormous noise eating their food. The men sit bent over their food like animals who feel that someone is going to take it away from them. They hold their bowl with their left arm part way around it, so that nobody can take it away, and they also protect it with their other elbow and with their head and mouth, while they move the spoon as fast as they can between their mouth and the bowl. . . .

We shuffle into the sleeping room, where each bed has a number painted in big letters on the wall over it. You must find the number that you have around your neck, and there is your bed, your home for one night. It stands in a row with fifty others and across the room there are fifty more in a row. . . .

I curl up in a ball for a few minutes and then see that the Saxon is lying the same way, curled up in the next bed. We look at each other with eyes that understand everything. . . .

. . . Only a few people, very few, move around at all. The others lie awake and still, staring at their blankets, wrapped up in themselves but not sleeping. Only an almost soldierly sense of comradeship, an inner self-control engendered by the presence of so many people, prevents the despair that is written on all these faces from expressing itself. The few who are moving about do so with the tormenting consciousness of men who merely want to kill time. They do not believe in what they are doing.

Going to sleep means passing into the unconscious, eliminating the intelligence. And one can read deeply into a man's life by watching the way he goes to sleep. For we have not always slept in municipal lodgings. There are men among us who still move as if they were in a bourgeois bedchamber. . . .

. . . The air is poisoned with the breath of men who have stuffed too much food into empty stomachs. There is also a sickening smell of lysol. It seems completely terrible to me, and I am not merely pitying myself. It is painful just to look at the scene. Life is no longer human here. Today, when I am experiencing this for the first time, I think that I should prefer to do away with myself, to take gas, to jump into the river, or leap from some high place, if I were ever reduced to such straits that I had to live here in the lodging house. But I have had too much experience not to mistrust even myself. If I ever were reduced so low, would I really come to such a decision? I do not know. Animals die, plants wither, but men always go on living.

---

4 The Rise of Hitler

Many extreme racist-nationalist and paramilitary organizations sprang up in postwar Germany. Adolf Hitler (1889–1945), a veteran of World War I, joined one of these organizations, which became known as the National Socialist German Worker's party (commonly called the Nazi party). Hitler's uncanny insight into the state of mind of many postwar Germans and his extraordinary oratorical gifts enabled him to gain control of the party.

Adolf Hitler
MEIN KAMPF

In the "Beer Hall Putsch" of November 1923, Hitler attempted to overthrow the state government in Bavaria as the first step in bringing down the Weimar Republic. But the Nazis quickly scattered when Bavarian police opened fire. Hitler was arrested and sentenced to five years' imprisonment—he served only nine months. While in prison, Hitler wrote *Mein Kampf (My Struggle),* in which he presented his views. The book came to be regarded as an authoritative

expression of the Nazi world-view and served as a kind of sacred writing for the Nazi movement.

Hitler's thought—a patchwork of nineteenth-century anti-Semitic, volkish, Social Darwinist, and anti-Marxist ideas—contrasted sharply with the core values of both the Judeo-Christian and the Enlightenment traditions. Central to Hitler's world-view was racial mythology: a heroic Germanic race was descended from the ancient Aryans, who once swept across Europe, and was now battling for survival against racial inferiors. In the following passages excerpted from *Mein Kampf,* Hitler presents his views of race, of propaganda, and of the National Socialist territorial goals.

[THE PRIMACY OF RACE]

Nature does not want a pairing of weaker individuals with stronger ones; it wants even less a mating of a higher race with a weaker one. Otherwise its routine labors of promoting a higher breed lasting perhaps over hundreds of thousands of years would be wiped out.

History offers much evidence for this process. It proves with terrifying clarity that any genetic mixture of Aryan blood with people of a lower quality undermines the culturally superior people. The population of North America consists to a large extent of Germanic elements, which have mixed very little with inferior people of color. Central and South America shows a different humanity and culture; here Latin immigrants mixed with the aborigines, sometimes on a large scale. This example alone allows a clear recognition of the effects of racial mixtures. Remaining racially pure the Germans of North America rose to be masters of their continent; they will remain masters as long as they do not defile their blood.

The result of mixing races in short is: a) lowering the cultural level of the higher race; b) physical and spiritual retrogression and thus the beginning of a slow but progressive decline.

To promote such a development means no less than committing sin against the will of the eternal creator. . . .

Everything that we admire on earth—science, technology, invention—is the creative product of only a few people, and perhaps originally of only *one* race; our whole culture depends upon them. If they perish, the beauties of the earth will be buried. . . .

All great cultures of the past perished because the original creative race was destroyed by the poisoning of its blood.

Such collapse always happened because people forgot that all cultures depend on human beings. In order to preserve a given culture it is necessary to preserve the human beings who created it. Cultural preservation in this world is tied to the iron law of necessity and the right to victory of the stronger and better. . . .

If we divide humanity into three categories: into founders of culture, bearers of culture, and destroyers of culture, the Aryan would undoubtedly rate first. He established the foundations and walls of all human progress. . . .

The mixing of blood and the resulting lowering of racial cohesion is the sole reason why cultures perish. People do not perish by defeat in war, but by losing the power of resistance inherent in pure blood.

All that is not pure race in this world is chaff. . . .

A state which in the age of racial poisoning dedicates itself to the cultivation of its best racial elements will one day become master of the world.

Modern anti-Semitism was a powerful legacy of the Middle Ages and the unsettling changes brought about by rapid industrialization; it was linked to racist doctrines that asserted the Jews were inherently wicked and bore dangerous racial qualities. Hitler grasped the political potential of anti-Semitism: by concentrating all evil in one enemy, he could provide non-Jews with an emotionally satisfying explanation for all their misfortunes and thus manipulate and unify the German people.

[ANTI-SEMITISM]

The Jew offers the most powerful contrast to the Aryan. . . . Despite all their seemingly intellectual qualities the Jewish people are without true culture, and especially without a culture of their own. What Jews seem to possess as culture is the property of others, for the most part corrupted in their hands.

In judging the Jewish position in regard to human culture, we have to keep in mind their essential characteristics. There never was—and still is no—Jewish art. The Jewish people made no original contribution to the two queen goddesses of all arts: architecture and music. What they have contributed is bowdlerization or spiritual theft. Which proves that Jews lack the very qualities distinguishing creative and culturally blessed races. . . .

The first and biggest lie of Jews is that Jewishness is not a matter of race but of religion, from which inevitably follow even more lies. One of them refers to the language of Jews. It is not a means of expressing their thoughts, but of hiding them. While speaking French a Jew thinks Jewish, and while he cobbles together some German verse, he merely expresses the mentality of his people.

As long as the Jew is not master of other peoples, he must for better or worse speak their languages. Yet as soon as the others have become his servants, then all should learn a universal language (Esperanto for instance), so that by these means the Jews can rule more easily. . . .

For hours the blackhaired Jewish boy lies in wait, with satanic joy on his face, for the unsuspecting girl whom he disgraces with his blood and thereby robs her from her people. He tries by all means possible to destroy the racial foundations of the people he wants to subjugate.

But a people of pure race conscious of its blood can never be enslaved by the Jew; he remains forever a ruler of bastards.

Thus he systematically attempts to lower racial purity by racially poisoning individuals.

In politics he begins to replace the idea of democracy with the idea of the dictatorship of the proletariat.

He found his weapon in the organized Marxist masses, which avoid democracy and instead help him to subjugate and govern people dictatorially with his brutal fists.

Systematically he works toward a double revolution, in economics and politics.

With the help of his international contacts he enmeshes people who effectively resist his attacks from within in a net of external enemies whom he incites to war, and, if necessary, goes on to unfurling the red flag of revolution over the battlefield.

He batters the national economies until the ruined state enterprises are privatized and subject to his financial control.

In politics he refuses to give the state the means for its self-preservation, destroys the bases of any national self-determination and defense, wipes out the faith in leadership, denigrates the historic past, and pulls everything truly great into the gutter.

In cultural affairs he pollutes art, literature, theatre, befuddles national sentiment, subverts all concepts of beauty and grandeur, of nobleness and goodness, and reduces people to their lowest nature.

Religion is made ridiculous, custom and morals are declared outdated, until the last props of national character in the battle for survival have collapsed. . . .

Thus the Jew is the big rabble-rouser for the complete destruction of Germany. Wherever in the world we read about attacks on Germany, Jews are the source, just as in peace and during the war the newspapers of both the Jewish stock market and the Marxists systematically incited hatred against Germany. Country after country gave up its neutrality and joined the world war coalition in disregard of the true interest of the people.

Jewish thinking in all this is clear. The Bolshevization of Germany, i.e., the destruction of the German national people-oriented intelligentsia and thereby the exploitation of German labor under the yoke of Jewish global finance are but the prelude for the expansion of the Jewish tendency to conquer the world. As so often in history, Germany is the turning point in this mighty struggle. If our people and our state become the victims of blood-thirsty and money-thirsty Jewish tyrants, the whole world will be enmeshed in the tentacles of this octopus. If, however, Germany liberates itself from this yoke, we can be sure that the greatest threat to all humanity has been broken. . . .

Hitler was a master propagandist and advanced his ideas on propaganda techniques in *Mein Kampf.* He mocked the learned and book-oriented German liberals and socialists who he felt were entirely unsuited for modern mass politics. The successful leader, he said, must win over the masses through the use of simple ideas and images, constantly repeated, to control the mind by evoking primitive feelings. Hitler contended that mass meetings were the most effective means of winning followers. What counted most at these demonstrations, he said, was will power, strength, and unflagging determination radiating from the speaker to every single individual in the crowd.

[PROPAGANDA AND MASS RALLIES]

The task of propaganda does not lie in the scientific training of individuals, but in directing the masses toward certain facts, events, necessities, etc., whose significance is to be brought to their attention.

The essential skill consists in doing this so well that you convince people about the reality of a fact, about the necessity of an event, about the correctness of something necessary, etc. . . . You always have to appeal to the emotions and far less to the so-called intellect. . . .

The art of propaganda lies in sensing the emotional temper of the broad masses, so that you, in psychologically effective form, can catch their attention and move their hearts. . . .

The attention span of the masses is very short, their understanding limited; they easily forget. For that reason all effective propaganda has to concentrate on very few points and drive them home through simple slogans, until even the simplest can grasp what you have in mind. As soon as you give up this principle and become too complex, you will lose your effectiveness, because the masses cannot digest and retain what you have offered. You thereby weaken your case and in the end lose it altogether.

The larger the scope of your case, the more psychologically correct must be the method of your presentation. . . .

The task of propaganda lies not in weighing right and wrong, but in driving home your own point of view. You cannot objectively explore the facts that favor others and present them in doctrinaire sincerity to the masses. You have to push relentlessly your own case. . . .

Even the most brilliant propaganda will not produce the desired results unless it follows this fundamental rule: You must stick to limiting yourself to essentials and repeat them endlessly. Persistence on this point, as in so many other cases in the world, is the first and most important precondition for success. . . .

Propaganda does not exist to furnish interesting diversions to blasé young dandies, but to convince above all the masses. In their clumsiness they always require a long lead before they are ready to take notice. Only by thousandfold repetition will the simplest concepts stick in their memories.

No variation of your presentation should change the content of your propaganda; you always have to come to the same conclusion. You may want to highlight your slogans from various sides, but at the end you always have to reaffirm it. Only consistent and uniform propaganda will succeed. . . .

Every advertisement, whether in business or politics, derives its success from its persistence and uniformity. . . .

The mass meeting is . . . necessary because an incipient supporter of a new political movement will feel lonely and anxiously isolated. He needs at the start a sense of a larger community which among most people produces vitality and courage. The same man as member of a military company or battalion and surrounded by his comrades will more lightheartedly join an attack than if he were all by himself. In a crowd he feels more sheltered, even if reality were a thousandfold against him.

The sense of community in a mass demonstration not only empowers the individual, but also promotes an esprit de corps. The person who in his business or workshop is the first to represent a new political creed is likely to be exposed to heavy discrimination. He needs the reassurance that comes from the conviction of being a member and a fighter in a large comprehensive organization. The sense of this organization comes first to him in a mass demonstration. When he for the first time goes from a petty workshop or from a large factory, where he feels insignificant, to a mass demonstration surrounded by thousands and thousands of like-minded fellows—when he as a seeker is gripped by the intoxicating surge of enthusiasm among three or four thousand others—when the visible success and the consensus of thousands of others prove the correctness of his new political creed and for the first time arouse doubts about his previous political convictions—then he submits to the miraculous influence of what we call "mass suggestion." The will, the yearning, and also the power of thousands of fellow citizens now fill every individual. The man who full of doubts and uncertain enters such a gathering, leaves it inwardly strengthened; he has become a member of a community. . . .

Hitler was an extreme nationalist who wanted a reawakened, racially united Germany to expand eastward at the expense of the Slavs, whom he viewed as racially inferior.

[LEBENSRAUM]

A people gains its freedom of existence only by occupying a sufficiently large space on earth. . . .

If the National Socialist movement really wants to achieve a hallowed mission in history for our people, it must, in painful awareness of its position in the world, boldly and methodically fight against the aimlessness and incapacity which have hitherto guided the foreign policy of the German people. It must then, without respect for "tradition" and prejudice, find the courage to rally the German people to a forceful advance on the road which leads from their present cramped living space to new territories. In this manner they will be liberated from the danger of perishing or being enslaved in service to others.

The National Socialist movement must try to end the disproportion between our numerous population and its limited living space, the source of our food as well as the base of our power—between our historic past and the hopelessness of our present impotence. . . .

The demand for restoring the boundaries of 1914 is a political nonsense with consequences so huge as to make it appear a crime—quite apart from the fact that our pre-war boundaries were anything but logical. They neither united all people of German nationality nor served strategic-political necessity. . . .

In the light of this fact we National Socialists must resolutely stick to our foreign policy goals, namely *to secure for the German people the territorial base to which they are entitled.* This is the only goal which before God and our German posterity justifies shedding our blood. . . .

Just as our forebears did not receive the soil on which we live as a gift from heaven—they had to risk their lives for it—so in future we will not secure the living space for our people by divine grace, but by the might of the victorious sword.

However much all of us recognize the necessity of a reckoning with France, it would remain ineffectual if we thereby limited the scope of our foreign policy. It makes sense only if we consider it as a rear-guard action for expanding our living space elsewhere in Europe. . . .

If we speak today about gaining territory in Europe, we think primarily of Russia and its border states. . . .

Kurt G. W. Ludecke
THE DEMAGOGIC ORATOR

Nazi popularity grew partly due to Hitler's power as an orator to play on the dissatisfactions of postwar Germans with the Weimar Republic. In the following selection, Kurt G. W. Ludecke, an early supporter of Hitler who later broke with the Nazis, describes Hitler's ability to mesmerize his audience.

. . . [W]hen the Nazis marched into the Koenigsplatz with banners flying, their bands playing stirring German marches, they were greeted with tremendous cheers. An excited, expectant crowd was now filling the beautiful square to the last inch and overflowing into surrounding streets. They were well over a hundred thousand. . . . I was close enough to see Hitler's face, watch every change in his expression, hear every word he said.

When the man stepped forward on the platform, there was almost no applause. He stood silent for a moment. Then he began to speak, quietly and ingratiatingly at first. Before long his voice had risen to a hoarse shriek that gave an extraordinary effect of an intensity of feeling. There were many high-pitched, rasping notes. . . .

Critically I studied this slight, pale man, his brown hair parted on one side and falling again and again over his sweating brow. Threatening and beseeching, with small, pleading hands and flaming, steel-blue eyes, he had the look of a fanatic.

Presently my critical faculty was swept away. Leaning from the tribune as if he were trying to impel his inner self into the consciousness of all these thousands, he was holding the masses, and me with them, under a hypnotic spell by the sheer force of his conviction.

He urged the revival of German honor and manhood with a blast of words that seemed to cleanse. "Bavaria is now the most German land in Germany!" he shouted, to roaring applause. Then, plunging into sarcasm, he indicted the leaders in Berlin as "November Criminals," daring to put into words thoughts that Germans were now almost afraid to think and certainly to voice.

It was clear that Hitler was feeling the exaltation of the emotional response now surging up toward him from his thousands of hearers. His voice rising to passionate climaxes, he finished his speech with an anthem of hate against the "Novemberlings" and a pledge of undying love for the Fatherland. "Germany must be free!" was his final defiant slogan. Then two last words that were like the sting of a lash:

"Deutschland Erwache!"

Awake, Germany! There was thunderous applause. Then the masses took a solemn oath "to save Germany in Bavaria from Bolshevism."

I do not know how to describe the emotions that swept over me as I heard this man. His words were like a scourge. When he spoke of the disgrace of Germany, I felt ready to spring on any enemy. His appeal to German manhood was like a call to arms, the gospel he preached a sacred truth. He seemed another Luther. I forgot everything but the man; then, glancing round, I saw that his magnetism was holding these thousands as one.

Of course I was ripe for this experience. I was a man of thirty-two, weary of disgust and disillusionment, a wanderer seeking a cause; a patriot without a channel for his patriotism, a yearner after the heroic without a hero. The intense will of the man, the passion of his sincerity seemed to flow from him into me. I experienced an exaltation that could be likened only to religious conversion.

I felt sure that no one who had heard Hitler that afternoon could doubt that he was the man of destiny, the vitalizing force in the future of

Germany. The masses who had streamed into the Koenigsplatz with a stern sense of national humiliation seemed to be going forth renewed.

The bands struck up, the thousands began to move away. I knew my search was ended. I had found myself, my leader, and my cause.

Thomas Mann
"AN APPEAL TO REASON"

In 1931, two years before Hitler took power, the internationally prominent German author Thomas Mann (1875–1955) wrote an article entitled "An Appeal to Reason," in which he discussed the crisis in the European soul that gave rise to fascism. He saw national socialism and the extreme nationalism it espoused as a rejection of the Western rational tradition and as a regression to primitive and barbaric modes of behavior. Some excerpts from Mann's article follow.

. . . The economic decline of the middle classes was accompanied—or even preceded—by a feeling which amounted to an intellectual prophecy and critique of the age: the sense that here was a crisis which heralded the end of the bourgeois epoch that came in with the French revolution and the notions appertaining to it. There was proclaimed a new mental attitude for all mankind, which should have nothing to do with bourgeois principles such as freedom, justice, culture, optimism, faith in progress. As art, it gave vent to expressionistic soul-shrieks; as philosophy it repudiated . . . reason, and the . . . ideological conceptions of bygone decades; it expressed itself as an irrationalistic throwback, placing the conception *life* at the centre of thought, and raised on its standard the powers of the unconscious, the dynamic, the darkly creative, which alone were life-giving. Mind, quite simply the intellectual, it put under a taboo as destructive of life, while it set up for homage as the true inwardness of life . . . the darkness of the soul, the holy procreative underworld. Much of this nature-religion, by its very essence inclining to the orgiastic and to . . . [frenzied] excess, has gone into the nationalism of our day, making of it something quite different from the nationalism of the nineteenth century, with its bourgeois, strongly cosmopolitan and humanitarian cast. It is distinguished in its character as a nature-cult, precisely by its absolute unrestraint, its orgiastic, radically anti-humane, frenziedly dynamic character. . . .

. . . And there is even more: there are other intellectual elements come to strengthen this national-social political movement—a certain ideology, a Nordic creed, a Germanistic romanticism, from philological, academic, professorial spheres. It addresses the Germany of 1930 in a highflown wishy-washy jargon full of mystical good feeling, with hyphenated prefixes like race- and folk- and fellowship-, and lends to the movement a . . . fanatical cult-barbarism, . . . dangerous and estranging, with . . . power to clog and stultify the brain. . . .

Fed, then, by such intellectual and pseudo-intellectual currents as these, the movement which we sum up under the name of national-socialism and which has displayed such a power of enlisting recruits to its banner, mingles with the mighty wave—a wave of anomalous barbarism, of primitive popular vulgarity—that sweeps over the world to-day, assailing the nerves of mankind with wild, bewildering, stimulating, intoxicating sensations. . . . Humanity seems to have run like boys let out of school away from the humanitarian, idealistic nineteenth century, from whose morality—if we can speak at all of morality in this connection—our time represents a wide and wild reaction. Everything is possible, everything permitted as a weapon against human decency; if we have got rid of the idea of freedom as a relic of the bourgeois state of mind, as though an idea so bound up with all European feeling, upon which Europe has been founded, for which she has made such sacrifices, could ever be utterly lost—it comes back again, this cast-off conception, in a guise suited to the time: as demoralization, as a mockery of all human authority, as a free rein to instincts, as the emancipation of brutality, the dictatorship of force. . . . In all this violence demonstrates itself, and demonstrates nothing but violence, and even that is unnecessary, for all other considerations are fallen away, man does not any longer believe in them, and so the road is free to vulgarity without restraint.

This fantastic state of mind, of a humanity that has outrun its ideas, is matched by a political scene in the grotesque style, with Salvation Army methods, hallelujahs and bell-ringing and dervishlike repetition of monotonous catchwords, until everybody foams at the mouth. Fanaticism turns into a means of salvation, enthusiasm into epileptic ecstasy, politics becomes an opiate for the masses, . . . and reason veils her face.

5 The Leader-State

Adolf Hitler came to power by legal means, appointed chancellor by President Paul von Hindenburg on January 30, 1933, according to the constitution of the Weimar Republic. Thereafter, however, he proceeded to dismantle the legal structure of the Weimar system and replace it with an inflexible dictatorship that revolved around his person. Quickly reacting to the popular confusion caused by the suspicious Reichstag fire, Hitler issued a decree on February 28 that suspended all guarantees of civil and individual freedom. In March, the Reichstag adopted the Enabling Act, which vested all legislative powers in his hands. Then Hitler proceeded to destroy the autonomy of the federal states, dissolve the trade unions, outlaw other political parties, and end freedom of the press. By the time he eliminated party rivals in a blood purge on June 30, 1934, the consolidation of power was complete. Meanwhile, much of Germany's public and institutional life fell under Party control in a process known as the *Gleichschaltung,* or coordination. The Third Reich was organized as a leader-state, in which Hitler the *Führer* (leader) embodied and expressed the real will of the German people, commanded the supreme loyalty of the nation, and had unlimited authority.

Ernst Huber
"THE AUTHORITY OF THE FÜHRER IS . . . ALL-INCLUSIVE AND UNLIMITED"

In *Verfassungsrecht des grossdeutschen Reiches (Constitutional Law of the Greater German Reich),* legal scholar Ernst Rudolf Huber (1903–1990) offered a classic explication of the basic principles of national socialism. The following excerpts from that work describe the nature of Hitler's political authority.

The Führer-Reich of the [German] people is founded on the recognition that the true will of the people cannot be disclosed through parliamentary votes and plebiscites but that the will of the people in its pure and uncorrupted form can only be expressed through the Führer. Thus a distinction must be drawn between the supposed will of the people in a parliamentary democracy, which merely reflects the conflict of the various social interests, and the true will of the people in the Führer-state, in which the collective will of the real political unit is manifested. . . .

It would be impossible for a law to be introduced and acted upon in the Reichstag which had not originated with the Führer or, at least, received his approval. The procedure is similar to that of the plebiscite: The lawgiving power does not rest in the Reichstag; it merely proclaims through its decision its agreement with the will of the Führer, who is the lawgiver of the German people.

The Führer unites in himself all the sovereign authority of the Reich; all public authority in the state as well as in the movement is derived from the authority of the Führer. We must speak not of the state's authority but of the Führer's authority if we wish to designate the character of the political authority within the Reich correctly. The state does not hold political authority as an impersonal unit but receives it from the Führer as the executor of the national will. The authority of the Führer is complete and all-embracing; it unites in itself all the means of political direction; it extends into all fields of national life; it embraces the entire people, which is bound to the Führer in loyalty and obedience. The authority of the Führer is not limited by checks and controls, by special autonomous bodies or individual rights, but it is free and independent, all-inclusive and unlimited. It is not, however, self-seeking or arbitrary and its ties are within itself. It is derived from the people; that is, it is entrusted to the Führer by the people. It exists for the people and has its justification in the people; it is free of all outward ties because it is in its innermost nature firmly bound up with the fate, the welfare, the mission, and the honor of the people.

6 The Nazification of Culture and Society

The Nazis aspired to more than political power; they also wanted to have the German people view the world in accordance with National Socialist ideology. Toward this end, the Nazis strictly regulated cultural life. Believing that the struggle of racial forces occupied the center of world history, Nazi ideologists tried to strengthen the racial consciousness of the German people. Numerous courses in "race science" introduced in schools and universities emphasized the superiority of the Nordic soul as well as the worthlessness of Jews and their threat to the nation.

Johannes Stark
"JEWISH SCIENCE" VERSUS "GERMAN SCIENCE"

Several prominent German scientists endorsed the new regime and tried to make science conform to Nazi ideology. In 1934, Johannes Stark (1874–1957), who had won a Nobel Prize for his work in electromagnetism, requested fellow German

Nobel Prize winners to sign a declaration supporting "Adolf Hitler . . . the savior and leader of the German people." In the following passage, Stark made the peculiar assertion that "German science" was based on an objective analysis of nature, whereas "Jewish science" (German Jews had distinguished themselves in science and medicine) sacrificed objectivity to self-interest and a subjective viewpoint.

But aside from this fundamental National Socialist demand, the slogan of the international character of science is based on an untruth, insofar as it asserts that the type and the success of scientific activity are independent of membership in a national group. Nobody can seriously assert that art is international. It is similar with science. Insofar as scientific work is not merely imitation but actual creation, like any other creative activity it is conditioned by the spiritual and characterological endowments of its practitioners. Since the individual members of a people have a common endowment, the creative activity of the scientists of a nation, as much as that of its artists and poets, thus assumes the stamp of a distinctive Volkish type. No, science is not international; it is just as national as art. This can be shown by the example of Germans and Jews in the natural sciences.

Science is the knowledge of the uniform interconnection of facts; the purpose of natural science in particular is the investigation of bodies and processes outside of the human mind, through observation and, insofar as possible, through the setting up of planned experiments. The spirit of the German enables him to observe things outside himself exactly as they are, without the interpolation of his own ideas and wishes, and his body does not shrink from the effort which the investigation of nature demands of him. The German's love of nature and his aptitude for natural science are based on this endowment. Thus it is understandable that natural science is overwhelmingly a creation of the Nordic-Germanic blood component of the Aryan peoples. Anyone who, in Lenard's classic work *Grosse Naturforscher (Great Investigators of Nature),* compares the faces of the outstanding natural scientists will find this common Nordic-Germanic feature in almost all of them. The ability to observe and respect facts, in complete disregard of the "I," is the most characteristic feature of the scientific activity of Germanic types. In addition, there is the joy and satisfaction the German derives from the acquisition of scientific knowledge, since it is principally this with which he is concerned. It is only under pressure that he decides to make his findings public, and the propaganda for them and their commercial exploitation appear to him as degradations of his scientific work.

The Jewish spirit is wholly different in its orientation: above everything else it is focused upon its own ego, its own conception, and its self-interest—and behind its egocentric conception stands its strong will to win recognition for itself and its interests. In accordance with this natural orientation the Jewish spirit strives to heed facts only to the extent that they do not hamper its opinions and purposes, and to bring them in such a connection with each other as is expedient for effecting its opinions and purposes. The Jew, therefore, is the born advocate who, unencumbered by regard for truth, mixes facts and imputations topsy-turvy in the endeavor to secure the court decision he desires. On the other hand, because of these characteristics, the Jewish spirit has little aptitude for creative activity in the sciences because it takes the individual's thinking and will as the measure of things, whereas science demands observation and respect for the facts.

It is true, however, that the Jewish spirit, thanks to the flexibility of its intellect, is capable, through imitation of Germanic examples, of producing noteworthy accomplishments, but it is not able to rise to authentic creative work, to great discoveries in the natural sciences. In recent times the Jews have frequently invoked the name of Heinrich Hertz as a counter-argument to this thesis. True, Heinrich Hertz made the great discovery of electromagnetic waves, but he was not a full-blooded Jew. He had a German mother, from whose side his spiritual endowment may well have been conditioned. When the Jew in natural science abandons the Germanic example and engages in scientific work according to his own spiritual particularity, he turns to theory. His main object is not the observation of facts and their true-to-reality presentation, but the view which he forms about them and the formal exposition to which he subjects them. In the interest of his theory he will suppress facts that are not in keeping with it and likewise, still in the interest of his theory, he will engage in propaganda on its behalf.

Jakob Graf
HEREDITARY AND RACIAL BIOLOGY FOR STUDENTS

The following assignments from a textbook entitled *Hereditary and Racial Biology for Students* (1935) shows how young people were indoctrinated with racist teachings.

HOW WE CAN LEARN TO RECOGNIZE A PERSON'S RACE

Assignments

1. Summarize the spiritual characteristics of the individual races.

2. Collect from stories, essays, and poems examples of ethnological illustrations. Underline those terms which describe the type and mode of the expression of the soul.

3. What are the expressions, gestures, and movements which allow us to make conclusions as to the attitude of the racial soul?

4. Determine also the physical features which go hand in hand with the specific racial soul characteristics of the individual figures.

5. Try to discover the intrinsic nature of the racial soul through the characters in stories and poetical works in terms of their inner attitude. Apply this mode of observation to persons in your own environment.

6. Collect propaganda posters and caricatures for your race book and arrange them according to a racial scheme. What image of beauty is emphasized by the artist (a) in posters publicizing sports and travel? (b) in publicity for cosmetics? How are hunters, mountain climbers, and shepherds drawn?

7. Collect from illustrated magazines, newspapers, etc., pictures of great scholars, statesmen, artists, and others who distinguish themselves by their special accomplishments (for example, in economic life, politics, sports). Determine the preponderant race and admixture, according to physical characteristics. Repeat this exercise with the pictures of great men of all nations and times.

8. When viewing monuments, busts, etc., be sure to pay attention to the race of the person portrayed with respect to figure, bearing, and physical characteristics. Try to harmonize these determinations with the features of the racial soul.

9. Observe people whose special racial features have drawn your attention, also with respect to their bearing when moving or when speaking. Observe their expressions and gestures.

10. Observe the Jew: his way of walking, his bearing, gestures, and movements when talking.

11. What strikes you about the way a Jew talks and sings?

Louis P. Lochner
BOOK BURNING

The anti-intellectualism of the Nazis was demonstrated on May 10, 1933, when the principal German student body organized students for a book-burning festival. In university towns, students consigned to the flames books that were considered a threat to the Germanic spirit. Louis P. Lochner (1887–1975), head of the Associated Press Bureau in Berlin, gave an eyewitness account of the scene in the German capital in *The Goebbels Diaries 1942–43.*

The whole civilized world was shocked when on the evening of May 10, 1933, the books of authors displeasing to the Nazis, including even those of our own Helen Keller, were solemnly burned on the immense Franz Joseph Platz between the University of Berlin and the State Opera on Unter den Linden. I was a witness to the scene.

All afternoon Nazi raiding parties had gone into public and private libraries, throwing onto the streets such books as Dr. [Joseph] Goebbels [Nazi Propaganda Minister] in his supreme wisdom had decided were unfit for Nazi Germany. From the streets Nazi columns of beer-hall fighters had picked up these discarded volumes and taken them to the square above referred to.

Here the heap grew higher and higher, and every few minutes another howling mob arrived, adding more books to the impressive pyre. Then, as night fell, students from the university, mobilized by the little doctor, performed veritable Indian dances and incantations as the flames began to soar skyward.

When the orgy was at its height, a cavalcade of cars drove into sight. It was the Propaganda Minister himself, accompanied by his bodyguard and a number of fellow torch bearers of the new Nazi *Kultur.*

"Fellow students, German men and women!" he said as he stepped before a microphone for all Germany to hear him. "The age of extreme Jewish intellectualism has now ended, and the success of the German revolution has again given the right of way to the German spirit. . . .

"You are doing the right thing in committing the evil spirit of the past to the flames at this late hour of the night. It is a strong, great, and symbolic act—an act that is to bear witness before all the world to the fact that the spiritual foundation of the November Republic has disappeared. From the ashes there will rise the phoenix of a new spirit. . . .

"The past is lying in flames. The future will rise from the flames within our own hearts. . . . Brightened by these flames our vow shall be: The Reich and the Nation and our Fuehrer Adolf Hitler: *Heil! Heil! Heil!*"

The few foreign correspondents who had taken the trouble to view this "symbolic act" were stunned. What had happened to the "Land of Thinkers and Poets"? they wondered.

Joseph Roth
"THE AUTO-DA-FÉ OF THE MIND"

Joseph Roth (1894–1939) was born to Jewish parents in the Austro-Hungarian Empire. He became a distinguished journalist in Berlin during the short-lived Weimar Republic. Until 1933, when the rise of the Nazis forced him into exile, he

worked uninterruptedly for major newspapers and wrote many novels, of which *The Radetzky March,* set in the Austro-Hungarian Empire, is the best known. Already in exile in Paris when the book burnings in Germany took place, Roth reflected on what the burning of those books meant for German cultural life. He described German-Jewish writers as having "fallen on the intellect's field of honor. All of them, in the eyes of the German murderer and arsonist, share a common fault: *their Jewish blood and their European intellect.*" The book burning, he declared, threatened European civilization. The following excerpts are from an essay he wrote immediately after the Nazi outrage. The term auto-da-fé in its title refers to the public burning of heretics in Spain during the Spanish Inquisition. Many of the heretics were forcibly converted Jews whom the Inquisition believed to be secretly practicing Judaism.

Very few observers anywhere in the world seem to have understood what the Third Reich's burning of books, the expulsion of Jewish writers, and all its other crazy assaults on the intellect actually mean. The technical apotheosis of the barbarians, the terrible march of the mechanized orangutans, armed with hand grenades, poison gas, ammonia, and nitroglycerine, with gas masks and airplanes, the return of the spiritual (if nor the actual) descendants of the Cimbri and Teutoni[1]—all this means far more than the threatened and terrorized world seems to realize: It must be understood. Let me say it loud and clear: The European mind is capitulating. It is capitulating out of weakness, out of sloth, out of apathy, out of lack of imagination (it will be the task of some future generation to establish the reasons for this disgraceful capitulation).

Now, as the smoke of our burned books rises into the sky, we German writers of Jewish descent must acknowledge above all that we have been defeated. Let us, who were fighting on the front line, under the banner of the European mind, let us fulfill the noblest duty of the defeated warrior: Let us concede our defeat.

Yes. we have been beaten. . . . We are proud of our defeat. We stood in the front row of the defenders of Europe, and we were the first to be defeated. Our comrades "of Aryan descent" can still hope to be pardoned (always assuming that they will be prepared to make some concession to the language of Goebbels and Göring). There is even a chance that the vandals of the Third Reich will try to exploit such "Aryan" writers of great renown as Thomas Mann and Gerhart Hauptmann (currently persecuted) for a while, in order to trick mankind into believing that National Socialism has some respect for the human spirit. But we writers of Jewish descent are, thank God, safe from any temptation to take the side of the barbarians in any way. We are the only representatives of Europe who are debarred from returning to Germany. Even if there were in our ranks a traitor, who, from personal ambition, stupidity, and blindness, wanted to conclude a shameful peace with the destroyers of Europe—he couldn't do it! That "Asiatic" and "Oriental" blood which the current wielders of power in the German Reich hold against us will quite certainly not permit us to desert from the noble ranks of the European army. God himself—and we are proud of the fact—will not allow us to betray Europe, Christendom, and Judaism. God is with the vanquished, not with the victors! At a time when His Holiness, the infallible Pope of Christendom, is concluding a peace agreement, a Concordat, with the enemies of Christ, when the Protestants are establishing a "German church" and censoring the Bible, we descendants of the old Jews, the forefathers of European culture, are the only legitimate

[1]The Cimbri and Teutoni were Germanic tribes who ravaged Europe in the second century B.C.

German representatives of that culture. Thanks to inscrutable divine wisdom, we are physically incapable of betraying it to the heathen civilization of poison gases, to the ammonia-breathing Germanic war god. . . .

It would be true to say that, from about 1900, German cultural life was largely defined, if not dominated by this "top class" of German Jews. To be fair, what they did was not wholly bad. Even their errors were sometimes salutary. In the whole of that large kingdom with a population of sixty million, among all those industrialists, there was—individual exceptions aside—no class that was actively interested in art and intellect. As far as the Prussian Junkers[2] are concerned, the civilized world will know that they were just about able to read and write. One of their representatives, President Hindenburg,[3] openly admitted *that he had never read a book in his life.* And, incidentally, it was this icon, ancient from early youth, that the workers, Social Democrats, journalists, artists, and Jews worshipped during the war, and that the German people (workers, Jews, journalists, artists, Social Democrats, and the rest of them) then reelected president. Is a people that elects as its president an icon that has never read a book all that far away from burning books itself? And are the Jewish writers, scholars, and philosophers who voted for Hindenburg really entitled to complain about the bonfire in which our thoughts are consumed?

As for the industrialists—their minds were taken up by iron and steel, by guns and "Big Berthas"; they were smelting the modern version of "Siegfried's sword." The big business-people were producing the cheap junk labeled "Made in Germany" with which they flooded an unhappy world. *Only the German Jews (doctors, lawyers, tradesmen, department store owners, artisans, or manufacturers) were interested in books, theater, museums, music.* Even if they were occasionally guilty of bad taste, it remains a fact that there was no one else in the whole of Germany capable of pointing out and correcting their errors. The magazines and newspapers were edited by Jews, managed by Jews, read by Jews! A swarm of intellectual Jewish critics and reviewers discovered and promoted numerous "pure Aryan" poets, writers, and actors! Does there exist—now that theater and literature have been "cleansed"—a single outstanding actor or writer who was not recognized and praised at a time when reviewing and public opinion were in the hands of Jews? I challenge the Third Reich to come up with a single example of a gifted "pure Aryan" poet, actor, or musician who was kept down by the Jews and emancipated by Herr Goebbels! It's only the feeblest dilettantes who flourish in the swastika's shadow, in the bloody glow cast by the ash heaps in which we are consumed. . . .

The threatened and terrorized world must understand that the arrival on the scene of Corporal Hitler does not mark the beginning of any new chapter in the history of anti-Semitism: Far from it! What the arsonists tell us is true, though not in the way they intended: This Third Reich is only the beginning of the end! By destroying Jews they are persecuting Christ. For the first time the Jews are not being murdered for crucifying Christ but for having produced him from their midst. If the books of Jewish or supposed Jewish authors are burned, what is really set fire to is the Book of Books: the Bible. If Jewish judges and attorneys are expelled or locked up, it represents a symbolic assault on law and justice.

---

[2]Prussian Junkers were aristocratic landowners.

[3]President Hindenburg (1847–1934) was a general in World War I and president of the Weimar Republic from 1925 until his death.

7 Nazi Persecution of the Jews

The Nazis deprived Jews of their German citizenship and instituted many anti-Jewish measures designed to make them outcasts. Thousands of Jewish doctors, lawyers, musicians, artists, and professors were barred from practicing their professions, and Jewish members of the civil service were dismissed. A series of laws tightened the screws of humiliation and persecution. Marriages or sexual encounters between Germans and Jews were forbidden. Universities, schools, restaurants, pharmacies, hospitals, theaters, museums, and athletic fields were gradually closed to Jews.

In November 1938, using, as a pretext, the assassination of a German official in Paris by a seventeen-year-old Jewish youth, whose family had been mistreated by the Nazis, the Nazis organized an extensive pogrom. Nazi gangs murdered scores of Jews and burned and looted thousands of Jewish businesses, homes, and synagogues all over Germany—an event that became known as Night of the Broken Glass *(Kristallnacht)*. Some thirty thousand Jews were thrown into concentration camps. The Reich then imposed on the Jewish community a fine of 1 billion marks. By the outbreak of the war in September 1939, approximately one-half of Germany's 600,000 Jews had fled the country. Those who stayed behind would fall victim to the last stage of the Nazi anti-Jewish campaign—the Final Solution.

Hertha Nathorff
A GERMAN JEWISH DOCTOR'S DIARY

Hertha Nathorff, niece of Albert Einstein, practiced medicine in Berlin. In her diary, she recorded the constant abuse and humiliation inflicted on Jews as a result of Nazi anti-Semitic policies. Dr. Nathorff managed to leave Germany in 1939 before the outbreak of war. Following are excerpts from her diary.

1 April 1933

Jewish Boycott.

This day is engraved in my heart in flames. To think that such things are still possible in the twentieth century. In front of all Jewish shops, lawyers' offices, doctors' surgeries and flats there are young boys with signs saying, 'Don't buy from Jews', 'Don't go to Jewish doctors', 'Anybody who buys from Jews is a traitor', 'Jews are the incarnation of lies and deceit.' Doctors' signs on the walls of houses are soiled, and sometimes damaged, and people have looked on, gawping in silence. They must have forgotten to stick anything over my sign. I think I would have reacted violently. It was afternoon before one of these young boys visited me at home and asked: 'Is this a Jewish business?' 'This isn't a business at all; it's a doctor's surgery', I said. 'Are you sick?' After these ironic words the youth disappeared without posting anybody in front of my door. Of course some patients who had appointments did not turn up. One woman rang to say that of course she couldn't come today, and I said that it would be better if she didn't come any more at all. For my own part, I shopped deliberately in places where such pickets were posted. One of them wanted to stop me going into a little soap shop, but I pushed him to one side, saying, 'I'll spend my money where I want.' Why doesn't everybody do that? That would soon settle the boycott. But people are a cowardly lot, as I know only too well.

In the evening we were with friends at the Hohenzollerndamm, three couples, all doctors. They were all quite depressed. One of the company, Emil, the optimist, tried to convince us: 'It'll all be over in a few days.' They don't understand my anger when I say, 'They should strike us dead instead. It would be more humane than the psychological death they have in mind . . .' But my instincts have always proved right.

25 April 1933

A letter from Charlottenburg municipal authorities: 'You are requested to cease your activity as senior doctor at the women's advice centre!' Full stop.

Thrown out then—full stop. My poor women, whose hands will they fall into now? I've run that place for five years, expanded it and made it well known, and now? It's all over. I have to repeat it again and again, in order to be able to grasp it.

30 August 1933

Back from holidays in southern Germany. How tense the atmosphere is there. The situation is completely changed in my home town, where everyone knows everyone else.

My family have lived in that small town for two hundred years, looked up to, respected and now. . . . My old father said to me in passing that he no longer goes to his local. Mother got rather worked up because nobody knows how to greet her properly any more.

A friend of my sister's, a lawyer's wife, comes to visit only in the evenings after dark, until my sister suggests she doesn't bother coming at all. The Catholics are beside themselves with fear and dread. Where will it all end?

2 October 1934

I have just come from the H. mental asylum. They rang to ask if I would come. A patient had arrived during the night who was calling for me. She had been picked up on the street, in front of a hospital. They thought she was drunk, the way she was behaving, talking, crying in the street, and giving away her possessions to passers-by. Then she was brought to the asylum. Did I know her? A young colleague who is not allowed to practise. Her licence has been taken away. A love affair with an Aryan colleague suddenly came to an end. Then she tried to work as a nurse, and it proved too much for her soul, for her intellect. As a result she had gone mad.

30 November 1934

I have been to southern Germany. My dear father was seriously ill. The things I had to do to get the doctor treating him—it would be unprofessional to comment on his medical ability—to agree to send him for a consultation with the capable specialist in Ulm! 'One can't consult a Jewish doctor!' He would rather treat the patient wrongly and badly! He should be grateful that he can get an Aryan doctor to come at all. There is no Jewish doctor left in the small town, and the other Nazi doctor does not treat Jews. It's almost like the camps where they have imprisoned innocent people. 'If one happens to be a Jew, one is either healthy or dead!'

One of the Catholic nurses looking after Father told me: 'Frau Doktor, we needn't fear hell any more. The devil is already abroad in the world.'

30 December 1934

Three more suicides by people who could no longer stand the continuing defamation and spite.

The boy is afraid to go on the ice rink. Yesterday Jewish children were chased away and beaten up.

9 October 1935

I met my former secretary today. She fixed me sharply with her short-sighted eyes, and then turned away. I was so nauseated I spat into my handkerchief. She was once a patient of mine. Later I met her in the street. Her boyfriend had left her and she was out of work and without money. I took her on, trained her for years and employed her in my clinic until the last day. Now she has changed so much that she can no longer greet me; me, who rescued her from the gutter!

I never go anywhere any more. I am so well known through my profession and my position; why should I make trouble for myself and for others? I'm happy to be at home in peace.

4 December 1935

Miss G. in the surgery, completely broken. She knows nothing of Jews and Jewry. Suddenly they've dug up her Jewish grandmother! She is no longer allowed to work as an artist, and she must give up her boyfriend, a senior officer. She wants something 'to end it all.' She can only groan pitifully, 'I can't go on living.' What can I do? I can no longer help my patients, it's a living death for me.

5 August 1938

There was a telephone call as we were sitting at the table with guests. I went to the telephone myself. A colleague, S., who asks: 'Have you been listening to the radio?' 'No', I say, 'what's happened now?' The colleague, usually so calm, says with a trembling, angry voice: 'What you always said would happen. They're taking away our licenses, we are no longer allowed to practise—it's just been on the radio.' 'On the radio.' This is how we learn that they are taking away from us what we earned through years of study, what we were taught by eminent professors, famous universities . . . I can't take it in . . . All I could think at that moment was: 'And now I have to tell my husband.' How I went calmly back to the dining table, drew the meal to a close, and told my guests, 'It's nothing much', I don't know; I know only that I sat at the desk, my hands clenched and said to my husband: 'It's over—over—over.' He went to get a paper, and it had already been reported. This is how we Jewish doctors learnt of our death sentence. In the clinic they are all in a state of complete despair.

Marta Appel
MEMOIRS OF A GERMAN JEWISH WOMAN

Marta Appel and her husband, Dr. Ernst Appel, a rabbi in the city of Dortmund, fled Germany in 1937. In 1940–1941, while in the United States, she wrote her memoirs, which described conditions in Dortmund after the Nazis took power.

The children had been advised not to come to school on April 1, 1933, the day of the boycott. Even the principal of the school thought Jewish children's lives were no longer safe. One night they placed big signs on every store or house owned by Jewish people. In front of our temple, on every square and corner, billboards were scoffing at us. Everywhere, and on all occasions, we read and heard that we were vermin and had caused the ruin of the German people. No Jewish store was closed on that day, none was willing to show fear in the face of the boycott. The only building which did not open its door as usual, since it was Saturday, was the temple. We did not want this holy place desecrated by any trouble.

I even went downtown that day to see what was going on in the city. There was no cheering crowd as the Nazis had expected, no running and smashing of Jewish businesses. I heard only words of anger and disapproval. People were massed before the Jewish stores to watch the Nazi guards who were posted there to prevent anyone from entering to buy. And there were many courageous enough to enter, although they were called rude names by the Nazi guards, and their pictures were taken to show them as enemies of the German people in the daily papers. . . .

Our gentile friends and neighbors, even people whom we had scarcely known before, came to assure us of their friendship and to tell us that these horrors could not last very long. But after some months of a regime of terror, fidelity and friendship had lost their meaning, and fear and treachery had replaced them. For the sake of our gentile friends, we turned our heads so as not to greet them in the streets, for we did not want to bring upon them the danger of imprisonment for being considered a friend of Jews.

With each day of the Nazi regime, the abyss between us and our fellow citizens grew larger. Friends whom we had loved for years did not know us anymore. They suddenly saw that we were different from themselves. Of course we were different, since we were bearing the stigma of Nazi hatred, since we were hunted like deer. Through the prominent position of my husband we were in constant danger. Often we were warned to stay away from home. We were no longer safe, wherever we went.

How much our life changed in those days! Often it seemed to me I could not bear it any longer, but thinking of my children, I knew we had to be strong to make it easier for them. From then on I hated to go out, since on every corner I saw signs that the Jews were the misfortune of the people. . . .

In the evenings we sat at home at the radio listening fearfully to all the new and outrageous restrictions and laws which almost daily brought further suffering to Jewish people. . . .

Since I had lived in Dortmund, I had met every four weeks with a group of women, all of whom were born in Metz, my beloved home city. We all had been pupils or teachers in the same high school. After the Nazis came, I was afraid to go to the meetings. I did not want the presence of a Jewess to bring any trouble, since we always met publicly in a café. One day on the street, I met one of my old teachers, and with tears in her eyes she begged me: "Come again to us; we miss you; we feel ashamed that you must think we do not want you anymore. Not one of us has changed in her feeling toward you." She tried to convince me that they were still my friends, and tried to take away my doubts. I decided to go to the next meeting. It was a hard decision, and I had not slept the night before. I was afraid for my gentile friends. For nothing in the world did I wish to bring them trouble by my attendance, and I was also afraid for myself. I knew I would watch them, noticing the slightest expression of embarrassment in their eyes when I came. I knew they could not deceive me; I would be aware of every change in their voices. Would they be afraid to talk to me?

It was not necessary for me to read their eyes or listen to the change in their voices. The empty table in the little alcove which always had been reserved for us spoke the clearest language. It was even unnecessary for the waiter to come and say that a lady phoned that morning not to reserve the table thereafter. I could not blame them. Why should they risk losing a position only to prove to me that we still had friends in Germany?

I, personally, did not mind all those disappointments, but when my children had to face them, and were not spared being offended everywhere, my heart was filled with anguish. It required a great deal of inner strength, of love and harmony among the Jewish families, to make our children strong enough to bear all that persecution and hatred. [. . .] My heart was broken when I saw tears in my younger child's eyes when she had been sent home from school while all the others had been taken to a show or some other pleasure. It was not because she was denied going to the show that my little girl was weeping—she knew her Mommy always could take her—but because she had to stay apart, as if she were not good enough to associate with her comrades any longer. It was this that made it hard and bitter for her. I think that even the Nazi teacher sometimes felt ashamed when she looked into the sad eyes of my little girl, since several times, when the class was going out for pleasure, she phoned not to send her to school. Maybe it was not right to hate this teacher so much, since everything she did had been upon orders, but it was she who brought so much bitterness to my child, and never can I forget it.

Almost every lesson began to be a torture for Jewish children. There was not one subject anymore which was not used to bring up the Jewish question. And in the presence of Jewish children the teachers denounced all the Jews, without exception, as scoundrels and as the most destructive force in every country where they were living. My children were not permitted to leave the room during such a talk; they were compelled to stay and to listen; they had to feel all the other children's eyes looking and staring at them, the examples of an outcast race.

Every day they had to face another degrading and offensive incident. As Mother's Day came near, the children were practicing songs at school to celebrate that day. Every year on that occasion the whole school gathered in a joint festival. It was the day before when my girls were ordered to see the music teacher. "You have to be present for the festival," the teacher told them, "but since you are Jewish, you are not allowed to join in the songs." "Why can't we sing?" my children protested with tears in their eyes. "We have a mother too, and we wish to sing for her." But it seemed the teacher did not want to understand the children's feelings. Curtly she rebuked their protest. "I know you have a mother," she said haughtily, "but she is only a Jewish mother." At that the girls had no reply; there was no use to speak any longer to the teacher, but seldom had they been so much disturbed as when they came from school that day, when someone had tried to condemn their mother. . . .

One day, for the first time in a long while, I saw my children coming back from school with shining eyes, laughing and giggling together. Most of the classes had been gathered that morning in the big hall, since an official of the new *Rasseamt,* the office of races, had come to give a talk about the differences of races. "I asked the teacher if I could go home," my daughter was saying, "but she told me she had orders not to dismiss anyone. You may imagine it was an awful talk. He said that there are two groups of races, a high group and a low one. The high and upper race that was destined to rule the world was the Teutonic, the German race, while one of the lowest races was the Jewish race. And then, Mommy, he looked around and asked one of the girls to come to him." The children again began to giggle about their experience. "First we did not know," my girl continued, "what he intended, and we were very afraid when he picked out Eva. Then he began, and he was pointing at Eva, 'Look here, the small head of this girl, her long forehead, her very blue eyes, and blond hair,' and he was lifting one of her long blond braids. 'And look,' he said, 'at her tall and slender figure. These are the unequivocal marks of a pure and unmixed Teutonic race.' Mommy, you should have heard how at this moment all the girls burst into laughter. Even Eva could not help laughing. Then from all sides of the hall there was shouting, 'She is a Jewess!' You should have seen the officer's face! I guess he was lucky that the principal got up so quickly and, with a sign to the pupils, stopped the laughing and shouting and dismissed the man, thanking him for his interesting and very enlightening talk. At that we began again to laugh, but he stopped us immediately. Oh, I was so glad that the teacher had not dismissed me and I was there to hear it."

When my husband came home, they told him and enjoyed it again and again. And we were thankful to know that they still had not completely forgotten how to laugh and to act like happy children.

"If only I could take my children out of here!" That thought was occupying my mind more and more. I no longer hoped for any change as did my husband. Besides, even a changed Germany could not make me forget that all our friends, the whole nation, had abandoned us in our need. It was no longer the same country for me. Everything had changed, not people alone—the city, the forest, the river—the whole country looked different in my eyes.

David H. Buffum
NIGHT OF THE BROKEN GLASS (*KRISTALLNACHT*)

The Nazi press depicted the terrible events of *Kristallnacht*—the burning and vandalizing of thousands of Jewish synagogues, homes, and businesses throughout Germany and the killing and maiming of Jews—as a "spontaneous wave of righteous indignation" directed at enemies of Germany. In reality the violence was planned and coordinated by the government, and many Germans were horrified by the destruction of property and the abuse inflicted on helpless people. The following account of the vicious onslaught in Leipzig was prepared by David H. Buffum, the American consul.

At 3 A.M. November 10, 1938 was unleashed a barrage of Nazi ferocity as had had no equal hitherto in Germany, or very likely anywhere else in the world since savagery, if ever. Jewish dwellings were smashed into and contents demolished or looted. In one of the Jewish sections an eighteen year old boy was hurled from a three story window to land with both legs broken on a street littered with burning beds and other household furniture and effects from his family's and other apartments. This information was supplied by an attending physician. It is reported from another quarter that among domestic effects thrown out of a Jewish dwelling, a small dog descended four flights to a broken spine on a cluttered street. Although apparently centered in poor districts, the raid was not confined to the humble classes. One apartment of exceptionally refined occupants known to this office, was violently ransacked, presumably in a search for valuables that was not in vain, and one of the marauders thrust a cane through a priceless medieval painting portraying a biblical scene. Another apartment of the same category is known to have been turned upside down in the frenzied course of whatever the invaders were after. Reported loss of looting of cash, silver, jewelry, and otherwise easily convertible articles, have been frequent.

Jewish shop windows by the hundreds were systematically and wantonly smashed throughout the entire city at a loss estimated at several millions of marks. There are reports that substantial losses have been sustained on the famous Leipzig "Bruhl," as many of the shop windows at the time of the demolition were filled with costly furs that were seized before the windows could be boarded up. In proportion to the general destruction of real estate, however, losses of goods are felt to have been relatively small. The spectators who viewed the wreckage when daylight had arrived were mostly in such a bewildered mood, that there was no danger of impulsive acts, and the perpetrators probably were too busy in carrying out their schedule to take off a whole lot of time for personal profit. At all events, the main streets of the city were a positive litter of shattered plate glass. According to reliable testimony, the debacle was executed by S. S. men and Storm Troopers not in uniform, each group having been provided with hammers, axes, crowbars and incendiary bombs.

Three synagogues in Leipzig were fired simultaneously by incendiary bombs and all sacred objects and records desecrated or destroyed, in most instances hurled through the windows and burned in the streets. No attempts whatsoever were made to quench the fires, functions of the fire brigade having been confined to playing water on adjoining buildings. All of the synagogues were irreparably gutted by flames, and the walls of the two that are in the close proximity of the consulate are now being razed. The blackened frames have been centers of attraction during the past week of terror for eloquently silent and bewildered crowds. One of the largest clothing stores in the heart of the city was destroyed by flames from incendiary bombs, only the charred walls and gutted roof having been left standing. As was the case with the synagogues, no attempts on the part of the fire brigade were made to extinguish the fire, although apparently there was a certain amount of apprehension for adjacent property, for the walls of a coffee house next door were covered with asbestos and sprayed by the doughty firemen. It is extremely difficult to believe, but the owners of the clothing store were actually charged with setting the fire and on that basis were dragged from their beds at 6 A.M. and clapped into prison.

Tactics which closely approached the ghoulish took place at the Jewish cemetery where the temple was fired together with a building occupied by caretakers, tombstones uprooted and graves violated. Eyewitnesses considered reliable report that ten corpses were left unburied at this cemetery for a week's time because all gravediggers and cemetery attendants had been arrested.

Ferocious as was the violation of property, the most hideous phase of the so-called "spontaneous" action has been the wholesale arrest and transportation to concentration camps of male German Jews between the ages of sixteen and sixty, as well as Jewish men without citizenship. This has been taking place daily since the night of horror. This office has no way of accurately checking the numbers of such arrests, but there is very little question that they have gone into several thousands in Leipzig along. Having demolished dwellings and hurled most of the moveable effects to the streets, the insatiably sadistic perpetrators threw many of the trembling inmates into a small stream that flows through the Zoological Park, commanding horrified spectators to spit at them, defile them with mud and jeer at their plight. The latter incident has been repeatedly corroborated by German witnesses who were nauseated in telling the tale. The slightest manifestation of sympathy evoked a positive fury on the part of the perpetrators, and the crowd was powerless to do anything but turn horror-stricken eyes from the scene of abuse, or leave the vicinity. These tactics were carried out the entire morning of November 10th without police intervention and they were applied to men, women and children.

There is much evidence of physical violence, including several deaths. At least half a dozen cases have been personally observed, victims with bloody, badly bruised faces having fled to this office, believing that as refugees their desire to emigrate could be expedited here. As a matter of fact this consulate has been a bedlam of humanity for the past ten days, most of these visitors being desperate women, as their husbands and sons had been taken off to concentration camps.

Similarly violent procedure was applied throughout this consular district, the amount of havoc wrought depending upon the number of Jewish establishments or persons involved. It is understood that in many of the smaller communities even more relentless methods were employed than was the case in the cities. Reports have been received from Weissenfels to the effect that the few Jewish families there are experiencing great difficulty in purchasing food. It is reported that three Aryan professors of the University of Jena have been arrested and taken off to concentration camps because they had voiced disapproval of this insidious drive against mankind.

8 The Spanish Civil War

One of the bitterest conflicts of the century, the civil war in Spain pitted conservative, traditional elements of the population (the Catholic Church, the military, large landowners) against disaffected groups seeking change (workers, peasants, regional separatists). The conflict began in July 1936 with a rebellion in the army led by General Francisco Franco (1892–1975). He sought to rid Spain of the republic, along with the radical and secular policies of its left-wing political parties. Outside of the country, meanwhile, the civil war took on the appearance of a struggle between fascism and communism. Franco's Nationalists benefited from large amounts of materiel and even manpower readily supplied by Mussolini and Hitler. The Loyalists received help from the Soviet Union, but the aid was limited, and Stalinist agents often seemed more concerned with hunting down Trotskyist supporters of the republic. Franco achieved victory in March 1939, conducted a blood purge, and instituted an authoritarian regime that ruled the country for the next four decades. In the end, the civil war cost hundreds of thousands of lives, rent asunder Spain's social fabric, and heightened international tensions.

Fred Thomas
TO TILT AT WINDMILLS

The fact that democracies such as Britain and France enforced a policy of nonintervention in the Spanish Civil War and a strict embargo against the Republicans gave Franco an important edge. Nevertheless, thousands of young people from Western Europe and the Americas volunteered for one of the international brigades that formed to support the Loyalist cause. One such volunteer was Fred Thomas, a member of the British Labor party, who eventually became a member of the Fifteenth International Brigade. Frustrated by his country's "hands-off" policy, Thomas decided to take matters into his own hands, which, in this case, meant working through the local Communist party. He described this experience in his memoir of the war, *To Tilt at Windmills,* which appeared in 1996 and is excerpted below.

It is easy now to recognize the unbroken but twisted chain of events that led, eventually, to my finding myself in Spain's Civil War. Nobody cajoled, coerced or bullied me into making the decision; certainly not the Communist party, even though, at my request, they provided the means. It was no easy decision reached on impulse. Indeed, I hesitated longer, perhaps much longer, than a good anti-fascist ought in the face of such a threat to all a young socialist stood for.

Since 1931 I had been an active member of the Hackney Labour Party in northeast London. Soon came Hitler's traumatic rise to power and the rapid, brutal, suppression of democracy and freedom in Germany. In Britain Mosley[1] formed his British Union of Fascists and, apeing

[1]Oswald Mosley (1896–1980) founded the British Union of Fascists (1932–1940), which attracted no more than a few thousand supporters during its brief lifespan.

his master, turned his thugs loose on Jews and all who opposed him. But there was no clarion call from Labour to the people of Britain to get out on the streets and fight this evil of fascism. It was to the communists that we had to look for leadership. "Anti-fascist Committees" were formed in almost every London borough, usually led or inspired by communists but supported by local Labour party people, liberals, churchmen and, of course, Jews. (Though the Jewish hierarchy seemed as reluctant to come out fighting as was the Labour Party). I was soon busy, speaking at meetings, adding my presence and voice to the vociferous opposition at fascist street-corner speakers. It was, frequently, a frightening and testing experience; Mosley's louts had been well drilled in the use of fists, boots and belts. Only once at Ridley Road, a favorite fascist meeting place, did I see the police act. Then, it was not to warn the speaker for making the customary obscene, ignorant, and certainly provocative attacks on Jews, but to pull out "troublemakers" from the crowd. I was one.

Many people have found it convenient to say we were used by the comrades. The truth is that their energy and initiative played a major part in rallying many thousands to show their detestation of Mosley and his mindless ones. At its very lowest evaluation, this surge of popular feeling countered the inclination of some important people (including at least one newspaper owner and more than one prominent leader of the Labour Party) to see in Mosley their looked-for strong man who would recognize their right to power and privilege.

So, politics then was a simple matter of being anti-fascist or fascist. Never has there been in England an issue creating such intense emotional fervor. When Franco and his Moors began their revolt in Spain in July 1936, at once it seemed everything crystallized into a glaringly simple truth. Fascism must be halted.

The situation in Spain called for every one of us who opposed fascism to do his utmost to defeat it. Meetings, demonstrations, collecting food, money, medical supplies, seemed no longer the answer. I determined to go to Spain myself. I had no wish for heroism, nor did I think Spain would live or die on my decision: I just knew I had to go.

In truth, I think emotion rather than cold reasoning determined the moment of decision. In the *Daily Express* I saw a picture of Franco's troops entering a captured village. Distraught women ran forward, arms outstretched in hopeless submission, pleading for the lives of their men. I could not bear the anguish in their eyes. Somewhere else, in another photo, a line of young militiamen, roped together, defeated, abject, were being marched off to immediate execution. I was obsessed by hate for the arrogant, swaggering Civil Guard officer, pistol in hand, at their head. Almost daily I read of massacres of men and women shot down in cold blood. The bombing of Guernica[2] followed, near the end of April. And, unexpectedly, Galsworthy![3] When and why he wrote these lines I do not know, but they struck an answering chord in me:

> Come, let us lay a lance in rest,
> And tilt at windmills under a wild sky;
> For who could live so petty and unblest
> That dare not tilt at something ere he die
> Rather than, screened by safe majority,
> Preserve his little life to little ends
> And never raise a rebel cry.

In April 1937 I made my first approach. The only way I knew of was through the Communist party, so I phoned their head office in King Street, London. Understandably, whomever I spoke to was scathing; did I really think such matters were discussed on the phone? I took a half day off from work and called there.

I've no idea whom I saw that first time, but he obviously shared my own view that the survival of the Spanish Republic did not depend

---

[2]Guernica, a small market town in the Basque region of Spain, was the scene of a notorious bombing raid by German planes in April 1937; the tragedy was immortalized by Pablo Picasso (1882–1973) in his painting of the same name.

[3]John Galsworthy (1867–1933) was an English author and Nobel Prize winner.

on my prompt arrival. Had I any military experience or training? I assured him I had been on the streets doing my bit in the struggle against Mosley. That smart answer brought a short, sharp lecture. The Spanish people were engaged in a life or death struggle, there was no place for any except trained men. At the time I felt fittingly rebuked. Later, when I had been in Spain long enough to get my bearings, I sometimes wondered about the strange "training" some of the veterans had received!

Daily the news from Spain became more alarming. Aided by the farce of Nonintervention, Franco's troops were advancing steadily, capturing town after town, whole provinces. Maps made depressing viewing, with considerably more than half the country in fascist occupation. Since November 1936 they had been at the very gates of Madrid; in the North, the Basque country was cut off, its troops being inexorably driven back. Seeking crumbs of comfort where we could we delighted in press reports—glamourized, dramatised, and largely inaccurate—of such exploits as those of "Potato Jones," captain of a British merchant ship who, we read, had successfully defied the blockading insurgent warships to land much-needed food for the people of Bilbao. In London and elsewhere hundreds of children, refugees from bombs and starvation, were arriving to be cared for by a wide variety of kindly organizations and individuals.

I decided to try again. This time, another interviewer and a very different response. Rightly, he was inquisitive and guarded. Why did I want to go to Spain? Was I in the Communist party? Was I in work? Was I married? Was there anyone who would vouch for me? I muddled through with platitudes, facts, and the name of a Hackney C.P. member whom I knew well. Then—"Come back on Thursday. Till then, keep your mouth shut!"

This seemed more like it. Something told me I was as good as on my way. On Thursday I was back at King Street. The Party man was brief and to the point. Apparently my contact had reported favourably and they obviously liked the fact that I was unmarried and in work. Anyway, I was accepted.

> Report here on Saturday morning, 10oc. You'll be given final instructions then. Remember, you still say nothing to anyone.

How different everything and everybody seemed as I stepped out into the street again. I think I remained in a haze of unreality until I found myself actually in Spain.

I made some few essential arrangements, being compelled in the process to let three or four people know my plans. On Saturday morning, I went back to King Street for a final briefing. It was more final than I had expected. A small party of volunteers was to go that same night! Plenty of time, though, for me to settle some remaining, personal matters and make my farewells.

Arthur Koestler
DIALOGUE WITH DEATH

Author Arthur Koestler, a Communist during the 1930s, was captured by the Nationalists while covering the Spanish Civil War. At the time, he was working for the *London News Chronicle* as well as the Loyalist Government's official news agency. While in solitary confinement, Koestler witnessed the executions of other prisoners and expected to be shot himself. Indeed, Koestler was sentenced to death; after several months of imprisonment, however, he was released in a prisoner exchange arranged by the International Red Cross. *Dialogue with Death,*

excerpted below, describes his incarceration. It was published in 1937 as part of a larger work entitled *Spanish Testament.*

I had spent the first two months in the Seville prison in complete isolation. Only now, when I came into contact with the other prisoners, did I learn what was going on around me.

I learned that in the week after my transfer to the prison thirty-seven men from the big patio had been executed.

In the last week of February no executions had taken place; in March, forty-five.

Most of the victims were prisoners of war from the various fronts. In every case the procedure had been the same as in that of Nicolás.

True, not a single man had been shot without trial. But these trials were far more disgraceful than the unceremonious slaughter of prisoners in the front lines, immediately after a battle.

In the case of every single prisoner of war, without exception, the charge was one of '*rebelión militar*'. Those who were defending the legal Government against open rebellion, were condemned for taking part in a rebellion—by an authority that claimed to be a court of law and to pronounce judgment in the name of justice.

The scenario of this sinister comedy was always the same. The proceedings lasted two or three minutes. The so-called Prosecutor demanded the death sentence; always and without exception. The so-called Defending Officer—always and without exception—asked for a life sentence in view of mitigating circumstances. Then the prisoner was marched off. He was never informed of his sentence. Sentence was passed the moment he was out of the door; it was one of death; always and without exception.

The record of the sentence was passed on to the Commander-in-Chief of the Southern Forces, General Queipo de Llano. The sentences were carried out in summary fashion. Twenty to twenty-five per cent of the prisoners—according to Queipo's mood or the situation at the front—were reprieved. The rest were shot.

Theoretically, the final decision lay with General Franco. In a few cases—especially if there were a risk of international repercussions—the Generalissimo granted a commutation. As for the *pobres y humildes,* he never even saw the lists of those condemned. Nicolás, for instance, had been shot on the fourth day after his trial; it is technically impossible that in such a short time his dossier should have travelled from the Court to Queipo, from Queipo to Franco's H.Q. in Salamanca or Burgos, and then back again.

From the moment he left the court-martial the accused was kept in uncertainty as to his fate. Were his sentence commuted to thirty years' imprisonment he was informed by letter—a week or a month or six months later. Were the death sentence confirmed, he learned of it only at the moment of execution.

In the interval he was left to play football and leap-frog in the patio, and count his buttons every morning to see whether he were going to be shot that night.

There were men in the patio who had been waiting for four months to be shot. The record was held by a Captain of the Militia—four and a half months. He was executed a few days before my release.

Nicolás had been lucky; he had had to wait only four days.

During March forty-five men were shot.

During the first thirteen days of April there were no executions.

During the night of April 13th to 14th seventeen men were shot, in celebration of the anniversary of the proclamation of the Republic. Nicolás was among them.

Two nights later, the night of Thursday, eight were shot. This was the first time I heard anything.

The proceedings were very subdued; perhaps that explains why I hadn't heard them before. But now I was on the watch.

I had learned that the critical time was between midnight and two in the morning. For some days I stood from midnight until two o'clock with my ear pressed to the door of my cell.

During the first night of my vigil, the night of Wednesday, nothing happened.

During the second night . . .

A feeling of nausea still comes over me when I remember that night.

I had gone to sleep, and I woke up shortly before midnight. In the black silence of the prison charged with the nightmarish dreams of thirteen hundred sleeping men, I heard the murmured prayer of the priest and the ringing of the sanctus bell.

Then a cell door, the third to the left of mine, was opened, and a name was called out, *'Qué?'*—What is the matter?—asked a sleepy voice, and the priest's voice grew clearer and the bell rang louder.

And now the drowsy man in his cell understood. At first he only groaned; then in a dull voice, he called for help: *'Socorro, socorro.'*

'Hombre, there's no help for you,' said the warder who accompanied the priest. He said this neither in a hostile nor in a friendly tone; it was simply a statement of fact. For a moment the man who was about to die was silent; the warder's quiet, sober manner puzzled him. And then he began to laugh. He kept slapping his knees with his hands, and his laughter was quiet and subdued, full of little gasps and hiccoughs. 'You are only pretending,' he said to the priest. 'I knew at once that you were only pretending.'

'Hombre, this is no pretence,' said the warder in the same dry tone as before.

They marched him off.

I heard him shouting outside. But the sound of the shots came only a few minutes later.

In the meantime the priest and the warder had opened the door of the next cell; it was No. 42, the second to my left. Again, *'Qué?'* And again the prayer and the bell. This one sobbed and whimpered like a child. Then he cried out for his mother: *'Madre, madre!'*

And again: *'Madre, madre!'*

'Hombre, why didn't you think of her before?' said the warder.

They marched him off.

They went on to the next cell. When my neighbour was called, he said nothing. Most probably he was already awake, and, like me, prepared. But when the priest had ended his prayer, he asked, as if of himself: 'Why must I die?' The priest answered in five words, uttered in a solemn voice but rather hurriedly: 'Faith, man. Death means release.'

They marched him off.

They came to my cell and the priest fumbled at the bolt. I could see him through the spy-hole. He was a little, black, greasy man.

'No, not this one,' said the warder.

They went on to the next cell. He, too, was prepared. He asked no questions. While the priest prayed, he began in a low voice to sing the 'Marseillaise'. But after a few bars his voice broke, and he too sobbed.

They marched him off.

And then there was silence again.

And now I realised why the merchant from Gibraltar had said that he and his friends would shortly be moving in to No. 39.

I frequently awoke during this night feeling my bed shaking, as though in an earthquake. Then I realised that it was my own body that was trembling from head to foot. The moment I awoke my body grew still; the moment I fell asleep the nervous trembling began again. I thought at first that it was a permanent affliction like shell shock: but I only had two further attacks in the next few days; then it passed off.

Carlos was in a far worse plight. He had heard all that I had heard. During the night of Friday, nine were shot; during Saturday night, thirteen. We heard everything, four nights running. On Monday morning I was called to Carlos's cell; he was lying on the ground by the door, foam on his lips, both legs stiff and paralysed.

In the space of five days they had shot forty-seven men. Even for this prison it was a record. The faces in the patio were grey; during a game of football two men had a set-to and pulled each other's hair out in handfuls. In the morning the warders who had been on night duty crept along the corridors, pale, scared, and troubled. Even Angelito, who had to open the doors of the condemned cells night after night, arrived one morning red-eyed. 'If this goes on,' he said, 'they'll finish us all off.' . . .

On the night of Tuesday seventeen were shot.

On Thursday night eight.

On Friday night nine.

On Saturday night thirteen.

I tore strips off my shirt and stuffed my ears with them so as not to hear anything during the night. It was no good. I cut my gums with a splinter of glass, and said they were bleeding, so as to obtain some iodised cotton wool. I stuffed the cotton wool in my ears; it was no good, either.

Our hearing became preternaturally sharp. We heard everything. On the nights of the executions we heard the telephone ring at ten o'clock. We heard the warder on duty answer it. We heard him repeating at short intervals: 'ditto . . . ditto . . . ditto. . . .' We knew it was someone at military headquarters reading out the list of those to be shot during the night. We knew that the warder wrote down a name before every 'ditto'. But we did not know what names they were and we did not know whether ours was among them.

The telephone always rang at ten. Then until midnight or one o'clock there was time to lie on one's bed and wait. Each night we weighed our lives in the balance and each night found them wanting.

Then at twelve or one we heard the shrill sound of the night bell. It was the priest and the firing squad. They always arrived together.

Then began the opening of doors, the ringing of the sanctus bell, the praying of the priest, the cries for help and the shouts of 'Mother'.

The steps came nearer down the corridor, receded, came nearer, receded. Now they were at the next cell; now they were in the other wing; now they were coming back. Clearest of all was always the priest's voice: 'Lord, have mercy on this man, Lord, forgive him his sins, Amen.' We lay on our beds and our teeth chattered.

On Tuesday night seventeen were shot.

On Thursday night eight were shot.

On Friday night nine were shot.

On Saturday night thirteen were shot.

Six days shalt thou labour, saith the Lord, and on the seventh day, the Sabbath, thou shalt do no manner of work.

On Sunday night three were shot.

9 The Anguish of the Intellectuals

A somber mood gripped European intellectuals in the postwar period. The memory of World War I and the hypernationalism behind it, the rise of totalitarianism, and the Great Depression caused intellectuals to have grave doubts about the nature and destiny of Western civilization. To many European liberals, it seemed that the sun was setting on the Enlightenment tradition, that the ideals of reason and freedom, already gravely weakened by World War I, could not endure the threats posed by resurgent chauvinism, economic collapse, and totalitarian ideologies.

Richard N. Coudenhove-Kalergi *PAN-EUROPE*

The Austrian Count Richard Coudenhove-Kalergi (1894–1972) was a lifelong advocate of European unity who believed that the competing nationalisms typical

of the prewar era threatened to bring about more conflict. In 1924, he founded the Pan-European Union and succeeded in winning over several European statesmen to his ideas, notably French Foreign Minister Aristide Briand, who launched his own plan of European federation a few years later. In *Pan-Europe,* which originally appeared in 1926, Coudenhove-Kalergi rejected the idea that Germans, French, Magyars, or any other national group represent a "community of blood" and warned that "national megalomania" fosters hatred of other peoples. To counter nationalism, which "is becoming the gravedigger of European civilization," he stressed the ties that bound the peoples of Europe to one another, necessitating the pursuit of their interests on a continental basis. In the process, he provided astute observations about the evolution and nature of European nationalism. Excerpts from his work follow.

1. THE ESSENCE OF THE NATION

The dogma of European nationalism declares the nations to be communities of blood. This dogma is a myth.

After the numerous migrations of peoples which the continent has witnessed in historic and prehistoric times, it is impossible that pure races should still exist. All the peoples of Europe (with the possible exception of the Icelanders) are mixed peoples: mixtures of Nordic, Alpine, and Mediterranean strains; of Aryan immigrant and Mongoloid autochthonous blood; of fair and dark, of long-skulled and short-skulled, races.

It is false dilettantism to conclude from the existence of Romanic, Germanic, and Slavic language-groups, the existence of Romanic, Germanic, and Slavic races. . . .

. . . the French are Gauls and Franks; the Italians are Etruscans, Celts, and Germans, with Greek and Albanian admixtures; the Greeks are compounded of Slavic, Germanic, and Albanian blood, and so likewise are the Serbs; . . . the Germans of the west and south are blended with Celtic elements, while east of the Elbe they are Germanized Slavs with a Germanic strain. . . .

Whoever upholds the thesis that a nation is a community of blood, stands helpless before the fact that eminent German-Bohemians have Czech names, and conversely; that the greatest Magyar national poet, Petöfi, was of Slavic descent; that of the three greatest German philosophers, Kant was of Scottish, Schopenhauer of Dutch, and Nietzsche of Polish extraction; that Napoleon, Gambetta, and Zola, in respect of blood, were not French; Bernard Shaw and Lloyd George not English. . . .

Thus, in whatever way you take it, the theory that the nation is a community of blood leads to internal contradictions.

And yet there *are* European nations, and it were folly to deny their existence. These nations, however, are not communities of blood, but communities of spirit; they derive, not physically from common ancestors, but spiritually from common teachers. . . .

Among all the peoples of Europe there grew up national literatures, which were multiplied and spread broadcast by the printing-press. Insofar as Europeans were not illiterate, they divided themselves into readers of the German, French, Spanish, and Italian literatures. Every one of these readers felt himself the pupil and disciple of his great writers, whose thoughts he enthusiastically accepted.

Thus through its national literatures Europe came to be divided into a number of great school communities, which in consequence of the diversity of languages could not attain to a mutual understanding. In the end, the introduction of compulsory school-attendance forced every European to join one or another of these national school communities.

These school communities of the European spirit are the nations. They are secular-religious communities, welded together by the sacrament of language and the cult of national poets and national heroes.

School, literature, and press are the organs of the modern nation, to which they communicate, in a diluted form, the thoughts and deeds of its great leaders, for the glorification of whom they work unceasingly. . . .

This chauvinism, which expresses itself in contempt for foreign nations, has its origin in the fact that the nationalist comes to know and to love only the works of his own literature, only the thoughts and deeds of his own heroes. The cultures which remain closed to him because he does not understand them, appear to him inferior and barbarous. The less he knows his neighbors, the more he despises them. He commits the perspective error of seeing his own culture larger, because it is nearer to him, than foreign and more remote cultures. Because, owing to his ignorance of foreign languages, he lacks a standard for estimating his own culture, he lapses into national megalomania and becomes blind to the merits of foreign nations.

Hence it comes about that today the nations have adopted the intolerant standpoint which formerly characterized the creeds. Every people considers itself the Chosen People: Frenchmen, "la Grande Nation"; Italians, the legitimate heirs of *Imperium Romanum*; Germans, the true repositories of culture, destined to make this a healthier and better world; the Slavs, the people of the future.

This national megalomania, which is also shared by the lesser nations, is artificially fomented by school and press, and does not fail to find expression in politics as well. Demagogs have long since learned that they can count on certain applause by flattering national pride and praising the superiority of their own nation to foreign nations. Of that knowledge they make full use; and accordingly, from the imagined superiority of their nation they deduce its moral right to force its higher culture upon its "barbarian" enemies, to denationalize and subdue them. . . .

Just as a past enlightenment overthrew fanaticism, so a future enlightenment will overthrow chauvinism and pave the way to national tolerance. This tolerance will supplement the love for one's own nation by respect for foreign nations, and lay the foundations for the cultural re-birth of Europe.

2. THE EUROPEAN NATION . . .

National chauvinism cannot be overcome by an abstract internationalism; it can be overcome only by deepening and broadening national cultures into a general European culture; by spreading the truth that all national cultures in Europe are closely interwoven parts of a great and homogeneous European culture.

In order to attain to this European cultural unity, the peoples of Europe must learn to know, as well as their own, the intellectual leaders of their neighbors, and to estimate how much they owe, or might owe, to them. The way to that goal leads through linguistic attainments and the production of numerous translations.

In the hearts of Europeans the national pantheon is to be widened till it becomes a European pantheon, in which Goethe would take his place beside Shakespeare, Voltaire beside Nietzsche, Hus beside Spinoza. If only the Germans, instead of . . . sneering at the superficiality of French culture, were to set about assimilating the thoughts of the great Encyclopædists,[1] they would soon become aware how many threads lead from the latter to the Weimar Classics, and how close are the bonds uniting all that is great in Europe. . . .

. . . Europe is bound together by the Christian religion, by European science, art and culture, which rest on a *Christian-Hellenic* basis. . . .

The constitutions and laws of the various European states are incomparably nearer akin to one another than once were the constitutions of the Greek city-states. The same style of writing, the same mode of life, and the same social stratifications unite the Europeans, the same views respecting morality and the family, the same customs and habits, the same manner of dress, the very fashions of which are subject to the same changes. Equally the artistic tendencies in European painting, literature, and music are international: Romanticism and Realism, Impressionism and Expressionism. . . .

[1]A reference to the writers of the French Encyclopédie (1751–1772), the great compendium of knowledge produced during the European Age of Enlightenment.

The cultural unity of the Occident gives us the right to speak of a European nation, which is linguistically and politically divided into a variety of groups. If that Pan-European cultural sense succeeds in asserting itself, then every good German, Frenchman, Pole, and Italian will also be a good European.

5. PAN-EUROPEAN UNION

Before it can start its existence on the political map, Pan-Europe must first take root in the hearts and minds of Europeans. Bridges of understanding, of common interest, and of friendship must be thrown from people to people, from industry to industry, from guild to guild, from literature to literature. The Pan-European sense of solidarity, the European sense of patriotism, must establish itself as the crown and complement of the national sentiment.

Europe cannot wait until its governments and party leaders recognize the need for such unification; every man and every woman, convinced of the necessity of Pan-Europe, must place himself or herself at the service of that work, upon the issue of which depends the fate of a continent. . . .

. . . [A] movement and an organization are starting in every European state, whose object will be the building-up, by joint endeavors, of Pan-Europe: the Pan-European Union.

Europe's youth are called upon to lead this movement—the young in years and in heart. They refuse to be driven into the War of the Future by politicians grown incapable, by a sort of mental sclerosis, of changing their ideas. They are being joined by Europe's women, who want to prevent their children, husbands, and themselves, from falling victims to the ambition of political adventurers.

The intellectual leaders of Europe are promoting that movement, in the knowledge that nationalist policy is becoming the grave-digger of European civilization, which can recover only by the establishment of a European brotherhood.

All well-intentioned Europeans are turning away from that policy of hate and envy which has brought Europe to the verge of utter ruin; they will flock to join the Pan-European movement because it is an honest attempt to realize what has long formed the substance of their dreams.

Men and women of all classes are coming forward, ready to make moral and material sacrifices to that great end. Just as the Pan-American movement owes a great part of its success to the generous spirit of Andrew Carnegie, so European Carnegies will also fulfil their duty toward Europe.

After this advance action will come the decisive struggle between the Anti-Europeans and the Pan-Europeans for the fate of Europe—the struggle between past and future, between purblindness and understanding, between barbarism and civilization.

The emblem under which the Pan-Europeans of all states will unite, is the Solar Cross: the red cross on a golden sun, the symbols of Humanity and of Reason.

This banner of love and of the spirit will wave one day, from Poland to Portugal, above a united World Empire of Peace and Freedom!

Johan Huizinga
IN THE SHADOW OF TOMORROW

Dutch historian Johan Huizinga (1872–1945) wrote that European civilization was at the breaking point in his book *In the Shadow of Tomorrow* (1936).

We are living in a demented world. And we know it. It would not come as a surprise to anyone if tomorrow the madness gave way to a frenzy which would leave our poor Europe in a state of distracted stupor, with engines still turning and flags streaming in the breeze, but with the spirit gone.

Everywhere there are doubts as to the solidity of our social structure, vague fears of the imminent future, a feeling that our civilization is on the way to ruin. They are not merely the shapeless anxieties which beset us in the small hours of the night when the flame of life burns low. They are considered expectations founded on observation and judgment of an overwhelming multitude of facts. How to avoid the recognition that almost all things which once seemed sacred and immutable have now become unsettled, truth and humanity, justice and reason? We see forms of government no longer capable of functioning, production systems on the verge of collapse, social forces gone wild with power. The roaring engine of this tremendous time seems to be heading for a breakdown. . . .

If, then, this civilization is to be saved, if it is not to be submerged by centuries of barbarism but to secure the treasures of its inheritance on new and more stable foundations, there is indeed need for those now living fully to realise how far the decay has already progressed.

It is but a little while since the apprehension of impending doom and of a progressive deterioration of civilization has become general. For the majority of men it is the economic crisis with its direct material effects (most of us being more sensitive in body than in spirit), which has first prepared the soil for thoughts and sentiments of this nature. Obviously those whose occupation it is to deal systematically and critically with problems of human society and civilization, philosophers and sociologists, have long ago realised that all was not well with our vaunted modern civilization. They have recognised from the outset that the economic dislocation is only one aspect of a transformation-process of much wider import.

The first ten years of this century have known little if anything in the way of fears and apprehensions regarding the future of our civilization. Friction and threats, shocks and dangers, there were then as ever. But except for the revolution menace which Marxism had hung over the world, they did not appear as evils threatening mankind with ruin. . . .

Today, however, the sense of living in the midst of a violent crisis of civilization, threatening complete collapse, has spread far and wide. Oswald Spengler's *Untergang des Abendlandes*[1] has been the alarm signal for untold numbers the world over. This is not to say that all those who have read Spengler's famous work have become converts to his views. But it has jolted them out of their unreasoning faith in the providential nature of Progress and familiarised them with the idea of a decline of existing civilization and culture in our own time. Unperturbed optimism is at present only possible for those who through lack of insight fail to realise what is ailing civilization, having themselves been affected by the disease, and for those who in their social or political creed of salvation think to have the key to the hidden treasure-room of earthly weal from which to scatter on humanity the blessings of the civilization to come. . . .

How naïve the glad and confident hope of a century ago, that the advance of science and the general extension of education assured the progressive perfection of society, seems to us today! Who can still seriously believe that the translation of scientific triumphs into still more marvelous technical achievements is enough to save civilization, or that the eradication of illiteracy means the end of barbarism! Modern society, with its intensive development and mechanisation, indeed looks very different from the dream vision of Progress! . . .

Delusion and misconception flourish everywhere. More than ever men seem to be slaves to a word, a motto, to kill one another with, to silence one another in the most literal sense. The world is filled with hate and misunderstanding. There is no way of measuring how great the percentage of the deluded is and whether it is greater than formerly, but delusion and folly

---

[1]Oswald Spengler was the author of *Untergang des Abendlandes (The Decline of the West;* volume 1, 1918; volume 2, 1922), which maintained that Western civilization was dying.

have more power to harm and speak with greater authority. For the shallow, semi-educated person the beneficial restraints of respect for tradition, form and cult are gradually falling away. Worst of all is that widely prevalent indifference to truth which reaches its peak in the open advocacy of the political lie.

Barbarisation sets in when, in an old culture which once, in the course of many centuries, had raised itself to purity and clarity of thought and understanding, the vapours of the magic and fantastic rise up again from the seething brew of passions to cloud the understanding: when the *muthos* [myth] supplants the *logos* [reason].

Again and again the new creed of the heroic will to power, with its exaltation of life over understanding, is seen to embody the very tendencies which to the believer in the Spirit spell the drift towards barbarism. For the "life-philosophy" does exactly this: it extols *muthos* over *logos*. To the prophets of the life-philosophy barbarism has no deprecatory implications. The term itself loses its meaning. The new rulers desire nothing else. . . .

. . . Against all that seems to presage decline and ruin, contemporary humanity, except for a few fatalists, for once unanimously [asserts] the energetic declaration . . . we *will* not perish. This world of ours is, with all its misery, too fine to allow it to sink into a night of human degradation and blindness of the spirit. We no longer count with an early end of all time. This heirloom of centuries called Western civilization has been entrusted to us to pass it on to coming generations, preserved, safeguarded, if possible enriched and improved, if it must be, impoverished, but at any rate as pure as it is in our power to keep it.

Arthur Koestler
"I WAS RIPE TO BE CONVERTED"

The economic misery of the Depression and the rise of fascist barbarism led many intellectuals to find a new hope, even a secular faith, in communism. They praised the Soviet Union for supplanting capitalist greed with socialist cooperation, for recognizing the dignity of work, for replacing a haphazard economic system marred by repeated depressions with one based on planned production, and for providing employment for everyone when joblessness was endemic in capitalist lands. Seduced by Soviet propaganda and desperate for an alternative to crisis-ridden liberal society, these intellectuals saw the Soviet Union as a champion of peace and social justice. To these intellectuals, it seemed that in the Soviet Union a vigorous and healthy civilization was emerging and that only communism could stem the tide of fascism. For many, however, the attraction was short-lived. Sickened by Stalin's purges and terror, the denial of individual freedom, and suppression of truth, they came to view the Soviet Union as another totalitarian state and communism as another "god that failed."

One such intellectual was Arthur Koestler (see also pages 133–134 and 177–178). Born in Budapest of Jewish ancestry and educated in Vienna, Koestler worked as a correspondent for a leading Berlin newspaper chain. He joined the Communist party at the very end of 1931 because he "lived in a disintegrating society thirsting for faith," was sensitized by the Depression, and saw communism as the "only force capable of resisting the inrush of the primitive [Nazi] horde." In 1938, he broke with the Party in response to Stalin's liquidations.

In the following passage, written in 1949, Koestler recalled the attraction communism had held for him.

A faith is not acquired by reasoning. One does not fall in love with a woman, or enter the womb of a church, as a result of logical persuasion. Reason may defend an act of faith—but only after the act has been committed, and the man committed to the act. Persuasion may play a part in a man's conversion; but only the part of bringing to its full and conscious climax a process which has been maturing in regions where no persuasion can penetrate. A faith is not acquired; it grows like a tree. Its crown points to the sky; its roots grow downward into the past and are nourished by the dark sap of the ancestral humus. . . .

I became converted because I was ripe for it and lived in a disintegrating society thirsting for faith. But the day when I was given my Party card was merely the climax of a development which had started long before I had read about the drowned pigs or heard the names of Marx and Lenin. Its roots reach back into childhood; and though each of us, comrades of the Pink Decade, had individual roots with different twists in them, we are products of, by and large, the same generation and cultural climate. It is this unity underlying diversity which makes me hope that my story is worth telling.

I was born in 1905 in Budapest; we lived there till 1919, when we moved to Vienna. Until the First World War we were comfortably off, a typical Continental middle-middle-class family: my father was the Hungarian representative of some old-established British and German textile manufacturers. In September, 1914, this form of existence, like so many others, came to an abrupt end; my father never found his feet again. He embarked on a number of ventures which became the more fantastic the more he lost self-confidence in a changed world. He opened a factory for radioactive soap; he backed several crank-inventions (everlasting electric bulbs, self-heating bed bricks and the like); and finally lost the remains of his capital in the Austrian inflation of the early 'twenties. I left home at twenty-one, and from that day became the only financial support of my parents.

At the age of nine, when our middle-class idyl collapsed, I had suddenly become conscious of the economic Facts of Life. As an only child, I continued to be pampered by my parents; but, well aware of the family crisis, and torn by pity for my father, who was of a generous and somewhat childlike disposition, I suffered a pang of guilt whenever they bought me books or toys. This continued later on, when every suit I bought for myself meant so much less to send home. Simultaneously, I developed a strong dislike of the obviously rich; not because they could afford to buy things (envy plays a much smaller part in social conflict than is generally assumed) but because they were able to do so without a guilty conscience. Thus I projected a personal predicament onto the structure of society at large.

It was certainly a tortuous way of acquiring a social conscience. But precisely because of the intimate nature of the conflict, the faith which grew out of it became an equally intimate part of myself. It did not, for some years, crystallize into a political creed; at first it took the form of a mawkishly sentimental attitude. Every contact with people poorer than myself was unbearable—the boy at school who had no gloves and red chilblains [inflamed swellings produced by exposure to cold] on his fingers, the former traveling salesman of my father's reduced to [begging] occasional meals—all of them were additions to the load of guilt on my back. The analyst would have no difficulty in showing that the roots of this guilt-complex go deeper than the crisis in our household budget; but if he were to dig even deeper, piercing through the individual layers of the case, he would strike the archetypal pattern which has produced millions of particular variations on the same theme—"Woe, for they chant to the sound of harps and anoint themselves, but are not grieved for the affliction of the people."

Thus sensitized by a personal conflict, I was ripe for the shock of learning that wheat was burned, fruit artificially spoiled and pigs were drowned in the depression years to keep prices up and enable fat capitalists to chant to the sound of harps, while Europe trembled under the torn boots of hunger-marchers and my father hid his frayed cuffs under the table. The frayed cuffs and drowned pigs blended into one emotional explosion, as the fuse of the archetype was touched off. We sang the "Internationale" [the communists' anthem], but the words might as well have been the older ones: "Woe to the shepherds who feed themselves, but feed not their flocks."

In other respects, too, the story is more typical than it seems. A considerable proportion of the middle classes in central Europe was, like ourselves, ruined by the inflation of the 'twenties. It was the beginning of Europe's decline. This disintegration of the middle strata of society started the fatal process of polarization which continues to this day. The pauperized bourgeois became rebels of the Right or Left; Schickelgrüber [Hitler] and Djugashwili [Stalin] shared about equally the benefits of the social migration. Those who refused to admit that they had become déclassé, who clung to the empty shell of gentility, joined the Nazis and found comfort in blaming their fate on Versailles and the Jews. Many did not even have that consolation; they lived on pointlessly, like a great black swarm of tired winterflies crawling over the dim windows of Europe, members of a class displaced by history.

The other half turned Left, thus confirming the prophecy of the "Communist Manifesto":

> Entire sections of the ruling classes are . . . precipitated into the proletariat, or are at least threatened in their conditions of existence. They . . . supply the proletariat with fresh elements of enlightenment and progress. . . .

I was ripe to be converted, as a result of my personal case-history; thousands of other members of the intelligentsia and the middle classes of my generation were ripe for it, by virtue of other personal case-histories; but, however much these differed from case to case, they had a common denominator: the rapid disintegration of moral values, of the pre-1914 pattern of life in postwar Europe, and the simultaneous lure of the new revelation which had come from the East.

I joined the Party (which to this day remains "the" Party for all of us who once belonged to it) in 1931. . . .

I lived at that time in Berlin. For the last five years, I had been working for the Ullstein chain of newspapers—first as a foreign correspondent in Palestine and the Middle East, then in Paris. Finally, in 1930, I joined the editorial staff in the Berlin "House." . . .

. . . With one-third of its wage-earners unemployed, Germany lived in a state of latent civil war, and if one wasn't prepared to be swept along as a passive victim by the approaching hurricane it became imperative to take sides. . . . The Communists, with the mighty Soviet Union behind them, seemed the only force capable of resisting the onrush of the primitive horde with its swastika totem. I began for the first time to read Marx, Engels and Lenin in earnest. By the time I had finished with *Feuerbach* and *State and Revolution,* something had clicked in my brain which shook me like a mental explosion. To say that one had "seen the light" is a poor description of the mental rapture which only the convert knows (regardless of what faith he has been converted to). The new light seems to pour from all directions across the skull; the whole universe falls into pattern like the stray pieces of a jigsaw puzzle assembled by magic at one stroke. There is now an answer to every question, doubts and conflicts are a matter of the tortured past—a past already remote, when one had lived in dismal ignorance in the tasteless, colorless world of those who *don't know.* Nothing henceforth can disturb the convert's inner peace and serenity—except the occasional fear of losing faith again, losing thereby what alone makes life worth living, and falling back into the outer darkness, where there is wailing and gnashing of teeth.

Nicolas Berdyaev
MODERN IDEOLOGIES AT VARIANCE WITH CHRISTIANITY

To Nicolas Berdyaev, a Russian Christian philosopher who fled the Soviet Union, communism and nazism were modern forms of idolatry in opposition to the core values of Christianity. Nationalism, he said, "dehumanizes ethics" and provokes hatred among peoples; Nazi racism, which demonizes Jews because of their genes, is "unworthy of a Christian." Only by a return to Christian piety, maintained Berdyaev, can we overcome the "collective demoniac possession" that is destroying European civilization. By Christian piety, he meant an active struggle for human dignity and social justice. Berdyaev expressed these views in *The Fate of Man in the Modern World* (1935), which is excerpted below.

Once the veil of civilization was torn aside by the war, the prime realities were revealed in all their nakedness. The faith in mankind which had existed for nineteen hundred years was finally shattered. Faith in God had been shaken earlier, and loss of one was followed by loss of the other. The humanist myth about man was exploded, and the abyss yawned at the feet of mankind. The wolf-like life of capitalist society was not able to encourage and support the faith in man. Man himself is left out of the picture. Economics, which should have aided man, instead of being for his service, is discovered to be that for which man exists: the non-human economic process. The war merely put into plain words what was already implicit in capitalism, that man is of no account, that he has not only ceased to be the supreme value, but value of any sort. And almost all the movements launched against capitalism since the war have accepted the same attitude toward man which characterized both capitalism and the war itself. This is the most characteristic process of our times. Man appears unable to withstand this process, to defend his own value, to find support within himself, and he grasps, as at a life-belt, at the collective, communist or national and racial, at the State as the Absolute here on earth, or at organized and technicalized forms of living. Man has lost his worth; it has been torn to tatters. Coming out of the war, there have appeared in the arena of history a series of human collectives, masses of men who have dropped out of the organized order and harmony of life, lost the religious sanctions for their lives and now demand obligatory organization as the sole means of avoiding final chaos and degeneration. . . .

. . . [W]e live in a very authoritarian epoch. The urge toward an authoritarian form of life is felt throughout the whole world: the liberal element seems completely discredited. . . .

The war was the catastrophic moment which disclosed that chaos moves beneath the false civilization of capitalism. The war was chaos, organized by forced labour. For chaos may wear an appearance of complete external organization. And since the war, man is not merely willing, but actively desires to live in the obligatorily-organized chaos which expresses itself in the authoritarian form of life. . . .

. . . The masses are easily subject to suggestion and often enter a state of collective demoniac possession. They may be possessed only by ideas which permit of a simple and elemental symbolism, a mode quite characteristic of our time. The search for leaders who can lead the masses, offer alleviation for woes, solve all problems, means simply that all the classic authorities have fallen, monarchy and democracy together, and that they must be replaced by new authorities, born of the collective "possession" of the mass. The leader must provide "bread and the theatre." . . .

. . . We are witnessing the process of dehumanization in all phases of culture and of social life. Above all, moral consciousness is being dehumanized. Man has ceased to be the supreme value: he has ceased to have any value at all. The youth of the whole world, communist, fascist, national-socialist or those simply carried away by technics . . . this youth is not only anti-humanistic in its attitudes, but often anti-human. . . .

. . . A bestial cruelty toward man is characteristic of our age, and this is more astonishing since it is displayed at the very peak of human refinement, where modern conceptions of sympathy, it would seem, have made impossible the old, barbaric forms of cruelty. Bestialism is something quite different from the old, natural, healthy barbarism; it is barbarism within a refined civilization. Here the atavistic, barbaric instincts are filtered through the prism of civilization, and hence they have a pathological character. . . . The bestialism of our time is a continuation of the war, it has poisoned mankind with the blood of war. The morals of wartime have become those of "peaceful" life, which is actually the continuation of war, a war of all against all. According to this morality, everything is permissible: man may be used in any way desired for the attainment of inhuman or anti-human aims. Bestialism is a denial of the value of the human person, of every human personality; it is a denial of all sympathy with the fate of any man. The new humanism is closing: this is inescapable.

We are entering an inhuman world, a world of inhumanness, inhuman not merely in fact, but in principle as well. Inhumanity has begun to be presented as something noble, surrounded with an aureole of heroism. Over against man there rises a class or a race, a deified collective or state. Modern nationalism bears marks of bestial inhumanity. No longer is every man held to be a man, a value, the image and likeness of God. For often even Christianity is interpreted inhumanly. The "Aryan paragraph" offered to German Christians is the project for a new form of inhumanity in Christianity. . . .

. . . The new world which is taking form is moved by other values than the value of man or of human personality, or the value of truth: it is moved by such values as power, technics, race-purity, nationality, the state, the class, the collective. The will to justice is overcome by the will to power. . . .

. . . National passion is tearing the world and threatening the destruction of European culture. This is one more proof of the strength of atavism in human society, of how much stronger than the conscious is the subconscious, of how superficial has been the humanizing process of past centuries. . . . [M]odern Nationalism means the dehumanization and bestialization of human societies. It is a reversion from the category of culture and history to that of zoology. . . .

. . . The results of the Christian-humanistic process of unifying humanity seem to be disappearing. We are witnessing the paganization of Christian society. Nationalism is polytheism: it is incompatible with monotheism.

This process of paganization takes shocking forms in Germany, which wishes no longer to be a Christian nation, has exchanged the swastika for the cross and demands of Christians that they should renounce the very fundamentals of the Christian revelation and the Christian faith, and cast aside the moral teaching of the Gospels. . . .

Nationalism turns nationality into a supreme and absolute value to which all life is subordinated. This is idolatry. The nation replaces God. Thus Nationalism cannot but come into conflict with Christian universalism, with the Christian revelation that there is neither Greek nor Jew, and that every man has absolute value. Nationalism uses everything as its own instrument, as an instrument of national power and prosperity. . . .

. . . Nationalism has no Christian roots and it is always in conflict with Christianity. . . .

. . . Nationalism involves not only love of one's own, but hatred of other nations, and hatred is usually a stronger motive than love.

Nationalism preaches either seclusion, isolation, blindness to other nations and culture, self-satisfaction and particularism, or else expansion at the expense of others, conquest, subjection, imperialism. And in both cases it denies Christian conscience, contraverts the principle and the habits of the brotherhood of man. Nationalism is in complete contradiction to a personal ethic; it denies the supreme value of human personality. Modern Nationalism dehumanizes ethics, it demands of man that he renounce humanity. It is all one and the same process, in Communism as in Nationalism. Man's inner world is completely at the mercy of collectivism, national or social. . . .

[R]acialism . . . has no basis at all in Christianity. The mere consideration of the "Aryan paragraph" is unworthy of a Christian, although it is now demanded of Christians in Germany. Racialist anti-Semitism inevitably leads to anti-Christianity, as we see in Germany today. That Germano-Aryan Christianity now being promoted is a denial of the Gospels and of Christ Himself. The ancient religious conflict between Christianity and Judaism, a real conflict by the way, has taken such a turn in our difficult and uncertain times, that militant anti-Judaism turns out to be anti-Christianity. Truly Christian anti-Judaism is directed, not against the Bible or the Old Testament, but against the Talmudic-rabbinic Judaism which developed after the Jews' refusal to accept Christ. But when religious anti-Judaism becomes racialist anti-Semitism, it inevitably turns into anti-Christianity, for the human origins of Christianity are Hebrew. . . . [I]t is impossible, it is forbidden, for a true Christian to be a racialist and to hate the Jews. . . .

. . . According to the race theory there is no hope of salvation, whatever: if you were born a Jew or a negro, no change of consciousness or belief or conviction can save you, you are doomed. A Jew may become a Christian: that does him no good. Even if he becomes a national-socialist, he cannot be saved.

WORLD WAR II

HEINRICH HIMMLER, head of the SS, inspects a POW camp. More than 3 million Russians perished in prisoner of war camps during WWII, most of them deliberate victims of starvation. Unlike the death camps which were administered by the SS, POW camps were run by the Wehrmacht, the regular army. *(Bettmann Corbis)*

From the early days of his political career, Hitler dreamed of forging a vast German empire in central and eastern Europe. He believed that only by waging a war of conquest against Russia could the German nation gain the living space and security it required and, as a superior race, deserved. War was an essential component of National Socialist ideology; it also accorded with Hitler's temperament. For the former corporal from the trenches, the Great War had never ended. Hitler aspired to political power because he wanted to mobilize the material and human resources of the German nation for war and conquest. Whereas historians may debate the question of responsibility for World War I, few would disagree with French historian Pierre Renouvin that World War II was Hitler's war:

> It appears to be an almost incontrovertible fact that the Second World War was brought on by the actions of the Hitler government, that these actions were the expression of a policy laid down well in advance in *Mein Kampf,* and that this war could have been averted up until the last moment if the German government had so wished.

Western statesmen had sufficient warning that Hitler was a threat to peace and the essential values of Western civilization, but they failed to rally their people and take a stand until Germany had greatly increased its capacity to wage aggressive war.

World War II was the most destructive war in history. Estimates of the number of dead range as high as 50 million, including 25 million Russians, who sacrificed more than the other participants in both population and material resources. The consciousness of Europe, already profoundly damaged by World War I, was again grievously wounded. Nazi racial theories showed that even in an age of sophisticated science the mind remains attracted to irrational beliefs and mythical imagery. Nazi atrocities proved that people will torture and kill with religious zeal and machinelike indifference. The Nazi assault on reason and freedom demonstrated anew the precariousness of Western civilization. This assault would forever cast doubt on the Enlightenment conception of human goodness, secular rationality, and the progress of civilization through advances in science and technology.

1 Prescient Observers of Nazi Germany

After Hitler took power in January 1933, many Western officials hoped that his radicalism would be tamed by the responsibilities of leadership. Moreover, these officials either never read *Mein Kampf* or did not take it seriously. But there were also astute observers who, within months after Hitler became chancellor,

warned that Nazi Germany constituted a threat to the European peace. They maintained that Hitler, who believed that a Darwinian struggle for existence governed relations between nations and races, would eventually launch a war in order to realize the territorial aims of Nazi ideology.

Horace Rumbold "PACIFISM IS THE DEADLIEST OF SINS"

On April 26, 1933, Horace Rumbold (1869–1941), Britain's ambassador to Germany, sent the following dispatch to London. It is clear that Rumbold had read and correctly discerned Hitler's goals.

The outlook for Europe is far from peaceful if the speeches of Nazi leaders, especially of the Chancellor, are borne in mind. The Chancellor's account of his political career in *Mein Kampf* contains not only the principles which have guided him during the last fourteen years, but explains how he arrived at these fundamental principles. Stripped of the verbiage in which he has clothed it, Hitler's thesis is extremely simple. He starts with the assertions that man is a fighting animal, therefore the nation is, he concludes, a fighting unit, being a community of fighters. Any living organism which ceases to fight for its existence is, he asserts, doomed to extinction. A country or a race which ceases to fight is equally doomed. The fighting capacity of a race depends on its purity. Hence the necessity for ridding it of foreign impurities. The Jewish race, owing to its universality, is of necessity pacifist and internationalist. Pacifism is the deadliest sin, for pacifism means the surrender of the race in the fight for existence. The first duty of every country is, therefore, to nationalise the masses; intelligence is of secondary importance in the case of the individual; will and determination are of higher importance. The individual who is born to command is more valuable than countless thousands of subordinate natures. Only brute force can ensure the survival of the race. Hence the necessity for military forms. The race must fight; a race that rests must rust and perish. The German race, had it been united in time, would now be master of the globe today. The new Reich must gather within its fold all the scattered German elements in Europe. A race which has suffered defeat can be rescued by restoring its self-confidence. Above all things, the army must be taught to believe in its own invincibility. To restore the German nation again, it is only necessary to convince the people that the recovery of freedom by force of arms is a possibility.

Hitler describes at great length in his turgid style the task which the new Germany must therefore set itself. Intellectualism is undesirable. The ultimate aim of education is to produce a German who can be converted with the minimum of training into a soldier. The idea that there is something reprehensible in chauvinism is entirely mistaken. Indeed, the greatest upheavals in history would have been unthinkable had it not been for the driving force of fanatical and hysterical passions. Nothing could have been effected by the *bourgeois* virtues of peace and order. The world is now moving towards such an upheaval, and the new (German) State must see to it that the race is ready for the last and greatest decisions on this earth (p. 475, 17th edition of *Mein Kampf*). Again and again he proclaims that fanatical conviction and uncompromising resolution are indispensable qualities in a leader.

The climax of education is military service (p. 476). A man may be a living lexicon, but unless he is a soldier he will fail in the great crises of life. . . . An army is indispensable to ensure the maintenance and expansion of the race. The recovery of lost provinces has never been effected by protest and without the use of force. To forge the necessary weapons is the task of the internal political leaders of the people.

. . . Germany's lost provinces cannot be gained by solemn appeals to Heaven or by pious hopes in the League of Nations, but only by force of arms (p. 708). Germany must not repeat the mistake of fighting all her enemies at once. She must single out the most dangerous in turn and attack him with all her forces. . . . It is the business of the Government to implant in the people feelings of manly courage and passionate hatred. The world will only cease to be anti-German when Germany recovers equality of rights and resumes her place in the sun. . . .

Still more disquieting is the fact that though Germany remains nominally a member of the League of Nations the official policy of the country so far as it has been translated into action or expounded by members of the Government is fundamentally hostile to the principles on which the League is founded. Not only is it a crime to preach pacificism or condemn militarism but it is equally objectionable to preach international understanding, and while politicians and writers who have been guilty of the one have actually been arrested and incarcerated, those guilty of the other have at any rate been removed from public life and of course from official employment. . . .

[Germany has] to rearm on land, and, as Herr Hitler explains in his memoirs, they have to lull their adversaries into such a state of coma that they will allow themselves to be engaged one by one. It may seem astonishing that the Chancellor should express himself so frankly, but it must be noted that his book was written in 1925, when his prospects of reaching power were so remote that he could afford to be candid. He would probably be glad to suppress every copy extant today. Since he assumed office, Herr Hitler has been as cautious and discreet as he was formerly blunt and frank. He declares that he is anxious that peace should be maintained for a ten-year period. What he probably means can be more accurately expressed by the [following] formula: Germany needs peace until she has recovered such strength that no country can challenge her without serious and irksome preparations. I fear that it would be misleading to base any hopes on a return to sanity or a serious modification of the views of the Chancellor and his entourage.

George S. Messersmith
"THE NAZIS WERE AFTER . . . UNLIMITED TERRITORIAL EXPANSION"

Two months after Rumbold's dispatch, George S. Messersmith, American consul general at Berlin, also reported on the "dangerous situation" developing in Germany. Appointed Minister to Austria in 1934, he continued to warn that the Nazis were serious about expanding Germany's territory.

CONSUL GENERAL MESSERSMITH'S REPORT FROM BERLIN

The United States Consul General at Berlin, George S. Messersmith, who had been at that post since 1930, reported frequently to the Department of State during this period on the menace inherent in the Nazi regime. Mr. Messersmith expressed the view, in a letter of June 26, 1933 to Under Secretary of State Phillips, that the United States must be exceedingly careful in its dealings with Germany as long as the existing Government was in power, as that Government had no spokesmen who could really be depended upon and those who held the highest positions were "capable of actions which really outlaw them from ordinary intercourse". He reported that some of the men who were running the German Government were "psychopathic cases"; that others were in a state of exaltation and in a frame of mind that knew no reason; and that those men in the party and in responsible positions who were really worthwhile were powerless because they had to follow the orders of superiors who were suffering from the "abnormal psychology" prevailing in Germany. "There is a real revolution here and a dangerous situation," he said.

Consul General Messersmith reported further that a martial spirit was being developed in Germany; that everywhere people were seen drilling, including children from the age of five or six to persons well into middle age; that a psychology was being developed that the whole world was against Germany, which was defenseless before the world; that people were being trained against gas and airplane attacks; and that the idea of war from neighboring countries was constantly harped upon. He emphasized that Germany was headed in directions which could only carry ruin to it and create a situation "dangerous to world peace." He said we must recognize that while Germany at that time wanted peace, it was by no means a peaceful country or one looking forward to a long period of peace; that the German Government and its adherents desired peace ardently for the time being because they needed peace to carry through the changes in Germany which they wanted to bring about. What they wanted to do was to make Germany "the most capable instrument of war that there has ever existed."

Consul General Messersmith reported from Berlin five months later, in a letter of November 23, 1933 to Under Secretary Phillips, that the military spirit in Germany was constantly growing and that innumerable measures were being taken to develop the German people into a hardy, sturdy race which would "be able to meet all comers." He said that the leaders of Germany had no desire for peace unless it was a peace in complete compliance with German ambitions; that Hitler and his associates really wanted peace for the moment, but only to have a chance to prepare for the use of force if it were found essential; and that they were preparing their way so carefully that the German people would be with them when they wanted to use force and when they felt that they had the "necessary means to carry through their objects". . . .

Mr. Messersmith, who had been appointed Minister to Austria in 1934, continued to send to the Department of State reports on the situation in Germany. In February 1935 he reported that the Nazis had their eyes on Memel, Alsace-Lorraine, and the eastern frontier; that they nourished just as strongly the hope to get the Ukraine for the surplus German population; that Austria was a definite objective; and that absorption or hegemony over the whole of southeastern Europe was a definite policy. A few weeks later he reported a conversation with William E. Dodd, United States Ambassador to Germany, in which they had agreed that no faith whatsoever could be placed in the Nazi regime and its promises, that what the Nazis were after was "unlimited territorial expansion," and that there was probably in existence a German-Japanese understanding, if not an alliance.

Douglas Miller
"THE NAZIS WERE DETERMINED TO SECURE MORE POWER AND MORE TERRITORY IN EUROPE"

In April 1934, Douglas Miller, acting commercial attaché, reported to Consul General Messersmith his views of the new Germany.

ACTING COMMERCIAL ATTACHÉ MILLER'S REPORT ON THE NAZIS

Consul General Messersmith transmitted to the Department of State on April 21, 1934 a report by Acting Commercial Attaché Douglas Miller on the situation in Germany. The Consul General noted that the conclusions of the Attaché had been arrived at independently and that they accorded entirely with his own appraisal of the situation.

Mr. Miller stated that the fundamental purpose of the Nazis "is to secure a greater share of the world's future for the Germans, the expansion of German territory and growth of the German race until it constitutes the largest and most powerful nation in the world, and ultimately, according to some Nazi leaders, until it dominates the entire globe". He expressed the view that the German people were suffering from a traditional inferiority complex, smarting from their defeat in the war and the indignities of the post-war period, disillusioned in their hopes of a speedy return to prosperity along traditional lines, and inflamed by irresponsible demagogic slogans and flattered by the statement that their German racial inheritance gave them inherent superior rights over other peoples. As a result the German people, who were "politically inept and unusually docile", had to a large measure adopted the Nazi point of view for the time being.

The most important objective of the Nazis, according to Mr. Miller's analysis, was to retain absolute control of the German people. This control, he said, had been gained by making irresponsible and extravagant promises; by the studied use of the press, the radio, public meetings, parades, flags, uniforms; and finally by the use of force. He said that the Nazis were at heart belligerent and aggressive; that although they desired a period of peace for several years in which to rearm and discipline their people, the more completely their experiments succeeded "the more certain is a large-scale war in Europe some day".

Mr. Miller warned that we must not place too much reliance on Nazi public statements designed for consumption abroad, which breathed the spirit of good-will and peace and asserted the intention of the Government to promote the welfare of the German people and good relations with their neighbors. The real emotional drive behind the Nazi program, he said, was not so much love of their own country as dislike of other countries. The Nazis would never be content in merely promoting the welfare of the German people; they desired to be feared and envied by foreigners and "to wipe out the memory of 1918 by inflicting humiliations in particular upon the French, the Poles, the Czechs and anybody else they can get their hands on". Hitler and the other Nazi leaders had capitalized on the wounded inferiority complex of the German people and had magnified their own bitter feelings "into a cult of dislike against the foreign world which is past the bounds of ordinary good sense and reason". Mr. Miller emphasized that the Nazis were building a tremendous military machine, physically very poorly armed, but morally aggressive and belligerent. The control of this machine was in the hands of "narrow, ignorant and unscrupulous adventurers who have been slightly touched with madness from brooding over Germany's real or imagined wrongs". Mr. Miller stated that the Nazis were determined to secure more power and more territory in Europe; that they would certainly use force if these were not given to them by peaceful means.

2 Fascist Aggression: Italy's Invasion of Ethiopia

Benito Mussolini (1883–1945) sought to create an Italian empire, partly to take people's minds off the lackluster performance of the domestic economy and to restore their faith in the fascist system. Moreover, an expansionist, militaristic nationalism was an essential component of his fascist credo. And what better object of his aggression than Ethiopia? It lay between two Italian colonies, Eritrea on the Red Sea and Italian Somaliland on the Indian Ocean; it also had been the scene of a disastrous Italian defeat in 1896, when the newly formed state had tried joining the club of imperialist powers. Now, artificially provoked border clashes with Italian soldiers in Eritrea set the stage for a full-scale invasion, which began in the autumn of 1935.

Ethiopia's protest caused the League of Nations to denounce the move and vote sanctions against Italy. But Italy continued to receive oil from American suppliers. Believing that the conquest of Ethiopia did not affect their vital interests and hoping to keep the Italians friendly in the event of a clash with Germany, neither Britain nor France sought to restrain Italy, despite its act of aggression against another member of the League. Ignoring the international body, Mussolini completed the takeover of the country, which was annexed to Italy, and had himself crowned emperor of Ethiopia. His successful defiance of the League weakened it as an instrument for keeping the peace; moreover, the campaign launched against a foreign land marked the first in a series of fascist acts of aggression.

Benito Mussolini
"A SOLEMN HOUR"

On October 2, 1935, Mussolini, speaking from the balcony of the Palazzo Venezia in Rome, addressed a receptive crowd about the Italian invasion of Ethiopia, which had just begun. His speech, delivered in his typically flamboyant style, is reproduced below.

"Blackshirts[1] of the revolution, men and women of all Italy, Italians scattered throughout the world, across the mountains and across the oceans, listen.

"A solemn hour is about to strike in the history of the Fatherland. Twenty million Italians are this moment gathered in the squares throughout the whole of Italy. It is the most gigantic demonstration which the history of mankind records. Twenty millions, a single heart, a single will, a single decision. This manifestation is to signify that the identity between Italy and Fascism is perfect, absolute, and unchangeable. Only brains weakened by puerile illusions or benumbed in a crass ignorance can think the contrary, because they do not know what this Fascist Italy of 1935 is. For many months the wheel of destiny, under the impulse of our calm determination, has been making towards the goal. In these last hours the rhythm has become more speedy and cannot now be arrested.

[1]The Blackshirts, so called because of their distinctive apparel, were the members of the paramilitary formation of the Italian Fascist party; roaming the streets in gangs, they beat up on alleged enemies of the nation, especially socialists and communists.

"Not only is an army marching towards its objectives, but 40,000,000 Italians are marching in unison with this army, all united because there is an attempt to commit against them the blackest of all injustices, to rob them of a place in the sun. When in 1915 Italy united its lot with those of the Allies, how many shouts of admiration and how many promises! But after the common victory, to which Italy had brought the supreme contribution of 670,000 dead, 400,000 disabled, 1,000,000 wounded, when it came to sitting around the table of the mean peace to us were left only the crumbs from the sumptuous colonial booty of others. During 20 years we have been patient while there tightened round us ever more rigidly the ring which wanted to suffocate our overflowing vitality. With Ethiopia we have been patient for 40 years. Now, enough! (Fierce shouts of assent from the crowd.)

"At the League of Nations, instead of recognizing the just rights of Italy, they dared to speak of sanctions. Now, until there is a proof to the contrary, I refuse to believe that the true people of France can associate themselves with sanctions against Italy. The dead of Bligny,[2] who perished in a heroic attack which drew admiration even from the enemy, would turn in their graves. Until there is a proof to the contrary I refuse to believe that the true people of Great Britain want to spill blood and push Europe on the road to catastrophe in order to defend an African country universally stamped as a barbarous country and unworthy of taking its place with the civilized peoples.

"At the same time, we must not pretend not to know the eventualities of tomorrow. To sanctions of an economic character we will reply with our discipline, with our sobriety, and with our spirit of sacrifice. To sanctions of a military character we will reply with orders of a military character. To acts of war we will reply with acts of war.

"Let nobody delude himself that he can deflect us. A people which is proud of its name and of its future cannot adopt a different attitude. But let it be said once again in the most categorical manner, as a sacred pledge which I take at this moment before all the Italians who are listening to me, that we will do everything possible to avoid a colonial conflict assuming the character and bearing of a European conflict. This may be the wish of those who see in a new war revenge for fallen temples, but it cannot be our wish.

"Never more than in this historic epoch has the Italian people revealed the force of its spirit and the power of its character. And it is against this people to which humanity owes the greatest of its conquests, it is against this people of heroes, poets, artists, navigators, and administrators, that they dare to speak of sanctions.

"Italy, proletarian and fascist Italy, . . . to your feet! To your feet! (Thunderous cheers.)

"Let the cry of your firm and unshakable decision reach the sky and be a comfort to the soldiers who are about to fight in Africa, and let this be a spur to them and a warning to enemies in all parts of the world, a cry of justice and a cry of victory." (Deafening cheers.)

[2]Bligny is the name of a village in western France where an Allied assault on the Germans occurred in June 1918, during one of the last campaigns of World War I.

Haile Selassie
"IT IS INTERNATIONAL MORALITY THAT IS AT STAKE"

After Ethiopia had fallen under Italian control, Emperor Haile Selassie (1892–1975) addressed the Assembly of the League of Nations in Geneva. He criticized

the barbaric methods deployed against his countrymen and warned the League that failure to defend the "small peoples" would only provoke other aggressors. Excerpts from his speech, which he delivered on June 30, 1936, appear below.

I, Haile Selassie I, Emperor of Ethiopia, am here to-day to claim that justice which is due to my people and the assistance promised to it eight months ago when 50 nations asserted that an aggression had been committed. None other than the Emperor can address the appeal of the Ethiopian people to these 50 nations.

It is my duty to inform the Governments assembled in Geneva of the deadly peril which threatens them by describing to them the fate which has been suffered by Ethiopia. It is not only upon warriors that the Italian Government has made war, it has above all attacked populations far removed from hostilities. Towards the end of 1935 Italian aircraft hurled upon my armies bombs of tear gas. Their effects were but slight. The soldiers learned to scatter. The Italian aircraft then resorted to mustard gas. Barrels of liquid were hurled upon armed groups, but this means also was not effective. The liquid affected only a few soldiers, and barrels upon the ground were themselves a warning to troops and to the population of the danger.

It was at the time when the operations for the encircling of Makale were taking place that the Italian Command followed the procedure which it is now my duty to denounce to the world. Special sprayers were installed on aircraft so that they could vaporize over vast areas of territory a fine death-dealing rain. Groups of nine, 15, and 18 aircraft followed one another so that the fog issuing from them formed a continuous sheet. It was thus that as from the end of January, 1936, soldiers, women, children, cattle, rivers, lakes, and pastures were drenched continually with this deadly rain.

In order to kill off systematically all living creatures, in order more thoroughly to poison waters and pastures, the Italian Command made its aircraft pass over and over again. That was its chief method of warfare. The very refinement of barbarism consisted of carrying ravage and terror into the most densely populated parts of the territory. The object was to scatter fear and death over a great part of the Ethiopian territory. These fearful tactics succeeded. Men and animals succumbed. The deadly rain that fell from the aircraft made all those whom it touched fly, shrieking with pain.

The emperor then recounted events leading up to the invasion of his country, in particular, acts of provocation by which the Italian government fomented revolt among armed rebels against his rule.

The Italian provocation was obvious and he had not hesitated to appeal to the League of Nations. Unhappily for Ethiopia this was the time when a certain Government considered that the European situation made it imperative at all costs to obtain the friendship of Italy. The price paid was the abandonment of Ethiopian independence to the greed of the Italian Government. This secret agreement, contrary to the obligations of the Covenant, had exerted a great influence over the course of events. . . .

I ask the 52 nations not to forget to-day the policy upon which they embarked eight months ago and on the face of which I directed the resistance of my people against the aggressor whom they had denounced to the world. . . . In December, 1935, the League Council made it quite clear that its feelings were in harmony with hundreds of millions of people who in all parts of the world had protested against the proposal to dismember Ethiopia. It was constantly repeated that there was not merely a conflict between the Italian Government and Ethiopia but also a conflict between the Italian Government and the League of Nations, and that is why I personally refused all proposals to my personal advantage made to me by the Italian Government if only I would betray my people and the Covenant of the League of Nations. I was defending the cause of all small peoples who are threatened with aggression.

The Ethiopian Government never expected other Governments to shed their soldiers' blood to defend the Covenant when their own immediate personal interests were not at stake. Ethiopian warriors asked only for means to defend themselves. On many occasions I have asked for financial assistance for the purchase of arms. That assistance has been constantly refused me. . . .

I assert that the problem submitted to the Assembly to-day is a much wider one than the removal of sanctions. It is not merely a question of the settlement of Italian aggression. It is collective. It is the very existence of the League of Nations. It is the confidence that each State is to place in international treaties, it is the value of promises made to small States that their integrity and their independence shall be respected and ensured. It is the principle of the equality of States on the one hand or, otherwise, the application laid down upon small Powers to accept the bonds of vassalship. In a word, it is international morality that is at stake. Apart from the Kingdom of the Lord there is not on this earth any nation that is superior to any other.

God and history will remember your judgment. It is my painful duty to note that the initiative has to-day been taken with a view to raising sanctions. Does this initiative mean in practice the abandonment of Ethiopia to its aggressor? . . . Placed by the aggressor face to face with the accomplished fact, are States going to set up a terrible precedent of bowing before force? Representatives of the world, I have come to Geneva to discharge in your midst the most painful of the duties of a Head of a State. What reply shall I have to take back to my people?

3 Remilitarization of the Rhineland

In the Locarno Pact (1925), Germany, France, and Belgium agreed not to change their existing borders, which meant, in effect, that Germany had accepted both the return of Alsace and Lorraine to France and the demilitarization of the Rhineland—two provisions of the Treaty of Versailles. On March 7, 1936, Hitler marched troops into the Rhineland, violating both the Versailles Treaty and the Locarno Pact. German generals had cautioned Hitler that such a move would provoke a French invasion of Germany and re-occupation of the Rhineland, which the German army still in the first stages of rearmament could not repulse. But Hitler gambled that France and Britain, lacking the will to fight, would take no action. He had assessed the Anglo-French mood correctly. British statesmen in particular championed a policy of appeasement: giving in to Hitler in the hope that Europe would not be dragged through another world war.

William L. Shirer
BERLIN DIARY

Immediately after the German army occupied the demilitarized zone, Hitler addressed the Reichstag. William L. Shirer, an American correspondent in Germany, witnessed the speech and recorded his observations, reproduced below, in his diary.

The Reichstag, more tense then I have ever felt it (apparently the hand-picked deputies on the main floor had not yet been told what had happened, though they knew something was afoot), began promptly at noon. The French, British, Belgian, and Polish ambassadors were absent, but the Italians were there and Dodd. General von Blomberg, the War Minister, sitting with the Cabinet on the left side of the stage, was as white as a sheet and fumbled the top of the bench nervously with his fingers. I have never seen him in such a state. Hitler began with a long harangue which he has often given before, but never tires of repeating, about the injustices of the Versailles Treaty and the peacefulness of Germans. Then his voice, which had been low and hoarse at the beginning, rose to a shrill, hysterical scream as he raged against Bolshevism.

"I will not have the gruesome Communist international dictatorship of hate descend upon the German people! This destructive Asiatic *Weltanschauung* strikes at all values! I tremble for Europe at the thought of what would happen should this destructive Asiatic conception of life, this chaos of the Bolshevist revolution, prove successful!" (Wild applause.)

Then, in a more reasoned voice, his argument that France's pact with Russia had invalidated the Locarno Treaty. A slight pause and:

"Germany no longer feels bound by the Locarno Treaty. In the interest of the primitive rights of its people to the security of their frontier and the safeguarding of their defence, the German Government has re-established, as from today, the absolute and unrestricted sovereignty of the Reich in the demilitarized zone!"

Now the six hundred deputies, personal appointees all of Hitler, little men with big bodies and bulging necks and cropped hair and pouched bellies and brown uniforms and heavy boots, little men of clay in his fine hands, leap to their feet like automatons, their right arms upstretched in the Nazi salute, and scream "*Heil's*," the first two or three wildly, the next twenty-five in unison, like a college yell. Hitler raises his hand for silence. It comes slowly. Slowly the automatons sit down. Hitler now has them in his claws. He appears to sense it. He says in a deep, resonant voice: "Men of the German Reichstag!" The silence is utter.

"In this historic hour, when in the Reich's western provinces German troops are at this minute marching into their future peace-time garrisons, we all unite in two sacred vows."

He can go no further. It is news to this hysterical "parliamentary" mob that German soldiers are already on the move into the Rhineland. All the militarism in their German blood surges to their heads. They spring, yelling and crying, to their feet. The audience in the galleries does the same, all except a few diplomats and about fifty of us correspondents. Their hands are raised in slavish salute, their faces now contorted with hysteria, their mouths wide open, shouting, shouting, their eyes, burning with fanaticism, glued on the new god, the Messiah. The Messiah plays his role superbly. His head lowered as if in all humbleness, he waits patiently for silence. Then, his voice still low, but choking with emotion, utters the two vows:

"First, we swear to yield to no force whatever in the restoration of the honour of our people, preferring to succumb with honour to the severest hardships rather than to capitulate. Secondly, we pledge that now, more than ever, we shall strive for an understanding between European peoples, especially for one with our western neighbour nations. . . . We have no territorial demands to make in Europe! . . . Germany will never break the peace."

It was a long time before the cheering stopped. Down in the lobby the deputies were still under the magic spell, gushing over one another. A few generals made their way out. Behind their smiles, however, you could not help detecting a nervousness.

Shirer recorded that Hitler "staked all on the success of his move and cannot survive if the French humiliate him" by taking action. The following day he made this entry in his diary.

Hitler has got away with it! France is not marching. Instead it is appealing to the League! No wonder the faces of Hitler and Göring and Blomberg and Fritsch were all smiles this noon as they sat in the royal box at the State Opera and for the second time in two years celebrated in a most military fashion Heroes Memorial Day, which is supposed to mark the memory of the two million Germans slain in the last war.

Oh, the stupidity (or is it paralysis?) of the French! I learned today on absolute authority that the German troops which marched into the demilitarized zone of the Rhineland yesterday had strict orders to beat a hasty retreat if the French army opposed them in any way. They were not prepared or equipped to fight a regular army. That probably explains Blomberg's white face yesterday. Apparently Fritsch (commander-in-chief of the Reichswehr) and most of the generals opposed the move, but Blomberg, who has a blind faith in the Führer and his judgment, talked them into it. It may be that Fritsch, who loves neither Hitler nor the Nazi regime, consented to go along on the theory that if the coup failed, that would be the end of Hitler; if it succeeded, then one of his main military problems was solved.

4 The Anschluss, March 1938

One of Hitler's aims was the incorporation of Austria into the Third Reich. The Treaty of Versailles had expressly prohibited the union of the two countries, but in *Mein Kampf,* Hitler had insisted that an Anschluss was necessary for German Lebensraum. In February 1938, under intense pressure from Hitler, Austrian Chancellor Kurt von Schuschnigg promised to accept Austrian Nazis in his cabinet and agreed to closer relations with Germany. Austrian independence was slipping away and, increasingly, Austrian Nazis undermined Schuschnigg's authority. Seeking to gain his people's support, Schuschnigg made plans for a plebiscite on the issue of preserving Austrian independence. An enraged Hitler ordered his generals to draw up plans for an invasion of Austria. Hitler then demanded Schuschnigg's resignation and the formation of a new government headed by Arthur Seyss-Inquart, an Austrian Nazi.

Believing that Austria was not worth a war, Britain and France informed the embattled chancellor that they would not help in the event of a German invasion. Schuschnigg then resigned, and Austrian Nazis began to take control of the government. Under the pretext of preventing violence, Hitler ordered his troops to cross into Austria, and on March 13, 1938, Austrian leaders declared that Austria was a province of the German Reich.

The Anschluss was supported by many Austrians: Nazis and their sympathizers, average people who hoped it would bring improved material conditions, and opportunists who had their eyes set on social and economic advancement. Even many opponents of the Nazis felt that Austrian unity with Germany was fated to be accomplished, even as they lamented that it meant incorporation into Hitler's regime.

In the first days after the Anschluss, anti-Nazis, particularly Social Democrats, were incarcerated; a wave of dissidents, politicians, and intellectuals fled the country; and Jews were subjected to torment and humiliation. Austrian

Nazis, often with the approval of their fellow citizens, plundered Jewish shops, pulled elderly Orthodox Jews around by their beards, and made Jews scour pro-Schuschnigg slogans off the streets with toothbrushes or their bare hands. One eyewitness recalled years later: "I saw in the crowd a well-dressed woman . . . holding up a little girl, a blond lovely little girl with these curls, so that the girl could see better how a . . . Nazi Storm Trooper kicked an old Jew who fell down because he wasn't allowed to kneel. He had to scrub and just bend down sort of, and he fell and he kicked him. And they all laughed and she laughed as well—it was wonderful entertainment—and that shook me."

Stefan Zweig
THE WORLD OF YESTERDAY

One of modern German-speaking Europe's most important authors, Stefan Zweig, was born into a well-to-do Viennese Jewish household, came of age during the waning years of the monarchy, and witnessed both the devastation of World War I and the chaos of the interwar years. A passionate European and a convinced Austrian patriot, Zweig was disgusted by national chauvinisms, particularly the virulent German nationalism clearly discernible in Austria after the collapse of the Habsburg monarchy. His *World of Yesterday* both laments the loss of European cosmopolitanism and offers biting criticism of the inability, or unwillingness, of many Austrians to come to terms with the violent intolerance in their own society and the spreading danger of nazism. Zweig's despair was all-consuming; he took his own life in South American exile, unable to reconcile himself to the changes in his beloved Europe and his Austrian homeland.

In the following selection from his autobiography, Zweig describes the orgy of hate that engulfed Vienna immediately after the Anschluss.

I thought that I had foreboded all the terror that would come to pass when Hitler's dream of hate would come true and he would triumphantly occupy Vienna, the city which had turned him off, poor and a failure, in his youth. But how timid, how petty, how lamentable my imagination, all human imagination, in the light of the inhumanity which discharged itself on that March 13, 1938, that day when Austria and Europe with it fell prey to sheer violence! The mask was off. The other States having plainly shown their fear, there was no further need to check moral inhibitions or to employ hypocritical pretexts about "Marxists" having to be politically liquidated. Who cared for England, France, for the whole world! Now there was no longer mere robbery and theft, but every private lust for revenge was given free rein. University professors were obliged to scrub the streets with their naked hands, pious white-bearded Jews were dragged into the synagogue by hooting youths and forced to do knee-exercises and to shout "Heil Hitler" in chorus. Innocent people in the streets were trapped like rabbits and herded off to clean the latrines in the S. A. barracks. All the sickly, unclean fantasies of hate that had been conceived in many orgiastic nights found raging expression in bright daylight. Breaking into homes and tearing earrings from trembling women may well have happened in the looting of cities, hundreds of years ago during medieval wars; what was new, however, was the shameless delight in public tortures, in spiritual martyrization, in the refinements of humiliation. All this has been recorded not by one but by thousands who suffered it; and a more peaceful day—not one already morally fatigued as ours is—will shudder to read what a single hate-crazed man perpetrated in that city of culture in the twentieth century. For amidst his military and political victories Hitler's most diabolic triumph was that he succeeded through progressive excesses in blunting every sense of law and order. Before this "New Order," the murder of a single man without legal process and without apparent reason would have shocked the world; torture was considered unthinkable in the twentieth century, expropriations were known by the old names, theft and robbery. But now after successive Bartholomew nights the daily mortal tortures in the S. A. prisons and behind barbed wire, what did a single injustice or earthly suffering signify? In 1938, after Austria, our universe had become accustomed to inhumanity, to lawlessness, and brutality as never in centuries before. In a former day the occurrences in unhappy Vienna alone would have been sufficient to cause international proscription, but in 1938 the world conscience was silent or merely muttered surlily before it forgot and forgave.

Those days, marked by daily cries for help from the homeland when one knew close friends to be kidnapped and humiliated and one trembled helplessly for every loved one, were among the most terrible of my life. These times have so perverted our hearts that I am not ashamed to say that I was not shocked and did not mourn upon learning of the death of my mother in Vienna; on the contrary, I even felt something like composure in the knowledge that she was now safe from suffering and danger. Eighty-four years old, almost completely deaf, she occupied rooms in our old home and thus could not, even under the new "Aryan" code, be evicted for the time being and we had hoped somehow to get her abroad after a while. One of the first Viennese ordinances had hit her hard. At her advanced age she was a little shaky on her legs and was accustomed, when on her daily laborious walk, to rest on a bench in the Ringstrasse or in the park, every five or ten minutes. Hitler had not been master of the city for a week when the bestial order forbidding Jews to sit on public benches was issued—one of those orders obviously thought up only for the sadistic purpose of malicious torture. There was logic and reason in robbing Jews for with the booty from factories, the home furnishings, the villas, and the jobs compulsorily vacated they could feather their followers' nests, reward their satellites; after all, Goering's picture-gallery owes its splendor mainly to this generously exercised practice. But to deny an aged woman or an exhausted old man a few minutes on a park bench to catch his breath—this remained reserved to the twentieth century and to the man whom millions worshiped as the greatest in our day.

Fortunately, my mother was spared suffering such brutality and humiliation for long. She died a few months after the occupation of Vienna and I cannot forbear to write about an episode in connection with her passing; it seems important to me to record just such details for a time in which such things will again seem impossible.

One morning the eighty-four-year-old woman suddenly lost consciousness. The doctor who was called declared that she could hardly live through the night and engaged a nurse, a woman of about forty, to attend her deathbed. Neither my brother nor I, her only children, was there nor could we have come back, because a return to the deathbed of a mother would have been counted a misdeed by the representatives of German culture. A cousin of ours undertook to spend the night in the apartment so that at least one of the family might be present at her death. He was then a man of sixty, and in poor health; in fact he too died about a year later. As he was uncovering his bed in an adjoining room the nurse appeared and declared her regret that because of the new National-Socialist laws it was impossible for her to stay overnight with the dying woman. To her credit be it said that she was rather shamefaced about it. My cousin being a Jew and she a woman under fifty, she was not permitted to spend a night under the same roof with him, even at a deathbed, because according to the Streicher mentality, it must be a Jew's first thought to practice race defilement upon her. Of course the regulation was extremely embarrassing, but she would have to obey the law. So my sixty-year-old cousin had to leave the house in the evening so that the nurse could stay with my dying mother; it will be intelligible, then, why I considered her almost lucky not to have to live on among such people.

5 The Munich Agreement

Hitler sought power to build a great German empire in Europe, a goal that he revealed in *Mein Kampf.* By 1938, he had successfully reintroduced military conscription, remilitarized the Rhineland, and incorporated Austria into the Third Reich without resistance from Britain and France. Now he threatened war if Czechoslovakia did not cede to Germany the Sudetenland with its large German population—of the 3.5 million people living in the Czech Sudetenland, some 2.8 million were Germans. In September 1938, Hitler met with other European leaders at Munich. Prime Minister Neville Chamberlain (1869–1940) of Great Britain and Prime Minister Édouard Daladier (1884–1970) of France agreed to Hitler's demands, despite France's mutual assistance pact with Czechoslovakia and the Czechs' expressed determination to resist the dismemberment of their country. Both Chamberlain and Daladier were praised by their compatriots for ensuring, as Chamberlain said, "peace in our time."

Neville Chamberlain
IN DEFENSE OF APPEASEMENT

Britain and France pursued a policy of appeasement—giving in to Germany in the hope that a satisfied Hitler would not drag Europe into another war. Appeasement expressed the widespread British desire to heal the wounds of World War I and to correct what many British officials regarded as the injustices of the Versailles Treaty. Some officials, lauding Hitler's anticommunism, regarded a powerful Germany as a bulwark against the Soviet Union. Britain's lack of military preparedness was another compelling reason for not resisting Hitler. On September 27, 1938, when negotiations between Hitler and Chamberlain reached a tense moment, the British prime minister addressed his nation. Excerpts of this speech and of another before the House of Commons, which appeared in his *In Search of Peace* (1939), follow.

First of all I must say something to those who have written to my wife or myself in these last weeks to tell us of their gratitude for my efforts and to assure us of their prayers for my success. Most of these letters have come from women—mothers or sisters of our own countrymen. But there are countless others besides—from France, from Belgium, from Italy, even from Germany, and it has been heartbreaking to read of the growing anxiety they reveal and their intense relief when they thought, too soon, that the danger of war was past.

If I felt my responsibility heavy before, to read such letters has made it seem almost overwhelming. How horrible, fantastic, incredible it is that we should be digging trenches and trying on gas masks here because of a quarrel in a far-away country between people of whom we know nothing. It seems still more impossible that a quarrel which has already been settled in principle should be the subject of war.

I can well understand the reasons why the Czech Government have felt unable to accept the terms which have been put before them in the German memorandum. Yet I believe after my talks with Herr Hitler that, if only time were allowed, it ought to be possible for the arrangements for transferring the territory that the Czech Government has agreed to give to Germany to be settled by agreement under conditions which would assure fair treatment to the population concerned. . . .

However much we may sympathise with a small nation confronted by a big and powerful neighbour, we cannot in all circumstances undertake to involve the whole British Empire in war simply on her account. If we have to fight it must be on larger issues than that. I am myself a man of peace to the depths of my soul. Armed conflict between nations is a nightmare to me; but if I were convinced that any nation had made up its mind to dominate the world by fear of its force, I should feel that it must be resisted. Under such a domination life for people who believe in liberty would not be worth living; but war is a fearful thing, and we must be very clear, before we embark on it, that it is really the great issues that are at stake, and that the call to risk everything in their defence, when all the consequences are weighed, is irresistible.

For the present I ask you to await as calmly as you can the events of the next few days. As long as war has not begun, there is always hope that it may be prevented, and you know that I am going to work for peace to the last moment. Good night. . . .

On October 6, 1938, in a speech to Britain's House of Commons, Chamberlain defended the Munich agreement signed on September 30.

Since I first went to Berchtesgaden [to confer with Hitler in Germany] more than 20,000 letters and telegrams have come to No. 10, Downing Street [British prime minister's residence]. Of course, I have only been able to look at a tiny fraction of them, but I have seen enough to know that the people who wrote did not feel that they had such a cause for which to fight, if they were asked to go to war in order that the Sudeten Germans might not join the Reich. That is how they are feeling. That is my answer to those who say that we should have told Germany weeks ago that, if her army crossed the border of Czechoslovakia, we should be at war with her. We had no treaty obligations and no legal obligations to Czechoslovakia and if we had said that, we feel that we should have received no support from the people of this country. . . .

. . . When we were convinced, as we became convinced, that nothing any longer would keep the Sudetenland within the Czechoslovakian State, we urged the Czech Government as strongly as we could to agree to the cession of territory, and to agree promptly. The Czech Government, through the wisdom and courage of President Benes, accepted the advice of the French Government and ourselves. It was a hard decision for anyone who loved his country to take, but to accuse us of having by that advice betrayed the Czechoslovakian State is simply preposterous. What we did was to save her from annihilation and give her a chance of new life as a new State, which involves the loss of territory and fortifications, but may perhaps enable her to enjoy in the future and develop a national existence under a neutrality and security comparable to that which we see in Switzerland today. Therefore, I think the Government deserve the approval of this House for their conduct of affairs in this recent crisis which has saved Czechoslovakia from destruction and Europe from Armageddon.

Does the experience of the Great War and of the years that followed it give us reasonable hope that, if some new war started, that would end war any more than the last one did? . . .

One good thing, at any rate, has come out of this emergency through which we have passed. It has thrown a vivid light upon our preparations for defence, on their strength and on their weakness. I should not think we were doing our duty if we had not already ordered that a prompt and thorough inquiry should be made to cover the whole of our preparations, military and civil, in order to see, in the light of what has happened during these hectic days, what further steps may be necessary to make good our deficiencies in the shortest possible time.

Winston Churchill
"A DISASTER OF THE FIRST MAGNITUDE"

On October 5, 1938, Britain's elder statesman Winston Churchill (1874–1965) delivered a speech in the House of Commons attacking the Munich agreement and British policy toward Germany.

. . . I will begin by saying what everybody would like to ignore or forget but which must nevertheless be stated, namely, that we have sustained a total and unmitigated defeat, and that France has suffered even more than we have. . . .

. . . And I will say this, that I believe the Czechs, left to themselves and told they were going to get no help from the Western Powers, would have been able to make better terms than they have got—they could hardly have worse—after all this tremendous perturbation. . . .

. . . I have always held the view that the maintenance of peace depends upon the accumulation of deterrents against the aggressor, coupled with a sincere effort to redress grievances. . . . After [Hitler's] seizure of Austria in March . . . I ventured to appeal to the Government . . . to give a pledge that in conjunction with France and other Powers they would guarantee the security of Czechoslovakia while the Sudeten-Deutsch question was being examined either by a League of Nations Commission or some other impartial body, and I still believe that if that course had been followed events would not have fallen into this disastrous state. . . .

France and Great Britain together, especially if they had maintained a close contact with Russia, which certainly was not done, would have been able in those days in the summer, when they had the prestige, to influence many of the smaller States of Europe, and I believe they could have determined the attitude of Poland. Such a combination, prepared at a time when the German dictator was not deeply and irrevocably committed to his new adventure, would, I believe, have given strength to all those forces in Germany which resisted this departure, this new design. They were varying forces, those of a military character which declared that Germany was not ready to undertake a world war, and all that mass of moderate opinion and popular opinion which dreaded war, and some elements of which still have some influence upon the German Government. Such action would have given strength to all that intense desire for peace which the helpless German masses share with their British and French fellow men. . . .

. . . I do not think it is fair to charge those who wished to see this course followed, and followed consistently and resolutely, with having wished for an immediate war. Between submission and immediate war there was this third alternative, which gave a hope not only of peace but of justice. It is quite true that such a policy in order to succeed demanded that Britain should declare straight out and a long time beforehand that she would, with others, join to defend Czechoslovakia against an unprovoked aggression. His Majesty's

Government refused to give that guarantee when it would have saved the situation. . . .

All is over. Silent, mournful, abandoned, broken, Czechoslovakia recedes into the darkness. She has suffered in every respect by her association with the Western democracies and with the League of Nations, of which she has always been an obedient servant. She has suffered in particular from her association with France, under whose guidance and policy she has been actuated for so long. . . .

We in this country, as in other Liberal and democratic countries, have a perfect right to exalt the principle of self-determination, but it comes ill out of the mouths of those in totalitarian States who deny even the smallest element of toleration to every section and creed within their bounds. . . .

What is the remaining position of Czechoslovakia? Not only are they politically mutilated, but, economically and financially, they are in complete confusion. Their banking, their railway arrangements, are severed and broken, their industries are curtailed, and the movement of their population is most cruel. The Sudeten miners, who are all Czechs and whose families have lived in that area for centuries, must now flee into an area where there are hardly any mines left for them to work. It is a tragedy which has occurred. . . .

I venture to think that in future the Czechoslovak State cannot be maintained as an independent entity. You will find that in a period of time which may be measured by years, but may be measured only by months, Czechoslovakia will be engulfed in the Nazi régime. Perhaps they may join it in despair or in revenge. At any rate, that story is over and told. But we cannot consider the abandonment and ruin of Czechoslovakia in the light only of what happened only last month. It is the most grievous consequence which we have yet experienced of what we have done and of what we have left undone in the last five years—five years of futile good intention, five years of eager search for the line of least resistance, five years of interrupted retreat of British power, five years of neglect of our air defences. Those are the features which I stand here to declare and which marked an improvident stewardship for which Great Britain and France have dearly to pay. We have been reduced in those five years from a position of security so overwhelming and so unchallengeable that we never cared to think about it. We have been reduced from a position where the very word "war" was considered one which would be used only by persons qualifying for a lunatic asylum. We have been reduced from a position of safety and power—power to do good, power to be generous to a beaten foe, power to make terms with Germany, power to give her proper redress for her grievances, power to stop her arming if we chose, power to take any step in strength or mercy or justice which we thought right—reduced in five years from a position safe and unchallenged to where we stand now.

When I think of the fair hopes of a long peace which still lay before Europe at the beginning of 1933 when Herr Hitler first obtained power, and of all the opportunities of arresting the growth of the Nazi power which have been thrown away, when I think of the immense combinations and resources which have been neglected or squandered, I cannot believe that a parallel exists in the whole course of history. So far as this country is concerned the responsibility must rest with those who have the undisputed control of our political affairs. They neither prevented Germany from rearming, nor did they rearm ourselves in time. . . . They neglected to make alliances and combinations which might have repaired previous errors, and thus they left us in the hour of trial without adequate national defence or effective international security. . . .

We are in the presence of a disaster of the first magnitude which has befallen Great Britain and France. Do not let us blind ourselves to that. It must now be accepted that all the countries of Central and Eastern Europe will make the best terms they can with the triumphant Nazi Power. The system of alliances in Central Europe upon which France has relied for her safety has been swept away, and I can see no means by which it can be reconstituted. . . .

. . . If the Nazi dictator should choose to look westward, as he may, bitterly will France and England regret the loss of that fine army of ancient Bohemia [Czechoslovakia] which was estimated last week to require not fewer than 30 German divisions for its destruction. . . .

. . . Many people, no doubt, honestly believe that they are only giving away the interests of Czechoslovakia, whereas I fear we shall find that we have deeply compromised, and perhaps fatally endangered, the safety and even the independence of Great Britain and France. . . . [T]here can never be friendship between the British democracy and the Nazi Power, that Power which spurns Christian ethics, which cheers its onward course by a barbarous paganism, which vaunts the spirit of aggression and conquest, which derives strength and perverted pleasure from persecution, and uses, as we have seen, with pitiless brutality the threat of murderous force. That Power cannot ever be the trusted friend of the British democracy. . . .

. . . [O]ur loyal, brave people . . . should know the truth. They should know that there has been gross neglect and deficiency in our defences; they should know that we have sustained a defeat without a war, the consequences of which will travel far with us along our road; they should know that we have passed an awful milestone in our history, when the whole equilibrium of Europe has been deranged, and that the terrible words have for the time being been pronounced against the Western democracies:

> Thou art weighed in the balance and found wanting.

And do not suppose that this is the end. This is only the beginning of the reckoning. This is only the first sip, the first foretaste of a bitter cup which will be proffered to us year by year unless by a supreme recovery of moral health and martial vigour, we arise again and take our stand for freedom as in the olden time.

---

6 World War II Begins

After Czechoslovakia, Hitler turned to Poland. In the middle of June 1939, the army presented him with a battle plan for an invasion of Poland, and on August 22, Hitler informed his leading generals that war with Poland was necessary. The following day, Nazi Germany signed a nonaggression pact with its ideological nemesis the Soviet Union which blocked Britain and France from duplicating their World War I alliance against Germany. The Nazi-Soviet pact was the green light for an attack on Poland. At dawn on September 1, German forces, striking with coordinated speed and power, invaded Poland, starting World War II.

Adolf Hitler
"POLAND WILL BE DEPOPULATED AND SETTLED WITH GERMANS"

An American journalist was given a copy of Hitler's speech to his generals at the August 22 conference. Probably the supplier was an official close to Admiral Canaris, an opponent of Hitler who had attended the conference. The journalist then gave it to the British ambassador. The speech is reproduced below.

Decision to attack Poland was arrived at in spring. Originally there was fear that because of the political constellation we would have to strike at the same time against England, France, Russia and Poland. This risk too we should have had to take. Göring had demonstrated to us that his Four-Year Plan is a failure and that we are at the end of our strength, if we do not achieve victory in a coming war.

Since the autumn of 1938 and since I have realised that Japan will not go with us unconditionally and that Mussolini is endangered by that nitwit of a King and the treacherous scoundrel of a Crown Prince, I decided to go with Stalin. After all there are only three great statesmen in the world, Stalin, I and Mussolini. Mussolini is the weakest, for he has been able to break the power neither of the crown nor of the Church. Stalin and I are the only ones who visualise the future. So in a few weeks hence I shall stretch out my hand to Stalin at the common German-Russian frontier and with him undertake to re-distribute the world.

Our strength lies in our quickness and in our brutality; Genghis Khan has sent millions of women and children into death knowingly and with a light heart. History sees in him only the great founder of States. As to what the weak Western European civilisation asserts about me, that is of no account. I have given the command and I shall shoot everyone who utters one word of criticism, for the goal to be obtained in the war is not that of reaching certain lines but of physically demolishing the opponent. And so for the present only in the East I have put my death-head formations[1] in place with the command relentlessly and without compassion to send into death many women and children of Polish origin and language. Only thus we can gain the living space that we need. Who after all is today speaking about the destruction of the Armenians?

Colonel-General von Brauchitsch has promised me to bring the war against Poland to a close within a few weeks. Had he reported to me that he needs two years or even only one year, I should not have given the command to march and should have allied myself temporarily with England instead of Russia for we cannot conduct a long war. To be sure a new situation has arisen. I experienced those poor worms Daladier and Chamberlain in Munich. They will be too cowardly to attack. They won't go beyond a blockade. Against that we have our autarchy and the Russian raw materials.

Poland will be depopulated and settled with Germans. My pact with the Poles was merely conceived of as a gaining of time. As for the rest, gentlemen, the fate of Russia will be exactly the same as I am now going through with in the case of Poland. After Stalin's death—he is a very sick man—we will break the Soviet Union. Then there will begin the dawn of the German rule of the earth. . . .

The opportunity is as favourable as never before. I have but one worry, namely that Chamberlain or some other such pig of a fellow ('Saukerl') will come at the last moment with proposals or with ratting ('Umfall'). He will fly down the stairs, even if I shall personally have to trample on his belly in the eyes of the photographers.

No, it is too late for this. The attack upon and the destruction of Poland begins Saturday[2] early. I shall let a few companies in Polish uniform attack in Upper Silesia or in the Protectorate. Whether the world believes it is quite indifferent ('Scheissegal'). The world believes only in success.

For you, gentlemen, fame and honour are beginning as they have not since centuries. Be hard, be without mercy, act more quickly and brutally than the others. The citizens of Western Europe must tremble with horror. That is the most human way of conducting a war. For it scares the others off.

The new method of conducting war corresponds to the new drawing of the frontiers. A war extending from Reval, Lublin, Kaschau to the mouth of the Danube. The rest will be

[1]The S.S. Death's Head formations were principally employed in peace-time in guarding concentration camps. During World War II, they became part of the Waffen SS, a key fighting force.

[2]August 26.

given to the Russians. Ribbentrop has orders to make every offer and to accept every demand. In the West I reserve to myself the right to determine the strategically best line. Here one will be able to work with Protectorate regions, such as Holland, Belgium and French Lorraine.

And now, on to the enemy, in Warsaw we will celebrate our reunion.

The speech was received with enthusiasm. Göring jumped on a table, thanked bloodthirstily and made bloodthirsty promises. He danced like a wild man. The few that had misgivings remained quiet. (Here a line of the memorandum is missing in order no doubt to protect the source of information.)[3]

During the meal which followed Hitler said he must act this year as he was not likely to live very long. His successor however would no longer be able to carry this out. Besides, the situation would be a hopeless one in two years at the most.

[3]This sentence in parentheses forms part of the original typescript.

7 The Fall of France

On May 10, 1940, Hitler launched his offensive in the West with an invasion of neutral Belgium, Holland, and Luxembourg. French troops rushed to Belgium to prevent a breakthrough, but the greater menace lay to the south, on the French frontier. Meeting almost no resistance, German panzer divisions had moved through the narrow mountain passes of Luxembourg and the dense Forest of the Ardennes in southern Belgium. On May 12, German units were on French soil near Sedan. Thinking that the Forest of the Ardennes could not be penetrated by a major German force, the French had only lightly fortified the western extension of the Maginot Line, the immense fortifications designed to hold back a German invasion.

The battle for France turned into a rout. Whole French divisions were cut off or in retreat. On June 10, Mussolini also declared war on France. With authority breaking down and resistance dying, the French cabinet appealed for an armistice, which was signed on June 22 in the same railway car in which Germany had agreed to the armistice ending World War I.

Several reasons explain the quick collapse of the French Republic. France possessed planes, but the high command either failed to use them or did not deploy them wisely. Indeed, France had fewer pilots and planes, particularly tactical bombers, than Germany; however, because French airfields lacked early warning systems and sufficient antiaircraft artillery protection, many French aircraft never even left the tarmac and the German Luftwaffe was able to destroy many of them on the ground. In contrast, the German air force was an integral part of an offensive operation, providing support for advancing tanks and infantry and bombing behind enemy lines. Dominating the air, the Luftwaffe disrupted Allied reconnaissance efforts and decimated tanks and infantry attempting to counterattack. Unlike the Germans, the French did not comprehend or appreciate the use of aviation in modern warfare.

As for tanks, the French had as many as the Germans, and some were superior, but they were spread among the infantry divisions, unlike the Germans, who deployed their tanks in massed formations that powered their way through enemy lines.

Nor was German manpower overwhelming. France met disaster largely because its military leaders, unlike the Germans, had not mastered the psychology and technology of motorized warfare. "The French commanders, trained in the slow-motion methods of 1918, were mentally unfitted to cope with panzer pace, and it produced a spreading paralysis among them," says British military expert Sir Basil Liddell Hart. One also senses a loss of will among the French people: a consequence of internal political disputes dividing the nation, poor leadership, the years of appeasement and lost opportunities, and German propaganda, which depicted nazism as irresistible and the Führer as a man of destiny. It was France's darkest hour.

Heinz Guderian
"FRENCH LEADERSHIP . . . COULD NOT GRASP THE SIGNIFICANCE OF THE TANK IN MOBILE WARFARE"

After the war, General Heinz Guderian (1888–1954), whose panzer divisions formed the vanguard of the attack through the Ardennes into France, analyzed the reasons for France's collapse.

The First World War on the Western Front, after being for a short time a war of movement, soon settled down to positional warfare. No massing of war material, on no matter how vast a scale, had succeeded in getting the armies moving again until, in November 1916, the enemy's tanks appeared on the battlefield. With their armour plating, their tracks, their guns and their machine-guns, they succeeded in carrying their crews, alive and capable of fighting, through artillery barrages and wire entanglements, over trench systems and shell craters, into the centre of the German lines. The power of the offensive had come back into its own.

The true importance of tanks was proved by the fact that the Versailles Treaty forbade Germany the possession or construction of armoured vehicles, tanks or any similar equipment which might be employed in war, under pain of punishment.

So our enemies regarded the tank as a decisive weapon which we must not be allowed to have. I therefore decided carefully to study the history of this decisive weapon and to follow its future development. For someone observing tank theory from afar, unburdened by tradition, there were lessons to be learned in the employment, organisation and construction of armour and of armoured units that went beyond the doctrines then accepted abroad. After years of hard struggle, I had succeeded in putting my theories into practice before the other armies had arrived at the same conclusions. The advance we had made in the organisation and employment of tanks was the primary factor on which my belief in our forthcoming success was based. Even in 1940 this belief was shared by scarcely anybody in the German Army.

A profound study of the First World War had given me considerable insight into the psychology of the combatants. I already, from personal experience, knew a considerable amount about our own army. I had also formed certain opinions about our Western adversaries which the events of 1940 were to prove correct. Despite the tank weapons to which our enemies owed in large measure their 1918 victory, they were preoccupied with the concepts of positional warfare.

France possessed the strongest land army in Western Europe. France possessed the numerically strongest tank force in Western Europe.

The combined Anglo-French forces in the West in May 1940 disposed of some 4,000 armoured vehicles: the German Army at that time had 2,800, including armoured reconnaissance cars, and when the attack was launched only 2,200 of these were available for the operation. We thus faced superiority in numbers, to which was added the fact that the French tanks were superior to the German ones both in armour and in gun-calibre, though admittedly inferior in control facilities and in speed. Despite possessing the strongest forces for mobile warfare the French had also built the strongest line of fortifications in the world, the Maginot Line. Why was the money spent on the construction of those fortifications not used for the modernisation and strengthening of France's mobile forces?

The proposals of de Gaulle, Daladier[1] and others along these lines had been ignored. From this it must be concluded that the highest French leadership either would not or could not grasp the significance of the tank in mobile warfare. In any case all the manœuvres and large-scale exercises of which I had heard led to the conclusion that the French command wanted its troops to be trained in such a way that careful movement and planned measures for attack or for defence could be based on definite, pre-arranged circumstances. They wanted a complete picture of the enemy's order of battle and intentions before deciding on any undertaking. Once the decision was taken it would be carried out according to plan, one might almost say methodically, not only during the approach march and the deployment of troops, but also during the artillery preparation and the launching of the attack or the construction of the defence as the case might be. This mania for planned control, in which nothing should be left to chance, led to the organisation of the armoured forces within the army in a form that would destroy the general scheme, that is to say their assignment in detail to the infantry divisions. Only a fraction of the French armour was organised for operational employment.

So far as the French were concerned the German leadership could safely rely on the defence of France being systematically based on fortifications and carried out according to a rigid doctrine: this doctrine was the result of the lessons that the French had learned from the First World War, their experience of positional warfare, of the high value they attached to fire power, and of their underestimation of movement.

These French strategic and tactical principles, well known to us in 1940 and the exact contrary of my own theories of warfare, were the second factor on which my belief in victory was founded.

By the spring of 1940 we Germans had gained a clear picture of the enemy's dispositions, and of his fortifications. We knew that somewhere between Montmédy and Sedan the Maginot Line changed from being very strong indeed to being rather weaker. We called the fortifications from Sedan to the Channel 'the prolonged Maginot Line.' We knew about the locations and, usually, about the strength of the Belgian and Dutch fortifications. They all faced only towards Germany.

While the Maginot Line was thinly held, the mass of the French army together with the British Expeditionary Force was assembled in Flanders, between the Meuse and the English Channel, facing northeast; the Belgian and Dutch troops, on the other hand, were deployed to defend their frontiers against an attack from the east.

From their order of battle it was plain that the enemy expected the Germans to attempt the Schlieffen Plan once again, and that they intended to bring the bulk of the allied armies against this anticipated outflanking movement through Holland and Belgium. A sufficient safeguard of the hinge of their proposed advance into Belgium by reserve units—in the area, say, of Charleville and Verdun—was not apparent. It seemed that the French High Command did not regard any alternative to the old Schlieffen Plan as even conceivable.

---

[1]General Charles de Gaulle (1890–1970) refused to accept the surrender of France to Germany in 1940 and escaped to Londan, where he organized the Free French forces and continued the fight against Hitler. Édouard Daladier (1884–1970) was premier of France from April 1938 until his resignation in March 1940. Although he participated in the Munich Agreement that ceded the Sudetenland to Germany, Daladier had no illusions as to Hitler's ultimate aims of conquest and expansion.

Our knowledge of the enemy's order of battle and of his predictable reactions at the beginning of the German advance was the third factor that contributed to my belief in victory.

In addition there were a number of other aspects in our general evaluation of the enemy which, though of less reliability, were still worth taking into consideration.

We knew and respected the French soldier from the First World War as a brave and tough fighter who had defended his country with stubborn energy. We did not doubt that he would show the same spirit this time. But so far as the French leaders were concerned, we were amazed that they had not taken advantage of their favourable situation during the autumn of 1939 to attack, while the bulk of the German forces, including the entire armoured force, was engaged in Poland. Their reasons for such restraint were at the time hard to see. We could only guess. Be that as it may, the caution shown by the French leaders led us to believe that our adversaries hoped somehow to avoid a serious clash of arms. The rather inactive behavior of the French during the winter of 1939–40 seemed to indicate a limited enthusiasm for the war on their part.

From all this I concluded that a determined and forcibly led attack by strong armoured forces through Sedan and Amiens, with the Atlantic coast as its objective, would hit the enemy deep in the flank of his forces advancing into Belgium; I did not think that he disposed of sufficient reserves to parry this thrust; and I therefore believed it had a great chance of succeeding and, if the initial success were fully exploited, might lead to the cutting off of all the main enemy forces moving up into Belgium.

Hans Habe
FRANCE'S INTERNAL WEAKNESSES

Was there more than a military explanation for the utter rout of the French army? Some analysts point to internal divisions that weakened France's will to fight; in particular they point to the conflict between Left and Right that continued to plague France for decades after the notorious Dreyfus affair (see the footnote on p. 218). The French Right, it has been suggested, hostile to the democratic republic and social reform and sympathetic to Fascist ideals, did not regard a German victory as unthinkable, an outlook that undermined French morale.

Hans Habe (1911–1977), a Hungarian Jew by birth and family, was a talented journalist who made the defeat of nazism a personal cause. Living in Geneva in September 1939, he immediately volunteered for service in the French army and was assigned to the 21st Infantry of Foreign Volunteers, where he rose to the rank of sergeant. Following the fall of France, Habe was imprisoned in a German camp with 22,000 other inmates. After two months, he managed to escape to unoccupied France. From there he made his way to Portugal and then to the United States. Shortly after his arrival, Habe wrote about his experiences in France and its surrender to Germany in *A Thousand Shall Fall,* from which the following selection comes.

We lay silent for a few minutes; then Saint-Brice[1] asked, 'What are you sighing about?'

'Did I sigh?'

'You did.'

He too sighed. Then he said, 'No, it's not a pretty sight.'

'What do you think?' I asked. 'How long are we going to keep running like this?'

'I've no idea! Maybe till the Germans occupy all France.'

'And what about the Maginot Line? And the Daladier Line that's supposed to be waiting somewhere? And the resistance that's being organized on the Loire? Why shouldn't this war have its Marne, too? Don't you believe in it?'

I felt in the darkness that he had turned towards me with his head in his hands.

'No,' he said, 'I don't believe in it.'

I did not want to ask questions, but he went on talking, as he seldom did.

'I have stopped believing,' he said. 'We had not prepared for this war. No, I don't speak of armaments. We could have caught up in nine months. But no Frenchman knew what he was fighting for. The Germans, over there, wrapped their foulest plans in ideological tissue-paper. And we? We did the opposite. We were really fighting for freedom and humanity, and we were ashamed of those two words. We acted as though nothing but territory were at stake. Did we hate the Germans? Our young people didn't even know what the Germans meant. Even today the blockheads think they'll survive a Hitler victory. Yes, they *will* survive! But as slaves. The purpose of this whole war is to bring slavery back to the world. And the world will regard us as voluntary slaves!'

His voice sounded hoarse. I stretched out on the narrow school bench. Between us lay a desk with an inkpot and drawer.

'We Frenchman forgot the meaning of freedom long ago,' he went on. 'Real freedom. We were in the midst of a civil war when the Germans overran us.'

'In times of war,' I objected, 'Frenchmen always dropped their internal quarrels.'

'That was true in the past,' said Saint-Brice. 'Patriotism is stronger than politics. It always was in our country. But philosophy is stronger than patriotism. The Germans armed themselves with a philosophy for this war. Their philosophy is a skeleton key that lets them into a country without resistance. But God help a country once the Germans have occupied it!'

Never before had he spoken like this. Despite our intimacy, we both had preserved the distance between superior and subordinate, between Frenchman and foreigner. This time Saint-Brice seemed to be speaking to himself.

'Recently,' he continued, 'a captain told me that he loved France more than he loved Hitler, but that he loved Hitler more than Leon Blum.[2] What more do you want?'

He was interrupted by a fit of coughing.

'Yes,' he said at last, 'I know the old story of our deficiency in arms. But do you think that was the decisive factor? Didn't we win the Great War despite our inferior armament? They say that the greatest part of our aircraft was destroyed on the ground. Do you know what that means? There were officers who prevented our pilots, at the point of a gun, from taking off. Can you conceive of such a thing?'

'No, I can't.'

'I am beginning to understand; we were not sold out, but we were betrayed. And that's the worst part of it. A couple of corrupted generals can always be dealt with by a firing-squad. But we had no corrupt generals. You can't prove anything against them. There is no

---

[1]Lieutenant Saint-Brice was Habe's commanding officer. Unlike many members of the French officer corps, he wanted to continue the military struggle against Germany.

[2]Léon Blum (1872–1950), a socialist and a Jew, became premier of a French Popular Front government in 1936 to rally the political forces opposing fascism at home and abroad. Blum introduced many progressive reforms that benefited the working class but also provoked the wrath of French conservatives. He resigned in 1937, and the Popular Front fell apart.

bordereau as in the Dreyfus Case.[3] They betrayed us without having exchanged a single word with the Germans. They did not want to fight against Germany. They liked Germany. Bought by the Germans? If only they had been bought! But they weren't even bought! Once I was told that the people of some Balkan state were always ready to sell their country, but never to deliver it. We did worse than that. We delivered our country without even getting paid for it.'

'Aren't you painting too black a picture?'

I said this without conviction. But he was tormenting me, just as he was tormenting himself. We had loved this country and this people more than anything in the world: each of us in his own way.

'No,' he said, 'it can't be painted too black.'

We tried to sleep. But the day and the conversation had been too much for us. And the thunder of the guns was drawing nearer.

'Artillery preparation,' said Saint-Brice. 'They still expect resistance.'

I took up the thread of his thought.

'On this lousy, clogged road resistance is unthinkable.'

'Right', said the officer. 'That's what they want to show us. It's the same men who sabotaged our armament. Always the same. They started the Dreyfus Case—and lost it. After that they were dethroned in France. Now they're taking revenge for the Dreyfus Case. Now they expect to stage a triumphal come-back on German bayonets. People won't understand that. Not for a long time. Because, by accident, war was declared between Germany and France. Because our generals were not as straightforward as General Franco. He, at least, openly invited the foreigners into his country. . . . In the streets of Sainte-Menehould, couldn't you feel that this is not a war between two states, but a civil war? You did feel it, didn't you? And doesn't that explain everything? On the one side, free France. Like free Spain. And against it, a gang of bandits leaning on foreign support! Only here the plot was much more diabolic, the whole thing was much more subtly conceived, much more treacherously carried out. In Spain civil war was openly proclaimed. The motives were clearly stated. No false slogans, no false banners! You could take one side or the other. Here they all sail under a false banner. They make it look as though Frenchmen are fighting Germans. Never, never, I'm telling you, would France have lost the war against Germany. We would have beaten them even with our medieval guns. But this was a war of Frenchmen against Frenchmen. And no one told us. . . .'

[3]In 1894 Captain Alfred Dreyfus, an Alsatian-Jewish artillery officer, was wrongly accused of selling military secrets to Imperial Germany. Anti-Semites made common cause with opponents of the Third Republic—including monarchists, army leaders, clerics, and nationalists—to denounce Dreyfus and secure his condemnation. Dreyfus was court-martialed and then sentenced to life imprisonment on Devil's Island. With the help of radical republicans, among them the writers Anatole France and Émile Zola, Dreyfus was finally cleared of the charges against him in 1906. His exoneration provided supporters of the Republic an opportunity to clamp down on anti-Republican forces, especially the army and Catholic Church. The *bordereau* (memorandum) refers to the incriminating evidence that helped expose the campaign against Dreyfus within higher military circles.

8 The Battle of Britain

Hitler expected that after his stunning victories in the West, Britain would make peace. The British, however, continued to reject Hitler's overtures, for they envisioned a bleak future if Nazi Germany dominated the Continent. With Britain unwilling to come to terms, Hitler proceeded in earnest with invasion plans.

A successful crossing of the English Channel and the establishment of beachheads on the English coast depended on control of the skies. In early August 1940, the Luftwaffe began massive attacks on British air and naval installations. Virtually every day during the Battle of Britain, hundreds of planes fought in the sky above Britain as British pilots rose to the challenge. On September 15, the Royal Air Force (RAF) shot down sixty aircraft; two days later Hitler postponed the invasion of Britain "until further notice." The development of radar by British scientists, the skill and courage of British fighter pilots, and the inability of Germany to make up its losses in planes saved Britain in its struggle for survival. With the invasion of Britain called off, the Luftwaffe concentrated on bombing English cities, industrial centers, and ports. Almost every night for months, the inhabitants of London sought shelter in subways and cellars to escape German bombs, while British planes rose time after time to make the Luftwaffe pay the price. British morale never broke during the "Blitz."

Winston Churchill
"BLOOD, TOIL, TEARS, AND SWEAT"

Churchill, at the age of sixty-six, proved to be an undaunted leader, sharing the perils faced by all and able by example and by speeches to rally British morale. When he first addressed Parliament as prime minister on May 13, 1940, he left no doubt about the grim realities that lay ahead. Excerpts from his speeches in 1940 follow.

May 13, 1940

I would say to the House, as I said to those who have joined this Government: "I have nothing to offer but blood, toil, tears, and sweat." We have before us an ordeal of the most grievous kind. We have before us many, many long months of struggle and suffering. You ask: "What is our policy?" I will say: "It is to wage war by sea, land, and air with all our might, and with all the strength that God can give us; to wage war against a monstrous tyranny, never surpassed in the dark lamentable catalogue of human crime." That is our policy.

You ask: "What is our aim?" I can answer in one word: "Victory!" Victory at all costs, victory in spite of all terror, victory however long and hard the road may be; for without victory there is no survival.

When Churchill spoke next, on May 19, the Dutch had surrendered to the Germans, and the French and British armies were in retreat. Still, Churchill promised that "conquer we shall."

May 19, 1940

This is one of the most awe-striking periods in the long history of France and Britain. It is also beyond doubt the most sublime. Side by side, unaided except by their kith and kin in the great Dominions and by the wide Empires which rest beneath their shield—side by side, the British and French peoples have advanced to rescue not only Europe but mankind from the foulest and most soul-destroying tyranny which has ever darkened and stained the pages of history.

Behind them—behind us—behind the armies and fleets of Britain and France—gather a group of shattered states and bludgeoned races: the Czechs, the Poles, the Norwegians, the Danes, the Dutch, the Belgians—upon all of whom the long night of barbarism will descend unbroken even by a star of hope, unless we conquer, as conquer we must; as conquer we shall.

By early June the Belgians had surrendered to the Germans, and the last units of the British Expeditionary Force in France had been evacuated from Dunkirk; the French armies were in full flight. Again Churchill spoke out in defiance of events across the Channel.

June 4, 1940

We shall not flag or fail. We shall go on to the end. We shall fight in France, we shall fight on the seas and oceans, we shall fight with growing confidence and growing strength in the air. We shall defend our island, whatever the cost may be. We shall fight on the beaches, we shall fight on the landing-grounds, we shall fight in the fields and in the streets, we shall fight in the hills. We shall never surrender; and even if, which I do not for a moment believe, this island or a large part of it were subjugated and starving, then our Empire beyond the seas, armed and guarded by the British Fleet, would carry on the struggle, until, in God's good time, the New World, with all its power and might, steps forth to the rescue and liberation of the Old.

By June 18 the battle of France was lost; on June 22 France surrendered. Now Britain itself was under siege. Churchill again found the right words to sustain his people.

June 18, 1940

What General [Maxime] Weygand [commander of the French army] called the Battle of France is over. . . . The Battle of Britain is about to begin. Upon this battle depends the survival of Christian civilization. Upon it depends our own British life and the long continuity of our institutions and our Empire. The whole fury and might of the enemy must very soon be turned upon us. Hitler knows that he will have to break us in this island or lose the war.

If we can stand up to him, all Europe may be free and the life of the world may move forward into broad sunlit uplands. But if we fail, then the whole world, including the United States, including all that we have known and cared for, will sink into the abyss of a new Dark Age made more sinister and perhaps more prolonged by the lights of a perverted science.

Let us therefore brace ourselves to our duty and so bear ourselves that if the British Empire and Commonwealth last for a thousand years, men will still say, "This was their finest hour."

The bombing of Britain began, in advance of the Germans' planned invasion, in July, reaching a climax in September with great raids on London and other cities. The Battle of Britain was fought in the air by British pilots defending their country. Early in the battle Churchill acknowledged the courage of British airmen and their contribution to Britain's survival.

August 20, 1940

The gratitude of every home in our island, in our Empire, and indeed throughout the world, except in the abodes of the guilty, goes out to the British airmen who, undaunted by odds, unwearied in their constant challenge and mortal danger, are turning the tide of world war by their prowess and by their devotion. Never in the field of human conflict was so much owed by so many to so few. All hearts go out to the fighter pilots whose brilliant actions we see with our own eyes day after day.

9 The Indoctrination of the German Soldier: For Volk, Führer, and Fatherland

After World War II, Germans maintained that the Wehrmacht (the German army) was an apolitical professional fighting force that remained free of Nazi ideology and was uninvolved in criminal acts perpetrated by Heinrich Himmler's SS, the elite units responsible for the extermination of Jews. It is now known that units of the German army assisted the SS in the rounding up of Jews and at times participated in mass murder. Recently, historians have argued that the regular army, far from being apolitical, was imbued with Nazi ideology and that many German officers and soldiers, succumbing to Nazi indoctrination, viewed the war, particularly on the Eastern Front, as a titanic struggle against evil and subhuman Jewish-led Bolsheviks who threatened the very existence of the German Volk. The following excerpts from German army propaganda and letters written by soldiers show how Nazi ideology influenced ordinary German troops. The first is a news-sheet published by the High Command of the Armed Forces in the spring of 1940 and distributed to all army units, which expressed quasi-religious fervor for the Führer.

[THE FÜHRER AS SAVIOR]

Behind the battle of annihilation of May 1940 stands in lone greatness the name of the Führer.

All that has been accomplished since he has taken the fate of our people into his strong hands!

. . . He gave the people back its unity, smashed the parties and destroyed the hydra of the organizations . . . he decontaminated the body of our people from the Jewish subversion, created a stock-proud, race-conscious *Volk,* which had overcome the racial death of diminishing births and was granted renewed [abundance of childbirths] as a carrier of the great future of the Fatherland. He subdued the terrible plight of unemployment and granted to millions of people who had already despaired of the *Volk* a new belief in the *Volksgemeinschaft* [community of the people] and happiness in a new Fatherland. . . .

His genius, in which the whole strength of Germandom is embodied with ancient powers, has animated the souls of 80,000,000 Germans, has filled them with strength and will, with the storm and stress [*Sturm und Drang*] of a renewed young people; and, himself the first soldier of Germany, he has entered the name of the German soldier into the book of immortality.

All this we were allowed to experience. Our great duty in this year of decision is that we do not accept it as observers, but that we, enchanted, and with all the passion of which we are capable, sacrifice ourselves to this Führer and strive to be worthy of the historical epoch molded by a heaven-storming will.

This same religious devotion to Hitler and Nazi ideology was expressed in literature given to company commanders to assist them in indoctrinating their troops.

Only the Führer could carry out what had not been achieved for a thousand years. . . . [He has] brought together all the German stock . . . for the struggle for freedom and living space . . . [and] directed all his thoughts and efforts toward the National Socialist education of the *Volk,* the inner cohesion of the state, the armament and offensive capability of the

Wehrmacht. . . . When the German Eastern Armies fought an unparalleled battle during the winter of 1941–42 in the snow and ice of the Russian winter, he said: "Any weakling can put up with victories. Only the strong can stand firm in battles of destiny. But heaven gives the ultimate and highest prize only to those who are capable of withstanding battles of destiny." In the difficult winter of 1942–43 the strength of the Führer was demonstrated once more, when . . . he called upon the German *Volk* at the front and in the homeland to stand firm and make the supreme effort. The Führer . . . clearly sees the goal ahead: a strong German Reich as the power of order in Europe and a firm root of the German *Lebensraum.* This goal will be achieved if the whole *Volk* remains loyal to him even in difficult times and as long as we soldiers do our duty.

Such words were not without their impact on German soldiers. In November 1940, one soldier expressed his feelings about Hitler in a letter home.

The last words of the Führer's radio address are over and a new strength streams through our veins. It is as if he spoke to each individual, to every one of us, as if he wanted to give everyone new strength. With loyalty and a sense of duty, we must fight for our principles and endure to the end. Our Führer represents our united German Fatherland. . . . What we do for him, we do for all of you; what we sacrifice in foreign lands, we sacrifice for our loved ones. When the Führer speaks on these festive occasions, I feel deep in my soul that you at home also feel that we must be ready to make all sacrifices. . . . German victory is as certain as our love for each other. Just as we believe in our love, so we believe in our final victory and in the future of our people and our Fatherland.

Similar sentiments were voiced by a private in a letter to his brother.

The Führer has grown into the greatest figure of the century, in his hand lies the destiny of the world and of culturally-perceptive humanity. May his pure sword strike down the Satanic monster. Yes, the blows are still hard, but the horror will be forced into the shadows through the inexorable Need, through the command which derives from our National Socialist idea. This [battle] is for a new ideology, a new belief, a new life! I am glad that I can participate, even if as a tiny cog, in this war of light against darkness.

[BOLSHEVIKS AND JEWS AS DEVILS]

German propaganda described Jews and Russian Communists in racial and religious terms, calling them a morally depraved form of humanity in the service of Satan. A tract from SS headquarters illustrates the mythical quality of nazism.

Just as night rises up against the day, just as light and darkness are eternal enemies, so the greatest enemy of world-dominating man is man himself. The sub-man—that creature which looks as though biologically it were of absolutely the same kind, endowed by Nature with hands, feet and a sort of brain, with eyes and mouth—is nevertheless a totally different, a fearful creature, is only an attempt at a human being, with a quasi-human face, yet in mind and spirit lower than any animal. Inside this being a cruel chaos of wild, unchecked passions: a nameless will to destruction, the most primitive lusts, the most undisguised vileness. A sub-man—nothing else! . . . Never has the sub-man granted peace, never has he permitted rest. . . . To preserve himself he needed mud, he needed hell, but not the sun. And this underworld of sub-men found its leader: the eternal Jew!

The news-sheet distributed to regular army units used similar language.

Anyone who has ever looked at the face of a red commissar knows what the Bolsheviks are like. Here there is no need for theoretical expressions. We would insult the animals if we described these mostly Jewish men as beasts. They are the embodiment of the Satanic and insane hatred against the whole of noble humanity. The shape of these commissars reveals to us the rebellion of the *Untermenschen* [sub-men] against noble blood. The masses, whom they have sent to their deaths [in this war against Germany] by making use of all means at their disposal such as ice-cold terror and insane incitement, would have brought an end to all meaningful life, had this eruption not been dammed at the last moment.

In October 1941, Walter von Reichenau, commander of the sixth army, appealed to his men in the language of Nazi racial ideology.

Regarding the conduct of the troops toward the Bolshevik system many unclear ideas still remain.

The essential goal of the campaign against the Jewish-Bolshevik system is the complete destruction of its power instruments and the eradication of the Asiatic influence on the European cultural sphere.

Thereby the troops too have *tasks,* which go beyond the conventional unilateral soldierly tradition [*Soldatentum*]. In the East the soldier is not only a fighter according to the rules of warfare, but also a carrier of an inexorable racial conception [*völkischen Idee*] and the avenger of all the bestialities which have been committed against the Germans and related races.

Therefore the soldier must have *complete* understanding for the necessity of the harsh, but just atonement of Jewish subhumanity. This has the further goal of nipping in the bud rebellions in the rear of the Wehrmacht which, as experience shows, are always plotted by the Jews.

In November 1941, General von Manstein, commander of the eleventh army, used much the same language.

Since 22 June the German *Volk* is in the midst of a battle for life and death against the Bolshevik system. This battle is conducted against the Soviet army not only in a conventional manner according to the rules of European warfare. . . .

Judaism constitutes the mediator between the enemy in the rear and the still fighting remnants of the Red Army and the Red leadership. It has a stronger hold than in Europe on all key positions of the political leadership and administration, it occupies commerce and trade and further forms cells for all the disturbances and possible rebellions.

The Jewish-Bolshevik system must be eradicated once and for all. Never again may it interfere in our European living space.

The German soldier is therefore not only charged with the task of destroying the power instrument of this system. He marches forth also as a carrier of a racial conception and as an avenger of all the atrocities which have been committed against him and the German people.

The soldier must show understanding for the harsh atonement of Judaism, the spiritual carrier of the Bolshevik terror.

And in the same month, Colonel-General Hoth also interpreted the war as a struggle between racial superiors and inferiors.

It has become increasingly clear to us this summer, that here in the East spiritually unbridgeable conceptions are fighting each other: German sense of honor and race, and a soldierly tradition of many centuries, against an Asiatic mode of thinking and primitive instincts, whipped up by a small number of mostly Jewish intellectuals: fear of the knout [whip used for flogging], disregard of moral values, levelling down, throwing away of one's worthless life.

More than ever we are filled with the thought of a new era, in which the strength of the German people's racial superiority and achievements entrust it with the leadership of Europe. We clearly recognize our mission to save European culture from the advancing Asiatic barbarism. We now know that we have to fight against an incensed and tough opponent. This battle can only end with the destruction of one or the other; a compromise is out of the question.

> The frontline soldier was affected by ideological propaganda.

I have received the "Stürmer" [a notoriously anti-Semitic newspaper] now for the third time. It makes me happy with all my heart. . . . You could not have made me happier. . . . I recognized the Jewish poison in our people long ago; how far it might have gone with us, this we see only now in this campaign. What the Jewish-regime has done in Russia, we see every day, and even the last doubters are cured here in view of the facts. We must and we will liberate the world from this plague. This is why the German soldier protects the Eastern Front, and we shall not return before we have uprooted all evil and destroyed the center of the Jewish-Bolshevik "world-do-gooders."

10 Stalingrad

In the summer of 1942, the Germans launched a new anti-Soviet offensive, one of whose goals was the conquest of Stalingrad, a vital transportation center located on the Volga River. Germans and Russians battled with dogged ferocity over every part of the city; 99 percent of Stalingrad was reduced to rubble. A Russian counteroffensive in November trapped the German Sixth Army. Realizing that the Sixth Army, exhausted and short of weapons, ammunition, food, and medical supplies, faced annihilation, German generals pleaded in vain with Hitler to permit withdrawal before the Russians closed the ring. On February 2, 1943, the remnants of the Sixth Army surrendered. More than a million people—Russian civilians and soldiers, Germans and their Italian, Hungarian, and Romanian allies—perished in the epic struggle for Stalingrad. The Russian victory was a major turning point in the war.

William Hoffman
DIARY OF A GERMAN SOLDIER

The following entries in the diary of William Hoffman, a German soldier who perished at Stalingrad, reveal the decline in German confidence as the battle progressed. While the German army was penetrating deeply into Russia, he believed that victory was not far away and dreamed of returning home with medals. Then the terrible struggles in Stalingrad made him curse the war.

Today, after we'd had a bath, the company commander told us that if our future operations are as successful, we'll soon reach the Volga, take Stalingrad and then the war will inevitably soon be over. Perhaps we'll be home by Christmas.

July 29 (1942). . . . The company commander says the Russian troops are completely broken, and cannot hold out any longer. To reach the Volga and take Stalingrad is not so difficult for us. The Führer knows where the Russians' weak point is. Victory is not far away. . . .

August 2. . . . What great spaces the Soviets occupy, what rich fields there are to be had here after the war's over! Only let's get it over with quickly. I believe that the Führer will carry the thing through to a successful end.

August 10. . . . The Führer's orders were read out to us. He expects victory of us. We are all convinced that they can't stop us.

August 12. We are advancing towards Stalingrad along the railway line. Yesterday Russian "katyushi" [small rocket launchers] and then tanks halted our regiment. "The Russians are throwing in their last forces," Captain Werner explained to me. Large-scale help is coming up for us, and the Russians will be beaten.

This morning outstanding soldiers were presented with decorations. . . . Will I really go back to Elsa without a decoration? I believe that for Stalingrad the Führer will decorate even me. . . .

August 23. Splendid news—north of Stalingrad our troops have reached the Volga and captured part of the city. The Russians have two alternatives, either to flee across the Volga or give themselves up. Our company's interpreter has interrogated a captured Russian officer. He was wounded, but asserted that the Russians would fight for Stalingrad to the last round. Something incomprehensible is, in fact, going on. In the north our troops capture a part of Stalingrad and reach the Volga, but in the south the doomed divisions are continuing to resist bitterly. Fanaticism. . . .

August 27. A continuous cannonade on all sides. We are slowly advancing. Less than twenty miles to go to Stalingrad. In the daytime we can see the smoke of fires, at nighttime the bright glow. They say that the city is on fire; on the Führer's orders our Luftwaffe [air force] has sent it up in flames. That's what the Russians need, to stop them from resisting. . . .

September 4. We are being sent northward along the front towards Stalingrad. We marched all night and by dawn had reached Voroponovo Station. We can already see the smoking town. It's a happy thought that the end of the war is getting nearer. That's what everyone is saying. If only the days and nights would pass more quickly. . . .

September 5. Our regiment has been ordered to attack Sadovaya station—that's nearly in Stalingrad. Are the Russians really thinking of holding out in the city itself? We had no peace all night from the Russian artillery and aeroplanes. Lots of wounded are being brought by. God protect me. . . .

September 8. Two days of non-stop fighting. The Russians are defending themselves with insane stubbornness. Our regiment has lost many men from the "katyushi," which belch out terrible fire. I have been sent to work at battalion H.Q. It must be mother's prayers that have taken me away from the company's trenches. . . .

September 11. Our battalion is fighting in the suburbs of Stalingrad. We can already see the Volga; firing is going on all the time. Wherever you look is fire and flames. . . . Russian cannon and machine-guns are firing out of the burning city. Fanatics. . . .

September 13. An unlucky number. This morning "katyushi" attacks caused the company heavy losses: twenty-seven dead and fifty wounded. The Russians are fighting desperately like wild beasts, don't give themselves up, but come up close and then throw grenades. Lieutenant Kraus was killed yesterday, and there is no company commander.

September 16. Our battalion, plus tanks, is attacking the [grain storage] elevator, from which smoke is pouring—the grain in it is burning, the Russians seem to have set light to it themselves. Barbarism. The battalion is suffering heavy losses. There are not more than sixty men left in each company. The elevator is occupied not by men but by devils that no flames or bullets can destroy.

September 18. Fighting is going on inside the elevator. The Russians inside are condemned men; the battalion commander says: "The commissars have ordered those men to die in the elevator."

If all the buildings of Stalingrad are defended like this then none of our soldiers will get back to Germany. I had a letter from Elsa today. She's expecting me home when victory's won.

September 20. The battle for the elevator is still going on. The Russians are firing on all sides. We stay in our cellar; you can't go out into the street. Sergeant-Major Nuschke was killed today running across a street. Poor fellow, he's got three children.

September 22. Russian resistance in the elevator has been broken. Our troops are advancing towards the Volga. . . .

. . . Our old soldiers have never experienced such bitter fighting before.

September 26. Our regiment is involved in constant heavy fighting. After the elevator was taken the Russians continued to defend themselves just as stubbornly. You don't see them at all, they have established themselves in houses and cellars and are firing on all sides, including from our rear—barbarians, they use gangster methods.

In the blocks captured two days ago Russian soldiers appeared from somewhere or other and fighting has flared up with fresh vigour. Our men are being killed not only in the firing line, but in the rear, in buildings we have already occupied.

The Russians have stopped surrendering at all. If we take any prisoners it's because they are hopelessly wounded, and can't move by themselves. Stalingrad is hell. Those who are merely wounded are lucky; they will doubtless be at home and celebrate victory with their families. . . .

September 28. Our regiment, and the whole division, are today celebrating victory. Together with our tank crews we have taken the southern part of the city and reached the Volga. We paid dearly for our victory. In three weeks we have occupied about five and a half square miles. The commander has congratulated us on our victory. . . .

October 3. After marching through the night we have established ourselves in a shrub-covered gully. We are apparently going to attack the factories, the chimneys of which we can see clearly. Behind them is the Volga. We have entered a new area. It was night but we saw many crosses with our helmets on top. Have we really lost so many men? Damn this Stalingrad!

October 4. Our regiment is attacking the Barrikady settlement. A lot of Russian tommy-gunners have appeared. Where are they bringing them from?

October 5. Our battalion has gone into the attack four times, and got stopped each time. Russian snipers hit anyone who shows himself carelessly from behind shelter.

October 10. The Russians are so close to us that our planes cannot bomb them. We are preparing for a decisive attack. The Führer has ordered the whole of Stalingrad to be taken as rapidly as possible.

October 14. It has been fantastic since morning: our aeroplanes and artillery have been hammering the Russian positions for hours on end; everything in sight is being blotted from the face of the earth. . . .

October 22. Our regiment has failed to break into the factory. We have lost many men; every time you move you have to jump over bodies. You can scarcely breathe in the daytime: there is nowhere and no one to remove the bodies, so they are left there to rot. Who would have thought three months ago that instead of the joy of victory we would have to endure such sacrifice and torture, the end of which is nowhere in sight? . . .

The soldiers are calling Stalingrad the mass grave of the Wehrmacht [German army]. There are very few men left in the companies. We have been told we are soon going to be withdrawn to be brought back up to strength.

October 27. Our troops have captured the whole of the Barrikady factory, but we cannot break through to the Volga. The Russians are not men, but some kind of cast-iron creatures; they never get tired and are not afraid of fire. We are absolutely exhausted; our regiment now has barely the strength of a company. The Russian artillery at the other side of the Volga won't let you lift your head. . . .

October 28. Every soldier sees himself as a condemned man. The only hope is to be wounded and taken back to the rear. . . .

November 3. In the last few days our battalion has several times tried to attack the Russian positions, . . . to no avail. On this sector also the Russians won't let you lift your head. There have been a number of cases of self-inflicted wounds and malingering among the men. Every day I write two or three reports about them.

November 10. A letter from Elsa today. Everyone expects us home for Christmas. In Germany everyone believes we already hold Stalingrad. How wrong they are. If they could only see what Stalingrad has done to our army.

November 18. Our attack with tanks yesterday had no success. After our attack the field was littered with dead.

November 21. The Russians have gone over to the offensive along the whole front. Fierce fighting is going on. So, there it is—the Volga, victory and soon home to our families! We shall obviously be seeing them next in the other world.

November 29. We are encircled. It was announced this morning that the Führer has said: "The army can trust me to do everything necessary to ensure supplies and rapidly break the encirclement."

December 3. We are on hunger rations and waiting for the rescue that the Führer promised. I send letters home, but there is no reply.

December 7. Rations have been cut to such an extent that the soldiers are suffering terribly from hunger; they are issuing one loaf of stale bread for five men.

December 11. Three questions are obsessing every soldier and officer: When will the Russians stop firing and let us sleep in peace, if only for one night? How and with what are we going to fill our empty stomachs, which, apart from 3½–7 ozs of bread, receive virtually nothing at all? And when will Hitler take any decisive steps to free our armies from encirclement?

December 14. Everybody is racked with hunger. Frozen potatoes are the best meal, but to get them out of the ice-covered ground under fire from Russian bullets is not so easy.

December 18. The officers today told the soldiers to be prepared for action. General Manstein is approaching Stalingrad from the south with strong forces. This news brought hope to the soldiers' hearts. God, let it be!

December 21. We are waiting for the order, but for some reason or other it has been a long time coming. Can it be that it is not true about Manstein? This is worse than any torture.

December 23. Still no orders. It was all a bluff with Manstein. Or has he been defeated at the approaches to Stalingrad?

December 25. The Russian radio has announced the defeat of Manstein. Ahead of us is either death or captivity.

December 26. The horses have already been eaten. I would eat a cat; they say its meat is also tasty. The soldiers look like corpses or lunatics, looking for something to put in their mouths. They no longer take cover from Russian shells; they haven't the strength to walk, run away and hide. A curse on this war! . . .

Anton Kuzmich Dragan
A SOVIET VETERAN RECALLS

Anton Kuzmich Dragan, a Russian soldier, describes the vicious street fighting in Stalingrad during late September 1942.

"The Germans had cut us off from our neighbours. The supply of ammunition had been cut off; every bullet was worth its weight in gold. I gave the order to economize on ammunition, to collect the cartridge-pouches of the dead and all captured weapons. In the evening the enemy again tried to break our resistance, coming up close to our positions. As our numbers grew smaller, we shortened our line of defence. We began to move back slowly towards the Volga, drawing the enemy after us, and the ground we occupied was invariably too small for the Germans to be able easily to use artillery and aircraft.

"We moved back, occupying one building after another, turning them into strongholds. A soldier would crawl out of an occupied position only when the ground was on fire under him and his clothes were smouldering. During the day the Germans managed to occupy only two blocks.

"At the crossroads of Krasnopiterskaya and Komsomolskaya Streets we occupied a three-storey building on the corner. This was a good position from which to fire on all comers and it became our last defence. I ordered all entrances to be barricaded, and windows and embrasures to be adapted so that we could fire through them with all our remaining weapons.

"At a narrow window of the semi-basement we placed the heavy machine-gun with our emergency supply of ammunition—the last belt of cartridges. I had decided to use it at the most critical moment.

"Two groups, six in each, went up to the third floor and the garret. Their job was to break down walls, and prepare lumps of stone and beams to throw at the Germans when they came up close. A place for the seriously wounded was set aside in the basement. Our garrison consisted of forty men. Difficult days began. Attack after attack broke unendingly like waves against us. After each attack was beaten off we felt it was impossible to hold off the onslaught any longer, but when the Germans launched a fresh attack, we managed to find means and strength. This lasted five days and nights.

"The basement was full of wounded; only twelve men were still able to fight. There was no water. Ail we had left in the way of food was a few pounds of scorched grain; the Germans decided to beat us with starvation. Their attacks stopped, but they kept up the fire from their heavy-calibre machine-guns all the time.

"We did not think about escape, but only about how to sell our lives most dearly—we had no other way out. . . .

"The Germans attacked again. I ran upstairs with my men and could see their thin, blackened and strained faces, the bandages on their wounds, dirty and clotted with blood, their guns held firmly in their hands. There was no fear in their eyes. Lyuba Nesterenko, a nurse, was dying, with blood flowing from a wound in her chest. She had a bandage in her hand. Before she died she wanted to help to bind someone's wound, but she failed . . .

"The German attack was beaten off. In the silence that gathered around us we could hear the bitter fighting going on for Mameyev Kurgan and in the factory area of the city.

"How could we help the men defending the city? How could we divert from over there even a part of the enemy forces, which had stopped attacking our building?

"We decided to raise a red flag over the building, so that the Nazis would not think we had given up. But we had no red material. Understanding what we wanted to do, one of the men who was severely wounded took off his bloody vest and, after wiping the blood off his wound with it, handed it over to me.

"The Germans shouted through a megaphone: 'Russians! Surrender! You'll die just the same!'

"At that moment a red flag rose over our building.

"'Bark, you dogs! We've still got a long time to live!' shouted my orderly, Kozhushko.

"We beat off the next attack with stones, firing occasionally and throwing our last grenades. Suddenly from behind a blank wall, from the rear, came the grind of a tank's caterpillar tracks. We had no anti-tank grenades. All we had left was one anti-tank rifle with three rounds. I handed this rifle to an anti-tank man, Berdyshev, and sent him out through the back to fire at the tank point-blank. But before he could get into position he was captured by German tommy-gunners. What Berdyshev told the Germans I don't know, but I can guess that he led them up the garden path, because an hour later they started to attack at precisely that point where I had put my machine-gun with its emergency belt of cartridges.

"This time, reckoning that we had run out of ammunition, they came impudently out of their shelter, standing up and shouting. They came down the street in a column.

"I put the last belt in the heavy machine-gun at the semi-basement window and sent the whole of the 250 bullets into the yelling, dirty-grey Nazi mob. I was wounded in the hand but did not leave go of the machine-gun. Heaps of bodies littered the ground. The Germans still alive ran for cover in panic. An hour later they led our anti-tank rifleman on to a heap of ruins and shot him in front of our eyes, for having shown them the way to my machine-gun.

"There were no more attacks. An avalanche of shells fell on the building. The Germans stormed at us with every possible kind of weapon. We couldn't raise our heads.

"Again we heard the ominous sound of tanks. From behind a neighbouring block stocky German tanks began to crawl out. This, clearly, was the end. The guardsmen said goodbye to one another. With a dagger my orderly scratched on a brick wall: 'Rodimatsev's guardsmen fought and died for their country here.' The battalion's documents and a map case containing the Party and Komsomol cards of the defenders of the building had been put in a hole in a corner of the basement. The first salvo shattered the silence. There were a series of blows, and the building rocked and collapsed. How much later it was when I opened my eyes, I don't know. It was dark. The air was full of acrid brickdust. I could hear muffled groans around me. Kohushko, the orderly, was pulling at me:

"'You're alive . . .'

"On the floor of the basement lay a number of other stunned and injured soldiers. We had been buried alive under the ruins of the three-storey building. We could scarcely breathe. We had no thought for food or water—it was air that had become most important for survival. I spoke to the soldiers:

"'Men! We did not flinch in battle, we fought even when resistance seemed impossible, and we have to get out of this tomb so that we can live and avenge the death of our comrades!'

"Even in pitch darkness you can see somebody else's face, feel other people close to you.

"With great difficulty we began to pick our way out of the tomb. We worked in silence, our bodies covered with cold, clammy sweat, our badly-bound wounds ached, our teeth were covered with brickdust, it became more and more difficult to breathe, but there were no groans or complaints.

"A few hours later, through the hole we had made, we could see the stars and breathe the fresh September air.

"Utterly exhausted, the men crowded round the hole, greedily gulping in the autumn air. Soon the opening was wide enough for a man to crawl through. Kozhushko, being only relatively slightly injured, went off to reconnoitre. An hour later he came back and reported:

" 'Comrade Lieutenant, there are Germans all round us; along the Volga they are mining the bank; there are German patrols nearby ...'

"We took the decision to fight our way through to our own lines."

11 The Holocaust

Over conquered Europe the Nazis imposed a "New Order" marked by exploitation, torture, and mass murder. The Germans took some 5.5 million Russian prisoners of war, of whom more than 3.5 million perished; many of these prisoners were deliberately starved to death. The Germans imprisoned and executed many Polish intellectuals and priests and slaughtered vast numbers of Gypsies. Using the modern state's organizational capacities and the instruments of modern technology, the Nazis murdered six million Jews, including 1.5 million children—two-thirds of the Jewish population of Europe. Gripped by the mythical, perverted world-view of nazism, the SS, Hitler's elite guard, carried out these murders with dedication and idealism; they believed that they were exterminating subhumans who threatened the German nation.

Hermann Graebe
SLAUGHTER OF JEWS IN UKRAINE

While the regular German army penetrated deeply into Russia, special SS units, the *Einsatzgruppen,* rounded up Jews for mass executions, killing an estimated 1 to 1.4 million people. Hermann Graebe, a German construction engineer, saw such a mass slaughter in Dubno in Ukraine. He gave a sworn affidavit before the Nuremberg tribunal, a court at which the Allies tried Nazi war criminals after the end of World War II.

Graebe had joined the Nazi party in 1931 but later renounced his membership, and during the war he rescued Jews from SS custody. Graebe was the only German citizen to volunteer to testify at the Nuremberg trials, an act that earned him the enmity of his compatriots. Socially ostracized, Graebe emigrated to the United States, where he died in 1986 at the age of eighty-five.

On October 5, 1942, when I visited the building office at Dubno, my foreman told me that in the vicinity of the site, Jews from Dubno had been shot in three large pits, each about 30 metres long and 3 metres deep. About 1,500 persons had been killed daily. All the 5,000 Jews who had still been living in Dubno before the pogrom were to be liquidated. As the shooting had taken place in his presence, he was still much upset.

Thereupon, I drove to the site accompanied by my foreman and saw near it great mounds of earth, about 30 metres long and 2 metres high. Several trucks stood in front of the mounds. Armed Ukrainian militia drove the people off the trucks under the supervision of an S.S. man. The militiamen acted as guards on the trucks and drove them to and from the pit. All these people had the regulation yellow patches on the front and back of their clothes, and thus could be recognized as Jews.

My foreman and I went directly to the pits. Nobody bothered us. Now I heard rifle shots in quick succession from behind one of the earth mounds. The people who had got off the trucks—men, women and children of all ages—had to undress upon the orders of an S.S. man, who carried a riding or dog whip. They had to put down their clothes in fixed places, sorted according to shoes, top clothing and undercloth-ing. I saw a heap of shoes of about 800 to 1,000 pairs, great piles of underlinen and clothing.

Without screaming or weeping, these people undressed, stood around in family groups, kissed each other, said farewells, and waited for a sign from another S.S. man, who stood near the pit, also with a whip in his hand. During the fifteen minutes that I stood near I heard no complaint or plea for mercy. I watched a family of about eight persons, a man and a woman both about fifty with their children of about one, eight and ten, and two grown-up daughters of about twenty to twenty-nine. An old woman with snow-white hair was holding the one-year-old child in her arms and singing to it and tickling it. The child was cooing with delight. The couple were looking on with tears in their eyes. The father was holding the hand of a boy about ten years old and speaking to him softly; the boy was fighting his tears. The father pointed to the sky, stroked his head, and seemed to explain something to him.

At that moment the S.S. man at the pit shouted something to his comrade. The latter counted off about twenty persons and instructed them to go behind the earth mound. Among them was the family which I have mentioned. I well remember a girl, slim and with black hair, who, as she passed close to me, pointed to herself and said "23." I walked around the mound and found myself confronted by a tremendous grave. People were closely wedged together and lying on top of each other so that only their heads were visible. Nearly all had blood running over their shoulders from their heads. Some of the people shot were still moving. Some were lifting their arms and turning their heads to show that they were still alive. The pit was already two-thirds full. I estimated that it already contained about 1,000 people.

I looked for the man who did the shooting. He was an S.S. man, who sat at the edge of the narrow end of the pit, his feet dangling into the pit. He had a tommy-gun on his knees and was smoking a cigarette. The people, completely naked, went down some steps which were cut in the clay wall of the pit and clambered over the heads of the people lying there, to the place to which the S.S. man directed them. They lay down in front of the dead or injured people; some caressed those who were still alive and spoke to them in a low voice.

Then I heard a series of shots. I looked into the pit and saw that the bodies were twitching or the heads lying motionless on top of the bodies which lay before them. Blood was running from their necks. I was surprised that I was not ordered away, but I saw that there were two or three postmen in uniform nearby. The next batch was approaching already. They went down into the pit, lined themselves up against the previous victims and were shot.

When I walked back round the mound, I noticed another truckload of people which had just arrived. This time it included sick and infirm persons. An old, very thin woman with terribly thin legs was undressed by others who were already naked, while two people held her up. The woman appeared to be paralyzed. The naked people carried the woman around the mound. I left with my foreman and drove in my car back to Dubno.

On the morning of the next day, when I again visited the site, I saw about thirty naked people lying near the pit—about 30 to 50 metres away from it. Some of them were still alive; they looked straight in front of them with a fixed stare and seemed to notice neither the chilliness of the morning nor the workers of my firm who stood around. A girl of about twenty spoke to me and asked me to give her clothes and help her escape. At that moment we heard a fast car approach and I noticed that it was an S.S. detail. I moved away to my site. Ten minutes later we heard shots from the vicinity of the pit. The Jews alive had been ordered to throw the corpses into the pit, then they had themselves to lie down in it to be shot in the neck.

Rudolf Hoess
COMMANDANT OF AUSCHWITZ

To speed up the "final solution of the Jewish problem," the SS established death camps in Poland. Jews from all over Europe were crammed into cattle cars and shipped to these camps to be gassed or worked to death. At Auschwitz, the most notorious of the concentration camps, the SS used five gas chambers to kill as many as 9,000 people in a day. Special squads of prisoners, called *Sonderkommandos,* were forced to pick over the corpses for gold teeth, jewelry, and anything else of value for the German war effort. Some 1.3 million Jews perished at Auschwitz. Rudolf Hoess (1900–1947), commandant of Auschwitz, described the murder process in a deposition at the trial in Nuremberg of major Nazi war criminals. He was executed by Polish authorities in 1947. An excerpt from Hoess's account follows.

The "final solution" of the Jewish question meant the complete extermination of all Jews in Europe. I was ordered to establish extermination facilities at Auschwitz in June 1941. At that time, there were already in the general government three other extermination camps: Belzek, Treblinka, and Wolzek. These camps were under the Einsatzkommando of the Security Police and SD. I visited Treblinka to find out how they carried out their extermination. The Camp Commandant at Treblinka told me that he had liquidated 80,000 in the course of one-half year. He was principally concerned with liquidating all the Jews from the Warsaw ghetto. He used monoxide gas and I did not think that his methods were very efficient. So when I set up the extermination building at Auschwitz, I used Cyclon B, which was a crystallized prussic acid which we dropped into the death chamber from a small opening. It took from 3 to 15 minutes to kill the people in the death chamber depending upon climatic conditions. We knew when the people were dead because their screaming stopped. We usually waited about one-half hour before we opened the doors and removed the bodies. After the bodies were removed our special commandos took off the rings and extracted the gold from the teeth of the corpses.

Another improvement we made over Treblinka was that we built our gas chambers to accommodate 2,000 people at one time, whereas at Treblinka their 10 gas chambers only accommodated 200 people each. The way we selected our victims was as follows: we had two SS doctors on duty at Auschwitz to examine the incoming transports of prisoners. The prisoners would be marched by one of the doctors who would make spot decisions as they walked by. Those who were fit for work were sent into the Camp. Others were sent immediately to the extermination plants. Children of tender years were invariably exterminated since by reason of their youth they were unable to work.

Still another improvement we made over Treblinka was that at Treblinka the victims almost always knew that they were to be exterminated and at Auschwitz we endeavored to fool the victims into thinking that they were to go through a delousing process. Of course, frequently they realized our true intentions and we sometimes had riots and difficulties due to that fact. Very frequently women would hide their children under the clothes but of course when we found them we would send the children in to be exterminated. We were required to carry out these exterminations in secrecy but of course the foul and nauseating stench from the continuous burning of bodies permeated the entire area and all of the people living in the surrounding communities knew that exterminations were going on at Auschwitz.

We received from time to time special prisoners from the local Gestapo office. The SS doctors killed such prisoners by injections of benzine. Doctors had orders to write ordinary death certificates and could put down any reason at all for the cause of death.

Y. Pfeffer
CONCENTRATION CAMP LIFE AND DEATH

Jews not immediately selected for extermination faced a living death in the concentration camp, which also included non-Jewish inmates, many of them opponents of the Nazi regime. The SS, who ran the camps, took sadistic pleasure in humiliating and brutalizing their helpless Jewish victims. In 1946, Y. Pfeffer, a Jewish survivor of Majdanek concentration camp in Poland, described the world created by the SS and Nazi ideology.

You get up at 3 A.M. You have to dress quickly, and make the "bed" so that it looks like a matchbox. For the slightest irregularity in bed-making the punishment was 25 lashes, after which it was impossible to lie or sit for a whole month.

Everyone had to leave the barracks immediately. Outside it is still dark—or else the moon is shining. People are trembling because of lack of sleep and the cold. In order to warm up a bit, groups of ten to twenty people stand together, back to back so as to rub against each other.

There was what was called a wash-room, where everyone in the camp was supposed to wash—there were only a few faucets—and we were 4,500 people in that section (no. 3). Of course there was neither soap nor towel or even a handkerchief, so that washing was theoretical rather than practical. . . . In one day, a person there [be]came a lowly person indeed.

At 5 A.M. we used to get half a litre of black, bitter coffee. That was all we got for what was called "breakfast." At 6 A.M.—a headcount (*Appell* in German). We all had to stand at attention, in fives, according to the barracks, of which there were 22 in each section. We stood there until the SS men had satisfied their game-playing instincts by "humorous" orders to take off and put on caps. Then they received their report, and counted us. After the headcount—work.

We went in groups—some to build railway tracks or a road, some to the quarries to carry stones or coal, some to take out manure, or for potato-digging, latrine-cleaning, barracks—or sewer—repairs. All this took place inside the camp enclosure. During work the SS men beat up the prisoners mercilessly, inhumanly and for no reason.

They were like wild beasts and, having found their victim, ordered him to present his backside, and beat him with a stick or a whip, usually until the stick broke.

The victim screamed only after the first blows, afterwards he fell unconscious and the SS man then kicked at the ribs, the face, at the most sensitive parts of a man's body, and then, finally convinced that the victim was at the end of his strength, he ordered another Jew to pour one pail of water after the other over the beaten person until he woke and got up.

A favorite sport of the SS men was to make a "boxing sack" out of a Jew. This was done in the following way: Two Jews were stood up, one being forced to hold the other by the collar, and an SS man trained giving him a knockout. Of course, after the first blow, the poor victim was likely to fall, and this was prevented by the other Jew holding him up. After the fat, Hitlerite murderer had "trained" in this way for 15 minutes, and only after the poor victim was completely shattered, covered in blood, his teeth knocked out, his nose broken, his eyes hit, they released him and ordered a doctor to treat his wounds. That was their way of taking care and being generous.

Another customary SS habit was to kick a Jew with a heavy boot. The Jew was forced to stand to attention, and all the while the SS man kicked him until he broke some bones. People who stood near enough to such a victim, often heard the breaking of the bones. The pain was so terrible that people, having undergone that treatment, died in agony.

Apart from the SS men there were other expert hangmen. These were the so-called Capos. The name was an abbreviation for "barracks police." The Capos were German criminals who were also camp inmates. However, although they belonged to "us," they were privileged. They had a special, better barracks of their own, they had better food, better, almost normal clothes, they wore special red or green riding pants, high leather boots, and fulfilled the functions of camp guards. They were worse even than the SS men. One of them, older than the others and the worst murderer of them all, when he descended on a victim, would not revive him later with water but would choke him to death. Once, this murderer caught a boy of 13 (in the presence of his father) and hit his head so that the poor child died instantly. This "camp elder" later boasted in front of his peers, with a smile on his beast's face and with pride, that he managed to kill a Jew with one blow.

In each section stood a gallows. For being late for the headcount, or similar crimes, the "camp elder" hanged the offenders.

Work was actually unproductive, and its purpose was exhaustion and torture.

At 12 noon there was a break for a meal. Standing in line, we received half a litre of soup each. Usually it was cabbage soup, or some other watery liquid, without fats, tasteless. That was lunch. It was eaten—in all weather—under the open sky, never in the barracks. No spoons were allowed, though wooden spoons lay on each bunk—probably for show, for Red Cross committees. One had to drink the soup out of the bowl and lick it like a dog.

From 1 P.M. till 6 P.M. there was work again. I must emphasize that if we were lucky we got a 12 o'clock meal. There were "days of punishment"—when lunch was given together with the evening meal, and it was cold and sour, so that our stomach was empty for a whole day.

Afternoon work was the same blows, and blows again. Until 6 P.M.

At 6 there was the evening headcount. Again we were forced to stand at attention. Counting, receiving the report. Usually we were left standing at attention for an hour or two, while some prisoners were called up for "punishment parade"—they were those who in the Germans' eyes had transgressed in some way during the day, or had not been punctilious in their performance. They were stripped naked publicly, laid out on specially constructed benches, and whipped with 25 or 50 lashes.

The brutal beating and the heart-rending cries—all this the prisoners had to watch and hear.

12 Resistance

Each occupied country had its collaborators who welcomed the demise of democracy, saw Hitler as Europe's best defense against communism, and profited from the sale of war material. Each country also produced a resistance movement that grew stronger as Nazi barbarism became more visible and prospects of a German defeat more likely. The Nazis retaliated by torturing and executing captured resistance fighters and killing hostages—generally, fifty for every German killed.

In western Europe, the resistance rescued downed Allied airmen, radioed military intelligence to Britain, and sabotaged German installations. Norwegians blew up the German stock of heavy water needed for atomic research. The Danish underground sabotaged railways and smuggled into neutral Sweden almost all of Denmark's eight thousand Jews just before they were to be deported to the death camps. The Greek resistance blew up a vital viaduct, interrupting the movement of supplies to German troops in North Africa. After the Allies landed on the coast of France in June 1944, the French resistance delayed the movement of German reinforcements and liberated sections of the country. Belgian resistance fighters captured the vital port of Antwerp.

The Polish resistance, numbering nearly 400,000 at its height, reported on German troop movements and interfered with supplies destined for the Eastern Front. In August 1944, with Soviet forces approaching Warsaw, the Poles staged a full-scale revolt against the German occupiers. The Poles appealed to the Soviets, camped ten miles away, for help. Thinking about a future Soviet-dominated Poland, Stalin ordered the Red Army to stay in place. After sixty-three days of street fighting, remnants of the Polish underground surrendered, and the Germans destroyed what was left of Warsaw.

Russian partisans numbered several hundred thousand men and women. Operating behind the German lines, they sabotaged railways, destroyed trucks, and killed thousands of German soldiers in hit-and-run attacks.

The mountains and forests of Yugoslavia provided excellent terrain for guerrilla warfare. The leading Yugoslav resistance army was headed by Josip Broz (1892–1980), better known as Tito. Moscow-trained, intelligent, and courageous, Tito organized the partisans into a disciplined fighting force, which tied down a huge German army and ultimately liberated the country from German rule.

Jews participated in the resistance movements in all countries and were particularly prominent in the French resistance. Specifically Jewish resistance organizations emerged in eastern Europe, but they suffered from shattering hardships. They had virtually no access to weapons. Poles, Ukrainians, Lithuanians, and other peoples of eastern Europe with a long history of anti-Semitism gave little or no support to Jewish resisters—at times, even denounced them to the Nazis, or killed them. The Germans responded to acts of resistance with savage reprisals against other Jews, creating a moral dilemma for any Jew who considered taking up arms. Nevertheless, revolts did take place in the ghettos and concentration camps. In the spring of 1943, the surviving Jews of the Warsaw ghetto, armed only with a few guns and homemade bombs, fought the Germans for several weeks.

Italy and Germany also had resistance movements. After the Allies landed in Italy in 1943, bands of Italian partisans helped to liberate Italy from fascism and the German occupation. In Germany, army officers plotted to assassinate the Führer. On July 20, 1944, Colonel Claus von Stauffenberg planted a bomb at a staff conference attended by Hitler, but the Führer escaped serious injury. In retaliation, some five thousand suspected anti-Nazis were imprisoned, and 200 were executed in exceptionally barbarous fashion.

Albert Camus
"I AM FIGHTING YOU BECAUSE YOUR LOGIC IS AS CRIMINAL AS YOUR HEART"

Reared and educated in French-ruled Algeria, Albert Camus (1908–1960) gained an instant reputation in 1942 with the publication of *The Stranger,* a short novel, and "The Myth of Sisyphus," a philosophical essay. For Camus, neither religion nor philosophy provides a sure basis for human values; neither can tell us with certainty what is right or wrong. Ultimately existence has no higher meaning, and the universe is indifferent to us.

While serving in the French Resistance, he wrote letters to an imaginary German friend, which were published clandestinely during the German occupation. These letters, said Camus years later, "had a purpose, which was to throw some light on the blind battle we were then waging and thereby to make our battle more effective." In the following letter, written in July 1944, Camus reveals an attitude that pervades his writings: a moralistic humanism that promotes fraternity and dignity and offers a worthwhile response to the absurdity of the human condition.

Now the moment of your defeat is approaching. I am writing you from a city known throughout the world which is now preparing against you a celebration of freedom. . . .

. . . I want to tell you how it is possible that, though so similar, we should be enemies today, how I might have stood beside you and why all is over between us now.

For a long time we both thought that this world had no ultimate meaning and that consequently we were cheated. I still think so in a way. But I came to different conclusions from the ones you used to talk about, which, for so many years now, you have been trying to introduce into history. I tell myself now that if I had really followed your reasoning, I ought to approve what you are doing. And this is so serious that I must stop and consider it, during this summer night so full of promises for us and of threats for you.

You never believed in the meaning of this world, and you therefore deduced the idea that everything was equivalent and that good and evil could be defined according to one's wishes. You supposed that in the absence of any human or divine code the only values were those of the animal world—in other words, violence and cunning. Hence you concluded that man was negligible and that his soul could be killed, that in the maddest of histories the only pursuit for the individual was the adventure of power and his only morality, the realism of conquests. And, to tell the truth, I, believing I thought as you did, saw no valid argument to answer you except a fierce love of justice which, after all, seemed to me as unreasonable as the most sudden passion.

Where lay the difference? Simply that you readily accepted despair and I never yielded to it. Simply that you saw the injustice of our condition to the point of being willing to add to it, whereas it seemed to me that man must exalt justice in order to fight against eternal injustice, create happiness in order to protest against the universe of unhappiness. Because you turned your despair into intoxication, because you freed yourself from it by making a principle of it, you were willing to destroy man's works and to fight him in order to add to his basic misery. Meanwhile, refusing to accept that despair and that tortured world, I merely wanted men to rediscover their solidarity in order to wage war against their revolting fate.

As you see, from the same principle we derived quite different codes, because along the way you gave up the lucid view and considered it more convenient (you would have said a matter of indifference) for another to do your thinking for you and for millions of Germans. Because you were tired of fighting heaven, you relaxed in that exhausting adventure in which you had to mutilate souls and destroy the world. In short, you chose injustice and sided with the gods. Your logic was merely apparent.

I, on the contrary, chose justice in order to remain faithful to the world. I continue to believe that this world has no ultimate meaning. But I know that something in it has a meaning and that is man, because he is the only creature to insist on having one. This world has at least the truth of man, and our task is to provide its justifications against fate itself. And it has no justification but man; hence he must be saved if we want to save the idea we have of life. With your scornful smile you will ask me: what do you mean by saving man? And with all my being I shout to you that I mean not mutilating him and yet giving a chance to the justice that man alone can conceive.

At present everything must be obvious to you; you know that we are enemies. You are the man of injustice, and there is nothing in the world that my heart loathes so much. But now I know the reasons for what was once merely a passion. I am fighting you because your logic is as criminal as your heart. And in the horror you have lavished upon us for four years, your reason plays as large a part as your instinct. This is why my condemnation will be sweeping; you are already dead as far as I am concerned. But at the very moment when I am judging your horrible behavior, I shall remember that you and we started out from the same solitude, that you and we, with all Europe, are caught in the same tragedy of the intelligence. And, despite yourselves, I shall still apply to you the name of man. In order to keep faith with ourselves, we are obliged to respect in you what you do not respect in others. For a long time that was your great advantage since you kill more easily than we do. And to the very end of time that will be the advantage of those who resemble you. But to the very end of time, we, who do not resemble you, shall have to bear witness so that mankind, despite its worst errors, may have its justification and its proof of innocence.

This is why, at the end of this combat, from the heart of this city that has come to resemble hell, despite all the tortures inflicted on our people, despite our disfigured dead and our villages peopled with orphans, I can tell you that at the very moment when we are going to destroy you without pity, we still feel no hatred for you. And even if tomorrow, like so many others, we had to die, we should still be without hatred. We cannot guarantee that we shall not be afraid; we shall simply try to be reasonable. But we can guarantee that we shall not hate anything. And we have come to terms with the only thing in the world I could loathe today, I assure you, and we want to destroy you in your power without mutilating you in your soul.

As for the advantage you had over us, you see that you continue to have it. But it likewise constitutes our superiority. And it is what makes this night easy for me. Our strength lies in thinking as you do about the essence of the world, in rejecting no aspect of the drama that is ours. But at the same time we have saved the idea of man at the end of this disaster of the intelligence, and that idea gives us the undying courage to believe in a rebirth. To be sure, the accusation we make against the world is not mitigated by this. We paid so dear for this new knowledge that our condition continues to seem desperate to us. Hundreds of thousands of men assassinated at dawn, the terrible walls of prisons, the soil of Europe reeking with millions of corpses of its sons—it took all that to pay for the acquisition of two or three slight distinctions which may have no other value than to help some among us to die more nobly. Yes, that is heart-breaking. But we have to prove that we do not deserve so much injustice. This is the task we have set ourselves; it will begin tomorrow. In this night of Europe filled with the breath of summer, millions of men, armed or unarmed, are getting ready for the fight. The dawn about to break will mark your final defeat. I know that heaven, which was indifferent to your horrible victories, will be equally indifferent to your just defeat. Even now I expect nothing from heaven. But we shall at least have helped save man from the solitude to which you wanted to relegate him. Because you scorned such faith in mankind, you are the men who, by thousands, are going to die solitary. Now, I can say farewell to you.

July 1944

Hans and Sophie Scholl
THE WHITE ROSE

In February 1943, Hans Scholl, aged twenty-five, a medical student, and his twenty-two-year-old sister, Sophie Scholl, who was studying biology and philosophy, were executed by the Nazis for high treason. The Scholls belonged to the White Rose, a small group of idealistic students at the University of Munich that urged passive resistance to the National Socialist regime. The White Rose hoped that if more Germans were aware of the Nazi regime's inhumane character they would withdraw their loyalty.

The Scholls had once been enthusiastic members of the Hitler Youth, but over the years they grew increasingly disillusioned with nazism. Their outlook was shaped by their anti-Nazi father, by a commitment to the German humanist tradition best represented by Schiller and Goethe, by their Christian faith, and by Kurt Huber, a professor of philosophy and psychology at their university, who spoke to trusted students of a duty "to enlighten those Germans who are still unaware of the evil intentions of our government." Hans was also swayed by the persecution of Jews he had witnessed when he was in transport through Poland to the Russian front.

On walls in Munich, the Scholls painted signs: "Down with Hitler" and "Freedom." Stowing their anti-Nazi leaflets in luggage, the students traveled by railroad to several German cities to drop them off.

On February 18, 1943, Hans and Sophie were spotted dropping leaflets in the university by the building superintendent, who reported them to the Gestapo. On February 23, Hans, Sophie, and Christoph Probst, also a medical student, were executed. Several days before she died, Sophie stated: "What does my death matter if through us thousands of people will be stirred to action and awakened?" Hans' last words, "Long live freedom," echoed through the prison. Kurt Huber and other members of the group were executed on July 13, 1943.

The following excerpts come from the White Rose's leaflets.

[SECOND LEAFLET]

We do not want to discuss here the question of the Jews, nor do we want in this leaflet to compose a defense or apology. No, only by way of example do we want to cite the fact that since the conquest of Poland *three hundred thousand* Jews have been murdered in this country in the most bestial way. Here we see the most frightful crime against human dignity, a crime that is unparalleled in the whole of history. For Jews, too, are human beings—no matter what position we take with respect to the Jewish question—and a crime of this dimension has been perpetrated against human beings. Someone may say that the Jews deserved their fate. This assertion would be a monstrous impertinence; but let us assume that someone said this—what position has he then taken toward the fact that the entire Polish aristocratic youth is being annihilated? (May God grant that this program has not fully achieved its aim as yet!) All male offspring of the houses of the nobility between the ages of fifteen and twenty were transported to concentration camps in Germany and sentenced to forced labor, and all girls of this age group were sent to Norway, into the bordellos of the SS! Why tell you these things, since you are fully aware of them—or if not of these, then of other equally grave crimes committed by this frightful sub-humanity? Because here we touch on a problem which involves us deeply and forces us all to take thought. Why do the German people behave so apathetically in the face of all these abominable crimes, crimes so unworthy of the human race? Hardly anyone thinks about that. It is accepted as fact and put out of mind. The German people slumber on in their dull, stupid sleep and encourage these fascist criminals; they give them the opportunity to carry on their depredations; and of course they do so. Is this a sign that the Germans are brutalized in their simplest human feelings, that no chord within them cries out at the sight of such deeds, that they have sunk into a fatal consciencelessness from which they will never, never awake? It seems to be so, and will certainly be so, if the German does not at last start up out of his stupor, if he does not protest wherever and whenever he can against this clique of criminals, if he shows no sympathy for these hundreds of thousands of victims. He must evidence not only sympathy; no, much more: a sense of *complicity* in guilt. For through his apathetic behavior he gives these evil men the opportunity to act as they do; he tolerates this "government" which has taken upon itself such an infinitely great burden of guilt; indeed, he himself is to blame for the fact that it came about at all! Each man wants to be exonerated of a guilt of this kind, each one continues on his way with the most placid, the calmest conscience. But he cannot be exonerated; he is *guilty, guilty, guilty*! It is not too late, however, to do away with this most reprehensible of all miscarriages of government, so as to avoid being burdened with even greater guilt. Now, when in recent years our eyes have been opened, when we know exactly who our adversary is, it is high time to root out this brown horde. Up until the outbreak of the war the larger part of the German people was blinded; the Nazis did not show themselves in their true aspect. But now, now that we have recognized them for what they are, it must be the sole and first duty, the holiest duty of every German to destroy these beasts. . . .

Please make as many copies as possible of this leaflet and distribute them.

[THIRD LEAFLET]

. . . Every individual human being has a claim to a useful and just state, a state which secures the freedom of the individual as well as the good of the whole. For, according to God's will, man is intended to pursue his natural goal, his earthly happiness, in self-reliance and self-chosen activity, freely and independently within the community of life and work of the nation.

But our present "state" is the dictatorship of evil. "Oh, we've known that for a long time," I hear you object, "and it isn't necessary to bring that to our attention again." But, I ask you, if you know that, why do you not bestir yourselves, why do you allow these men who are in power to rob you step by step, openly and in secret, of one domain of your rights after another, until one day nothing, nothing at all will be left but a mechanized state system presided over by criminals and drunks? Is your spirit already so crushed by abuse that you forget it is your right—or rather, your *moral duty*—to eliminate this system? But if a man no longer can summon the strength to demand his right, then it is absolutely certain that he will perish. . . .

. . . At *all* points we must oppose National Socialism, wherever it is open to attack. We must soon bring this monster of a state to an end. A victory of fascist Germany in this war would have immeasurable, frightful consequences. The military victory over Bolshevism dare not become the primary concern of the Germans. The defeat of the Nazis must *unconditionally* be the first order of business. . . .

And now every convinced opponent of National Socialism must ask himself how he can fight against the present "state" in the most effective way, how he can strike it the most telling blows. Through passive resistance, without a doubt. We cannot provide each man with the blueprint for his acts, we can only suggest them in general terms, and he alone will find the way of achieving this end:

Sabotage in armament plants and war industries, sabotage at all gatherings, rallies, public ceremonies, and organizations of the National Socialist Party. Obstruction of the smooth functioning of the war machine (a machine for war that goes on solely to shore up and perpetuate the National Socialist Party and its dictatorship). *Sabotage* in all the areas of science and scholarship which further the continuation of the war—whether in universities, technical schools, laboratories, research institutes, or technical bureaus. *Sabotage* in all cultural institutions which could potentially enhance the "prestige" of the fascists among the people. *Sabotage* in all branches of the arts which have even the slightest dependence on National Socialism or render it service. *Sabotage* in all publications, all newspapers, that are in the pay of the "government" and that defend its ideology and aid in disseminating the brown lie. Do not give a penny to public drives. . . . Do not contribute to the collections of metal, textiles, and the like. Try to convince all your acquaintances, including those in the lower social classes, of the senselessness of continuing, of the hopelessness of this war; of our spiritual and economic enslavement at the hands of the National Socialists; of the destruction of all moral and religious values; and urge them to *passive resistance*! . . .

Please duplicate and distribute!

[FOURTH LEAFLET]

Every word that comes from Hitler's mouth is a lie. When he says peace, he means war, and when he blasphemously uses the name of the Almighty, he means the power of evil, the fallen angel, Satan. His mouth is the foul-smelling maw of Hell, and his might is at bottom accursed. True, we must conduct the struggle against the National Socialist terrorist state with rational means; but whoever today still doubts the reality, the existence of demonic powers, has failed by a wide margin to understand the metaphysical background of this war. Behind the concrete, the visible events, behind all objective, logical considerations, we find the irrational element: the struggle against the demon, against the servants of the Antichrist. . . .

. . . Has God not given you the strength, the will to fight? We *must* attack evil where it is strongest, and it is strongest in the power of Hitler.

Marek Edelman
THE GHETTO FIGHTS: THE WARSAW GHETTO UPRISING, 1943

Three million Jews lived in Poland at the time of the Nazi invasion in 1939. In 1940, the Nazis began herding Jews from all over the country into densely packed ghettos—six or seven to a room in Warsaw—located in a number of cities. There the Jews worked as slave laborers for the German war effort. Many died of beatings, shootings, disease, and starvation before being transported to death camps. The largest of the ghettos was in Warsaw, the Polish capital, where 450,000 Jews were confined behind a ten-foot wall, sealing them off from the rest of the Polish population—the "Aryan side". The Germans killed anyone they found trying to escape from the ghetto, including starving children desperate to smuggle food in from beyond the wall. Between July and October 1942 the Germans deported in freight cars some 300,000 Jews from the Warsaw Ghetto to be gassed in the death camp at Treblinka.

By the beginning of 1943, a remnant of 60,000 Jews remained in the Warsaw Ghetto. Jewish underground organizations now resolved to resist the final deportations to the gas chambers. They knew they had no chance to succeed; their hope was stated in the Jewish Resistance Organization's (ZOB) "Manifesto to the Poles": "We, as well as you, are burning with the desire to punish the enemy for all his crimes, with a desire for vengeance. It is a fight for our freedom, as well as yours; for our human dignity and national honour, as well as yours." Armed with a few pistols, rifles, automatic firearms, and several hundred homemade bottled explosives, the insurgents battled the German troops from April 19 to May 16. From their hiding places in buildings, the Jews reigned grenades and bullets on Nazi patrols. Unable to dislodge the Jews from their positions, the Nazis block by block systematically set fire to and blew up the buildings in the ghetto. In this ghastly inferno, the Jewish partisans continued their desperate struggle until resistance was no longer possible. Some 14,000 Jews perished in the uprising; many of them were burned alived or perished from smoke inhalation. The Germans rounded up surviving Jews, executing large numbers on the spot and transporting the remaining mainly to Treblinka, where most were exterminated. A few Jews escaped to the "Aryan side" through the sewers and continued their struggle in the forests. Some were imprisoned in a concentation camp in the ghetto and, when liberated by Polish forces in the second Warsaw Uprising the following year, fought alongside their fellow Poles. German losses are estimated at 400 dead, including their Ukrainian and Latvian auxiliaries, and 1,000 wounded. News of the Jewish revolt in the Warsaw Ghetto quickly spread throughout Poland and occupied Europe, inspiring Jews and non-Jews to resist their Nazi overlords. Hundreds of the Warsaw Ghetto survivors participated in the Warsaw Uprising of 1944 (see next selection).

The following selection is from *The Ghetto Fights*, first published in Warsaw in 1945. The author, Marek Edelman, is the last surviving leader of the Warsaw Ghetto uprising. After the war Edelman became a prominent cardiologist; in the 1980s he was a leading supporter of Solidarity, the independent trade union movement that helped bring down the Communist regime.

Finally, the Germans decided to liquidate the Warsaw Ghetto completely, regardless of cost. On 19 April 1943, at 2am, the first messages concerning the Germans' approach arrived from our outermost observation posts. These reports made it clear that German gendarmes, aided by Polish 'navy-blue' policemen, were encircling the outer Ghetto walls at 30-yard intervals. An emergency alarm to all our battle groups was immediately ordered, and at 2.15am, that is 15 minutes later, all the groups were already at their battle stations. We also informed the entire population of the imminent danger, and most of the Ghetto inhabitants moved instantly to previously prepared shelters and hide-outs in the cellars and attics of buildings. A deathly silence enveloped the Ghetto. The ZOB was on the alert.

At 4am the Germans, in groups of threes, fours, or fives, so as not to arouse the ZOB's or the population's suspicion, began penetrating into the 'inter-Ghetto' areas. Here they formed into platoons and companies. At seven o'clock motorised detachments, including a number of tanks and armoured vehicles, entered the Ghetto. Artillery pieces were placed outside the walls. Now the SS men were ready to attack. In closed formations, stepping haughtily and loudly, they marched into the seemingly dead streets of the Central Ghetto. Their triumph appeared to be complete. It looked as if this superbly equipped modern army had scared off the handful of bravado-drunk men. . . .

But no, they did not scare us and we were not taken by surprise. We were only awaiting an opportune moment. Such a moment presently arrived. The Germans chose the intersection at Mila and Zamenhofa Streets for their bivouac area, and battle groups barricaded at the four corners of the street opened concentric fire on them. Strange projectiles began exploding everywhere (the hand grenades of our own make), the lone machine pistol sent shots through the air now and then (ammunition had to be conserved carefully), rifles started firing a bit further away. Such was the beginning.

The Germans attempted a retreat, but their path was cut. German dead soon littered the street. The remainder tried to find cover in the neighbouring stores and house entrances, but this shelter proved insufficient. The 'glorious' SS, therefore, called tanks into action under the cover of which the remaining men of two companies were to commence a 'victorious' retreat. But even the tanks seemed to be affected by the Germans' bad luck. The first was burned out by one of our incendiary bottles, the rest did not approach our positions. The fate of the Germans caught in the Mila Street-Zamenhofa Street trap was settled. Not a single German left this area alive. . . .

Simultaneously, fights were going on at the intersection of Nalewki and Gesia Streets. Two battle groups kept the Germans from entering the Ghetto area at this point. The fighting lasted more than seven hours. The Germans found some mattresses and used them as cover, but the partisans' well-aimed fire forced them to several successive withdrawals. German blood flooded the street. German ambulances continuously transported their wounded to the small square near the Community buildings. Here the wounded lay in rows on the sidewalk awaiting their turn to be admitted to the hospital. At the corner of Gesia Street a German air liaison observation post signalled the partisans' positions and the required bombing targets to the planes. But from the air as well as on the ground the partisans appeared to be invincible. The Gesia Street-Nalewki Street battle ended in the complete withdrawal of the Germans.

At the same time heavy fighting raged at Muranowski Square. Here the Germans attacked from all directions. The cornered partisans defended themselves bitterly and succeeded, by truly superhuman efforts, in repulsing the attacks. Two German machine guns as well as a quantity of other weapons were captured. A German tank was burned, the second tank of the day.

At 2pm, not a single live German remained in the Ghetto area. It was the ZOB's first complete victory over the Germans. The remaining hours of the day passed in 'complete quiet', that is with the exception of artillery fire (the guns were in positions at Krasinskich Square) and several bombings from the air.

The following day there was silence until 2pm. At that time the Germans, again in closed formation, arrived at the brushmakers' gate. They did not suspect that at that very moment an observer lifted an electric plug. A German factory guard walked toward the gate wanting to open it. At precisely the same moment the plug was placed in the socket and a mine, waiting for the Germans for a long time, exploded under the SS men's feet. Over one hundred SS men were killed in the explosion. The rest, fired on by the partisans, withdrew.

Two hours later the Germans tried their luck once again. In a different manner now, carefully, one after another, in extended order formations, they attempted to penetrate into the brushmakers' area. Here, however, they were again suitably received by a battle group awaiting them. Of the thirty Germans who succeeded in entering the area, only a few were able to leave it. Once again the Germans withdrew from the Ghetto. Once again the partisans' victory was complete. It was their second victory.

The Germans tried again. They attempted to enter the Ghetto at several other points, and everywhere they encountered determined opposition. Every house was a fortress. . . .

The partisans' stand was so determined that the Germans were finally forced to abandon all ordinary fighting methods and to try new, apparently infallible tactics. Their new idea was to set fire to the entire brushmakers' block from the outside, on all sides simultaneously. In an instant fires were raging over the entire block, black smoke choked one's throat, burned one's eyes. The partisans, naturally, did not intend to be burnt alive in the flames. We decided to gamble for our lives and attempt to reach the Central Ghetto area regardless of consequences. . . .

The flames cling to our clothes, which now start smouldering. The pavement melts under our feet into a black, gooey substance. Broken glass, littering every inch of the streets, is transformed into a sticky liquid in which our feet are caught. Our soles begin to burn from the heat of the stone pavement. One after another we stagger through the conflagration. From house to house, from courtyard to courtyard, with no air to breathe, with a hundred hammers clanging in our heads, with burning rafters continuously falling over us, we finally reach the end of the area under fire. We feel lucky just to stand here, to be out of the inferno.

We continued the fight in the Central Ghetto in cooperation with the battle groups existing in that area. As in the brushmakers' area before, it was almost impossible to move freely through the area. Entire streets were sometimes blocked by tremendous fires. The sea of flames flooded houses and courtyards, wooden beams burned noisily, walls collapsed. There was no air, only black, choking smoke and heavy, burning heat radiating from the red hot walls, from the glowing stone stairs.

The omnipotent flames were now able to accomplish what the Germans could not do. Thousands of people perished in the conflagration. The stench of burning bodies was everywhere. Charred corpses lay around on balconies, in window recesses, on unburned steps. The flames chased the people out from their shelters, made them leave the previously prepared safe hideouts in attics and cellars. Thousands staggered about in the courtyards where they were easy prey for the Germans who imprisoned them or killed them outright. Tired beyond all endurance, they would fall asleep in driveways, entrances, standing, sitting, lying and were caught asleep by a passing German's bullet. Nobody would even notice that an old man sleeping in a corner would never again wake up, that a mother feeding her baby had been cold and dead for three days, that a baby's crying and sucking was futile since its mother's arms were cold and her breast dead. Hundreds committed suicide jumping from fourth or fifth stories of apartment houses. Mothers would thus save their children from terrible death in flames. The Polish population saw these scenes from Sto Jerska Street and from Krasinskich Square. . . .

In this area, like in the others, the Germans finally 'saved' their military honour by setting house after house on fire.

In view of the changed conditions, the ZOB now resolved to change its tactics, namely to attempt the protection of larger groups of the population hidden in bunkers and shelters. Thus two ZOB detachments (Hochberg's and Sznadjmil's) escorted a few hundred people from the ruined shelter at 37 Mila Street to 7 Mila Street in broad daylight. The partisans were able to hold this latter hide-out, where several thousand people found shelter for over a week.

The burning of the Ghetto came to an end. There simply weren't any more living quarters and, still worse, there was no water. The partisans themselves now descended to the underground shelters occupied by the civilian population to defend whatever could still be defended.

The partisans' situation was becoming more grave every hour. Not only were there shortages of food and water, but ammunition was also becoming scarce. We no longer had any communications with the 'Aryan side' and we were, therefore, unable to arrange for the transportation of additional weapons that we had received (on the 'Aryan side') from the People's Army while the fighting in the Ghetto was going on (twenty rifles and ammunition).

The Germans now tried to locate all inhabited shelters by means of sensitive sound-detecting devices and police dogs. On 3 May they located the shelter on 30 Franciszkanska Street, where the operation base of those of our groups who had formerly forced their way from the brushmakers' area was at the time located. Here one of the most brilliant battles was fought. The fighting lasted for two days and half of all our men were killed in its course. A hand grenade killed Berek Sznajdmil. But even in the most difficult moments, when there was almost nothing left, Abrasha Blum kept our spirits up. His presence among us meant more to us and gave us more strength than the possession of the best possible weapon. One can hardly speak of victories when Life itself is the reason for the fight and so many people are lost, but one thing can surely be stated about this particular battle: we did not let the Germans carry out their plans. They did not evacuate a single living person.

On 8 May detachments of Germans and Ukrainians surrounded the Headquarters of the ZOB Command. The fighting lasted two hours, and when the Germans convinced themselves that they would be unable to take the bunker by storm, they tossed in a gas-bomb. Whoever survived the German bullets, whoever was not gassed, committed suicide, for it was quite clear that from here there was no way out, and nobody even considered being taken alive by the Germans. Jurek Wilner called upon all partisans to commit suicide together. Lutek Rotblat shot his mother, his sister, then himself. Ruth fired at herself seven times.

Thus 80 per cent of the remaining partisans perished, among them the ZOB Commander, Mordchaj Anilewicz.

At night the remnants, who had miraculously escaped death, joined the remaining few of the brushmakers' detachments now deployed at 22 Franciszkanska Street.

That very same night two of our liaison men (S Ratajzer—'Kazik', and Franek) arrived from the 'Aryan side'.

Ten days previously the ZOB Command had dispatched Kazik and Zygmunt Frydrych to our representative on the 'Aryan side', Icchak Cukierman ('Antek'), to arrange the withdrawal of the fighting groups through the sewer mains. Now these liaison men arrived.

Unfortunately, it was too late. For one thing, the ZOB was already almost non-existent, but even the remnants that had remained could not all be taken out of the Ghetto together.

All night we walked through the sewers, crawling through numerous entanglements built by the Germans for just such an emergency. The entrance traps were buried under heaps of rubble, the throughways booby-trapped with hand-grenades exploding at a touch. Every once in a while the Germans would let gas into the mains. In similar conditions, in a sewer 28 inches high, where it was impossible to stand up straight and where the water reached our lips, we waited 48 hours for the time to get out. Every minute someone else lost consciousness.

Thirst was the worst handicap. Some even drank the thick slimy sewer water. Every second seemed like months.

On 10 May, at 10am, two trucks halted at the trap door on the Prosta Street-Twarda Street intersection. In broad daylight, with almost no cover whatsoever (the promised Home Army cover failed and only three of our liaison men and Comrade Krzaczek—a People's

Army representative specially detailed for this assignment—patrolled the street), the trap door opened and one after another, with the stunned crowd looking on, armed Jews appeared from the depths of the dark hole (at this time the sight of *any* Jew was already a sensational occurrence). Not all were able to get out. Violently, heavily the trap-door snapped shut, the trucks took off at full speed.

"Two battle groups remained in the Ghetto. We were in contact with them until the middle of June. From then on every trace of them disappeared.

Those who had gone over to the 'Aryan side' continued the partisan fight in the woods. The majority perished eventually. The small group that was still alive at the time took an active part in the 1944 Warsaw Uprising as the 'ZOB Group'.

Tadeusz Bor-Komorowski
THE WARSAW RISING, 1944

Nazi policy toward defeated Poland was especially harsh. To counter this brutality and maintain their national identity, the Poles created an underground, alternative society. Perhaps their most notable institution was the Home Army, an amalgamation of all of the resistance units in Poland. With 380,000 members at its height, the Home Army represented the fourth-largest Allied army, after the Soviet, U.S., and British. It carried out numerous intelligence and guerrilla operations against the German occupiers while awaiting the proper moment for a general revolt. That moment seemed to have arrived in the summer of 1944. Nazi armies were in flight throughout Europe, and the Red Army stood just across the Vistula. Fearful of Stalin's intention to install a puppet government in Poland after the war, the Home Army decided to take matters into its own hands and rid Warsaw of the Nazis, in effect declaring themselves masters in their own house. The Warsaw Rising began on August 1, 1944. In the opening days of the battle, the Home Army, which numbered about 50,000 fighters, defeated the Germans in several bloody skirmishes, and the citizens of Warsaw were jubilant when the Polish national flag was unfurled. Several other partisan groups and volunteers, including Jews in hiding on the "Aryan Side" and recently freed by Polish insurgents from a concentration camp standing in the ruins of the Warsaw Ghetto, fought with the Home Army. Reinforced German troops counterattacked, and special murder squads went house to house massacring some 40,000 civilians, including women and children, in the Wola district alone. Despite these and other German atrocities—using civilians as human shields for tanks and killing outright captured insurgents—the Poles continued their heroic resistance. However, defying the expectations of the insurgents' leaders, the Red Army provided no support. Seeing an opportunity to rid himself of political opponents, Stalin prevented Soviet troops from assisting the insurgents. Shortages of food, water, and ammunition and the great los of life—some 2,000 a day were perishing—forced the capitulation of the Home Army on October 2, 1944. An enraged Hitler ordered the total destruction of the city, particularly its historic religious and cultural centers. The Nazis evacuated the remainder of Warsaw's population and then street by street reduced the once beautiful Polish capital to rubble and ruins. It is estimated that more than 200,000 Poles died in the Rising and many

survivors were sent to concentration camps; some 25,000 Germans were killed. After the war, the Communist leadership imposed by Stalin deported to Siberia or executed many of the leaders of the Uprising, and until the demise of communism in Poland it was prohibited to honor the insurgents. Today the Poles commemorate the 63-day Uprising as a symbol of national pride and inspiration.

Tadeusz Bor-Komorowski was one of the organizers of the Home Army and, from 1943 until its disbandment late in 1944, its commander. His history of this underground military organization, *The Secret Army,* appeared in 1950. The following excerpts from that work provide a thumbnail sketch of the Warsaw Rising.

. . . Warsaw by now was fully aware that the battle would not pass it by. The hope that it would be fought for the dignity, freedom, and sovereignty of the Polish nation gave the inhabitants a strength of spirit capable of the greatest valour and sacrifice. The general lust of revenge for the years of tragedy and humiliation suffered under the Germans was overwhelming and practically impossible to check. The whole town was waiting breathlessly for a call to arms, and the vast majority of the population would have considered a passive attitude as a betrayal of the Polish cause. . . .

Having decided to fight, we faced a situation without precedent in the carrying out of full mobilisation in a town occupied by an enemy. For the first time a revolution was worked out as a military operation, according to a prearranged plan. Our strength amounted to nearly 40,000 Underground soldiers and about 4,200 women. The majority were workers, railwaymen, artisans, students and clerks in factories, railways and offices. These men had to be informed verbally of the place, date and hour to muster. It was only after many rehearsals and thanks to a continuously improved system of warning that we achieved the rate at which an order given by me reached the lower ranks in two hours. This enabled us to decide the rising no more than twenty-four hours before it was to start. But the task of informing 40,000 men, of giving them the code word and fixing hours and places of assembly was not the whole work. There was also liaison between the fighting groups to be established. Commanders of all ranks had to be constantly furnished with information and orders, and thousands of instructions had to be distributed throughout the city. All these tasks were carried out by girl messengers. From dawn till dusk they covered the length and breadth of the city, climbed numberless stairs and repeated orders and reports, mostly by word of mouth. . . .

. . . Thirty minutes before zero hour, all preparations were completed. The soldiers brought out their arms and put on white-and-red armbands, the first open sign of a Polish army on Polish soil since the occupation. For five years they had all awaited this moment. Now the last seconds seemed an eternity. At five o'clock they would cease to be an underground resistance movement and would become once more Regular soldiers fighting in the open.

At exactly five o'clock thousands of windows flashed as they were flung open. From all sides a hail of bullets struck passing Germans, riddling their buildings and their marching formations. In the twinkling of an eye, the remaining civilians disappeared from the streets. From the entrances of houses, our men streamed out and rushed to the attack. In fifteen minutes an entire city of a million inhabitants was engulfed in the fight. . . .

My first message to the soldiers in the capital read:

> Soldiers of the capital!
>
> I have to-day issued the order which you desire, for open warfare against Poland's age-old enemy, the German invader. After nearly five years of ceaseless and determined struggle, carried on in secret, you stand to-day openly with arms in hand, to restore freedom to our country and to mete out fitting punishment to

the German criminals for the terror and crimes committed by them in Polish soil.

Bor.
Commander-in-Chief, Home Army.

. . . People in the streets reacted with shouts and applause at the sight of the Polish eagle or the uniform which they had not seen for five years and when they saw German prisoners or captured arms. In this case, a window was flung open and a loud-speaker started up the song "Warszawianka," the Polish revolutionary song composed 114 years before. Everyone in the street, whether passing by or busy at the barricades, stood to attention and joined in the song. I was deeply affected by the fervour of the crowd. I think those moments were my happiest of the whole war. Unfortunately, they were short-lived.

On my return to the Kammler Factory, I found reports awaiting me on the incredible bestialities being practised by the Germans on civilians. This cruelty affected all the civilians in districts and buildings still in German hands. At the beginning, the Germans had set fire to most of the houses in these districts. The city was covered by a smoky glow. In many cases the inhabitants were not allowed to leave their houses or else not given sufficient time to do so. Thousands of people were burned alive. . . .

. . . Actually, there was not a single place in Warsaw which was out of range of artillery fire, incendiaries and mines, or grenades and bombs. Raid followed raid in such quick succession that from dawn to dusk the whole city lived in a state of continual alert. Every day, in nearly every street, more houses fell victim to the Luftwaffe. . . .

Meanwhile, the prolongation of the fight in the city forced us to more intensive use of the sewers for communication purposes. These dark, underground tunnels, mysterious and forbidding, stretching for miles, were the scene of a human effort of the greatest self-sacrifice—an effort to link up the torn shreds of fighting Warsaw so that all our isolated battles could form one whole and united operation fought in common. The network of sewers carried water and sewage to the Vistula. Built sixty years before, they formed a complicated labyrinth under the houses and streets of the city.

They had previously been used when fighting was going on in the Ghetto, which the Germans had surrounded by a wall and a cordon of police. By this route food, arms and ammunition had been smuggled in. Special organisations were formed at the time and provided with a suitable means of transport to ensure the supply of food for the Jewish population over a period of several months. Handcarts on rubber wheels, built to a width which would allow them to be pushed along the tunnels, were used. During the massacre of the Ghetto, many young Jews managed to flee by the same route.

When the Ghetto had been liquidated and destroyed, the sewers were forgotten, but now that our present fight was continuing, we were obliged once more to use these underground lines of communication. . . .

The tunnels were pitch dark, because for security reasons lights were either severely restricted or completely banned. The acrid air was asphyxiating and brought tears to the eyes. The size of the passages varied. The smallest which could be negotiated were 3 feet high and 2 wide. Sharp debris, such as broken glass, strewed the semicircular floor of the passages, making hand support impossible when crawling. The most superficial scratch would have caused septicæmia. Two sticks had to be used as supports and progress was made in short jumps, rather like the motion of a kangaroo. It was extremely tiring and slow. To give an example, one of the routes leading from Stare Miasto to the centre of the city through one of the narrowest tunnels took as long as nine hours to negotiate, although the distance was no more than a mile. To advance along a narrow passage of this sort in pitch darkness, with mud up to the shoulders, often caused stark terror. I knew many men, in no way lacking courage, who would never have hesitated to attack enemy tanks with a bottle of petrol, who nevertheless lost their nerve and were overcome by complete exhaustion after only a few hundred yards in one of these narrow passages. The feeling of panic was increased by the difficulty of breathing in the fœtid atmosphere and by the fact that it was impossible to turn round. If an immovable obstacle was encountered, the only course was to back out.

Great help was given to the traffic now moving along the sewers by women's units. The women who volunteered for it were known as *Kanalarki* (*kanal,* in Polish, is a sewer). They carried messages and orders, reconnoitred new passages and removed obstacles.

In September the tunnels became the route of withdrawal for units being evacuated from overrun positions. Even wounded were transported underground, a proof of the greatest self-sacrifice and devotion on the part of the soldiers who refused to allow their officers and comrades to be left to fall into enemy hands. . . . In the beginning the Germans did not realise that we were using the sewers. They were as puzzled as they were infuriated to know that isolated districts were in touch and able to help each other and co-ordinate their activities. It took them some time to realise that the means of contact was running just beneath their positions. . . .

. . . After a time, however, they heard the rumbling echo of movements in the sewer and soon realised what was going on. It was thus that the fight for the sewers began, characterised by cunning and ruses on both sides.

All the manholes in German-occupied areas were opened and down them were thrown hand-grenades, mines and tins of acrid gas. Other passages were blocked with rubble and bags of cement. Many *Kanalarki* engaged in the work of removing these barriers were drowned in the flood of water which had accumulated behind the obstacles. The enemy hung hand-grenades in the tunnels with the pins removed. If a man, crawling along, hit one of these, he was immediately blown to pieces. These ambushes and other similar tricks were an additional danger to anyone venturing into the passages. In some cases, real battles developed underground against German engineers. The fights went on in the darkness in an incredibly fœtid atmosphere between men up to the waist in excrement. They fought within hand-grenade distance, even hand to hand with knives, and failing weapons they drowned each other in the slime. . . .

The last hours were hard for all of us. It was not easy to give up the last bit of the city on which we had lived for sixty-three days as free men and where, beneath the ruins, now lay so many of our comrades of the Underground days.

On the previous evening, Blyskawica had broadcast its farewell programme. Broken with emotion, the voice of the speaker had announced: ". . . We have been free for two months; to-day once more we must go into captivity, but at least the Germans cannot take Warsaw again. All that is left is a heap of rubble. . . . Warsaw no longer exists."

13 D-Day, June 6, 1944

On June 6, 1944, the allied forces launched their invasion of Nazi-occupied France. The invasion, called Operation Overlord, had been planned with meticulous care. Under the supreme command of General Dwight D. Eisenhower (1890–1969), the Allies organized the biggest amphibious operation of the war. It involved 5,000 ships of all kinds, 11,000 aircraft, and 2 million soldiers, 1.5 million of them Americans, all equipped with the latest military gear. Two artificial harbors and several oil pipelines stood ready to supply the troops once the invasion was under way.

Historical Division, War Department
OMAHA BEACHHEAD

Allied control of the air was an important factor in the success of D-Day. A second factor was the fact that the Germans were caught by surprise. Although expecting an invasion, they did not believe that it would take place in the Normandy area of France, and they dismissed June 6 as a possible date because weather conditions were unfavorable.

Ultimately the invasion's success depended on what happened during the first few hours. If the Allies had failed to secure beachheads, the operation would have ended in disaster. As the following reading illustrates, some of the hardest fighting took place on Omaha Beach, which was attacked by the Americans. The extract, published in 1945, comes from a study prepared in the field by the 2nd Information and Historical Service attached to the First Army, and by the Historical Section, European Theater of Operations.

As expected, few of the LCVP's and LCA's [amphibious landing craft] carrying assault infantry were able to make dry landings. Most of them grounded on sandbars 50 to 100 yards out, and in some cases the water was neck deep. Under fire as they came within a quarter-mile of the shore, the infantry met their worst experiences of the day and suffered their heaviest casualties just after touchdown. Small-arms fire, mortars, and artillery concentrated on the landing area, but the worst hazard was produced by converging fires from automatic weapons. Survivors from some craft report hearing the fire beat on the ramps before they were lowered, and then seeing the hail of bullets whip the surf just in front of the lowered ramps. Some men dove under water or went over the side to escape the beaten zone of the machine guns. Stiff, weakened from seasickness, and often heavily loaded, the debarking troops had little chance of moving fast in water that was knee deep or higher, and their progress was made more difficult by uneven footing in the runnels crossing the tidal flat. Many men were exhausted before they reached shore, where they faced 200 yards or more of open sand to cross before reaching cover at the sea wall or shingle bank. Most men who reached that cover made it by walking, and under increasing enemy fire. Troops who stopped to organize, rest, or take shelter behind obstacles or ranks merely prolonged their difficulties and suffered heavier losses. . . .

Perhaps the worst area on the beach was Dog Green, directly in front of strongpoints guarding the Vierville draw [gully] and under heavy flanking fire from emplacements to the west, near Pointe de la Percée. Company A of the 116th was due to land on this sector with Company C of the 2d Rangers on its right flank, and both units came in on their targets. One of the six LCA's carrying Company A foundered about a thousand yards off shore, and passing Rangers saw men jumping overboard and being dragged down by their loads. At H+6[1] minutes the remaining craft grounded in water 4 to 6 feet deep, about 30 yards short of the outward band of obstacles. Starting off the craft in three files, center file first and the flank files peeling right and left, the men were enveloped in accurate and intense fire from automatic weapons. Order was quickly lost as the troops attempted to dive under water or dropped over the sides into surf over their heads. Mortar fire scored four direct hits on one LCA, which "disintegrated." Casualties were suffered all the way to the sand,

[1]H indicates the start of an operation.

but when the survivors got there, some found they could not hold and came back into the water for cover, while others took refuge behind the nearest obstacles. Remnants of one boat team on the right flank organized a small firing line on the first yards of sand, in full exposure to the enemy. In short order every officer of the company, including Capt. Taylor N. Fellers, was a casualty, and most of the sergeants were killed or wounded. The leaderless men gave up any attempt to move forward and confined their efforts to saving the wounded, many of whom drowned in the rising tide. Some troops were later able to make the sea wall by staying in the edge of the water and going up the beach with the tide. Fifteen minutes after landing, Company A was out of action for the day. Estimates of its casualties range as high as two-thirds. . . .

As headquarters groups arrived from 0730 on, they found much the same picture at whatever sector they landed. Along 6,000 yards of beach, behind sea wall or shingle embankment, elements of the assault force were immobilized in what might well appear to be hopeless confusion. As a result of mislandings, many companies were so scattered that they could not be organized as tactical units. At some places, notably in front of the German strongpoints guarding draws, losses in officers and noncommissioned officers were so high that remnants of units were practically leaderless. . . .

There was, definitely, a problem of morale. The survivors of the beach crossing, many of whom were experiencing their first enemy fire, had seen heavy losses among their comrades or in neighboring units. No action could be fought in circumstances more calculated to heighten the moral effects of such losses. Behind them, the tide was drowning wounded men who had been cut down on the sands and was carrying bodies ashore just below the shingle. Disasters to the later landing waves were still occurring, to remind of the potency of enemy fire. . . .

At 0800, German observers on the bluff sizing up the grim picture below them might well have felt that the invasion was stopped at the edge of the water. Actually, at three or four places on the four-mile beachfront, U.S. troops were already breaking through the shallow crust of enemy defenses.

The outstanding fact about these first two hours of action is that despite heavy casualties, loss of equipment, disorganization, and all the other discouraging features of the landings, the assault troops did not stay pinned down behind the sea wall and embankment. At half-a-dozen or more points on the long stretch, they found the necessary drive to leave their cover and move out over the open beach flat toward the bluffs. Prevented by circumstance of mislandings from using carefully rehearsed tactics, they improvised assault methods to deal with what defenses they found before them. In nearly every case where advance was attempted, it carried through the enemy beach defenses. . . .

Various factors, some of them difficult to evaluate, played a part in the success of these advances. . . . But the decisive factor was leadership. Wherever an advance was made, it depended on the presence of some few individuals, officers and noncommissioned officers, who inspired, encouraged, or bullied their men forward, often by making the first forward moves. On Easy Red a lieutenant and a wounded sergeant of divisional engineers stood up under fire and walked over to inspect the wire obstacles just beyond the embankment. The lieutenant came back and, hands on hips, looked down disgustedly at the men lying behind the shingle bank. "Are you going to lay there and get killed, or get up and do something about it?" Nobody stirred, so the sergeant and the officer got the materials and blew the wire. On the same sector, where a group advancing across the flat was held up by a marshy area suspected of being mined, it was a lieutenant of engineers who crawled ahead through the mud on his belly, probing for mines with a hunting knife in the absence of other equipment. When remnants of an isolated boat section of Company B, 116th Infantry, were stopped by fire from a well-concealed emplacement, the lieutenant in charge went after it single-handed. In trying to grenade the rifle pit he was hit by three rifle bullets and eight grenade fragments, including some from his own grenade. He turned his map and compass over to a sergeant and ordered his group to press on inland. . . .

. . . Col. George A. Taylor arrived in the second section at 0815 and found plenty to do on the beach. Men were still hugging the embankment, disorganized, and suffering casualties from mortar and artillery fire. Colonel Taylor summed up the situation in terse phrase: "Two kinds of people are staying on this beach, the dead and those who are going to die—now let's get the hell out of here." Small groups of men were collected without regard to units, put under charge of the nearest non-commissioned officer, and sent on through the wire and across the flat, while engineers worked hard to widen gaps in the wire and to mark lanes through the minefields.

14 The End of the Third Reich

In January 1945, the Red Army launched a major offensive, which ultimately brought them into Berlin. In February, American and British forces were battling the Germans in the Rhineland, and in March they crossed the Rhine into the interior of Germany. In April, the Russians encircled Berlin. After heavy artillery and rocket-launchers inflicted heavy damage on the besieged city, Russian infantry attacked and engaged in vicious street fighting. The siege took the lives of some 125,000 Berliners, many of them suicides. Russian dead, wounded, and missing totaled about 305,000. From his underground bunker near the chancellery in Berlin, a physically exhausted and emotionally unhinged Hitler engaged in wild fantasies about new German victories.

The last weeks of the war were chaotic and murderous. Many German soldiers fought desperately against the invaders of the Fatherland, particularly the Russians, who had been depicted by Nazi propaganda as Asiatic barbarians. SS officers, still loyal to Hitler and national socialism, hunted down and executed reluctant fighters as a warning to others. The misery of the Jews never abated. As the Russians neared the concentration camps, the SS marched the inmates into the German interior. It was a death march, for many of them, already human skeletons, could not endure the long trek, the weather, and the brutality of guards who shot stragglers.

Nerin E. Gun
THE LIBERATION OF DACHAU

In the closing weeks of the war, the Allies liberated German concentration camps, revealing the full horror of Nazi atrocities to a shocked world. On April 29, 1945, American soldiers entered Dachau. One of the liberated prisoners was Nerin E. Gun, a Turkish Catholic journalist, who had been imprisoned by the Nazis during the war for his reports about the Warsaw ghetto and his prediction

that the German armies would meet defeat in Russia. Gun described the liberation of Dachau in *The Day of the Americans* (1966), from which the following selection is taken.

[An American scout spots the camp. The inmates see him.]

The silence was broken again by a burst of hurrahs, *vivas, siegs* and *dobres,* but all these Tower of Babel voices harmonized to express the same cry of gratitude. We stood before the fence, up on the roofs; some of us had climbed into trees and raised our arms to the heavens, waving berets, handkerchiefs, some even jackets, shirts, or any random rag; and this mass of humanity, only a few minutes earlier so apathetic, so somnolent, indifferent, exhausted, was now alive with wild enthusiasm.

The GI with the somber uniform became aware of our presence. He stopped, nonplused. He must have seen nothing but a multitude of skeletons dressed in tatters, organized into a frightful dance of death. He was dispatched as a scout and now here he was in the entryway of a gehenna peopled by phantoms straight out of the second act of *Fidelio.* He discovered there the emaciated, desiccated, haggard faces whose boniness was even more accentuated by the contortions which tried to express happiness; the atrophied bodies covered with rags—for zebra-striped prison uniforms were still a sign of great luxury at Dachau—climbing up one on the other like tipsy cockroaches; the bleating, the nauseating stench of our bodies and our clothing mingled with that of charred flesh coming from the fallout of the crematorium smokestacks, which clung to the nostrils. All of this must have struck him like a hallucination.

And the man in the olive-drab uniform with the big helmet covered with leaves and branches, who had crossed all of Europe to get to us, shrank back, turned, and went to hide behind the cement-mixer. We had frightened our liberator.

First GI at Dachau, we will never forget those first few seconds. Even those of us who have died since you freed them must have carried with them into the other world the memory of that unique, magnificent moment of your arrival. We had prayed, we had waited, we had lost all hope of ever seeing you, but you had finally come, Messiah from across the seas, angel and demon. You had come at the risk of your life, into an unknown country, for the sake of unknown people, bringing us the most precious thing in the world, the gift of freedom. . . .

The GI's hesitation didn't last long. He retraced his steps, accompanied now by some fifty foot soldiers. Then there was a burst of shots from up on the watchtower. We threw ourselves to the ground, terrified again at the thought of a possible massacre. Lying thus, face down in the dirt, we saw nothing of the advance of the Americans. One of the prisoners, in a sudden fit of madness, threw himself against the electrified fence, trying to scale it. He was immediately electrocuted and stayed there, the last scarecrow of our nightmare, his hands welded to the wires, his clothing singed black, his naked feet dangling. . . .

We started getting up, one by one, even before the firing had stopped. The Americans were now almost within reach, on the other side of the moat. They had forced the SS men to come down from their watchtower and line up one behind the other, hands on their heads. . . .

Contact having finally been cut off between the high-tension plant and the wire fences, the prisoners were at last able to get out and go to shake the hands of the American soldiers outside. The first wave of Americans had been followed by a second, which must have broken into the camp either through the crematorium or through the marshaling-yard, where the boxcars loaded with thousands of corpses had been parked. For, as soon as they saw the SS men standing there with their hands on their heads, these Americans, without any other semblance of trial, without even saying a warning word, turned their fire on them. Most of the inmates applauded this summary justice, and those who had been able to get over the ditch rushed out to strip the corpses of the Germans. Some even hacked their feet off, the more quickly to be able to get their boots. . . .

Many SS officers had fled the camp just prior to the arrival of the Americans. Command was given to Lieutenant Heinrich Skodzensky, a decorated hero from the Russian front, who had arrived just two days earlier. At this point in the narrative, Gun quotes a Belgian inmate who witnessed the meeting between Skodzensky and an American officer.

"At this point, the young Teutonic lieutenant, Heinrich Skodzensky, emerges from the guard post and comes to attention before the American officer. The German is blond, handsome, perfumed, his boots glistening, his uniform well-tailored. He reports, as if he were on the military parade grounds near the Unter den Linden during an exercise, then very properly raising his arm he salutes with a very respectful 'Heil Hitler!' and clicks his heels.

"'I hereby turn over to you the concentration camp of Dachau, 30,000 residents, 2,340 sick, 27,000 on the outside, 560 garrison troops.'

"Am I dreaming? It seems that I can see before me the striking contrast of a beast and a god. Only that the Boche is the one who looks divine.

"The American major does not return the salute. He hesitates for a moment, as if he were trying to make sure that he is remembering the adequate words. Then, he spits into the face of the German,

"'Du Schweinehund!'

"And then, 'Sit down there!'—pointing to the rear seat of one of the jeeps which in the meantime have driven in." . . .

"The major gave an order, the jeep with the young German officer in it went outside the camp again. A few minutes went by, my comrades had not yet dared to come out of their barracks, for at that distance they could not tell the outcome of the negotiations between the American officer and the SS men.

"Then I hear several shots.

"'The bastard is dead!' the American major says to me. . . ."

Gun continues with his account.

The detachment under the command of the American major had not come directly to the Jourhaus. It had made a detour by way of the marshaling yard, where the convoys of deportees normally arrived and departed. There they found some fifty-odd cattle cars parked on the tracks. The cars were not empty.

"At first sight," said [Lieutenant Colonel Will] Cowling, "they seemed to be filled with rags, discarded clothing. Then we caught sight of hands, stiff fingers, faces. . . ."

The train was full of corpses, piled one on the other, 2,310 of them, to be exact. The train had come from Birkenau, and the dead were Hungarian and Polish Jews, children among them. Their journey had lasted perhaps thirty or forty days. They had died of hunger, of thirst, of suffocation, of being crushed, or of being beaten by the guards. There were even evidences of cannibalism. They were all practically dead when they arrived at Dachau Station. The SS men did not take the trouble to unload them. They simply decided to stand guard and shoot down any with enough strength left to emerge from the cattle cars. The corpses were strewn everywhere—on the rails, the steps, the platforms.

The men of the 45th Division had just made contact with the 42nd, here in the station. They too found themselves unable to breathe at what they saw. One soldier yelled: "Look, Bud, it's moving!" He pointed to something in motion among the cadavers. A louse-infested prisoner was crawling like a worm, trying to attract attention. He was the only survivor.

"I never saw anything like it in my life," said Lieutenant Harold Mayer. "Every one of my men became raving mad. We turned off toward the east, going around the compound, without even taking the trouble to reconnoiter first. We were out to avenge them." . . .

The ire of the men of the First Battalion, 157th Regiment, was to mount even higher as they got closer to the Lager of the deportees. The dead were everywhere—in the ditches, along the side streets, in the garden before a small building with chimneys—and there was a huge mountain of corpses inside the yard of this building, which they now understood to be the crematorium. And finally there was the ultimate horror—the infernal sight of those thousands and thousands of living skeletons, screaming like banshees, on the other side of the placid poplars.

When some of the SS men on the watchtowers started to shoot into the mobs of prisoners, the Americans threw all caution to the winds. They opened fire on the towers with healthy salvos. The SS men promptly came down the ladders, their hands reaching high. But now the American GI saw red. He shot the Germans down with a telling blast, and to make doubly sure sent a final shot into their fallen bodies. Then the hunt started for any other Germans in SS uniforms. Within a quarter of an hour there was not a single one of the Hitler henchmen alive within the camp.

In the SS refectory, one soldier had been killed while eating a plate of beans. He still held a spoonful in his hand. At the signal center, the SS man in charge of the switchboard was slumped over his panel, blood running down to the receiver, the busy signal from Munich still ringing in his unheeding ear. At the power plant, the SS foreman had been beaten to death with shovels by a Polish prisoner and his Czech assistant. After that, they had been able to cut the high-voltage current from the barbed-wire fences around the camp.

Margaret Freyer
"THEY FAINTED AND THEN BURNED TO CINDERS"

In an attempt to shatter German morale and to support the Russians who were advancing west into Germany, in early 1945 the Allies planned to mass bomb several large cities in Eastern Germany. They believed that such attacks, particularly if they destroyed railyards, would hinder the movement of German reinforcements to the Russian front. On February 13 and 14, Allied planes dropped tons of high explosive bombs and incendiaries packed with highly combustible chemicals on the relatively defenseless city of Dresden. The bombings created a firestorm that turned the city into an inferno. A landmark cultural center, famous for its splendid architecture, was totally devastated and some 40,000 inhabitants—many of them refugees fleeing the advancing Russians—perished, and thousands of others suffered horrific wounds.

The massive destruction of Dresden has aroused a historical controversy regarding the morality of terror bombing civilians. The German far Right has maintained that the firebombings of German cities, particularly Dresden, were war crimes that equalled or exceeded what the Nazis had done, and that the Allied leadership should be labeled war criminals. And some British and American commentators have called the bombing a criminal

act. Dresden, they argue, was of no military importance; and with the war nearly won, its destruction was totally unnecessary. Defenders of the raid point out that Dresden was a major railway junction that could be used for transporting troops to fight the Russians; its factories produced military gunsights, radar equipment, gas masks and parts for the German airforce, and fuses for anti-aircraft shells; and with the Germans offering strong resistance on both fronts, there was no certainty that the war would end shortly. Moreover, Allied bombing of German cities was the price Germany paid for initiating this policy of destroying civilian targets—Guernica (1937) during the Spanish Civil War, Warsaw (1939), Rotterdam (1940), London (1940)—in order to terrorize the population.

Margaret Freyer (b. 1920), who barely escaped being sent to a concentration camp by the Gestapo for telling political jokes, took shelter in a cellar during the first wave of the attack. During a lull in the bombing, she left the damaged building and went to her friend Cenci's apartment. When the sirens sounded again, she and Cenci, thirty-nine other women, and Cenci's husband fled to the building's cellar. In the following excerpt, Freyer describes the horror of the firebombing.

I sat next to Cenci on a box while a non-stop hail of bombs seemed to last an eternity. The walls shook, the ground shook, the light went out and our heavy iron door was forced open by blast. In this cellar now, there were the same scenes as had occurred before in the Ferdinandstrasse cellar: a crowd of crying, screaming, or praying women, throwing themselves on top of each other. Cenci and I tried to disentangle them and calm them down. We longed for the 'All Clear', but it never came—the sirens had stopped working. But eventually the earth stopped shaking and now we believed that it was really all over. Cenci and I exchanged a glance of thankfulness. Our cellar had held.

Out of here—nothing but out! Three women went up the stairs in front of us, only to come rushing down again, wringing their hands. 'We can't get out of here! Everything outside is burning!' they cried. Cenci and I went up to make sure. It was true.

Then we tried the 'Breakthrough' which had been installed in each cellar, so people could exit from one cellar to the other. But here we met only thick smoke which made it impossible to breathe.

So we went upstairs. The back door, which opened on to the back yard and was made partly of glass, was completely on fire. It would have been madness to touch it. And at the front entrance, flames a metre and a half high came licking at short intervals into the hall.

In spite of this, it was clear that we could not stay in the building unless we wanted to suffocate. So we went downstairs again and picked up our suitcases. I put two handfuls of handkerchiefs into a water tub and stuffed them soaking wet into my coat pocket. They probably saved my life later on.

But as we went up the stairs out of the cellar, Cenci's husband came up and said: 'Cenci, please stay here, you must help my sister. She's ill.'

I made a last attempt to convince everyone in the cellar to leave, because they would suffocate if they did not; but they didn't want to. And so I left alone—and all the people in that cellar suffocated. Most died down there, but three women were found outside the door, amongst them Cenci. I cried bitterly when I found out that I was the only one who had escaped from that cellar.

I stood by the entrance and waited until no flames came licking in, then I quickly slipped through and out into the street. . . . A witches' cauldron was waiting for me out there: no street, only rubble nearly a metre high, glass, girders, stones, craters. I tried to get rid of the sparks by constantly patting them off my coat. It was useless. I stopped doing it, stumbled, and someone behind me called out: 'Take your coat off, it's started to burn.' In the pervading extreme heat I hadn't even noticed. I took off the coat and dropped it.

Next to me a woman was screaming continually: 'My den's burning down, my den's burning down,' and dancing in the street. As I go on, I can still hear her screaming but I don't see her again. I run, I stumble, anywhere. I don't even know where I am any more, I've lost all sense of direction because all I can see is three steps ahead.

Suddenly I fall into a big hole—a bomb crater, about six metres wide and two metres deep, and I end up down there lying on top of three women. I shake them by their clothes and start to scream at them, telling them that they must get out of here—but they don't move any more. I believe I was severely shocked by this incident; I seemed to have lost all emotional feeling. Quickly, I climbed across the women, pulled my suitcase after me, and crawled on all fours out of the crater.

To my left I suddenly see a woman. I can see her to this day and shall never forget it. She carries a bundle in her arms. It is a baby. She runs, she falls, and the child flies in an arc into the fire. It's only my eyes which take this in; I myself feel nothing. The woman remains lying on the ground, completely still. Why? What for? I don't know, I just stumble on. The firestorm is incredible, there are calls for help and screams from somewhere but all around is one single inferno. I hold another wet handkerchief in front of my mouth, my hands and my face are burning; it feels as if the skin is hanging down in strips.

On my right I see a big, burnt-out shop where lots of people are standing. I join them, but think: 'No, I can't stay here either, this place is completely surrounded by fire.' I leave all these people behind, and stumble on. Where to? No idea! But every time towards those places where it is dark, in case there is no fire there. I have no conception of what the street actually looked like. But it is especially from those dark patches that the people come who wring their hands and cry the same thing over and over again: 'You can't carry on there, we've just come from there, everything is burning there!' Wherever and to whomsoever I turn, always that same answer.

In front of me is something that might be a street, filled with a hellish rain of sparks which look like enormous rings of fire when they hit the ground. I have no choice. I must go through. I press another wet handkerchief to my mouth and almost get through, but I fall and am convinced that I cannot go on. It's hot. Hot! My hands are burning like fire. I just drop my suitcase, I am past caring, and too weak. At least, there's nothing to lug around with me any more.

I stumbled on towards where it was dark. Suddenly, I saw people again, right in front of me. They scream and gesticulate with their hands, and then—to my utter horror and amazement—I see how one after the other they simply seem to let themselves drop to the ground. I had a feeling that they were being shot, but my mind could not understand what was really happening. Today I know that these unfortunate people were the victims of lack of oxygen. They fainted and then burnt to cinders. I fall then, stumbling over a fallen woman and as I lie right next to her I see how her clothes are burning away. Insane fear grips me and from then on I repeat one simple sentence to myself continuously: 'I don't want to burn to death—no, no burning—I don't want to burn!' Once more I fall down and feel that I am not going to be able to get up again, but the fear of being burnt pulls me to my feet. Crawling, stumbling, my last handkerchief pressed to my mouth . . . I do not know how many people I fell over. I knew only one feeling: that I must not burn. . . .

I try once more to get up on my feet, but I can only manage to crawl forward on all fours. I can still feel my body, I know I'm still alive. Suddenly, I'm standing up, but there's something wrong, everything seems so far away and I can't hear or see properly any more. As I found out later, like all the others, I was suffering from lack of oxygen. I must have stumbled forwards roughly ten paces when I all at once inhaled fresh air. There's a breeze! I take another breath, inhale deeply, and my senses clear. . . .

I walk on a little and discover a car. I'm pleased and decide to spend the night in it. The car is full of suitcases and boxes but I find enough room on the rear seats to squeeze in. Another stroke of good luck for me is that the car's windows are all broken and I have to keep awake putting out the sparks which drifted in. I don't know how long I sat there, when a hand suddenly descended on my shoulder and a man's voice said: 'Hello! You must get out of there.' I got such a fright, because obviously someone was determined to force me away from my safe hiding place. I said, with great fear in my voice: 'Please, allow me to stay here, I'll give you all the money I've got on me.' (If I think about this now it almost sounds like a joke.) But the answer I got was: 'No, I don't want your money. The car is on fire.'

Good God! I leapt out immediately and could see that indeed all four tyres were burning. I hadn't noticed because of the tremendous heat. . . .

We walk on a little way and discover two crouching figures. They were two men, one a railwayman who was crying because (in the smoke and debris) he could not find the way to his home. The other was a civilian who had escaped from a cellar together with sixty people, but had had to leave his wife and children behind, due to some dreadful circumstances. All three men were crying now but I just stood there, incapable of a single tear. It was as if I was watching a film. We spent half the night together, sitting on the ground too exhausted even to carry on a conversation. The continuous explosions didn't bother us, but the hollow cries for help which came continuously from all directions were gruesome. Towards 6 o'clock in the morning, we parted.

I spent all the daylight hours which followed in the town searching for my fiance. I looked for him amongst the dead, because hardly any living beings were to be seen anywhere. What I saw is so horrific that I shall hardly be able to describe it. Dead, dead, dead everywhere. Some completely black like charcoal. Others completely untouched, lying as if they were asleep. Women in aprons, women with children sitting in the trams as if they had just nodded off. Many women, many young girls, many small children, soldiers who were only identifiable as such by the metal buckles on their belts, almost all of them naked. Some clinging to each other in groups as if they were clawing at each other.

From some of the debris poked arms, heads, legs, shattered skulls. The static water-tanks were filled up to the top with dead human beings, with large pieces of masonry lying on top of that again. Most people looked as if they had been inflated, with large yellow and brown stains on their bodies. People whose clothes were still glowing . . . I think I was incapable of absorbing the meaning of this cruelty any more, for there were also so many little babies, terribly mutilated; and all the people lying so close to together that it looked as if someone had put them down there, street by street, deliberately.

I then went through the Grosser Garten and there is one thing I did realise. I was aware that I had constantly to brush hands away from me, hands which belonged to people who wanted me to take them with me, hands which clung to me. But I was much too weak to lift anyone up. My mind took all this in vaguely, as if seen through a veil. In fact, I was in such a state that I did not realise that there was a third attack on Dresden. Late that afternoon I collapsed in the Ostra-Alle, where two men took me to a friend who lived on the outskirts of the city.

I asked for a mirror and did not recognise myself any more. My face was a mass of blisters and so were my hands. My eyes were narrow slits and puffed up, my whole body was covered in little black, pitted marks. I cannot understand to this day how I contracted these marks, because I was wearing a pair of long trousers and a jacket. Possibly the fire-sparks ate their way through my clothing.

Joseph Goebbels
"THE MORALE OF THE GERMAN PEOPLE, BOTH AT HOME AND AT THE FRONT, IS SINKING EVER LOWER"

In his diary, Joseph Goebbels (1897–1945), the cynical and sinister head of the propaganda ministry, recorded his impressions of Germany in the last weeks of the war. The following selections from his diary show Goebbels' concern with German morale, particularly as affected by devastating air raids.

March 8 (1945)

During the last 24 hours the air war has again raged over Reich territory with devastating effect. It was the turn of Magdeburg and even more of Dessau. The greater part of Dessau is a sheet of flame and totally destroyed; yet another German city which has been largely flattened. In addition reports coming in from towns recently attacked, Chemnitz in particular, make one's hair grow grey. Yet once more it is frightful that we have no defence worth mentioning with which to oppose the enemy air war.

The Party Chancellery is now planning a special operation to raise the troops' morale. . . . Evidence of demoralization is now to be seen. . . . Desertions have reached a considerable level. . . . Again and again one hears that the enemy air bombardment is at the bottom of it all. It is understandable that a people which has been subjected for years to the fire-effect of a weapon against which it has no defence, should gradually lose its courage.

March 12

The morale of the German people, both at home and at the front, is sinking ever lower. The Reich propaganda agencies are complaining very noticeably about this. The people thinks that it is facing a perfectly hopeless situation in this war. Criticism of our war strategy does not now stop short even of the Führer himself. . . . It must always be pointed out, however, that the present level of morale must not be confused with definite defeatism. The people will continue to do their duty and the front-line soldier will defend himself as far as he has a possibility of doing so. These possibilities are becoming increasingly limited, however, primarily owing to the enemy's air superiority. The air terror which rages uninterruptedly over German home territory makes people thoroughly despondent. One feels so impotent against it that no one can now see a way out of the dilemma. The total paralysis of transport in West Germany also contributes to the mood of increasing pessimism among the German people.

March 13

. . . [P]eople in Eisenhower's headquarters are clear that they still face a titanic struggle in the West. They declare that on both sides war is being waged without mercy and that there is no question whatsoever of the German Wehrmacht yielding. Above all people in Eisenhower's headquarters are deeply impressed by the fact that all German prisoners of war still have faith in victory and—as they explicitly state—believe in Hitler with well-nigh mystical fanaticism. . . .

The Jews are re-emerging. Their spokesman is the well-known notorious Leopold Schwarzschild [former newspaper editor, who had emigrated to America]; he is now arguing in the American press that under no circumstances should Germany be given lenient treatment. Anyone in a position to do so should kill these Jews off like rats. In Germany, thank God, we have already done a fairly complete job. I trust that the world will take its cue from this.

March 16

Mail received testifies to a deep-seated lethargy throughout the German people degenerating almost into hopelessness. There is very sharp criticism of the Luftwaffe but also of the entire national leadership. The latter is accused of being over-ambitious in its policy and strategy, of having been negligent in its conduct of the war, particularly in the air, and this is given as the main reason for our misfortunes.

March 21

The number killed in air raids up to December inclusive is reported as 353,000—a horrifying figure which becomes even more terrible when one adds the 457,000 wounded. This is a war within a war, sometimes more frightful than the war at the front. The homeless are simply innumerable. The air war has turned the Reich into one great heap of ruins. In the last 24 hours a further crazy series of air raids has been reported, particularly on the west of the Reich.

March 23

The letters I receive evince profound apathy and resignation. All refer quite openly to the leadership crisis. All the letter-writers show marked aversion to Göring, Ley and Ribbentrop.[1] Unfortunately even the Führer is now more frequently referred to in critical terms. I get off somewhat more lightly in the letters I receive but that must not be over-estimated. Everything must be looked at relatively. I think that my work too is no longer being totally effective today. A fateful development seems to me to be that now neither the Führer in person nor the National-Socialist concept nor the National-Socialist movement are immune from criticism. Many Party members, moreover, are now beginning to waver. All our set-backs are unanimously ascribed to Anglo-American air superiority.

March 26

As we know, the Americans succeeded in taking our Saar front in rear. The Army fighting on the Siegfried Line was withdrawn too late and largely fell into enemy hands. The troops' morale was correspondingly low. That of the civil population was even worse; in many places people opposed the troops and placed obstacles in the way of the defence. To a great extent the tank barriers constructed in the hinterland were captured by the enemy without a fight. I [blame] Slesina [head of the propaganda office in Westmark] with the fact that not a single symbol of resistance has emerged in the West, like Breslau or Königsberg, for instance, in the East. His explanation is that people in the West have been so worn down by the months and years of enemy air raids that they prefer an end to this horror rather than an endless horror.

March 29

The military situation in the West is characterised mainly by sinking morale both among the civil population and among the troops. This loss of morale implies great danger for us since a people and an army no longer prepared to fight cannot be saved, however great the reinforcements in men and weapons. In Siegburg, for instance, a women's demonstration took place outside the Town Hall demanding the laying down of arms and capitulation.

March 30

As far as morale is concerned, I am firmly convinced that, now that the Führer has removed from me the impediment of the Reich Press Officer, I can get going again. I shall very quickly purge the Press Section of refractory and defeatist

---

[1]Reichsmarschall Hermann Göring headed the German airforce. Robert Ley headed the Nazi German Labor Front. Joachim von Ribbentrop was the Nazi foreign minister from 1938 to 1945.

elements and can now carry on propaganda against the West which will be in no way inferior to that against the East. Anti-Anglo-American propaganda is now the order of the day. Only if we can demonstrate to our people that Anglo-American intentions towards them are no different from those of the Bolshevists will they adopt a different attitude to the enemy in the West. If we succeeded in stiffening the German people against the bolshevists and instilling hatred into them, why should we not succeed in doing so against the Anglo-Americans!

Charles Fuhrmann
"IN THE RUINS OF THE BURNING CITY SS-MEN AND HITLER YOUTH WERE HOLDING OUT FANATICALLY"

In mid-April 1945 the Red Army's spearhead pushed into Berlin, which Hitler had ordered defended "to the last man and the last shot." The greatly outnumbered defenders—army remnants, elderly recruits, and fanatical Hitler Youth—fought tenaciously block by block. As the Russians stormed through the devastated city, SS squads hunted down and lynched deserters and ordinary soldiers for the flimsiest of reasons. The Russians suffered over 300,000 dead and wounded. German casualties were also in the hundreds of thousands, many of them civilians. Hundreds of thousands of Berliners fled west to escape revengeful Russians, who murdered, mutilated, raped, and looted in random acts of savagery.

Baptized as a Lutheran, Claus Fuhrmann (b. 1919) discovered as a teenager that his mother, who died before he was two years old, was Jewish. During the war he was assigned various manual labor duties and spent time in prison for the crime of sexual pollution—having sexual relations with a German girl. In February 1945, Fuhrmann, his "girlfriend," and their baby were in Berlin, where he was drafted into the *Volkssturm* battalion, which, he recalls, "consisted of a couple of hundred old gaffers, most of them over sixty." Furhmann informed the battalion commander that he had been called up by mistake. "As a 'Mischling' {half-Jew designated by Nazi law} military service was 'verboten' {forbidden} to me; Mischlings, as he knew, were unworthy of military service." Fearful of violating the law, the commander released him. Following is Fuhrmann's account of the battle of Berlin.

In March all normal life ceased in Berlin. The factories were hardly working at all. We spent more time in the cellars than out of them. The Nazis became even more anxious, raved hysterically about the "wonder weapons" soon to go into operation, and of the immense hidden might of the Werewolf,* while Russian tanks stood on the Oder and the American and British armies were pushing east across the Rhine. . . .

---

*Secret Nazi Organisation.

Several dozen people were crowded into the few inadequate cellar rooms. It was hot, stuffy and foetid with the smell of human bodies. The only light was from flickering candles. Children screamed, fought and fell over each other in the chaos. Nina never stopped crying; she was teething.

Panic had reached its peak in the city. Hordes of soldiers stationed in Berlin deserted and were shot on the spot or hanged on the nearest tree. A few clad only in underclothes were dangling on a tree quite near our house. On their chests they had placards reading: "We betrayed the Führer." The Werewolf pasted leaflets on the houses:

> "Dirty cowards and defeatists
> We've got them all on our lists!"

The S.S. went into underground stations, picked out among the sheltering crowds a few men whose faces they did not like, and shot them then and there.

The scourge of our district was a small one-legged Hauptscharführer of the S.S., who stumped through the street on crutches, a machine pistol at the ready, followed by his men. Anyone he didn't like the look of he instantly shot. The gang went down cellars at random and dragged all the men outside, giving them rifles and ordering them straight to the front. Anyone who hesitated was shot.

The front was a few streets away. At the street corner diagonally opposite our house Walloon Waffen S.S. had taken up position; wild, desperate men who had nothing to lose and who fought to their last round of ammunition. Armed Hitler Youth were lying next to men of the Vlassov White Russian Army.

The continual air attacks of the last months had worn down our morale; but now, as the first shells whistled over our heads, the terrible pressure began to give way. It could not take much longer now, whatever the Walloon and French Waffen S.S. or the fanatic Hitler Youth with their 2-cm. anti-aircraft guns could do. The end was coming and all we had to do was to try to survive this final stage.

But that was by no means simple. Everything had run out. The only water was in the cellar of a house several streets away. To get bread one had to join a queue of hundreds, grotesquely adorned with steel helmets, outside the baker's shop at three a.m. At five a.m. the Russians started and continued uninterruptedly until nine or ten. The crowded mass outside the baker's shop pressed closely against the walls, but no one moved from his place. Often the hours of queuing had been spent in vain; bread was sold out before one reached the shop. Later one could only buy bread if one brought half a bucket of water.

Russian low-flying wooden biplanes machine-gunned people as they stood apathetically in their queues and took a terrible toll of the waiting crowds. In every street dead bodies were left lying where they had fallen.

At the last moment the shopkeepers, who had been jealously hoarding their stocks, not knowing how much longer they would be allowed to, now began to sell them. Too late! For a small packet of coffee, half a pound of sausages, thousands laid down their lives. A salvo of the heavy calibre shells tore to pieces hundreds of women who were waiting in the market hall. Dead and wounded alike were flung on wheel-barrows and carted away; the surviving women continued to wait, patient, resigned, sullen, until they had finished their miserable shopping.

The pincers began to narrow on the capital. Air raids ceased; the front lines were too loose now for aircraft to distinguish between friend and foe. Slowly but surely the T.52 tanks moved forward through Prenzlauer Allee, through Schonhauser Allee, through Kaiserstrasse. The artillery bombardment poured on the city from three sides in unbroken intensity. Above it, one could hear sharply close and distinct, the rattling of machine-guns and the whine of bullets. . . .

We left the cellar at longer and longer intervals and often we could not tell whether it was night or day. The Russians drew nearer; they advanced through the underground railway tunnels, armed with flame throwers; their advance snipers had taken up positions quite near us; and their shots ricochetted off the houses opposite. Exhausted German soldiers would stumble in and beg for water—they were practically children; I remember one with a pale, quivering face who said: "We shall do it all right; we'll make our way to the north west yet." But his eyes belied his words and he looked at me despairingly. What he wanted to say was: "Hide me, give me shelter. I've had enough of it." I should have liked to help him; but neither of us dared to speak. Each might have shot the other as a "defeatist".

An old man who had lived in our house had been hit by a shell splinter a few days ago and had bled to death. His corpse lay near the entrance and had already began to smell. We threw him on a cart and took him to a burnt-out school building where there was a notice: "Collection point for Weinmeisterstrasse corpses." We left him there; one of us took the opportunity of helping himself to a dead policeman's boots. . . .

Whilst the city lay under savage artillery and rifle fire the citizens now took to looting the shops. The last soldiers withdrew farther and farther away. Somewhere in the ruins of the burning city S.S. men and Hitler Youth were holding out fanatically. The crowds burst into cellars and storehouses. While bullets were whistling through the air they scrambled for a tin of fish or a pouch of tobacco. . . .

From the street corner Russian infantry were slowly coming forward, wearing steel helmets with hand grenades in their belts and boots. The S.S. had vanished. The Hitler Youth had surrendered. . . .

After the first wave of combatant troops there followed reserves and supply troops who "liberated" us in the true Russian manner. At our street corner I saw two Russian soldiers assaulting a crying elderly woman and then raping her in full view of a stunned crowd. I ran home as fast as I could. Bunny was all right so far. We had barricaded the one remaining room of our flat with rubble and charred beams in such a manner that no one outside could suspect that anyone lived there.

Every shop in the district was looted. As I hurried to the market I was met by groups of people who were laden with sacks and boxes. Vast food reserves belonging to the armed forces had been stored there. The Russians had forced the doors open and let the Germans in. . . .

But now things were getting out of hand. In order not to be trampled down themselves the Russians fired at random into the crowds with machine pistols, killing several.

I cannot remember how I extricated myself from this screaming, shouting chaos; all I remember is that even here in this utter confusion, Russian soldiers were raping women in one of the corners.

Bunny had meanwhile made me promise not to try to interfere if anything were to happen to her. There were stories in our district of men being shot trying to protect their wives. In the afternoon two Russians entered our flat, while Bunny was sitting on the bed with the child. They looked her over for some time; evidently they were not very impressed with her. We had not washed for a fortnight, and I had expressly warned Bunny not to make herself tidy, for I thought the dirtier and more neglected she looked the safer.

But the two gentlemen did not seem to have a very high standard as far as cleanliness was concerned. With the usual words "Frau komm!" spoken in a menacing voice, one of them went towards her. I was about to interfere; but the other shouted "Stoi" and jammed his machine pistol in my chest. In my despair I shouted "Run away, quick"; but that was, of course, impossible. I saw her quietly lay the baby aside, then she said:

"Please don't look, darling." I turned to the wall.

When the first Russian had had enough they changed places. The second was chattering in Russian all the time. At last it was over. The man patted me on the shoulder:

"Nix angst! Russki Soldat gut!"

Marie Neumann
"WE'RE IN THE HANDS OF A MOB, NOT SOLDIERS, AND THEY'RE ALL DRUNK OUT OF THEIR MINDS"

As Soviet troops advanced into Germany, many terrified German civilians fled westward and not without reason. The invading Russians, seeking vengeance for the misery and ruin the Nazis had inflicted on their homeland and kinfolk, committed numerous atrocities against the conquered enemy. It quickly became official Soviet policy to prevent the perpetration of such personal acts of revenge and mayhem.

Marie Neumann of Baerwalde in Pomerania was one of the victims of this "terrible revenge." She put her nightmare in writing in 1948. Thirty years later, after reading *Nemesis at Potsdam* by Alfred-Maurice de Zayas, she sent the author her story. Following an exchange of letters and two personal visits, de Zayas was convinced she was telling the truth and later incorporated her testimony into a book about the postwar fate of Germans in Eastern Europe. Frau Neumann eventually left the Soviet zone of occupation and began a new life in West Germany. Unlike many others, she survived the acts of cruelty carried out against her and her family, described in the following passages from her 1948 account.

. . . My sister was on one side of the house with her seven-year-old daughter, and I was on the other side with her two other children and my husband. Someone had pressed a burning candle into his hand. My sister and I were raped again and again. The beasts lined up for us. During this time one of the military policemen held the door shut. I saw this because I was finally left alone before my sister was. Once she and her daughter both screamed in a most unnatural way, so that I thought they were being killed; and I wanted to go over to them when the policeman standing guard burst into our room and knocked my husband to the ground with his rifle. My niece Ilschen was crying and threw herself on my husband while the boy and I held the policeman's arm crying loudly, otherwise he would probably have killed my husband.

When we were finally granted a little peace and my husband had regained his senses, my sister came over to us and begged my husband to help her, asking, "Karl, what's going to happen to us?" My husband said, "I can't help any of you; we're in the hands of a mob, not soldiers, and they're all drunk out of their minds." I said, "Karl has to hide himself or they'll beat him to death; they've already beaten him half to death." My husband agreed with me and wanted to hide, but Grete held him back and begged him to think of her poor children. My husband then answered: "Grete, I just can't help anybody, but I'll stay with you; all we can do is hide, all of us, out in the hayloft." No sooner said than done. But just as we were climbing up into the loft, three men appeared; since there was snow outside, they had seen our tracks. We had to climb down; the two little girls were kissed and their mother raped again. She and her children cried so that it broke my heart. She cried out desperately: "O God, O God, why is this happening?" The men left, and my husband said: "They're going to kill me, they're going to kill all of you, and what they'll do to the children you can well imagine." My husband said that hiding now made no sense, we don't have any time to do it. I said: "Everybody get up there.

I'll lock all the doors and they'll have to break them down first," hoping that it would give us the time to hide ourselves. But I had forgotten in the excitement that the yard gates had been broken down already because we had been closing them whenever we could. We had just gotten into the loft when there came a howling and yelling of rabble in our yard, shooting like crazy into the ground, and then they came after us. It had gotten dark in the meantime and they had flashlights. They were civilians and some military wearing cornered hats with pompoms. What happened next I can barely write down, the pen sticks in my hand. They hanged us all in that hayloft, from the rafters, except for the children. The mob strangled them by hand with a rope.

Later I was told by the people who had taken shelter in the Hackbarth family's cellar on Polziner Street that they had heard our unnatural screams, even down in the cellar; but no one had the courage to come for us, they were all fighting for their own lives at the time. I came to on the floor, lying next to my loved ones. I didn't know yet what had happened to them, although I had a good idea, it was the details I lacked. Because I was first thrown to the floor when the mob caught us, hit on the head and raped, after which I was hanged. I had lost consciousness immediately. Later I heard voices. I was lying on the floor, four men kneeling around me. They said, "Frau komm," and when I tried to stand, I fell down at once. Later I found myself in the yard being held up by two men. They took me inside and laid me on a bed. One of the four men, a civilian, a Pole, stayed by me and asked: "Frau, who did?" I said: "The Russians." Then he hit me and said: "Russians, good soldiers. German SS, pigs, hang women and children." I fell into a fit of crying; it was impossible to stop. Then the other three came back in, but when they saw me, they left my apartment. Shortly thereafter a Russian came in carrying a whip, constantly yelling at me. Apparently he wanted me to be still, but I just couldn't. So he hit me once with the whip, then kept hitting the side of the bed. When that didn't work, he gave up and left my house. Then I heard voices in front of the house and got more scared than I was ever before or since. Seized by a cold panic I ran out to the little creek next to our garden, where the geese used to swim. I wanted to drown myself and tried for a long time until I was faint. But even that didn't bring my life to an end.

How I got through all this I don't know to this day. In any case someone had hauled me out of the creek. When I regained my senses I made my way to Fraulein Bauch's room on the ground floor of Schmechel's, the shopkeeper. Dear God how I was freezing because there were no windows or doors left in the place, and my clothes were wet; it was the night of March 4th to 5th and there was still snow and ice about. After a while I saw there was a bed in the room, so I laid down thinking I was alone in the place. But I quickly saw that someone had been sitting at the table and was now standing up, coming over to my bed, and, oh no, it was a Russian. Suddenly my whole miserable plight came before my eyes. I cried again and begged him if he wouldn't please shoot me. He shined a flashlight into my face, took off his coat and showed me his medals, saying that he was a first lieutenant and that I need not be afraid. He took a hand towel down from the wall and began to rub me dry. When he saw my throat, he asked: "Who did?" I said, the Russians. "Yes, yes," he said, "Was the Bolsheviks, but now not Bolsheviks, now White Russians; White Russians good." He then took his bayonet and cut off my panties, whereupon I again was ready to die, for I didn't know what to expect anymore. He rubbed my legs dry; but I was still freezing and didn't know what I should do if I had frostbite. But then he took off my wedding ring and put it in his pocket. He asked me where my husband was, and then raped me in spite of my miserable condition. Afterwards he promised to send me to a German doctor. I was happy about that, but then I remembered there were no more German doctors in our area.

Shortly after he left four 18- to 20-year-old Russians appeared. Totally drunk, they pulled me out of bed and raped me in an unnatural way. In my condition I wasn't able to do more and fell beside the bed, so they kicked me with their boots, getting me just in the worst spot. I fainted again. When I came to, I crawled back into the bed. Then two more such bums showed up, but they left me alone as I was more dead than alive. I learned back then how much a human being can endure; I couldn't talk, couldn't cry, couldn't even utter a sound. They hit me a bit, which didn't matter to me since I couldn't feel anything, and then left me alone. I fell asleep out of sheer exhaustion.

When I awoke very early next morning, I realized again where I was. I quickly noticed an open wardrobe door, and inside was a dress. There was also a shirt and some underwear. So even though the things were much too small, I put them on; what was left of my clothes was still wet. I had to put the dress on leaving the back unfastened, to make it fit. There were no stockings to be found; mine had been wound up so tight they were like bones. Then I was visited by the Russians again. First one who apparently thought the room was empty, because when he saw me in bed, he left the room immediately. He came back with three more men; that first one wanted to hit me, but the officer wouldn't let him. So the first man pointed to the Hitler portrait on the wall which was full of bullet holes, and he said I was a Hitler fascist. I said, "No! This isn't my house." He said, "Come! Go your house!" I had to walk ahead of them to my house and must have been a pretty sight. When I got there I saw a truck parked in front, and Russian soldiers were loading my slaughtered livestock into a car. The soldiers almost laughed themselves to death when they saw me. They indicated to their officer, their fingers tapping their heads, that I was probably crazy, and when four female soldiers appeared, they wanted to shoot me. But the officer didn't permit it. He asked about my neck, and I said, "Russian soldiers; my husband, sister, children, too." When he heard the word children, he was shocked. I asked him to come to the barn with me but he didn't want to, and I wasn't allowed to go back either. So I asked to go to the commandant. He agreed at once with that and sent a soldier with me. But when we got to the corner by Kollatz, he indicated to me that I should continue along Neustettiner Street by myself. There were several men already in the marketplace, clearing things away. When I got to the butcher, Albert Nass's place, a Russian soldier told me to go in: Commander's Headquarters.

Inside the courtyard. . . .

[A] Russian soldier said, "German woman! Stairs there, go up." I was immediately made a prisoner for my effort, locked into a room with others.

When evening arrived, it was hell itself. One woman after another in our group was hauled out. The shoemaker's wife, Frau Graf, who was in her last month of pregnancy, was taken, also a woman from Wusterhausen, and the Peters' daughter Frau Schmidt. They were driven away by some soldier. The women screamed as they were being forced into the car, and the prisoners' room was full of screaming. Our nerves were raw. Then we heard the motor revving up, the Russians shone searchlights into the room through the window, so bright that several women screamed out that they were using flame throwers against us. The children cried miserably; it was horrible. Toward morning the women came back. Two came into the room and collapsed; the other woman was raped once more by the door before they let her in. They came to get me once during the night. I was taken into the slaughterhouse and assaulted on a feather bed right on the soil. When I came to, my neighbor Herr Held was crying over me. My neck had swollen so much over the past hours that I had trouble moving my mouth, and I was spitting blood.

Adolf Hitler
"POLITICAL TESTAMENT"

On April 30, 1945, with the advancing Red Army only blocks away, Hitler took his own life. In his "Political Testament," which is printed below, he again resorted to the vile lie.

More than thirty years have now passed since I in 1914 made my modest contribution as a volunteer in the first world-war that was forced upon the Reich.

In these three decades I have been actuated solely by love and loyalty to my people in all my thoughts, acts, and life. They gave me the strength to make the most difficult decisions which have ever confronted to mortal man. I have spent my time, my working strength, and my health in these three decades.

It is untrue that I or anyone else in Germany wanted the war in 1939. It was desired and instigated exclusively by those international statesmen who were either of Jewish descent or worked for Jewish interests. I have made too many offers for the control and limitation of armaments, which posterity will not for all time be able to disregard for the responsibility for the outbreak of this war to be laid on me. I have further never wished that after the first fatal world war a second against England, or even against America, should break out. Centuries will pass away, but out of the ruins of our towns and monuments the hatred against those finally responsible whom we have to thank for everything, International Jewry and its helpers, will grow.

Three days before the outbreak of the German-Polish war I again proposed to the British ambassador in Berlin a solution to the German-Polish problem—similar to that in the case of the Saar district, under international control. This offer also cannot be denied. It was only rejected because the leading circles in English politics wanted the war, partly on account of the business hoped for and partly under influence of propaganda organized by international Jewry.

I also made it quite plain that, if the nations of Europe are again to be regarded as mere shares to be bought and sold by these international conspirators in money and finance, then that race, Jewry, which is the real criminal of this murderous struggle, will be saddled with the responsibility. I further left no one in doubt that this time not only would millions of children of Europe's Aryan peoples die of hunger, not only would millions of grown men suffer death, and not only hundreds of thousands of women and children be burnt and bombed to death in the towns, without the real criminal having to atone for this guilt, even if by more humane means.

After six years of war, which in spite of all set-backs, will go down one day in history as the most glorious and valiant demonstration of a nation's life purpose, I cannot forsake the city which is the capital of this Reich. As the forces are too small to make any further stand against the enemy attack at this place and our resistance is gradually being weakened by men who are as deluded as they are lacking in initiative, I should like, by remaining in this town, to share my fate with those, the millions of others, who have also taken upon themselves to do so. Moreover I do not wish to fall into the hands of an enemy who requires a new spectacle organized by the Jews for the amusement of their hysterical masses.

I have decided therefore to remain in Berlin and there of my own free will to choose death at the moment when I believe the position of the Fuehrer and Chancellor itself can no longer be held.

I die with a happy heart, aware of the immeasurable deeds and achievements of our soldiers at the front, our women at home, the achievements of our farmers and workers and the work, unique in history, of our youth who bear my name.

That from the bottom of my heart I express my thanks to you all, is just as self-evident as my wish that you should, because of that, on no account give up the struggle, but rather continue it against the enemies of the Fatherland, no matter where, true to the creed of the great Clausewitz. From the sacrifice of our soldiers and from my own unity with them unto death, will in any case spring up in the history of Germany, the seed of a radiant renaissance of the National-Socialist movement and thus of the realization of a true community of nations.

Many of the most courageous men and women have decided to unite their lives with mine until the very last. I have begged and finally ordered them not to do this, but to take part in the further battle of the Nation. I beg the heads of the Armies, the Navy and the Air Force to strengthen by all possible means the spirit of resistance of our soldiers in the National-Socialist sense, with special reference to the fact that also I myself, as founder and creator of this movement, have preferred death to cowardly abdication or even capitulation.

May it, at some future time, become part of the code of honour of the German officer—as is already the case in our Navy—that the surrender of a district or of a town is impossible, and that above all the leaders here must march ahead as shining examples, faithfully fulfilling their duty unto death.

Before my death I expel the former Reichsmarschall Hermann Goering from the party and deprive him of all rights which he may enjoy by virtue of the decree of June 29th, 1941, and also by virtue of my statement in the Reichstag on September 1st, 1939, I appoint in his place Grossadmiral Doenitz, President of the Reich and Supreme Commander of the Armed Forces.

Before my death I expel the former Reichsfuehrer-SS and Minister of the Interior, Heinrich Himmler, from the party and from all offices of State. In his stead I appoint Gauleiter Karl Hanke as Reichsfuehrer-SS and Chief of the German Police, and Gauleiter Paul Giesler as Reich Minister of the Interior.

Goering and Himmler, quite apart from their disloyalty to my person, have done immeasurable harm to the country and the whole nation by secret negotiations with the enemy, which they conducted without my knowledge and against my wishes, and by illegally attempting to seize power in the State for themselves.

In order to give the German people a government composed of honourable men,—a government which will fulfill its pledge to continue the war by every means—I appoint the following members of the new Cabinet as leaders of the nation:

President of the Reich: Doenitz.

Chancellor of the Reich: Dr. Goebbels.

Party Minister: Bormann. . . .

Several other appointees are listed; then the text resumes.

Although a number of these men, such as Martin Bormann, Dr. Goebbels, etc., together with their wives, have joined me of their own free will and did not wish to leave the capital of the Reich under any circumstances, but were willing to perish with me here, I must nevertheless ask them to obey my request, and in this case set the interests of the nation above their own feelings. By their work and loyalty as comrades they will be just as close to me after death, as I hope that my spirit will linger among them and always go with them. Let them be hard, but never unjust, above all let them never allow fear to influence their actions, and set the honour of the nation above everything in the world. Finally, let them be conscious of the fact that our task, that of continuing the building of a National Socialist State, represents the work of the coming centuries, which places every single person under an obligation always to serve the common interest and to subordinate his own advantage to this end. I demand of all Germans, all National Socialists, men, women and all the men of the Armed Forces, that they be faithful and obedient unto death to the new government and its President.

Above all I charge the leaders of the nation and those under them to scrupulous observance of the laws of race and to merciless opposition to the universal poisoner of all peoples, international Jewry.

Given in Berlin, this 29th day of April 1945. 4:00 A.M.

Adolf Hitler.

Witnessed by

Dr. Josef Fuhr. Wilhelm Buergdorf.

Martin Bormann. Hans Krebs.

CHAPTER SIX

WESTERN EUROPE: THE DAWN OF A NEW ERA

When the war in Europe ended in May 1945, many areas lay devastated, none more so than the once-picturesque German city of Dresden, in which at least 50,000 people had perished in a terror bombing by Allied planes in February 1945. Europe was faced with the awesome task of reconstructing a continent in ruins. *(dpa/Corbis)*

By the war's end in 1945, there were tens of millions of dead, many more maimed or displaced, and the infrastructure of the lands touched by war was shattered or greatly damaged. Europeans were faced with the Herculean task of reconstructing the Continent. In Western Europe, the work of reconstruction was multifaceted. It required efforts to provide shelter, fresh water, and food to refugees; repair lines of communication; and restore functioning administrations and peacetime economies. National socialism had visited a war like no other in history upon the peoples of Europe. To underscore that aggressive war and genocide would not be tolerated again, initiatives to promote international dialogue and punish the architects of Nazi atrocities met with near-universal approbation.

Unlike the circumstances of 1918, when economic chaos, civil war, and international tensions continued to put peace to the test, after 1945 an American determination to avoid withdrawing into isolationism and an emerging recognition within the United States and Western Europe that Germany needed to be integrated, not marginalized, provided a basis for recovery and integration. Moreover, a totally defeated, devastated, and demoralized German nation had relinquished the dream of forging a greater Germany. These tendencies were reinforced by massive deliveries of American aid in the late 1940s and early 1950s—an effort to nip fascist and especially communist extremism in the bud by removing the root of disaffection. Moreover, it had become apparent during the war in Britain, and shortly after the war ended on the Continent, that an effective social security net would help prevent the appeal of extremist political movements. Comprehensive welfare would require sound economies, however. Partly toward this end, Western European states began to embrace economic cooperation, laying the basis for the European Community (later, the European Union); German recovery prompted less acrimony and jealousy than would have been expected, and more admiration.

Two decades after the war ended the physical and emotional effects of the Second World War were still evident in European society and felt by many individuals, but the basis of recovery had been successfully established. The first postwar generation began to face the future with a sense of hope, although many intellectuals, scarred by war and genocide, continued to speak of the fragility of reason, the reality of human evil, and the precariousness of civilization.

1 The Aftermath: Devastation and Hope

Unlike the mood following World War I, the two decades after 1945 witnessed no quibbling over territorial revisions, no glorification of the front-line experience—in short, no palpable desire for revenge that expressed itself in an eagerness for another, future conflict. The nightmare of death, physical injury, loss of human dignity, and material destruction left most Europeans bereft of energy for anything other than piecing their lives back together during the initial postwar years. If conflict were to return to the Continent, it threatened to be the result of Soviet-American geopolitical differences, rather than the work of those in Western Europe. The wounds of war would take years to heal and require the earnest efforts and moral force of Europeans, as well as large-scale international engagement.

Stephen Spender
EUROPEAN WITNESS

The British poet, essayist, and journalist Stephen Spender (1909–1995) undertook a continental journey in the summer and autumn of 1945, and took stock of the impact of the fighting on lands that he knew before the war. Spender offered compelling eyewitness to a Europe in ruins. His observations, published in 1946, provide a benchmark against which to gauge the progress of European recovery over the ensuing two decades.

In the selection below, from *European Witness* (1946), Spender describes the physical destruction in the heavily bombed German city of Cologne.

My first impression on passing through [Cologne] was of there being not a single house left. There are plenty of walls but these walls are a thin mask in front of the damp, hollow, stinking emptiness of gutted interiors. Whole streets with nothing but the walls left standing are worse than streets flattened. They are more sinister and oppressive.

Actually, there are a few habitable buildings left in Cologne; three hundred in all, I am told. One passes through street after street of houses whose windows look hollow and blackened—like the open mouth of a charred corpse; behind these windows there is nothing except floors, furniture, bits of rag, books, all dropped to the bottom of the building to form there a sodden mass.

Through the streets of Cologne thousands of people trudge all day long. These are crowds who a few years ago were shop-gazing in their city, or waiting to go to the cinema or to the opera, or stopping taxis. They are the same people who once were the ordinary inhabitants of a great city when by what now seems an unbelievable magical feat of reconstruction in time, this putrescent corpse-city was the hub of the Rhineland, with a great shopping centre, acres of plate-glass, restaurants, a massive business street containing the head offices of many banks and firms, an excellent opera, theatres, cinemas, lights in the streets at night.

Now it requires a real effort of the imagination to think back to that Cologne which I knew well ten years ago. Everything has gone. In this the destruction of Germany is quite different from even the worst that has happened in England (though not different from Poland and from parts of Russia). In England there are holes, gaps and wounds, but the surrounding life of the people themselves has filled them up, creating a scar which will heal. In towns such as Cologne and those of the Ruhr, something quite different has happened. The external destruction is so great that it cannot be healed and the surrounding life of the rest of the country cannot flow into and resuscitate the city which is not only battered but also dismembered and cut off from the rest of Germany and from Europe. The ruin of the city is reflected in the internal ruin of its inhabitants who, instead of being lives that can form a scar over the city's wounds, are parasites sucking at a dead carcase, digging among the ruins for hidden food, doing business at their black market near the cathedral—the commerce of destruction instead of production.

The people who live there seem quite dissociated from Cologne. They resemble rather a tribe of wanderers who have discovered a ruined city in a desert and who are camping there, living in the cellars and hunting amongst the ruins for the booty, relics of a dead civilization.

The great city looks like a corpse and stinks like one also, with all the garbage which has not been cleared away, all the bodies still buried under heaps of stones and iron. Although the streets have been partly cleared, they still have many holes in them and some of the side streets are impassable. The general impression is that very little has been cleared away. There are landscapes of untouched ruin still left.

. . . But it is the comparatively undamaged cathedral which gives Cologne what it still retains of character. One sees that this is and was a great city, it is uplifted by the spire of the cathedral from being a mere heap of rubble and a collection of walls, like the towns of the Ruhr. Large buildings round the cathedral have been scratched and torn, and, forming a kind of cliff beneath the spires, they have a certain dignity like the cliffs and rocks under a church close to the sea.

. . . In the destroyed German towns one often feels haunted by the ghost of a tremendous noise. It is impossible not to imagine the rocking explosions, the hammering of the sky upon the earth, which must have caused all this.

The effect of these corpse-towns is a grave discouragement which influences everyone living and working in Germany, the Occupying Forces as much as the German. The destruction is *serious* in more senses than one. It is a climax of deliberate effort, an achievement of our civilization, the most striking result of cooperation between nations in the twentieth century. It is the shape created by our century as the Gothic cathedral is the shape created by the Middle Ages. Everything has stopped here, that fusion of the past within the present, integrated into architecture, which forms the organic life of a city, a life quite distinct from that of the inhabitants who are, after all, only using a city as a waiting-room on their journey through time: that long, gigantic life of a city has been killed. The city is dead and the inhabitants only haunt the cellars and basements. Without their city they are rats in the cellars, or bats wheeling around the towers of the cathedral. The citizens go on existing with a base mechanical kind of life like that of insects in the crannies of walls who are too creepy and ignoble to be destroyed when the wall is torn down. The destruction of the city itself, with all its past as well as its present, is like a reproach to the people who go on living there. The sermons in the stones of Germany preach nihilism. . . .

Theodore H. White
"GERMANY: SPRING IN THE RUINS"

Political journalist Theodore H. White (1915–1986) covered postwar reconstruction and European politics during a more than five-year residence on the Continent in the late 1940s and early 1950s. In the following account, excerpted from *Fire in the Ashes: Europe in Mid-Century* (1953), White recounted circumstances in Germany during the initial postwar years with an eye to the transformation he witnessed by 1951–52 (see p. 298).

Here and there in this Germany of 1945 lay little pockets or unscarred village and hamlet, bypassed by encircling armies or ignored by maranding bombers, their brown and gray church spires rising like accusing fingers to the sky from the sturdy, field-stone house of the peasants. But the roads that ran from village to town, from town to city were torn and ruptured by the passage of war; tanks had disemboweled the roadbeds, artillery and planes had shattered the bridges. And the roads led to cities, one more appalling than the other—rubble heaps of stone and brick, rank with the smell of sewage and filth, dirty with the dust of destruction working its way into clothes, linen, skin and soul. The forlorn people who lived in the ruins in those Winter Years could feel little beyond hunger. The clear German skin which glows so pink and ruddy in health shrunk sallow over shriveled bodies, or puffed over the unhealthy putty of children bloated by hunger edema. By April of 1947 even the conquerors' statisticians admitted that the daily German ration had fallen to 1,040 calories, or thirty-three per cent below the scientific calculation of the minimum necessary to sustain life. Allied health teams stopped Germans on street corners and weighed them bodily to confirm these figures, and found the nation decaying. White-faced men and women collapsed at their jobs for lack of food. Dignified people sought jobs as clerks or servants in the offices of the occupying armies because in the barracks of the conquerors they got one hot meal of stew a day, which kept them alive. The United States government appropriated money to give every German school child one hot meal a day in his classroom. When Germans could think of anything beyond food they thought of clothes; the leather jerkins of German workingmen and their black leather boots had frayed and cracked; the ugly woolen stockings of German women were thin and holed; children played in the streets in the cut-down Wehrmacht jackets and pants of their fathers. The search for shelter was a nightmare; for this country, forty per cent of whose homes had been smashed, was being forced to absorb and shelter eight million refugees thrust back into it. For a German the perspective of ambition was the search to find for his family two rooms with a toilet and running water, and, if this were found, he dreamed cautiously of a home where the toilet would not be in the kitchen where the food was cooked, but in a real toilet compartment of remembered privacy.

Values withered: Girls roamed the streets, sleeping with the conquering soldiers for a candy bar, a cake of soap, a tin of Quaker Oats, coming home to once-chaste beds dirty with disease. Money was meaningless, cigarettes were currency; two cartons of American cigarettes bought a set of Meissen china, three cartons bought a Leica camera, two cigarettes were a tip. Businessmen became pirates. Families dissolved.

By an enormous, instinctive act of national resolution Germans put thinking out of their minds and concentrated on simple things: how to find a job, and how to work. For only by working could one find food, find clothes, find a roof. Even work was difficult; Germany could make only a strictly limited quantity of steel, of aluminum, of sulfur, of copper. She was forbidden to make again the vast range of intricate machinery in which lay her commercial strength; she could not build airplanes, could not fly airplanes, could not synthesize rubber or gasoline. One worked at what came to hand. In the Ruhr workmen stood in sullen silence and watched the dismantlers surveying for removal of generators, rolling mills and steel ovens. Krupp sat in his prison and British engineers carefully paced the jungle of his Essen works marking with white chalk the machine tools, the drop forges, the presses to be taken away. At the Bochumer Verein, which had made both submarine assemblies and the finest crucible steels, the newest and most efficient shops were dismantled.

Gerold Frank
THE TRAGEDY OF THE DPs

The term "Displaced Persons" was coined at the end of World War II to describe the unprecedented number of people who were uprooted by almost six years of violence. The geographic and personal circumstances of these individuals, who numbered in the millions, was extraordinarily diverse: Jewish and non-Jewish concentration camp survivors; laborers from the agricultural, mining, and heavy industrial sectors forced to toil for the Nazi war effort or willing to pursue employment within the Third Reich; German nationals who fled their homes in eastern Germany, Poland, Hungary, Czechoslovakia, and Romania to escape the advancing Red Army, or who suddenly found themselves within redrawn borderlands (East Prussia, Silesia, the Sudetenland) that were no longer part of Germany; and German and non-German members of the Wehrmacht who either could not return to their homes in Soviet-occupied Eastern Europe, or sought to traverse war-torn Germany to rejoin their families.

DP camps were established by the Allies to feed and house these refugees until they could move on, but the problem was so vast that the newly founded United Nations was compelled to create a UN Relief and Rehabilitation Commission to coordinate DP assistance. The following description deals specifically with the problems confronting Jewish refugees who wished to emigrate to Palestine, then still a mandate of Britain, which restricted immigration of Jews.

Prague

One overwhelming truth emerges from a tour of investigation through displaced-persons camps in Germany. It is that these people must be taken out—at once. If we fail to act, within six months we shall run the risk of having 100,000 psychiatric cases on our hands, plus the complete demoralization of a people; and it will take not only psychiatric help but the Army to prevent the possibility not only of their killing Germans but of killing themselves. There is a limit to how long a human being can be told "no" and be denied everything he needs and on which he counts.

Constant denial, constant frustration, unending disillusion—these are driving Jews who survived concentration camps to a point beyond despair. They are on the verge of moral collapse. The only substance on which they exist is Palestine. It dominates their every waking moment. The word itself is incandescent with meaning to them. One is appalled even to contemplate what might now be taking place among them if there were no Palestine on which to fasten their hopes and with which to identify their future.

The actual liberation was a miraculous event. For the Jewish DP's it was almost like the Messianic deliverance, and with it they expected a kind of universal welcome and universal repentance by the world which had permitted them to suffer such monstrous cruelties. There was no welcome. There was no repentance. Instead, there came to them the dawning realization that they were nuisances, problems, pariahs.

So far, I've heard no talk of vengeance—only this grim determination to go to Palestine—but the path may become too difficult; the world may have learned the art of keeping them out of Palestine better than they have learned the art of getting into it. In such an event it is possible that the determination to have their own way for once, if allowed no other outlet, will explode disastrously.

No one who has visited a DP center is likely to have any illusions about it. Physically it is a transient overnight camp in which people are sitting on packed bags with no alternative but to remain day after day. Psychologically it is an institution where creative instincts are thwarted, where there is no real opportunity for work, no incentive to build, no possibility of saving for the future. What German marks a DP can earn are worthless outside Germany. Within Germany, there is virtually nothing buyable. His immediate needs which are not supplied by the Army or UNRRA are suppliable on the black market. Everybody in Germany—officers, soldiers, Germans and DP's—is engaged in black-marketing on a wide scale. The army acknowledges this by the admission that the daily ration for Germans—1,500 calories—is somehow supplemented by most Germans with from 500 to 1,500 extra calories daily. The black market is the only source for this supplement. There are raids by army MP's now and then on DP camps because of black-marketing. DP's see them only as a new form of tyrannical oppression. A DP found with a package of American cigarettes is liable to be thrown into jail, even though he intends to barter it for a pair of rubbers for his child—unobtainable in any other way.

The diet given DP's, though medically sufficient, is so monotonous and unfilling that hunger strikes have occurred in some camps. I have visited a camp where supper consisted of a slice of black bread, a spoonful of marmalade, and coffee with powdered milk. That living conditions are crowded, and certainly below present German standards, that diets are almost unendurable, that leisure activities are severely limited or nonexistent, that the DP's are not surrounded by the normal laughter of children (an average camp of 2,500 may have less than 60 children, nearly all orphans)—all this is dwarfed by the denial of the consuming wish to "return home"—to go to Palestine.

And why is Palestine, as the subcommittee of the Anglo-American Committee of Inquiry on Palestine repeatedly asked DP's in camp after camp, why is Palestine uppermost in their minds—not the United States or Britain, with their millions of free Jewish citizens? These men and women and young people replied in words not soon forgotten that Palestine has become to them a symbol with infinite meanings, of which, perhaps, the most significant is personal dignity. This is the quality of which Hitler robbed the survivors of his massacres in the eyes of the world. Palestine means security for them, not in the sense of safety but in the sense of being wanted by those among whom they live. The committee questioned a group of a dozen ragged Jewish boys and girls who infiltrated into the American zone after they returned to Poland and found none of their families alive. Who organized these youngsters into a group, the committee asked, remembering tales of well fed Jews with pockets full of money.

"Organized?" repeated a 20-year-old girl, puzzled. "We met on the road, first three of us and then two more, and so on. Our mothers, fathers, brothers and sisters were all burned by the Germans and so we became brothers and sisters to each other." Individually they are wanted by each other, these DP's, and by no one else; collectively they are wanted by no one save the Jews of Palestine. This symbol of Palestine has in it the desire to stand up proudly, to cast off the stigma of an inferior race, to cease being objects of contempt and toleration. "When will you let us go home to Palestine and no longer hear all these terrible things said about us?" asked a 13-year-old boy at the Fahrenwald camp near Munich. "When shall I be able to be a Jew again?" In this symbol of Palestine there is above all else a desire to go to the end of the line, to cease being a wanderer, to reach *home.*

This helps to explain the poll of their attitudes on emigration taken under UNRRA auspices at the request of the committee. It resulted in more than 18,700 of 19,000 answering "Palestine"; when asked to list their second choice, 98 percent renamed Palestine. This is no rationalization of the fact that there is no chance to emigrate to the democracies. They are convinced that their only hope is to begin life anew on their own soil. "Yes," said Israel Wilence of the Greifenberg camp, 25 miles from Augsburg, "I know that six million Jews are living happily in America. They lived happily in Germany. I don't say what happened in Germany will happen in America, but I don't want even to take the chance that it will happen."

In the words of Dr. Zelman Greenberg, chairman of the Central Committee of Liberated Jews in Bavaria, they cannot be fully understood unless you take into account "their horrible yesterday, their impossible today, their uncertain tomorrow." The truth of this is now realized by the subcommittee as it could not be realized in Washington and London, no matter how eloquent the witnesses were.

It is true that the problems faced by both the Army and UNRRA are staggering: Germany is a battered, ruined country. Her transportation system was the special object of very accurate bombing. Her roads are pockmarked with craters; bridges are out, railways wrecked. There is not sufficient railway space to carry to Munich or Nuremberg or Frankfort supplies which the United States would be willing to make available. There is a tremendous housing shortage. Of the 50,000 Jewish DP's in the American zone alone, 40,000 live in DP centers ranging from camp barracks to private dwellings, built by slave labor, in which each room, even the kitchen, is bedroom and living quarters for from four to seven persons.

In contrast to the life of the Jewish DP's is that of the Germans, who not only eat well despite all the reports—any GI will tell you that German cellars today are among the best stocked in Europe—but are among the best-dressed people in Europe. Nothing fills the heart of the Jewish DP with more resentment than to be presented with patched and tattered cast-off clothing collected in an American salvage campaign while he watches German women parade in finery filched from millions of slave laborers and concentration-camp inmates in the years of Nazi power. When the DP sleeps on his straw mattress in wooden barracks, he knows the German across the road is sleeping between sheets on a bed of down, and wonders who was vanquished and who was liberated. He sees the attitude of newly arrived American soldiers who have not seen the Germany of concentration camps, whose conception of the DP's problem is that given them by the fraulein with whom they last slept.

The Jewish DP's hate Germany with a pathological hate. They detest Europe and they distrust the world. The one in seven who survived starvation, torture, slave camps, gas chambers and crematoria has had agonizing time to think and draw conclusions. They wrote "Palestine" as first choice and second choice, but when they were told, as in the Fürth DP center near Nuremberg, not to make the second choice the same as the first, 500 of the 2,000 there wrote as second choice the single word "crematorium."

The Jewish DP's in Germany, as the committee noted admiringly time and time again, possess a pent-up reservoir of energy and creativeness—which turned the desert into a vineyard in Palestine. But this is a precious and perishable commodity. It must be utilized beneficently now or it will be utilized tragically tomorrow.

These people must be taken out. Even if physical conditions improve, to keep them in these camps means the spiritual and moral desolation of the remnants of European Jewry, as Bartley Crum, a member of the committee, asserts. This is also the conviction of Judge Simon Rifkind, adviser to General McNarney on Jewish affairs. Here is how he sums it up: "The solution of the problem of displaced persons is to place them. Jewish DP's cannot be placed without mass migration to Palestine. That is manifest to everyone who has learned to know them intimately. The overwhelming majority of Jewish DP's will accept no other solution. Every day's delay compounds Hitler's crimes against his first victim. The time is rotten ripe for action."

These people—the world must know it now lest it know it too late—these people must be taken out.

Bruno Foa
EUROPE IN RUINS

Shortly after the end of World War II, international economic experts in Europe and the United States began to evaluate the difficulties posed by social and economic dislocation and material destruction. The following report, authored by Bruno Foa, a specialist in Inter-American Affairs and member of the Board of Governors of the Federal Reserve System, isolated the central challenges to European recovery. His conclusions proved prescient; the European Recovery Program announced by Secretary of State Marshall only two years later was formulated to address the problems that Foa pointed out so clearly.

The present situation of the liberated countries of Europe is governed, to an overwhelming extent, by facts and realities from which there is no escape. These facts are hunger, unemployment, economic dislocation of unprecedented scope, and destruction and damage on an appalling scale. . . .

. . . [I]t is already clear that the economic and social disturbances which followed the last war were child's play in comparison with the crisis Europe is now facing. . . . [T]he experiences of this war, and of the new dark age which began on January 30, 1933, have destroyed old frames of references and created conditions favorable to nihilism and despair.

The lights which Sir Edward Grey saw dimming all over Europe in the fateful August of 1914, and which went out once more twenty-five years later, are being rekindled over a desolate landscape of death and ruins. The living skeletons who are emerging from German concentration camps, and the millions of "displaced persons" to whom liberation means rescue from certain death but holds no promise of real life and happiness, symbolize the depths to which Europe has fallen. . . .

ECONOMIC CONSEQUENCES OF WAR

It is unnecessary to dwell on the dreary catalogue of the economic consequences of war for the liberated countries of Europe. There have been the effects of actual war damage and destruction. There have been the effects of the ruthless economy of spoliation and slavery enforced by the Germans. . . .

War Damage and Destruction

The physical destruction wrought by this war is beyond description. It is reported that in France over a million buildings have been destroyed or badly damaged, a number considerably in excess of the damage produced in World War I. In France thousands of bridges have also been demolished. Railroad equipment, both fixed installations and rolling stock, has suffered great destruction and depletion. Practically all major French ports have been either destroyed or badly damaged. Italy has suffered perhaps even more—countless cities, towns and villages from Salerno to Bologna are heaps of ruins; extensive damage has been wreaked on such great cities as Milan, Genoa, Naples and Turin. Bridges and railroad lines were sabotaged by the Germans in the course of their slow retreat across the Italian peninsula. First reports from liberated Holland, although less catastrophic than expected, are grim. As to eastern Europe and the Balkans, the tale of destruction due to actual fighting, guerrilla warfare and enemy ruthlessness is now generally familiar. . . .

It can be confidently predicted that, in some areas at least, reconstruction will be carried on with vigor and speed. This was the case after World War I, although it must be noted that the damage caused by World War II is far in excess of anything previously experienced. Among other things destruction of railroad lines and equipment has been incomparably heavier, and their rebuilding will require massive imports of expensive and specialized equipment and materials. Reconstruction of permanent port installations in places like Antwerp, Rotterdam, Bordeaux, Marseilles, Genoa and Naples will entail enormous cost and effort. . . .

Impact on Human Potential

The war and German occupation have had an incalculable impact on the human potential of the subjugated lands of Europe. German policies have followed a single criminal pattern—a slave Europe ruled by the [master race]. These policies have been implemented in varying ways and degrees in the different countries. Extermination was applied against the Jews of all occupied territories, and millions of Poles, Russians and other peoples of eastern Europe were murdered. By holding in bondage over two and a half million young Frenchmen for five years, the Germans struck a heavy blow at France's birth rate. Outright starvation killed hundreds of thousands, and indeed millions, in Greece, Poland and the Balkans. In most occupied countries malnutrition, tuberculosis and a high rate of infant mortality have sapped the human potential. All this is bound to have lasting effects not only on population statistics but also on the vitality, the physical and mental balance, and the productivity of at least two generations.

German Depredation

German depredation varied in degree and methods in different countries, but was uniformly far-reaching. In Poland and Russia it took the form of outright robbery, confiscation, and the dismantlement and removal to Germany of industrial and productive assets. In Czechoslovakia the ownership of most basic industries was transferred to German hands, and Germans penetrated into practically the entire economic life of the country. In Italy depredation and destruction of foodstuffs, cattle, etc., were extensive. In western and northern Europe spoliation was thinly clothed under financial and other manipulations, which deceived no one. . . .

Heavy occupation costs and other equivalent contributions were levied on France, Belgium, Holland, Czechoslovakia, Norway and Poland. The most significant case in point was that of France, which paid to Germany for occupation costs . . . the enormous sum of 860 billion francs—the equivalent of more than $17 billion. The amounts levied by Germany on other countries, although lower, were proportionately even heavier. . . . [T]he damaging effects of these tributes, in terms of inflation and public finance, are irreparable. . . .

Hunger: Legacy of War

With few exceptions, liberated Europe is starving or semi-starving. The situation is worse in Greece, Yugoslavia and Poland, but also disastrous in Italy, France—with the exception of a few well-stocked rural districts such as Normandy—Belgium and Holland. The average caloric intake of people in Greece, France and Italy is far below the minimum subsistence level. Death rates have risen to exceptionally high levels, in particular infant mortality, which in France and Italy is said to exceed 50 per cent. Even those who escape outright starvation are suffering from the effects of an unbalanced diet and deficiencies in fats, iron, calcium and vitamins. . . .

Coal and Transportation

Everywhere in liberated western Europe coal and transportation are pressing problems of the day, on which almost everything else depends. . . .

Prices, Wages, and Black Markets

Europe [is], from one end to the other, a single, giant black market. . . .

[T]here is no incentive at present for a worker to stick to his job or look for a new one. For, wages being what they are, the worker is better off . . . supplementing his income by engaging in black-market or other illegal activity which lends itself to exploitation of the consumer. In general, and this applies both to entrepreneurs and to laborers, there is hardly a legitimate activity that pays. While some of these illegal activities—such as outright racketeering, dealings in Allied stolen properties, etc.—are still considered criminal by a majority of the people, the line of demarcation between what is legal and what is illegal has become increasingly blurred. To survive, one has literally to push around, cheat or exploit the other fellow. It is the law of the jungle. The white collar, professional and lower middle classes are the hardest hit; and the proletarianization of large strata of the population, which played havoc with central Europe in the early twenties and contributed powerfully to the rise of Hitler, is spreading throughout the continent.

George C. Marshall
LAYING THE FOUNDATIONS FOR RECOVERY

If European societies were to rebound from the destruction and dislocation of total war, it was abundantly clear that the European states themselves lacked the financial and administrative resources to engineer recovery on their own. As U.S. Army Chief of Staff during the war and now Secretary of State, George C. Marshall appreciated the severity of the problem better than most observers. His now-famous speech before an audience at Harvard University in June 1947, printed below, outlined the central humanitarian, economic, and political issues inherent in the question of U.S. aid to Europe. Historians have subsequently weighed in with various emphases concerning their evaluations of the American government's principal objectives. Was it to feed, clothe, and rebuild Europe for the sake of its inhabitants' survival? A strategy to develop future markets, which would receive U.S. manufactured goods? An effort to forestall the appeal of communism by largely eliminating the sources of material discontent upon which its adherents solicited new supporters? A combination of these or other concerns? There is little doubt, however, that the European Recovery Program—or "Marshall Plan"—was instrumental in promoting recovery and integration for those Central and Western European states that elected to participate in it.

The Soviet Union and the Eastern European states were also extended an invitation to participate, but the Soviet government dismissed the American initiative as a barely concealed expression of U.S. imperialism. The only state in the Soviet sphere of influence to respond favorably to the invitation was Czechoslovakia; after making their intentions known, the Czechoslovak leaders were summoned to Moscow and warned ominously to reverse their course or suffer the consequences. In the end, between 1948 and 1951 over $10 billion in foodstuffs, fuel, machinery, and various grants, loans, and credits helped Western Europe along the path to recovery, whereas Eastern Europe fell behind and remained comparatively underdeveloped for the remainder of the century.

Thus, the Marshall Plan must be seen as a contributing factor to both the reconstruction of Western Europe and a significant development in the early stages of the Cold War.

I need not tell you gentlemen that the world situation is very serious. That must be apparent to all intelligent people. I think one difficulty is that the problem is one of such enormous complexity that the very mass of facts presented to the public by press and radio make it exceedingly difficult for the man in the street to reach a clear appraisement of the situation. Furthermore, the people of this country are distant from the troubled areas of the earth and it is hard for them to comprehend the plight and consequent reactions of the long-suffering peoples, and the effect of those reactions on their governments in connection with our efforts to promote peace in the world.

In considering the requirements for the rehabilitation of Europe the physical loss of life, the visible destruction of cities, factories, mines and railroads was correctly estimated, but it has become obvious during recent months that this visible destruction was probably less serious than the dislocation of the entire fabric of European economy. For the past ten years conditions have been highly abnormal. The feverish preparation for war and the more feverish maintenance of the war effort engulfed all aspects of national economies. Machinery has fallen into disrepair or is entirely obsolete. Under the arbitrary and destructive Nazi rule, virtually every possible enterprise was geared into the German war machine. Long-standing commercial ties, private institutions, banks, insurance companies and shipping companies disappeared, through loss of capital, absorption through nationalization or by simple destruction. In many countries, confidence in the local currency has been severely shaken. The breakdown of the business structure of Europe during the war was complete. Recovery has been seriously retarded by the fact that two years after the close of hostilities a peace settlement with Germany and Austria has not been agreed upon. But even given a more prompt solution of these difficult problems, the rehabilitation of the economic structure of Europe quite evidently will require a much longer time and greater effort than had been foreseen.

There is a phase of this matter which is both interesting and serious. The farmer has always produced the foodstuffs to exchange with the city dweller for the other necessities of life. This division of labor is the basis of modern civilization. At the present time it is threatened with breakdown. The town and city industries are not producing adequate goods to exchange with the food-producing farmer. Raw materials and fuel are in short supply. Machinery is lacking or worn out. The farmer or the peasant cannot find the goods for sale which he desires to purchase. So the sale of his farm produce for money which he cannot use seems to him an unprofitable transaction. He, therefore, has withdrawn many fields from crop cultivation and is using them for grazing. He feeds more grain to stock and finds for himself and his family an ample supply of food, however short he may be on clothing and the other ordinary gadgets of civilization. Meanwhile people in the cities are short of food and fuel. So the governments are forced to use their foreign money and credits to procure these necessities abroad. This process exhausts funds which are urgently needed for reconstruction. Thus a very serious situation is rapidly developing which bodes no good for the world. The modern system of the division of labor upon which the exchange of products is based is in danger of breaking down.

The truth of the matter is that Europe's requirements for the next three or four years of foreign food and other essential products—principally from America—are so much greater than her present ability to pay that she must have substantial additional help, or face economic, social and political deterioration of a very grave character.

The remedy lies in breaking the vicious circle and restoring the confidence of the European people in the economic future of their own countries and of Europe as a whole. The manufacturer and the farmer throughout wide areas must be able and willing to exchange their products for currencies the continuing value of which is not open to question.

Aside from the demoralizing effect on the world at large and the possibilities of disturbances arising as a result of the desperation of the people concerned, the consequences to the economy of the United States should be apparent to all. It is logical that the United States should do whatever it is able to do to assist in the return of normal economic health in the world, without which there can be no political stability and no assured peace. Our policy is directed not against any country or doctrine but against hunger, poverty, desperation and chaos. Its purpose should be the revival of a working economy in the world so as to permit the emergence of political and social conditions in which free institutions can exist. Such assistance, I am convinced, must not be on a piece-meal basis as various crises develop. Any assistance that this Government may render in the future should provide a cure rather than a mere palliative. Any government that is willing to assist in the task of recovery will find full cooperation, I am sure, on the part of the United States Government. Any government which maneuvers to block the recovery of other countries cannot expect help from us. Furthermore, governments, political parties or groups which seek to perpetuate human misery in order to profit therefrom politically or otherwise will encounter the opposition of the United States.

It is already evident that, before the United States Government can proceed much further in its efforts to alleviate the situation and help start the European world on its way to recovery, there must be some agreement among the countries of Europe as to the requirements of the situation and the part those countries themselves will take in order to give proper effect to whatever action might be undertaken by this Government. It would be neither fitting nor efficacious for this Government to undertake to draw up unilaterally a program designed to place Europe on its feet economically. This is the business of the Europeans. The initiative, I think, must come from Europe. The role of this country should consist of friendly aid in the drafting of a European program and of later support of such a program so far as it may be practical for us to do so. The program should be a joint one, agreed to by a number, if not all European nations.

An essential part of any successful action on the part of the United States is an understanding on the part of the people of America of the character of the problem and the remedies to be applied. Political passion and prejudice should have no part. With foresight, and a willingness on the part of our people to face up to the vast responsibility which history has clearly placed upon our country, the difficulties I have outlined can and will be overcome.

2 The Recent Past and Western Consciousness

The Nazi era had a profound impact on Western consciousness. It showed how fragile is the Western tradition of freedom, reason, and human dignity. The popularity of fascism in many European lands demonstrated that liberty is not appealing to many people—that, at any rate, there are many things they consider more important. It seems that without much reluctance people will trade freedom for security, a feeling of solidarity with their fellows, or national grandeur. A painful lesson of the Nazi era is that the irrational cannot be underestimated or neglected. Nazi racist ideology and Nazi atrocities demonstrated that the

liberals' confidence in the primacy of reason, in the essential goodness of human nature, and in the march of progress constituted a rather naive view of both human nature and the human condition. For many thinkers, the recent past bore out Walter Lippmann's insight that "men have been barbarians much longer than they have been civilized. They are only precariously civilized, and within us there is the propensity, persistent as the force of gravity, to revert under stress and strain, under neglect or temptation, to our first natures." Both the Christian and the Enlightenment traditions had failed the West. The future envisioned by the *philosophes* seemed further away than ever.

In the immediate aftermath of the war, some intellectuals, shocked by the irrationality and horrors of the Hitler era, drifted into despair. Nevertheless, this profound disillusionment was tempered by hope. Democracy had, in fact, prevailed over Nazi totalitarianism and terror. Perhaps, then, democratic institutions and values would spread throughout the globe, and the newly established United Nations would promote world peace.

Ernst Cassirer
THE MYTH OF THE STATE

Nazism's idolization of the leader, the race, the party, and the state was a striking example of human irrationality, a triumph of mythical thinking over reason. That many Germans, including many of the intellectual elite, succumbed to these myths unnerved Western liberals who were heirs to the Enlightenment tradition of reason. To safeguard civilized life from political ideologies that arouse and mobilize potentially dangerous human emotions became a principal concern of several thinkers.

A staunch defender of the Enlightenment tradition, Ernst Cassirer (1874–1945), a prominent German philosopher of Jewish lineage, emigrated after Hitler came to power, eventually settling in the United States. In 1932, just prior to Hitler's triumph, Cassirer wrote about the need to uphold and reenergize that tradition: "The age which venerated reason and science as man's highest faculty cannot and must not be lost even for us. We must find a way not only to see that age in its own shape but to release again those original forces which brought forth and molded that shape."

In his posthumous work, *The Myth of the State* (1946), excerpted below, Cassirer explored how the Nazis cleverly manufactured myths that disoriented the intellect. Germans who embraced these myths, he said, surrendered their capacity for independent judgment, leaving themselves vulnerable to manipulation by the Nazi leadership. To contain the destructive powers of political myths, Cassirer urged strengthening the rational-humanist tradition and called for the critical study of political myths, "for in order to fight an enemy you must know him."

In the last thirty years, in the period between the first and the second World Wars, we have not only passed through a severe crisis of our political and social life but have also been confronted with quite new theoretical problems. We experienced a radical change in the forms of political thought. New questions were raised and new answers were given. Problems that had been unknown to the political thinkers of the eighteenth and nineteenth centuries came suddenly to the fore. Perhaps the most important and the most alarming feature in this development of modern political thought is the appearance of a new power: the power of mythical thought. The preponderance of mythical thought over rational thought in some of our modern political systems is obvious. After a short and violent struggle mythical thought seemed to win a clear and definitive victory. How was this victory possible? How can we account for the new phenomenon that so suddenly appeared on our political horizon and in a sense seemed to reverse all our former ideas of the character of our intellectual and our social life?

If we look at the present state of our cultural life we feel at once that there is a deep chasm between two different fields. When it comes to political action man seems to follow rules quite different from those recognized in all his mere theoretical activities. No one would think of solving a problem of natural science or a technical problem by the methods that are recommended and put into action in the solution of political questions. In the first case we never aim to use anything but rational methods. Rational thought holds its ground here and seems constantly to enlarge its field. Scientific knowledge and technical mastery of nature daily win new and unprecedented victories. But in man's practical and social life the defeat of rational thought seems to be complete and irrevocable. In this domain modern man is supposed to forget everything he has learned in the development of his intellectual life. He is admonished to go back to the first rudimentary stages of human culture. Here rational and scientific thought openly confess their breakdown; they surrender to their most dangerous enemy. . . .

. . . In politics we are always living on volcanic soil. We must be prepared for abrupt convulsions and eruptions. In all critical moments of man's social life, the rational forces that resist the rise of the old mythical conceptions are no longer sure of themselves. In these moments the time for myth has come again. For myth has not been really vanquished and subjugated. It is always there, lurking in the dark and waiting for its hour and opportunity. This hour comes as soon as the other binding forces of man's social life, for one reason or another, lose their strength and are no longer able to combat the demonic mythical powers. . . .

Myth has always been described as the result of an unconscious activity and as a free product of imagination. But here we find myth made according to plan. The new political myths do not grow up freely; they are not wild fruits of an exuberant imagination. They are artificial things fabricated by very skilful and cunning artisans. It has been reserved for the twentieth century, our own great technical age, to develop a new technique of myth. Henceforth myths can be manufactured in the same sense and according to the same methods as any other modern weapon—as machine guns or airplanes. That is a new thing—and a thing of crucial importance. It has changed the whole form of our social life. . . .

. . . Every political action has its special ritual. And since, in the totalitarian state, there is no private sphere, independent of political life, the whole life of man is suddenly inundated by a high tide of new rituals. They are as regular, as rigorous and inexorable as those rituals that we find in primitive societies. Every class, every sex, and every age has a rite of its own. No one could walk in the street, nobody could greet his neighbor or friend without performing a political ritual. And just as in primitive societies the neglect of one of the prescribed rites has meant misery and death. Even in young children this is not regarded as a mere sin of omission. It becomes a crime against the majesty of the leader and the totalitarian state.

The effect of these new rites is obvious. Nothing is more likely to lull asleep all our active forces, our power of judgment and critical discernment, and to take away our feeling of personality and individual responsibility than the steady, uniform, and monotonous performance of the same rites. . . .

Our primitive ancestors, says Cassirer, were bound by tribal customs based on immemorial tradition. In contrast, civilized persons are often too restless and too eager for change to acquiesce permanently to ancient ways. The totalitarian regime, with its stress on unquestioned obedience to a leader and ideological myths, is a regression to our precivilized past.

. . . [W]e have learned a new lesson, a lesson that is very humiliating to our human pride. We have learned that modern man, in spite of his restlessness, and perhaps precisely because of his restlessness, has not really surmounted the condition of savage life. When exposed to the same forces, he can easily be thrown back to a state of complete acquiescence. He no longer questions his environment, he accepts it as a matter of course.

Of all the sad experiences of these last twelve years this is perhaps the most dreadful one. . . .

. . . [H]ere are men, men of education and intelligence, honest and upright men who suddenly give up the highest human privilege. They have ceased to be free and personal agents. Performing the same prescribed rites they begin to feel, to think, and to speak in the same way. Their gestures are lively and violent; yet this is but an artificial, a sham life. In fact they are moved by an external force. They act like marionettes in a puppet show—and they do not even know that the strings of this show and of man's whole individual and social life, are hence-forward pulled by the political leaders.

For the understanding of our problem this is a point of crucial importance. Methods of compulsion and suppression have ever been used in political life. But in most cases these methods aimed at material results. Even the most fearful systems of despotism contented themselves with forcing upon men certain laws of action. They were not concerned with the feelings, judgments, and thoughts of men. . . . Now the modern political myths proceeded in quite a different manner. They did not begin with demanding or prohibiting certain actions. They undertook to change the men, in order to be able to regulate and control their deeds. The political myths acted in the same way as a serpent that tries to paralyze its victims before attacking them. Men fell victims to them without any serious resistance. They were vanquished and subdued before they had realized what actually happened. . . .

. . . Freedom is not a natural inheritance of man. In order to possess it we have to create it. If man were simply to follow his natural instincts he would not strive for freedom; he would rather choose dependence. Obviously it is much easier to depend upon others than to think, to judge, and to decide for himself. That accounts for the fact that both in individual and in political life freedom is so often regarded much more as a burden than a privilege. Under extremely difficult conditions man tries to cast off this burden. Here the totalitarian state and the political myths step in. The new political parties promise, at least, an escape from the dilemma. They suppress and destroy the very sense of freedom: but, at the same time, they relieve men from all personal responsibility. . . .

It is beyond the power of philosophy to destroy the political myths. A myth is in a sense invulnerable. It is impervious to rational arguments; it cannot be refuted by syllogisms. But philosophy can do us another important service. It can make us understand the adversary. In order to fight an enemy you must know him. That is one of the first principles of a sound strategy. To know him means not only to know his defects and weaknesses; it means to know his strength. All of us have been liable to under-rate this strength. When we first heard of the political myths we found them so absurd and incongruous, so fantastic and ludicrous that we could hardly be prevailed upon to take them seriously. By now it has become clear to all of us that this was a great mistake. We should not commit the same error a second time. We should carefully study the origin, the structure, the methods, and the technique of the political myths. We should see the adversary face to face in order to know how to combat him.

John H. Hallowell "THE SICKNESS OF THE MODERN WORLD"

Some thinkers, adopting a Christian orientation, attributed the crisis of our times to a false confidence in human goodness and the achievements of reason, particularly in the realm of science, and to human beings' moving away from God. Focusing on the limitations of secular humanism and the reality of sin, they questioned the core values of the liberal tradition.

In 1950, John Hallowell, an American political theorist, published *Main Currents in Modern Political Thought,* which, written from a Christian perspective, pointed out the deficiencies of modern secular ideologies, including liberalism. In the chapter "The Crisis of Our Times," Hallowell presented his interpretation of the ills confronting modern Western civilization.

It requires no great seer or prophet to discern today the signs of decadence that are everywhere manifest. Only the most stubborn and obtuse would venture optimistic predictions for the future of the world and its civilization. The complacent optimism of the last century has given way to a deep-rooted despair and men everywhere are gripped by fear and insecurity. Anxiety gnaws at their vitals. Everywhere men tremble, whether they are yet conscious of the cause of their fears, before the judgment of God.

The sickness of the modern world is the sickness of moral confusion, intellectual anarchy, and spiritual despair. The revolution of nihilism, born of this confusion and despair, is peculiar not alone to any one country or people but in varying degrees is taking place everywhere. With almost frantic zeal we search for the political or economic panacea that will save us and the world from disaster, not seeing, apparently, that the disaster is already upon us and that for the cure we must examine the state of our own souls. The political and economic crises from which the world suffers are not causes but symptoms of a crisis that is even more profound—a spiritual crisis within the soul of man. Having alienated himself from God, having discredited the reason with which he was endowed by God, unable or unwilling to identify the evil with which the world of man is infected—modern man oscillates between extravagant optimism and hopeless despair. As his optimism is shattered more and more by the force of events he sinks lower and lower into the slough of despondency. In his despondency he is tempted to strike out against the enemy he cannot identify, whose name he does not know, in desperate action. In his anxiety to escape from utter futility and meaningless existence he is tempted to give up his most priceless heritage—his freedom—to any man who even promises deliverance from insecurity. He is tempted to put his faith in the most absurd doctrine, to submit his will to the most brutal dictator, if only in such a way he can find that for which he longs with all the passion of his being—a meaningful existence, a life worth living, a life worth dying to preserve.

Modern man's great lack is lack of conviction, particularly the conviction that good and evil are real. . . .

Lulled into complacent self-satisfaction by the liberal positivistic doctrine of the nineteenth century modern man became a blind devotee of the Goddess Progress who, he believed, bestowed her blessings upon man in the form of increased knowledge and control over nature through an automatic and impersonal process, in which man, at best, was but a passive tool of Nature or of History. Where formerly men looked to God for the salvation of their souls, they now looked to science and technology for the gratification of their desires. Paradise on earth was substituted for eternal spiritual salvation as an aspiration worthy of men's efforts. The method for bringing about this paradise, moreover, had been found to lie within the power of man: paradise on earth waited only upon the proper execution of a plan to be discovered in the truths and with the methods of the natural sciences. It required no sacrifice on the part of man, no change in his behavior, no moderation of his appetites—it required simply the application of intelligence, directed by science, to social problems. Progress was conceived as automatic, irreversible, and inevitable. Time alone would heal all wounds, cure all evil and solve all problems. In his search for bodily well being and comfort, in his search for economic security and political utopia, modern man appears not simply to have lost his soul but to have forgotten that he has a soul to lose. Everyday in every way, until very recently at least, modern man believed, the world is getting better and better. Through increased knowledge of and control over nature, through education and technology, man through science would overcome all the evil with which the world is infected and live in perpetual peace and harmony with his neighbor. This, at least, was his fervent hope and his faith.

The optimism that characterized the nineteenth century has given way in the twentieth to a deep-rooted despair. The very Science upon which the nineteenth century pinned its hopes for the realization of Utopia has led many individuals in the twentieth century to the brink of meaninglessness. Man is but a chance product of the earth, his aspirations and his ideals products of vain imagination—only a kind of desperate bravado serves to keep him afloat in a sea of meaningless existence, . . .

Most men today no longer believe that progress is automatic, irreversible, and inevitable though many still cling, if with much less assurance than formerly, to a belief in education, science and technology as the way out of our difficulties. With the invention of the atom bomb modern man realizes that the blessings of science are not unmixed, that science can be used for evil purposes as well as good and that science itself is silent on the question as to what purposes its knowledge should be put. Man's technical knowledge and capacity has outstripped his moral capacity. Evil has manifested itself so unmistakably in the twentieth century that modern man finds it increasingly difficult to deny its reality, even if he still has considerable difficulty calling it by name.

The liberals of the last century ascribed evil to men's ignorance and to their faulty political institutions. Evil was to be overcome by education and political reform. Equating evil with intellectual error the liberals were led, as Lewis Mumford points out, "to the flattering conclusion that the intelligent cannot sin and that the mentally adult can do no evil." The inability or unwillingness of the liberal to recognize the reality of evil lulled him into a false sense of security. . . .

While the liberals denied the reality of evil and ascribed the appearance of evil in the world to faulty political institutions and lack of "enlightenment," the Marxians explained the appearance of evil in the world to the prevailing capitalistic mode of production, to the institution of private property and to the class conflict engendered by that institution. Evil would disappear, they predicted, inevitably and automatically, with the establishment of a classless society through the medium of revolution and the dictatorship of the proletariat. With the distribution of material goods in accordance with men's needs, men would no longer be frustrated in their search for material satisfaction and all evil would disappear.

However profoundly liberalism may differ from Marxism in details and in conclusions both start from the assumption that human nature is essentially good and ascribe whatever evil there is in the world to bad or faulty institutions. But why these institutions, political and economic, should be so bad, and so much in need of reform, if men are essentially good is a question to which neither has a very satisfactory answer. Or why men should believe that they will be able to do in the future what they have never succeeded in doing in the past, namely, to establish a perfect political and economic system, is never explained.

In recent years one of America's most astute thinkers, Reinhold Niebuhr, has recalled to our consciousness a fact which both liberalism and Marxism have ignored with almost fatal consequences to our civilization. Evil, he points out, is something real and the name for it is sin. Its locus is not in institutions, which are but a reflection of human purposes, but in human nature itself. . . .

The crisis of our times stems from this inability or unwillingness to recognize the evil in the world for what it is, the sin of man. What describes more accurately the evil that is rampant in the world today if it be not the perversion of men's wills? What describes more realistically the evils we must seek to overcome by God's grace if not pride, self-righteousness, greed, envy, hatred, and sloth? What has for centuries brought men to catastrophe if it has not been their attempt to create a god in their own image rather than seeking to make their own image more like that of God? What is the root of all evil if it is not that man seeks to make himself God? . . .

But if modern man has lost sight of the sinfulness of man he has also lost sight, in his despair, of the image of God in man; and man has become progressively dehumanized. The inhumanity of man to man has manifested itself in varying degrees throughout the ages man has lived but not until modern times has man's inhumanity to man been pursued as a matter of principle. . . .

An English writer and publisher, Victor Gollancz, believes that we are experiencing something quite new in the history of Western civilization, not simply the rejection of the values traditionally associated with that civilization but something even more ominous—the complete reversal of those values and the glorification of their opposites. This reversal of the values traditionally associated with Western civilization finds its most characteristic expression in the twentieth century in contempt for human personality, in the denial of "the *essential* spiritual equality of all human beings." Having lost sight of the fact that God created all men in His image, that God is the Father of all men and that consequently all men are brothers, the modern world has no basis for believing that men *are* equal. Where individuals still cling to the belief in individual equality it is often without any understanding of the basis for that belief and consequently without any rational means of defending it. . . .

It is in fascism, of course, that contempt for personality reaches its final expression; for it passes beyond contempt, and becomes hatred. . . .

Hitler is dead and Germany is in ruins. But has the horror passed? I do not think so. Nazism was not an isolated phenomenon, it was merely the final expression, so far, of tendencies which had for a long time been growing stronger. Those tendencies are still at work; some of them are more widespread than ever; and even here in England there are disquieting signs that respect for personality, which we have guarded, and in spite of everything still guard, more devotedly perhaps than other people, is growing weaker.

Jean-Paul Sartre
"EXISTENCE PRECEDES ESSENCE"

The philosophical movement that best exemplified the anxiety and uncertainty of Europe in an era of world wars and totalitarianism was existentialism. Like Nietzsche, existentialists maintained that the universe is devoid of any overarching meaning. Reality defies ultimate comprehension; there are no timeless truths, or essences, that exist independently of and prior to the individual human being. One becomes less than human in permitting one's life to be determined by a

mental outlook—a set of rules and values—imposed by others. For the existentialist, the human being is alone and life is absurd. The universe is indifferent to our expectations and needs, and death is ever stalking us. There is no purpose to our presence in the universe. We simply find ourselves here; we do not know and will never find out why. When we face squarely the fact that existence is purposeless, we can give our life meaning. It is in the act of choosing freely from among different possibilities that the individual shapes an authentic existence. There is a dynamic quality to human existence; the individual has the potential to become more than he or she is.

Jean-Paul Sartre (1905–1980), the leading French existentialist, defined himself as an atheist and saw existentialism as a means of facing the consequences of a godless universe. For Sartre, existence precedes essence, that is, there are no values that precede the individual metaphysically or chronologically to which he or she must conform. There exists no higher realm of Being and no immutable truths that serve as ultimate standards of virtue. It is unauthentic to submit passively to established values that one did not participate in making. It is the first principle of existentialism, said Sartre, that we must each choose our own ethics, define ourselves, and give our own meaning to our existence. In Sartre's view, a true philosophy does not engage in barren discourses on abstract themes. Rather it makes commitments and incurs risks. The realization that we have the freedom to decide for ourselves what meaning we give to our lives can be liberating and exhilarating. But it can also fill us with dread that immobilizes or that leads us to seek refuge in a role selected for us by others. When we abdicate this responsibility of choosing a meaning for our lives, said Sartre, we live in "bad faith." The selection below, drawn from a work published immediately after the war, summarizes the core principles of Sartre's existentialist philosophy.

Atheistic existentialism, which I represent . . . states that if God does not exist, there is at least one being in whom existence precedes essence, a being who exists before he can be defined by any concept, and that this being is man, or, as Heidegger says, human reality. What is meant here by saying that existence precedes essence? It means that, first of all, man exists, turns up, appears on the scene, and, only afterwards, defines himself. If man, as the existentialist conceives him, is indefinable, it is because at first he is nothing. Only afterward will he be something, and he himself will have made what he will be. Thus, there is no human nature, since there is no God to conceive it. Not only is man what he conceives himself to be, but he is also only what he wills himself to be after this thrust toward existence.

Man is nothing else but what he makes of himself. Such is the first principle of existentialism. . . .

. . . [I]f existence really does precede essence, man is responsible for what he is. Thus, existentialism's first move is to make every man aware of what he is and to make the full responsibility of his existence rest on him. And when we say that a man is responsible for himself, we do not only mean that he is responsible for his own individuality, but that he is responsible for all men. . . .

. . . When we say that man chooses his own self, we mean that every one of us does likewise; but we also mean by that that in making this choice he also chooses all men. In fact, in creating the man that we want to be, there is not a single one of our acts which does not at the same time create an image of man as we think he ought to be. To choose to be this or that is to affirm at the same time the value of what we choose. . . .

If . . . existence precedes essence, and if we grant that we exist and fashion our image at one and the same time, the image is valid for everybody and for our whole age. Thus, our responsibility is much greater than we might have supposed, because it involves all mankind. . . . [I]f I want to marry, to have children; even if this marriage depends solely on my own circumstances or passion or wish, I am involving all humanity in monogamy and not merely myself. Therefore, I am responsible for myself and for everyone else. I am creating a certain image of man of my own choosing. In choosing myself, I choose man. . . .

. . . The existentialists say at once that man is anguish. What that means is this: the man who involves himself and who realizes that he is not only the person he chooses to be, but also a law-maker who is, at the same time, choosing all mankind as well as himself, can not help escape the feeling of his total and deep responsibility. Of course, there are many people who are not anxious; but we claim that they are hiding their anxiety, that they are fleeing from it. Certainly, many people believe that when they do something, they themselves are the only ones involved, and when someone says to them, "What if everyone acted that way?" they shrug their shoulders and answer, "Everyone doesn't act that way." But really, one should always ask himself, "What would happen if everybody looked at things that way?" There is no escaping this disturbing thought except by a kind of double-dealing. A man who lies and makes excuses for himself by saying "not everybody does that," is someone with an uneasy conscience, because the act of lying implies that a universal value is conferred upon the lie. . . .

The existentialist . . . thinks it very distressing that God does not exist, because all possibility of finding values in a heaven of ideas disappears along with Him; there can no longer be an *a priori* Good, since there is no infinite and perfect consciousness to think it. Nowhere is it written that the Good exists, that we must be honest, that we must not lie; because the fact is we are on a plane where there are only men. Dostoievsky said, "If God didn't exist, everything would be possible." That is the very starting point of existentialism. Indeed, everything is permissible if God does not exist, and as a result man is forlorn, because neither within him nor without does he find anything to cling to. He can't start making excuses for himself.

If existence really does precede essence, there is no explaining things away by reference to a fixed and given human nature. In other words, there is no determinism, man is free, man is freedom. On the other hand, if God does not exist, we find no values or commands to turn to which legitimize our conduct. So, in the bright realm of values, we have no excuse behind us, nor justification before us. We are alone, with no excuses.

That is the idea I shall try to convey when I say that man is condemned to be free. Condemned, because he did not create himself, yet, in other respects is free; because, once thrown into the world, he is responsible for everything he does. The existentialist does not believe in the power of passion. He will never agree that a sweeping passion is a ravaging torrent which fatally leads a man to certain acts and is therefore an excuse. He thinks that man is responsible for his passion. . . .

. . . The doctrine I am presenting is the very opposite of quietism, since it declares, "There is no reality except in action." Moreover, it goes further, since it adds, "Man is nothing else than his plan; he exists only to the extent that he fulfills himself, he is therefore nothing else than the ensemble of his acts, nothing else than his life."

According to this, we can understand why our doctrine horrifies certain people. Because often the only way they can bear their wretchedness is to think, "Circumstances have been against me. What I've been and done doesn't show my true worth. To be sure, I've had no great love, no great friendship, but that's because I haven't met a man or woman who was worthy. The books I've written haven't been very good because I haven't had the proper leisure. I haven't had children to devote myself to because I didn't find a man with whom I could have spent my life. So there remains within me, unused and quite viable, a host of propensities, inclinations, possibilities, that one wouldn't guess from the mere series of things I've done."

Now, for the existentialist there is really no love other than one which manifests itself in a person's being in love. There is no genius other than one which is expressed in works of art; the genius of Proust is the sum of Proust's works; the genius of Racine is his series of tragedies. Outside of that, there is nothing. Why say that Racine could have written another tragedy, when he didn't write it? A man is involved in life, leaves his impress on it, and outside of that there is nothing. To be sure, this may seem a harsh thought to someone whose life hasn't been a success. But, on the other hand, it prompts people to understand that reality alone is what counts, that dreams, expectations, and hopes warrant no more than to define a man as a disappointed dream, as miscarried hopes, as vain expectations. In other words, to define him negatively and not positively. However, when we say, "You are nothing else than your life," that does not imply that the artist will be judged solely on the basis of his works of art; a thousand other things will contribute toward summing him up. What we mean is that a man is nothing else than a series of undertakings, that he is the sum, the organization, the ensemble of the relationships which make up these undertakings. . . .

Thus, I think we have answered a number of the charges concerning existentialism. You see that it can not be taken for a philosophy of quietism, since it defines man in terms of action; nor for a pessimistic description of man—there is no doctrine more optimistic, since man's destiny is within himself; nor for an attempt to discourage man from acting, since it tells him that the only hope is in his acting and that action is the only thing that enables a man to live. Consequently, we are dealing here with an ethics of action and involvement.

3 The New West Germany: Democratic Government, The Nazi Past, and the Economic Miracle

May 1945 has long been referred to in Germany as *Stunde Null,* or "zero hour." This designation would suggest that everything prior to the end of the war had been eliminated by the defeat of the Third Reich—that the terrible destruction visited upon Germany as a result of the war launched by the Nazi government had wiped the slate clean, that Germans could only go forward, not backward. Most Germans had little inclination to reflect upon the meaning of Nazi aggression and crimes against humanity. Their priorities included clearing rubble, restoring economic life, and creating a sense of normalcy.

The consensus among the victorious Allied powers and most European leaders was that the potential for future German aggression had to be checked and that the best way to do this was to integrate Germany into broader Western European economic and security arrangements. As Cold War considerations began to determine the administration of the Allied occupation zones in Germany, however, competing visions for Germany's—and Europe's—future development manifested themselves. In the West, the reestablishment of democratic political parties, elimination of the black market, and the introduction of a market economy were central considerations. German leaders and their Anglo-American and French occupiers sought to guide Germany between the Scylla of resurgent fascism and the Charybdis of Communist expansion. In the East, preparations were quickly undertaken to create a Soviet-style regime, in which the Communists sought to ground their state organization upon the principles of antifascist solidarity. Regardless of zonal administration and ideological orientation, Germans were generally more interested in rebuilding than coming to terms with the past, despite the occasional admonitions of intellectuals and critical historians.

Konrad Adenauer
DEMOCRATIC POLITICS AND CHRISTIAN IDEALS

Konrad Adenauer (1876–1967) is widely regarded as the founding father of the Federal Republic of Germany. After many years of service as the mayor of Cologne, Adenauer was forced into retirement by the Nazis. Once the Nazi regime was toppled, his political experience and sober commitment to a Western-oriented German democracy made him one of the Western occupation zones' most prominent politicians. Because he had direct experience of the Imperial period, the Weimar Republic, and the Nazi era, his insights into what was necessary for the reestablishment of postwar German political and civil society—and the pitfalls to be avoided—allowed him to make a good claim to leadership of the Christian Democratic Union. Moreover, his firm Catholic convictions led him to conclude that moral force was necessary to guide and temper power politics. Adenauer served as federal chancellor from 1949 to 1963, and his policies played a leading role in West German reconstruction and integration into the Western European community of states.

. . . I had seen that the parties of the Weimar Republic were unable to withstand National Socialism. . . . The failure lay in the behaviour of these parties in the period prior to the so-called seizure of power by the NSDAP. At that time parties with a democratic basis could have successfully opposed National Socialism by legal means. . . . I mention the failure of the parties under the Weimar Republic only in order to explain the fact that a large number of people who thought as I did believed that only a new party based on the broadest Christian foundations, on firm ethical principles, and able to draw on all strata of the German electorate, would be in a position to re-animate Germany.

The National Socialists had opened our eyes to the power wielded by a dictatorial state. I had seen the atrocities of National Socialism, the consequences of dictatorship. I had lost the vocation to which I had devoted my life; my wife was hopelessly ill as a result of a stay in the Gestapo prison at Brauweiler. I had seen the consequences of the war. Three of my sons had served at the front and I had suffered constant anxiety for them; one of them had been severely wounded.

I had heard about the crimes committed against Jews and by Germans against their fellow-Germans. I had seen where an atheistic dictatorship could lead. I had seen Germany plunged into chaos.

From the East we were menaced by the atheist, communist dictatorship. The Soviet Union showed us that a dictatorship of the Left is at least as dangerous as one of the Right. As a result of the war the Soviet Union had advanced deep into central Germany, up to the Elbe, and was a great danger to us.

We had seen in the National Socialist state, and we saw again in Communist Russia, the dangers inherent in a party that disregarded ethical principles. This convinced most of the adherents of the former Centre, and many members of the former parties of the Right, of the necessity for us to unite into a new party founded on an ethical basis.

The conviction began to spread that only a great party with its roots in Christian-Western thinking and ethics could educate the German people for their resurgence, and build a strong dyke against the atheist dictatorship of communism. We were not alone in this view. All over Germany, including the Soviet occupied zone, political groups and associations based on these principles sprang up quite spontaneously. They may have differed in some of their political and economic demands, but they were agreed in essentials. The most important feature of these groups was their common adherence to democratic political convictions and Christian loyalties developed over the centuries in our country. The proposition that the dignity of the individual must be the paramount consideration, even above the power of the state, is one that derives naturally from occidental Christianity. During the National Socialist period it seemed to be buried. National Socialism, despite its suppression of individual liberty, had found so large a following because political awareness and responsibility were very poorly developed in a great many people. Moreover, owing to their history, the Germans were all too inclined to submit to the power of the state. To this must be added the pressure of deteriorating material conditions and, in particular, large-scale unemployment. The majority of Germans did not recognize the dangers of National Socialism in its first years. They did not see that it put the power of the state above the claims of the individual. When they did see, it was too late.

Western Christianity denies the dominance of the state, and insists on the dignity and liberty of the individual. Only this traditional Christian principle could now help us to show the German people a new political goal, to recall them to a new political life. This conviction would give our party the strength to raise Germany from the depths. Hence the new party had to be a Christian party, and one that would embrace all denominations. Protestant and Catholic Germans, indeed all who knew and valued the importance of Christianity in Europe, should be able to join—and it goes without saying that this also applied to our Jewish fellow-citizens.

Only a very great party that included all strata of society could rebuild prostrate, broken Germany. It must be a party which could appeal to employers and employed, the middle classes, farmers, civil servants, intellectuals, people from the North and the South, those driven from their homes and those who had simply fled. The ethical foundations adopted by the CDU must be strong and elastic enough to contain and ease the tensions that exist in a big party.

It was not easy to found a new party in the sombre situation of post-war Germany. Material misery was great and it was easy to be discouraged by the political indifference then prevalent. For us the present was oppressive and the future without hope. The German people were regarded as the heirs of the crimes of National Socialism and were hated throughout the world. Party politics seemed quite pointless. It took a lot of courage to refound an old party; it took much more to found a new one.

When I look back to those dark days it seems to me almost a miracle that everywhere, all over Germany, groups were being formed to demand a new Christian party. They demanded it because of the experience of the National Socialist period. Such groups were formed in all four zones of Germany. Gradually they forged tenuous links amongst themselves. It took years before a tight organization could be developed.

These groups wanted their name to include the word 'Christian': they wanted to indicate their essential aims and their opposition to National Socialism. At the first so-called 'Reich Meeting' of the Christian Democratic party groups which took place at Bad Godesberg in December 1945, it was decided to adopt the name of 'Union'. This was to underline the fact that it was to be a rallying point for all who shared our political principles—whatever their denomination or occupation.

This was the origin of the Christian Democratic Union in the whole of Germany. In Bavaria the same Christian party developed under the name of 'Christian Social Union'.

We were well aware that the creation of a new party was a difficult task; the new edifice could not be built in a day. Inter-denominational tensions in Germany could be overcome only by deliberate and painstaking work. The Social Democrats, based on the trade unions, would strongly oppose the formation of a new great popular Christian party. We knew that very hard work lay ahead of us, work that would require much patience.

The CDU was a new party that drew on old traditions. But it had to begin by drawing up a detailed programme and by creating an organization. This put it at an initial disadvantage compared with the other political parties, which were content to continue where they had left off in 1933. In addition the CDU was at a special disadvantage in the British zone compared with the Social Democrats. In July 1945 the government of Britain had passed to the Labour Party. It was often fairly obvious that the British occupation authorities favoured the Social Democrats. The KPD (Communist Party) and the Centre were also well treated by the British and American occupation forces. At first no one quite trusted the CDU, the new party.

The state of mind of the Germans was very precarious at that time. Not only were the people suffering great material hardships, but much psychological damage had also been done and the education of the younger generation had been neglected.

The framework of family life had cracked under the strain of the flight and expulsion of many millions of people, the evacuation of the big cities, and the large-scale destruction of housing. Another disturbing factor was the uncertainty about the fate of hundreds of thousands of German prisoners of war. The nation was labouring under an enormous burden, and it was necessary to awaken the deepest intellectual and spiritual forces if any resurgence was to be made possible. Such forces were to come especially from the Christian foundation of our party.

There was, too, the danger of atheistic Soviet communism. The Soviets had penetrated deep into central Germany, up to the Elbe. A German party founded on Christian principles would be able to combat this new threat.

That was how we saw the great tasks before us and we went to work full of courage and idealism.

Friedrich Meinecke
THE GERMAN CATASTROPHE

Friedrich Meinecke (1862–1954) ranks as one of the most prominent German historians of the late nineteenth and early twentieth centuries, a decidedly Prussian liberal who held that the liberal tradition could only develop properly within the context of a strong nation-state. During the course of the First World War and the turbulent interwar republic, Meinecke became disillusioned with the ways in which he perceived that power cut itself free from the burden of ethics when it became opportune to do so. Popular sentiment, expressed in mass hysteria, he concluded, had derailed the state from the principled application of power. Not surprisingly, he regarded the Nazi regime disdainfully, even as he found himself impressed with the ways in which Germany projected its power in the international arena.

Meinecke's *The German Catastrophe,* first published in 1946, attempted to come to terms with the conundrums of the relationships between ethics and power, individual freedom and the higher good represented in the national collective, and the relationship between politics and culture. He concluded that between 1918 and 1945 Germany had traveled a special path characterized by "inner foreign rule, that is, by an ideology and leaders that did not represent the true German spirit." This approach represented an attempt to uncouple Germans collectively from responsibility for Hitler's rise to power and Nazi barbarism. As a result, the book became an important marker in broader postwar discussions concerning German historical development in the modern era, the nature of German identity, and the thorny matter of culpability for Nazi crimes against humanity.

So the task of eradicating the poisonous growth of National Socialism passed into the hands of the victors. That made it psychologically difficult for those of us Germans who had privately hoped to accomplish this by our own strength. Many a troubled mind unable to think things through to the end and moved by a feeling of national pride might reject the idea of pulling on the same rope with the former enemies of his country. . . .

So far as the victors try to eradicate National Socialist influences and thereby provide the atmosphere for Christian Occidental sound morals, we must not only recognize that they are fundamentally right but must ourselves help them. . . .

Our task then is to give them a real understanding of our conditions. The number of people who compromised with National Socialism—persons without much judgment but at bottom harmless, decent, and even wanting to be idealistic—was enormously large. In their case not only strict justice but also human understanding must be exercised. Not all party members were alike—*distinguendum est*—we cry to our judges, especially we who from the beginning condemned Nazism. It is a matter not only of exercising moderation in individual cases and preserving many private existences from ruin, but also of preventing a general embitterment of the people. Embitterment might spring from a feeling of being treated unjustly, might hinder our inner recovery, and might make Germany into a center of disease of the worst sort. Very great also was the number of those who protested inwardly against Hitler but outwardly yielded for existence's sake. Many who would have mustered up courage for martyrdom for themselves did not do so in order not to plunge their families into misfortune. It was a feature of the Nazi party's refined technique in punishment always to make all one's relatives suffer also.

Now, however, the victors have announced that they intend to eradicate not only National Socialism, but also militarism, as the source of disturbance for the world. Our great power of defense, our system of universal military service, must end. . . . But does it not happen in the case of all great and fruitful ideas in world history that in the course of their historical evolution both good and evil can develop out of them? One effect of what we have experienced is that the demonic element hidden in human and historical life rises before our eyes more clearly and disturbingly than previously. So also in the evolution of Prussian-German militarism, as we have already shown, both good and evil are certainly to be distinguished from one another. . . . A higher and a lower principle were always struggling with one another, and the lower principle won. This we must today quite honestly admit to ourselves, and draw our conclusions from it. The lower and degenerate militarism, which could blindly become the tool of a Hitler and which finally reached its last vicious peak in Himmler's *Waffen-SS,* is hopeless. It can, indeed it must, disappear in order to purify of bad germs a soil in which a future and nobler conception of self-defense can take root. For in Central Europe no nation without a sound conception of self-defense can in the long run live and maintain itself as a nation.

Certainly countless brave soldiers in Germany possessed such a sound idea of defense in the last war and tried to do their duty under the hardest circumstances. They are now faced with the equally hard task of struggling to realize that their idea of defense was outrageously misused and that in order to prevent a similar misuse again the former militarism must come to an end. That will be unspeakably painful, especially for those men in the officer corps who carry in themselves the nobler traditions of the Scharnhorst period. In cutting loose from the old traditions which embody much fame and pride, they lose something which to them means home and the breath of life. But have we all not lost something of home today? Let us be deeply conscious of the pain, but not allow it to oppress us, nor obscure our insight into the inevitable, nor weaken our will to life and to revival.

To be defenseless now does not mean that we shall always be defenseless. It is humiliating enough for us that when we may enjoy the rights of a free nation depends on the decision of foreign powers. Today, however, the anger over our humiliation should be turned primarily against those who are to blame for it, against the overweening pride of those who led us to the abyss, and against the lack of judgment of those who subjected themselves to this leadership without any inner protest.

The radical break with our military past that we must now accept faces us with the question about what is to become of our historical traditions in general. It would be impossible and suicidal to throw them wholesale into the fire and behave as apostates. But our customary picture of the history under which we grew to greatness needs at any rate a fundamental revision in order to discriminate between what was valuable and what was valueless. To do this, according to our conviction, only that type of historical thinking is adequate which perceives the close demonic connection between the valuable and the valueless in history. . . .

Even a partitioned Germany robbed of her national political existence, which is our lot today, ought to remember with sorrowful mourning the unity and strength that she previously enjoyed. Her former striving for unity and strength was not merely, as Burckhardt saw it in his *Reflections on History,* a blind striving of the masses to whom culture meant nothing. Rather was it borne along, as Burckhardt was not quite fully able to understand, by that great idea of an inner union of spirit and power, by humanity and nationality. Great cultural values emerged for us from it. But this union, as we must make clear to ourselves, was disrupted through our own fault. Now the question arises, shall we immediately work for it anew? In the first place, we are at present prevented from doing so by the external control by foreign powers. To attempt at present to win back a part of the strength of such a union would today lead only to impotent convulsions. For inner reasons also, it must be renounced at present. Our conception of power must first be purified from the filth which came into it during the Third Reich before it can again be capable of forming a union with spirit and culture. The purpose of power must be reflected upon and wisely limited. The desire to become a world power has proven to be a false idol for us. Our geopolitical and geophysical situation alone forbids it. To be a world power is furthermore an adventure which cuts in two directions leading to temptations in which culture is too much the loser.

People may protest to us saying: But did not our now-shattered former world policy have a positive sense in that it furnished a livelihood for our mightily increased population? And now is it not to be feared that our eastern provinces, on whose agricultural produce we depended, will be completely lost and that there will be a severe shrinkage of our industry from which our working classes gained their livelihood. In this respect anxieties of the very darkest sort press upon us. One may indeed reproach our former world policy and the sudden striving of the Third Reich for world power with the fact that they pursued the correct aim of assuring Germany's food supply for the future but used false and finally utterly false methods. As a result, we are not brought to the lamentable situation of having our physical existence depend solely upon the insight and wisdom of the victors.

For us power has hitherto been too much of an end in itself, and furthermore, not merely for ourselves alone, but for nationalism in general. Power, however, can justify itself, outside the service that it performs for a people's needs of life, just by the service that it renders to the highest spiritual and ethical values—to culture and religion. That it is otherwise in reality and that the power of the state ever and again acts and behaves as an end in itself, the historian knows very well. But it behooves him after every necessary look at reality to lift his gaze again to mankind's highest stars. Tragic will appear the contrast that he perceives between the reality and the ideal. Tragic indeed is the history that he will have to write.

Hannah Vogt
THE BURDEN OF GUILT

Until the 1960s, German secondary school history courses generally ended with the beginning of the twentieth century. Few teachers discussed the Nazi regime, and appropriate books about nazism and the Holocaust were lacking. Moreover, many teachers found the subject uncomfortable, for only a few years earlier they had faithfully served the Third Reich and embraced its ideology. Distressed by a sudden outburst of anti-Semitic incidents that afflicted Germany in 1959, notably desecrated cemeteries and swastikas smeared on the walls of synagogues, German educational authorities made a concerted effort to teach young people about the Nazi past. These same anti-Semitic outrages moved Hannah Vogt, a civil servant concerned principally with education, to write a book for students about the Nazi past. Published in 1961, *The Burden of Guilt* became a widely used text in secondary schools. In the Preface, Vogt stated the book's purpose:

> **[S]elf-examination and a repudiation of false political principles are the only means we have of winning new trust among those peoples who were forced to suffer fearful things under Hitler's brutal policy of force. . . . Only if we draw the right conclusions from the mistakes of the past and apply them to our thought and action can we win new trust. . . . Anyone who makes an effort to understand recent political history will learn that in politics not every means is just [and] that law and the dignity of man are not empty phrases.**

The book's conclusion, excerpted below, showed a sincere effort of German schools to come to grips with the darkest period in German history.

A nation is made up of individuals whose ideas—right or wrong—determine their actions, their decisions, and their common life, and for this reason a nation, too, can look back at its history and learn from it. As Germans, we should not find it too difficult to understand the meaning of the fourteen years of the Weimar Republic and the twelve years of the Hitler regime.

The ancient Greeks already knew and taught that no state can remain free without free citizens. If the citizens of a commonwealth are not prepared to make sacrifices for their liberty, to take matters into their own hands and participate in public affairs, they deliver themselves into the hands of a tyrant. They do not deserve anything but tyrannical rule: "A class which fails to make sacrifices for political affairs may not make demands on political life. It renounces its will to rule, and must therefore be ruled." These words of a German liberal about the educated class are valid for people everywhere.

The Greeks called a man who abstained from politics "idiotēs." The Oxford English Dictionary translates this as "private person," "ignorant," "layman," or "not professionally learned." And what are we to call those who have learned nothing from our recent history but the foolish slogan "without me" *(Ohne mich)*? Are they not like fish who expect to improve their condition by jumping from the frying pan into the fire?

We have paid dearly once before for the folly of believing that democracy, being an ideal political arrangement, must function automatically while the citizens sit in their parlors berating it, or worrying about their money. Everybody must share in the responsibility and must be prepared to make sacrifices. He must also respect the opinions of others and must curb his hates, which are too blinding to be good guides for action. In addition, we need to be patient, we must have confidence in small advances and abandon the belief in political miracles and panaceas.

Only if the citizens are thoroughly imbued with democratic attitudes can we put into practice those principles of political life which were achieved through centuries of experience, and which we disregarded to our great sorrow. The first such principle is the need for a continuous and vigilant control of power. For this, we need not only a free and courageous press but also some mechanism for shaping a vital political opinion in associations, parties, and other organizations. Equally necessary are clearly drawn lines of political responsibility, and a strong and respected political opposition. Interest groups must not be diffused too widely but must aim at maximum cohesiveness. Present developments appear to indicate that we are deeply aware of at least this necessity.

More than anything else we must base our concept of law on the idea of justice. We have had the sad experience that the principle "the law is the law" does not suffice, if the laws are being abused to cover up for crimes and to wrap injustices in a tissue of legality. Our actions must once again be guided by that idea which is the basis of just life: no man must be used as a means to an end.

This principle must also be applied to our relationships with other nations. Although, on the international scene, there is as yet no all-inclusive legal body that would have enough power to solve all conflicts peacefully, still there are legal norms in international affairs which are not at all the "sound and smoke" (Faust) Hitler had presumed them to be. In no other matter was he as divorced from reality as in his belief that it was shrewd to conclude treaties today and "to break them in cold blood tomorrow," and that he could undo 2000 years of legal evolution without having such action recoil upon him. He considered force the one and only means of politics, while, in reality, it had always been the worst. Hitler's so-called *Realpolitik* was terrifyingly unreal, and brought about a catastrophe which has undone the gains Bismarck had made through moderation. Bismarck gave Germany its unity. Hitler, goaded by his limitless drive for world power, divided Germany and destroyed the work of generations.

Thus we are now faced with the difficult task of regaining, by peaceful means, the German unity that Hitler has gambled away. We must strive for it tirelessly, even though it may take decades. At the same time, we must establish a new relationship, based on trust, with the peoples of Europe and the nations of the world. Our word must again be believed, our commitment to freedom and humanity again be trusted. Our name has been used too much for lies and treachery. We cannot simply stretch out our hands and hope that all will be forgotten.

These are the questions which should touch the younger generation most deeply: What position could and should we have among the nations? Can we restore honor to the German name? Can we shape a new and better future? Or shall we be burdened with the crimes of the Hitler regime for generations to come?

However contradictory the problem may look at first sight, there can be no shilly-shallying, but only a clear Yes to these questions. The past cannot be erased, but the future is free. It is not predetermined. We have the power to re-examine our decisions and mend our wrong ways; we can renounce force and place our trust in peaceful and gradual progress; we can reject racial pride. Instead of impressing the world with war and aggression, we can strive for world prestige through the peaceful solution of conflicts, as the Swiss and the Scandinavians have done for centuries to their national glory. For us, the choice is open to condemn Hitler's deluded destructiveness and to embrace Albert Schweitzer's message—respect for life.

If we are really serious about this new respect for life, it must also extend to the victims of the unspeakable policy of extermination. Ever since human beings have existed, respect for life has included respect for the dead. Everywhere it is the duty of the living to preserve the memory of the dead. Should we listen to insinuations that the time has come to forget crimes and victims because nobody must incriminate himself? Is it not, rather, cowardly, mean, and miserable to deny even now the dead the honor they deserve, and to forget them as quickly as possible?

We owe it to ourselves to examine our consciences sincerely and to face the naked truth, instead of minimizing it or glossing over it. This is also the only way we can regain respect in the world. Covering up or minimizing crimes will suggest that we secretly approve of them. Who will believe that we want to respect all that is human if we treat the death of nearly six million Jews as a "small error" to be forgotten after a few years?

The test of our change of heart should be not only the dead but the living. There are 30,000 Jewish fellow-citizens living among us. Many of them have returned only recently from emigration, overwhelmed with a desire for their old homeland. It is up to all of us to make sure that they live among us in peace and without being abused, that their new trust in us, won after much effort, is not destroyed by desecrated cemeteries, gutter slogans, or hate songs. Those who will never learn must not be allowed to take refuge in the freedom of opinion. A higher value is at stake here, the honor of the dead, and respect for the living. But it is not up to the public prosecutor to imbue our lives with new and more humane principles. This is everybody's business. It concerns us all! It will determine our future.

Theodore H. White
"GERMANY IS ALIVE AND VIGOROUS AGAIN"

Upon defeat of the Nazi regime in May 1945, Germany's economy lay in ruins. Bridges, railroad lines, factories and mining operations, and urban centers had received considerable damage; in some cases much of entire cityscapes had been reduced to rubble. Damage to infrastructure was compounded by a workforce that was scattered by invasion and air raids; and millions of laborers had been killed, maimed, or taken prisoner during the course of military service, while hundreds of thousands of demobilized German servicemen found the return home delayed

by transportation problems. Disruptions in foodstuff production and in distribution networks meant virtually all Germans suffered from hunger. Moreover, Soviet, British, and American officials determined in a series of meetings, which culminated in a gathering of the Big Threes' leaders at Potsdam in the summer of 1945, that a USSR devastated by four years of savage warfare would help itself to reparations of salvageable industrial infrastructure. This decision had the net effect of further depleting Germany's own industrial base. In order to stave off mass starvation, the victorious powers resolved to transfer German resources across their respective occupation zone boundaries and deliver food aid.

By 1947, mounting tensions—the new, "cold" war—led to increased suspicions and the separation of economic cooperation between the Soviets and the Western Allies in Germany. The United States began to increase its relief aid, particularly as British contributions became more constrained by the United Kingdom's own domestic needs. The United States extended grants, credits, and loans that culminated formally in the European Recovery Program (ERP) or Marshall Plan aid (see George C. Marshall, "Laying the Foundations for Recovery," page 277 in this volume). The western zones of occupation in Germany, which became the Federal Republic of Germany in 1949, were a principal beneficiary of this assistance. While ERP aid amounted to a relatively small percentage of Western Germany's gross domestic product between 1948 and 1951, together with the creation of a central bank, currency reform, and integration into Western European economic networks, the importance of this assistance for foodstuffs and raw materials cannot be overemphasized. During the mid and late 1950s, the West German economy took advantage of its newly established stability and began to grow steadily as a manufacturing and consumer-based economy with a strong agricultural sector, soon becoming the most dynamic economy in Western Europe.

As of the early 1960s, the Federal Republic's "economic miracle," or *Wirtschaftswunder*, became an object of admiration for its neighbors. West German economic success, like that of Japan, helped to ensure social stability; this, in turn, worked against any potential embrace of communism or a return to violent, intolerant nationalism. By the time Ludwig Erhard extolled the virtues of the Federal Republic's social market economy in 1960 (see page 364 in this volume), West Germany had undergone a transformation that no one would have dared imagine possible in the spring of 1945.

Stephen Spender's observations of German circumstances immediately after the war's conclusion and Theodore White's overview of conditions between 1945–47 stand in marked contrast to what White encountered by the time Marshall Plan aid and initial Western European economic integration helped infuse life into the West German economy in 1952. The following selection reveals the astonishment White felt upon each of his periodic visits during his extended reportage on developments across postwar Europe.

No traveler making the seasonal circuit of Europe's political centers has failed to describe how swiftly the face of Germany has changed since the ending of the Winter Years. Once set on its upward course in 1949, Germany changed from month to month. People in the streets filled out visibly. Their clothes changed from rumpled rags to decent garments, to neat business suits, to silk stockings. Cigarettes disappeared as currency, then became available everywhere, then, finally, were sold from slot machines on every corner. Food returned, food as the Germans love it, with whipped cream beaten thick in the coffee, on cake, with fruit. The streets changed face as buildings rose, as neon signs festooned them, as their windows shone with goods. For a number of years I have visited Frankfurt twice a year, staying at the Park Hotel opposite the railway station. On my first visit I could look out of the window on a hot day and still smell the dust of rubble rising from the ruins up and down the street, ruins all down the curving Bahnhof square, ruins on every side of the railway station. At each visit thereafter, some patch of rubble was cleared, some new construction sprouted into the sky, some long stretch of broken cobblestone yielded to smooth asphalt until, finally, on my last spring visit I woke and heard the sound of hammers under my window and looked out to see the last red walls of the last red ruin on my street crumbling under the wrecker's sledge, to be cleared for what new hotel or new office building only the next visit will reveal.

The revival offered its most dramatic contrasts in Düsseldorf, the capital both of Ruhr industry and the British Occupation of that province. Down Koenigsallee, the beautiful main street of the city, luxury shops blossomed year by year to offer the steel barons and coal merchants the delights they have always enjoyed. Today, the cigar stores of Koenigsallee and Flingerstrasse offer the greatest collection of yellow, black, tan, brown, half-white stogies in Europe, gathered from Brazil, Manila, Havana, Hamburg. The Konditorei decorate their shop-fronts in midwinter with bananas and oranges, pineapples from the tropics, cheeses from Denmark, champagne and Burgundy from France, grapes from Italy, hams from Scandinavia. Gradually, as this happened, the British Occupiers of Düsseldorf began to wonder who had won and who had lost the war. The first season it became obvious that the German ration had passed the British ration, a group of British women, wives of Occupation officials, demonstrated in the main streets outside British military headquarters to protest that the Germans they had defeated were eating fatter than British soldiers' families, who themselves were eating better than Britons back home. But no housewifely protest could stop the surge. It was the next season that Americans, visiting Cologne and stopping at one of its larger hotels, noticed that its dining room was divided in two halves—one for the British Occupation officials, living on the dull, juiceless, meat-thin rations of the Ministry of Food; the other for German civilians, eating rich, heavy, stomach-filling German food. The American visitors preferred to sit on the German or conquered side of the dining room, rather than on the side of the victorious British.

Revival throbbed on all the roads and arteries of communications. Bridges went up and spans were sutured. On my first visit to Germany, in an early Winter Year, the smooth concrete paths of the autobahns were dominated by vehicles of the Occupation. The Army's olive-drab trucks purring in convoy formation, the American jeeps wasping in and out, the glittering, shimmering sedans of the American families with white Occupation plates made the wheezing old German sedans, the bumbling old German trucks—so frequently overturned, so frequently wrecked, so frequently waiting idly by the road in breakdown—seem like strangers on their own roads. But each succeeding visit has shown the roads reconquered by Germans, even though there are now three times as many Americans and troops in Germany than on my first visit. New Kapitans, Opels, Volkswagens, Porsches, Mercedes-Benzes whiz by, obscuring from sight American sedans in the procession of the autobahn; huge German double and triple trailers with their trailing black exhaust becloud the occasional American convoys. Rhine barges, furrowing the busy waters, are new again, spick and span in gleaming brass fittings, and red, white, green coats of paint. The railways run on time, efficiently, the dining cars proud with white stiff linen and solid plentiful food.

Germany is alive and vigorous again—to the sight, to the ear, to the touch. Nor is this only a matter of appearances, for statistically the profile of German effort now traces the outline of an industrial power again equal to England, and greater than any other in Western Europe.

Economists estimate that Germany's gross national product has increased by seventy per cent since the year 1948–1949; that her industrial production is two-thirds again higher than it was in 1936, Hitler's peak peacetime year; that her wage-earners are now numbered at an all-time high. Germany's exports have multiplied by seven times in the five years since currency reform; her Dollar Gap should vanish in 1953; her credits in the European Payments Union stand at almost half a billion dollars, higher than any other of the Marshall Plan countries.

Each set of statistics bears its own story, but none reflect the phenomenon of Germany's Renaissance better than the figures of her steel production. In 1946, the year after Germany's collapse, she poured 2,500,000 tons of steel; in 1947, 3,000,000 tons. Those were the years in which the Allies had sworn that Germany should never produce more than 5,600,000 tons again. At the end of 1947, when the Western Allies lifted Germany's limit to 11,100,000 tons, their experts assured them it would take at least five years for Germany to reach the distant level of 10,000,000 tons. By 1949, however, the Germans were pouring 9,000,000 tons of steel and had drawn abreast of the French. In the fall of 1950 the Western Allies tore up the 11,100,000 ton limit and urged Germany to go all out in producing steel for the Western defense effort. At that time Western engineers gave their solemn opinion that the old, outmoded plants of the Ruhr could not be overhauled to produce more than an outer technical maximum of 13,500,000 tons. By the end of 1951 Germany was producing 13,500,000 tons and was racing after Britain, the leading steel producer in Western Europe. In 1953 the Germans let another notch out of their belt and poured 14,500,000 tons, in some months equaling and surpassing British production. German engineers now figure that if business holds good they can pour 18,000,000 tons in the next twelve-month period, to make them the senior steel producer of Western Europe. At that point they will be pouring more than the Ruhr ever produced before, or just slightly more than three times as much as the Allies swore, seven years ago, she would ever produce again.

All other statistics crackle with the same energy. Coal production in Germany has jumped from 60,000,000 to 100,000,000 to 125,000,000 tons. The production of radios doubled Germany's prewar production by the spring of 1951, and by the beginning of 1953 Germany was producing almost twice as many automobiles as in 1936. Starting in the rubble and disaster of defeat, the Germans began to build houses. Slowly at first, as the cramped economy put itself together again, then more swiftly German craftsmen began to house their countrymen until, by 1951, Germany was building over 400,000 dwelling units a year, or more than the total number France had built in the eight years since Liberation. Germany's home-building rate per capita is, indeed, the only major European housing effort that can match America's.

4 The Cold War

The Allied coalition of the British Empire, the United States, and the Soviet Union was one of pure political expediency. Although drawn together to defeat the common Nazi enemy, the Anglo-American governments on the one side, and the Soviet regime on the other, had long regarded each other's social, economic, and political systems with suspicion and disdain. Neither camp could envision a place in the world for the other—indeed, the success of liberal capitalism precluded the

existence of Soviet-style socialism, and vice versa. These sentiments were evident in the rhetoric of the 1930s and in the mutual distrust with which Joseph Stalin and Winston Churchill regarded one another during the war years, despite Franklin D. Roosevelt's well-intentioned efforts to focus on the Allies' common goal.

After the war's end, mistrust rapidly eclipsed cooperation in the Anglo-American and Soviet relationship. Churchill had always been reluctant to see a Soviet presence in East Central Europe; Stalin, for his part, regarded possession of these territories as both a form of security against another attack on the Soviet Union and as the fruits of hard-fought victory. The Berlin Blockade and Airlift, the Marshall Plan, the Communist coup in Czechoslovakia, and the formal division of Germany in the late 1940s, followed by the creation of adversarial alliances and the definitive division of Eastern and Western Germany through the Berlin Wall and barbed-wire fringed free-fire zones, manifested irreconcilable differences and served as powerful symbols of potential conflict between the two camps.

Winston Churchill
THE IRON CURTAIN

In a famous speech at Fulton, Missouri, in early March 1946, when he was no longer in office, Churchill articulated his views on the duty of Western democracies in the face of Soviet expansion. Significant passages from that speech, in which the term "iron curtain" was first used, follow.

A shadow has fallen upon the scenes so lately lighted by the Allied victory. Nobody knows what Soviet Russia and its Communist international organization intends to do in the immediate future, or what are the limits, if any, to their expansive and proselytizing tendencies. I have a strong admiration and regard for the valiant Russian people and for my wartime comrade, Marshal Stalin. There is sympathy and good will in Britain—and I doubt not here also—toward the peoples of all the Russias and a resolve to persevere through many differences and rebuffs in establishing lasting friendships. We understand the Russian need to be secure on her western frontiers from all renewal of German aggression. We welcome her to her rightful place among the leading nations of the world. Above all we welcome constant, frequent and growing contacts between the Russian people and our own people on both sides of the Atlantic. It is my duty, however, to place before you certain facts about the present position in Europe—I am sure I do not wish to, but it is my duty, I feel, to present them to you.

From Stettin in the Baltic to Trieste in the Adriatic, an iron curtain has descended across the Continent. Behind that line lie all the capitals of the ancient states of central and eastern Europe. Warsaw, Berlin, Prague, Vienna, Budapest, Belgrade, Bucharest and Sofia, all these famous cities and the populations around them lie in the Soviet sphere and all are subject in one form or another, not only to Soviet influence but to a very high and increasing measure of control from Moscow. . . . The Communist parties, which were very small in all these eastern states of Europe, have been raised to pre-eminence and power far beyond their numbers and are seeking everywhere to obtain totalitarian control. Police governments are prevailing in nearly every case. . . . Turkey and Persia are both profoundly alarmed and disturbed at the claims which are made upon them and at the pressure being exerted by the Moscow government. An attempt is being made by the Russians in Berlin to build up a quasi-Communist party in their zone of occupied Germany. . . . Whatever conclusions may be drawn from these facts—and facts they are—this is certainly not the liberated Europe we fought to build up. Nor is it one which contains the essentials of permanent peace. . . . What we have to consider here today while time remains, is the permanent prevention of war and the establishment of conditions of freedom and democracy as rapidly as possible in all countries. Our difficulties and dangers will not be removed by closing our eyes to them. They will not be removed by mere waiting to see what happens; nor will they be relieved by a policy of appeasement. What is needed is a settlement and the longer this is delayed the more difficult it will be and the greater our dangers will become. From what I have seen of our Russian friends and allies during the war, I am convinced that there is nothing they admire so much as strength, and there is nothing for which they have less respect than for military weakness. . . . If the western democracies stand together in strict adherence to the principles of the United Nations Charter, their influence for furthering these principles will be immense and no one is likely to molest them. If, however, they become divided or falter in their duty, and if these all-important years are allowed to slip away, then indeed catastrophe may overwhelm us all.

Nikita S. Khrushchev
REPORT TO THE TWENTIETH PARTY CONGRESS

After World War II, the Korean War, and the escalation of the nuclear arms race into the deployment of hydrogen bombs, the Soviets perceived themselves to be in a worldwide struggle with the Western capitalists. In the Soviet view, the socialist system was advancing, whereas the capitalist system was in decline; the cold war represented a desperate effort to preserve capitalism. Communists especially attacked the American desire to deal with the socialist countries from a position of superior strength.

Soviet international policy gave special attention to the aspirations of "the people of the East," the Asians and Africans emerging from colonial rule. Soviets described American aid to developing countries as a new form of imperialism, whereas Soviet aid was pictured as humanitarian assistance in the struggle against colonialism.

Nikita Khrushchev (1894–1971) summed up the Soviet perspective on world affairs for the benefit of a new generation of Soviet citizens. As first secretary of the Communist party, he delivered a report to the Twentieth Party Congress in February 1956, on the eve of his famous denunciation of the crimes of the Stalin era (see page 126). He sounded an optimistic but militant note. Alarmed by the progress of the arms race, Khrushchev gave vigorous support to an old Soviet plea for the peaceful coexistence of the two competing sociopolitical systems—a coexistence in which victory would inevitably go to communism.

Soon after the Second World War ended, the influence of reactionary and militarist groups began to be increasingly evident in the policy of the United States of America, Britain and France. Their desire to enforce their will on other countries by economic and political pressure, threats and military provocation prevailed. This became known as the "positions of strength" policy. It reflects the aspiration of the most aggressive sections of present-day imperialism to win world supremacy, to suppress the working class and the democratic and national-liberation movements; it reflects their plans for military adventures against the socialist camp.

The international atmosphere was poisoned by war hysteria. The arms race began to assume more and more monstrous dimensions. Many big U.S. military bases designed for use against the U.S.S.R. and the People's Democracies [East European countries under Soviet control] were built in countries thousands of miles from the borders of the United States. "Cold war" was begun against the socialist camp. International distrust was artificially kindled, and nations set against one another. A bloody war was launched in Korea; the war in Indo-China dragged on for years.

The inspirers of the "cold war" began to establish military blocs, and many countries found themselves, against the will of their peoples, involved in restricted aggressive alignments—the North Atlantic bloc, Western European Union, SEATO (military bloc for South-East Asia) and the Baghdad pact.

The organizers of military blocs allege that they have united for defence, for protection against the "communist threat." But that is sheer hypocrisy. We know from history that when planning a redivision of the world, the imperialist powers have always lined up military blocs. Today the "anti-communism" slogan is again being used as a smokescreen to cover up the claims of one power for world domination. The new thing here is that the United States wants, by means of all kinds of blocs and pacts, to secure a dominant position in the capitalist world for itself, and to reduce all its partners in the blocs to the status of obedient executors of its will. . . .

The winning of political freedom by the peoples of the former colonies and semi-colonies is the first and most important prerequisite of their full independence, that is, of the achievement of economic independence. The liberated Asian countries are pursuing a policy of building up their own industry, training their own technicians, raising the living standards of the people, and regenerating and developing their age-old national culture. History-making prospects for a better future are opening up before the countries which have embarked upon the path of independent development. . . .

[T]he colonial powers . . . have recourse to new forms of colonial enslavement under the guise of so-called "aid" to underdeveloped countries, which brings colossal profits to the colonialists. Let us take the United States as an example. The United States renders such "aid" above all in the form of deliveries of American weapons to the underdeveloped countries. This enables the American monopolies to load up their industry with arms orders. . . . States receiving such "aid" in the form of weapons, inevitably fall into dependence. . . .

Naturally, "aid" to underdeveloped countries is granted on definite political terms, terms providing for their integration into aggressive military blocs, the conclusion of joint military pacts, and support for American foreign policy aimed at world domination, or "world leadership," as the American imperialists themselves call it. . . .

[In contrast,] the exceptionally warm and friendly welcome accorded the representatives of the great Soviet people has strikingly demonstrated the deep-rooted confidence and love the broad masses in the Eastern countries have for the Soviet Union. Analyzing the sources of this confidence, the Egyptian *Al Akhbar* justly wrote: "Russia does not try to buy the conscience of the peoples, their rights and liberty. Russia has extended a hand to the peoples and said that they themselves should decide their destiny, that she recognizes their rights and aspirations and does not demand their adherence to military pacts or blocs." Millions of men and women ardently acclaim our country for its uncompromising struggle against colonialism, for its policy of equality and friendship among all nations and for its consistent peaceful foreign policy. *(Stormy, prolonged applause.)*

. . . The Leninist principle of peaceful coexistence of states with different social systems has always been and remains the general line of our country's foreign policy. . . . To this day the enemies of peace allege that the Soviet Union is out to overthrow capitalism in other countries by "exporting" revolution. It goes without saying that among us Communists there are no supporters of capitalism. But this does not mean that we have interfered or plan to interfere in the internal affairs of countries where capitalism still exists. . . . It is ridiculous to think that revolutions are made to order. We often hear representatives of bourgeois countries reasoning thus: "The Soviet leaders claim that they are for peaceful co-existence between the two systems. At the same time they declare that they are fighting for communism, and say that communism is bound to win in all countries. Now if the Soviet Union is fighting for communism, how can there be any peaceful co-existence with it?". . . .

When we say that the socialist system will win in the competition between the two systems—the capitalist and the socialist—this by no means signifies that its victory will be achieved through armed interference by the socialist countries in the internal affairs of the capitalist countries. Our certainty of the victory of communism is based on the fact that the socialist mode of production possesses decisive advantages over the capitalist mode of production. Precisely because of this, the ideas of Marxism-Leninism are more and more capturing the minds of the broad masses of the working people in the capitalist countries, just as they have captured the minds of millions of men and women in our country and the People's Democracies. *(Prolonged applause.)* We believe that all working men in the world, once they have become convinced of the advantages communism brings, will sooner or later take the road of struggle for the construction of socialist society.

Paul-Henri Spaak
WHY NATO?

Well before the creation of the North Atlantic Treaty Organization (NATO), Western Europe had begun moving in the direction of greater regional unity and cooperation with the United States. The Marshall Plan had introduced economic integration. The presence of Anglo-American forces in Western Germany, the brinkmanship exhibited through the Berlin Blockade and Airlift, and the West German currency reform contributed to growing mistrust between the West and the Soviet Union. The formation of NATO in the spring of 1949 confirmed these trends emphatically.

In 1959, NATO Secretary General Paul-Henri Spaak (1899–1972) published a think-piece, *Why NATO?,* commemorating the tenth anniversary of the alliance. His central points express the fundamental thinking behind NATO, which had contributed to the maintenance of a vigilant peace *despite* the eruption of cold war tension into open hostilities in Korea and elsewhere during the 1950s. The following are excerpts from Spaak's book.

The word alliance brings to mind, I know, a long history of bloody conflict; it implies division, rivalry, and suspicion. Many of us had hoped that the lesson learned in two World Wars would force humanity to end the state of anarchy in which world society lives, and that it would no longer be necessary to resort to this traditional solution. However, the failure of the United Nations, even if it is only temporary, illustrates the difficulties such a revolution would face in a world which is divided by ideologies, partly conquered by Soviet imperialism, and torn by nationalist passions. But I am convinced that the day will come when the very excess of disorder and, above all, the danger of death which a nuclear conflict would mean, will force us to establish a world order which gives effective guarantees of peace and security for all.

Until that day, statesmen can but see things as they are and make the best of such possibilities as exist of establishing, in the interest of their peoples, at least some kind of order through which the essentials can be safeguarded.

This is the primary aim of the Atlantic Alliance. It is based on the elementary principle underlying the whole of society, namely, the incontestable right of self-defence. Since it is not possible in the international field to rely on the police or the law courts, this right can only be effectively exercised by collective action guaranteed by a treaty of mutual assistance and organized in advance. The Charter of the United Nations expressly sanctions the right to 'individual or collective self-defence if an armed attack occurs'.

The alliances of the past were, of course, based on the same principle; but their authors were certainly more intent upon ensuring victory in the event of conflict than upon preventing the conflict itself. This is clear from the extreme secrecy which surrounded the terms, and often even the very existence, of alliances in Europe before 1914. Naturally, the governments which negotiated the North Atlantic Treaty also wished to give their countries the best chance of successfully resisting a possible aggressor, and of finally defeating him. But their highest aim was, by declaring their common purpose, actually to prevent aggression. They had to ensure that there was no repetition of the disastrous gamble which always ended in the adversary throwing in his hand without a word, or in world war.

If the victorious alliances of 1918 and 1945 had been set up in peace-time, the Central Powers and Hitler's Germany would have hesitated to embark upon ventures which were doomed in advance to failure. There would have been no World War; there would have been neither *Anschluss,* nor Munich. The fundamental idea of the Atlantic Alliance is to unite sooner to ensure peace, so as to avoid having to unite later to win a war.

How does NATO act as a preventive?

First of all, the point at which hostile action would provoke a collective reaction is laid down. The essential point about this is that no doubt can exist as to the obligations of each member state. These are laid down by Article 5 of the Treaty, according to which the parties agree 'that an armed attack against one or more of them in Europe or North America shall be considered an attack against them all' and that 'if such an armed attack occurs, each of them . . . will assist the Party or Parties so attacked by taking forthwith, individually and in concert with the other Parties, such action as it deems necessary, including the use of armed force.'

Nevertheless, the Alliance derived insufficient preventive powers from this mutual assistance clause. In view of the disparity between our forces and those of the USSR in 1949, a declaration of solidarity was not enough to deter a potential aggressor; he would probably not have considered the price too high. We had, therefore, to replace the mere desire for collective defence with deeds; in other words, we had to set up the required force and define a common strategy.

The first and most urgent task of the Alliance was, therefore, to build up its defences. This process was an essential part of its evolution towards what is today not merely a classic alliance, but a real community served by permanent organs which prepare and discuss collective action, and which constitute the North Atlantic Treaty Organization.

The supreme organ of NATO, the Council, composed of the Foreign Ministers of the member countries, should, according to Article 9, 'consider matters concerning the implementation of this Treaty'—that is, it must ceaselessly adapt the action and resources of the fifteen member countries to the Soviet threat. The Council therefore had to create specialized agencies to work out a common defence system.

Its first task was to evaluate Soviet military strength, and then, on the basis of this evaluation, to establish common strategy, a plan of the forces required, and a coordinated military production programme. It was up to the governments of the fifteen countries to put the plans into effect.

The common strategy to be pursued was plain—the NATO countries had to be defended along the line of the Iron Curtain itself. For obvious moral reasons, there could be no question of surrendering part of an ally's territory and population. For military reasons, it was equally imperative not to fall back westwards and thereby reduce yet further the already dangerously limited depth of our defence area.

The 'shield' forces, which were to defend the Alliance along its frontiers, were supported by another all-important element in Western strategy—atomic weapons. Carried by the American and British air forces, these constituted both a compelling argument against aggression (the 'deterrent') and a potential means of reprisal.

If the 'shield' forces were to be effective, however, they must be based on strength. They needed far more than the 14 divisions which they comprised in 1950, as against the 200 odd Soviet divisions; but a whole series of difficulties had to be overcome before the necessary forces could be raised.

Rearmament is costly, and when NATO's military authorities had made an evaluation of the forces considered necessary to an efficient 'shield', and to common defence in general, it appeared that it would be difficult to carry out their recommendations without endangering the economic and financial stability of member countries. The principle of mutual assistance written into the Treaty had, of course, been put into effect since 1950 through a programme of military and financial aid laid down in a series of agreements between the United States and their European partners. Nevertheless, however generous this assistance might be, it could not provide more than a partial solution.

It would have been unrealistic and dangerous to sacrifice the economy to rearmament. Inflation and social disorder would immediately have undermined the very basis of the military effort; and in any event it would also have encouraged the spread of Communism.

The Alliance, therefore, sought for the solution which would best harmonize defence requirements with those of the economy. . . .

NATO's military strategy also created a political problem. In view of the effort which was required, it was essential that all the peoples covered by the 'shield' forces should participate in the common defence system: a means therefore had to be found of associating the Federal German Republic with the Atlantic Treaty partners. This question was put to the Atlantic Council in November 1950, after the Communist aggression in Korea; but it was only solved four years later, by the actual entry of Germany into the Alliance.

Finally, the accession of Greece and Turkey to NATO in 1952 extended the frontiers of our defence system to the Caucasus.

This, then, is how the broad lines of our defence policy have been laid down. In order to achieve our principal objective, that of deterring the potential aggressor, we do not aim at achieving complete parity with the adversary's forces. It is enough for us to have at our disposal sufficient means of reprisal for the price of aggression to become exorbitant.

Government of the German Democratic Republic "WHAT YOU SHOULD KNOW ABOUT THE WALL"

When the Federal Republic of Germany (West) and the German Democratic Republic (East) came into being in 1949, the city of Berlin's status became a curious one. Once occupied by the U.S., U.K., and French victors in World War II,

West Berlin was now protected by them; East Berlin became the capital of the new GDR. Travel between the two sectors of Berlin continued after 1949 as it had between 1945 and 1949; it was not uncommon for people to reside in one half of the city and work in the other. As the West German economy began to prosper through the "economic miracle" of the mid and late 1950s, for those East Germans critical of shortages and regimentation of their lives the attractions of a Western lifestyle and democratic freedoms seemed irresistible. Between 1949 and 1961, many East Germans "voted with their feet" and crossed into West Germany, most notably through West Berlin. No less than two million GDR citizens (over 15 percent of the population) seized this opportunity; many of them were skilled workers, professionals, and mainly younger people, which raised among GDR leaders the concern of a "brain drain" that could retard East German efforts to build a socialist society.

Intermittent attempts to negotiate a peace settlement for Germany during the 1950s came to naught, as both German states and their allies remained suspicious of the other side. East German leaders had hoped that resolution of the "German Question" would help resolve their emigration problem, which they couched as a West German effort to undermine peace and stability in the heart of Europe. In a last-ditch effort to cut off this exodus, the GDR Council of Ministers resolved on 12 August 1961 that:

> Maintaining peace calls for putting a stop to the activities of West German revanchists and militarists and, by concluding a German peace treaty, opening the way for securing peace and for Germany's rebirth as a peace-loving, anti-imperialist, neutral state. The position of the government in Bonn—that the Second World War has not yet ended—is tantamount to a demand for license for militaristic provocations and civil war-type measures. This imperialistic policy, which is conducted under the guise of anti-Communism, continues the aggressive aims of fascist German imperialism from the period of the Third Reich. From the defeat of Hitler's Germany in the Second World War, the Bonn government has concluded that the rapacious politics of German monopoly capitalism and its Hitler-generals should be given one more try—by renouncing a national policy for Germany and transforming West Germany into a NATO state, a satellite of the USA.

Plans to seal off West Berlin had been developed within the Ministry of State Security (Stasi) under the direction of its no-nonsense minister Erich Mielke. During the early morning hours of 13 August 1961, workers under Stasi and military supervision unrolled barbed wire along the line that would become the Berlin Wall.

In the following selection, a brochure entitled "What You Should Know About the Wall" and published in English for foreign distribution in 1962, the GDR government explained why it considered the barrier essential. Perhaps the most prominent symbol of Cold War division, the Berlin Wall would stand for twenty-eight years. East Germans hatched bold and sometimes ingenious schemes to cross over it into the West. At least 136 people were killed by East German border guards as they tried to cross; some estimates cite even higher figures.

Newspapers, radio and television report daily about Berlin and West Berlin in many languages throughout the world. They often speak or write of a state frontier, or of a wall.

It may be very difficult for you to form a valid picture from all these reports which frequently contradict each other. We want to help you to do so.

We tried to imagine what would be the considerations of a citizen of a foreign state if he wanted to gain clarity about the problems in West Berlin. And we would like to reply to these considerations.

1ST CONSIDERATION. WHERE, EXACTLY, IS BERLIN SITUATED?

A glance at the map suffices: Berlin lies in the middle of the German Democratic Republic, exactly 180 kilometres (112.5 miles) to the east of its western frontier. A quite normal locality for the capital of a state. Only one thing is not normal at all: that a hostile, undermining policy and disruptive acts have for years been carried on from the western part of this city against the surrounding state territory. West Berlin Mayor Willi Brandt called West Berlin a "thorn in the side of the GDR". Would you like to have a thorn in your side? We don't either! But Brandt even proclaims quite frankly: "We want to be the disturber of the peace."

2ND CONSIDERATION. DID THE WALL FALL OUT OF THE SKY?

No. It was the result of developments of many years standing in West Germany and West Berlin. Let us recall preceding events: In 1948 a separate currency reform was introduced in West Germany and West Berlin—the West German reactionaries thereby split Germany and even west Berlin into two currency areas.

The West German separatist state was founded in 1949—Bonn thereby turned the zonal border into a state frontier.

In 1954 West Germany was included in NATO—Bonn thereby converted the state frontier into the front-line between two pact systems.

The decision on the atomic armament of the West German Bundeswehr was made in 1958—thus, Bonn continues to aggravate the situation in Germany and Berlin. Repeatedly the annexation of the GDR is proclaimed as the official aim of Bonn policy, most recently in a statement of the Adenauer Christian Democratic Union (CDU), on 11 July 1961.

Thus did the anti-national, aggressive NATO policy create the wall which today separates the two German states and also goes through the middle of Berlin. The Bonn government and the West Berlin Senate have systematically converted West Berlin into a centre of provocation from where 90 espionage organizations, the RIAS American broadcasting station in West Berlin (Radio in American Sector) and revanchist associations organize acts of sabotage against the GDR and the other socialist countries. Through our protective measures of 13 August 1961 we have only safeguarded and strengthened that frontier which was already drawn years ago and made into a dangerous front-line by the people in Bonn and West Berlin. How high and how strongly fortified a frontier must be, depends, as is common knowledge, on the kind of relations existing between the states of each side of the frontier.

3RD CONSIDERATION. DID THE WALL HAVE TO COME?

Yes and no. We have submitted more than one hundred proposals for understanding, on the renunciation of atomic armament, and on the withdrawal of the two German states from NATO or the Warsaw Treaty. If things had gone according to our proposals the situation in Germany would not have been aggravated and, consequently, there would have been no wall. Especially since 1958 the GDR and the Soviet Union have repeatedly told the West Berlin Senate, the Bonn government, and the western powers: Be reasonable! Let us eliminate the abnormal situation in West Berlin together. Let us start negotiations. Why did Bonn and West Berlin reject these proposals? Why did they, instead, step up agitation to an unprecedented degree before 13 August?—The wall had to come because they were bringing about the danger of a conflict. Those who do not want to hear, must feel.

4TH CONSIDERATION. WHAT DID THE WALL PREVENT?

We no longer wanted to stand by passively and see how doctors, engineers, and skilled workers were induced by refined methods unworthy of the dignity of man to give up their secure existence in the GDR and work in West Germany or West Berlin. These and other manipulations cost the GDR annual losses amounting to 3.5 thousand million marks.

But we prevented something much more important with the wall—West Berlin's becoming the starting point for a military conflict. The measures we introduced on 13 August in conjunction with the Warsaw Treaty states have cooled off a number of hotheads in Bonn and West Berlin. For the first time in German history the match which was to set fire to another war was extinguished before it had fulfilled its purpose.

5TH CONSIDERATION. WAS PEACE REALLY THREATENED?

Indian journalists R. K. Karanjia shall give you the answer to the question. He published a sensational report from Berlin in the biggest Indian weekly, Blitz, in which the world public is warned against the West Berlin powder-keg. K. R. Karanjia wrote:

"It (the protective wall of the GDR) served the cause of world peace since it halted the advance of the German neo-Hitlerites toward the East, forced the world to recognize the reality of the division of Germany and thus supports negotiation." (retranslated from German)

If further evidence of the aggressive intentions of the West German government is needed it is provided by the authoritative West German employers' newspaper, the Industriekurier, which regretfully wrote, exactly 19 days after 13 August 1961: "A reunification with the Bundeswehr marching victoriously through the Brandenburg Gate to the beating of drums—such a reunification will not take place in the foreseeable future."

Bonn heads were really haunted by ideas of such a victorious entry. That would have meant war.

6TH CONSIDERATION. WHO IS WALLED IN?

According to the exceedingly intelligent explanations of the West Berlin Senate we have walled ourselves in and are living in a concentration camp. But in that case why are the gentlemen so excited? Obviously, because in reality their espionage centres, their revanchist radio stations, their fascist solders' associations, their youth poisoners, and their currency racketeers have been walled in. They are excited because we have erected the wall as an antifascist, protective wall against them.

Does something not occur to you? West Berlin Mayor Brandt wails that half of the GDR, including the workers in the enterprise militia groups, is armed. What do you think of a concentration camp whose inmates have weapons in their hands?

7TH CONSIDERATION. WHO BREAKS OFF HUMAN CONTACTS?

Of course, it is bitter for many Berliners not to be able to visit each other at present. But it would be more bitter if a new war were to separate them forever. Moreover, when the GDR was forced to introduce compulsory entry permits for West Berlin citizens on 23 August in the interests of its security we at the same time offered to open up entry permit offices in municipal railway stations in West Berlin. In fact we opened them and issued the first permits.

Who closed them by force? The same Senate of that Mr. Brandt who is today shedding crocodile tears about "contacts being broken"! The GDR has maintained its offer. If we had our way Berliners could visit each other despite the wall.

8TH CONSIDERATION. DOES THE WALL THREATEN ANYONE?

Bonn propaganda describes the wall as a "monstrous evidence of the aggressiveness of world communism". Have you ever considered it to be a sign of aggressiveness when someone builds a fence around his property?

9TH CONSIDERATION. WHO IS AGGRAVATING THE SITUATION?

The wall? It stands there quite calmly. Former French Premier Reynaud said already on 19 August 1961, according to UPI: "The sealing-off measures of the East Berlin government did not increase, but lessened, the danger of a third world war." In reality, the situation is being aggravated by persons who play at being the strong man on our state frontier, who are turning West Berlin into a NATO base and daily inciting West Berliners against the GDR. Municipal railway cars are being destroyed, frontier guards attacked and brutally shot, tunnels dug for agents and bomb attacks made on the GDR's frontier security installations. Does that serve relaxation? One must really ask why attacks on the GDR state frontier in West Berlin are not subject to court prosecution as in other states. The Brandt Senate even presents "its respects" to the provocateurs.

10TH CONSIDERATION. IS THE WALL A GYMNASTIC APPARATUS?

The wall is the state frontier of the German Democratic Republic. The state frontier of a sovereign state must be respected. That is so the world over. He who does not treat it with respect can not complain if he comes to harm. West German and West Berlin politicians demand that "the wall be removed". We are not particularly fond of walls, either. But please consider where the actual wall runs in Germany, the wall which must be pulled down in your and our interest. It is the wall which was erected because of the fateful Bonn NATO policy. On the stones of this wall stand atomic armament, entry into NATO, revanchist demands, anti-communist incitement, non-recognition of the GDR, rejection of negotiations, the front-line city of West Berlin.

So, make your contribution to the pulling down of this wall by advocating a reasonable policy of military neutrality, peaceful co-existence, normal relations between the two German states, the conclusion of a peace treaty with Germany, a demilitarized Free City of West Berlin. That is the only way to improve the situation in Berlin, to safeguard peace, a way which can one day also lead to the reunification of Germany. The wall says to the warmongers:

He who lives on an island should not make an enemy of the ocean.

{Here the brochure reproduces a map of the German Democratic Republic.}

Decide in favour of the recognition of realities. Don't join in the row over the wall. Perhaps YOU don't want socialism. That is your affair.

But should we not come to an agreement jointly to refrain from doing anything that leads to war and do everything that serves peace?

CHAPTER SEVEN

THE EASTERN BLOC, 1945–1981

IN 1956, HUNGARIAN PATRIOTS, resentful of Russian domination and Communist dictatorship, rose in rebellion, forcing Soviet troops to withdraw. Here Hungarians express their resentment by throwing Stalin's picture into the flames. A Soviet counterattack crushed the revolution and drove 200,000 Hungarians into exile. *(Erich Lessing/Magnum Photos)*

Even more than Western Europe, the eastern part of the continent had suffered staggering human and material losses as a result of the Second World War. Hard on the heels of the conflict another casualty proved to be freedom, surrendered to a Soviet Union bent on guarding against future aggression by installing friendly (and compliant) Communist regimes throughout the region. These states were known as the "People's Democracies," although it was difficult to find anything democratic about their creation or operation. In the late 1940s, the People's Democracies all underwent Stalinization. Party rule became a fact of political life; command economies reorganized industry and agriculture in a top-down manner; and all formerly independent activity passed under the control of an omnipotent state. Meanwhile, the Soviet Union created international mechanisms to oversee and exploit the region's economic production and military resources, so that the phrase "Eastern Bloc" became entirely fitting. Other phenomena familiar from the U.S.S.R. of the 1930s appeared as well, such as the purge, the show trial, and collective terrorism. There was no need to be an outright enemy of the regime in order to be targeted for persecution or elimination.

The spirit of resistance survived nevertheless. At first, it took the form of individual attempts at unmasking the brutal and self-serving nature of these regimes. More organized efforts—still modest in scope—developed later, when person-to-person contacts once again became possible in the post-Stalin era. The Soviet political leadership even proved capable of criticizing and reforming itself, as Nikita Khrushchev demonstrated during the heyday of de-Stalinization. Such official "thaws" were likely to be partial and temporary, but they whetted the popular appetite for liberalization of a more substantial kind. In particular, the quest for political change in Hungary and Czechoslovakia tested the limits of Soviet tolerance for alternate paths to socialism—and found those limits still in place.

Even during the Cold War, however, the peoples of Eastern Europe sometimes found it possible to pursue their dreams of autonomy with a measure of success. Such was the case in Poland, whose workers kept up an insistent drumbeat for an independent labor union and benefited from the special interest of the Polish pope. Although Solidarity's radicals provoked an official reaction that withdrew their hard-won gains, their example demonstrated that mass movements would not necessarily draw the fire of Soviet tanks. In addition to Poland, other Eastern European societies—never fully Sovietized or divorced from their national roots—were quietly beginning to assert their identities and press their claims. The final outcome for them would depend, as it had ever since 1945, on the prevailing leader in the Kremlin. By the mid 1980s, a reformer, Mikhail Gorbachev, was waiting in the wings.

1 The "People's Democracies"

Even before the conclusion of World War II, Joseph Stalin was preparing to transform Eastern Europe into a zone of Soviet influence, which would protect the U.S.S.R. from yet another German military assault as had occurred in both 1914 and 1941. Using Eastern European Communists who had sought refuge in the Soviet Union after fleeing their own countries, the Soviet dictator created "National Liberation Committees"; they were, in fact, the bases for postwar Communist governments that would obediently toe the Kremlin's party line. The National Liberation Committees rode into Eastern Europe in the train of the victorious Red Army, which not only smashed the retreating Wehrmacht but also oversaw the growth of Soviet power in the years immediately following the war. Before long, Eastern Europe had become the Eastern Bloc, an alliance dominated by the Soviet Union and fashioned to serve the economic, military, and political interests of its "protector."

G. E. R. Gedye
WITNESS TO THE CZECHOSLOVAK COUP (1948)

The installation of Communist power in Eastern Europe proceeded at varying rates. In the case of Poland, for example, the process occurred swiftly and was essentially complete by 1946. In the case of Czechoslovakia, by contrast, events moved more slowly. Several factors may help account for the gap. Unlike other Eastern European "successor" states established after World War I, Czechoslovakia had maintained generally good relations with the Soviet Union. In addition, the Western democracies regarded the country with a mixture of admiration, solicitude, and guilt. In the years prior to the war, Czechoslovakia had maintained its devotion to representative government while its neighbors embraced fascist-style authoritarianism. Moreover, during the war itself the Czechs had not collaborated with the Nazis in the manner of other Eastern European peoples. Indeed, Czechoslovakia had been an early victim of Hitler's territorial designs, aided and abetted by Britain and France at Munich in 1938. Aware of the special interest of the West in the country, Stalin may have acted more cautiously toward Czechoslovakia. For several years following the Second World War, it even appeared as though Czechoslovakia might maintain its independence. Eventually, however, the mounting tensions of the Cold War sealed its fate. With the Communists installed in Prague, Soviet hegemony over Eastern Europe had reached its height.

In the following selection, which originally appeared in the periodical *Commentary,* English-born journalist G. E. R. Gedye (1890–1970) offers an eyewitness account of the Communist takeover in Czechoslovakia. Gedye had earlier witnessed the Anschluss in Austria in 1938 and the military takeover of

Czechoslovakia in March 1939. Now, reporting from Prague in February 1948, Gedye describes the tactics that Communists already had used to their advantage in other Eastern European countries.

The Czechs have learned their bitter lesson: that democratic liberties are things which a little country set amidst mammoth states may cherish, but for which it is impossible to fight—at least, unaided. . . .

In 1938 they suffered for daring to demand independence and democracy in the area claimed as *Lebensraum* by totalitarian Germany. Today they have been taught the futility of such dreams in the "outer zone" of totalitarian Russia. . . .

The curtain rose on the prelude to this new tragedy of Czechoslovakia last June, when she shocked the Kremlin by accepting the invitation to the Marshall Plan Conference. With the strong Communist parliamentary minority of thirty-eight per cent assisted by crypto-Communists running the Social Democrats, Russia had believed the country was in the bag. It was good propaganda to allow her only satellite where Communists had gained strength through democratic, instead of through fraudulent, elections to play at democracy for some years. Czechoslovakia was Russia's shop window, where a real parliament and democracy were temptingly displayed.

Overnight the Czechs' illusions were smashed. They had forgotten that these goods in the window were only dummies to attract woolly-minded Western customers. They thought they were free to decide that they needed the Marshall Plan. Among those who thought this were even some Communist ministers. No wonder the Kremlin was shocked. Not even all Czech Communists could be trusted! At a word from Stalin, acceptance of the invitation was cancelled.

The Kremlin was placated but not reassured. Elections were approaching. Russia's grip must be so strengthened that it could never again be challenged. The Communists, though strong, were still a minority. They enjoyed socialist support through a working arrangement which sometimes failed to work. People were restive in the factories. In 1945 the Communists had seized key factory positions, having been the best organized, best armed, and the most daring of the resistance groups. The Red Army had increased their armaments. Their Moscow-trained organizers had been given precise objectives and seized them before the other parties realized what was afoot. At the outset the Communists had captured URO—the single, centralized Revolutionary Trade Union. Hence the big Communist poll in 1946. But now the workers were grumbling about Moscow's rigid grip. The innate Czech instinct for democracy was reasserting itself and strengthening democratic socialism. The Communists countered with factory terror—workers were forced to join the party, to remain within the Communist camp.

But after a preliminary rush to cover within the Communist party, there was a reverse movement into the opposite camp when it seemed that surrender to Russia on the Marshall Plan might not mean surrender to Communism at home. The Communists decided on a coup.

The leader of the Social Democrats was Zdenek Fierlinger, a trained diplomat. I knew him well when, as minister to Vienna, and still a democratic socialist, he did his utmost in February 1934 to save arrested Austrian Social Democrats from the gallows. . . . When I met him in Moscow in 1939, where he was Czechoslovak minister, he was disillusioned and embittered by the betrayal of democratic Czechoslovakia by France and Britain. Representatives of the countries which had facilitated Hitler's rape of Czechoslovakia ignored him. Not so the Narkomindel, Russia's Foreign Office. Its astute chiefs kept up close unofficial relations with Fierlinger until the Russo-German Pact, and when that Nazi-Communist honeymoon ended, Fierlinger returned as Czechoslovak ambassador—and as a whole-hearted backer of Soviet policy and Communism. As such he was Czechoslovakia's first postwar premier.

Here then was an enthusiastic ally. On September 29 last, the Communist Premier, Clement Gottwald, and Fierlinger moved swiftly. Without consulting the Socialist party executive, they issued a totally unauthorized declaration that "the two parties" had agreed to present a single front on all political questions. Jubilantly the Communists cried out that fusion was on the way—as indeed it was. At the same time they tried an unsuccessful putsch against the Democratic party in Slovakia. But a Socialist congress met at Brno in November, and the democratic Socialists purged their ranks of the "cryptos." Fierlinger was turned out of the chairmanship of the party and many of his followers lost office with him. The party wanted to elect Dr. Majer, a right-wing Socialist, but feared to provoke the Communists too far. A left-winger, Minister of Industry Bohumil Lausman, was finally chosen.

Now the Kremlin was seriously alarmed. The Socialists were no longer struggling behind the scenes to ensure the survival of a measure of independence and democracy. They had nailed their colors to the masthead and had mutinied against the Communists' fifth column. Soon after Brno, Lausman authorised me to quote him: "You need have no fears for the independence of the Czech Social Democrats. Since Brno, the workers are flocking to our colors. This will be reflected in the May election results." He was confirmed by the unofficial polls which most Czechoslovak parties and some foreign embassies hold from time to time. The highest percentage which even the Communist polls forecast for their party at the elections was 35 per cent instead of the existing 38 per cent. For their plans to succeed they needed at least 51 per cent and had boasted that they would get it. In January there began a steady decrease in the estimates of their strength, the lowest estimate being 30 per cent. "Free and unfettered" elections would spell disaster for the Communists.

Early in February the non-Communist parties realized that something was brewing. The Communist "cold putsch" appeared to have been fixed for February 29. . . .

The Communists arrested a number of Czechs who had served in Britain during the war, accusing them of the usual "plot" in the service of "foreign powers." The "plot" lost its allure when Dr. Drtina and the Deputy Premier Petr Zenkl revealed that a convict had been "borrowed" from prison by officers of the secret police. They had introduced him to two pseudo "American-Czechs" and told him: "You will go with these men and try secretly to recruit people to resist an expected Communist putsch, saying that Zenkl and Drtina are backing you. Your sentence is remitted."

The full crisis broke over what has been the cornerstone of Communist triumphs in every country in the Russian orbit—the "Communizing" of the police through a Communist Minister of the Interior. On February 12 the Czech Socialist party's Secretary-General, Krajina, told Parliament that a Cabinet meeting had established that the "agents of foreign powers" were really *agents provocateurs* of the secret police. Another deputy revealed that police officials had to pay weekly visits to Communist headquarters for instructions. On February 16 the Communist chairman of URO, Antonin Zapotocky (today a Deputy Premier), said: "If Parliament does not accept URO's demands, away with Parliament!"

By a majority decision the Cabinet decided on February 13 that Nosek[1] must cancel the dismissal of eight leading Prague police officials whom he had replaced by Communists, and instructed him to report in a Cabinet meeting on February 17 that he had complied. When that day came, Nosek failed to appear, pleading ill-health. The Communist Minister of Information, Vaclav Kopecky (Nosek's deputy in his absence), refused to speak for him. Next day the non-Communist

[1]Václav Nosek (1892–1955), a coal miner by trade, later joined the Czech Communist Party and served as Czech Minister of the Interior from 1945 until 1953.

ministers stated that they would not appear at Cabinet meetings until Nosek complied with orders and the plan to "Communize" the police was halted. On February 20, the crisis came to a head with the resignation of twelve non-Communist ministers (who are believed to have been advised to do so by President Benes with the promise that their resignations would not be accepted; meantime Benes would try to heal the breach with the Communists).

The Communists rejected every effort of the sick and failing President, and presented their ultimatum. The ministers must be replaced by men of Gottwald's own choice; his press poured out accusations that the ministers had planned an armed putsch. Soon arms were indeed seen on the streets of Prague—in the hands of the Communist work-militia, mobilized to exert pressure. In vain did the twelve ministers insist that they had no desire to drive the Communists from office but only objected to their dictatorship. In vain did Benes announce that no other Premier than Gottwald, leader of the strongest party, would be acceptable to him. The Social-Democratic leader, Lausman, insisted on compromise. But the Communists had seen their chance to establish the dictatorship they intended and yet to put responsibility on their opponents. Gottwald and Nosek called for the notorious—and quite illegal and unconstitutional—"action committees" of Communists to go into action.

When Nosek sent his police to invade the Social Democrats' (and other parties') headquarters, Lausman surrendered, while armed Communist bands tramped the streets. . . . The Communists never let up their pressure on the frail President, who was bullied as was President Hacha in Berlin in 1939. In vain did Benes publicly plead that he could not violate "my sincerely democratic creed." To the Communists he wrote on February 24: "Without betraying myself I cannot do other than insist on parliamentary government and democracy as the only basis for a decent and dignified way of life." By 4:30 PM next day, the Communists had got him down: he accepted the resignations and gave Gottwald *carte blanche.* "It has been very difficult for me," he apologized when Gottwald's men were sworn in three days later. "After long and grave reflection I decided that I could not persist in rejecting your demands. The crisis might have led on to the splitting of the nation and complete chaos. You want to conduct the state in a new way. I wish it may prove a happy way for all."

At once the Communist witch hunt rose to its zenith. Before the purges of the "action committees" there went down the flower of the democratic Republic—diplomats, statesmen, great writers and editors, the expert technicians of industry and commerce, rectors, professors, and students of the universities, scientists, famous socialists, famous liberals, the great colleagues of Benes and Thomas Masaryk—all who would not kiss the hands of the new dictators. It is not too much to say that the blow thus dealt to the country—with its currency already tottering, and the importation of essential raw materials an almost insoluble problem—by depriving it of nearly all its capable guides, will cripple it economically for years to come.

The figure for those deprived of their means of livelihood overnight runs into hundreds of thousands. How many have been arrested the government will not reveal. As happened after Hitler, a suicide wave set in, headed by Jan Masaryk.[2] Thousands of desperate fugitives tried to escape across the closely guarded frontiers. Many who were caught were lodged, to the delight of Nazi war criminals, in the Prague prisons in cells adjoining their own.

There is one feature of the Communist coup which everyone praises—its brilliant stage management. How far the producers have progressed beyond the crudities of the Nazis, the shameless electoral terrorism of the Communists which

---

[2]Jan Masaryk (1888–1948), the son of Czechoslovakia's founder and first president Thomas Masaryk, had been serving as the country's foreign minister. His suicide may have been a political murder.

I saw in the Rumanian elections of 1946, the patent falsification of the electoral register and the lorry columns of Communist multiple voters whom I watched in Hungary last year! If the farce of elections is staged in Czechoslovakia there will be no opposition, no free press, and everything will run smoothly. Thanks to meticulous preparation, the coup was completed almost without bloodshed. Within two days of its enslavement, the population was going about its business, cowed and depressed—but unresisting.

Yet the Czechs are at heart as democratic as the British, the Swedes, the Austrians, or the Swiss. The betrayal of 1939 had destroyed faith in the power of the West to help. The preliminary capture of the trade unions; the network of fellow travelers established in key posts in the press—including foreign correspondents—the lessons learned from earlier Communist mistakes, the Russian alliance, and, above all, Communist control of the police through the Minister of the Interior, made victory easy for the Communists. *It is for those countries where democracy still survives to examine each of these factors and secure their elimination while there is yet time—if there is time.* Otherwise there is nothing to do but wait for the triumph of the man with the tommy-gun and the loud-speaker over those, no matter how great their majority, who have lost control of both.

Wolfgang Leonhard
THE COMMUNIST TAKEOVER OF EAST GERMANY

The preliminary organization of a Soviet-style socialist German republic—the state that would later become East Germany—was undertaken in the middle of 1943 by the "National Committee for a Free Germany," a Moscow-based, Soviet-controlled association of German Communists in exile and German POWs disillusioned with the Third Reich. The goals of the committee were the creation of an anti-fascist state committed to the ideas of Leninism-Stalinism and the integration of this new Germany into a fraternal, Soviet-led, European community of socialist nations.

Wolfgang Leonhard was one of the German Communist functionaries entrusted with the work of creating this new state. The son of an idealistic woman whose Communist sympathies prompted her to emigrate to the U.S.S.R. in the 1920s, Leonhard was raised in a party-run school after one of Stalin's xenophobic crackdowns on foreigners led to his mother's removal to Siberia. In time, Leonhard internalized the idealism and discipline instilled in him by the Soviet system and became an active participant in the National Committee for a Free Germany. Members of this group took part in ideological and organizational training courses that would enable them to lay the groundwork for a Soviet-style German state, with the Red Army as their guarantor. Central to this ideological training was the notion that the defeat of nazism had been brought about by the Allied armies, and not by internal resistance led by Germans themselves. Consequently, the reeducation of Germans and the reorganization of political,

social, economic, and cultural activities could be undertaken only by individuals associated with the Allied authorities.

In the following selection, Leonhard discusses the Communists' organizational work for the first elections in the Soviet sector of Berlin, held in October 1946. He touches upon the integration of former Nazi party members and the increasing heavy-handedness of the Soviet authorities. By the time the German Democratic Republic was declared a separate German state in 1949, Leonhard had become disillusioned with Stalinism and found refuge in non-aligned Yugoslavia. He moved to the West in 1950, where he remained an outspoken left-wing critic of the Western system. However, once safely in the West, he directed his energies equally to the vigorous criticism of Stalinism and advocacy of the more independent, democratic form of communism favored by Communist parties in France and Italy.

In September the first local elections were to be held, and then on 20th October, 1946, the elections for the provincial parliaments, and in all four sectors of the City of Berlin.

As the date of the elections drew near, the S.E.D.[1] authorities published an announcement clarifying their attitude towards what were known as "nominal Nazis." This statement had been prepared a long time beforehand. In private, the decisive argument in the S.E.D.'s attitude was that we must not repeat the errors of the Austrian Communist Party in the elections of autumn, 1945, when our Austrian comrades had been carried away by their crude anti-Nazism to the point of rejecting the great mass of minor Nazis, and thus isolating themselves from the population as a whole. Officially, however, the argument was that "the S.E.D. considers the time has arrived to incorporate those who were nothing more than simple members of fellow-travellers of the former Nazi Party into the democratic structure." This led, however, to a storm of angry protest in our own ranks, going far beyond anything we had expected. Whatever subject might be announced for discussion at Party meetings, without fail the first speaker would start angrily on the question of the Nazis.

There was only one thing to be done: education. At once the S.E.D. began to organise and encourage meetings with former "nominal Nazis." Many officials said that this was really going too far, but others were very favourably impressed by these meetings. They said there were some splendid people among them, who would do well with us—vigorous, constructive and not inclined to grumble.

Waldemar Schmidt, who had almost ten years of concentration camps behind him, came home one evening very amused from one of these meetings with "nominal Nazis."

"I've seen a lot in my time," he said, "but I should never have dreamed of anything like this. They're downright enthusiastic about the S.E.D.'s announcement. One of them made a very excitable speech and ended up with a slogan he had invented himself." Waldemar Schmidt looked at me and said with a mischievous smile: "You've made up a lot of slogans. What do you think his was?"

I suggested several possibilities, but he only shook his head. "No, our nominal Nazi's slogan

---

[1]*Sozialistische Einheitspartei Deutschlands*, or Socialist Unity party of Germany. Created in 1946 in the Soviet Zone, the SED was the result of a forced union of the SPD with the KPD [*Kommunistische Partei Deutschlands*, or German Communist party]. Social Democrats who spoke out against this Communist-engineered amalgamation were threatened with violence, and in some cases were attacked; many were arrested, and often deported to the East by Soviet agents. Rather than sacrifice their democratic principles, many SPD members in Eastern Germany fled to one of the Western Allied-controlled occupation zones.

was much better. He shouted out: 'Long live the S.E.D.—the little Nazi's greatest friend!'"

As soon as the uneasiness over our new Party line towards the "nominal Nazis" had died down, our Party members and officials turned all their efforts to the election campaign. Despite all their efforts, however, the S.E.D. received on the average less than half of the votes cast. Out of a total of 519 deputies elected to the regional parliaments in the Soviet Zone, only 249 belonged to the S.E.D. There was some help from the mass organisations, for 12 out of their 16 deputies were members of the S.E.D., thus bringing the actual total of S.E.D. deputies up to 261. This gave the S.E.D. a narrow overall majority in the regional parliaments of the Soviet Zone. The electoral regulations provided that the next local election should take place two years later, in 1948, and the next district and regional parliamentary elections three years later, in 1949. "By the next elections, things will go better," said many of the more optimistic officials after 20th October, 1946: but there were no next elections. The elections of October, 1946, were the first and the last in the Soviet Zone at which a political choice was open to the electors. From that time onwards there were only single lists.

We realised that the regional elections in the Soviet Zone were only a preliminary. The real decision would be made at the Berlin elections on 20th October, 1946. I spent the night of the 20th–21st October at the editorial offices of *Neues Deutschland.* Every report came in here, and we could at once form the best possible picture of what was going on. In expectation of our victory at the elections, huge loud-speakers had been put up in front of the editorial building to publish the results to the crowds assembled outside. Soon the reports came in: one piece of bad news after another. Our faces became longer and longer. The announcer who was to publish the results to the crowds waiting outside was tearing his hair. Despairingly he tried to pick out from the flow of reports such as were favourable to the S.E.D. With every few minutes that passed, the situation grew worse. The first reports to be put together showed a catastrophic defeat for the S.E.D. and a gigantic victory for the S.P.D., which only six months before we had been referring to as the "Zehlendorf Hospital Club" and in the last few weeks as the "S.P.D. splinter."

We heard the final results in the early hours of the morning. The Social Democratic Party had received 48.7% of the votes; the Christian Democratic Union, 22.1%: the S.E.D., 19.8%; and the Liberal Democratic Party, 9.4%. The cause of our defeat was perfectly clear to me and to many other officials. To the man in the street, we were known as the "Russian" party. Theoretically, of course, we had evolved the line of a separate German road to Socialism, but only a narrow circle of the population knew or understood this. In practice, we had supported and defended all measures taken by the Soviet occupation authorities. They had supplied us with paper, vehicles, buildings and special food rations. Our leading officials lived in large country houses hermetically sealed from the rest of the population and guarded by soldiers of the Red Army. They travelled in cars which, in some cases, carried Russian marks of identification. The result of the elections was the logical consequence of our dependence on the Soviet occupation authorities. I told myself that the population of Berlin had not voted against us because we were in favour of Socialism, nor had they voted against Party members and officials who had done what they could, at considerable cost to themselves, to relieve the needs of the population. They had voted against us because they saw in us a Party dependent on the Soviet Union; and unfortunately they were not wrong.

Now only one thing could save us: a clear dissociation from the Soviet occupation authorities, and a public avowal of our intention from now on to function as an independent German Socialist Party. That night I hoped that perhaps the electoral defeat of 20th October would finally lead to our taking this step, and thus work eventually to our advantage. I hoped that the Party leadership would now openly recognise the real reasons for our defeat, and would draw the appropriate conclusions.

Despite the electoral disappointment of October 20, 1946, the position of the S.E.D. in the Soviet Zone was never in jeopardy; the Red Army and the Soviet political police saw to it that the other parties did not become powerful. On the contrary, between early 1947 and the autumn of 1948, as "Sovietization" proceeded in neighboring Czechoslovakia and in Poland, harassment of Social Democrats in the Soviet Zone of Germany increased, and police surveillance and interference of parties in competition with the S.E.D. reduced them to mere nameplate organizations whose existence was entirely dependent upon the Soviet and East German authorities. In September 1948, less than two years after its creation, German Communists declared the Soviet road to socialism to be the only viable option open to Eastern Germany, and, with the help of their Soviet patrons, East Germany effectively became a one-party state. Although the German Democratic Republic was proclaimed after the West German Federal Republic came into being, S.E.D. officials had long since prepared a Soviet-style regime.

Communist Information Bureau
COMINFORM RESOLUTION ON YUGOSLAVIA (1949)

In 1947, at Stalin's behest, the Communist parties of the Eastern Bloc created the Communist Information Bureau or Cominform, an agency designed to consolidate Soviet power in Eastern Europe. Eventually, the Cominform dutifully pursued the Soviet campaign against Yugoslavia, which grew out of a rift between Stalin and Yugoslav Communist party leader Josef Broz Tito (1892–1980). During the war, Tito had led a partisan movement that liberated most of the country prior to the arrival of the Red Army; thus, unlike other Communist leaders in Eastern Europe, he was not beholden to Soviet military power for Yugoslavia's liberation or his own political authority. In addition, Tito deeply resented the increasing interference of Stalin in Yugoslavia's postwar political affairs, which included dispatching Kremlin spies to the country. In 1948, the Tito-Stalin split became public, both sides trading insults and denunciations with each other. World communism was no longer a monolith directed from the Kremlin. Tito—no democrat himself—had nonetheless successfully defied Stalin and thereby pioneered the notion of "alternate roads to communism." Until his death in 1980, he cannily guided Yugoslavia between the capitalist and socialist camps, often taking advantage of material support from both, and maintained a precarious unity among the country's fractious nationalities.

The following document—entitled "The Communist Party of Yugoslavia in the Power of Murderers and Spies"—appeared in the Cominform organ *For a Lasting Peace, For a People's Democracy!* in November 1949. A year earlier the agency, as usual taking its cues from Moscow, had expelled Yugoslavia from its ranks. Here it virtually calls on "loyal" (i.e., Stalinist) Yugoslav Communists to overthrow the Tito regime.

The information bureau, consisting of representatives of the Communist Party of Bulgaria, Rumanian Workers' Party, Working People's Party of Hungary, United Workers' Party of Poland, Communist Party of the Soviet Union (Bolsheviks), Communist Party of France, and the Czechoslovak and Italian Communist Parties, having considered the question "The Yugoslav Communist Party in the power of murderers and spies," unanimously reached the following conclusions:

Whereas, in June 1948 the meeting of the Information Bureau of the Communist Parties noted the changeover of the Tito-Rankovic[1] clique from democracy and socialism to bourgeois nationalism, during the period that has elapsed since the meeting of the Information Bureau this clique has travelled all the way from bourgeois nationalism to fascism and outright betrayal of the national interests of Yugoslavia.

Recent events show that the Yugoslav Government is completely dependent on foreign imperialist circles and has become an instrument of their aggressive policy, which has resulted in the liquidation of the independence of the Yugoslav Republic.

The Central Committee of the Party and the Government of Yugoslavia have merged completely with the imperialist circles against the entire camp of socialism and democracy; against the Communist Parties of the world; against the New Democracies, and the U.S.S.R.

The Belgrade clique of hired spies and murderers made a flagrant deal with imperialist reaction and entered its service. . . .

. . . [T]he present Yugoslav rulers, having fled from the camp of democracy and socialism to the camp of capitalism and reaction, have become direct accomplices of the instigators of a new war, and, by their treacherous deeds, are ingratiating themselves with the imperialists and kowtowing to them. . . .

The brutality with which staunch fighters for Communism are being annihilated in Yugoslavia, can be compared only with the atrocities of the Hitler fascists or . . . Franco in Spain.

Expelling from the ranks of the Party those Communists loyal to proletarian internationalism, annihilating them, the Yugoslav fascists opened wide the doors of the Party to bourgeois and kulak elements.

As a result of the fascist terror of the Tito gangs against the healthy forces in the Yugoslav Communist Party, leadership of the party is wholly in the hands of spies and murderers, mercenaries of imperialism.

The Information Bureau of Communist and Workers' Parties considers, therefore, that the struggle against the Tito clique—hired spies and murderers, is the international duty of all Communist and Workers' Parties.

It is the duty of Communist and Workers' Parties to give all possible aid to the Yugoslav working class and working peasantry who are fighting for the return of Yugoslavia to the camp of democracy and socialism.

A necessary condition for the return of Yugoslavia to the socialist camp is active struggle on the part of the revolutionary elements both inside the Yugoslav Communist Party and outside its ranks, for the regeneration of the revolutionary, genuine Communist Party of Yugoslavia, loyal to Marxism-Leninism, to the principles of proletarian internationalism, and fighting for the independence of Yugoslavia from imperialism.

The loyal Communist forces in Yugoslavia who, in the present brutal conditions of fascist terror, are deprived of the possibility of engaging in open action against the Tito-Rankovic clique, were compelled in the struggle for the cause of Communism, to follow the path taken by the Communists of those countries where legal work is forbidden.

The Information Bureau expresses the firm conviction that, among the workers and peasants of Yugoslavia, forces will be found capable of ensuring victory over the bourgeois-restoration

[1]Alexander Rankovic (1909–83) was vice-president of Yugoslavia and head of its security services.

espionage Tito-Rankovic clique; that the toiling people of Yugoslavia led by the working class will succeed in restoring the historical gains of People's Democracy, won at the price of heavy sacrifice and heroic struggle by the peoples of Yugoslavia, and that they will take the road of building socialism.

[Signed by 22 representatives of Cominform member parties.]

2 Repression in the Soviet Union and Its Satellites

To encourage widespread participation in the struggle against Hitler, Stalin had eased up on party control during the war. With Nazism vanquished, however, dictatorial repression returned. No doubt, Stalin's domestic policies reflected the international climate. With the Cold War now under way, the Soviet dictator may have feared that a hostile West would discover the exhausted condition of the U.S.S.R. and seize the opportunity to launch an invasion, in the manner of the interventionists during the Russian Civil War. Ringing down the "Iron Curtain," therefore, would enable the Soviet people to get on with the business of rebuilding their devastated country free from the snooping of foreign enemies. It also would prevent those under Communist rule from making unfavorable comparisons between their spartan existence and the much higher standard of living abroad.

Of course, what was good for the goose was good for the gander, so that the Eastern European satellites had to undergo not merely Sovietization but Stalinization in the immediate postwar years. Economic transformation was accompanied by the severe regimentation of society and culture. Creativity and independent thinking were brutally suppressed. If "Trotskyist" had been the most dangerous label in the Soviet Union of the 1930s, that honor was now held by "Titoist." Not until after Stalin's death in March 1953 would some light begin to appear on the horizon.

Roy Medvedev
STALIN'S LAST YEARS

One of the most remarkable interpreters of the Soviet past is the philosopher and historian Roy Medvedev (b. 1925). The twin brother of biologist Zhores Medvedev, Roy has maintained a staunch belief in democratic socialism; for this reason, he has rigorously criticized those phenomena of Soviet history—Stalinism, in particular—that not only prevented its realization but also threatened to despoil it as an ideal. He spent years amassing research for his magisterial analysis of the Stalinist era, much of it from interviews with survivors. The work appeared in the West in 1972 under the title *Let History Judge.* In 1989, Medvedev released a revised and expanded edition of the book which drew on materials recently made available under Mikhail Gorbachev.

In the following selection from the 1989 edition of the work, Medvedev describes the resumption of political repression in the Soviet Union following the Second World War.

The victory of the Soviet people in the Great Patriotic War, though won at the price of enormous sacrifices, engendered great exaltation. People tried to heal the wounds of war as quickly as possible; they lived on the hope of a better and happier future. The land was so bloodsoaked that any thought of new deaths seemed unbearable. So strong was this sentiment that immediately after the war the Presidium of the Supreme Soviet decreed an end to the death penalty, even for the most serious crimes. The spy mania and universal suspicion that prevailed before the war tended to disappear, especially in view of the drastic change in the international situation. The Soviet Union was no longer isolated. It had become a superpower, and both its friends and its enemies abroad closely followed events inside the USSR. All this set limits on the arbitrary measures Stalin and his circle could indulge in.

Still, repression continued in the postwar period, though on a somewhat smaller scale than in the prewar years. In 1947, for example, many prominent figures in the Soviet air force and aviation industry, who had been heroes in the war, were arrested on trumped-up charges. . . . A large number of officials in the aviation industry and military aviators were also arrested on charges of producing airplanes of "poor quality," of stopping military production too soon and switching aircraft factories over to consumer production too quickly. Stalin's own son Vasily took a hand in this affair. He was a coarse, semiliterate alcoholic, who began the war as a captain and rose to lieutenant general by the end of the war, being placed in charge of the air force of the Moscow Military District, a position totally incommensurate with his abilities.

A number of other prominent military men were arrested on false charges, including major figures in the Soviet navy. . . .

Even Marshal Zhukov, who after the war remained minister of defense and deputy to the supreme commander in chief, as well as being the chief in command of the Soviet forces in Germany, fell into disfavor. . . .

Until after Stalin's death Zhukov was obliged to stay far from Moscow, at first in Odessa, later in the Urals Military District. The press stopped writing about him; people stopped talking about him. Some thought he had been arrested. On the other hand, rumors circulated . . . that he was leading the People's Liberation Army in China. . . .

In 1949–1951 some oblast[1] party organizations were decimated. The "Leningrad Affair" was the most serious of such cases. . . . Indeed, nearly the entire staff of the Leningrad obkom[2] was arrested, and mass repression fell on officials of the local Komsomol, the Soviet executive committee, on raikom[3] leaders, factory managers, scientific personnel, and people in higher education. Thousands of innocent people were arrested, and many of them died in confinement.

Many of the officials who were cut down in 1949–1952 . . . belonged to the new generation of leaders who rose to prominence after 1936–1937 and distinguished themselves during the war. They were significantly different from the preceding generation. As a rule, they completely accepted the cult of Stalin's personality. As their careers progressed, some of them acquired the characteristic features of Stalinists: rudeness and unjustified abruptness in their treatment of subordinates, dictatorial manners, vanity. But many of these younger officials knew little about the crimes Stalin had committed. They took a creative attitude toward their work, displaying great energy and

---

[1]An oblast is a province or large administrative unit of the Communist party.
[2]An obkom is the party committee of an oblast.
[3]A raikom is the party committee of a raion, or district, several of which make up an oblast.

organizational talent. They were basically honorable people who tried to do their jobs as well as possible, and with increasing frequency they came into conflict with such figures in Stalin's inner circle. . . .

In the first years following the war the influence of these younger officials, who had distinguished themselves during the war, increased markedly. Voznesensky,[4] for example, was made first deputy chairman of the USSR Council of Ministers. . . . Sooner or later some of them were bound to become a nuisance to Stalin, as people who might diminish his own authority. That is how death came to Voznesensky, after he had been in charge of Gosplan[5] for eleven years, since December 1937.

A major factor creating a conflict with Stalin was Voznesensky's book on the war economy of the Soviet Union, which was issued in 1947. Its detailed analysis was based on much new factual material, and despite certain mistakes, it soon became popular among economists, who began to cite it on the same level as Stalin's works. Although Stalin had read the manuscript in 1947 and had even signed the authorization for publication, the book was suddenly declared to be anti-Marxist and was withdrawn. At the beginning of 1949 Stalin removed Voznesensky from all his posts, including membership in the Central Committee. Stalin also refused to see his former aide and hear him out.

Voznesensky remained at liberty for several months following his "disgrace." Apparently there was not even a pretext for his arrest. Beria[6] tried to create one—an excuse for decimating the Gosplan leadership—by concocting a case about the loss of some secret papers in Gosplan. . . . Voznesensky spoiled the show by flatly denying the charges and exposing the provocative nature of the trial in his first statement. Fearing further exposure, Beria ordered that Voznesensky appear in court no more and that the other defendants be condemned.

This was only a postponement for Voznesensky. Yet even then, out of office, with Beria after him, he did not lose faith in Stalin. His wife relates that he repeatedly phoned Poskrebyshev, Stalin's secretary, asking him to send over a courier, with whom he sent back memoranda pleading for work and assuring Stalin of his devotion and honesty. But he did not get an answer. He believed that there was some sort of misunderstanding. "While Stalin is getting to the bottom of his," he told his family, "I must not lose time." He continued to work on a new book, "The Political Economy of Communism," which he had begun in 1948, but it remained unfinished. In 1950 he was arrested and shot.

In the postwar period the Soviet intelligentsia was struck some particularly hard blows. Instead of serious, dispassionate analysis of both the achievements and certain errors of Soviet writers, composers, theater people, and so on, Stalin and Zhdanov[7] launched pogrom-style campaigns of denunciation, one after another, which severely damaged Soviet culture at home and its prestige abroad. The persecution began in 1946–1947 with a series of speeches by Zhdanov, resulting in the expulsion of Mikhail Zoshchenko and Anna Akhmatova from the Union of Writers. Other artists were subjected to mudslinging. . . .

Soon the arrests began. . . .

The Jewish theater was in fact destroyed by the security police, the MGB (Ministry of State Security). Many leading actors of this theater were arrested. . . . The head of the theater, Solomon Mikhoels, a prominent public figure as well as a great actor, was killed. . . . Stalin, on Kaganovich's advice, invited Mikhoels to

[4]Nikolai Voznesensky (1903–1950) was a Soviet economist whose rise to administrative prominence began in the late 1930s.

[5]Gosplan is the State Planning Commission, the agency which oversees the Soviet economy and prepares Five-Year Plans for it.

[6]Lavrenty P. Beria (1899–1953) was, from 1938, the head of Stalin's secret police organization and a figure so feared that, following the dictator's death in 1953, the other members of the ruling Politburo engineered his ouster and execution.

[7]Andrei A. Zhdanov (1896–1948) was a junior member of the Politburo who, after the war, became Stalin's chief aide and heir apparent. He is best known for leading the ideological assault on "cosmopolitanism" in the late 1940s.

play the role of King Lear for him in 1946. This remarkable actor was repeatedly invited to give private performances of Shakespearean roles for Stalin. Each time Stalin thanked Mikhoels and praised his acting. But in 1948, with Stalin's knowledge, if not on his initiative, Beria's agents killed Mikhoels in Minsk, then made up the story that he died in an auto accident. A few years later he was posthumously labeled a spy for Anglo-American intelligence.

Those were also the years of an ugly campaign against "cosmopolitanism" and "worship of things foreign," bringing dozens of arrests and thousands of dismissals. It was dangerous even to quote foreign sources, to say nothing of corresponding with foreign scholars. . . .

After the meetings of the Agricultural Academy and the Academy of Medical Sciences in 1948 and 1950 the medical and biological sciences were subjected to unprecedented devastation. Dozens of leading scientists were repressed and thousands were fired or demoted. . . .

Attached to prisoners' dossiers were coded initials describing their "crimes"—for example, KRTD meaning "counter revolutionary Trotskyist activity." In the postwar period new initials appeared: VAT for "praising American technology"; VAD, "praising American democracy"; and PZ, "kowtowing to the West."

In the years 1946–1949 many émigrés who had returned to the Soviet Union after the war were arrested. An intensive campaign for return to the homeland had begun in 1945–1946 among émigrés living in Western Europe and Manchuria. Several thousand people responded to these appeals, of whom most were by this time children of the émigrés of the early twenties. Yet there were some former Russian officers as well. Most of the arrests before 1950 were on the standard charges of "espionage" or "anti-Soviet activity while in residence abroad." . . .

In late 1949 the MGB cooked up a story about the existence of a "pro-American Jewish conspiracy" in the Soviet Union, which was followed by the arrests of leading officials and public figures of Jewish origin. Solomon Lozovsky (Dridzo), who had just turned seventy-four, an Old Bolshevik member of the Central Committee and deputy minister of foreign affairs, was arrested and shot. Almost all the members of the Jewish Antifascist Committee were arrested, and most were shot. . . . In the summer of 1952 a large group of Jewish poets and writers who had been arrested earlier were also shot.

Early in 1949 Mikhail Borodin was arrested and soon shot. In the twenties he had been the Soviet Communist Party's chief political adviser to the Kuomintang revolutionary nationalist movement in China and a personal friend of Sun Yat-sen. From 1941 to 1949 Borodin had worked as editor in chief of the English-language newspaper *Moscow News* as well as chief editor of the Soviet Information Bureau. . . .

The repression of former political prisoners in 1948 and 1949 deserves special attention. While the war was on, they remained in confinement, even those whose terms ended in 1942–1945. The great victory, one would think, should have relieved the tension and permitted a general amnesty. It was expected, and an amnesty was in fact declared—but not for "enemies of the people." On the contrary, in the first years after the war a wave of terror swept through the camps. A vast number of prisoners received illegal extensions of their sentences by five, eight, or ten years. Many politicals were transferred from general to special camps with an "intensified regime." On completion of their sentences some were released from the camps but condemned to "eternal settlement" in northern areas, in the Kolyma region, Siberia, and Kazakhstan. A very few received permission to return to European Russia, but not, as a rule, to the big cities. . . . Although the "lucky ones" were relatively few, almost all were rearrested in 1948–1949. They were sent back to prisons and camps, often without any concrete charges, simply for preventive custody, as it was called. Those few who by some oversight were not rearrested found themselves in a terrible position. No one would hire them or register their right to live anywhere; they often wandered through the country for months and years without roofs over their heads. Some were so desperate they committed suicide; others became beggars; there were even some who returned to "their" camps, hoping to find work as wage laborers.

On November 26, 1948, the Presidium of the USSR Supreme Soviet passed a decree that stated: "Those exiled during the Great Patriotic War to remote districts of the Soviet Union on suspicion of treason, Germans, Chechens, Ingush, Crimean Tatars, . . . are to remain in those places forever, and in the case of flight from their place of registration will be sentenced to twenty years hard labor."

In late 1951 the MGB issued an order which placed all exiles and resettled persons, regardless of how or why they had come to be in that situation, under the terms of the decree of November 26, 1948. The period of exile for all was made permanent, so that those convicted for political reasons during the Stalin years had no hope of ever returning to their families or home towns.

I have been discussing arrests and executions of completely innocent persons, but I shall also take note of a special trend in the postwar years—the emergence of small conspiratorial groups among young people in Leningrad, Moscow, and Georgia whose aim was to fight the cult of Stalin and his dictatorship and to promote the "revival of Leninism." Sometimes group members took on theoretical tasks, such as writing a true history of the party or a critique of Stalin's philosophical and political statements. But in some cases the possibility of Stalin's or Beria's assassination was considered. In Moscow, for example, there was a group of sixteen students who called themselves the "Union of Struggle for the Cause of Revolution" (SBDR—Soyuz Borby za Delo Revoliutsii). . . . As a rule, these groups had strictly Marxist programs; sometimes they put out journals and composed manifestos. . . .

Under conditions of mass terror, all-embracing surveillance, and the universal cult of Stalin these groups were usually quickly discovered and their members arrested. Although matters had never gone beyond plans and discussions and the drafting of programs with any of these groups, the sentences handed down at closed trials were very severe. Three leaders of the SBDR group, . . . who were only nineteen or twenty years old, were shot. The other members of the group were sentenced to twenty-five years imprisonment. They were freed only after the Twentieth Party Congress.

Some writers and Old Bolsheviks also spoke out clandestinely against the crimes of the Stalinist dictatorship. . . .

All such uncoordinated individual protests could not of course disturb the foundations of Stalin's despotism in the slightest.

Heda Margolius Kovály
UNDER A CRUEL STAR

Early in 1948, a Communist-dominated government came to power in Prague, marking the completion of Soviet hegemony throughout Eastern Europe. Czechoslovakia, along with the other members of the newly formed Eastern Bloc, was subjected to severe Stalinization on the political, economic, social, and cultural levels. Only two decades later, with the coming of the Prague Spring in 1968, would the liberalization of the regime appear a viable alternative.

Heda Margolius Kovály's memoir offers compelling insights into the grand hopes, frustrations, challenges, and terror of everyday life during this crucial period in postwar Czechoslovakia. Born into a well-to-do Czech Jewish family, Heda was only a teenager when the Nazis deported her family to a ghetto in

Poland. Although her family perished, she survived the horrors of camp life and managed to escape during an evacuation of concentration camp inmates west, away from the advancing Red Army, to a location where their toil on behalf of the Third Reich could continue. Heda eventually made her way back to Prague and went from one old friend to another until she found someone willing to hide her until the time, a few weeks later, when the Soviets chased the Germans out of the city. Shortly thereafter, Heda was reunited with her beloved Rudolf, a former Czech army officer and university-educated economist. Rudolf was determined to contribute to the rebuilding of Czechoslovak society, and his idealism led him to seek membership in the Communist party. A dedicated patriot and advocate of social justice, Rudolf lent his services to the state through employment in the economics ministry, where he worked on foreign trade issues and specialized in exchange with Western European lands. Heda and Rudolf married, brought a son into the world, and lived the lives of privileged Communist party elites.

In 1952, however, the couple's happiness came to an abrupt end. Police officials arrested Rudolf during a Stalinist-style crackdown within the Communist party. Party leaders had begun the process of "sanitizing" the party when they ordered the arrests of a group of fourteen people a few weeks earlier, which included the highly-placed CP functionary Rudolf Slánský. All of those seized in this purge were accused of "cosmopolitanism"—international connections and an intention to actively undermine socialism. ("Cosmopolitanism" in Soviet-influenced parlance often carried with it connotations of "Jewish global conspiracy," sometimes the international—i.e., non-Soviet-oriented socialist allegiances—associated with Titoism.) Once Rudolf disappeared into police custody, Heda became persona non grata in her formerly comfortable social circle and at her job in a publishing firm. She desperately sought assistance from party bureaucrats and other potentially helpful people in an increasingly hostile climate.

The following afternoon I was sitting in the office of the chairman of the Economic Commission of the Party, Ludvik Frejka. I knew him only slightly, but he had always seemed a kind man and vaguely reminded me of one of my uncles. In fact, he now received me as an older relative might, hunching despondently behind his huge desk. He had already heard about Rudolf's arrest, and I had the feeling that he knew much more, none of it good. He sighed and said, "My dear girl, you have no idea how much I appreciate Rudolf and how much I would like to help both of you. Only a year ago, I might have been able to pull a few strings. Then I was still a deserving old Communist. Today they think of me only as a dirty Jew. I'm in no position to help you. I can't even help myself."

A few weeks later, he, too, was arrested.

It was the same story with Pavel Kavan, Rudolf's friend at the Ministry of Foreign Affairs. He was fired shortly after I saw him and arrested a few months later.

The only other official who agreed to see me was Bohumil Sucharda, then a deputy minister of finance. I knew he could do nothing for Rudolf but I was grateful to him for receiving me courageously in his office and for speaking of my husband with confidence and trust.

Other doors remained firmly closed. Of all the high-ranking comrades who were my husband's colleagues, the only one to pay me a visit was Ota Klicka, our Ambassador to Finland. One day he appeared at the door of our apartment, unexpectedly, and said, "I've known Rudolf since we went to school together and I will never believe he did anything dishonest. I'd stake my life on it. All this is utter nonsense!"

By that time, I had become like a leper, to be avoided by anyone who valued his life. Even the most casual encounter with me could arouse suspicion and invite disaster. I understood that and could bear the isolation better than most people in the same situation. The war had inured me to it and, besides, I knew that I had no right to expose other people to danger. Why should anyone risk his job or the safety of his family or, perhaps, his freedom, just to talk to me? It is natural for people to think first of those for whom they are responsible. If everyone were a hero, what would courage be worth? And so it was largely without bitterness that I watched people suddenly cross the street when they saw me coming or, if they spotted me too late to cross, avert their eyes. To those few who insisted on continuing their acquaintance with me, I myself would say, "Don't stop. Don't talk to me. It makes no sense."

Several good friends, all people I had known for years, stood by me. They believed in Rudolf and it did not occur to them to condemn him, although none were Party members and none had ever agreed with his political views. Almost all of them had already lost their jobs and were living from one day to the next. So far, the parents of the children living in our building still allowed my child to play with theirs, so that he, at least, did not suffer from loneliness. State Security kept tabs on everyone I had met, and as a result some of these people—such as the family of the publisher for whom I had worked before the coup—were ruthlessly interrogated. Not to turn away from me required enormous courage. . . .

My position at the publishing house became more and more unpleasant. No one spoke an unnecessary word to me. Conversations stopped and faces froze whenever I entered a room. These embarrassments, however, did not last very long. About a month after Rudolf's arrest, my editor-in-chief called me into his office and, gently, explained that he had received instructions "from above" to fire me.

I had, of course, been expecting to lose my job for some time but, until it happened, I had refused to worry about it. I knew that if I was to keep my sanity, I had to resolve problems as they came up, one by one, that I had to force myself to think no more than one day ahead. But now there could be no more stalling.

The loss of my job meant not only being unable to support myself and my child. It also provided the police with an excuse to arrest me as a "parasite," an individual who refused to contribute to the building of socialist society. In Czechoslovakia, as in all the Communist countries of Europe at the time, being unemployed was not merely unfortunate; it was illegal. But in a country where all jobs had become government jobs, who would employ an outcast like myself?

I lived a few days of utter horror before help arrived, again through friends. Otto and Milena had managed to persuade the manager of a machine shop which already employed several people with questionable political profiles to give me a job. The wages were minuscule; they did not even suffice to pay my rent. But, at least, I was not unemployed. . . .

Life in Prague, from which I was almost entirely excluded by this time, had acquired a totally negative character. People no longer aspired toward things but away from them. All they wanted was to avoid trouble. They tried not to be seen anywhere, not to talk to anyone, not to attract any attention. Their greatest satisfaction would be that nothing happened, that no one had been fired or arrested or questioned or followed by the secret police. Some fifty thousand people had so far been jailed in our small country. More were disappearing every day. . . .

During this time, I was notified that Rudolf had been expelled from the Party. That was a bad sign; evidently his interrogation had taken a turn for the worse. Because his ouster was announced in the local Party organization, my own situation worsened as well. Until then, the people on our street had simply ignored or avoided me; now a wave of hatred began to swell.

Women particularly would stop and stare at me with venom, whispering among themselves as I walked by. Sometimes a comrade concierge would spit onto the sidewalk after I passed her door, loudly, making sure I noticed. . . .

Under the strain of advocating on Rudolf's behalf against a system determined to see him as an enemy, Heda faced new personal pressures. She lost her job and was forced to scramble to find work in industrial jobs, which paid little and for which she had no previous training. Her status was low, and she bounced from one job to the next. One evening, party officials visited her at home and confiscated almost all of the family's belongings. Soon she would be evicted, and be forced to find a cheap apartment in which she and her son could live. Faced with no work, she feared being labeled a "parasite"—a useless drag on society—that could consign her to death through deprivation of the basic necessities of life. In the midst of these tribulations, Heda fell terribly ill and wound up in hospital care. It was there that she learned of the show trial in which Rudolf entered his "confession"; he would be sentenced to death.

On November 20, 1952, the old lame woman who brought in the newspapers every morning came by as usual. The headlines on the front page swam before my eyes and an odd silence settled over the ward. THE TRIAL FOR THE ANTI-STATE CONSPIRACY OF RUDOLF SLANSKY. For God's sake, what conspiracy? I thought. Those poor people . . . At least my Rudolf could not be involved in this, thank God! He had never had anything to do with Slansky.

Then I skimmed down to the list of the accused. There were fourteen names. Eleven of them were followed by the note "of Jewish origin." Then came the words "sabotage," "espionage," "treason," like salvoes at dawn.

One of the names on the list was Rudolf Margolius. Rudolf Margolius, of Jewish origin.

With unusual clarity I heard the woman in the bed beside me whispering to her neighbor, "You have to read this—it's *Der Stuermer*[1] all over again!" and then the voice of the lame news vendor in the corridor, "You have to read this to see how those swine sold us out to the imperialists, the bastards! They should all be hung! In public!". . .

Day after day, the newspapers carried detailed testimony from the accused, who not only made no attempt to defend themselves, confessing to all crimes as charged, but even kept introducing new accusations against themselves, heaping one on top of another.

Is this all or is there more you did to betray your country? Did you sell out your people to the enemy in other ways?

There is more. In my limitless hatred for the popular democratic order, I also committed the crime of . . .

Aside from the official record of the courtroom proceedings, there was other reading matter, often more shocking than the trial itself. There was the letter-to-the-editor from Lisa London, the wife of one of the three men tried who would be sentenced to life imprisonment. She wrote about a man with whom she had lived for sixteen years, with whom she had raised children and fought against the Nazis in the French Resistance, and the authenticity of her sorrow and despair was clear, "I lived with a traitor . . ."

Another letter-to-the-editor came from a child, from Ludvik Frejka's sixteen-year-old son Thomas: "I demand that my father receive the highest penalty, the death sentence . . . and it is my wish that this letter be read to him."

I cannot be sure now whether those were his exact words, but their meaning is exact. It is hard to say whose fate was more tragic, that of the father who went to his death accompanied by those words or that of the son who would have to go through life with the memory of having written them.

Every day, *Rude Pravo*, the Party newspaper, also carried commentaries on the trials from the pens of various intellectuals. Some were incompetent hacks such as Ivan Skala, a so-called

[1]Notorious propaganda publication from the Nazi era that trafficked in a most vulgar form of anti-Semitism.

poet whose sole claim to immortality lies in the vulgarity of his outbursts against the accused, and whose article about Rudolf ended with the line. "To a dog, a dog's death!" But even noted, respected writers such as Karel Konrad, Ivan Obracht, and Jarmila Glazerova volunteered their poisonous opinions. . . .

The trial in its entirety was being broadcast over the radio. I waited in the corridor until the nurse whom I had overheard talking the night before came in and pleaded with her to let me listen in her private room. Reluctantly, she agreed. That evening, she picked me up in a wheelchair and took me there.

Up until that evening, I had managed to hold on to a glimmer of hope. Rudolf was the only man on trial who was not a veteran Communist; he had joined the Party only after the war. He had never been part of the group around Slansky; he had never held a high position in the Party. There were many other ways in which he did not fit into the group of the accused.

And then, after almost a year, I heard his voice.

As soon as he began to speak, I knew things were very bad. He spoke in such an odd, tense, monotonous voice that, at first, I thought he had been drugged. Then I realized that he was simply reciting something he had memorized. A few times he stopped short, as though he were trying to remember his lines, and then he started up again, like a robot.

The things he said! First about his parents, then about himself, finally about his work. Lie after lie. He had joined the Party only in order to betray it. He had devoted his energies to nothing but espionage and sabotage. He had enriched himself by taking bribes and, as a mercenary in the employ of the imperialists, he had plotted far-reaching conspiracies against the Republic and its people.

Then came the unfortunate trade agreement with England, for which he had received the congratulations of Gottwald himself. This had now been transformed into the most treacherous act of his career, an act of sabotage which had dealt a near-fatal blow to the Czechoslovak economy.

How could they have forced him to such testimony, my Rudolf who had never, in all the years I had known him, ever lied about anything? How could they have made him vilify his parents, who had been murdered in Auschwitz? What had he suffered before he broke down? How had they crushed him? At one point, I heard Rudolf's voice say that he had been trained in espionage in London during the war when, of course, he had spent the entire war as a prisoner in German concentration camps. This item was dutifully reported in the Party newspaper the following day, but later edited out of a book in which the transcript of the trial was published.

Toward the end of the broadcast, I could no longer take it in. The nurse wheeled me back into my ward without a word.

The next morning, Dr. Hulek had me brought into his office. He looked at me unhappily. "please forgive me," he said. "But I've received an order to discharge you immediately. It's a terrible thing to do. You still are in serious need of hospital care. But I don't have the power to keep you here. I have to obey orders."

"Don't worry," I said. "I'll be better off at home. But could you send me in an ambulance?"

"I'm so sorry. Unfortunately . . ."

Later I learned what had happened. The Party had ordered general meetings of employees at all institutions and enterprises, including the hospitals, where a resolution had been read demanding the death penalty for all those accused in what came to be known as the Slansky Trial. At the hospital where I was a patient, the vote was taken by a show of hands, and Dr. Hulek alone did not raise his hand in favor of the resolution.

That did not escape the attention of the comrades. Among the most vehement was Dr. Wicklicka, the physician who had shown me such concern until she discovered my identity. She had attacked Dr. Hulek in public, accusing him of keeping me in the hospital to shield me from the rightful wrath of the people, thereby helping an enemy of the Party and of the working class. This was such a dangerous accusation that even the chief surgeon became frightened. Poor Dr. Hulek, a mere staff physician and the father of three children, had no choice but to act on their orders. . . .

The trip home sapped all my remaining energy. In order to manage the few steps from the front door to the elevator, I had to crawl on all fours. But when I finally lay down in my own bed, I felt relieved. I no longer had to pretend. I no longer had to control my anxiety. At last I was alone. I could prepare for whatever was coming.

The trial of the fourteen men took only one week. Now it was over and everyone waited for the verdict. On November 27, I got up in the morning, put on Rudolf's robe, and shuffled into the abandoned nursery. I lay down on Ivan's bed and switched on the radio. By that time I had become totally oblivious to the things around me, to myself, even to the pain that had returned in full force. And then a voice spurted out of the radio set, flooding the room from floor to ceiling until it forced out the last glimmer of light, the last bubble of air.

"In the trial of the Anti-State Conspiracy . . . Rudolf Slansky, death penalty . . . Vlado Clementis, death penalty . . . Ludvik Frejka, death penalty . . . death penalty . . . death penalty . . . Rudolf Margolius, death penalty."

I do not know how long I lay there, motionless, without a thought, without pain, in total emptiness.

In 1963 the communist party rehabilitated Rudolf posthumously. A new climate of openness gradually began to materialize in Czechoslovakia, and culminated in the Prague Spring of 1968. Heda was among the vocal advocates of the "socialism with a human face" that reformers surrounding the progressive new premier, Alexander Dubček, sought to introduce into the country. This was precisely the form of socialism that had inspired her and Rudolf two decades earlier. Rather than live through yet another repressive phase, Heda joined many other Czechs and Slovaks who fled west after the Soviet-led Warsaw Pact crackdown on the Dubček government. She came to the United States and worked for many years at the Harvard Law School Library, then returned to the Czech Republic after the collapse of communism.

Jozsef Cardinal Mindszenty
"THE POLICE WRENCHED ME AWAY"

Soviet-style attempts to control the most important aspects of people's lives were bound to bring the new Communist regimes of Eastern Europe into conflict with the major churches of the region. Moreover, the Catholic Church—in view of its international ties and claims to universalism, not to mention the Vatican's staunch anti-communism—was bound to be singled out for persecution. In the years following World War II, several prominent members of the Catholic hierarchy in Eastern Europe were put on trial and imprisoned, sometimes on the grounds of collusion with the Nazis.

Jozsef Cardinal Mindszenty (1892–1975), since 1945 the Catholic primate of Hungary, was no Nazi; indeed, he had been imprisoned by the fascist Arrow Cross party during its brief reign of terror toward the end of the war. He came from a conservative and wealthy landowning family, however, and his devout nature took offense at the materialist ideology of Hungary's new rulers. As the Communist party stepped up its efforts to seize Church lands and assert its control over education, Cardinal Mindszenty resorted to militant methods, calling on the faithful to support non-Communist political parties at the polls (while they still existed) and to stage mass demonstrations. When government attempts

to force his resignation proved fruitless, the authorities decided on a kangaroo court to remove the problem.

In the following excerpts from his *Memoirs,* Cardinal Mindszenty describes his arrest and trial. The book appeared in 1974, three years after he left Hungary and went into exile.

The attacks on me and the slanders directed against me continued throughout the summer of 1948. In the autumn, as an immediate preliminary to my arrest, a new campaign was launched under the slogan: "We will annihilate Mindszentyism! The well-being of the Hungarian people and peace between Church and state depend on it." School children and the factory workers were ordered into the streets to demonstrate against me. Communist agents led the demonstrators to the episcopal palace and demanded that the bishops help remove me, "the obstinate and politically short-sighted" cardinal-primate from his position as head of the Church. The bishops rejected these demands. . . .

As had happened previously, before the secularization of the schools, armies of agents appeared in offices and factories to extract signatures to petitions demanding that I be removed from office and tried before a people's court. Village, town, and county governments, all of them under Communist direction, sent letters to the cabinet and Parliament declaring that it was the people's wish that I be punished. On November 18 I responded to this shameless falsification of public opinion in an appeal to the people. . . . I ended with a reminder that some of my predecessors in the office of primate had been martyrs, and added a word of forgiveness for my persecutors.

The edition of the *Magyar Kurir* that carried my appeal was confiscated. Parish priests were forbidden by the police to read it aloud. But the press reported, contrary to the truth, that the clergy had been unwilling to read it because they disagreed with me and would condemn my position. . . .

About 1:30 P.M. on December 23, 1948, squads of policemen surrounded my house. They had driven up in a long column of cars under the command of Police Colonel Gyula Décsi. Without permission, in fact without a warrant, they forced their way into the archiepiscopal palace and conducted a search. . . .

On the eve of the feast of St. Stephen,[1] the first martyr, in whose honor was built my titular church in Rome, Santo Stefano Rotondo, I was arrested. Once again an unusually large police squadron came to the house under the direction of Police Colonel Décsi. . . .

The police wrenched me away, dragged me down to the gate, and forced me into a big car with curtained windows. On my right sat Colonel Décsi, on my left a major. Beside the driver, and facing me, sat policemen with submachine guns. In this way I was taken from my archiepiscopal see and driven through the night to Budapest. . . .

The column of police cars stopped in front of 60 Andrássy Street. I was ordered to get out of the car. Then I was led between two closely packed rows of policemen into the notorious building. Here Hungarians who had been taught their trade by Hitler's Gestapo had already created, during the period of the German occupation, a gruesome place of torture, a true center of terror. Even then passers-by who had business in the vicinity gave the building as wide a berth as possible, or turned their heads if they had to pass in front of it. Now the whole neighborhood was given its character by the movement of prisoners and police cars. The number of arrests was rising to a fearful extent, so that all the buildings in the neighborhood had been made into jails. . . .

In the fourth week of my detention I was required to choose a defense attorney. Right from the start I had demanded one, and as I have mentioned I wanted to entrust my friend József Gróh with this task. But he himself

[1]December 26.

was already under arrest. I therefore asked the president of the bar association to take the case. Colonel Décsi informed me, however, that he had refused. Later I learned that in the meantime my mother had asked Endre Farkas, a well-known Budapest lawyer, to defend me. But he was not allowed to see me at all during the investigation. Finally, during the fourth week Décsi spoke of the necessity for defense counsel and recommended Dr. Kálmán Kiczkó. "Do as you like," I said, for my spirit was already broken, and I signed a letter authorizing Kiczkó to take the case. That must have been some time around January 20. The lawyer did not come to see me until the end of the month, after the interrogation was over. I did not know him, but later heard that he had played a part in Hungary's first period of communism in 1919. There could be no doubt concerning what side he was on.

I met with this "defense" attorney in a room on the first floor of the prison. A guard was present at our conference. The conversation lasted for no more than fifteen minutes. . . . I told him about the nocturnal interrogations, about the demand that I sign statements already drawn up, about the beatings and the torture of sleeplessness.

He promptly declared: "If you want to bring up such matters at the trial, I won't take your case. None of that can be proved. Talking about it would only worsen your situation. The only hope of obtaining a more lenient sentence is to keep quiet about such incidents. That is much wiser." In other words, a defense counsel's function in a show trial is to further the interests of the authorities. I imagine that Kiczkó never even read the records of my interrogation. He was simply given a text for the part he was to play, so that he could quickly get it letter-perfect in time for the trial. The files on my case were by now so vast that it would in any case have been impossible for him to look the material over in so short a time. . . .

We defendants sat opposite the judges. To our right were the places for the defense attorneys, to our left the police. . . . The stenographers had their seats behind the judges. Alongside them, separated by a glass wall, were the radio technicians who took care of the microphones and passed on the "confessions" to the reporters. These confessions must all have been prepared beforehand, for the tape recordings and the newspaper stories frequently contained contradictory statements and invariably showed great differences. . . .

Kiczkó demonstrated his talents for the last time when he answered the prosecution's summation. I scarcely think any of his colleagues abroad is likely to match this particular "masterpiece" of his. For to my disadvantage, but to the great advantage of those who staged the trial, my counsel stated:

1. At all times, including the period he was in Andrássy Street and during the trial itself, the defendant had the opportunity to conduct his defense without interference.
2. He confessed fully to all the charges.
3. He must be regarded as a victim of the Vatican.
4. The Church is an enemy of the state because the latter deprived it of land and took away its schools. "My client erred when he thought that the secularization of the schools would promote religious and moral decadence among the youth."
5. The defendant lived in a kind of ivory tower and therefore failed to observe the great progress and reconstruction in the country.
6. He was an inexperienced cleric who rose to the highest office in the church.
7. He confirms what the prosecutor has frequently stressed: There is no religious persecution in Hungary.
8. He affirms the necessity of an agreement between Church and state.
9. In view of extenuating circumstances the defense moves that the sentence of life imprisonment be granted instead of the death penalty demanded by the prosecution.

Kiczkó several times referred to my "repentance." Before this altogether astonishing defense summation the prosecutor had delivered his summation, demanding the defendant's execution. . . .

The public proceedings lasted for three days. At their end the court was convinced we were all guilty and imposed severe prison sentences on all of us.

I was sentenced to life imprisonment and Jusztin Baranyay to fifteen years, since we were regarded as the leaders of the organization that had aimed at overthrowing the Republic—the crime specified in the notorious "hangman's law." András Zakár was sentenced to six years for participation in the organization. Pál Esterházy was given fifteen years because he had provided the organization with financial aid. . . .

According to the court, there was not the slightest doubt that we were guilty. No evidence of armed uprisings or riot was required, for any opposition to the Republic was regarded as an infraction of the law. Thus any attempt to change the form of government by peaceful and legal means was also a criminal offense. In reality we had not aimed at overthrowing the Republic either by peaceable or by violent means. The prosecution had only cunningly twisted some of my acts to make it seem so. My actual crimes consisted in having fought against the illegalities of the communist rulers, in having defended the religious freedom the laws solemnly guaranteed, and in having attempted to preserve the Catholic schools and religious instruction and to prevent the introduction of atavist monopoly in education. . . .

The authorities tried to cover up their lack of evidence and legality by shrill propaganda. From the moment of my arrest to the last scene in the judicial spectacle, the controlled press kept up its ranting about "traitors" who meant to rob the Hungarian people of their newly won democratic freedoms.

Czesław Miłosz
THE CAPTIVE MIND

The postwar creation of the Eastern Bloc under Soviet auspices was accompanied by its Stalinization. That meant the concentration of political power in the hands of a single party subservient to Moscow and a centralized command economy overseeing the processes of heavy industrialization and collectivization. Significantly, it also entailed the imposition of a uniform culture yoked to the dictates of "socialist realism," an artistic ideology hammered out in the USSR in the 1930s. Socialist realism required works of art—whether in literature, music, painting, or film—that were immediately accessible to the masses and ideologically edifying. Artists were charged with depicting reality as it underwent its inevitably triumphant changeover to socialism. The impact of such rigidly enforced didacticism on creative endeavor was deadly. Intellectual life throughout Eastern Europe became arid and stultifying as well as dangerous.

No more acute an analysis of the cultural Sovietization of Eastern Europe exists than *The Captive Mind*. It came from the pen of Czesław Miłosz (1911–2004), one of the greatest poets of the twentieth century. Milosz was born in Lithuania but identified with the multiethnic character of pre-partition Poland. He spent the Second World War in German-occupied Warsaw, where he participated in the remarkable cultural life sponsored by the Polish underground. After the war, he became the cultural attaché of the People's Republic of Poland in Paris. In 1951

he defected and settled in France. *The Captive Mind* appeared two years later. Miłosz emigrated to the United States in 1960 and later became a U.S. citizen. In 1961 he accepted a professorship in the Department of Slavic Languages and Literatures at the University of California at Berkeley. In 1980 Miłosz received the Nobel Prize for Literature. After the fall of communism in Eastern Europe, he divided his time between Berkeley and Kraków, where he died in 2004.

The following excerpts from *The Captive Mind* come from the penultimate chapter in the book, which is entitled "Man, this Enemy."

In the people's democracies, a battle is being waged for mastery over the human spirit. Man must be made to understand, for then he will accept. Who are the enemies of the new system? The people who do not understand. They fail to understand because their minds work feebly or else badly.

In every capital of Central and Eastern Europe the windows in the Central Committee buildings are illuminated late into the night. Behind their desks sit men well-versed in the writings of Lenin and Stalin. Not the least of their tasks is to define the position of the enemy. . . .

Different groups of people are the main object of study. The least important is the propertied class which was dispossessed by the nationalization of factories and mines and by the agricultural reform. Their number is insignificant; their way of thinking amusingly old-fashioned. They are no problem. In time they will die off—if need be, with a little help.

The petty bourgeoisie, that is the small merchants and craftsmen, cannot be taken so lightly. They constitute a powerful force, one that is deeply rooted in the masses. Hardly is one clandestine workshop or store liquidated in one neighborhood or city than another springs up elsewhere. Restaurants hide behind a sliding wall of a private house; shoemakers and tailors work at home for their friends. In fact, everything that comes under the heading of speculation sprouts up again and again. And no wonder! State and municipal stores consistently lack even the barest essentials. . . .

What is worse, this matter involves the peasant problem. Peasants, who make up the majority of the population of the country, have a middle-class mentality. They are more deeply attached to their few little hectares of field than the storekeepers due to their little shops. As late as the nineteenth century they were still living in bondage. They oppose collectivization because they see it as a return to a state their fathers found unbearable. To leap out of bed at the signal of an official on a collective farm is just as hateful as to do so at the sound of a gong rung by the overseer of an estate. . . .

But the peasants are not dangerous. They may beat up a Party boss or even kill him in a burst of desperation, but nothing more. When the state is the sole buyer of their produce, and when they cannot voice their protest at the amount of tribute the state demands of them, they are powerless. The security police can easily handle recalcitrants, especially since it can complain of no lack of informers, now that informing has become an excellent means of saving oneself. The peasants are a leaderless mass. . . .

Workers are far more important than peasants. Most of them are antagonistic to the new system. That is understandable. They resent the norms they must fill. Those norms are constantly rising. . . .

. . . [W]orkers are told that a strike is a crime. Against whom are they to strike? Against themselves? After all, the means of production belong to them, the state belongs to them. But such an explanation is not very convincing. The workers, who dare not state aloud what they want, know that the goals of the state are far from identical with their own. . . .

A strike requires a certain minimum of organization. That is why nothing else makes Party dialecticians so uneasy. The workers are the only class capable of organized action—that Marxist principle has never been forgotten. No action, however, is possible without leaders. If the leaders reason correctly, that is, if they understand the necessities of the historic process, then the workers as a mass will be unable to protest.

Everything, thus, takes us back to the question of mastery over the mind. Every possible opportunity for education and advancement is offered to the more energetic and active individuals among the workers. The new, incredibly extensive bureaucracy is recruited from among the young people of working-class origin. The road before them is open, open but guarded; their thinking must be based on the firm principles of dialectical materialism. Schools, theaters, films, painting, literature, and the press all shape their thinking. . . .

Dialectical materialism, Russian-style, is nothing more than nineteenth-century science vulgarized to the second power. Its emotional and didactic components are so strong that they change all proportions. Although the Method was scientific at its origins, when it is applied to humanistic disciplines it often transforms them into edifying stories adapted to the needs of the moment. But there is no escape once a man enters upon these convenient bridges. Centuries of human history, with their thousands upon thousands of intricate affairs, are reduced to a few, most generalized terms. Undoubtedly, one comes closer to the truth when one sees history as the expression of the class struggle rather than a series of private quarrels among kings and nobles. But precisely because such an analysis of history comes closer to the truth, it is more dangerous. It gives the illusion of *full knowledge;* it supplies answers to all questions, answers which merely run around in a circle repeating a few formulas. . . .

The son of a worker, subjected to such an education, cannot think otherwise than as the school demands. Two times two equals four. The press, literature, painting, films, and theater all illustrate what he learns, just as the lives of saints and martyrs serve as illustrations of theology. It would be wrong to assert that a dual set of values no longer exists. The resistance against the new set of values is, however, emotional. It survives, but it is beaten whenever it has to explain itself in rational terms. A man's subconscious or not-quite-conscious life is richer than his vocabulary. His opposition to this new philosophy of life is much like a toothache. Not only can he not express the pain in words, but he cannot even tell you which tooth is aching. . . .

Above all, there exists the question of religion. This problem still persists despite the many weak points in Christianity that can be attacked successfully. . . . [R]eligious needs exist in the masses and it would be a mistake, from the Party's point of view, to deny them. Perhaps they will disappear once the entire population has been transformed into workers; but no one knows when that will happen. We are dealing here with imponderable elements. Mysterious, indeed, is the instinct which makes man revolt against a reasonable explanation of all phenomena. Christianity's armor is so thin in the twentieth century, a child in school is so deeply immersed in the new way of thinking, and yet the zone of shadow eludes the light of reason. We suddenly stumble upon puzzles. . . .

. . . [T]he masses in the people's democracies behave like a man who wants to cry out in his sleep and cannot find his voice. They not only dare not speak, they do not know *what* to say. Logically, everything is as it should be. From the philosophical premises to the collectivization of the farms, everything makes up a single closed whole, a solid and imposing pyramid. The lone individual inevitably asks himself if his antagonism is not wrong; all he can oppose to the entire propaganda apparatus are simply his irrational desires. Should he not, in fact, be ashamed of them?

The Party is vigilantly on guard lest these longings be transmuted into new and vital intellectual formulas adapted to new conditions and therefore capable of winning over the masses. Neither the reaction nor the Church are as great a menace as is *heresy*. If men familiar with dialectics and able to present dialectical materialism in a new light appear, they must be rendered harmless at once. A professor of philosophy who clings to obsolete "idealistic" concepts is not particularly dangerous. He loses his lectureship, but he is allowed to earn a living by editing texts, etc. Whereas a professor who, using the names of Marx and Engels, permits himself departures from orthodoxy sows seeds from which alarming crops may grow. . . .

When one considers the matter logically, it becomes obvious that intellectual terror is a principle that Leninism-Stalinism can never forsake, even if it should achieve victory on a world scale. The enemy, in a potential form, will *always* be there; the only friend will be the man who accepts the doctrine 100 per cent. If he accepts only 99 per cent, he will necessarily have to be considered a foe, for from that remaining 1 per cent a new church can arise. . . .

To forestall doubt, the Party fights any tendency to delve into the depths of a human being, especially in literature and art. Whoever reflects on "man" in general, on his inner needs and longings, is accused of bourgeois sentimentality. Nothing must ever go beyond the description of man's behavior as a member of a social group. This is necessary because the Party, treating man exclusively as the by-product of social forces, believes that he becomes the type of being he pictures himself to be. He is a social monkey. *What is not expressed does not exist*. Therefore if one forbids men to explore the depths of human nature, one destroys in them the urge to make such explorations; and the depths in themselves slowly becomes unreal. . . .

. . . [I]f the literature of socialist realism is useful, it is so only to the Party. It is supposed to present reality not as a man *sees* it (that was the trait of the previous realism, the so-called "critical"), but as he *understands* it. Understanding that reality is in motion, and that in every phenomenon what is being born and what is dying exist simultaneously—dialectically speaking, this is the battle between the "new" and the "old"—the author should praise everything that is budding and censure everything that is becoming the past. In practice, this means that the author should perceive elements of the class struggle in every phenomenon. Carrying this reasoning further, the doctrine forces all art to become didactic. Since *only* the Stalinists have the right to represent the proletariat, which is the rising class, everything that is "new" and therefore praiseworthy results from Party strategy and tactics. "Socialist realism" depends on an identification of the "new" with the proletariat and the proletariat with the Party. It presents model citizens, i.e. Communists, and class enemies. Between these two categories come the men who vacillate. Eventually, they must—according to which tendencies are stronger in them—land in one camp or the other. When literature is not dealing with prefabricated figures of friends and foes, it studies the process of metamorphosis by which men arrive at total salvation or absolute damnation in Party terms.

This way of treating literature (and every art) leads to absolute conformism. Is such conformism favorable to serious artistic work? That is doubtful. The sculptures of Michelangelo are completed acts that endure. There was a time when they did not exist. Between their non-existence and existence lies the creative act, which cannot be understood as a submission to the "wave of the future." The creative act is associated with a feeling of freedom that is, in its turn, born in the struggle against an apparently invincible resistance. Whoever truly creates is alone. . . .

This is the framework within which life develops in the people's democracies; but it is a life that moves at a frenzied tempo. "Socialist construction" is not merely a slogan; it is taken in a quite literal sense. The observer's eye meets scaffolding everywhere; new factories, offices, and government buildings spring up almost overnight; production curves rise; the masses change character with unheard-of rapidity; more and more persons become state functionaries and acquire a certain minimum of "political education." The press, literature, films, and theater magnify these attainments. If a man from Mars, knowing nothing of earthly affairs, were to judge the various countries of the world on the basis of Soviet books, he would conclude that the East is inhabited by rational, intelligent beings, while the West is peopled by dwarfs and degenerates. Small wonder that so many intelligent Westerners, for whom the Soviet Union and its satellites are the legendary isles of happiness, arrive at a similar conclusion.

The citizen of the people's democracies is immune to the kind of neurosis that takes such manifold forms in capitalist countries. In the West a man subconsciously regards society as unrelated to him. Society indicates the limits he must not exceed; in exchange for this he receives a guarantee that no one will meddle excessively in his affairs. If he loses it's his own fault; let psychoanalysis help him. In the East there is no boundary between man and society. His game, and whether he loses or wins, is a public matter. He is never alone. If he loses it is not because of indifference on the part of his environment, but because his environment keeps him under such minute scrutiny. Neuroses as they are known in the West result, above all, from man's aloneness; so even if they were allowed to practice, psychoanalysts would not earn a penny in the people's democracies. . . .

The supreme goal of doing away with the struggle for existence—which was the theoretician's dream—has not been and cannot be achieved while every man fears every other man. The state which, according to Lenin, was supposed to wither away gradually is now all-powerful. It holds a sword over the head of every citizen; it punishes him for every careless word. The promises made from time to time that the state will begin to wither away when the entire earth is conquered lack any foundation. Orthodoxy cannot release its pressure on men's minds; it would no longer be an orthodoxy. There is always some disparity between facts and theories. The world is full of contradictions. Their constant struggle is what Hegel called dialectic. That dialectic of reality turns against the dialectic fashioned by the Center; but then so much the worse for reality. It has been said that the twentieth century is notable for its synthetic products—synthetic rubber, synthetic gasoline, etc. Not to be outdone, the Party has processed an artificial dialectic whose only resemblance to Hegel's philosophy is purely superficial. The Method is effective just so long as it wages war against an enemy. A man exposed to its influence is helpless. How can he fight a system of symbols? In the end he submits; and this is the secret of the Party's power, not some fantastic narcotic. . . .

The philosophy of History emanating from Moscow is not just an abstract theory, it is a material force that uses guns, tanks, planes, and all the machines of war and oppression. All the crushing might of an armed state is hurled against any man who refuses to accept the New Faith. At the same time, Stalinism attacks him from within, saying his opposition is caused by his "class consciousness," just as psychoanalysts accuse their foes of wanting to preserve their complexes.

Still, it is not hard to imagine the day when millions of obedient followers of the New Faith may suddenly turn against it. That day would come the moment the Center lost its material might, not only because fear of military force would vanish, but because success is an integral part of this philosophy's argument. If it lost, it would prove itself wrong by its own definition; it would stand revealed as a false faith, defeated by its own god, reality. The citizens of the Imperium of the East long for nothing so much as liberation from the terror their own thought creates.

3 Dissidence and Popular Revolt

Opportunities to oppose the Communist regimes of the Eastern Bloc—even by peaceful means—were virtually nonexistent during Stalin's lifetime. Control was thorough, punishment severe. The sole way to criticize Party rule and survive seemed to be publishing abroad while already living within the safe confines of a foreign country. Only after Stalin's death in 1953 did Communist authorities begin to relax their grip on society, allowing for a measure of artistic freedom and political discussion that the U.S.S.R. had not experienced since the 1920s. When

Soviet leader Nikita Khrushchev initiated a de-Stalinization campaign in 1956, moreover, criticism of his predecessor's crimes and excesses began to receive official encouragement and support. This state-sponsored effort, however, did not last. Khrushchev's successors—above all, Leonid Brezhnev (1906–1982)—led a crackdown on dissidents as part of their neo-Stalinist program.

If full-fledged dissidents in the Eastern Bloc remained few, discontent with Communist rule was widespread. That it could, on occasion, assume organized form on a mass scale is most convincingly demonstrated by the events of 1956 in Hungary and of 1968 in Czechoslovakia. While different from one another in certain respects (Hungary proved much bloodier then Czechoslovakia, for example), the similarities of the two situations are noteworthy. In both cases, an Eastern European people confidently asserted its autonomy with respect to the Soviet Union, in the belief that it was safe to do so. The Hungarians were bolstered in their desire for reform by Nikita Khrushchev's "Secret Speech" earlier in the same year and its repudiation of Stalinism. Khrushchev's decision to pay a call on Tito also acknowledged the mistakenness of past Soviet policies and even hinted at an endorsement of the idea of "alternate paths to communism." The Czechs were encouraged by the toleration that the Soviet leadership initially demonstrated toward their "Prague Spring," a series of reforms that reduced party control. In both cases, too, the move toward change eventually proved too radical for the Kremlin. The introduction of political alternatives threatened Communist domination, while withdrawal from the Warsaw Pact was bound to undermine Soviet military hegemony in the region. The possibility that a successful break with communism or the Red Army could lead other Bloc members to follow suit made a third parallel inevitable—namely, the use of military force to restore the old order. A Soviet-led invasion crushed the Hungarian Revolution and "socialism with a human face," followed by repressive measures that at least temporarily set back the cause of reform. The fate of Hungary in 1956 and of Czechoslovakia in 1968 demonstrated that the Soviet Union was determined on remaining the master of Eastern Europe; the crisis of 1968 even occasioned an official pronouncement to that effect—the Brezhnev Doctrine. For the time being, fundamental change in the Eastern Bloc was not an option.

Milovan Djilas
THE NEW CLASS

Milovan Djilas's book *The New Class: An Analysis of the Communist System* (1957), from which the following excerpts are taken, provides helpful insights into the explosion of discontent in Hungary, Czechoslovakia, and Poland under Soviet control. Djilas (1911–1995), a Yugoslav author and political commentator, became a communist after finishing his studies in 1933. Although he began as a close friend of Marshal Tito, the all-powerful leader of Yugoslavia, in 1953 he turned critic, not only of his friend, but also of Communist practice and ideology. Jailed for his heresies in 1956, he wrote his assessment of the Communist system, showing its connection to the unprecedented new class of political bureaucrats dominating state and society. Under communism, the state did not wither away,

as early theorists had expected. On the contrary, it grew more powerful, thanks to that highly privileged "exploiting and governing class." Aware of the dynamics of nationalism at work underneath each Communist regime, Djilas pointed to the weaknesses of Communist rule and the growing desire for national self-assertion among the peoples of the Soviet satellite states.

Earlier revolutions, particularly the so-called bourgeois ones, attached considerable significance to the establishment of individual freedoms immediately following cessation of the revolutionary terror. Even the revolutionaries considered it important to assure the legal status of the citizenry. Independent administration of justice was an inevitable final result of all these revolutions. The Communist regime in the U.S.S.R. is still remote from independent administration of justice after forty years of tenure. The final results of earlier revolutions were often greater legal security and greater civil rights. This cannot be said of the Communist revolution. . . .

In contrast to earlier revolutions, the Communist revolution, conducted in the name of doing away with classes, has resulted in the most complete authority of any single new class. Everything else is sham and an illusion. . . .

This new class, the bureaucracy, or more accurately the political bureaucracy, has all the characteristics of earlier ones as well as some new characteristics of its own. Its origin had its special characteristics also, even though in essence it was similar to the beginnings of other classes. . . . The new class may be said to be made up of those who have special privileges and economic preference because of the administrative monopoly they hold. . . .

The mechanism of Communist power is perhaps the simplest which can be conceived, although it leads to the most refined tyranny and the most brutal exploitation. The simplicity of this mechanism originates from the fact that one party alone, the Communist Party, is the backbone of the entire political, economic, and ideological activity. The entire public life is at a standstill or moves ahead, falls behind or turns around according to what happens in the party forums. . . .

. . . Communist control of the social machine . . . restricts certain government posts to party members. These jobs, which are essential in any government but especially in a Communist one, include assignments with police, especially the secret police; and the diplomatic and officers corps, especially positions in the information and political services. In the judiciary only top positions have until now been in the hands of Communists. . . .

Only in a Communist state are a number of both specified and unspecified positions reserved for members of the party. The Communist government, although a class structure, is a party government; the Communist army is a party army; and the state is a party state. More precisely, Communists tend to treat the army and the state as their exclusive weapons.

The exclusive, if unwritten, law that only party members can become policemen, officers, diplomats, and hold similar positions, or that only they can exercise actual authority, creates a special privileged group of bureaucrats. . . .

The entire governmental structure is organized in this manner. Political positions are reserved exclusively for party members. Even in non-political governmental bodies Communists hold the strategic positions or oversee administration. Calling a meeting at the party center or publishing an article is sufficient to cause the entire state and social mechanism to begin functioning. If difficulties occur anywhere, the party and the police very quickly correct the "error." . . .

The classes and masses do not exercise authority, but the party does so in their name. In every party, including the most democratic, leaders play an important role to the extent that the party's authority becomes the authority of the leaders. The so-called "dictatorship of the proletariat," which is the beginning of and under the best circumstances becomes the authority of the party, inevitably evolves into the dictatorship of the leaders. In a totalitarian government of this type, the dictatorship of the proletariat is a theoretical justification, or ideological mask at best, for the authority of some oligarchs. . . .

Freedoms are formally recognized in Communist regimes, but one decisive condition is a prerequisite for exercising them: freedoms must be utilized only in the interest of the system of "socialism," which the Communist leaders represent, or to buttress their rule. This practice, contrary as it is to legal regulations, inevitably had to result in the use of exceptionally severe and unscrupulous methods by police and party bodies. . . .

. . . It has been impossible in practice to separate police authority from judicial authority. Those who arrest also judge and enforce punishments. The circle is closed: the executive, the legislative, the investigating, the court, and the punishing bodies are one and the same. . . .

Communist parliaments are not in a position to make decisions on anything important. Selected in advance as they are, flattered that they have been thus selected, representatives do not have the power or the courage to debate even if they wanted to do so. Besides, since their mandate does not depend on the voters, representatives do not feel that they are answerable to them. Communist parliaments are justifiably called "mausoleums" for the representatives who compose them. Their right and role consist of unanimously approving from time to time that which has already been decided for them from the wings. . . .

Though history has no record of any other system so successful in *checking* its opposition as the Communist dictatorship, none ever has *provoked* such profound and far-reaching discontent. It seems that the more the conscience is crushed and the less the opportunities for establishing an organization exist, the greater the discontent. . . .

In addition to being motivated by the historical need for rapid industrialization, the Communist bureaucracy has been compelled to establish a type of economic system designed to insure the perpetuation of its own power. Allegedly for the sake of a classless society and for the abolition of exploitation, it has created a closed economic system, with forms of property which facilitate the party's domination and its monopoly. At first, the Communists had to turn to this "collectivistic" form for objective reasons. Now they continue to strengthen this form—without considering whether or not it is in the interest of the national economy and of further industrialization—for their own sake, for an exclusive Communist class aim. They first administered and controlled the entire economy for so-called ideal goals; later they did it for the purpose of maintaining their absolute control and domination. That is the real reason for such far-reaching and inflexible political measures in the Communist economy. . . .

A citizen in the Communist system lives oppressed by the constant pangs of his conscience, and the fear that he has transgressed. He is always fearful that he will have to demonstrate that he is not an enemy of socialism, just as in the Middle Ages a man constantly had to show his devotion to the Church. . . .

. . . Tyranny over the mind is the most complete and most brutal type of tyranny; every other tyranny begins and ends with it. . . .

History will pardon Communists for much, establishing that they were forced into many brutal acts because of circumstances and the need to defend their existence. But the stifling of every divergent thought, the exclusive monopoly over thinking for the purpose of defending their personal interests, will nail the Communists to a cross of shame in history. . . .

In essence, Communism is only one thing, but it is realized in different degrees and manners in every country. Therefore it is possible to speak of various Communist systems, i.e., of various forms of the same manifestation.

The differences which exist between Communist states—differences that Stalin attempted futilely to remove by force—are the result, above all, of diverse historical backgrounds. . . . When ascending to power, the Communists face in the various countries different cultural and technical levels and varying social relationships, and are faced with different national intellectual characters. . . . Of the former international proletariat, only words and empty dogmas remained. Behind them stood the naked national and international interests, aspirations, and plans of the various Communist oligarchies, comfortably entrenched. . . .

. . . The Communist East European countries did not become satellites of the U.S.S.R. because they benefited from it, but because they were too weak to prevent it. As soon as they become stronger, or as soon as favorable conditions are created, a yearning for independence and for protection of "their own people" from Soviet hegemony will rise among them.

The subordinate Communist governments in East Europe can, in fact must, declare their independence from the Soviet government. No one can say how far this aspiration for independence will go and what disagreements will result. The result depends on numerous unforeseen internal and external circumstances. However, there is no doubt that a national Communist bureaucracy aspires to more complete authority for itself. This is demonstrated . . . by the current unconcealed emphasis on "one's own path to socialism," which has recently come to light sharply in Poland and Hungary. The central Soviet government has found itself in difficulty because of the nationalism existing even in those governments which it installed in the Soviet republics (Ukraine, Caucasia), and still more so with regard to those governments installed in the East European countries. Playing an important role in all of this is the fact that the Soviet Union was unable, and will not be able in the future, to assimilate the economies of the East European countries.

The aspirations toward national independence must of course have greater impetus. These aspirations can be retarded and even made dormant by external pressure or by fear on the part of the Communists of "imperialism" and the "bourgeoisie," but they cannot be removed. On the contrary, their strength will grow.

Andor Heller
THE HUNGARIAN REVOLUTION, 1956

In 1956, the Hungarian yearning for escape from Soviet domination exploded. On October 23, a student demonstration in Budapest, the capital, provided the spark. Throughout the country, Communist officials were ousted and the Soviet troops forced to withdraw. A coalition government under Imre Nagy was formed to restore Hungary's independence; it even appeared that the country would withdraw from the newly formed Warsaw Pact controlled by Moscow. In Budapest especially, the popular excitement over the country's liberation from the Soviet yoke knew no bounds, as described in the following eyewitness account.

I saw freedom rise from the ashes of Communism in Hungary: a freedom that flickered and then blazed before it was beaten down—but not extinguished—by masses of Russian tanks and troops.

I saw young students, who had known nothing but a life under Communist and Russian control, die for a freedom about which they had only heard from others or from their own hearts.

I saw workers, who had been pushed to the limit of endurance by their hopeless existence under Communism, lay down their tools and take up arms in a desperate bid to win back freedom for our country.

I saw a girl of fourteen blow up a Russian tank, and grandmothers walk up to Russian cannons.

I watched a whole nation—old and young, men and women, artists and engineers and doctors, clerks and peasants and factory workers—become heroes overnight as they rose up in history's first successful revolt against Communism.

Tuesday, October 23, 1956

No Hungarian will forget this day. . . .

. . . In spite of the cold and fog, students are on the streets early in the morning, marching and singing. No one shows up for classes at the universities. After a decade of Communist control over our country, we are going to show our feelings spontaneously, in our own way—something never allowed under Communist rules.

The students carry signs with slogans that until now we have never dared express except to members of our own family—and not in every family. The slogans read:

RUSSIANS GO HOME!

LET HUNGARY BE INDEPENDENT!

BRING RAKOSI TO JUSTICE!

WE WANT A NEW LEADERSHIP!

SOLIDARITY WITH THE POLISH PEOPLE!

WE TRUST IMRE NAGY—BRING IMRE NAGY INTO THE GOVERNMENT!

The walls of Budapest are plastered with leaflets put up by the students during the night. They list the fourteen demands adopted at the stormy meetings held at the universities:

1. Withdrawal of all Soviet troops from Hungary.
2. Complete economic and political equality with the Soviet Union, with no interference in Hungary's internal affairs.
3. Publication of Hungary's trade agreements, and a public report on Hungary's reparations payments to the U.S.S.R.
4. Information on Hungary's uranium resources, their exploitation, and the concessions given to the U.S.S.R.
5. The calling of a Hungarian Communist Party congress to elect a new leadership.
6. Reorganization of the government, with Imre Nagy as Premier.
7. A public trial of Mihaly Farkas and Matyas Rakosi [notorious Stalinists].
8. A secret general multi-party election.
9. The reorganization of Hungary's economy on the basis of her actual resources.
10. Revision of the workers' output quotas, and recognition of the right to strike.
11. Revision of the system of compulsory agricultural quotas.
12. Equal rights for individual farmers and cooperative members.
13. Restoration of Hungary's traditional national emblem and the traditional Hungarian army uniforms.
14. Destruction of the giant statue of Stalin.

During the morning a radio announcement from the Ministry of Interior bans all public meetings and demonstrations "until further notice," and word is sent to the universities that the student demonstrations cannot be held. At that moment the students decide that the will to freedom is greater than the fear of the A. V. H.—the Russian-controlled Hungarian secret police. The meeting will be held! . . .

At 3 P.M. there are 25,000 of us at the Petofi Monument. We weep as Imre Sinkovits, a young actor, declaims the *Nemzett Dal* ("National Song"), Sandor Petofi's [a great Hungarian poet and revolutionary hero in the anti-Austrian rebellion of 1848–1849] ode to Hungary and our 1848 "freedom revolution." With tears in our eyes, we repeat the refrain with Sinkovits: . . .

We swear, we swear, we will no longer remain slaves.

The student voices are tense with feeling. No policeman or Communist official is in sight. The young people are keeping order on their own.

. . . [W]e have swelled to some 60,000. Someone grabs a Hungarian flag and cuts out the hated hammer and sickle that the Communists had placed at its center.

One after another of the purified Hungarian flags appear. Suddenly someone remembers to put the old Kossuth [Lajos Kossuth was the leader of the Hungarian uprising of 1848–1849] coat-of-arms on the flag, in place of the Communist emblem.

We have created a new flag of freedom!

Meantime we all sing the . . . *Appeal to the Nation,* and the *Hungarian National Hymn* that begins "God Bless the Magyar"—both of which had been banned under the Communist rule.

We cannot get enough. The actor Ferenc Bessenyei recites the *National Song* again, and follows once more with *Appeal to the Nation.* Peter Veres, the head of the Hungarian Writers Federation, leaps to the top of a car equipped with a loudspeaker. He reads the Hungarian writers' demands for more freedom—many of them the same as those in the fourteen points of the students.

The day is ending. We begin to march toward the Parliament Building. The crowds are peaceful, marching in orderly lines. We carry the new Hungarian flag.

As we march we are joined by workers leaving their jobs. By the time we arrive in Kossuth Lajos Square there are at least 150,000 of us, in front of the Parliament Building. On the square, all traffic stops.

Suddenly everyone makes torches of newspapers, and lights them. It is a marvelous spectacle—ten thousand torches burning in the Square before the Parliament Building.

But finally, Imre Nagy appears on the balcony. "Comrades!" he begins, but the crowd interrupts him with a roar: "There are no more comrades! We are all Hungarians!"

The crowd grows still bigger, and we head for the Stalin statue. Now the demonstration has spread so large that it is going on simultaneously in three places: at the Parliament Building; in Stalin Square, where the crowd is trying to pull down the huge Stalin statue with tractors and ropes; and at the building of Radio Budapest, where part of the crowd has gone to demand the right of patriots to be heard over the air.

I go with the group that heads for Stalin Square. Some of the workers have got hold of acetylene torches. They and the students are trying to cut down the dictator's twenty-five-foot metal figure. At the edge of the crowd the first Russian tanks appear, but at the moment they are only onlookers. The crowd pulls hard at the cables that have been attached to the Stalin statue. It leans forward, but is still held by its boots—a symbol, we feel. The cables are now being pulled by tractors, and the men with the torches work feverishly. The statue, though still in one piece, begins to bend at the knees. The crowds burst into cheers.

. . . [W]e watch the Stalin statue, cut off at the knees, fall to the ground with a thunderous crash. . . .

Suddenly shooting breaks out from all sides. The security police—the A.V.H.—are firing into the crowds. In minutes the streets are strewn with the dying and wounded. News of the A.V.H. attack spreads. All over Budapest the workers and students are battling the hated A.V.H.

The peaceful demonstrations of the youth and the workers have been turned by Communist guns into a revolution for national freedom.

For four days—from October 31 to November 3, 1956—Hungary was free. Although the Russian forces were still in our country, they had withdrawn from the cities and the fighting had stopped. The whole nation recognized the Imre Nagy government, which, knowing it had no other alternative, was ready to carry out the will of the people. . . .

On November 3, Radio Free Kossuth summed up: "The over-whelming weight of Hungarian public opinion sees the result of the revolution as the establishment of a neutral, independent and democratic country, and just as it was ready to sweep out Stalinist tyranny, so it will protect with the same determination and firmness its regained democratic achievement." . . .

In those four days of freedom, political liberty came quickly to life.

Before October 23 there had been only five newspapers in Budapest, all under complete Communist control. On November 4 there were twenty-five. Neither news nor opinions could be suppressed any longer.

Plans for a free general election were speeded.

Religious freedom, like political freedom, came back to strong life in those four days. . . .

In the countryside, the peasants and their spokesmen were mapping the changes of the farm laws and regulations. All were agreed on the goal of a free farm economy based on the individual working farmers and peasants. Peasants would be free to join or leave the farm collectives. If the collectives were dissolved, the land, tools and stock were to be distributed to the individual peasants. Compulsory deliveries at government fixed prices were abolished.

The factory committees and workers groups were putting forward the needs and demands of the workers, not the government. The right to strike—a criminal act under the Communists—was upheld. Wages, prices, pension rights, working conditions were eagerly discussed and debated.

The economy was slowly getting on its feet. Everyone wanted to be on the streets together.

RETURN OF THE RUSSIANS

At dawn on November 4, 1956, Soviet Russia attacked Hungary with 6,000 tanks, thousands of guns and armoured cars, squadrons of light bombers, 200,000 soldiers—and a tidal wave of lies.

The Communist Party of Czechoslovakia "ACTION PROGRAM (1968)"

The political trials of the early 1950s left Czechoslovakia one of the most Stalinist of Soviet satellite states. Even the subsequent "thaw" in the U.S.S.R. had no liberalizing effect on the country. Party Secretary Antonin Novotny (1904–1975) belittled de-Stalinization and ruled with an iron fist, presuming that material prosperity would keep the populace on his side. In the 1960s, however, an economic slowdown and the growing restiveness of the Slovaks—traditionally resentful of Czech domination—forced Novotny to incorporate a few reformers into his administration and entertain ideas of change. Exasperated by the need to court Party liberals, Novotny attempted a coup late in December 1967. Its failure—preordained by lack of support from Moscow—spelled an end to his rule; in January 1968, he was replaced by one of his critics, Alexander Dubček (1921–1992), who was a Slovak. Dubček was reform-minded but hardly radical; while intent on opening up the country's political system and bolstering its economy, he was committed to doing so through the agency of the Communist party and thus avoiding the mistakes that had cost the Hungarians so dearly in 1956. Nevertheless, in a gesture that anticipated Mikhail Gorbachev's *glasnost* ("openness") by nearly twenty years, Dubček encouraged public policy discussions. Censorship was abolished, and officials became answerable to the voters. Such were only a few of the highlights of the "Prague Spring," a period of eight months during which the Czechs sought to achieve "socialism with a human face."

In April 1968, the Czech Communist party adopted the "Action Program," excerpts from which appear below. The program might be considered the political platform of the Prague Spring. Restrained in tone, this document nonetheless represents a challenge to traditional party primacy and thus points toward an inevitable showdown with hardliners at home and in the Kremlin.

At the end of the fifties our society entered another stage of development. On this fact was gradually formed the political line which we want to apply in a creative way and to develop. Characteristic of the present stage are:

antagonistic classes no longer exist and the main feature of internal development is becoming the process of bringing all socialist groupings in society closer together;

methods of direction and organization hitherto used in the national economy are outdated and urgently demand changes, i.e., an economic system of management able to enforce a turn towards intensive growth;

it will be necessary to prepare the country for joining in the scientific-technical revolution in the world, which calls for especially intensive cooperation of workers and agricultural workers with the technical and specialized intelligentsia, and which will place high demands upon the knowledge and qualifications of people, on the application of science;

a broad scope for social initiative, frank exchange of views and democratization of the whole social and political system becomes virtually the condition for the dynamics of socialist society—the condition for us being able to hold our own in competition with the world, and to honourably fulfill our obligations towards the international workers' movement.

We stand resolutely on the side of progress, democracy and socialism in the struggle of the socialist and democratic forces against the aggressive attempts of world imperialism. It is from this point of view that we determine our attitude to the most acute international problems of the present, and our share in the world-wide struggle against the forces of imperialist reaction.

The basic orientation of Czechoslovak foreign policy was born and verified at the time of the struggle for national liberation and in the process of the socialist reconstruction of this country—*it is in alliance and cooperation with the Soviet Union and the other socialist states. We shall strive for friendly relations with our allies—the countries of the world socialist community—to continue, on the basis of mutual respect, to intensify sovereignty and equality, and international solidarity.* In this sense we shall contribute more actively and with a more elaborated concept to the joint activities of the Council of Mutual Economic Aid and the Warsaw Treaty.

A full development of the international role of socialist Czechoslovakia is inseparable from the education of citizens in the spirit of internationalism, which comprises both the grasping of common interests and aims of the world progressive forces and understanding of specific national needs. This is linked with the necessity of making prompt and detailed information on international problems and the course of our foreign policy available to the public and thus creating conditions for an active participation of Czechoslovak citizens in the shaping of foreign political attitudes.

The Communist Party of Czechoslovakia will be more active in the sphere of the international communist and workers' movement. *We shall put special emphasis on friendly ties, mutual consultations and exchange of experiences with the Communist Party of the Soviet Union, with the communist and workers' parties of the socialist community, with all the other fraternal communist parties.*

The Communist Party of Czechoslovakia will continue taking an active part in the struggle for the unity of the international communist movement, for strengthening the active cooperation of communist parties with all the progressive forces while regarding a resolute struggle against the aggressive policy of American imperialism as the most important task. The Communist Party of Czechoslovakia will take full advantage of its specific possibilities of establishing contacts with the socialist, peaceful and democratic forces in the capitalist and developing countries. It will contribute to expanding the forms of cooperation and co-ordinating the work of communist parties while attaching great importance to international party consultative meetings. From this point of view it welcomes and supports the outcomes of the Consultative Meeting of Communists and Workers Parties in Budapest. With dozens of fraternal parties the Communist Party of Czechoslovakia supports the proposal for convening an international communist consultative meeting in Moscow late in 1968.

We are not changing our fundamental orientation; in the spirit of our traditions and former decisions we want to develop to the utmost in this country an advanced socialist society rid of class antagonisms, economically, technologically and culturally highly advanced, socially and nationally just, democratically organized, with a qualified management, by the wealth of its resources, giving the possibility of dignified human life, comradely relations of mutual cooperation among people and free scope for the development of the human personality. We want to start building up a new intensely democratic model of a socialist society, which would fully correspond to Czechoslovak conditions. But our own experiences and Marxist scientific cognition lead us jointly to the conclusion that these aims cannot be achieved along the old paths while using means which have long been obsolete and harsh methods, which are always dragging us back. We declare with full responsibility that our society has entered a difficult period when we can no longer rely on traditional schemes. We cannot squeeze life into patterns, no matter how well-intended. It is now also up to us to make our way through unknown conditions, to experiment, to give the socialist development a new look, while leaning upon creative Marxist thinking and the experiences of the international workers' movement, relying on the true understanding of the conditions of the socialist development of Czechoslovakia as a country which assumes responsibility to the international communist movement for improving and taking advantage of the relatively advanced material base, unusually high standards of education and culture of the people and undeniable democratic traditions to the benefit of socialism and communism. No one could forgive us were we to waste this chance, were we to give up our opportunities.

We are not taking the outlined measures to make any concessions from our ideals—let alone to our opponents. On the contrary: we are convinced that they will help us to get rid of the burden which for years provided many advantages for the opponent by restricting, reducing and paralysing the efficiency of the socialist idea, the attractiveness of the socialist example. We want to set new penetrating forces of socialist life in motion in this country to give them the possibility of a much more efficient confrontation of the social systems and world outlooks and allowing a fuller application of the advantages of socialism.

4 Solidarity

Soviet-occupied in 1945 and fully Stalinized in 1948, Poland was officially a Marxist-socialist workers' state led by the Polish United Workers party. It was therefore not surprising that major political changes there since World War II resulted from workers' protests against poor living conditions and lack of freedom, most often expressed in strikes. In 1956, after Khrushchev's anti-Stalin speech, striking workers in the city of Poznan forced a relaxation of Soviet-style

totalitarianism, returning to power Wladyslaw Gomulka (who had previously led the country from 1945 to 1948). In 1970, major strikes broke out along the Baltic coast, provoked by price hikes; they were violently suppressed, with several hundred workers killed—ironically, within a "workers' state." In the turmoil, Gomulka, who had turned authoritarian and rigid, was ousted and replaced by Edward Gierek, who promised improvements in the material welfare of the country. Yet the workers' unrest continued, supported by intellectuals in Warsaw, the capital. The Roman Catholic Church was an even more significant ally, with added prestige after Cardinal Wojtyla became Pope John Paul II in 1978.

As the Polish economy continued in crisis, Gierek was forced to announce new price hikes in July 1980. The workers immediately protested, striking for higher wages and greater influence at their places of work; by August 8, 150 strikes had been reported. A few days later, the strike wave hit the city of Gdansk on the Baltic coast, the location of the Lenin shipyard (employing 16,000 workers), and the nearby city of Gdynia with its Paris Commune shipyard (employing 12,000 workers). Though these workers were the best paid in Poland, they too were dissatisfied with their harsh living conditions and their inability to make their grievances heard; they wanted more freedom for themselves and their fellow citizens as well.

One employee at the Lenin shipyard was an electrician named Lech Walesa. Of peasant background and a devout Catholic, he had worked there since 1967 and emerged as a leader in the strikes of 1970. Dismissed and banned from the shipyard in 1976, he continued his agitation, watching events locally and nationally while gaining the respect of his fellow workers. In August 1980, agitation for higher wages and anger against the dismissal of Anna Walentynowicz, a fifty-one-year-old widow, crane operator, and political activist, escalated into a resounding political protest. Thus was born the Solidarity movement, the first independent trade-union federation in the Eastern Bloc.

Inter-Factory Strike Committee of Gdansk Shipyard "THE TWENTY-ONE DEMANDS"

The name that striking Polish workers seized upon for their movement—Solidarity—was as much an ironic commentary on what their government lacked as it was a proud declaration of what they possessed. Confident of their strength, the leaders of Solidarity drew up a political program called the Twenty-One Demands. On August 31, Lech Walesa signed an agreement with the Gierek government that granted most of the strikers' demands. Less than a week later, the party replaced the discredited Gierek as first secretary with Stanislaw Kania.

"The Twenty-One Demands" are reproduced below.

The following are the Committee Demands:

1. Acceptance of free trade unions independent of the Communist Party and of enterprises, in accordance with convention No. 87 of the International Labour Organisation concerning the right to form free trade unions, which was ratified by the Communist Government of Poland.
2. A guarantee of the right to strike and of the security of strikers and those aiding them.
3. Compliance with the constitutional guarantee of freedom of speech, the press and publication, including freedom for independent publishers, and the availability of the mass media to representatives of all faiths.
4. (a) A return of former rights to:
   —People dismissed from work after the 1970 and 1976 strikes.
   —Students expelled from school because of their views.
   (b) The release of all political prisoners, among them Edmund Zadrozynski, Jan Kozlowski and Marek Kozlowski.
   (c) A halt in repression of the individual because of personal conviction.
5. Availability to the mass media of information about the formation of the Interfactory Strike Committee and publications of its demands.
6. The undertaking of actions aimed at bringing the country out of its crisis situation by the following means:
   (a) Making public complete information about the social-economic situation.
   (b) Enabling all sectors and social classes to take part in discussion of the reform programme.
7. Compensation of all workers taking part in the strike for the period of the strike, with vacation pay from the Central Council of Trade Unions.
8. An increase in the base pay of each worker by 2,000 zlotys [$50.00] a month as compensation for the recent rise in prices.
9. Guaranteed automatic increases in pay on the basis of increases in prices and the decline in real income.
10. A full supply of food products for the domestic market, with exports limited to surpluses.
11. The abolition of "commercial" prices and of other sales for hard currency in special shops.
12. The selection of management personnel on the basis of qualifications, not party membership. Privileges of the secret police, regular police and party apparatus are to be eliminated by equalizing family subsidies, abolishing special stores, etc.
13. The introduction of food coupons for meat and meat products (during the period in which control of the market situation is regained).
14. Reduction in the age for retirement for women to 50 and for men to 55, or after 30 years' employment in Poland for women and 35 years for men, regardless of age.
15. Conformity of old-age pensions and annuities with what has actually been paid in.
16. Improvements in the working conditions of the health service to insure full medical care for workers.
17. Assurances of a reasonable number of places in day-care centres and kindergartens for the children of working mothers.
18. Paid maternity leave for three years.
19. A decrease in the waiting period for apartments.
20. An increase in the commuter's allowance to 100 zlotys from 40, with a supplemental benefit on separation.
21. A day of rest on Saturday. Workers in the brigade system or round-the-clock jobs

are to be compensated for the loss of free Saturdays with increased leave or other paid time off.

For more than a year afterward, Solidarity continued to dominate the political scene in Poland. In October 1981, General Wojciech Jaruzelski (b. 1923) succeeded Kania as party secretary. Jaruzelski opened a dialogue with Walesa and the Catholic Church, but lingering suspicions between Solidarity and the government, not to mention food shortages and veiled threats of Soviet intervention, all served to thwart progress. Finally, on December 13, 1981, Jaruzelski declared martial law and created a Military Council of National Salvation to govern the country. He also suspended Solidarity and jailed thousands of its members. Nevertheless, the organization continued to survive underground, ready to reemerge when circumstances once again became favorable. In 1989 Jaruzelski—his stature by now much diminished and his governing options exhausted—granted Solidarity political recognition. Less than a decade after its founding, this extraordinary organization helped Poland complete its transformation into the first post-Communist state in the former Eastern Bloc.

CHAPTER EIGHT

WESTERN EUROPE SINCE THE 1960s

DEMONSTRATORS RALLY AGAINST RACISM. Xenophobia combined with economic difficulties prompted record incidences of skinhead violence in Germany in 1993, including the firebombing of hostels for asylum-seekers and the homes of resident Turks. In this photo, Turkish demonstrators react with anger against the killing of a Turkish family by neo-Nazi arsonists. *(David Turnley/Corbis)*

By the later 1960s, reconstruction of war-torn economies, the establishment of political democracy, and integration into the NATO alliance had created a significant degree of stability in Western Europe. A growing consensus had begun to emerge over the previous two decades that, while the conflicts and war-related crimes against humanity that had ravaged the Continent earlier in the century should not be forgotten, greater integration and the necessity of containing threats to democracy would ensure peace among neighbors. Quite simply stated, most Europeans seemed to want to put the chaos of the past securely behind them. A new generation found its voice by the end of the sixties, and expressed dissatisfaction with the conservative social order in which their elders had been raised—an order characterized by what critical youth perceived as a desire on the part of the older generation to repress rather than confront the failures of their past, a refusal to allow more extensive democratization of society, and a willingness to ignore injustices in lands seeking to liberate themselves from colonial bondage. Generational conflict, together with the oil crisis and recession of the early 1970s, made it clear—despite hopes that the hard work of reconstruction would not be beset with new challenges—that the growth phase and the relative social peace of the first postwar decades had come to an end.

New challenges to European stability manifested themselves in several forms. Growth rates fell during the 1970s, and traditional heavy industry and certain manufacturing sectors found themselves less competitive under the changed economic circumstances—a trend that would continue periodically well into the 1990s. The resultant unemployment led to resurgent tensions between conservative and social democratic segments of society and a new political divisiveness. Across Northern and Western Europe, residents from lesser-developed or war-torn regions, citizens from former colonial possessions, "guest workers" (who had come from South or Southwest Asia, Southeast or Southern Europe during the years of economic upsurge to fill jobs deemed largely undesirable by the indigenous population), and political refugees all found themselves the targets of verbal, even physical assault, as both legal far right-wing parties and illegal neo-Nazi groups emerged to combat the "flood" of foreigners who allegedly took jobs away from the home population. It appeared that stability was slowly being undermined by the sorts of circumstances that had been so carefully avoided during the reconstruction years.

At the same time, the memory of the Nazi past, particularly the industrialized murder of six million Jews, continued to burden the European conscience. Thoughtful people struggled to comprehend the meaning of the Holocaust and genocide for Western civilization.

Despite—or, perhaps, *because* of—these developments, Western Europeans continued to engage in active, critical discussion of their understanding of (and responses to) genocide; meanwhile, they advanced the delicate work of integration. Tightening the bonds of

European union, the end of the Cold War, the collapse of the Soviet bloc, and the reunification of Germany changed the Continent's political and economic landscape.

1 Social and Cultural Criticism

Economic reconstruction and the creation of stable, democratic state structures formed the principal concerns for Western European lands during the first two postwar decades. Once a significant degree of prosperity had been achieved and the foundations of government had been securely established, however, the preoccupation with comfort and accepted practices of government, business, and social relations found themselves increasingly under attack. The vanguard of this challenge came chiefly—but not exclusively—from the first postwar generation—i.e., those who came of age in the later 1960s. Targets of their criticisms included social injustice, ecologically irresponsible practices, and women's lack of equality with men. These criticisms, in turn, prompted others to challenge Westerners to recognize the historic achievements of European civilization.

Simone de Beauvoir *THE SECOND SEX*

Simone de Beauvoir (1908–1986), the French philosopher and feminist, published *The Second Sex* in 1949. It described the role of women in a traditional society, in which the majority of women were married, depended on men for their role in society, and were tied to their home and their children; only a minority of women (including the author) led independent lives. De Beauvoir traced the role of women through history and through their contemporary life cycle as evidence for her thesis: because the forces of social tradition are controlled by men, women have been relegated to a secondary place in the world.

In the excerpts that follow, de Beauvoir argued that despite considerable change in their social status, women of her time were still prevented from becoming autonomous individuals and taking their places as men's equals. Marriage was still expected to be women's common destiny, with their identity defined in relation to their husbands. In discussing the status of newly independent women, de Beauvoir implied that because of their failure to escape the psychological trap of secondary status, they lacked confidence and creativity in their work.

. . . Woman has always been man's dependent, if not his slave; the two sexes have never shared the world in equality. And even today woman is heavily handicapped, though her situation is beginning to change. Almost nowhere is her legal status the same as man's, and frequently it is much to her disadvantage. Even when her rights are legally recognized in the abstract, long-standing custom prevents their full expression in the mores. In the economic sphere men and women can almost be said to make up two castes; other things being equal, the former hold the better jobs, get higher wages, and have more opportunity for success than their new competitors. In industry and politics men have a great many more positions and they monopolize the most important posts. In addition to all this, they enjoy a traditional prestige that the education of children tends in every way to support, for the present enshrines the past—and in the past all history has been made by men. At the present time, when women are beginning to take part in the affairs of the world, it is still a world that belongs to men—they have no doubt of it at all and women have scarcely any. To decline to be the Other, to refuse to be a party to the deal—this would be for women to renounce all the advantages conferred upon them by their alliance with the superior caste. Man-the-sovereign will provide woman-the-liege with material protection and will undertake the moral justification of her existence; thus she can evade at once both economic risk and the metaphysical risk of a liberty in which ends and aims must be contrived without assistance. Indeed, along with the ethical urge of each individual to affirm his subjective existence, there is also the temptation to forgo liberty and become a thing. This is an inauspicious road, for he who takes it—passive, lost, ruined—becomes henceforth the creature of another's will, frustrated in his transcendence and deprived of every value. But it is an easy road; on it one avoids the strain involved in undertaking an authentic existence. When man makes of woman the *Other,* he may, then, expect to manifest deep-seated tendencies towards complicity. Thus, woman may fail to lay claim to the status of subject because she lacks definite resources, because she feels the necessary bond that ties her to man regardless of reciprocity, and because she is often very well pleased with her role as the *Other.* . . .

Marriage is the destiny traditionally offered to women by society. It is still true that most women are married, or have been, or plan to be, or suffer from not being. The celibate woman is to be explained and defined with reference to marriage, whether she is frustrated, rebellious, or even indifferent in regard to that institution. We must therefore continue this study by analysing marriage.

Economic evolution in woman's situation is in process of upsetting the institution of marriage: it is becoming a union freely entered upon by the consent of two independent persons; the obligations of the two contracting parties are personal and reciprocal; adultery is for both a breach of contract; divorce is obtainable by the one or the other on the same conditions. Woman is no longer limited to the reproductive function, which has lost in large part its character as natural servitude and has come to be regarded as a function to be voluntarily assumed; and it is compatible with productive labour, since, in many cases, the time off required by a pregnancy is taken by the mother at the expense of the State or the employer. In the Soviet Union marriage was for some years a contract between individuals based upon the complete liberty of the husband and wife; but it would seem that it is now a duty that the State imposes upon them both. Which of these tendencies will prevail in the world of tomorrow will depend upon the general structure of society, but in any case male guardianship of woman is disappearing. Nevertheless, the epoch in which we are living is still, from the feminist point of view, a period of transition. Only a part of the female population is engaged in production, and even those who are belong to a society in which ancient forms and antique values survive. Modern marriage can be understood only in the light of a past that tends to perpetuate itself.

Marriage has always been a very different thing for man and for woman. The two sexes are necessary to each other, but this necessity has never brought about a condition of reciprocity between them; women, as we have seen, have never constituted a caste making exchanges and contracts with the male caste upon a footing of equality. A man is socially an independent and complete individual; he is regarded first of all as a producer whose existence is justified by the work he does for the group: we have seen why it is that the reproductive and domestic role to which woman is confined has not guaranteed her an equal dignity. Certainly the male needs her; in some primitive groups it may happen that the bachelor, unable to manage his existence by himself, becomes a kind of outcast; in agricultural societies a woman co-worker is essential to the peasant; and for most men it is of advantage to unload certain drudgery upon a mate; the individual wants a regular sexual life and posterity, and the State requires him to contribute to its perpetuation. But man does not make this appeal directly to woman herself; it is the men's group that allows each of its members to find self-fulfilment as husband and father; woman, as slave or vassal, is integrated within families dominated by fathers and brothers, and she has always been given in marriage by certain males to other males. In primitive societies the paternal clan, the gens, disposed of woman almost like a thing: she was included in deals agreed upon by two groups. The situation is not much modified when marriage assumes a contractual form in the course of its evolution; when dowered or having her share in inheritance, woman would seem to have civil standing as a person, but dowry and inheritance still enslave her to her family. During a long period the contracts were made between father-in-law and son-in-law, not between wife and husband; only widows then enjoyed economic independence. The young girl's freedom of choice has always been much restricted; and celibacy—apart from the rare cases in which it bears a sacred character—reduced her to the rank of parasite and pariah; marriage is her only means of support and the sole justification of her existence. It is enjoined upon her for two reasons.

The first reason is that she must provide the society with children; only rarely—as in Sparta and to some extent under the Nazi régime—does the State take woman under direct guardianship and ask only that she be a mother. But even the primitive societies that are not aware of the paternal generative role demand that woman have a husband, for the second reason why marriage is enjoined is that woman's function is also to satisfy a male's sexual needs and to take care of his household. These duties placed upon woman by society are regarded as a *service* rendered to her spouse: in return he is supposed to give her presents, or a marriage settlement, and to support her. Through him as intermediary, society discharges its debt to the woman it turns over to him. The rights obtained by the wife in fulfilling her duties are represented in obligations that the male must assume. He cannot break the conjugal bond at his pleasure; he can repudiate or divorce his wife only when the public authorities so decide, and even then the husband sometimes owes her compensation in money; the practice even becomes an abuse in Egypt under Bocchoris [Egyptian King] or, as the demand for alimony, in the United States today. Polygamy has always been more or less openly tolerated: man may bed with slaves, concubines, mistresses, prostitutes, but he is required to respect certain privileges of his legitimate wife. If she is maltreated or wronged, she has the right—more or less definitely guaranteed—of going back to her family and herself obtaining a separation or divorce.

Thus for both parties marriage is at the same time a burden and a benefit; but there is no symmetry in the situations of the two sexes; for girls marriage is the only means of integration in the community, and if they remain unwanted, they are, socially viewed, so much wastage. . . .

It must be said that the independent woman is justifiably disturbed by the idea that people do not have confidence in her. As a general rule, the superior caste is hostile to newcomers from the inferior caste: white people will not consult a Negro physician, nor males a woman doctor; but individuals of the inferior caste, imbued with a sense of their specific inferiority and often full of resentment towards one of their kind who has risen above their usual lot, will also prefer to turn to the masters. Most women, in particular, steeped in adoration for man, eagerly seek him out in the person of the doctor, the lawyer, the office manager, and so on. Neither men nor women like to be under a woman's orders.

Her superiors, even if they esteem her highly, will always be somewhat condescending; to be a woman, if not a defect, is at least a peculiarity. Woman must constantly win the confidence that is not at first accorded her: at the start she is suspect, she has to prove herself. If she has worth she will pass the tests, so they say. But worth is not a given essence; it is the outcome of a successful development. To feel the weight of an unfavourable prejudice against one is only on very rare occasions a help in overcoming it. The initial inferiority complex ordinarily leads to a defence reaction in the form of an exaggerated affectation of authority.

Most women doctors, for example, have too much or too little of the air of authority. If they act naturally, they fail to take control, for their life as a whole disposes them rather to seduce than to command; the patient who likes to be dominated will be disappointed by plain advice simply given. Aware of this fact, the woman doctor assumes a grave accent, a peremptory tone; but then she lacks the bluff good nature that is the charm of the medical man who is sure of himself.

Man is accustomed to asserting himself; his clients believe in his competence; he can act naturally: he infallibly makes an impression. Woman does not inspire the same feeling of security; she affects a lofty air, she drops it, she makes too much of it. In business, in administrative work, she is precise, fussy, quick to show aggressiveness. As in her studies, she lacks ease, dash, audacity. In the effort to achieve she gets tense. Her activity is a succession of challenges and self-affirmations. This is the great defect that lack of assurance engenders: the subject cannot forget himself. He does not aim gallantly towards some goal: he seeks rather to make good in prescribed ways. In boldly setting out towards ends, one risks disappointments; but one also obtains unhoped-for results; caution condemns to mediocrity.

We rarely encounter in the independent woman a taste for adventure and for experience for its own sake, or a disinterested curiosity; she seeks "to have a career" as other women build a nest of happiness; she remains dominated, surrounded, by the male universe, she lacks the audacity to break through its ceiling, she does not passionately lose herself in her projects. She still regards her life as an immanent enterprise: her aim is not at an objective but, through the objective, at her subjective success. This is a very conspicuous attitude, for example, among American women; they like having a job and proving to themselves that they are capable of handling it properly; but they are not passionately concerned with the *content* of their tasks. Woman similarly has a tendency to attach too much importance to minor setbacks and modest successes; she is turn by turn discouraged or puffed up with vanity. When a success has been anticipated, one takes it calmly; but it becomes an intoxicating triumph when one has been doubtful of obtaining it. This is the excuse when women become addled with importance and plume themselves ostentatiously over their least accomplishments. They are for ever looking back to see how far they have come, and that interrupts their progress. By this procedure they can have honourable careers, but not accomplish great things. It must be added that many men are also unable to build any but mediocre careers. It is only in comparison with the best of them that woman—save for very rare exceptions—seems to us to be trailing behind. The reasons I have given are sufficient explanation, and in no way mortgage the future. What woman essentially lacks today for doing great things is forgetfulness of herself; but to forget oneself it is first of all necessary to be firmly assured that now and for the future one has found oneself. Newly come into the world of men, poorly seconded by them, woman is still too busily occupied to search for herself.

Daniel Cohn-Bendit
THE FRENCH STUDENT REVOLT

A major sign of the growing dissatisfaction of youth with Western European society was the uprising of Parisian students in May and June 1968. Disgusted with the bureaucratic structure of the university system and highly critical of capitalist society and what they regarded as the hypocrisy of bourgeois values, left-wing students took to the streets. Over the ensuing days, they voiced their opposition to the overwhelmingly conservative mindset of their professors, the bureaucratic structure of university administration policies that excluded student input, the failure of the government to engage in good-faith negotiations with labor unions concerning issues of fair pay and social benefits, and the foreign policy of France and its allies regarding both divided Europe and the less-developed regions of the world. On May 3, a confrontation between police and student demonstrators triggered a period of violent street fighting in the Latin Quarter, during which the students and their supporters erected barricades, much as had been done in the revolutionary years of 1848 and 1871. Parisian public transportation employees and workers from a number of factories throughout the city showed their support through strikes and sit-ins.

The vehemence of the Parisian student uprising came as a surprise to the French national government and to Paris municipal authorities, and the protests very nearly brought down the government of Charles de Gaulle (1890–1970). President de Gaulle accused the French Communist party of trying to undermine the government; the Communists responded by urging the students and strikers to express their dissatisfaction through the ballot box, rather than in the streets. The unrest subsided by the end of June, and in the subsequent vote de Gaulle won the support of an overwhelming majority of the electorate. The French student revolt did not bring about its desired aims of a far-reaching democratization of society and a governmental commitment to pursuing greater social justice; nonetheless, it energized many young people and workers, and it became a beacon for similar expressions of social and cultural criticism throughout Europe.

In the following selection, the student leader Daniel Cohn-Bendit offers his evaluation of "the events" and the students' goals for a far-reaching transformation of French society. This interview was conducted by the philosopher Jean-Paul Sartre (see pages 285–286) and published on May 20, 1968, in *Le Nouvel Observateur.*

JEAN-PAUL SARTRE: Within a few days, although no one called for a general strike, France has been practically paralyzed by work stoppages and factory occupations. And all because the students took control of the streets in the Latin Quarter. What is your analysis of the movement you have unleashed? How far might it go?

DANIEL COHN-BENDIT: It has grown much larger than we could have foreseen at the start. The aim is now the overthrow of the regime. But it is not up to us whether or not this is achieved. If the Communist Party, the CGT,[1] and the other union headquarters shared it there would be no problem; the regime would fall

---

[1]CGT, Confédération générale du travail—the major French trade union confederation, dominated by the French Communist party since 1945.

within a fortnight, as it has no counterthrust against a trial of strength supported by all working-class forces.

J-P. S.: For the moment there is an obvious disproportion between the massive nature of the strike movement, which does, indeed, make possible a direct confrontation with the regime, and the demands the trade unions have presented, which are still limited ones: for wages, work organization, pensions, etc.

D. C-B.: There has always been a disjunction in workers' struggles between the strength of the action and the initial demands. But it might be that the success of the action, the dynamism of the movement, could alter the nature of the demands *en route.* A strike launched for a partial victory may change into a movement for insurrection.

Even so, some of the demands put forward by the workers today are very far-reaching: a real 40-hour week, for example, and, at Renault's, a minimum wage of 1,000 francs per month. The Gaullist regime cannot accept them without a total loss of face and, if it holds out, then there will be a confrontation. Suppose the workers hold out, too, and the regime falls. What will happen then? The left will come to power. Everything will then depend on what it does. If it really changes the system—I must admit I doubt if it will—it will have an audience, and all will be well. But if we have a Wilson-style government,[2] with or without the Communists, which only proposes minor reforms and adjustments, then the extreme left will regain its strength and we shall have to go on posing the real problems of social control, workers' power, and so on.

But we have not reached that stage yet, and it is not at all certain even that the regime will fall.

J-P. S.: When the situation is a revolutionary one, a movement like your own may not be stopped, but it may be that its impetus will fade. In that case you will have to try to go as far as possible before you come to a halt. What irreversible results do you think the present movement will achieve, supposing that it soon stops?

D. C-B.: The worker will obtain the satisfaction of a number of material demands, and the moderates in the student movement and the teachers will put through important university reforms. These will not be the radical reforms we should like to see, but we shall still be able to bring some pressure to bear: we will make particular proposals, and no doubt a few of them will be accepted because they won't dare refuse us everything. That will be some progress, of course, but nothing basic will have changed and we shall continue to challenge the system as a whole.

Besides, I don't believe the revolution is possible overnight like that. I believe that all we can get are successive adjustments of more or less importance, but these adjustments can only be imposed by revolutionary action. That is how the student movement, which, even if it does temporarily lose its energy, will still have achieved an important university reform, can act as an example to many young workers. By using the traditional means of action of the workers' movement—strikes, occupations of the streets and workplaces—we have destroyed the first barrier: the myth that "nothing can be done about the regime." We have proved that this is not true. And the workers rushed into the breach. Perhaps this time they won't go right to the end. But there will be other explosions later on. What matters is that the effectiveness of revolutionary methods has been proved.

The union of workers and students can only be achieved in the dynamics of action if the student's movement and the workers' movement each sustain their own impetus and converge on one aim. At the moment, naturally and understandably enough, the workers distrust the students.

J-P. S.: This distrust is not natural, it has been acquired. It did not exist at the beginning of the nineteenth century, and did not appear until after the massacres of June 1848.

[2]Reference to the Labour government led by James Harold Wilson in Great Britain (1964–1970), which Cohn-Bendit and his codemonstrators felt did not advance the interests of workers with sufficient vigor.

Before that, republicans—who were intellectuals and petty bourgeois—and workers marched together. This unity has been out of the question ever since, even in the Communist Party, which has always carefully separated workers and intellectuals.

D. C-B.: But something did happen during the crisis. At Billancourt, the workers would not let the students into the factories. But even the fact that students went to Billancourt was new and important. In fact, there were three stages. First, open mistrust, not only in the working-class press, but among the workers themselves. They said, "Who are all these father's boys who have come here to annoy us?" Then, after the street battles, the students' struggle with the police, this feeling disappeared and solidarity was effectively achieved.

Now we are in a third stage: the workers and peasants have entered the struggle in their turn, but they tell us, "Wait a little, we want to fight our own battles for ourselves!" That is to be expected. Union can only take place later on if the two movements, the students' movement and the workers' movement, maintain their impetus. After fifty years of distrust, I don't think what is called "dialogue" is possible. It is not just a matter of talk. We should not expect the workers to welcome us with open arms. Contact will only be made when we are fighting side by side. We might for example set up common revolutionary action groups in which workers and students raise problems and act together. There are places where that will work, and others where it won't.

J-P. S.: The problem remains the same: adjustments or revolution. As you have said, everything you do by force is recovered positively by the reformists. Thanks to your action, the university will be readjusted, but only within the framework of a bourgeois society.

D. C-B.: Obviously, but I believe that is the only way to advance. Take the examinations, for example. There can be no doubt that they will take place. But certainly not in the way they used to. A new formula will be found. And once they take place in an unusual way, an irreversible process of reforms will have been set moving. I don't know how far it will go, and I know it will be a slow process, but it is the only possible strategy.

I am not interested in metaphysics, in looking for ways to "make the revolution." As I have said, I think that we are moving toward a perpetual change of society, produced by revolutionary actions at each stage. A radical change in the structure of our society would only be possible if, for example, a serious economic crisis, the action of a powerful workers' movement and vigorous student activity suddenly converged. These conditions have not all been realized today. At best we can hope to bring down the government. We must not dream of destroying bourgeois society. That does not mean that there is nothing to be done; on the contrary, we must struggle step by step, on the basis of a global challenge. . . .

J-P. S.: What many people cannot understand is the fact that you have not tried to work out a program or to give your movement a structure. They attack you for trying to "smash everything" without knowing—or at any rate saying—what you would like to put in place of what you demolish.

D. C-B.: . . . Our movement's strength is precisely that it is based on an "uncontrollable" spontaneity, that it gives an impetus without trying to canalize it or use the action it has unleashed to its own profit. There are clearly two solutions open to us today. The first would be to bring together half-a-dozen people with political experience, ask them to formulate some convincing immediate demands, and say, "Here is the student movement's position, do what you like with it!" That is the bad solution. The second is to try to give an understanding of the situation not to the totality of the students nor even to the totality of demonstrators, but to a large number of them. To do so we must avoid building an organization immediately, or defining a program; that would inevitably paralyze us. The movement's only chance is the disorder that lets men speak freely, and which can result in a form of self-organization. For example, we should now give up mass-spectacular meetings and turn to the formation of work and action groups. That is what we are trying to do at Nanterre.

But now that speech has been suddenly freed in Paris, it is essential first of all that people should express themselves. They say confused, vague things and they are often uninteresting things, too, for they have been said a hundred times before, but when they have finished, this allows them to ask "So what?" This is what matters, that the largest possible number of students say "So what?" Only then can a program and a structure be discussed. To ask us today, "What are you going to do about the examinations?" is to wish to drown the fish, to sabotage the movement, and interrupt its dynamics. The examinations will take place and we shall make proposals, but give us time. First we must discuss, reflect, seek new formulae. We shall find them. But not today.

J-P. S.: You have said that the student movement is now on the crest of a wave. But the vacation is coming, and with it a deceleration, probably a retreat. The government will take the opportunity to put through reforms. It will invite students to participate and many will accept, saying either, "Reformism is all we want," or, "It is only reformism, but it is better than nothing, and we have obtained it by force." So you will have a transformed university, but the changes may be merely superficial ones, dealing particularly with the development of material facilities, lodgings, university restaurants. These things would make no basic changes in the system. They are demands that the authorities could satisfy without bringing the regime into question. Do you think that you could obtain any "adjustments" that would really introduce revolutionary elements into the bourgeois university—for example, that would make the education given at the university contradictory to the basic function of the university in the present regime: the training of cadres who are well integrated into the system?

D. C-B.: First, purely material demands may have a revolutionary content. On university restaurants we have a demand which is basic. We demand their abolition as university restaurants. They must become youth restaurants in which all young people, whether students or not, can eat for 1.40 francs. No one can reject this demand: if young workers are working during the day, there seems no reason why they should not dine for 1.40 francs in the evening. Similarly, with the university cities. There are many young workers and apprentices who would rather live away from their parents but who cannot take a room because that would cost them 30,000 francs per month; let us welcome them to the cities, where the rent is from 9,000 to 10,000 francs per month. And let the well-to-do students in law and post-graduate students in political science go elsewhere.

Basically, I don't think that any reforms the government might make would be enough to demobilize the students. There obviously will be a retreat during the vacation, but they will not "break" the movement. Some will say: "We have lost our chance," without any attempt to explain what has happened. Others will say: "The situation is not yet ripe." But many militants will realize that we must capitalize on what has just taken place, analyze it theoretically and prepare to resume our action next term. For there will be an explosion then, whatever the government's reforms. And the experience of disorderly, unintentional, authority-provoked action we have just been through will enable us to make any action launched in the autumn more effective. The vacation will enable students to come to terms with the disarray they showed during the fortnight's crisis, and to think about what they want to and can do.

As to the possibility of making the education given at the university a "counter-education" manufacturing not well-integrated cadres but revolutionaries, I am afraid that seems to me a somewhat idealist hope. Even a reformed bourgeois education will still manufacture bourgeois cadres. People will be caught in the wheels of the system. At best they will become members of a right-thinking left, but objectively they will remain cogs ensuring the functioning of society.

Our aim is to pursue successfully a "parallel education" which will be technical and ideological. We must launch a university ourselves, on a completely new basis, even if it only lasts a few weeks. We shall call on left and extreme left teachers who are prepared to work with us in seminars and assist us with their knowledge—renouncing their "professional" status—in the investigations we shall undertake.

In all faculties we shall open seminars—not lecture courses, obviously—on the problems of the workers' movement, on the use of technology in the interests of man, on the possibilities opened up by automation. And all this not from a theoretical viewpoint (every sociological study today opens with the words: "Technology must be made to serve man's interests"), but by posing concrete problems. Obviously, this education will go in the opposite direction to the education provided by the system and the experiment could not last long; the system would quickly react and the movement give way. But what matters is not working out a reform of capitalist society, but launching an experiment that completely breaks with that society, an experiment that will not last, but which allows a glimpse of a possibility: something which is revealed for a moment and then vanishes. But that is enough to prove that that something could exist.

Joschka Fischer
THE ALTERATION OF INDUSTRIAL SOCIETY

Joschka Fischer (b. 1948) came of age politically as a student in 1968, when enthusiasm for the student protests in France manifested itself on the campuses of West German universities. Fischer expressed his commitment to grass-roots democracy and his criticism of the prevailing German political and business establishments most successfully as a co-organizer of the "Realos"—the realistic, or pragmatic wing of the environmentalist Green movement in the later 1970s and early 1980s. A response to the largely indifferent attitude of the mainstream Christian Democrats and Social Democrats to ecological concerns and grass-roots democracy, the Greens drew their membership primarily from young and disaffected members of these established parties. Although he was willing to use established channels to disseminate the Greens' message, Fischer demonstrated great oratorical skills, a keen intellect, and a sharp tongue to press for responsible management of natural resources and the establishment of rigorous environmental safeguards.

Fischer joined the first Green delegation to the West German Federal Parliament as an elected deputy in 1983; in 1985, he made history again by being named the first Green minister for environmental affairs, in his native state of Hesse. Between 1987 and 1998, he served first as a Green deputy to the Hesse state parliament, then again as a representative in the federal parliament. In the federal elections of 1998, Fischer took another historic step; as federal leader of the Green party, he negotiated a coalition agreement with the majority Social

Democrats, bringing the Greens to power at the federal level for the first time in their short history, and for the first time anywhere in Europe. Fischer himself became the German Vice Chancellor and Minister of Foreign Affairs, offices that he held until the Social Democrats were defeated at the polls in 2005.

In addition to his political work, since the mid 1980s Fischer has authored numerous books and articles on environmental politics. The following selection, written in 1989, represents perhaps his most comprehensive statement of Green goals: the environmental dangers posed by nuclear energy, automobiles, and chemical dumping. He pleads for a systematic reevaluation of prevailing energy policy and calls for the formulation of a well-conceived, ecologically minded energy system.

The ecological imperatives are well-known on all sides, on the basis of numerous analyses and descriptions of environmental crisis. Aside from their leading role in impassioned ecologically-oriented preaching, these ecological needs have virtually no significance in prevailing policy, even in environmental policy. And this shameful deficiency is repressed daily in society, too. The reason for the success of this collective repression is easy to understand: all concerned feel and suspect that a serious-minded policy of modifying industry, politics, society, and culture would necessarily affect lifestyles—and the fact that over the next thirty years a vast sum would have to be raised, and that a revolutionary structural transformation achieved through peaceful, democratic means would be required which would call the dearly-held matter of property ownership into question. . . . However, we cannot escape the compulsion to strategically define our environmental policy goals, otherwise this definition will be called to account through the blunt and fatal imperative of technological catastrophe and its impact upon entire ecosystems. The financial cost of proceeding in this fashion will be egregiously high, not to mention the victims and the injured. Let us attempt, then, to arrive at a definition of our ecological goals with practical intent.

Are we prepared to continue accepting an energy system that rests upon a massive, consciously-planned—or at least easily-dismissed—waste of resources, and thus, consequently, on the unmasterable risks of atomic energy? We know today, after Chernobyl, Harrisburg[1] and numerous other accidents and near-misses, that reactor safety is entirely insufficient. And nuclear power plants will be built and operated in order to produce electricity, and to earn money with this electricity. The limits of economic performance determine the limits of safety, and not vice-versa. . . . Throughout the world, 700 million people live in a 160 kilometer radius of a nuclear power plant (in Central Europe and especially in West Germany the numbers are even more ominous, given the significantly higher population density), and this fact establishes a challenging perspective on energy for the populations in question. Moreover, the question of nuclear waste remains entirely unsolved. . . . Besides that, there remains the standing danger of the dissemination of weapons-grade nuclear material and technological knowledge, as well as the risk of nuclear terrorism. . . .

The modification of our energy system means: breaking away from nuclear energy and development of an effective system of energy conservation, [including] appropriate, decentralized systems of heating power based on fossil fuels with an optimum of clean-burning gas. . . . Coal and nuclear fuel are not alternatives, given the mounting problem of global warming, even though proponents of nuclear energy, in particular, never tire of making claims to the

[1]Fischer refers here to the Three Mile Island nuclear power plant in Pennsylvania.

contrary. The actual alternatives to the present policy of energy squandering are *no* nuclear energy and *as little* coal as possible—and the latter with an optimal degree of clean-burning gas and the highest technically-attainable degree of energy through heat conversion.

Fischer cites 1980 statistics detailing that roughly 80 percent of the world's energy was used in the industrial lands of the East and West, home to approximately one-quarter of the world's population. According to his figures, the average person in the United States consumed 1,000 times more energy (and the average West German 600 times more) than the average person in the "Third World." He adds that the average amount of energy consumed by West German automobiles alone was higher than the entire energy consumption of the more than 300 million inhabitants of Sub-Saharan Africa.

If we want to part ways with a wasteful and environmentally hazardous pattern of energy production and consumption, if we are not prepared to accept the damaging substances in our air, acid rain, and dying forests as God's curse upon us, if streets are again to be a part of our social space and not the site of what they have come to be . . . long stretches of traffic gridlock. If we are not prepared to accept the monotonous compilation of annual statistics for traffic deaths, injuries, and material damage without protest, then we must be prepared to fundamentally transform our automobile-dominated traffic system. . . .

The construction and maintenance of efficient public transportation systems and, thereby, the corresponding deemphasis on the function of the automobile within the larger traffic system . . . the effective ban on further construction of roads (with additional construction undertaken as exceptions only), effective noise control . . . shifting of freight from trucks to rail, and an increase in the mineral oil tax to sustain ecological initiatives—these are the points of departure for an ecological restructuring of the traffic system. Parting with the dominant position of the automobile will be the most difficult part of such an ecological restructuring policy in the industrial lands. . . . For millions, the car is bound up with feelings of self-worth, of ego, freedom, power, prestige, self-expression, adventure, sex. . . . Thus, it is this parting that will be the most difficult and the most painful, but it is nonetheless inescapable.

Do we want to reconcile ourselves over the long run to the fact that our brooks, rivers, and streams remain overloaded channels for waste? Do we simply want to gaze upon the ruin of our drinking-water reserves, polluted by the excrement of our industrial civilization?

The ecological goals formulated here, when actually implemented, will bring with them far-reaching structural changes in industrial society. They will affect a fundamental transformation in the industry-mediated relationship between means of production and environment, and will pose the greatest of challenges to the efficiency of the economy, to the state, and to society. Naturally that also means that the individual will be drawn into difficult conflicts of interest, as is the case under the conditions of any structural transformation. The automobile industry is the largest industry, the chemical industry the third largest; together they represent the largest profit-makers and employers. Together with the energy industry, they are also responsible for the worst environmental burden and destruction. Indeed, parting ways with nuclear energy will be no walk in the park, not even for the most utopian, satisfied Green majorities [in a future] federal government. For most people, in the end, it will be all the same how their electricity is produced. . . . If energy is correspondingly safely produced and proffered with respect to the environment, or if even frugal energy-saving measures lower electricity consumption, most consumers would actually be pleased. Electricity, energy in general, is much too abstract for people, and is only concretely perceived in terms of its use and its cost. For the majority of people, the matter will become much more concrete with respect to traffic, to the automobile, to gasoline prices—to the pervasive blessings of our thoroughly chemical-oriented lifestyle.

Quite apart from the issue of environmental catastrophes that no one wishes for, the line of confrontation between economic and environmental policies appears to have solidified: here profit and jobs, there environment, health, and self-preservation; here short-term gain and the preoccupation with income, there the long-term concern with survival. The art of an ecologically-minded economic policy will thus lie in breaking down the rigidity of these positions and make employment and profitability compatible with environmentalist concerns. If this is not possible, an ecological restructuring policy will have failed from the very start.

In the concluding passage, Fischer alludes to the entrenched positions of both big business and organized labor, noting that the interests of both sides in economic growth and full employment stand in opposition to a careful examination of responsible environmental policy. Ever the pragmatist, he offers a synthesis that remains consistent with the essence and substance of his principles.

---

2 Conflicting Approaches to Industrial Relations

Most politicians and ordinary citizens in much of Western Europe were acutely aware of the importance of social peace for economic recovery during the first two decades after 1945. Indeed, the emergence of "social partnerships" between labor and business interests in societies such as Germany, Austria, Belgium, Holland, and Scandinavia precluded a return to the dislocation experienced in the wake of the First World War or during the Great Depression—dislocations that had led to serious street fighting between rival paramilitary groups, outright civil war, and the emergence of Fascist regimes between the wars. At the very least, the social fabric had been weakened to the extent that Communist subversion might have become possible. In these societies, the course chosen was a middle path between the seemingly unbridled freedom of the capitalist marketplace and the limits imposed by governmental planning under socialism. The result was a "social market economy" that may not have preempted the expression of acrimonious industrial relations, but certainly limited their negative impact by providing mechanisms through which business and labor representatives could remain in continuous contact. These arrangements promoted first recovery and later prosperity, despite occasional setbacks, well into the 1990s.

Just as Great Britain was the first state to embrace the industrial revolution wholesale, it too was the first to experience the profound decline of long-established industrial sectors from the 1960s onward. Steel, coal-mining, and other branches that had been the backbone of the British economy began feeling the pinch as a result of recession and cheaper foreign imports—distinct threats to the livelihood of workers in Labour Party–dominated trade unions. Labour sought to preserve these sectors from being undermined by broader international economic developments through determined maintenance of state control of the largest steel manufacturer, British Steel, whereas the Conservatives sought to deregulate the state-owned sector and force the affected industries to adapt to an open market or fold.

The absence of a spirit of social partnership in Britain created considerable mistrust between labor and management, and mounting tensions threatened to paralyze much of the British economy. Differences came to a head in the 1980s, during Margaret Thatcher's tenure as prime minister, when tensions between Labour and the Conservative government arguably reached their most acrimonious level since the General Strike of 1926. The dynamism exhibited by Thatcher—which placed her in the vanguard of a revitalized series of conservative successes throughout Europe—forced Labour to reconsider its long string of electoral failures. In the end, the Labour Party reevaluated its message and distanced itself from the stridency that had characterized its collective voice since the interwar years; in turn, Labour's subsequent electoral success in May 1997 under Tony Blair served as a compelling example for social democratic parties in France and even in Germany.

Ludwig Erhard
WEST GERMANY'S SOCIAL MARKET ECONOMY

West Germany's "economic miracle" is indelibly linked with the efforts of Ludwig Erhard (1897–1977), the Federal Republic's first economics minister (a post he held from 1949 to 1963) and second federal chancellor (1963–1966). Erhard sought to find a "Third Way" in the realm of social and economic policy, one that avoided the Social Darwinistic tendencies of unregulated market capitalism and the strict controls associated with state-directed socialism. The concept of the social market economy allowed for incentives and enough room for entrepreneurs to maneuver without permitting them to run roughshod over the working class. In short, Erhard and Adenauer's Christian Democratic government strived to create a socially responsible market economy capable of integrating the German population—rather than pursuing policies that would "atomize" it (a clear reference often employed by Christian Democrats and Liberals at the time to distinguish their policy from that of socialists of the democratic or Soviet variety).

Erhard's successful strategy served as the engine for West German recovery, making it a kind of model for many Western European states. The following selection is an excerpt from a speech Erhard delivered before the Federal Congress of the Christian Democratic Union on April 28, 1960, in which he outlined the features of his policy and emphasized the mutual responsibilities owed to one another by the individual and society. Erhard admonished those who looked to profit from the benefits of West German economic recovery without accepting the moral responsibility associated with the common task of reconstruction. (This may very well have been a reference to those who embraced what Erhard considered the "decadence" of 1920s material culture, i.e., those prosperous and

self-indulgent people who scorned the preoccupation of others with pressing social and economic problems.) Erhard also emphasized the importance of developing a safety net that rewarded people for participating in the reconstruction of Germany for future generations and that provided assistance to those thrown out of work due to shifts in the market economy.

No truly sincere person can deny, after the experiences of the past twelve years, that anything we have not so far achieved is in process of achievement, and that any further progress we make in the economic field will, in the first instance, benefit the broad mass of the people. To take only one example, the total of private incomes available for consumption and saving rose by 122 percent between 1950 and 1958. The net incomes of self-employed have increased by 71 percent, while the earnings of the mass of the people have gone up by 142 percent. In making these comparisons, however, we must bear in mind that invisible profits are not included and that the numbers of employed persons increased between 1949 and 1959 from 13.6 millions to 20.1 millions. But this in itself seems to me to be not the least of the achievements of our German economic policy, and it is also worth pointing out that the obvious success of a free economic and social system in Germany has produced a more and more pronounced trend towards market economy methods in other parts of the free world. One can, indeed, say that . . . the basic pattern . . . has so far proved itself as to be generally accepted today as the prototype of a worldwide system of free trading.

What then is lacking? Why is it that, for all the achievements and the almost grandiose triumphs of the Social Market Economy, people are still not entirely content and society is not entirely satisfied? How is one to explain the fact that, despite security of employment and growing production in a steadily expanding economy, people are still not satisfied? The prevailing and all too obvious unrest in our democratic society is alarming. When times were bad it was barely noticeable, whereas today it is quite apparent and, as an endemic weakness of any free society, seems hard to counteract. . . .

On closer reflection we may come to the conclusion that, where a democratic society such as ours has undergone tremendous industrial expansion and has been shaken to its foundations, a special effort is needed to evolve a social policy which will encourage a new approach to life in keeping with the times. Probably all that is needed in many cases is a conscious reappraisal of the bonds that still exist between the individual and his environment, 'his' world. Let us not overlook the fact, however, that industrialization, the development of our transport system, the loosening of traditional bonds with the home or the job, and a loss of independence have all had a serious, adverse effect on our society. Our form of society has been described figuratively as a 'classless society'. This concept, which has undergone a considerable historical change, can be taken to indicate not merely that the rise of the working class led to a process of deproletarization which is still going on, but also that the property-owning and professional layers of society have become fluid and that, throughout the whole range of modern consumer goods right up to the motorcar, the television set and all gadgets designed to lighten the burden of housework, a highly desirable trend, the market for consumer goods is widening, with the result that class privileges are disappearing and will continue to disappear. In this 'classless society' the great problem is one not of class but of the individual, the average man, who feels that he is subordinate to the community and therefore has a sense of insecurity. The problem of how and where he finds his rightful place in professional and social life is undoubtedly much more difficult to solve than it was in *dirigiste* [state-directed] systems. There is also the fact that trade cycles, market fluctuations and changes in production appear to involve him in mechanical processes which are impersonal and leave him dissatisfied because he finds it hard to understand how these forces work. The more such uncertainty leads to a vague feeling of anxiety, the less surprising it is that people escape from their sense of isolation by forming groups and organizations, which in their turn give public expression, in amplified form, to the individual's inner disquiet.

A process such as this naturally not only produces effects which heighten the danger both of atomizing and of collectivising life, but also intensifies the desire of the individual for some kind of bond in which he can find warmth and security. . . . It is asking too much of the Social Market Economy to expect it to break down the visible social manifestations of our present-day life and recreate them on an idealistic basis. But it does have an obligation to live up to the precepts of a Christian social policy and to implement them in a better society.

Seen in terms of economic policy, the problem is one of working towards a humanization of our environment in all spheres of life but particularly in the economic sphere. . . .

Of course the policy of the Social Market Economy has come to stay. I would even emphasize that we and the Western world as a whole have every justification for claiming the birthright to a far better economic policy, which is based on the principle that industry must, first and foremost, serve man, and which, in view of the sharpening competition with the collectivist world, must not be sacrificed or betrayed. . . .

It follows from all this that, in the future development of the Social Market Economy, problems of social policy will rank equally with economic problems. . . .

A social policy which aims to be more than just an ideology and to be realistic and progressive must have as its basis the actual conditions of our economic environment, and this means developing aims which also do justice to the large industrial organizations that have kept pace with modern technology. However clear our purpose might be, we would be frittering away our energy in a purely *pro forma* struggle against concentration of power if we were not prepared to admit that the large industrial units in our economy have achieved a great deal and can rightly claim to have made a major contribution to the general growth of prosperity. It is not the large concern as such but the unbridled lust for power that tends to produce the sort of concentration which is harmful to our national economy and socially undesirable and to which we are therefore opposed. So it is our intention to restrict, and indeed to suppress, all restrictive or monopolistic control of markets by introducing further legislation to protect competition and by pursuing an appropriate taxation policy. But wherever the market is influenced by a lowering of prices and society benefits, then we should acknowledge that such an influence is indispensable. This implies, of course, that even large concerns must recognize that they too have social obligations, especially as they can do much to expand the independent, self-supporting sector of industry. To take only one example, they can leave certain functions and services to independent suppliers. The more liberal our economic system becomes the more importance will accrue to the larger industrial concerns, but this certainly does not mean that intermediate enterprises must go to the wall. . . .

Several attempts have been made, particularly during the last few years, to benefit certain sectors of our society by adjusting taxes. It seems to me, however, that such a social policy, which confines itself to technical measures, is not sufficient to meet the psychological situation we are confronted with. The social blueprint we have to develop must do more than just prescribe certain individual measures to be taken; it must open up a complete vista of social policy, the aims of which can command the moral support of the mass of the people. What this means can best be imagined if we think of the appalling developments in East Germany, where free peasants are enslaved and the independent artisan is deprived of his livelihood.

No one would now deny that the Social Market Economy has provided this kind of comprehensive blueprint, more particularly during the period when our economic policy was undergoing a complete transformation. But today we have a new responsibility, namely to evolve a social policy for the future which will supplement and also perpetuate the functions of the Social Market Economy. As I have said time and again, the focal point of our economy is the individual. It is now up to us to translate this incontrovertible general principle into concrete terms, and in so doing we will find the economic basis established by the Social Market Economy can serve as the foundation for a continuing process of development.

Margaret Thatcher
THE FREE MARKET VERSUS STATE INTERVENTION

Margaret Thatcher (b. 1925), a lower-middle-class grocer's daughter, was an anomaly in the upper-class, male-dominated Conservative party, of which she became leader in 1975. The Conservative victory in the 1979 election made Thatcher the first woman prime minister in British history. Thatcher aspired to overcome economic stagnation by crushing the power of the trade unions, decreasing public spending, and privatizing government-owned utilities and industries. (This last measure was successfully copied by several countries throughout the world.) She aroused hostility by her personal style and by her willingness to increase unemployment in order to expand economic growth, yet under "Thatcherism" the country prospered. Because it fostered individual responsibility, the free market, according to Thatcher, would also contribute to Britain's moral renewal. These ideas were powerfully expressed in a lecture she gave at Cambridge University on July 6, 1979. Excerpts of this lecture, entitled "The Renewal of Britain," appear below.

Theorists of Socialism, like Laski, Tawney and their followers, motivated by a genuine desire for social justice, elevated the State as an instrument of social regeneration. Simultaneously, Keynes and later various schools of neo-Keynesian economists, exalted the role of Government and humbled the role of the individual in their pursuit of economic stability and prosperity. The events that we witnessed last winter mark, I believe, the failure of these collectivist approaches.

The desire to bring about a society which promotes greater human fulfilment is not the monopoly of any one political party. I acknowledge, readily, the sincerity and generosity of some Socialists. However, I believe that the Socialist approach is based upon a moral confusion which in practice is profoundly damaging. The moral fallacy of Socialism is to suppose that conscience can be collectivized. One sees this fallacy most plainly in Marxist theory. Marxists are quite unable to say why a proletarian revolution, a hate-filled and violent act of expropriation, should be morally cleansing and lead to a better society. Their failure in theory has been heavily and tragically underlined by the reality of life in twentieth-century Marxist States.

But the gentler proponents of Socialism, who stop short of subscribing to the full Marxist view of history, are equally unconvincing in their view of human nature. Experience has shown the practical failure of two fundamental

Socialist arguments: that nationalization is justified because it makes economic power accountable to the people whose lives it affects; and that State planning can point to better ways forward than can be charted by free enterprise. The Socialists had grossly expanded State intervention in the economy. They were going so far as to claim that the State should have monopoly rights in the provision of health and education.

It is certainly the duty of Government to do all it can to ensure that effective succour is given to those in need, and this is a Conservative principle as much as a Socialist one. Where Conservatives part company from Socialists is in the degree of confidence which we can place in the exclusive capacity of a Welfare State to relieve suffering and promote well-being. Charity is a personal quality—the supreme moral quality, according to St. Paul—and public compassion, State philanthropy and institutionalized charity can never be enough. There is no adequate substitute for genuine caring for one another on the part of families, friends and neighbours.

I think that this proposition would be widely accepted. And yet the collectivist ethos has made individuals excessively prone to rely on the State to provide for the well-being of their neighbours and indeed of themselves. There cannot be a welfare system in any satisfactory sense which tends, in this way, to break down personal responsibility and the sense of responsibility to family, neighbourhood and community. The balance has moved too far towards collectivism. In recent years, it has been quite widely held to be morally wrong for the individual to choose to make his own provision for the education of his children or the health of his family.

Yet if the State usurps or denies the right of the individual to make, where he is able to do so, the important decisions in his life and to provide the essentials for himself and his family, then he is demeaned and diminished as a moral being. We need, therefore, to achieve a better balance between the spheres of public and private activity. . . .

The wanton expansion of the State's responsibilities had been accompanied by a great drop in public spirit. Excessive public spending had (as usual) bred great private discontent. In the meantime, it was widely assumed that no large enterprise could be managed successfully without the help of the State. Private philanthropy and voluntary organizations were undermined. Heavy taxation had lowered fiscal morality. The malignant tumour of the so-called black economy was growing. We seemed to be losing our moral standards as well as our competence.

Then, partly as a result of high taxation, the idea of work well done had almost been forgotten. "Try to do any bit of work as well as it can be done for the work's sake," wrote C. S. Lewis. But that injunction seemed, in the last few years, to have become little more than a memory. Foreigners visiting this country shook their heads sadly when they remembered a resolute, industrious and great-hearted Britain which once had seemed to be able to move both "Earth and Heaven." Our industrial life seemed marked by petty labour disputes which were often both self-destructive and humiliating. The time spent by works managers upon trade union matters of a non-productive nature might be half of their day's work. That was one reason for the failure of Britain both to gain and to fulfill export orders. . . .

What did all this mean for our country? It meant that the 1960s and the early 1970s became the great age of the countries which suffered defeat in the 1939/45 War. The peoples of Germany and Japan, and also of France, worked together to restore their countries, and then to move ahead. They did not behave as if the world owed them a living. In Britain, we spent too much time dividing up the cake and pursuing petty sectional interests. So, although we had won the war, we let other countries win the peace.

For a long time, too, many leaders of the Labour Party refused to recognize the reality of British decline, to which they had contributed more than their fair share. They seemed blind to the evident truth that, all over the world, capitalism was achieving improvements in living standards and the quality of life, while Socialism was causing economic decay, bureaucracy and, when it took authoritarian or totalitarian forms, cruelty and repression. . . .

At the heart of a new mood in the nation must be a recovery of our self-confidence and our self-respect. Nothing is beyond us. Decline is not inevitable. But nor is progress a law of nature. The ground gained by one generation may be lost by the next.

The foundation of this new confidence has to be individual responsibility. If people come to believe that the State, or their employer, or their union, owe them a living, and that, in turn, the world owes Britain a living, we shall have no confidence and no future. It must be quite clear that the responsibility is on each of us to make the full use of our talents and to care for our families. It must be clear, too, that we have a responsibility to our country to make Britain respected and successful in the world.

The economic counterpart of these personal and national responsibilities is the working of the market economy in a free society. I am sure that there is wide acceptance in Britain, going far beyond the supporters of our party, that production and distribution in our economy is best operated through free competition.

A basic function of Government is to ensure that this market remains in being. The Government must be responsible, too, for ensuring the maintenance of social cohesion through the support of established customs and traditions. Governments can animate industry but they should not seek indefinitely to sustain it. Governments can purify the stagnant and corrupt parts of an economy and correct irregularities in the market, but they should not seek to regulate the market itself. Governments may provide certain goods or services which cannot easily be supplied competitively, but they should accept that one of their essential tasks is to define their limitations and those of the State.

Conservatives must work to make the idea of society so defined and so inspired as attractive as once it used to be and as it still is in other more successful nations. We need, for example, to create a mood where it is everywhere thought morally right for as many people as possible to acquire capital; not only because of the beneficial economic consequences, but because the possession of even a little capital encourages the virtues of self-reliance and responsibility, as well as assisting a spirit of freedom and independence.

Tony Blair
NEW LABOUR AND THE UNIONS

The British Labour Party's restoration of good fortune coincided with the emergence of Tony Blair (b. 1953) as party leader in 1994. By 1997, Blair engineered Labour's return to national leadership, combining an emphasis upon adapting Great Britain's work force to the needs of a predominantly information-age economy *without* abandoning the party's traditional working-class constituency. Blair walked this political tightrope masterfully during the initial years of his period as prime minister, bringing youthful exuberance to his emphasis upon social responsibility among Britons and a new willingness on the part of the United Kingdom for a cooperative and collegial role in a new, unifying Europe. In the following selection, excerpted from a speech delivered before the unions' conference in London on November 19, 1994, Blair emphasizes the commitment a future Labour government would have to restoring strength and pride to trade union membership, but he stresses simultaneously the responsibility union organizations and their members would have to accept in adapting to the exigencies of a changed world of work.

There is no bigger threat to people's quality of life today than insecurity in employment. Many millions of people will still work in traditional secure employment, but the level and spread of insecurity are greater than ever before. Teenagers leave school with little chance of finding a career with prospects. Graduates find qualifications are no longer a passport to a good job. Those in work fear for their jobs or are working under poorer terms and conditions than before.

In part these problems are derived from the recessions we have experienced. But we are fooling ourselves if we do not see that in part this insecurity derives from fundamental insecurity in the labour market and the economy.

These problems require a radically different approach to the labour market—one that centres on the individual within it. The answer is not to resist change—which is impossible—or to ignore it and have a market free-for-all with no attempt to respond to the change—which will result in precisely the insecurity we face. The answer is to empower the individual to survive and prosper through change.

I want to set out clearly the Labour Party's approach to this new labour market. It is not to try to re-create a labour market which is gone. Neither is it the new Right's approach of stripping away all rights and protection for employees and operating a labour market based on fear and insecurity. It is instead to empower workers to adapt to change and to guarantee a labour market that works within a sensible framework of rules and standards.

That approach, I believe, represents the best option for a competitive economy. It is in the interests of employers to have a flexible workforce. It is in the interests of employees to have choice and flexibility throughout their working lives and to acquire the skills to help them adapt to change. What neither employees nor employers want is the fear and insecurity which result from the Right's approach to these questions.

The last fifteen years have seen profound changes in the way people work:

- More of us than ever before are working part-time, are self-employed or have a temporary contract. Four out of ten of us in the workforce—almost 10 million people—now fall into one of those categories.
- Low-skill jobs are disappearing, and new ones are being created which demand new and different skills. Some industries are employing ever fewer people; other, new industries are expanding.
- Year by year the number of women in the labour force grows—a million more in 1994 than in the mid-1980s, and soon probably as many women as men.

The revolution in working life has destroyed the old certainties about career patterns, about what is men's work and what is women's work, and about income.

The Tories are content merely to abandon people to the effect of global change in the labour market. No minimum wage, no Social Chapter, no minimum standards. They call it deregulation, but this is a complete misnomer. It is instead a deliberate strategy to ensure that employees have no rights and the labour market has no rules. And the result is a low-wage workforce, poorly motivated and badly trained, combined with long-term mass unemployment.

Labour, by contrast, seeks both to reduce unemployment and to help those who are in work adapt to the new labour market. While the government is trying to shift people from one benefit to another, we are determined to get people off benefit altogether and into productive work. It is absurd, for example, that when a man loses his job his wife often has to give up her job—particularly if it is part-time—or the family will lose so much benefit it makes no sense for her to continue working. We want to build second-generation welfare, which gives people a hand-up and not just a handout, which provides child care as well as child benefit, training as well as unemployment benefit, and which—most importantly of all—will be a springboard to success, not just a safety net to cushion failure. The Commission on Social Justice addressed this problem in its report by recommending a Jobs, Education and Training plan to tackle long-term unemployment and to take people out of what in too many parts of Britain has become 'Giroland'.

We know that many of those who are in work welcome flexibility in the way they lead their working lives. When people are juggling the responsibilities of work and family life, and when more and more people want to go back to college or to retrain, it makes sense for individuals as well as for industry to have flexibility in employment. But flexibility should not mean stripping away of employment rights or a trend towards discrimination against people who choose to work part-time or are on temporary contracts. Unlike the Tories, we believe genuine flexibility will work only in a labour market which has rules and standards.

Labour will not simply press the rewind button when it comes to union legislation—ballots before strikes and other measures to improve the internal democracy of trade unions are here to stay. The issue today is not law or no law, but fair or unfair law—a positive framework of right which ensures that people who work hard and play by the rules get a fair deal at work.

If more people are choosing to work part-time, why should that result in a loss of rights? The same question applies to temporary work. And where a majority of employees want to organise in a trade union then employers should have a legal duty to recognise those unions and to work with them.

And of course a crucial rule in today's labour market should be a national minimum wage. It is both just and efficient. A minimum wage will stop the taxpayer having to subsidise low pay through the ballooning family-credit bill. It will decrease employee turnover, encourage investment in training, and help motivate employees.

But the case for the minimum wage must be fought and won among the public. I believe we have to go out and campaign on the principle of a minimum wage, to show that it is both efficient and just, and really to make it a winner for Labour. And if we are going to do that we should not make the mistake of getting bogged down in a discussion of this figure or that figure at this stage.

These are some of the rights Labour will guarantee to all employees. But government cannot and should not do it all. As John Prescott has said, 'We should be creating a fair framework in which all parties can coexist. And leave them to get on with sorting their relationships out for themselves.'

That means unions themselves have a responsibility to adapt to the new circumstances:

- they have to speak out as effectively for the part-time woman in the new labour market as they have done for the full-time man in the traditional labour market;
- they have to ensure that they take trade-unionism into new sectors, and recruit and represent members in areas where unions have traditionally been weak; and
- they have to play a positive role in creating the partnerships at work which can help Britain become a more successful and competitive economy.

These are major challenges for trade unions. The new environment is not an easy one for them. But, just as political parties have to change if they are to survive in the modern world, so too do unions if they are to represent their members effectively.

There are already signs of optimism that unions are rising to the challenge . . . to defend a highly popular public service. They highlighted the essential role the Post Office plays in communities up and down the country, and built maximum public support for the sensible case of keeping the Post Office in the public sector but freeing it up to face the challenges of increased competition. They have every right to be proud of their well-organised and successful campaign. It showed that unions can operate in a tough environment and can win.

And that has not been the only progress unions have made. United Biscuits, a company with a long history of financial donations to the Conservative Party, have announced an agreement with the GMB[1] to establish a works council, making a mockery of the government's opt-out from the Social Chapter. They did not have to reach such an agreement, but they realise it is in their own interests to have a workforce which is involved in how the company is run.

This shows yet again just how out of touch this government has become. While the Tories leave Britain on the sidelines in Europe, and in an increasingly weak position from which to influence future events, both industrialists and unions realise we have nothing to gain from such posturing and seek instead to exercise real influence in the mainstream of the debate.

Let me quote in support of our case the Business News section of *The Times.* Commenting on the United Biscuits move, it argued, cogently, 'It gives a strong incentive to plan continuously, rather than manage by crisis, or grandly operate as portfolio managers rather than business managers. And that could help raise the performance of industry as a whole.'

And we will continue to press for the adoption of the Social Chapter on grounds of both justice and efficiency. There is simply no reason why working people in this country cannot have the same basic rights as working people in every other state in the European Union—rights which are also supported by each of the four newest member states.

Unions have been active at both a British and a European level in their support for the Social Chapter, and in pressing for real improvements for working people. They have taken the Home Secretary to the Appeal Court and successfully exposed the yawning gap between his rhetoric of concern for victims of crime and the seedy reality of his illegal changes to the Criminal Injuries Compensation Scheme.

For some time now the GMB have been campaigning for a better deal for members of occupational pension schemes. They have launched a helpline for the many people who have been victims of poor advice on personal pensions, some of whom have lost a great deal through ill-advised transfers from occupational schemes to personal schemes.

And the T&G's[2] new 24-hour legal helpline means that all T&G members have access to initial legal advice whatever the time of day, which will be of real benefit to union members.

These are real, concrete examples of unions making a positive difference for their members and for working people in general. But there is a great deal more to be done. And I hope that, working together, we can argue the case for productive economic investment, for increased employment, for education and training, and for social justice.

There is a bond of belief between Labour and the unions that is more than a few lines in the rule-book. Unions know and accept that from a Labour government they can expect fairness not favours. But fairness will be a big advance on the open hostility they have had from government in the past fifteen years.

It will give unions a fair chance to adapt to the new world of work. It will give them an opportunity to work for new members and in new areas, and to campaign for the future in new areas of concern to people at work.

Government will provide the framework. It is up to unions themselves to take advantage of the opportunities that that framework provides.

---

[1]GMB—General Municipal Boilermakers

[2]T&G—Transport and General Workers' Union

3 The New Right

Although fascism was widely discredited in the wake of World War II and the crimes against humanity perpetrated by the National Socialist regime and its minions, a small core of obdurate extremists continued to harbor xenophobic and racist views well after 1945. Once the dynamic economic growth associated with reconstruction was tempered by serious recession in the early 1970s, radical right-wing rumblings were discernible in much of Western Europe. Targets of rightist anger included a wide range of "outsiders": foreign-born laborers (the so-called guest workers), immigrants from former colonial possessions, Jews (a traditional target of the extreme right), and the domestic left. Additionally, an increasingly dangerous phenomenon into the 1980s and 1990s was the emergence of extremism among the younger generation. Usually unemployed or under-employed youth who resented the welfare state's inability to provide the level of comfort and security they demanded, these young people began to flock to established far-right political organizations. They also organized their own new parties, formed new neo-Nazi groups, or expressed themselves through outbursts of skinhead violence against "outsiders," whom they regarded as parasites draining away scarce resources and diluting the "national character" of their respective host countries. As unrepentant members of the wartime generation felt comfortable reasserting their fascist convictions and younger, postwar rightists joined in the chorus of hate-mongering, Western European societies were forced to come to terms with the most sinister threat to both domestic stability and human rights since the 1930s and 1940s.

Jean-Marie Le Pen
"THE FIRST HORSEMAN OF THE APOCALYPSE: INTERNATIONAL COMMUNISM"

A career military man-turned politician, Jean-Marie Le Pen (b. 1928) organized the right-wing extremist National Front in the early 1980s. By 1984 the National Front had been elected to represent several French districts in the European parliament; by 1986 it had won as many seats in the French National Assembly as the Communists, and in 1988 Le Pen received ca. 14.5 percent of the vote in the first round of the French presidential elections. Although Le Pen has rejected virulently any claims that he embraces the anti-Semitism of the Vichy government of 1940–1944, he has made disparaging remarks about French politicians of Jewish background and has referred to Auschwitz as "a minor point in the history of World War II." Le Pen and the National Front have been vicious critics of a liberal immigration policy that has allowed a significant minority population of North and sub-Saharan Africans and Asians to settle in France. The core base of National Front supporters has generally been lower-middle-class shopkeepers and semi-skilled or unskilled workers whose lower-rent neighborhoods in major

cities have become more diverse via immigration, or whose job security has been challenged—or might be threatened—as a result of employers hiring immigrants for lower wages than French workers would be paid.

Le Pen's anti-Semitism and xenophobia was, up to the collapse of the Soviet bloc, matched in intensity only by his hatred of communism and personal enmity toward the Soviet Union. In the following selection, written near the end of the Cold War, which could not have been foreseen at that time, he discusses the necessity for developing a strong defense against the Soviet threat. Although the extreme right was not alone in its advocacy of military readiness, emphasis upon national strength as the only reliable way to resist communism was characteristic of extreme right-wing parties throughout Western Europe. In this respect, the National Front and other Western European ultra-rightists adopted the rhetoric of an anti-Communist "life-or-death" struggle in some respects reminiscent of the language of Italian fascism, national socialism, or the Action Française. Le Pen concludes this piece with a rhetorical flourish adapted from Emile Zola's "J'accuse," the famous document written in defense of Captain Alfred Dreyfus, the French officer of Jewish background wrongly convicted of spying for Germany in the 1890s. With the collapse of the Soviet bloc, Le Pen's attentions have returned to immigration issues, and have focused incresasingly on opposition to closer integration within the European Union.

A recent poll claims to demonstrate that in the case of a mobilization, only 17 percent of young Frenchmen would answer the call [to duty]. If that were true, it would be the end of our liberty and even of our existence. It is for this that we fight, precisely to wake up the energy of the French. It is evident that such a poll reflect the [softness], the general degradation of our system of education and training. Yet, in my opinion, out of a hundred well-born, normal, young Frenchmen, there are no more than a few who would refuse to face their obligations and, when all is said and done, to defend their personal interest, given the fact that their liberty, their life, and the life of their own are directly linked to the life of the Nation. It is this link that we are trying to reestablish in public opinion. One would think this would go without saying, but no, it must be said; it must constantly be recalled. Each Frenchman and each Frenchwoman must know that there is no individual salvation, that we are all linked together, and that, just as the history of our homeland [*patrie*] has shown throughout centuries, it is only in the unity of our defense that we have a chance to face the threats weighing against us.

The first horseman of the Apocalypse, the one that almost everyone knows at least by name, without daring to confront it with clarity and firmness, is international communism. The most fantastic aggressive military force in all the areas of armament has been gathered in the USSR, as much thermo-nuclear as classical, as much political as subversive. For seventy years, Soviet hegemony has not hidden its pitiless desire to dominate the world and to submit all peoples to its slavery.

We are from now in range of SS-20 missiles. If there is a threat in the world, it is Soviet. [. . .] Who would be made to believe that the current French government, any more than the previous one, has the intention of threatening the integrity of Soviet territory—nor even the unjust property, gotten through the Helsinki accords, of that part of Europe stolen through violence after the Second World War?[1] Who would be made to believe that it is possible to carry out

[1]Le Pen refers to eastern part of prewar Poland as well as the Baltic states of Lithuania, Latvia, and Estonia. After the Red Army had chased the Germans out of these lands, the Soviet Union refused to relinquish them.

politics that are in agreement with the [French] Communists, even as the allies of the Communists threaten our people with extermination?

In short, it is time not to choose between being "red or dead," not to let our anguish or fear take the form of capitulation, but rather [to opt for] resistance[2] [. . .] by preparing ourselves intelligently for a confrontation that could be military, subversive, or revolutionary, but about which one should know that there will be a victor and a vanquished, and that the vanquished risks being our country, Europe, and the West if we do not know how to mobilize our forces to survive and to win. [. . .]

The imperatives of modern war, characterized by short, decisive conflicts, does not allow for any delay in mobilizing troops. Moreover, the notion of "equality of citizens" with respect to military service is no longer respected: some are spared for vague medical reasons while others are given uneven, disappointing, and ill-adapted instruction as punishment. Let us point out in conclusion that pressure on recruits remains an excellent method for neutralizing the morale and patriotism of civilians. From Madame Thatcher's standpoint, would she have led the Falkland conflict to victory if her army had been made up of recruits whose families, full of tears and anger, had demonstrated every day in front of Buckingham Palace?

Only an army of career soldiers, based on short term contracts—three to five years—would allow the constitution of a flexible fighting force. In the France of today, it is reasonable to put the army into the hands of those who truly plan on defending their country. Ceasing to be an obligation passively endured by everyone, participation in the National Defense will constitute a voluntary, dynamic enterprise bringing together the best elements of the National youth.

There is no credible National Defense in a country whose people no longer feels national stirrings and whose individuals no longer have the sentiment of human dignity.

[2]A deliberate reference to the French resistance movement of World War II.

I ACCUSE Soviet communism to have given itself, in order to submit the world to its dictatorship, an aggressive force—nuclear, biological and chemical, as well as classical and subversive—unprecedented in history, putting into deathly peril all of humanity.

I ACCUSE the West, which has nonetheless saved its civilization over the course of centuries by opposing barbarism with the intelligence of its thinkers, the strength of its arms, and the heroism of its soldiers, of abandoning itself to decadence and of heading to subservience.

I ACCUSE the French governments who have succeeded each other over the past twenty-five years, and today that of the left, to have betrayed their essential mission: the national defense of France, which is not only that of her territories and her borders, but also that of her people, of her life, of her liberty.

I ACCUSE the military staff, in the area of the defense of populations, of being not one, but two, wars behind [in terms of military technology and training], and of sacrificing the survival of the French to a risky strategy of dissuasion.

I ACCUSE the parliament and the political parties, with only few exceptions, of having been and continuing to be accomplices in a veritable national suicide.

I ACCUSE the religious authorities whose natural vocations includes the defense of life, and above all of the lives of the weak and pacifistic, of preoccupying itself with nuclear strategy while allowing the incredible destitution of civil defense go unnoticed.

I ACCUSE the media of having established a curtain of skepticism and sarcasm around the problem of the defense of populations, and of having thus failed in their essential duty of informing citizens about the risks they run.

I ACCUSE the educational sector, so ready to mobilize its forces for trade union interests, and whose mission is to teach the youth how to live, of having done nothing to help [youth] not to die.

I ACCUSE veterans' organizations of confining themselves to commemorations and of sterilizing the immense force of devotion and mutual aid constituted by their members.

I ACCUSE ecologist movements of having shifted public opinion by polarizing its attention on the genuine, but limited, dangers of industrial pollution and civilian nuclear facilities, while overshadowing the [. . .] formidable dangers of a N[uclear] B[iological]C[hemical] war.

I ACCUSE the pacifists of making themselves into objective accomplices of warmongers by bleating about peace with the wolves instead of acting effectively to help the threatened innocents.

I ACCUSE all authorities of the Nation of continuing to hide from the country:

a) That nuclear, biological, or chemical war is not only possible but probable.

b) That in the current state of underpreparation, an attack, even a limited one, would cause immense losses of human life.

c) That, on the other hand, these lives could be mostly spared if the population were informed, organized, and protected as are already the populations of Israel (100 percent), of Sweden (95 percent), of Switzerland (90 percent), of the USSR (75 percent), of China (70 percent), of the United States (65 percent), France 0.1 percent.

d) That it is totally false that one can not effectively protect oneself in case of a NBC war.

I ACCUSE THEM of not assisting a people in danger of dying but also of felony since certain authorities (police, National Assembly, senate, Communist Party) have built shelters for themselves while the people are definitively exposed to a genocide. History will judge them!

There is still time, there is always time for refusing annihilation and slavery.

A sudden start by the French can still push the Apocalypse back.

Survival is not only a right, but a duty for all. Protecting one's own is the law of the species. But defend oneself, it is necessary to know. This is why nothing is more useful than crying out the truth. Truth is in action, nothing will stop it.

Jörg Haider
MULTICULTURALISM AND LOVE OF ONE'S COUNTRY

Jörg Haider (1950–2008) was arguably the most successful right-wing political leader in the democratic countries of Central and Western Europe since 1945. Trained as a lawyer, the telegenic Haider was raised by parents who had embraced national socialism enthusiastically in the Austrian province of Carinthia—a border region in which native Slovene speakers and German speakers had lived in an often uneasy state of coexistence for hundred of years. Hider emerged as leader of the right-wing Austrian Freedom Party during the mid 1980s, the result of his skillful orchestration of the established leadership's demise. The organization he inherited was a problematic one; its origins lay in the 1949 extension of full rights of Austrian citizenship to those former Nazis who had been political pariahs as a consequence of denazification legislation. During the 1980s, a traditional liberal wing had come to dominate a party that for the previous three decades had strongly emphasized Austria's German cultural identity. Upon his assumption of leadership, Haider steered the Freedom Party back toward a German-Austrian nationalism that at

times appeared to flirt with the "blood and soil" principles of the Third Reich. On the strength of Haider's personality—a blend of crowd-pleasing demagogue, dynamic and rugged outdoorsman, and slippery-glib news and talk show guest—the Freedom party won approximately 25 percent of the vote by the early 1990s and seemed poised to become the second-largest political party in Austria. Much of Haider's success came from his ability to mobilize young right-leaning protest voters and a number of middle-class voters who feared that immigration and European integration would threaten Austrian prosperity. He proved equally adept in addressing professional associations as he did speaking to adoring crowds at beer-soaked taverns and at SS and Wehrmacht veterans' gatherings.

Haider came very close to achieving his ambitions of national political prominence when the center-right conservative People's party formed a coalition government with the Freedom party after the 2000 federal elections. This prompted the leaders of the European Union states to condemn the new Austrian government, and for several months Austria was a pariah within Europe. Haider agreed not to play a role in the federal government, content to remain governor of Carinthia, but the coalition was highly criticized both inside the country and abroad. In 2005, Haider took a bold step by founding a new, far right splinter party, the Alliance for Austria's Future (BZÖ)—in no small measure an effort to separate himself from an increasingly unpopular Freedom party with which his name had been inexorably linked for almost two decades. This small party drew support from Haider loyalists, but failed to bring the Freedom party, represented by a host of new leaders with federal political experience, to its knees. The two far right parties have feuded bitterly since the BZÖ's founding. Pundits speculated that the two parties would reunite in the wake of Haider's accidental death in a high-speed car crash after an evening of drinking, but at the time this volume went to press, no such step had been announced.

The following selection is taken from Haider's 1993 political manifesto, published in English as *The Freedom I Mean*. He emphasized that the vital cultural roots of Austrian identity should be understood as decidedly German. Thus, there was no room for foreign cultural influences in a future Austria to be governed by what was then his Freedom party. It should be noted that the Freedom party suffered a notable setback in 1993 when Haider's "petition for a popular referendum against foreigners"—i.e., those outsiders whom some Austrians considered "undesirable," largely Turkish and Yugoslav guest workers and refugees from the Yugoslav civil wars—was met with candlelight vigils in favor of tolerance in most major Austrian towns and cities. In the end, the measure failed to gain sufficient signatures, but did not serve as a brake on Haider's popularity among his core constituency.

The concept of a "multi-cultural society" has become an ideology. After the pitiful Socialist utopia of a classless society proved itself to be a flop, a new dogma pops up to force us to be "happy." Since the Left failed to convert people to Marxist Socialism it has been in search of a new ideology, and new enemies. They found their new ideology in the idea of a multi-cultural society which to some has the same appeal as a classless society. But the experiment of a multi-cultural society has never worked anywhere in practice. Wherever and whenever it was tried, immense social problems, ghettos, slums, crime and social unrest ensued. The USA is the best example of this. In the American "melting pot" neither a social nor a cultural balance has been successful. The disturbances in Los Angeles are just an example of many. Every immigration wave creates an "elbow society"—discrimination and social injustice are never far behind.

Order in a state requires a minimal consensus on basic values. This is endangered when incompatible norms meet each other in an enclosed area. This is the crux of the problem of a multi-cultural society. This is most plain the more diverse the cultures and values are. In many European cities this is best illustrated by immigrants of Islamic faith. In France there are over three million Moslems, in Britain about a million, in Germany roughly 1.7 million. The social order of Islam is diametrically opposed to Western values. Our concept of human rights and democracy are about as compatible with the Moslem teachings as equal rights for women. The individual and freedom, as perceived by us, count for nothing, the fight for the faith, the Jihad, is everything. No religion on earth is spreading so fast at the moment as Islam. The German *Süddeutsche Zeitung* only recently asked whether "700 years after the crusades, Arabic Muslims would stage a counter-attack and storm the citadels of affluence, freedom and democracy."

However one assesses the danger of Islamic fundamentalism, the problems posed by the encounter of two very different cultural spheres remain. This is not easy to overcome as we could see from the dispute in France over whether Islamic schoolgirls should wear head-scarves. In Austria there was an outcry when Islamic parents demanded that the crucifix be removed from schoolrooms because it offended the religious feelings of their children!

This is the kernel of the problem of a would-be multi-cultural society. It is not the immigrants who integrate into the society and culture they find themselves in; instead they expect from the natives that they should accept their customs. Peaceful integration on these terms is not likely.

A society which does not rest on a shared value system leads inexorably into chaos and the breakup of law and order. This may be alright for the fans of leftist teaching with its anarchist tendencies. For citizens who want to live in peace in their country, such "utopian" dreams quickly turn into a nightmare. The arguments of the advocates of a multi-cultural society are not only naive and divorced from the real world but for the most part are plain cynical. This is especially true for the argument that we need large immigration to offset the decline in the birth rate. The same people who are for abortion on demand and constantly devalue the family justify unrestricted immigration to compensate for the results.

The mismanaged family policy of recent decades has meant that decisions to have children or not are taken largely for financial reasons. For the poor it is a question of survival, while for the affluent it means a decline in their standard of living and less leisure time. We need action which will make it attractive to say "yes" to children and "yes" to the family.

Both the extreme Left and Right have debauched the question of immigration and abuse it for their own dogma. The extreme Left hope for a new class struggle and the extreme Right for a new race warfare. These apologists for civil war have to be resolutely opposed. Whoever thinks the immigration problem can be solved with violence is either politically or emotionally unstable. The state must counter them with all the means at its disposal in no uncertain terms.

Every democratic, responsible politician is confronted with the question: How many foreigners can we take in without endangering social peace and security? Who gives us the right to make people strangers in their own country? When we mounted our popular initiative "Austria first" the argument was made that immigration was not an issue you should put to a vote. It was not "suitable".

Those who opposed the idea of an initiative on immigration thus implied that Austrians were either not competent enough to judge or hostile to foreigners. The historic facts prove the contrary. Austrians took in refugees fleeing from Hungary during the revolution in 1956 as they did for Czechs in 1968 when the Prague Spring was crushed. The same generosity was shown after the military putsch in Poland. No other country has taken in so many refugees from former Yugoslavia as

Austria. Humanitarian aid for Slovenia, Croatia, and above all for Bosnia, has served as a model for all Europe.

In the discussion on immigration and multiculturalism two factors stand out—the refugee problem on the one hand and the question of economic immigrants on the other. Austria was, and is, an exemplary country when it comes to providing asylum for those being persecuted. Austria, however, is not and cannot be a land of immigration. We are simply not in the position to let everyone who is in search of social and economic benefits settle here. We are, as the Austrian president Thomas Klestil put it, "a country of hospitality but no beaten track for unnecessary transit traffic and no dropping off point for all those without hope on our continent. . . . It would be a false understanding of humanity to keep the borders open for so long that social stability will be endangered."

We can only accept immigrants to the degree that we can offer jobs, apartments, and schools for their children. The German sociologist Horst Afheldt believes that Europe should only take in as many people as it can integrate in its social structures. That way it has a better chance of achieving harmony than a basically open society with ongoing immigration evoking fear amongst ethnic groups of being overwhelmed by others. "This can only lead to aggression," he said.

The question is, who should decide which path to take? In my opinion: the people. Whoever doubts the role of the people as the highest sovereign questions the very essence of democracy. People have the right not just to go to the polls every four years but are entitled to have a say in questions which are decisive for the future of their country. For this reason I and my party introduced at the beginning of 1993 the popular initiative "Austria first", which included the following 12 points:

1. *A constitutional provision: "Austria is no country of immigration."*

On account of its size and density of population, Austria is no country of immigration. Whereas on average in Europe there are 100 inhabitants per square kilometer of settled land, this amounts to 230 inhabitants in Austria.

2. *An end to immigration until a satisfactory solution to the problem of illegal foreigners has been found, until the accommodation shortage has been resolved and until unemployment goes down to 5 percent.*

In Vienna about 100,000 foreigners live illegally. This puts extra pressure on the labor market and accommodation. Only through an end to immigration can further social conflicts between the indigenous population and foreigners be prevented.

3. *An ID requirement for foreign employees at the work place which should be presented for the work permit and for registration for health insurance.*

Only controls can put a stop to the illegal hiring of foreigners, which has meant not only tax evasion and the bypassing of compulsory social insurance contributions, but has also led to a decline in wage levels. The need for an appropriate regulation was acknowledged by the government in the 1990 program but it now rejects its implementation.

4. *An expansion of the police-force (aliens and criminal branches) as well as better pay and resources to trace illegal foreigners and to effectively combat crime, especially organized crime.*

To be effective, it is necessary to increase manpower. This can only be achieved through making the profession more attractive. In the first instance this includes an increase in pay.

5. *Immediate creation of permanent border controls (customs-police) in place of the army.*

The auxiliary employment of the army on Austria's borders has become a long-term feature. The creation of a separate border patrol from the police and customs officials is absolutely vital.

6. *A reduction of tension in schools by limiting the percentage of pupils with a foreign mother tongue in elementary and vocational schools to a maximum of 30 percent; in case of more than 30 percent of foreign-speaking children, special classes for foreigners should be set up.*

The preservation of our cultural identity, the achievement of educational goals and the need for integration all make a limitation on the percentage of foreign-speaking children in classes indispensable.

7. *Reduction of tension in schools through participation in regular education by those with only adequate knowledge of German.*

In preparatory classes children of school age with a foreign mother tongue should be taught German in order to enable them to take part in education in the regular school classes.

8. *No right to vote for foreigners in general elections.*

The opposite demand of the government coalition and the Greens is primarily aimed at new votes, gaining to compensate for recent losses.

9. *No premature granting of Austrian citizenship.*

We demand that the 10-year period laid down in the law should be kept and exceptions should be kept to a minimum.

10. *Rigorous measures against illegal business activities of foreigners and the abuse of social benefits.*

Many associations of foreigners run restaurants and clubs which do not meet commercial, health or legal requirements. Some serve as centres for the black market.

11. *Immediate deportation and residence ban for foreign offenders of the law.*

The crime rate among foreigners, especially in Vienna, has soared, making it necessary to provide extra detention cells. In practice deportees cannot be detained because of the acute lack of cells.

12. *The establishment of an Eastern Europe Foundation to prevent migration.*

The lasting improvement of conditions of life in Eastern European countries should be provided by specially targeted economic help to prevent emigration for economic reasons.

The government was mobilized against this initiative in an unprecedented manner. Ruling parties, trade unions, representatives of the churches, teachers, artists, newspapers and television—all opposed the initiative as "totally reprehensible." A joint action group "SOS for fellow humans" organized a torchlit parade in downtown Vienna. Its slogan was "decency first"—implying that those who signed the initiative were somehow dishonest and disreputable. "Bring the Nazis here tonight, they will burn in our torchlight" chanted the demonstrators.

We called for this referendum because it is the right of citizens of my country to decide how many immigrants to take in. History teaches us the bitter lesson that often action is taken too late in response to events which could have been anticipated and prevented. Attacks on foreigners in Germany, France and elsewhere in Europe are terrible evidence. "No people in the world would stand for it if every year half a million foreigners came as they do to us . . . 500,000 people, that's simply too many" said the former German chancellor, Helmut Schmidt. The Mayor of Munich likewise warned that "an uncontrolled influx of immigrants to Germany could lead to an uprising."

It was exactly this development we wanted to stop through our initiative. We did not have to wait long for confirmation of the correctness of our policy. Within six months the government parties demanded a general requirement for foreigners to carry ID cards, as proposed by us. The trade unions came out for a reduction in the number of foreign workers, even beyond our demands.

Of course no country alone can solve the global problem of migration. The discrepancies in wealth between North and South and between East and West have triggered monumental migration movements, which challenge all the states in Europe. Mass poverty in the Third World, a population explosion and dramatic destruction of the environment, mean that in Africa alone more than 40 million people cannot live in their home countries, but are in search of some other place to survive.

Just as problematic are the pressures in the East. If economic and political stability in Eastern Europe cannot be established, millions of people will emigrate from the territory of the former Soviet Union alone, if they have the chance.

Our job is to tackle the reasons behind migration. Whoever in his own country has no hope for the future will naturally look to go somewhere else. Those who do this, however, should recognize that they come as guests and should behave as such, respecting their host country accordingly.

All the states in the West should try to help people in need so that it is possible for them to stay in their Home Lands and encourage them to rebuild their countries. Let us not forget the generation of our parents, who amidst the ruins and rubble of bombed Germany and Austria did not run away in search of the golden West. With guts, hard work and grit, they rebuilt their countries. They could serve as an example for the youth of Eastern Europe. Or should they all run away, leaving a generation behind whose lives have been ruined by Communism, to face further misery?

Ingo Hasselbach
INSIDE THE NEO-NAZI SCENE

The son of members of the Communist elite in East Germany, Ingo Hasselbach spent much of his adolescence in jail for petty crimes. After sharing a cell with the former Dresden Gestapo chief and hearing the old man blame Germany's division and weakness on the stale, but still emotionally appealing, myth of a global Jewish conspiracy, Hasselbach formed East Germany's first neo-Nazi party upon his release in 1988. Over the next five years, first in the East and then in the newly unified Germany, he led a violent, extremist group that engaged in street violence and organized and indoctrinated a small, but tightly organized cadre. The neo-Nazi movement's activities increased dramatically after unification, as splinter groups in the East and the West knitted together and began to plan terrorist attacks against foreigners and leftist opponents.

After confronting the human cost of the movement's activities—i.e., the firebombing of foreign refugee hostels in Solingen and Mölln—Hasselbach underwent a change of heart. He renounced neo-Nazi activities in 1993 and dedicated himself to working with German youths to steer them away from hatred and violence. The following selection details the depth of organization of the movement, sheds light on its support network within Germany and Austria, and describes the violent groundwork deemed necessary for the creation of a "Fourth Reich."

I happened to arrive in the United States from Germany for the first time two days before the bombing in Oklahoma City in April 1995. I was sitting in a hotel room in the middle of Manhattan finishing work on the pages that follow. It was one of the first times I'd had a chance to rest and pause in the two years since I'd left the neo-Nazi movement. America represented everything I'd come to love since quitting—a society of all nationalities, a strong democracy, a land of liberty—everything I'd worked to destroy when I was in the Movement.

The news in the weeks that followed linked the bombing with the existence of a far-right subversive movement, fueled by paranoid conspiracy theories and hatred of the federal government. That there was such a movement didn't come as news to me. As the founder of the former East Germany's first neo-Nazi political party, I'd been the main contact for several American far-right organizations in Europe and one of the main distributors of their propaganda. Before I got out of the Movement in 1993, I organized teach-ins, ran paramilitary camps, and indoctrinated young people at marches and meetings.

I began developing right-wing extremist ideas in 1987, when I was nineteen years old and sitting in an East German prison for shouting "the Wall must fall!" in a public place. When I got out, I began working secretly with a small militant group opposed to the Communist government.

After the government fell, I didn't simply quit being a troublemaker and rejoice in my newfound freedom. Prison, youthful rebellion, and the intense study of the most evil ideology known to mankind had already begun to change me. The peaceful revolution going on in the streets of Berlin in November 1989 had nothing to do with the violent revolution going on in my head. I didn't want a part of this capitalist West Germany where I could buy a Walkman or a bunch of bananas. I wanted the German empire a former Gestapo officer had told me about in prison, the one whose medals and slogans and insignia were the ultimate taboos in both East and West Germany—and whose embrace confirmed my opposition to both those systems. . . .

. . . Those looking for a new Führer saw me as a pure "blond beast" risen from the ashes of the Iron Curtain, and, along with the drug of never-ending rebellion, I began to crave the fix of power I got from handing out hate literature, planning attacks, and standing at the head of hundreds of other equally angry young people, egging them on, pushing them further over the edges of decency.

I made contact with a flourishing international network of neo-Nazis and racist movements and began building up caches of weapons and starting paramilitary camps. Like the extremists in America, the common attitude we shared was a hatred for the government (especially federal government agents), a belief that our freedoms and traditions as white men (or, as we said, Aryans) were being infringed on by a multicultural society, and a general anti-Semitism that held that the Jews ran a conspiracy that emanated from New York and Washington.

While most of these ideas could have come from European anti-Semitic tracts from before World War II, they didn't. Virtually all of our propaganda and training manuals came from right-wing extremist groups in Nebraska and California. Such materials are legal to print in the United States under the First Amendment. In Germany they are not, under the Constitution passed after the defeat of the Third Reich.

We also received illegal materials from our friends in Nebraska—the world headquarters of the NSDAP/AO, the successor to the original National Socialist German Workers' Party, or Nazi Party—like a U.S. Army training manual entitled *Explosives and Demolitions,* which has since been copied and circulated (still with the TOP SECRET stamp across the title page) to thousands of right-wing extremists all over Europe. A computer program we received from the NSDAP/AO, entitled "A Movement in Arms," described how to build bombs and wage a war of right-wing terrorism against a democratic government. Before I quit, I'd become the leader of an NSDAP/AO terrorist cell, taking my orders directly from Lincoln, Nebraska.

I'd had plenty of contact with America. But it was an America populated by men who hated their country and found the swastika a more appealing symbol than the Statue of Liberty, who saw great affinities between their Founding Fathers and Adolf Hitler. It was an America oddly obsessed with Germany and the Third Reich. . . .

I don't know if whoever blew up the Alfred P. Murrah Federal Building in Oklahoma read the army manual we worked from. If they didn't, I'm sure we had some other reading material in common. The right-wing extremist movement is a loose network of people with a great deal of hatred and potential for violence, and all over the world they are constantly exchanging information. Of course, lots of people in the Movement may have been horrified by the sight of burned children in the Oklahoma bombing, but my experience as a neo-Nazi taught me that enough militant ideology and conspiracy thinking can destroy even the most basic human sympathy.

I began the slow and difficult process of getting out of the Movement after the fatal firebombing in 1992 of a Turkish family in the city of Mölln in northern Germany by two young men in the middle of the night. It had killed two young girls and the grandmother of one of the girls. My group had had nothing to do with the attack, but for the first time the deadly potential of our rhetoric was driven home to me. The police investigation showed that the perpetrators had connections with and had received propaganda from a group like mine in Hamburg, as well as from an American neo-Nazi group. Yet in prosecuting the case the authorities viewed these connections as secondary and treated the bombing as a case of isolated, if deadly, juvenile delinquency.

I never personally built a bomb or set fire to anyone's house. I justified my role in the Movement much as the leaders of the American militias or any of the other militant groups do. I was trying to "defend" my society against rampant crime, too much immigration, racial and cultural "alienation," and control by a world conspiracy. I organized paramilitary camps and taught guerrilla warfare only to prepare Germans to defend themselves and the cultural traditions of northern Europeans. I knew the arguments well, and I taught them to many others.

I know now that during all that time I was deceiving myself. Morally, I was just as responsible as anyone who planted a fuse or drove a truck with explosives in it—because my messages of hatred against the larger society influenced who knows how many potentially violent young men. The first step for me in rejoining the civilized world was realizing that. . . .

Hasselbach describes the movement's contact with old Nazis still loyal to Hitler and Nazi party principles.

While the backbone of our organization was young men in their teens and twenties, we also got many visits from older people (our oldest member was seventy, an old Nazi, now, of course, retired). They often provided us with propaganda from the Third Reich that they'd carefully saved at home. These old Nazis—some from the SS, others from the Wehrmacht—would speak about the principles of national socialism in a way that made the concepts seem real and immediate. They could convey an enthusiasm for the SS, Hitler, and the Cause that simply could not be duplicated by someone who had not lived through the time.

These were not "important" Nazis, by and large, but that didn't matter. They were the living embodiment of not only Nazi glory but *German* glory. I came to realize then how fully Hitler had succeeded in merging the concepts of nationalism and Nazism in Germany and what a benefit that was to us. . . .

One man who came to us had belonged to the SS Leibstandarte, the elite SS bodyguards who were always around Adolf Hitler. This man educated us about race, about the system of national socialism and its entire program, about everything. He was still completely fixated on Hitler.

. . . He came to our organization through the West Berlin neo-Nazis, and he was probably about eighty years old.

[The old SS man] began our race education by making us aware of the racial characteristics of others. We started to pay attention to the size of everyone's head, the shades of color in their eyes, the shape of their hands. We learned to recognize the typical features of a Jew. For example, [he] taught us that a short back of the hand is typical for Jews and that a Jew will never have a straight body. Such things.

For the neo-Nazis, the Jew was still the main enemy. There was more violence against foreigners simply because Jews were harder to find. You would not see any recognizable Jews nowadays in the street. I thought I'd met a few people who were Jews—I wondered about it and tried to check the signs—but I couldn't be sure. There were hardly any Jews left in Germany, so we got little chance to practice our knowledge. But our Movement was always about the past and the future more than the present. It was important to learn about the racial characteristics of Jews in order to be able to understand the original Nazism, the history of our Movement, and it was also important for the future, when we might need to spot and segregate Jews again. The present was merely a stepping-stone between the Third and Fourth Reichs. . . .

If we really needed money badly, a telephone call to a well-to-do "friend" was all it took. One time there was a transport problem: one call, and the next day I had 5,000 marks in hand to buy a car.

This money was the gift of an elderly woman whose husband had been very influential in the National Socialists but had died during the war. These Nazi widows were usually well off because they got pensions from the State; in the case of the more fervent ones, their husbands had usually been rather high-ranking Nazis, and, as pensions were based on rank, this made them very rich indeed. It is an irony of the West German system that the widows of resistance fighters often didn't get any pension at all, while the widows of SS generals lived in luxury.

These old ladies all treated Michael Kühnen with great respect. He'd stop by their meetings, which would take place in individual homes or rented rooms, where they'd always serve coffee and lots of sweet cakes; the atmosphere was dainty compared to the meetings of the establishment professionals in the German Cultural Community.

Kühnen would stop by to shake the old ladies' hands and to gossip with them about their health and the Jews. And they would gawk like a movie star was in their presence, for they knew Kühnen was the Führer of the Movement, even if he wasn't their Führer, because that title would forever remain in the hands of their girlhood passion—Adolf Hitler, the *Führer!* In return, Kühnen had a deep respect for these militant Nazi widows. Partly because of this, he founded an organization called the HNG—the Help Organization for National Prisoners—to give old Nazi widows something useful to do: take care of young neo-Nazis sitting in prison. The HNG WAS explicitly devoted to the rights and comforts of imprisoned neo-Nazis. . . .

These Nazi widows send prisoners food and cigarettes and keep them supplied with propaganda material. In dark moments, they encourage them to hang on so they can fight the Jew another day. The HNG also publishes a monthly newsletter, the *HNG News,* which is distributed to all "political prisoners"—only neo-Nazis, not Communists, of course—to keep them abreast of all the goings-on in the scene. . . .

[T]hese old ladies were actually ideologically harder and more ruthless than most neo-Nazis of my generation.

In their youth, they had been hard-core Nazis, and they held stubbornly to this ideology. Bitterness and old age had only further hardened their love of the Führer and hatred of the Jews. A meeting with them was no ordinary coffee klatch. When these women began to gossip, they would talk about Auschwitz—or rather, the "Auschwitz lie"—and about the Jews and foreign pigs and Communists who should all be kicked out of Germany.

But first and always, they talked about Jews. Hatred of Jews was their deepest conviction, and Jews were their favorite topic of conversation. I don't think I ever talked about Jews as much as with these venomous little old ladies.

But they didn't just talk. They distributed propaganda and Holocaust denial literature—and they had a distinct advantage in that they were inconspicuous. They also worked as secret agents and spies for the Movement. They did come under surveillance, and about once a year some action was taken against the HNG. But usually the authorities would simply take the propaganda material away from an HNG member and tell her to stop passing it out in the future. It was a tough call for the cops because one couldn't very well put old ladies behind bars, though many of them really belonged there.

For one thing, they also held big meetings in which they would give speeches not *directly* calling for arson. But they might say, "It's about time something is done against foreigners, something our cowardly, corrupt democratic government in Bonn has neither the will nor the morality to do. . . ." Officially they would oppose the bombings and fires, while praising the young men who set foreigners' shelters on fire as being brave and patriotic in a land of cowardly democrats and multicultural mongrels.

And eventually they would express regret that they had to fight foreigners instead of the Jews. They'd say, "Nowadays there are only the foreigners, it is important to fight them . . . but we should not forget the Jews! We should not forget the Jews," they would always add, hopefully. . . .

Somehow, it seemed more natural for young people to have these beliefs. I know that sounds crazy. But it is a uniquely sinister sensation to be sitting next to an eighty-year-old woman who is eating a piece of cake and dribbling coffee onto her blouse, and saying, "We absolutely should desecrate more Jewish cemeteries this month." And somehow I hated them for trying to incite a young person like me to do such things. . . .

Military training and ideological indoctrination were cardinal concerns of the movement.

By far the most serious war games I observed were in Austria. They were organized by . . . trainers from the Austrian Federal Army, the Bundesheer. I went as an observer for the north German neo-Nazis. We took video cameras so we could film their camp for our own training exercises. What I saw in Austria made me realize that our exercises had all been childish games.

The exercises were held in Langleuten, a town where the far-right Austrian Freedom Party was very strong. The Austrian trainees arrived on Friday evening and practiced until Sunday afternoon—without sleep. It was total round-the-clock paramilitary training. During the day they practiced target shooting, grenade attacks, and laying explosives.

At night more specialized training took place. Night marches were accompanied by hand-to-hand combat in the dark and training in the art of silent killing. . . .

. . . What was unusual were the straw dummies used for the killing exercises. These were all dressed as concentration camp inmates, with striped uniforms and yellow Jewish stars on their breasts.

The Austrians would line up a row of these macabre scarecrows, and by the end of the practice there'd be little left of them. They practiced shooting them, stabbing them, and then, when they were mostly destroyed, putting them into a pile and blowing them up with grenades or timed charges.

The sadistic nostalgia for concentration camp tortures could hardly have been lost on anyone, but everyone participated cheerfully, taking the costumes as an amusing joke.

"Jews die!" a row of troops would scream as they led a bayonet charge against the scarecrows or shot them. Before blowing them up, there was simply mechanical efficiency, because it was a purely "technical" operation and they were clocking one another. They seemed to have an infinite supply of these striped concentration camp uniforms. I have no idea where they got them. . . .

The basic requirement for indoctrination was youth. We accepted older members, of course, but far fewer and treated them differently. It was assumed that if you joined an organization like ours when you were over, say, twenty-two, you were aware of what the Movement's history and implications were. You had at the very least the foundation of hatred and loyalty, a basic understanding of who the enemy was and why you wanted to fight him. This is not to say that older members weren't indoctrinated—in the Movement it was a permanent, ongoing process; you were never too old to indoctrinate or be indoctrinated—but we focused on indoctrinating teenagers. . . .

. . . We taught them about Germany in their grandparents' era, Germany the last time it had been a great power in the world—and we gave them a map of Europe at the time.

Together we'd look at the map showing Germany in 1937 and Germany today, and

I'd say, "Look at the Poles, they took this from us . . . the Czechs took this . . . and Austria too belonged to the German Reich. All this is gone. It was stolen, taken unlawfully from us Germans." You inflamed the recruit's feeling of injustice. And you began to draw all the strings connecting everything to the Jews. The land was gone because the Jews had stabbed Germany in the back in the First World War and then created the lie of the Holocaust in the Second. We'd begin to spend a lot of time on the *results* of the Holocaust lie, even before proving it was a lie. That way you first established Jewish guilt and made the idea suspect without having to confront the evidence. The Holocaust myth was simply a way to weaken Germans, as well as how the Jews had swindled Germany into financing the State of Israel.

And you could watch a fourteen-year-old quickly develop a total feeling of injustice. This could have been someone who'd never thought about the Jews before, and in a way that was even better, because he'd had no time to develop perspective or counterarguments.

What you wanted was a fresh tablet upon which to write. With the exception of someone whose grandparents had been concentration camp guards and who had been a ruthless Jew-hating Nazi from the cradle on, anyone who had thought much about the Holocaust before you got to him was basically disqualified from indoctrination. We didn't want to waste our time on him because he'd have too many questions in his head, too many doubts. But if you took a real blank slate and you worked on him, the result would often be someone who was soon filled with hate and prepared to either commit violent acts or at least express his anger in some other way.

4 Ethnic Minorities

Although the gradual movement in Europe toward the creation of nation-states since at least the French Revolution had established specific criteria for citizenship (ranging from language, to ethnicity, to residency), virtually no European state community has been able to make a serious claim to homogeneity. Moreover, by the 1960s Western European states had become new homes for an increasing number of people from outside the Continent. In the case of West Germany, most came as guest workers, largely from Turkey; in France and Great Britain, these new residents, searching for economic opportunity, came from former colonial possessions in North and sub-Saharan Africa, and from South Asia and the Caribbean, respectively. In these and other states, people came as asylum-seekers from regimes that had violated their human rights. Members of these new ethnic minorities brought with them very different cultural influences and often new languages, providing a truly cosmopolitan influence on host country residents, who reacted with a range of sentiment, from openness, to reluctant acceptance, to xenophobia. As long as the economies were healthy, Europeans generally expressed rather few xenophobic concerns. However, when competition for scarce jobs, competing claims on health and welfare services, and criminality increased during periods of recession, these foreigners often found themselves the objects of criticism, even physical attacks. The creation of the European Union has been successful thus far in promoting greater understanding and a sense of commonality among its member communities—yet the place of ethnic minorities in these states is far from uniformly secure.

Enoch Powell
BRINGING THE IMMIGRATION ISSUE TO THE CENTER OF POLITICS

Fear of being overwhelmed by immigrants from the West Indies, Africa, and South Asia became a serious political issue in Great Britain during the later 1960s, and the chief spokesman of those in favor of suspending immigration and assisting in re-immigration was the Conservative politician Enoch Powell. Powell was anything but a fire-breathing xenophobe along the lines of Jean-Marie Le Pen or Jörg Haider. Nonetheless, he was a darling of staunch British Tories, both because of his oratorical skill and his willingness to advance a politically sensitive issue such as immigration control. He was a controversial figure to the moderate center and left on account of his willingness to challenge the Labour government's progressive Race Relations Bill (1968) through a clear association of ethnic homogeneity with a stable Britain.

In the following speech, delivered in Birmingham on April 20, 1968, against the impending Race Relations Bill vote, Powell conjured up the image of a United Kingdom beset by people of color, and warned that his country might come to suffer the sorts of racial problems popularly associated with American society if measures were not taken to prevent an "untenable" influx of foreigners.

A week or two ago I fell into conversation with a constituent, a middle-aged, quite ordinary working man employed in one of our nationalised industries. After a sentence or two about the weather, he suddenly said: 'If I had the money to go, I wouldn't stay in this country.' I made some deprecatory reply, to the effect that even this government wouldn't last for ever; but he took no notice, and continued: 'I have three children, all of them been through grammar school and two of them married now, with family. I shan't be satisfied till I have seen them all settled overseas. In this country in fifteen or twenty years time the black man will have the whip hand over the white man.'

I can already hear the chorus of execration. How dare I say such a horrible thing? How dare I stir up trouble and inflame feelings by repeating such a conversation? The answer is that I do not have the right not to do so. Here is a decent, ordinary fellow Englishman, who in broad daylight in my own town says to me, his Member of Parliament, that this country will not be worth living in for his children. I simply do not have the right to shrug my shoulders and think about something else. What he is saying, thousands and hundreds of thousands are saying and thinking—not throughout Great Britain, perhaps, but in the areas that are already undergoing the total transformation to which there is no parallel in a thousand years of English history.

In fifteen or twenty years, on present trends, there will be in this country 3½ million Commonwealth immigrants and their descendants. That is not my figure. That is the official figure given to Parliament by the spokesman of the Registrar General's office. There is no comparable official figure for the year 2000; but it must be in the region of 5–7 million, approximately one-tenth of the whole population, and approaching that of Greater London. Of course, it will not be evenly distributed from Margate to Aberystwyth and from Penzance to Aberdeen. Whole areas, towns and parts of towns across England will be occupied by different sections of the immigrant and immigrant-descended population.

As time goes on, the proportion of this total who are immigrant descendants, those born in England, who arrived here by exactly the same route as the rest of us, will rapidly increase. Already by 1985 the native-born would constitute the majority. It is this fact above all which creates the extreme urgency of action now, of just that kind of action which is hardest for politicians to take, action where the difficulties lie in the present but the evils to be prevented or minimised lie several Parliaments ahead.

The natural and rational first question with a nation confronted by such a prospect is to ask: 'how can its dimensions be reduced?' Granted it be not wholly preventable, can it be limited—bearing in mind that numbers are of the essence: the significance and consequences of an alien element introduced into a country or population are profoundly different according to whether that element is 1 percent or 10 percent. The answers to the simple and rational question are equally simple and rational: by stopping, or virtually stopping, further inflow, and by promoting the maximum outflow. Both answers are part of the official policy of the Conservative Party.

It almost passes belief that at this moment twenty or thirty additional immigrant children are arriving from overseas in Wolverhampton alone every week—and that means fifteen or twenty additional families of a decade or two hence. Those whom the gods wish to destroy, they first make mad. We must be mad, literally mad, as a nation to be permitting the annual inflow of some 50,000 dependents, who are for the most part the material of the future growth of the immigrant-descended population. It is like watching a nation busily engaged in heaping up its own funeral pyre. So insane are we that we actually permit unmarried persons to immigrate for the purpose of founding a family with spouses and fiancés whom they have never seen. Let no one suppose that the flow of dependents will automatically tail off. On the contrary, even at the present admission rate of only 5000 a year by voucher, there is sufficient for a further 25,000 dependents per annum *ad infinitum,* without taking into account the huge reservoir of existing relations in this country—and I am making no allowance at all for fraudulent entry. In these circumstances nothing will suffice but that the total inflow for settlement should be reduced at once to negligible proportions, and that the necessary legislative and administrative measures be taken without delay. I stress the words 'for settlement'. This has nothing to do with the entry of Commonwealth citizens, any more than of aliens, into this country for the purposes of study or of improving their qualifications, like (for instance) the Commonwealth doctors who, to the advantage of their own countries, have enabled our hospital service to be expanded faster than would otherwise have been possible. These are not, and never have been, immigrants.

I turn to re-emigration. If all immigration ended tomorrow, the rate of growth of the immigrant and immigrant-descended population would be substantially reduced, but the prospective size of this element in the population would still leave the basic character of the national danger unaffected. This can only be tackled while a considerable proportion of the total still comprises persons who entered this country during the last ten years or so. Hence the urgency of implementing now the second element of the Conservative Party's policy: the encouragement of re-emigration. Nobody can make an estimate of the numbers which, with generous grants and assistance, would choose either to return to their countries of origin or to go to other countries anxious to receive the manpower and the skills they represent. Nobody knows, because no such policy has yet been attempted. I can only say that, even at present, immigrants in my own constituency from time to time come to me, asking if I can find them assistance to return home. If such a policy were adopted and pursued with the determination which the gravity of the alternative justifies, the resultant outflow could appreciably alter the prospects for the future.

It can be no part of any policy that existing families should be kept divided; but there are two directions in which families can be reunited, and if our former and present immigration laws have brought about the division of families, albeit voluntary or semi-voluntary, we ought to be prepared to arrange for them to be reunited in their countries of origin. In short, suspension of immigration and encouragement of re-emigration hang together, logically and humanly, as two aspects of the same approach.

The third element of the Conservative Party's policy is that all who are in this country as citizens should be equal before the law and that there shall be no discrimination or difference made between them by public authority. As Mr. Heath[1] has put it, we will have no 'first-class citizens' and 'second-class citizens'. This does not mean that the immigrant and his descendants should be elevated into a privileged or special class or that the citizen should be denied his right to discriminate in the management of his own affairs between one fellow-citizen and another or that he should be subjected to inquisition as to his reasons and motives for behaving in one lawful manner rather than another. . . .

The other dangerous delusion from which those who are wilfully or otherwise blind to realities suffer, is summed up in the word 'integration'. To be integrated into a population means to become for all practical purposes indistinguishable from its other members. Now, at all times, where there are marked physical differences, especially of colour, integration is difficult though, over a period, not impossible. There are among the Commonwealth immigrants who have come to live here in the last fifteen years or so, many thousands whose wish and purpose is to be integrated and whose every thought and endeavour is bent in that direction. But to imagine that such a thing enters the heads of a great and growing majority of immigrants and their descendants is a ludicrous misconception, and a dangerous one to boot.

We are on the verge here of a change. Hitherto it has been force of circumstance and of background which has rendered the very idea of integration inaccessible to the greater part of the immigrant population—that they never conceived or intended such a thing, and that their numbers and physical concentration meant the pressures towards integration which normally bear upon any small minority did not operate. Now we are seeing the growth of positive forces acting against integration, of vested interests in the preservation and sharpening of racial and religious differences, with a view to the exercise of actual domination, first over fellow-immigrants and then over the rest of the population. The cloud no bigger than a man's hand, that can so rapidly overcast the sky, has been visible recently in Wolverhampton and has shown signs of spreading quickly. The words I am about to use, verbatim as they appeared in the local press on 17 February, are not mine, but those of a Labour Member of Parliament who is a Minister in the present Government. 'The Sikh community's campaign to maintain customs inappropriate in Britain is much to be regretted. Working in Britain, particularly in the public services, they should be prepared to accept the terms and conditions of their employment. To claim special communal rights (or should one say rites?) leads to a dangerous fragmentation within society. This communalism is a canker; whether practised by one colour or another it is to be strongly condemned.' All credit to John Stonehouse for having had the insight to perceive that, and the courage to say it.

For these dangerous and divisive elements the legislation proposed in the Race Relations Bill is the very pabulum they need to flourish. Here is the means of showing that the immigrant communities can organise to consolidate their members, to agitate and campaign against their fellow citizens, and to overawe and dominate the rest with the legal weapons which the ignorant and the ill-informed have provided. As I look ahead, I am filled with foreboding. Like the Roman, I seem to see 'the River Tiber foaming with much blood'. That tragic and intractable phenomenon which we watch with horror on the other side of the Atlantic but which there is interwoven with the history and existence of the States itself, is coming upon us here by our own volition and our own neglect. Indeed, it has all but come. In numerical terms, it will be of American proportions long before the end of the century. Only resolute and urgent action will avert it even now. Whether there will be the public will to demand and obtain that action, I do not know. All I know is that to see, and not to speak, would be the great betrayal.

[1]Edward Heath—Conservative politician and prime minister from 1970 to 1974.

Zehra Onder
"MUSLIM-TURKISH CHILDREN IN GERMANY: SOCIOCULTURAL PROBLEMS"

During the early 1960s, the economy of the Federal Republic of Germany experienced enormous growth—the era of the so-called "economic miracle." There was more work than could be done by Germans alone, prompting the West German government to enter into labor recruitment agreements with Spain, Italy, Greece, Yugoslavia, and Turkey. Up until the recession of 1973 and the onset of widespread unemployment, there was ample work for these "guest-workers"; it was also expected that at some point they would return home. Turkish guest-workers proved the most reluctant to leave Germany and the most willing to bring their families with them to their new residences.

In 1961, the non-German population comprised 1.2 percent of the FRG's entire population, with the Turkish minority representing only one percent of that total; by 1970 this number increased to a non-German population of 4.3 percent and a Turkish minority of 16.5 percent. By 1992, the numbers had increased to 8 percent and more than 28.5 percent, respectively. When recruitment of foreign labor ended in 1973, this Turkish-dominated body of guest-workers became a resident minority overnight. Today, approximately 10 percent of all residents of Germany are considered foreigners, the overwhelming majority of them of Turkish origin. At the time of publication of this book, German authorities have been engaged in heated debate over the revision of citizenship laws—which have been based on ethnic, rather than residency principles since the beginning of the twentieth century—to allow for the possibility of naturalizing members of foreign minorities under specific circumstances as yet to be determined.

The following selection explores the challenges that children of Turkish guest-worker families face in socializing into *both* their particular ethnic subculture and the dominant culture of broader German society. The author explores the tensions between acculturation and ghettoization for primarily first and second-generation Turks born in Germany.

Although Germans of ethnic Turkish ancestry continue to play an ever-growing role in the arts, business, and politics at the local, state, and federal levels into the twenty-first century, debate persists in German society over the extent to which a multicultural Germany is desirable if immigrants from Muslim and other diverse backgrounds, and their descendants, seem unwilling to embrace mainstream values.

The circumstances of being torn between two cultures is most often a severe problem for Islamic families. Attempts made by these families to analyze and understand their situation are frequently inadequate. The issues are so complex that external help can only partially clarify certain aspects of them. Many relate to the private sphere of life, and there simply is not much that officials can do to help.

Most of the Turkish children who were born in and who have grown up in Germany are confused. They are torn between the family on the one side and the German environment and school on the other. They are disoriented because they seem to belong nowhere, like the Turkish schoolchildren who were interviewed in Duisburg, Germany in the district (Stadteil) Bruckhausen.

Why is this the case? [One Turk] explains: "In Turkey we are the Almanci (those coming from Germany) and in Germany 'the damned foreigners.' I don't know where I belong." It's a hard life to be torn between two cultures. We have interviewed children who feel happy and at ease neither in German schools, in their family, nor in their homeland. And everyone expects those children to be successful in German schools. . . .

Fatma Kurt, who has to take care of her eight siblings, says: "The parents take little care of their children. They are mainly interested in making money in order to return home sooner." This has an especially hard impact on girls. Sons are almost invariably the favorite ones in their families. For example, if the son becomes ill, he is immediately taken to a doctor. But, if this happens to the daughter, she is usually left to her own fate. This reflects conditions in Turkey, where thousands of children, especially girls, die because of this attitude and reasoning. It is usually said that if God wishes, the girl will get well without seeing the doctor anyway. This is not so important because many of the girls are just born accidentally, while a son is expected to be born.

One is usually unwillingly reminded of the times before Islam—times in which daughters were buried alive. Much has changed since then but the principal reaction of joy at birth of a son has remained.

Many marriages in Turkey fail just because the woman cannot give a son to her husband. A woman who has given birth to several sons has fulfilled her main duty and the only thing she expects from then on is the respect of her sons and the financial and other support of her husband and his family. The governing belief is that a girl will marry and leave the family so anything done for her will help others, not the family. The son, it is expected, will remain in the family and will eventually take care of his parents, if necessary. That is why many Turkish parents do not care about the education of their daughters. Fatma Kurt's mother says about the education of her daughters: "They will finally marry, what is the use of going to school; it is enough for them to know how to read and write."

On the other hand, the sons are so spoiled that it is hard for them to accept the authority of the teacher. They often begin to fight and so they remain at odds with the school education process. If there were not the fines of DM1000-1500 and other measures, such as cutting off the school-related payments for the children, there would not be any foreign children, especially girls, going to school. For, as noted, girls have a special negative shame within the family, as well as in the Islamic environment of Turkey or among relatives and friends in Germany.

These factors make the integration of foreign children into the German school environment very difficult and they are usually left alone and isolated. Thus, the so called integration of foreign children into German schools is unfortunately only seemingly successful. "Germany and German schools are not a natural environment for foreign children. From birth on, like all children, they are influenced by their close social and cultural identity, as far as their own orientation and behavior are concerned."

As elsewhere, these foreign children are exposed to certain prejudices. "The prejudices against the foreign children do them much harm. Their learning interest sinks, they get isolated, get autistic or aggressive and their socialization gets blocked." As a result, spiritual stress and conflicts follow. Many foreign children feel overwhelmed and view school as a burden and as an obligation. This often means for them withdrawal or special school. "The prejudice phenomenon, however, can also involve the teacher."

Though the foreign children try to mix with the German children of the same age, ". . . they do not succeed. Being labelled as 'foreigners' leads to an isolation in school as well as out of school."

For foreign children, the family progressively loses its role as an identity institution. Usually they can expect little if any help from parents in solving their problems because the parents themselves cannot become oriented in the new environment. So the parents are overwhelmed in their function as a socialization and identification institution. "Obliged to the cultural traditions they have brought with themselves concerning language and religion, the parents have to witness how their children develop away from their own values."

All these factors promote the aggressiveness of both the German and Turkish children in classrooms. The foreign children often become isolated at school. They feel like outsiders. For example, Temel Kurt, from Duisburg-Bruckhausen, looks troubled in saying: "I know the value which I have in the eyes of the Germans."

It is especially hard for the foreign children because their socialization has to take place in the background of two societies. The foreign family is not able to give the children strategies to cope with both social structures. The socialization performance of the foreign family is limited because they do not possess a strategy for confronting German society and because of their own background they are themselves lost. The parents are confused about the education of their children because they themselves have lost their orientation and the demands made on them by their children are very different from those for which they are more or less prepared.

In such situations, families often try to give their children what they have received from former generations. "The foreign children are torn between the traditional norms in their families and the new norms at school. These situations result in spiritual burdens and conflicts. They are overwhelmed and perceive the school as a burden and obligation only."

Identity problems of foreign children are complex. Both personal as well as social identity are concerned. Because both of them are lacking, this often leads to isolation from the German environment. This leads to behavioral problems. Foreign children . . . suffer much more insecurity and fear compared to German ones. Excessive sensitivity, depression and concentration problems, all being related to contact difficulties, are often obviously observable in the foreign children. . . .

The Islamic value-norm system determines what is right and what is wrong, what is good and what is bad. The new social environment turns all this upside down through another value-norm system. As time elapses, a great conflict grows that can in no way be managed.

The majority try to live as they did in Turkey. Otherwise there would be disputes about daily life which may result in difficulties for families and in school education.

It follows that the social change in the family in their new environment can follow slowly. For many families, this identity crisis turns into a debilitating permanent condition. Many of them prefer to keep their personal problems suppressed and do not apply to consultation centers. Their only help in such cases is relatives and friends. However, in very important matters like, for example, looking for a job, for a dwelling, for problems in kindergarten or school, they require the experienced help of consultation and education centers.

Neighbors and acquaintances from the same cultural milieu can help each other more through regular meetings. Often only women meet for exchange of information and mutual support, giving advice for example. The problems should first be discussed in this milieu before the Islamic family decides to apply for public assistance.

Eventual friendships between Turkish and German families are not without their problems. They demand mutual knowledge and understanding. Ordinary social contacts (mutual help in different fields; going to schools, officials; childcare; cooking now and then a common dinner) do not require a close relationship. A real exchange of private problems, such as school problems, does not take place. When families do not speak German, a dialogue is much more difficult. A Turkish woman, who lives in a neighborhood with no other Turkish women speaking German, remains widely isolated—together with her children. The husband often spends his free time with other men. The woman cannot go out into a society where German men and women commingle. Her freedom of movement outside the home is restricted by the separation of the sexes. She often spends all evening in front of the TV and is engaged in housework or other indoor activities for most of the other time.

Since traditionally a Turkish woman is not free to make her own decisions and is economically dependent on her husband, she fears that the husband will leave her because of inappropriate behavior. In a foreign society, because of her isolation, she is much more strongly attached to her family and would rather not undertake the risk of deciding what she is free to do.

The man who insists on his hierarchical position of primary importance in the family will not freely give this up. Traditionally he possesses the authority to decide and penalize. Moreover, the man tries to compensate for his lack of confidence in foreign surroundings by insisting on his position in the family. The foreign surrounding is often considered as "immoral." The man believes it to be his duty to keep the female members of the family away from society.

In this way German society and not a man's behavior becomes for both the mother and the daughter, the "enemy."

It is a success when mother and daughter can overcome this isolation through contacts with neighbors coming from their own country. These contacts should not be underestimated because in a purely German, i.e., "hostile," environment the isolation of the woman is absolute. In Duisburg-Bruckhausen we were able to establish that the families from Turkey contact other Turkish families exclusively.

Foreign families not only suffer identity crisis but also generation conflicts. As far as returning home is concerned, a very delicate situation exists. The question arises whether Turkish children (second and third generation) who have had their education in Germany, and in this way have adopted German culture, have any real relationship with the sociocultural environment in Turkey.

Within the family relations between the parents and children are characterized by respect and surrender to the parents; contacts with the sociocultural environment outside the family are reduced to a minimum degree.

When the children enter another sociocultural environment, they fall into a crisis situation "because their value and norm-system is tested in a totally different sociocultural environment. In such a stressful situation, their orientation is confused; there is nothing which can serve as a reliable basis for behavior and decisionmaking. In this way a permanent situation comes into existence in which all values are tested and questioned."

In their search for identity the foreign children are mostly left alone to fend for themselves between two cultures.

Joachim Krautz
"THE GRAPES OF NEGLECT—VIOLENCE AND XENOPHOBIA IN GERMANY"

While Germany is not the only European country to have experienced racist violence against foreigners particularly since the fall of communism, the specter of neo-nazism has led the international media to focus much of their attention upon xenophobia and crimes against foreigners by ultra-rightists in the Federal Republic. During the 1990s, some forty-nine foreigners—almost all of them Turks, Africans, or Asians—were killed by neo-Nazis in firebombings of guest-worker or refugee dwellings, or as a result of beatings and stabbings. In the following selection, the

journalist Joachim Krautz sought the causes of violence and hatred of foreigners in the post-reunification malaise of unemployment, inflation, and economic dislocation, particularly in Eastern Germany. If paroxysms of violence have abated during the first decade of the twenty-first century, xenophobia remains a concern in Germany, as in other Euopean lands—particularly in the wake of terror attacks on U.S., Spanish, and British targets. Heightened perceptions of vulnerability to terror in the wake of foiled Isalamist plots against German targets seems to factor into the antipathy against foreigners among some members of German society.

The arsonists came at night. Fully aware of the likelihood that people might be in their bedrooms they set fire to the apartment house, in which—according to the nameplates near the doorbells—a couple of Turkish families lived. The fact that Turks were the sole inhabitants of that house had been the precise reason for the murderers' choice of their target. In the night from Saturday to Whitsunday five people—all of them women and girls—became the victims of this treacherous crime which took place in Solingen, a small, until then very ordinary town in the west of Germany. It was the climax of a whole series of violent attacks against foreigners since the reunification of Germany. A deadly series which claimed 49 lives so far. All these assaults had in common that the perpetrators were led by racist or right-extremist motives. Pictures went around the world showing young men with tattoed arms and closely shorn haircuts, instigated by beer and rock music with explicitly fascist texts, hurling petrol bombs at houses while honest citizens stood by and watched. And the politicians, apparently, are not able or—as terrified foreigners in Germany claim—not willing to halt this development. Chancellor Helmut Kohl did not even think it appropriate to be present at the memorial ceremonies. What is happening in Germany at the moment? Has Nazism risen from its grave? Or will Germany turn once more into the scourge of Europe?

The current events make up a very complex issue. Over the past few years facts and statistics with regard to foreigners, aggressors and right-extremism in Germany have been perpetually blurred and distorted—both at home and abroad—to serve various interest groups. Right-extremism, nationalism and the ugly face of racism are by no means confined to Germany. But because of her historical peculiarity these phenomena have always been ascribed a specific significance in the country which made Auschwitz happen. . . .

For the majority of the young Germans who grew up in the sixties, seventies, and early eighties nationalism was out. And so were all its symbols like the national flag or the national anthem. It would have been unthinkable to sing the latter in school or to play it in cinemas after the performance as it is the custom in some other countries. Intoxicated fans bawled the national anthem and waved the country's flag in the football stadiums. But young (West) Germans who wanted to be politically fashionable defined their politics by the absence of patriotism and their national pride consisted of criticism of their country—if they were proud of it at all.

The situation in the other German state was different from the start. There the Communist government by definition had seen themselves as not having any links with the brown-shirted past. As a result there had never been any attempt at dealing with the past as there had been in the West.

Consequently, the notion of the nation had retained its positive connotation for the people in the former German Democratic Republic. National pride for socialist achievements was not only condoned but even encouraged by the government. After all, one lived in the better part of the two Germanies. The general public, however, saw it differently. After having been fed—or rather brainwashed—with West German advertisements and TV commercials for decades they, indeed, imagined paradise, the land of milk and honey, as the epitomy of

German ingeniousness—but on the other side of the Wall. Whether identifying themselves with or rebelling against the system and embracing the world view of the class enemy—none of the generations in East Germany ever felt obliged to suppress the sentiment of patriotism. . . .

No wonder the enticers of West German right-extremist groups met with such a fertile ground for their propaganda when the Wall fell in November 1989. While the legal right-wing parties NPD and the Republikaner (Republicans—REP) have tried to attract conservative petitbourgeois citizens the group which openly profess their loyalty to National Socialism have recruited their followers among East German skinheads and hooligans (a social phenomenon, by the way, which had been anything but unknown in the former German Democratic Republic). . . .

In spite of the fact that there were hardly any foreigners living in East Germany the various right-wing fringe groups and splinter parties were highly successful in spreading their message of the threat of 'foreignization'. In 1989 less than 200,000 foreign workers and students lived in the East—representing a mere 1.2 per cent of the entire population—compared to 5.2 million foreigners in the West—i.e., 8.2 per cent of the population there. And yet the first violent assaults against Vietnamese workers and Polish tourists in the East were reported as early as December 1989. Shocking pictures of attacks against hostels for asylum seekers in Hoyerswerda (in September 1991) and in Rostock (in August 1992) seemed only to confirm the worst prejudices West Germans hold against their brethren in the East: their society had been inferior, they are not used to hard work in a capitalist world, and now they even turn out to be prone to long-buried ideologies of hatred and violence.

However, the spectacular events of Mölln, a West German town where neo-Nazis murdered three Turks by setting their house alight in November last year, or of Solingen now, showed that all is not well in the old Republic either. But the good citizens in the West are only too willing to lay the blame on the sudden popularity of nationalist and neo-Nazi ideas in the East, to call West German evil-doers 'imitators', and to lament a spread of xenophobia coming from the former internationalist workers' paradise. On the one hand the East: a hotbed for terror and violence because of all its deficiencies? On the other hand the West: a natural realm of tolerance and understanding because of the long-standing dialogue and exchange of views in its society? Does this picture hold good?

A recent poll among A-level candidates in the West German city of Munich showed that the majority of them believed the actual rate of asylum seekers among the population amounted to a menacing 30 per cent or more, whereas in fact it is less than 1 per cent. Those interviewed were neither neo-Nazis nor skinheads but they belonged to the intellectual elite of the young generation. Such grossly wrong estimates about figures concerning asylum seekers, refugees, and foreigners in general are 'common knowledge' nowadays. This cannot be the work of a few splinter parties alone. . . .

Until May this year Germany had the world's most liberal legislation granting every political refugee an individual right to political asylum. The experience of the Nazi-dictatorship encouraged the Founding Fathers of the Federal Republic of Germany to write down this right into the German constitution. As a result of the political changes and upheavals in Eastern Europe and of the growing misery in the Third World but also because of improved international transportation the numbers of asylum seekers from all over the world have been increasing over the past few years.

Soon the right-extremist parties focused their attention on this alleged threat to society. At first, coming up with completely arbitrary figures, a differentiation was made between 'genuine' political refugees and 'economic migrants'. Using very emotional language the latter were denigrated as 'scroungers' or even as 'parasites'. Then, right-wing propaganda tried to create an atmosphere of fear using the absolute numbers of asylum seekers arriving in Germany every year. A horror scenario was conjured up claiming that within a few years foreigners would outnumber the native population. According to these figures from 1989 to 1991 alone about 650,000 refugees applied for political asylum.

But these statistics are faulty. . . . [A]bove all these figures grossly misrepresent the increase of the number of foreigners living in Germany because they do not take into account that in the same period of time almost 1.5 million foreigners left Germany for good. With other groups of migrants coming to the country—relatives of foreign workers, members of EC countries, etc., and because children born of foreign parents in Germany are nevertheless foreigners due to an atavistic law concerning nationality, the overall 'foreign' population is, however, still slightly on the rise.

Right-wing groups have constantly dwelt upon these statistics using terrifying images of 'floods of asylum parasites', etc. Germany has been compared to a 'boat [which] is full'. Appealing to basic instincts like fear and distrust, providing easy answers to complex problems, offering a clear profile of the enemy to project one's hate and frustration on—all this won them wide sympathies at a time when cries abound. . . .

Of all the immigrant nationalities the Turks have a culture the most foreign to German sensibilities. And yet it is not only their Muslim religion and their extremely patriarchal family structure but their sheer number—with 1.8 million the Turks represent the largest minority in Germany—which has kindled a subliminal anxiety within many Germans. The foreign loses its exotic facination if it becomes common and usual. It needs malicious incitement, however, to turn this anxiety into fear and hatred: fear of losing one's own cultural identity and hatred of those who appear to threaten this culture. . . .

The subconscious fear of an uncertain national identity has resulted in a concept of citizenship based upon descent ('ius sanguinis') or upon the profession of German culture reflecting the definition given by the Nazi-German's Home Secretary, Wilhelm Frick, in 1939. This can lead to the absurd situation that a Latvian SS-man's grandson who does not speak a single word of German but whose grandfather had proclaimed his loyalty to German culture by joining the SS can be entitled to German nationality. On the other hand a young Turk, who has been born in Germany and who speaks German better than Turkish, still has no right to it. This law governing nationality ensures a steady increase in 'homemade' foreigners. . . .

The damage right-extremist violence has done to Germany's image abroad is tremendous. Big business has long since realized that the current development runs against their interest. The tourist trade fears losses, export figures plummeted already, and Japanese investments fell off to a record low in 1992. And they reacted swiftly: companies started to fire employees who molested foreign workmates in word or in deed (measures which the women's rights movement has been fighting for for years). It was mainly their initiative which brought about the large turnoff of concerned citizens protesting against xenophobia at the nationwide candlelight vigils last December. All this reminded one of the 'public breast-beating contests', as Max Horkheimer used to call the mass abjurations after World War II. And while honest middle-class citizens—in accordance with the government—call the perpetrators 'a few demented criminals', the Left—in accordance with the press abroad—is busy in conjecturing the scare of reviving Nazism. Who is right?

It is a fact that since the reunification right-extremist terror and aggression have claimed at least 49 lives. The victims were not only foreigners; 15 homeless and disabled were among them. Pretending to feel a call to 'cleanse' Germany from its 'impurities' the young perpetrators insist that they only perform the will of the majority. And in a horrifying way they are right. Xenophobic, racist, and eugenic ideas and prejudices are widespread even if they mostly remain tacit. Although there have always been violent crimes committed by youths the nature of the tidal wave of aggression currently sweeping over Germany is altogether different. Above all, it is the brutality of the assaults which is shocking. The youths—two out of three are younger than 21—aim at maiming and killing their victims. Where does their readiness to commit acts of violence stem from? . . .

Frustration and disappointment prevail with unemployment soaring in a country whose citizens had not known anything but full employment for 40 years and whose self-respect had always been based upon work. Only anti-social elements, who refused to work, used to be without a job. Furthermore, despite the snooper activities of the 'Stasi' (the former East German Secret Service) there has been a sense of solidarity among the citizens against the bigwigs and party bosses of the ruling SED. Now with jobs scarce and uncertainty everywhere mistrust and envy govern people's minds. Young people are deprived of any perspective for the future. Besides, now that the euphoria about the reunification has long since abated and its true costs are presented by an only too evasive government, East Germans feel more and more excluded as second-class citizens by West Germans. They in their turn exclude those whom they deem even further down on the social scale. And so they fall back on the only identity which they think they can be sure of, i.e., their national identity: Germany for the Germans! . . .

What would be the cure of this crisis? First, it would be necessary to focus the attention of the masses on Germany's real problems: the decline of ethical standards, the devastation of the environment, the decrease of work, and the reunification which has virtually failed. Equally important would be to restrain the media from offering a forum for the perpetrators. The former were often rightly accused of depicting the crimes as if there were no victims or rather of portraying the aggressors, the 'misled youths', as the actual victims. Assaulting people is a safe bet to make it into the headlines of nationwide newspapers—but only if the motives are right-extremist. Some TV teams have been rumoured of having even paid Nazi hooligans to hurl stones or raise their arms with the illegal Hitler salute.

Commission for the Abolishment of Sexual Mutilations

AFRICAN IMMIGRANTS IN FRANCE: THE CONTROVERSY OVER FEMALE CIRCUMCISION

Language barriers, skin color, religion, diet, and practices such as the wearing of head scarves are among the most prominent of the cultural differences between immigrants to Western Europe from Africa, the Middle East, South Asia, or the Caribbean. In recent years, the practice of female circumcision—also referred to as female genital mutilation (or FGM) by critics—has been outlawed under Articles 310 of the French Penal Code. Since the criminalization of inflicting mutilation on a person in the 1980s, some two dozen cases of FGM cases have been heard by French criminal courts. By the early twenty-first century, the practice has been all but eliminated within France. However, the French Women's Association for the Abolition of Sexual Mutilations has become increasingly involved in advocating for asylum in cases where women from sub-Saharan and North African societies with fundamentalist interpretations of Islam seek to protect their daughters from FGM.

The following document from the late 1990s demonstrates the lack of understanding between French society and a number of African immigrants when it comes to this contentious cultural practice.

France is the only country to date to engage in legal proceedings when a child has been excised, providing that the case is reported to the police or to a Judge. It has now been over fifteen years that the French authorities have been compelled to deal with FGM.

It all began with three-month-old Bobo Traore's death in July 1982 who died of severe hemorrhage as a result of excision performed in a Parisian suburb, at her parents' request. The infant had bled for two days. The parents said that they did not seek medical care for their child, being aware that the practice was forbidden in France. This tragedy caused public outcry. . . . Doctors and social workers in contact with the African population started asking for guidelines from the authorities. Statistics showed a great number of African little girls had been mutilated and brought to hospitals.

The French Penal Code punishes violence all the harder when the victim is a child under the age of fifteen. When the violences cause permanent infirmity or a mutilation, it is a major criminal offense. The penalty incurred goes up to ten years of imprisonment, and is increased when the persons responsible for the harm done to the child are its own parents.

Linda Weil-Curiel, a lawyer, established that the mutilation of an African infant is a major criminal offense falling within the jurisdiction of the Criminal Court and convinced the Court to rule that excision should be punished no matter the motives invoked. The first penalties consisted in suspended prison sentences for the parents (three to five years) but they are harsher now and in 1991 an excisor was condemned to serve five years. One objective was to give visibility to that issue by numerous press reports of the trials.

The parents pleaded that they only had done what was expected of good parents among their kinfolks pleading the cultural gap. The fact is that this is not legally valid; all families in France including African families are required to visit childcare centers with their babies/children where they receive information from the doctors that it is unlawful to excise children in France.

At the trials in France many testimonies have been heard of how the young African girls react when they learn that they have been submitted to the practice by their parents. They feel humiliated to have been mutilated without their consent, and they are full of anger as they understand that they will never regain what has been taken from them.

The next excision trial scheduled will take place this autumn because a young girl has complained to a Judge about her mutilation and that of her sisters and gave the name of her excisor, who is now in prison. She will ask for damages in court. She feels she has been abused and betrayed by those who should have protected and taken the best care of her, that is to say her own parents.

The younger generation is now in favor of prosecution in excision cases. They want examples to be set and harsh punishment for those who won't respect their integrity and their right to live. . . . Since 1984, when an excisor was put in jail and African families acknowledged that prison might really lie ahead, the number of excisions has decreased in France: prosecution equals protection in the excision cases. A woman from Mali living in France when a journalist after a trial asked her: 'Is it acceptable to bring all these parents to trial?' answered: 'What is not acceptable is to allow children to be tortured.'

5 Coming to Terms with the Past: Reflections on the Holocaust

Material prosperity, participatory democracy, and substantial steps toward integration by the 1980s represented significant ways in which Western European societies had recovered from the cataclysm of World War II, but the moral and emotional legacy could not be easily surmounted. This was particularly true for

West German society, but also for the veterans, survivors, and victims of the conflict across the Continent. In Western Europe, however, the level of comfort achieved near the century's end suggested to some that events of the 1930s and the first half of the 1940s should, indeed, be relegated to the past—that efforts to assess responsibility or guilt for inhuman behavior or the origins, not to mention uniqueness, of past oppressive systems should be abandoned in the interests of the future, or that only from the perspective of several decades' distance could the past be examined free from taboos or emotional turmoil. Lively, sometimes heated, debate concerning the importance of the Holocaust during the 1980s indicated its enduring importance. Politicians, religious authorities, scholars, and activists, survivors, and members of societies that had been perpetrators emphasized in the end that acknowledgment of past misdeeds was essential, and that the assumption of moral responsibility to ensure that such actions would not occur again—or at the very least not go uncondemned—was required if integration and healing were to be achieved and justice served.

Richard von Weizsäcker "A GERMAN PLEA FOR REMEMBRANCE AND RECONCILIATION"

In a speech during a commemorative ceremony on May 8, 1985, Richard von Weizsäcker (b. 1920), then president of the Federal Republic of Germany, reflected on the Holocaust and the need for remembrance.

May 8th is a day of remembrance. Remembering means recalling an occurrence honestly and undistortedly so that it becomes a part of our very beings. This places high demands on our truthfulness.

Today we mourn all the dead of the war and tyranny. In particular we commemorate the six million Jews who were murdered in German concentration camps. . . .

At the root of the tyranny was Hitler's immeasurable hatred of our Jewish compatriots. Hitler had never concealed this hatred from the public, and made the entire nation a tool of it. Only a day before his death, on April 30, 1945, he concluded his so-called "will" with the words: "Above all, I call upon the leaders of the nation and their followers to observe painstakingly the race laws and to oppose ruthlessly the poisoners of all nations: international Jewry." Hardly any country has in its history always remained free from blame for war or violence. The genocide of the Jews is, however, unparalleled in history.

The perpetration of this crime was in the hands of a few people. It was concealed from the eyes of the public, but every German was able to experience what his Jewish compatriots had to suffer, ranging from plain apathy and hidden intolerance to outright hatred. Who could remain unsuspecting after the burning of the synagogues, the plundering, the stigmatization with the Star of David, the deprivation of rights, the ceaseless violation of human dignity? Whoever opened his eyes and ears and sought information could not fail to notice that Jews were being deported. The nature and scope of the destruction may have exceeded human imagination, but in reality there was, apart from the crime itself, the attempt by too many people, including those of my generation, who were young and were not involved in planning the events and carrying them out, not to take note of what was happening. There were many ways of not burdening one's conscience, of shunning responsibility, looking away, keeping mum. When the unspeakable truth of the Holocaust then became known at the end of the war, all too many of us claimed that they had not known anything about it or even suspected anything.

There is no such thing as the guilt or innocence of an entire nation. Guilt is, like innocence, not collective, but personal. There is discovered or concealed individual guilt. There is guilt which people acknowledge or deny. Everyone who directly experienced that era should today quietly ask himself about his involvement then.

The vast majority of today's population were either children then or had not been born. They cannot profess a guilt of their own for crimes that they did not commit. No discerning person can expect them to wear a penitential robe simply because they are Germans. But their forefathers have left them a grave legacy. All of us, whether guilty or not, whether old or young, must accept the past. We are all affected by its consequences and liable for it. The young and old generations must and can help each other to understand why it is vital to keep alive the memories. It is not a case of coming to terms with the past. This is not possible. It cannot be subsequently modified or made undone. However, anyone who closes his eyes to the past is blind to the present. Whoever refuses to remember the inhumanity is prone to new risks of infection.

The Jewish nation remembers and will always remember. We seek reconciliation. Precisely for this reason we must understand that there can be no reconciliation without remembrance. The experience of millionfold death is part of the very being of every Jew in the world, not only because people cannot forget such atrocities, but also because remembrance is part of the Jewish faith.

"Seeking to forget makes exile all the longer; the secret of redemption lies in remembrance." This oft quoted Jewish adage surely expresses the idea that faith in God is faith in the work of God in history. Remembrance is experience of the work of God in history. It is the source of faith in redemption. This experience creates hope, creates faith in redemption, in reunification of the divided, in reconciliation. Whoever forgets this experience loses his faith.

If we for our part sought to forget what has occurred, instead of remembering it, this would not only be inhuman. We would also impinge upon the faith of the Jews who survived and destroy the basis of reconciliation. We must erect a memorial to thoughts and feelings in our own hearts.

Elie Wiesel
REFLECTIONS OF A SURVIVOR

Elie Wiesel (b. 1928), survivor of Auschwitz, author of numerous books and articles on the Holocaust and Jewish culture, human rights activist, and the 1986 Nobel Peace Prize winner, has also stressed the need for remembrance. In November 1987, Wiesel spoke at a conference center built inside the shell of the destroyed Reichstag, the seat of parliamentary government during the Weimar era that the Nazis so reviled. The following is a journalistic report of his speech.

GHOSTS IN THE PARLIAMENT OF DEATH

. . . Elie Wiesel . . . delivered this speech from the rostrum of the Reichstag building in West Berlin. . . . The occasion was a planning conference for a museum to be built at Wannsee, the Berlin suburb where the formal decision to murder European Jewry was taken 45 years ago.

Elie Wiesel began his address in Yiddish. A literal translation follows.

"Hush, hush, let us be silent; tombs are growing here. Planted by the foe, they are green and turning to blue. . . . Hush, my child, don't cry, crying won't do us any good: the foe will never understand our plight. . . ."

This lullaby was written in the ghetto by Shmelke Katchegirsky. Grieving Jewish mothers would chant it, trying to put to sleep their hungry, weakened and agonizing children.

Tombs? These children—these innocent little children, perhaps the best our people ever had—were deprived of everything: their lives and even a burial place.

And so, hush, little children, one million of you, hush, come: we invite you. We invite you into our memory.

(The rest of Wiesel's speech was in English.)

Yiddish in the Reichstag? There is symbolism in using this warm, melancholy and compassionate language in a place where Jewish suffering and Jewish agony—some 50 years ago—aroused neither mercy nor compassion.

Yiddish was the tongue of many if not most of the Jewish victims who perished during the dark period when the Angel of Death seemed to have replaced God in too many hearts in this country.

There is symbolism, too—as there is irony and justice—in my speaking to you this afternoon from this very rostrum where my own death, and the death of my family, and the death of my friends, and the death of my teachers and the death of my entire people, was decreed and predicted by the legally elected leader of Germany.

I would betray the dead were I not to remind you that his poisonous words did *not* make him unpopular with his people. Most applauded with fervor; some, very few, remained silent. Fewer still objected.

How many Jews found shelter in how many German homes during the Kristallnacht? How many Germans tried to help extinguish the synagogues in flames? How many tried to save holy scrolls?

In those days and nights, humanity was distorted and twisted in this city, the capital of a nation proud of its distant history, but struggling with its recent memories.

Everything human and divine was perverted then. The law itself became immoral. Here, in this city, on this rostrum, it was made legal and commendable to humiliate Jews simply for being Jews—to hunt down children simply because they were Jewish children.

It became legal and praiseworthy to imprison, shame and oppress and, ultimately, to destroy human beings—sons and daughters of an ancient people—whose very existence was considered a crime.

The officials who participated in the Wannsee conference knew they acted on behalf of their government and in the name of the German people.

The atrocities committed under the law of the Third Reich *must* not and *will* not be forgotten; nor will they be forgiven.

I have no right to forgive the killers for having exterminated six million of my kinsmen. Only the dead can forgive, and no one has the right to speak on their behalf.

Still, not all Germans alive then were guilty. As a Jew, I have never believed in collective guilt. Only the guilty were guilty.

Children of killers are not killers but children. I have neither the desire nor the authority to judge today's generation for the unspeakable crimes committed by the generation of Hitler.

But we may—and we must—hold it responsible, not for the past, but for the way it remembers the past. And for what it does with the memory of the past.

Memory is the keyword. To remember is to forge links between past and present, between past and future.

It is in the name of memory that I address myself to Germany's youth. "Remember" is the commandment that dominates the lives of young Jews today; let it dominate your lives as well. Challenged by memory, we can move forward together. Opposed to memory, you will remain eternally opposed to us and to all we stand for.

I understand: of course, I understand: it is not easy to remember. It may be even more difficult for you than it is for us Jews. We try to remember the dead, you must remember those who killed them. Yes—there is pain involved in both our efforts. Not the same pain. Open yourselves to yours, as we have opened ourselves to ours.

You find it hard to believe that your elders did these deeds? So do I. Think of the tormentors as I think of their victims. I remember every minute of their agony. I see them constantly. I am afraid: if I stop seeing them, they will die. I keep on seeing them, and they died nevertheless.

I remember: 1942, in my childhood town, somewhere in the Carpathian Mountains. Jewish children were playing in the snow, others studied hard at school. They were already decreed dead here in Berlin, and they did not know it.

There is something in all this I do not understand—I never will. Why such obstinacy on the part of the killer to kill so many of my people? Why the old men and women? Why the children?

You, young men and women in Germany, must ask yourselves the same questions.

A people that has produced Goethe and Schiller, Bach and Beethoven, chose suddenly to put its national genius at the service of evil—to erect a monument to its dark power called Auschwitz.

A community that contributed to culture and education, as few nations have, called all of culture and education into question. After all: many of the killers had college degrees. And were products of the best universities in Germany. Many came from distinguished families.

Although I often wonder about the theological implications of Auschwitz, I must recognize that Auschwitz was not sent down from heaven. Auschwitz was conceived and built by human beings.

After Auschwitz, hope itself is filled with anguish.

But after Auschwitz, hope is necessary. Where can it be found? In remembrance alone.

How was remembrance handled after the war? Admit it, it took many Germans far too long to begin to confront their past.

Teachers did not teach, and pupils did not learn, the most tragic and important chapter in German and world history. Too painful, came the explanation.

It took the Eichmann trial in Jerusalem for German courts to indict 88 murderers who, after the war, had quietly returned to their homes and resumed their trades—as if nothing had happened.

True, the situation in East Germany is worse. Unlike the Federal Republic, which did make a serious effort, under Konrad Adenauer, to compensate the survivors and to help Israel, East Germany is hostile to Israel and refused to pay reparations. East Germany, like Austria, shows not the slightest trace of remorse.

The Federal Republic has chosen a more honest and enlightened course. In just a few decades, you have traveled from brutal totalitarianism to true democracy.

The freedom of the individual is respected here. Your commitment to the Western alliance is firm.

Among you are individuals and groups to whom we feel especially close. They have been seeking atonement, in word and in deed; some have gone to work in Israel; others are involved in religious dialogues.

Writers, artists, poets, novelists, statesmen: there are among them men and women who refuse to forget—and, make no mistake, the best books by German authors deal with the trauma of the past.

Now the museum. . . . What will it be?

Show pictures of Jews before they died.

Show the cold brutality of those who killed them.

Show the passivity, the cowardly indifference of the bystanders.

Remember the Jewishness of the Jewish victims, remember the uniqueness of their tragedy. True, not all victims were Jews, but all Jews were victims.

Be the conscience of your nation. And remember, a conscience that does not speak up when injustices are being committed is betraying itself. A mute conscience is a false conscience.

In remembering, you will help your own people vanquish the ghosts that hover over its history. Remember: a community that does not come to terms with the dead will continue to traumatize the living.

We remember Auschwitz and all that it symbolizes because we believe that, in spite of the past and its horrors, the world is worthy of salvation; and salvation, like redemption, can be found only in memory.

Vatican Commission for Religious Relations with the Jews "WE REMEMBER: A REFLECTION ON THE 'SHOAH' "

A continuing sore point in Jewish-Christian relations concerns accusations that Christians essentially left Europe's Jews to their fate at the hands of the Third Reich during the Second World War. The Catholic Church in particular has borne much of this criticism, due to the silence of Pope Pius XII (r. 1939–1958) on the issue, that is, his failure to denounce the genocide and summon Catholics to oppose it. The bitterness receded somewhat with the election of Pope John XXIII and his convening of the Second Vatican Council, which officially condemned anti-Semitism and recognized the common roots of Christianity and Judaism. In 1978, the naming of a Pole—Cardinal Karol Wojtyla, the archbishop of Cracow—as Pope John Paul II held out the promise of a further improvement in Jewish-Christian understanding. Poland, with its large prewar Jewish population, had been the Nazis' chief killing ground, and John Paul himself had lost Jewish friends to the slaughter. As pope, he demonstrated considerable sensitivity to the feelings of Jews; in 1987 he told an audience of American rabbis that he planned to commission a study on Catholicism, anti-Semitism, and the Holocaust.

Originally envisioned as a two-year project, the church's statement on the Final Solution took a decade to complete. Entitled "We Remember: A Reflection on the 'Shoah'" [the Hebrew term for the Holocaust], the document was prepared by the Vatican Commission for Religious Relations with the Jews and issued in March 1998. It forthrightly condemned the wartime extermination of Europe's Jews as "an unspeakable tragedy, which can never be forgotten." The statement

also described itself as an act of "teshuva" (the Hebrew word for repentance) and urged building new bridges of understanding between Christians and Jews. The reaction of Jewish groups to the document, however, was decidedly mixed. While grateful for the significant step that "We Remember" represents, they criticized its refusal to acknowledge the relationship between historic Christian anti-Judaism and Nazi anti-Semitism and the indifference of the Christian community as a whole—and, more specifically, the institutional church—to the Holocaust. The report's failure to take Pius XII to task came as another disappointment.

The text of "We Remember" follows.

. . . This reflection concerns one of the main areas in which Catholics can seriously take to heart the summons which Pope John Paul II has addressed to them in his apostolic letter *Tertio Millennio Adveniente:*

"It is appropriate that as the second millennium of Christianity draws to a close the church should become more fully conscious of the sinfulness of her children, recalled all those times in history when they departed from the spirit of Christ and his Gospel and, instead of offering to the world the witness of a life inspired by the values of faith, indulged in ways of thinking and acting which were truly forms of counter-witness and scandal."

This century has witnessed an unspeakable tragedy which can never be forgotten: the attempt by the Nazi regime to exterminate the Jewish people, with the consequent killing of millions of Jews. Women and men, old and young, children and infants, for the sole reason of their Jewish origin were persecuted and deported. Some were killed immediately, while others were degraded, ill-treated, tortured and utterly robbed of their human dignity, and then murdered. Very few of those who entered the camps survived, and those who did remained scarred for life. This was the *Shoah.* It is a major fact of the history of this century, a fact which still concerns us today.

Before this horrible genocide, which the leaders of nations and Jewish communities themselves found hard to believe at the very moment when it was being mercilessly put into effect, no one can remain indifferent, least of all the church, by reason of her very close bonds of spiritual kinship with the Jewish people and her remembrance of the injustices of the past. The church's relationship to the Jewish people is unlike the one she shares with any other religion. However, it is not only a question of recalling the past. The common future of Jews and Christians demands that we remember, for "there is no future without memory." History itself is *memoria futuri.*

In addressing this reflection to our brothers and sisters of the Catholic Church throughout the world, we ask all Christians to join us in meditating on the catastrophe which befell the Jewish people and on the moral imperative to ensure that never again will selfishness and hatred grow to the point of sowing such suffering and death. Most especially we ask our Jewish friends, "whose terrible fate has become a symbol of the aberrations of which man is capable when he turns against God," to hear us with open hearts.

WHAT WE MUST REMEMBER

While bearing their unique witness to the Holy One of Israel and to the Torah,[1] the Jewish people have suffered much at different times and in many places. But the *Shoah* was certainly the worst suffering of all. The inhumanity with which the Jews were persecuted and massacred during this century is beyond the capacity of words to convey. All this was done to them for the sole reason that they were Jews.

---

[1]The collected body of wisdom and law found in Jewish Scripture and other sacred literature and oral tradition.

The very magnitude of the crime raises many questions. Historians, sociologists, political philosophers, psychologists and theologians are all trying to learn more about the reality of the *Shoah* and its causes. Much scholarly study still remains to be done. But such an event cannot be fully measured by the ordinary criteria of historical research alone. It calls for a "moral and religious memory" and, particularly among Christians, a very serious reflection on what gave rise to it.

The fact that the *Shoah* took place in Europe, that is, in countries of long-standing Christian civilization, raises the question of the relation between the Nazi persecution and the attitudes down the centuries of Christians toward the Jews.

RELATIONS BETWEEN JEWS AND CHRISTIANS

The history of relations between Jews and Christians is a tormented one. His Holiness Pope John Paul II has recognized this fact in his repeated appeals to Catholics to see where we stand with regard to our relations with the Jewish people. In effect, the balance of these relations over 2,000 years has been quite negative.

At the dawn of Christianity, after the crucifixion of Jesus, there arose disputes between the early church and the Jewish leaders and people who, in their devotion to the law, on occasion violently opposed the preachers of the Gospel and the first Christians. In the pagan Roman Empire, Jews were legally protected by the privileges granted by the emperor, and the authorities at first made no distinction between Jewish and Christian communities. Soon, however, Christians incurred the persecution of the state. Later, when the emperors themselves converted to Christianity, they at first continued to guarantee Jewish privileges. But Christian mobs who attacked pagan temples sometimes did the same to synagogues, not without being influenced by certain interpretations of the New Testament regarding the Jewish people as a whole.

"In the Christian world—I do not say on the part of the church as such—erroneous and unjust interpretations of the New Testament regarding the Jewish people and their alleged culpability have circulated for too long, engendering feelings of hostility toward this people." Such interpretations of the New Testament have been totally and definitively rejected by the Second Vatican Council.

Despite the Christian preaching of love for all, even for one's enemies, the prevailing mentality down the centuries penalized minorities and those who were in any way "different." Sentiments of anti-Judaism in some Christian quarters and the gap which existed between the church and the Jewish people led to a generalized discrimination, which ended at times in expulsions or attempts at forced conversions. In a large part of the "Christian" world, until the end of the 18th century those who were not Christian did not always enjoy a fully guaranteed juridical status. Despite that fact, Jews throughout Christendom held on to their religious traditions and communal customs. They were therefore looked upon with a certain suspicion and mistrust. In times of crisis such as famine, war, pestilence or social tensions, the Jewish minority was sometimes taken as a scapegoat and became the victim of violence, looting, even massacres.

By the end of the 18th century and the beginning of the 19th century, Jews generally had achieved an equal standing with other citizens in most states and a certain number of them held influential positions in society. But in that same historical context, notably in the 19th century, a false and exacerbated nationalism took hold. In a climate of eventful social change, Jews were often accused of exercising an influence disproportionate to their numbers. Thus there began to spread in varying degrees throughout most of Europe an anti-Judaism that was essentially more sociological and political than religious.

At the same time, theories began to appear which denied the unity of the human race, affirming an original diversity of races. In the 20th century, National Socialism in Germany used these ideas as a pseudoscientific basis for a distinction between so-called Nordic-Aryan races and supposedly inferior races. Furthermore, an extremist form of nationalism was heightened in Germany by the defeat of 1918 and the demanding conditions imposed by the victors, with the consequence that many saw in National Socialism a solution to their country's problems and cooperated politically with this movement.

The church in Germany replied by condemning racism. The condemnation first appeared in the preaching of some of the clergy, in the public teaching of the Catholic bishops and in the writings of lay Catholic journalists. Already in February and March 1931, Cardinal Bertram of Breslau, Cardinal Faulhaber and the bishops of Bavaria, the bishops of the province of Cologne and those of the province of Freiburg published pastoral letters condemning National Socialism, with its idolatry of race and of the state. The well-known Advent sermons of Cardinal Faulhaber in 1933, the very year in which National Socialism came to power, at which not just Catholics but also Protestants and Jews were present, clearly expressed rejection of the Nazi anti-Semitic propaganda. In the wake of the Kristallnacht,[2] Bernhard Lichtenberg, provost of Berlin cathedral, offered public prayers for the Jews. He was later to die at Dachau and has been declared blessed.

Pope Pius XI too condemned Nazi racism in a solemn way in his encyclical letter *Mit Brennender Sorge,* which was read in German churches on Passion Sunday 1937, a step which resulted in attacks and sanctions against members of the clergy. Addressing a group of Belgian pilgrims on Sept. 6, 1938, Pius XI asserted: "Anti-Semitism is unacceptable. Spiritually, we are all Semites." Pius XII, in his very first encyclical, *Summi Pontificatus* of Oct. 20, 1939, warned against theories which denied the unity of the human race and against the deification of the state, all of which he saw as leading to a real "hour of darkness."

NAZI ANTI-SEMITISM AND THE SHOAH

Thus we cannot ignore the difference which exists between *anti-Semitism,* based on theories contrary to the constant teaching of the church on the unity of the human race and on the equal dignity of all races and peoples, and the long-standing sentiments of mistrust and hostility that we call *anti-Judaism,* of which, unfortunately, Christians also have been guilty.

The National Socialist ideology went even further, in the sense that it refused to acknowledge any transcendent reality as the source of life and the criterion of moral good. Consequently, a human group, and the state with which it was identified, arrogated to itself an absolute status and determined to remove the very existence of the Jewish people, a people called to witness to the one God and the law of the covenant. At the level of theological reflection we cannot ignore the fact that not a few in the Nazi Party not only showed aversion to the idea of divine providence at work in human affairs, but gave proof of a definite hatred directed at God himself. Logically such an attitude also led to a rejection of Christianity and a desire to see the church destroyed or at least subjected to the interests of the Nazi state.

It was this extreme ideology which became the basis of the measures taken first to drive the Jews from their homes and then to exterminate them. The *Shoah* was the work of a thoroughly modern neopagan regime. Its anti-Semitism had its roots outside of Christianity, and in pursuing its aims, it did not hesitate to oppose the church and persecute her members also.

But it may be asked whether the Nazi persecution of the Jews was not made easier by the anti-Jewish prejudices imbedded in some Christian minds and hearts. Did anti-Jewish

[2]"Crystal Night" (November 9, 1938), a coordinated assault on Jewish persons and property throughout Germany, is often regarded as the first instance of large-scale anti-Semitic persecution in the Third Reich.

sentiment among Christians make them less sensitive or even indifferent to the persecutions launched against the Jews by National Socialism when it reached power?

Any response to this question must take into account that we are dealing with the history of people's attitudes and ways of thinking, subject to multiple influences. Moreover, many people were altogether unaware of the "final solution" that was being put into effect against a whole people; others were afraid for themselves and those near to them; some took advantage of the situation; and still others were moved by envy. A response would need to be given case by case. To do this, however, it is necessary to know what precisely motivated people in a particular situation.

At first the leaders of the Third Reich sought to expel the Jews. Unfortunately, the governments of some Western countries of Christian tradition, including some in North and South America, were more than hesitant to open their borders to the persecuted Jews. Although they could not foresee how far the Nazi hierarchs would go in their criminal intentions, the leaders of those nations were aware of the hardships and dangers to which Jews living in the territories of the Third Reich were exposed. The closing of borders to Jewish emigration in those circumstances, whether due to anti-Jewish hostility or suspicion, political cowardice or shortsightedness or national selfishness, lays a heavy burden of conscience on the authorities in question.

In the lands where the Nazis undertook mass deportations, the brutality which surrounded these forced movements of helpless people should have led to suspect the worst. Did Christians give every possible assistance to those being persecuted and in particular to the persecuted Jews?

Many did, but others did not. Those who did help to save Jewish lives, as much as was in their power, even to the point of placing their own lives in danger, must not be forgotten. During and after the war, Jewish communities and Jewish leaders expressed their thanks for all that had been done for them, including what Pope Pius XII did personally or through his representatives to save hundreds of thousands of Jewish lives. Many Catholic bishops, priests, religious and laity have been honored for this reason by the state of Israel.

Nevertheless, as Pope John Paul II has recognized, alongside such courageous men and women, the spiritual resistance and concrete action of other Christians was not that which might have been expected from Christ's followers. We cannot know how many Christians in countries occupied or ruled by the Nazi powers or their allies were horrified at the disappearance of their Jewish neighbors and yet were not strong enough to raise their voices in protest. For Christians, this heavy burden of conscience of their brothers and sisters during the Second World War must be a call to penitence.

We deeply regret the errors and failures of those sons and daughters of the church. We make our own what is said in the Second Vatican Council's declaration *Nostra Aetate,* which unequivocally affirms: "The church . . . mindful of her common patrimony with the Jews and motivated by the Gospel's spiritual love and by no political considerations, deplores the hatred, persecutions and displays of anti-Semitism directed against the Jews at any time and from any source."

We recall and abide by what Pope John Paul II, addressing the leaders of the Jewish community in Strasbourg in 1988, stated: "I repeat again with you the strongest condemnation of anti-Semitism and racism, which are opposed to the principles of Christianity." The Catholic Church therefore repudiates every persecution against a people or human group anywhere, at any time. She absolutely condemns all forms of genocide as well as the racist ideologies which give rise to them. Looking back over this century, we are deeply saddened by the violence that has enveloped whole groups of peoples and nations. We recall in particular the massacre of the Armenians, the countless victims in Ukraine in the 1930s, the genocide of the Gypsies, which was also the result of racist ideas, and similar tragedies which have occurred in America, Africa and the Balkans. Nor do we forget the millions of victims of totalitarian ideology in the Soviet Union, in China, Cambodia and elsewhere. Nor can we forget the drama of the Middle East, the elements of which are well known. Even as we make this reflection, "many human beings are still their brothers' victims."

LOOKING TOGETHER TO A COMMON FUTURE

Looking to the future of relations between Jews and Christians, in the first place we appeal to our Catholic brothers and sisters to renew the awareness of the Hebrew roots of their faith. We ask them to keep in mind that Jesus was a descendant of David; that the Virgin Mary and the apostles belonged to the Jewish people; that the church draws sustenance from the root of that good olive tree onto which have been grafted the wild olive branches of the gentiles (cf. Rom. 11:17–24); that the Jews are our dearly beloved brothers, indeed in a certain sense they are "our elder brothers."

At the end of this millennium the Catholic Church desires to express her deep sorrow for the failures of her sons and daughters in every age. This is an act of repentance *(teshuva),* since as members of the church we are linked to the sins as well as the merits of all her children. The church approaches with deep respect and great compassion the experience of extermination, the *Shoah,* suffered by the Jewish people during World War II. It is not a matter of mere words, but indeed of binding commitment. "We would risk causing the victims of the most atrocious deaths to die again if we do not have an ardent desire for justice, if we do not commit ourselves to ensure that evil does not prevail over good as it did for millions of the children of the Jewish people. . . . Humanity cannot permit all that to happen again."

We pray that our sorrow for the tragedy which the Jewish people have suffered in our century will lead to a new relationship with the Jewish people. We wish to turn awareness of past sins into a firm resolve to build a new future in which there will be no more anti-Judaism among Christians or anti-Christian sentiment among Jews, but rather a shared mutual respect as befits those who adore the one Creator and Lord and have a common father in faith, Abraham.

Finally, we invite all men and women of good will to reflect deeply on the significance of the *Shoah.* The victims from their graves and the survivors through the vivid testimony of what they have suffered have become a loud voice calling the attention of all of humanity. To remember this terrible experience is to become fully conscious of the salutary warning it entails: The spoiled seeds of anti-Judaism and anti-Semitism must never again be allowed to take root in any human heart.

March 16, 1998.

Cardinal Edward Idris Cassidy
President

Bishop Pierre Duprey
Vice President

Rev. Remi Hoeckman, OP
Secretary

CHAPTER NINE

THE COLLAPSE OF COMMUNISM

THE BERLIN WALL FALLS. The fall of the Berlin Wall on November 11, 1989 ended the division between the East and West sides of the city; Berliners reacted with unrestrained joy. *(Raymond Depardon/Magnum Photos)*

Until the Communist governments of the Warsaw Pact nations began to fall like dominoes late in 1989—followed two years later by the Soviet Union—the Eastern Bloc appeared to be a permanent fixture on the international landscape. Western observers by and large failed to predict the impending collapse. Perhaps the transformation of the USSR that began under Mikhail Gorbachev should have sounded the alarm. For this was the most substantive and sustained series of liberalizing reforms ever to rock the country. Earlier initiatives—Khrushchev's de-Stalinization comes to mind—may have been significant, but they were always partial and temporary, eventually ending in retrenchment and re-Stalinization. Gorbachev ultimately proved unable to break with the Communist party (and ended up paying for that allegiance with his political career); nevertheless, for most of his time in office he diligently traveled a learning curve, moving from exclusively economic reforms aimed at improving the system to increasingly political changes that challenged the foundations on which that system rested. Moreover, his willingness to undertake so radical a program points to a realization on his part that nothing less would do.

Even if Gorbachev's motives were entirely self-serving, *glasnost* (openness) and *perestroika* (restructuring) opened the floodgates, inspiring (perhaps even demanding) a public response. As before, the response was first heard where hatred of Soviet control was most profound, that is, the satellite countries and the non-Russian republics of the USSR. Gorbachev could have signaled his displeasure with such efforts; instead, he tolerated the demands and demonstrations and expressed increasing impatience with anti-reformist Eastern Bloc leaders. When it became clear that he was not prepared to use force in order to halt reform, Eastern Europeans seized the opportunity and began pushing for a fundamental transformation of their societies. In short, they staged a revolution, often velvet, sometimes violent. By the end of 1989, the former satellites had achieved their independence. It would take another couple of years for matters to come to a head within the USSR, whose dissolution Gorbachev surely did not seek but now found himself powerless to arrest. By the end of 1991, the one-time monolith of Eastern European communism seemed near extinction.

The journey, however, had only begun. The changes of 1989–91—initially so promising and hopeful—often had unexpected and even painful repercussions. The removal of the political and social straitjackets was welcome, but it resulted in an inevitably awkward period of adjustment. People who for decades had been forced to take orders, now found that they had to make plans. Along with participatory democracy, many who supported reform called for the introduction of a market economy based on private enterprise. There was some question, however, as to whether the transition should be gradual or immediate. The former risked a loss of momentum; the latter meant a rise in social hardship. With capitalism, furthermore, came not only entrepreneurs but also outlaws, the "comrade criminals" who profited in the absence (or violation) of strict regulations and threatened harm to anyone who got in their way. Still another problem to be dealt with was the conversion of industries that were mainstays of the old socialist system but had become no more than millstones around the neck of an economy nearing the millenium. The fall of communism also allowed old demons to resurface, including prejudices based on religion and ethnicity, which offered a sinister solace to those bewildered by the transition to personal freedom and responsible citizenship.

As the Soviet Union neared its end in 1991, demonstrators marching through Moscow's Red Square in the annual May Day parade carried banners with the denunciation, "75 Years on the Road to Nowhere." For much of the former USSR and Eastern Bloc, the road is not necessarily that much clearer twenty years later.

1 A Tottering Old Regime

By the late 1980s, the Eastern Bloc was no longer the Communist monolith of earlier decades. The Jaruzelski government had outlawed Solidarity in Poland, and Czechoslovakia continued to languish under the oppressive regime that succeeded the Prague Spring, but changes were afoot nevertheless. For example, the economies of East Germany and Hungary (the latter propelled by the New Economic Mechanism instituted in the late 1960s) were becoming the consumerist showcases of Eastern Europe. In addition, the gradual reassertion by the Eastern European peoples of their national identities proceeded apace, now aided by increasing links with the West. A fresh breeze had begun to blow through the Soviet Union as well, the result of the changes introduced by Mikhail Gorbachev. Where all of these phenomena might lead, however, there was no telling. Few people could have predicted that the end of an era was at hand.

Mikhail Gorbachev
PERESTROIKA

The Soviet Union had been dealing with the legacy of Stalinism ever since the dictator's demise in 1953. Nikita Khrushchev made considerable progress in dismantling the system of terror that Stalin had put in place, but his successor Leonid Brezhnev, who ruled from 1964 until his death in 1982, halted the de-Stalinization process and placed renewed emphasis on authoritarian methods. Brezhnev's attempts to satisfy Soviet consumers while keeping the country militarily strong strained the economy to the breaking point. At the same time, bureaucratic corruption and ideological decrepitude turned his regime into an "era of stagnation," as official accounts would later describe it.

Following Brezhnev's death, the Soviet Union floundered under two caretaker regimes until Mikhail Gorbachev (b. 1931) assumed the leadership of the country in 1985. Boldly proclaiming that "everything is rotten through and through," Gorbachev faced the task of reforming the dilapidated Soviet system and upholding the allegiance of the Soviet satellite states. After testing the political realities, he outlined a program for restructuring Soviet society in *Perestroika: New Thinking for Our Country and the World* (1987). It signified a bold break from Communist ideology. At home he wanted to transform the Communist party into an agent of democracy, stimulate popular creativity, and follow Lenin's example of forever learning from new circumstances. Abroad, he hoped to end the Cold War.

In the following excerpt, Gorbachev analyzes what went wrong with the Soviet system.

Perestroika is an urgent necessity arising from the profound processes of development in our socialist society. This society is ripe for change. It has long been yearning for it. Any delay in beginning perestroika could have led to an exacerbated internal situation in the near future, which, to put it bluntly, would have been fraught with serious social, economic and political crises.

We have drawn these conclusions from a broad and frank analysis of the situation that has developed in our society by the middle of the eighties. This situation and the problems arising from it presently confront the country's leadership, in which new people have gradually appeared in the last few years. . . .

. . . Over the past seven decades—a short span in the history of human civilization—our country has traveled a path equal to centuries. One of the mightiest powers in the world rose up to replace the backward semi-colonial and semi-feudal Russian Empire. Huge productive forces, a powerful intellectual potential, a highly advanced culture, a unique community of over one hundred nations and nationalities, and firm social protection for 280 million people on a territory forming one-sixth of the earth—such are our great and indisputable achievements and Soviet people are justly proud of them. . . .

. . . [I]t is equally clear that my country's progress became possible only thanks to the Revolution. It is the product of the Revolution. It is the fruit of socialism, the new social system, and the result of the historical choice made by our people. Behind them are the fears of our fathers and grandfathers and millions of working people—workers, farmers and intellectuals—who seventy years ago assumed direct responsibility for the future of their country. . . .

At some state—this became particularly clear in the latter half of the seventies—something happened that was at first sight inexplicable. The country began to lose momentum. Economic failures became more frequent. Difficulties began to accumulate and deteriorate, and unresolved problems to multiply. Elements of what we call stagnation and other phenomena alien to socialism began to appear in the life of society. A kind of "braking mechanism" affecting social and economic development formed. And all this happened at a time when scientific and technological revolution opened up new prospects for economic and social progress. . . .

Analyzing the situation, we first discovered a slowing economic growth. In the last fifteen years the national income growth rates had declined by more than a half and by the beginning of the eighties had fallen to a level close to economic stagnation. A country that was once quickly closing on the world's advanced nations began to lose one position after another. Moreover, the gap in the efficiency of production, quality of products, scientific and technological development, the production of advanced technology and the use of advanced techniques began to widen, and not to our advantage. . . .

It became typical of many of our economic executives to think not of how to build up the national asset, but of how to put more material, labor and working time into an item to sell it at a higher price. Consequently, for all "gross output," there was a shortage of goods. We spent, in fact we are still spending, far more on raw materials, energy and other resources per unit of output than other developed nations. . . .

As time went on, material resources became harder to get and more expensive. On the other hand, the extensive methods of fixed capital expansion resulted in an artificial shortage of manpower. In an attempt to rectify the situation somehow, large, unjustified, i.e. in fact unearned, bonuses began to be paid and all kinds of undeserved incentives introduced under the pressure of this shortage, and that led, at a later stage, to the practice of padding reports merely for gain. Parasitical attitudes were on the rise, the prestige of conscientious and high-quality labor began to diminish and a "wage-leveling" mentality was becoming widespread. . . .

So the inertia of extensive economic development was leading to an economic deadlock and stagnation.

The economy was increasingly squeezed financially. The sale of large quantities of oil and other fuel and energy resources and raw materials on the world market did not help. It only aggravated the situation. Currency earnings thus made were predominantly used for tackling problems of the moment rather than on economic modernization or on catching up technologically. . . .

. . . Our society has ensured full employment and provided fundamental social guarantees. At the same time, we failed to use to the full the potential of socialism to meet the growing requirements in housing, in quality and sometimes quantity of foodstuffs, in the proper organization of the work of transport, in health services, in education and in tackling other problems which, naturally, arose in the course of society's development.

An absurd situation was developing. The Soviet Union, the world's biggest producer of steel, raw materials, fuel and energy, has shortfalls in them due to wasteful or inefficient use. One of the biggest producers of grain for food, it nevertheless has to buy millions of tons of grain a year for fodder. We have the largest number of doctors and hospital beds per thousand of the population and, at the same time, there are glaring shortcomings in our health services. Our rockets can find Halley's comet and fly to Venus with amazing accuracy, but side by side with these scientific and technological triumphs is an obvious lack of efficiency in using scientific achievements for economic needs, and many Soviet household appliances are of poor quality.

This, unfortunately, is not all. A gradual erosion of the ideological and moral values of our people began.

It was obvious to everyone that the growth rates were sharply dropping and that the entire mechanism of quality control was not working properly; there was a lack of receptivity to the advances in science and technology; the improvement in living standards was slowing down and there were difficulties in the supply of foodstuffs, housing, consumer goods and services.

On the ideological plane as well, the braking mechanism brought about ever greater resistance to the attempts to constructively scrutinize the problems that were emerging and to the new ideas. Propaganda of success—real or imagined—was gaining the upper hand. Eulogizing and servility were encouraged; the needs and opinions of ordinary working people, of the public at large, were ignored. In the social sciences scholastic theorization was encouraged and developed, but creative thinking was driven out from the social sciences, and superfluous and voluntarist assessments and judgments were declared indisputable truths. Scientific, theoretical and other discussions, which are indispensable for the development of thought and for creative endeavor, were emasculated. Similar negative tendencies also affected culture, the arts and journalism, as well as the teaching process and medicine, where mediocrity, formalism and loud eulogizing surfaced, too. . . .

. . . Decay began in public morals; the great feeling of solidarity with each other that was forged during the heroic times of the Revolution, the first five-year plans, the Great Patriotic War and postwar rehabilitation was weakening; alcoholism, drug addiction and crime were growing; and the penetration of the stereotypes of mass culture alien to us, which bred vulgarity and low tastes and brought about ideological barrenness increased. . . .

At some administrative levels there emerged a disrespect for the law and encouragement of eyewash and bribery, servility and glorification. Working people were justly indignant at the behavior of people who, enjoying trust and responsibility, abused power, suppressed criticism, made fortunes and, in some cases, even became accomplices in—if not organizers of—criminal acts. . . .

Naturally, Party organizations worked and the overwhelming majority of communists did their duty to the people sincerely and selflessly. And still it has to be recognized that there was no effective effort to bar dishonest, pushy, self-seeking people. In general, practical steps which were taken by Party and state bodies lagged behind the requirements of the times and of life itself. Problems snowballed faster than they were resolved. On the whole, society was becoming increasingly unmanageable. We only thought that we were in the saddle, while the actual situation that was arising was one that Lenin warned against: the automobile was not going where the one at the steering wheel thought it was going. . . .

I think I have said enough for you to realize how serious the situation was and how urgent a thorough change was. The Party has found the strength and the courage to soberly appraise the situation and recognize that fundamental changes and transformations are indispensable. . . .

Gorbachev tried securing popular support for his reforms by removing some of the traditional limits on freedom of expression. At the same time, he sought to make the Soviet economy work by stressing labor discipline and productivity and by eliminating bureaucratic inefficiency and corruption. Eventually realizing that the success of his policies hinged on changes of a more fundamental nature, Gorbachev cautiously began to open up the political system.

An uncompromising struggle was launched against violations of the principles of socialist justice with no account being taken of who committed these violations. A policy of openness was proclaimed. Those who spoke in favor of Party, government and economic bodies and public organizations conducting their activities openly were allowed to have their say and unwarranted restrictions and bans were removed. . . .

People, human beings with all their creative diversity, are the makers of history. So the initial task of restructuring—an indispensable condition, necessary if it is to be successful—is to "wake up" those people who have "fallen asleep" and make them truly active and concerned, to ensure that everyone feels as if he is the master of the country, of his enterprise, office, or institute. This is the main thing. . . .

We need wholesome, full-blooded functioning by all public organizations, all production teams and creative unions, new forms of activity by citizens and the revival of those which have been forgotten. In short, *we need broad democratization of all aspects of society*. That democratization is also the main guarantee that the current processes are irreversible.

We know today that we would have been able to avoid many of these difficulties if the democratic process had developed normally in our country. . . . Perestroika itself can only come through democracy. . . .

The new atmosphere is, perhaps, most vividly manifest in glasnost.[1] We want more openness about public affairs in every sphere of life. . . .

---

[1]*Glasnost,* the other of the two watchwords associated with Gorbachev's reforms, is popularly translated as "openness"; more literally, it means "publicity" or "the quality of being public."

. . . People are becoming increasingly convinced that glasnost is an effective form of public control over the activities of all government bodies, without exception, and a powerful lever in correcting shortcomings. As a result, the moral potential of our society has been set in motion. Reason and conscience are beginning to win back ground from the passiveness and indifference that were eroding hearts. . . .

We have begun drafting bills that should guarantee glasnost. These bills are designed to ensure the greatest possible openness in the work of government and mass organizations and to enable working people to express their opinion on any issue of social life and government activity without fear. . . .

The current democratization process is reflected not only in publications, it is increasingly influencing the activities of the mass media. Gradually, as though thawing, our newspapers, magazines, radio and television are uncovering and handling new topics. One of the signs of the general revitalization is that our press is increasingly preferring dialogue to monologue. . . .

It is no longer a question of whether the CPSU Central Committee will continue the policy of glasnost through the press and the other mass media and with the active participation of citizens. We need glasnost as we need the air. . . .

Glasnost, criticism and self-criticism are not just a new campaign. They have been proclaimed and must become a norm in the Soviet way of life. No radical change is possible without it. There is no democracy, nor can there be, without glasnost. And there is no present-day socialism, nor can there be, without democracy.

Václav Havel
"FARCE, REFORMABILITY, AND THE FUTURE OF THE WORLD"

Gorbachev's reforms blew the lid off of Soviet society, allowing people to express opinions about previously "forbidden" subjects without fear of reprisal. As a result, Gorbachev achieved enormous personal popularity abroad and, initially, at home. Not all observers of *glasnost* and *perestroika,* however, were enthusiastic. An especially insightful critic was the Czech playwright and political dissident Václav Havel (b. 1936). Havel's involvement in Charter 77, an organization of Czech intellectuals devoted to the cause of human rights, resulted in a four-and-a-half-year prison term late in the 1970s. In November 1989, he joined in the founding of the Civic Forum, the first legal opposition movement in Czechoslovakia since its takeover by Communists. Within a few weeks, he became president of the country and helped usher it into a new era.

Havel's article, "Farce, Reformability, and the Future of the World" (1987), which is excerpted below, was published around the same time as Gorbachev's *Perestroika.* It was written as part of a Czechoslovak-German anthology marking the twentieth anniversary of the Prague Spring (see page 378). The tragic fate of that enterprise—in retrospect, a harbinger of *perestroika*—inclined Havel to take a dim view of Gorbachev's efforts. Why should the Soviet program earn applause when the Czech reforms had elicited only reprisals? At the same time, Havel—writing two years before his own country's Velvet Revolution (see page 429) and four years before the collapse of the Soviet Union—held out the possibility that communism might one day lose "its totalitarian essence."

It is an amusing coincidence: the twentieth anniversary of the Soviet invasion that suppressed the Prague Spring has come at a time when Gorbachev is trying to institute wide-ranging reforms in the Soviet Union and when even in Czechoslovakia, the satraps who were installed by the Soviets and still follow them blindly find themselves obliged to talk of reforms. . . .

In the wake of the Soviet intervention, when they were looking around for people to run the country and "normalize" it, there were not a lot to choose from. The team that was finally assembled consisted largely of a motley assortment of leftovers from the distant past—hardline Stalinists and a few life-long toadies who could have worked for any side. It undoubtedly included a few intelligent individuals who had a clear idea where things stood, but these people had little influence, most likely because they lacked the courage to use what little influence they might have had. This team of normalizers has spent twenty years persecuting anyone associated in any way with the attempted reforms of the Prague Spring, as well as all those who were not one hundred percent loyal to the regime. The country's present leadership, in other words, is thoroughly antireformist, and over the past twenty years it has managed to create one of the most rigid, sterile, and stagnant types of communism in the world. When they now start babbling on about reforms, they make themselves a laughingstock. No one takes them seriously. No one believes them. Everyone knows it is empty talk that hides an unbending determination not to change, and not to let anyone else take control. The people who have spent twenty years ruining this country, and who now begin to criticize the devastation and talk about the need for remedies and changes without any intention of giving up their own power and privilege, must be regarded with derision by all sensible people. That is quite simply the way it is.

The Czechs and Slovaks are not passionate people. They seldom get worked up about anything. In 1968, though, they passionately believed that things could get better and they started getting actively involved. But they got burned, and they have been paying for their enthusiasm for twenty years now. Only a fool would expect that after such a bitter experience they could be worked up again and persuaded to risk an analogous fate for their involvement, especially since they are being asked to get involved by the very people who have for so long been systematically punishing them for their past enthusiasm.

Skepticism is now so general and so deep-seated that I find it impossible to imagine the kind of leader it would take to . . . get this society moving again. . . . History has taught [the people] not to trust communists in any way. As a result, yet another farcical aspect of the situation in Czechoslovakia today is the government's never-ending calls for nationwide discussions—whether of a new "enterprise law," a new constitution, or whatever it is—while people maintain stony silence at all meetings where such discussions are supposed to take place. Don't get me wrong: I am not advocating skepticism—I simply note its existence.

I have two more general points to make about what has become a regular recurrence of "revivals," "reforms," and "perestroikas," and their repeated suppression.

First, the Kronstadt Mutiny [see page 112], the Hungarian Revolution, the Prague Spring, the Solidarity era, Khrushchev's thaw, and now Gorbachev's version of it, and so on—all these attempts at "doing something about it"—despite thousands of individual differences, are variations of a single historical trend: society's desire to limit, moderate, or eliminate the totalitarian nature of the communist system. It is no coincidence that, sooner or later, all these events give rise, in one form or another, to the same basic demands: greater intellectual freedom, less centralism, political plurality, a workers' voice in industry, the independence of firms, economic competition, small private enterprise, authentic trade union rights, limits to the omnipotence of the ruling party or of its apparat, curbing the omnipotence of the police, the eliminating of historical and other taboos, the rehabilitation of all victims of tyrannical cruelty, greater respect for national independence and minority rights, and so on.

The communist system is—or, more precisely, has always been so up to now—a totalitarian system, whether it had the "human face" of Dubček's time (when it was even possible to live well) or the gangsterism of Pol Pot's regime (under which death seems to have been the only option).[1] The system's totalitarian character conflicts with life's own intrinsic tendency toward heterogeneity, diversity, uniqueness, autonomy—in a word, toward plurality. This is why life inevitably obstructs and resists a totalitarian system. And it does so in a whole range of ways: on one occasion it might take the form of a bloody uprising, on another the nonviolent creation of parallel structures, while on a third occasion, life's natural demands can infiltrate the very brains and organs of the regime. A fourth kind of resistance is the extraordinary capacity of some people to ignore the regime and its ideology. In all instances, however, it is basically the same resistance to the same phenomenon: it is life versus totalitarianism.

There are some who respect the Kronstadt Mutiny and the Hungarian Revolution and regard all the rest—and most of all Gorbachev's perestroika—as downright fraud, because in their view it should be all or nothing, and because a gun is the only thing communists understand. Then there are those who respect the Prague Spring and rave over Gorbachev but regard everything else, including the Polish Solidarity movement, as indefensible anticommunist, bourgeois-reactionary, extremist nonsense. Both attitudes come from unhappy individuals locked inside their own political and ideological paradigms, dogmas, and clichés, or alternatively, in their pragmatism (which is meant to display their extraordinary political perspicacity). To the latter, the former are pitiful slaves of anticommunist ideological fanaticism, who see only one possible solution: the extermination of the communists. To the former, the latter are equally pitiful slaves of Marxist Utopias, and their natural counterparts; they walk a dialectical tightrope, skillfully "differentiating" between what it is advisable and possible to say, and what is inadvisable to say if one does not want to risk losing one's left-wing credentials. But it's hard to persuade history to run according to somebody's ideological dreams. It takes every possible twist and turn, usually quite different from the course prescribed by ideological prophets of all hues. This is why life's resistance to totalitarianism takes so many different forms. . . .

Second, in recent years, the Czech and Slovak press—by which I mean that published both abroad by exiles and at home in *samizdat*[2]—has frequently got worked up over a controversy which I find rather quaint and have never been able to understand. . . .

. . . This controversy is comical because it is a quarrel between two groups of prophets, one of which is convinced that communism—being unreformable—cannot be reformed, while the other is convinced that communism—being reformable—is open to reform.

In the first place, much depends on what meaning is attached to the word "reform." Where does reform begin and where does it end? What fits the category and what falls outside it? For instance, if we say that communism of a more bearable kind—one in which we can breathe more freely and lead a happier existence, one in which there is greater freedom and rational behavior, one in which the police cannot do whatever they like—is "reformed," "reformist," or "reforming," then the answer is so obvious it makes no sense to waste any more time on it. We all know, for instance, that it makes a difference whether we live under Stalin's communism,

[1]Alexander Dubček (1921–1992) was first secretary of the Czechoslovak Communist party who oversaw the reforms of the Prague Spring (see page 378). Pol Pot led the Communist Khmer Rouge forces that took over Cambodia and instituted a reign of terror there in the late 1970s, resulting in millions of deaths.

[2]*Samizdat*, literally "self-published," refers to the carbon-copy format in which political dissidents circulated their writings throughout the Eastern Bloc.

Dubček's communism, Kádár's communism, Mao's communism, Pol Pot's communism, or Novotný's communism.[3] Clearly, some of these are more bearable than others, and if the degree of bearableness is an indicator of reform, then communism is certainly reformable, otherwise all forms of communism would be equally unbearable. . . .

If, however, we are debating about the totalitarian basis of communism, that is quite a different matter. Totalitarianism is intrinsic to communism, a tendency it has always had, irrespective of whether a local variant is bearable or totally unbearable. The external manifestation of this totalitarian basis is the familiar principle of the "leading role of the Communist Party." In more bearable communisms, this principle is easier to put up with. In fact, it might be said that such communisms are less totalitarian than others. But nowhere is there such a thing as nontotalitarian communism, nor has there ever been. Thus, if the notion that communism is nonreformable is asserted by someone who understands reform to mean communism's abandoning its totalitarian basis, then I have to admit that I fully sympathize with them. So far, no communist state has ever opened itself up to full political pluralism. The totalitarian essence of communism has an enormous inertia and such complex mechanisms of manipulation that any attempt so far to challenge it has always been severely suppressed. But the fact that such protagonists of nonreformability have my sympathy does not mean I share their view. They are probably right about how things have happened so far. But I deny them their claim to certainty that the communist system will never ever abandon its totalitarian nature. How can they possibly tell? What if powerful forces (a deepening economic and social crisis, international pressures, autonomous self-organization of society, a change of heart on the part of political leaders, and so on) should one day combine into one mighty force, so powerful that it overcomes the totalitarian inertia? It might happen dramatically, in the space of a few days, or it might be a gradual process that lasts several decades. But how can one be so arrogant as to maintain with total assurance that something like that could simply never, ever occur?

Anything can happen.

It is hardly likely that in the foreseeable future a communist state will utterly abandon totalitarianism of its own accord (and possibly then only due to the enlightenment of its leaders!). That is more or less obvious. But it seems equally obvious that history is unlikely to remain static, either.

Of course, there could be a world war (though I don't think it very likely). That could lead to communism everywhere—or alternatively, nowhere at all. The most probable result, though, would be neither communism nor democracy, because there would be quite simply nothing left.

But are these really the only alternatives: that history either stands still or comes to an end? Surely this is nonsense. Equally nonsensical, it seems to me, is the assertion that it is entirely out of the question that some bearable form of communism should go on getting more bearable until one day—though God knows when, how, and under what influence—it finally loses its totalitarian essence. . . .

Where does that leave us?

The way I see it, the only possible alternative for us is not to worry about ideological nonissues, but instead to make practical efforts—here and now, whatever we are doing, and wherever we are—to change things for the better, to try to win more freedom, more respect for human dignity, to work for an economy that functions better, less destruction of the earth, government by more sensible politicians, the right to speak the truth—and finally, to ensure that people do not lose hope when confronted with the truth, but instead try to draw the practical lessons from it.

[3]First secretary of the Communist party of Hungary, Janos Kádár (1912–1989) helped pacify the country after the 1956 Revolution; later, he instituted economic reforms resulting in a consumer-oriented semi-capitalism. Antonin Novotný (1904–1975) led the Czechoslovak Communist party between 1956 and 1968, when his ouster cleared the way for Alexander Dubček and the Prague Spring.

STASI REPORT ON MOTIVES FOR EMIGRATION, SEPTEMBER 9, 1989

The changes associated with *perestroika* were viewed enviously by East German critics of the GDR's hard-line gerontocracy. During the first six months of 1989, some 36,484 East Germans obtained permission to emigrate, another 4,849 sought to leave without the regime's permission, and 2,070 of them were apprehended. Mounting criticism of ruling Communist regimes elsewhere in East Central and Eastern Europe began to undermine the stability of these states as well. During the autumn of 1989, large numbers of East German vacationers in Hungary sought to escape over the increasingly open border to Austria and continue on to West Germany; East German travelers in Czechoslovakia and in Poland rushed to find safe haven in the Federal Republic's embassies in Prague and Warsaw, respectively, and travel to West Germany. In the following selection, the East German Ministry for State Security, or Stasi, frankly analyzes the reasons for this flight.

The overwhelming majority of these people has an essentially negative view of problems and failures in the development of society, especially in their private lives, personal living standards, and so-called everyday shortcomings; based on this attitude and on comparisons with conditions in the FRG and West Berlin, they assess developments in the GDR negatively.

The advantages of socialism, such as social security and protection, are acknowledged; however, they are no longer seen as decisive factors in comparison with the problems and failures that have emerged. To some extent, they are taken for granted; thus they are no longer included in these assessments at all, or are completely negated. Doubt and disbelief exist as to the achievability of goals and the correctness of party and government policies, especially in regard to domestic developments, guarantee of appropriate living standards, and satisfaction of personal needs. This is accompanied by the view that developments have not brought any perceptible improvements for the people and that, in many areas, things in the GDR had once been better. Such viewpoints are observed in particular in people who were once socially active, but who, for the aforementioned reasons, became "tired," resigned themselves, and in the end capitulated.

There is insufficient understanding of the complexity and objective contradictions involved in building socialism; from their point of view, goals and results that have not been attained, as well as existing problems, shortcomings, and defects, are interpreted and judged as mistakes in policy.

As the result of a long-term process, these people come to the conclusion that a perceptible, rapid, and permanent change in their living standards, especially pertaining to satisfaction of personal desires, is only attainable in the FRG or West Berlin.

Although in each individual case, a complex of concrete, individual facts, manifestations, events, etc. helps create the motive for leaving the GDR, a summary of the essential factors leading to such motives is attempted in the following:

The essential reasons for, and causes of, efforts to leave the GDR, either illegally or through emigration—which are echoed in numerous petitions to central and local organs or institutions—are:

- dissatisfaction with the supply of consumer goods;
- annoyance at inadequate services;
- impatience with problems of medical care and treatment;

- limited opportunities for travel within and outside the GDR;
- unsatisfactory working conditions and discontinuity in the production process;
- inadequacy and inconsistency in applying or carrying out the principle of merit pay, as well as dissatisfaction with the development of wages and salaries;
- annoyance at bureaucratic behavior by the heads and employees of state organs, industries, and institutions, and at unfeeling treatment of citizens;
- lack of understanding of the GDR's media policy.

In greater detail:

Dissatisfaction with the supply of consumer goods.

Criticism of distribution of goods to the population is the most significant factor in the motivational structure. In particular, there is little understanding of continuing problems with consistent supply of quality consumer goods (cars, furniture, textiles, shoes, home electronics, etc.), as well as spare parts, construction materials, and certain everyday goods (for example, quality groceries, fresh fruit, vegetables, and items on the continually changing list of "1,000 little things"). This includes distribution of goods, freshness of groceries, gaps in supply, a lack of constant availability until store closing time, and the related transport problems.

The persons concerned point in particular to the "standing in line" caused by this, the need to run around and search for particular items, the "procuring and organizing" that goes on even during working hours, and the possibility of obtaining certain goods only through "connections"; they conclude that they can no longer bear all this.

The chief complaint revolves around the fact that those who possess foreign currency can obtain almost anything (not only in Intershop* stores).

*Special hard currency stores for Western goods.

There is criticism of the so-called double currency system, of Intershops, luxury hotels and "privileges" for those with foreign currency.

The aforementioned persons—often pointing to the continuation or increase in such phenomena—doubt the possibility of a solution to these problems of concern to citizens.

ANNOYANCE AT INADEQUATE SERVICES

Closely related to the views regarding the supply situation are various problems in the service sector. In particular, reference is made to a lack of, or limits on, available facilities for repairs and services. Shortages of spare parts, long waiting periods and unfriendly treatment of citizens in the service sector, in restaurants and in stores are the main focus of criticism.

In summary, it must be pointed out that the motivational factors mentioned are in part linked with:

- illusions about "Western" lifestyle, especially expectations of a life with "better" material security and "better" earnings, more "freedom," enabling one to attain a lifestyle based on selfish striving for consumption and ownership;
- attitudes, viewpoints and characteristics such as selfishness, greed, careerism, immorality, overestimation of self, etc.

These factors are inseparably linked to current developments in other socialist states, in particular the Hungarian People's Republic, the People's Republic of Poland, and the Soviet Union; through these, significant doubts have arisen as to the unity, and thus the strength, of the community of socialist states, which lead increasingly to doubts about the prospects and chances of victory of socialism itself.

Additional motives for leaving the GDR are based to a small extent on truly humanitarian reasons (for example, marriage, reuniting families), "solutions" to family or personal conflicts, a yearning for adventure, and efforts to escape legal punishment.

In making an overall assessment, it must be taken into account that those applying for emigration or persons who leave the GDR illegally are, as a rule, no longer politically bound to the GDR in any way. However, the majority does not act out of a basically hostile attitude.

Manifestation of hostile attitudes can in many cases be explained by the fact that the citizens involved believe this improves their chances of having permanent emigration authorized. As a rule, they use the arguments of opponents without being able to explain them convincingly, for example, to the responsible organs of state.

2 Popular Protest and Dissolution

Glasnost and *perestroika* emboldened Eastern Europeans who had been living in the Kremlin's shadow since the Second World War. A wide array of civic groups, students, religious organizations, and individuals fed up with more than four decades of tyranny joined demonstrations, seeking greater freedom and political change. Growing in size and frequency, they acquired an unstoppable momentum. Most remarkable of all, they evoked no military response from the Russian bear to the east; Gorbachev apparently realized that the Soviet Union would have to accept the inevitable and that the use of physical force abroad threatened to undermine his reforms at home while destroying his reputation in the West. By the end of 1989, the Communist regimes of East Central Europe had largely ceased to exist, and the Berlin Wall was rubble. Even within the "homeland of communism," rumblings of dissatisfaction began to be heard. Not surprisingly, they sounded first among the non-Russian nationalities, many of whom had suffered under Moscow's oppression since the days of the tsars. When inept plotters tried bringing down Gorbachev in August 1991, Soviet Russians too finally took to the streets; a few months later the party-state that had governed them for seventy-four years had become a thing of the past.

Alfred Erich Senn
LITHUANIA AWAKENING

Among the non-Russian nationalities residing in the USSR, the Baltic peoples of Estonia, Latvia, and Lithuania were arguably the most Westernized and therefore the most resistant to Soviet rule. While criticism of the political situation in the Soviet Baltic republics had not been unknown in earlier years, only in the late 1980s did it begin to assume mass public forms. To put their case before Moscow, the Balts used solemn anniversary observances of a tragic turning point in their history—the Nazi-Soviet Pact of August 1939. A secret section of the pact called for the partition of Poland between the two signatories and Russian control over Latvia and Estonia (later the agreement was amended to include

Lithuania as well). These commemorations galvanized public opinion as never before and laid the basis for a movement that eventually ended in freedom after a half-century of Russian domination.

In the summer and fall of 1988, American historian Alfred Erich Senn, a specialist on Russia and the Baltic, was visiting Lithuania at the invitation of its Institute of History. Of Lithuanian descent, Senn witnessed many groundbreaking developments in the contemporary Lithuanian independence movement and spoke with numerous participants. He recounted his experiences in *Lithuania Awakening,* which was published in 1990, the same year in which that Baltic republic became the first to declare its independence from Soviet control. The following excerpts deal with events in the capital city of Vilnius surrounding the commemoration of the Nazi-Soviet Pact in August 1988.

. . . Lithuanians focused their attention on the upcoming anniversary of the Molotov-Ribbentrop Non-Aggression Pact of 1939 and the question of the "secret protocols" by which the Germans and the Soviets in 1939 had divided East Central Europe between themselves. In the first agreement of August 23, Lithuania had been consigned to Germany, but in the second agreement of September 28, 1939, the Germans had traded most of Lithuania to the Soviet Union. After the incorporation of Lithuania into the USSR in 1940, a third agreement, dated January 10, 1941, had assigned one last portion of Lithuania to the Soviet Union.

The Western powers had introduced the documents at the Nuremberg War Crimes Trial after World War II but, following their publication in the United States, Soviet historians had denounced them as forgeries. "Falsifiers of history," they called historians who accepted the documents as genuine. In 1987, working up to the observance of the anniversary of the Molotov-Ribbentrop pact, Radio Free Europe's Lithuanian service had broadcast a number of items pertaining to the protocols but, since the Soviets jammed this frequency, few in Lithuania seemed to have heard the programs.

Among Lithuanian writers and historians, discussion of the protocols had begun even before the 1987 anniversary. . . . [M]ost intellectuals seemed to have some idea of their existence, but many apparently had no idea of what the protocols might actually say. Soviet historians in Moscow insisted that they could not find the protocols in Soviet archives and that they therefore must not exist. Accordingly, Moscow declared, they should not be discussed. The press in Lithuania dutifully remained silent.

The Estonians finally broke the silence and published the texts in the summer of 1988. *Sajudžio žinios*[1] soon followed suit, using a *samizdat* translation of the original American publication, *Nazi-Soviet Relations.* Bronius Kuzmickas, a philosopher, put his name to the publication of the protocols and several key telegrams between Molotov and Ribbentrop. "Absolute openness about these agreements is essential," wrote Kuzmickas: silence served only to weaken popular belief in glasnost and democracy in the Soviet Union. . . .

. . . [T]here could be no doubt that something would happen in Vilnius on August 23, 1988; the question was "What?"

. . . Would a meeting be permitted? Perhaps there should just be some articles in the press; people could wear black ribbons that day. Were the people tired of having meetings and rallies?

The Initiative Group[2] finally decided in favor of a demonstration. A letter to the Party Central Committee, signed by twenty-three members of the group, declared that the Soviet government

[1] *Sajudis News,* the irregularly published organ of Sajudis, a popular front movement led by intellectuals that spearheaded the drive for independence.

[2] The directing committee of the Sajudis organization.

should publish the 1939 treaty with all its attachments and take a clear position on it based on "today's juridical, political, and ideological evaluation." Sajudis, it assured the party, viewed "Lithuania's place in the USSR as a historical reality," but it wanted to improve that place by establishing a state governed by laws and by amending the constitution. . . .

Conservatives still denied the protocols' existence, and they received support from Moscow. . . .

The Lithuanian press discussed the issue of the protocols more critically, but still cautiously. . . . In *Tiesa*[3] of August 20, Regina Žepkaite argued that even without the original text in hand historians had to recognize that evidence pointed to their existence and concluded that Germany gained more from the pact than did the Soviets. Although it did not satisfy those who wanted a blanket condemnation of Stalin and the Soviet government, Žepkaite's article could not have been published three months earlier.

TASS, the official Soviet news agency, contributed to the discussion with an anonymous article, written in the offices of TASS-ELTA in Vilnius and published in *Literatura ir menas*[4] on August 20. After reviewing the history of 1938 and 1939 and insisting that the Soviet Union took territory only to defend itself, the TASS dispatch printed the text of the protocol of August 23 as it had been introduced in the Nuremberg trial. . . .

[On August 23,] the public that gathered in Vingis Park entertained no doubts about the authenticity of the protocols as published. They came in carrying tricolor flags of all sizes, most with black ribbons attached. No one could be sure how many people were there. Moscow radio spoke of 100,000, Sajudis claimed "at least 150,000," and Voice of America reported 200,000. Months later, people tended to say 150,000 to 200,000. Formally they came "to commemorate" the pact and its consequences; in fact they were there to condemn the pact.

After the meeting had opened with . . . [the singing of] *Lithuania Beloved,* Vytautas Landsbergis[5] offered his own portrait of August 23, 1939: "That day two men signed one document. Their names were Ribbentrop and Molotov. But behind them, who were evil-enough criminals, stood two others, Hitler and Stalin, whom mankind has not yet found words to describe." He pictured Stalin as having enslaved his own country first and then having carried his system to other lands: "The earlier assertions of some historians that this murderer of his own family went into the street as the caring protector of the weak cannot even convince the paper on which they were written." Historians now have "more nerve, more freedom. We will hear their word." He declared that "Soviet Lithuania, as we know it today, is the result of many circumstances and actions" and that the population of the Soviet Union still suffered from "the virus of Stalinism . . . the AIDS of Stalinism. We have to get well or else we will die." . . .

[Philosopher] Arvydas Juozaitis took the microphone to give the briefest but at the same time most impassioned statement of the evening: "Today is the day of our great rebirth and cleansing. Therefore I wish that from today we would not see such slander about our people's history as Robertas Žiugžda[6] and his flunkies spread in our periodical and academic press."

[Historian] Liudas Truska then undertook to rehabilitate history and challenged historians' traditional interpretations of the pact of 1939, arguing that signing the pact was in fact not in the best interests even of the Soviet Union. The three Baltic republics, moreover, were the only states to disappear from the map of Europe as a result of World War II, and it was ridiculous

[3]The major organ of the Lithuanian Communist party.

[4]*Life and Art,* the weekly organ of the Lithuanian Writers' Union.

[5]A musicologist by training and staunch nationalist by inclination, Vytautas Landsbergis (b. 1932) became a Sajudis leader and, in March 1990, president of Lithuania.

[6]A historian at the University of Vilnius who viewed Lithuania's past from a pro-Soviet perspective.

to say that any people would willingly give up their independence. It was now time for historians to tell the truth about the costs that Lithuania had had to pay for that pact: "As a historian, I am ashamed that for so long we did not tell the public the entire truth, at times less than half, and that is the biggest lie."

The crowd so enthusiastically received Truska's confession that Landsbergis again had to call on it to keep order. The spectators responded by giving the next speaker, Vladislovas Mikučiauskas, the foreign minister of Soviet Lithuania, so much mock applause that he had to end his speech prematurely.

[Poet] Sigitas Geda then delivered a history lesson, reading the definition of *annexation* written into the Soviet government's decree on peace in November 1917: "the incorporation of any small or weak nationality by a large and strong state" without the indisputable consent of the small nationality. Conjuring up a biblical parable, he spoke of two strong neighbors' visiting a weak but free man and saying to him: "We will take your roof from above your head, we will take your land, and your woman, your children. . . . We will share your property, everything that here belonged to your ancestors, but you will be happy for it." Lithuania, he concluded, can still recover: "Not to believe today in Lithuania means not to believe in sense, conscience, freedom, and honor."

As darkness settled on the park, the spectators lit candles: according to the printed account of the meeting they represented "the eternal light remembering the senseless victims of Stalinism and Hitlerism." . . . After several more speakers, Virgilius Čepaitis, a translator, returned to the theme of history, asserting, "We must know our history. And not just know it, but also remember that each of us is there and participating." The meeting ended with . . . the singing of the *National Hymn.*

On television the previous Saturday Landsbergis had spoken of the meeting lasting an hour. In fact it continued for almost three. As rain started to fall, the spectators left in groups as they had come, discussing the speeches, evaluating who had made good points, who had failed. The speakers had raised many issues that in the past people would have feared to mention in public; no one could now dare to suggest that the protocols had not existed.

Timothy Garton Ash
"BERLIN: WALL'S END"

Among the most enduring images of the revolutionary autumn of 1989 are those associated with the fall of the Berlin Wall. Television broadcasts of this euphoric reunion of Berliners—and, by extension, East and West Germans on the whole—brought the festive atmosphere into homes throughout the world. This represented the first step toward the eventual disintegration of the East German regime and the reunification of Germany—a clear indication that the Cold War atmosphere had changed decisively, even though the Cold War would not be declared over until the Communist party of the Soviet Union was compelled to relinquish its hold on power almost two years later. The following selection comes from *The Magic Lantern,* a firsthand account of the revolutions of 1989 in East Central Europe by the British journalist Timothy Garton Ash. Here he describes the opening of the Wall and the celebration surrounding it.

Once upon a time, and a very bad time it was, there was a famous platform in West Berlin where distinguished visitors would be taken to stare at the Wall. American Presidents from Kennedy to Reagan stood on that platform looking out over the no man's land beyond. They were told that this, the Potsdamer Platz, had once been Berlin's busiest square, its Piccadilly Circus. Their hosts pointed out a grassy mound on the far side: the remains of Hitler's bunker. East German border-guards watched impassively, or rode up and down the death strip on their army motorbikes.

On the morning of Sunday, 12 November I walked through the Wall and across that no man's land with a crowd of East Berliners, a watchtower to our left, Hitler's bunker to our right. Bewildered border-guards waved us through. (As recently as February their colleagues had shot dead a man trying to escape.) Vertical segments of the wall stood at ease where the crane had just dumped them, their multicoloured graffiti facing east for the first time. A crowd of West Berliners applauded as we came through, and a man handed out free city plans. Then I turned round and walked back again, past more bewildered border-guards and customs officers. Ahead of me I noticed a tall man in an unfamiliar green uniform. He turned out to be the US commandant in Berlin, one General Haddock.

By nightfall, West Berlin workers had dismantled the famous platform, like an unneeded prop. Europe's *Mousetrap*[1] had ended its twenty-eight-year run. Clear the stage for another show.

Everyone has seen the pictures of joyful celebration in West Berlin, the vast crowds stopping the traffic on the Kürfurstendamm, *Sekt* corks popping, strangers tearfully embracing—the greatest street-party in the history of the world. Yes, it was like that. But it was not only like that. Most of the estimated two million East Germans who flooded into West Berlin over the weekend simply walked the streets in quiet family groups, often with toddlers in pushchairs. They queued up at a bank to collect the 100 Deutschmarks 'greeting money' (about thirty-five pounds) offered to visiting East Germans by the West German government, and then they went, very cautiously, shopping. Generally they bought one or two small items, perhaps some fresh fruit, a Western newspaper and toys for the children. Then, clasping their carrier-bags, they walked quietly back through the Wall, through the grey, deserted streets of East Berlin, home.

It is very difficult to describe the quality of this experience because what they actually did was so stunningly ordinary. In effect, they just took a bus from Hackney or Dagenham to Piccadilly Circus, and went shopping in the West End. Berliners walked the streets of Berlin. What could be more normal? And yet, what could be more fantastic! 'Twenty-eight years and ninety-one days,' says one man in his late thirties strolling back up Friedrichstrasse. Twenty-eight years and ninety-one days since the building of the Wall. On that day, in August 1961, his parents had wanted to go to a late-night Western in a West Berlin cinema, but their eleven-year-old son had been too tired. In the early hours they woke to the sound of tanks. He had never been to West Berlin from that day to this. A taxi-driver asks me, with a sly smile: 'How much is the ferry to England?' The day before yesterday his question would have been unthinkable.

Everyone, but everyone, on the streets of East Berlin has just been, or is just going to West Berlin. A breathless, denim-jacketed couple stop me to ask, 'Is this the way out?' They have come hot-foot from Leipzig. 'Our hearts are going pitter-pat,' they say, in broad Saxon dialect. Everyone looks the same as they make their way home—except for the tell-tale Western carrier-bag. But everyone is inwardly changed, changed utterly. 'Now people are standing up straight,' says a hotel porter. 'They are speaking their minds. Even work is more fun. I think the sick will get up from their hospital beds.' And it was

---

[1]A reference to the play of the same name by mystery writer Agatha Christie. Performed in the same London theater since opening in 1952, it holds the world's record for the longest single theatrical run.

in East rather than West Berlin that this weekend had the magic, pentecostal quality which I last experienced in Poland in autumn 1980. Ordinary men and women find their voice and their courage—*Lebensmut,* as the porter puts it. These are moments when you feel that somewhere an angel has opened his wings.

They may have been ordinary people doing very ordinary things, but the Berliners immediately grasped the historical dimensions of the event. 'Of course the real villain was Hitler,' said one. A note stuck to a remnant of the Wall read: 'Stalin is dead, Europe lives.' The man who counted twenty-eight years and ninety-one days told me he had been most moved by an improvised poster saying: 'Only today is the war really over.'

Bild newspaper—West Germany's *Sun*—carried a black-red-gold banner headline declaring 'Good Morning, Germany', and underneath it an effusive thank-you letter from the editors to Mikhail Gorbachev. The East Germans also felt grateful to Gorbachev. But more important, they felt they had won this opening for themselves. For it was only the pressure of their massive, peaceful demonstrations that compelled the Party leadership to take this step. 'You see, it shows Lenin was wrong,' observed one worker. 'Lenin said a revolution could succeed only with violence. But this was a peaceful revolution.' And even the Party's Central Committee acknowledged at the beginning of its hastily drafted Action Programme that 'a revolutionary people's movement has set in motion a process of profound upheavals.'

Why did it happen? And why so quickly? No one in East Germany predicted it. To be sure in July, . . . Church and opposition activists remained deeply pessimistic. The State Security Service—the 'Stasi'—still seemed all-powerful, the population at large not prepared to risk its modest prosperity. Above all, the ranks of the opposition had been continuously thinned by emigration to West Germany. For taking part in a demonstration, a young man would be threatened with a long prison term; then he would be taken into another room of the police station where another officer would present him with a neatly completed application to emigrate. Prison or the West. As one friend put it: 'It's like being asked to choose between heaven and hell.' 'Soon,' he added bitterly, 'there'll be nobody left in this country but a mass of stupid philistines and a few crazy idealists.'

With hindsight we may be a little wiser. At the very least, one can list in order some factors that brought the cup of popular discontent to overflowing. In the beginning was the Wall itself: the Wall and the system it both represented and preserved. The Wall was not round the periphery of East Germany, it was at its very centre. And it ran through every heart. It was difficult even for people from other East European countries to appreciate the full psychological burden it imposed. An East Berlin doctor wrote a book describing the real sicknesses—and of course the suicides—that resulted. He called it *The Wall Sickness.* In a sense, the mystery was always why the people of East Germany did not revolt.

The second causal factor, both in time and importance, was Gorbachev. The 'Gorbachev effect' was strongest in East Germany because it was more strongly oriented towards—and ultimately dependent on—the Soviet Union than any other East European state. . . . East Germany's young people had for years been told, *Von der Sowjetunion lernen heisst siegen lernen*—'To learn from the Soviet Union is to learn how to win.' So they did! For several years East Germans had been turning the name of Gorbachev, and the Soviet example, against their rulers. And Gorbachev personally gave the last push—on his visit to join the fortieth-anniversary celebrations of the GDR on 7 October—with his carefully calculated utterance that 'Life itself punishes those who delay', the leaked news that he had told Honecker[2] Soviet troops would not be used for internal repression and (according to

[2]Erich Honecker headed the East German Communist party from May 1971 until his forced resignation in October 1989.

well-informed West German sources) his direct encouragement to the likes of Egon Krenz[3] and the Berlin Party chief Günter Schabowski, to move to depose Honecker. . . .

Church-protected opposition activity had been increasing through the summer. There had been independent monitoring of the local elections in May, which clearly showed that they were rigged. In June, the East German authorities' emphatic endorsement of the repression in China brought another round of protests. It is important to recall that right up to, and during, the fortieth-anniversary celebrations on 7 October, the police used force, indeed gratuitous brutality, to disperse these protests and intimidate any who might have contemplated joining in. Young men were dragged along the cobbled streets by their hair. Women and children were thrown into prison. Innocent bystanders were beaten.

If one can identify a turning-point it was perhaps Monday, 9 October, the day after Gorbachev left. Since the late summer, the regular Monday evening 'prayers for peace' in Leipzig's church of St. Nicholas had been followed by small demonstrations on the adjacent Karl-Marx-Platz. At the outset, most of the demonstrators were people who wanted to emigrate. But on 25 September there were between 5,000 and 8,000 people, with the would-be emigrants now in a minority, and on 2 October, as the emigration crisis deepened, there were perhaps 15,000 to 20,000—the largest spontaneous demonstration in East Germany since the uprising of 17 June 1953. They sang the Internationale and demanded the legalization of the recently founded 'citizens' initiative', New Forum. The police were baffled, and in places peacefully overwhelmed.

On Monday, 9 October, however, following the violent repression during the fortieth anniversary celebrations two days earlier, riot police, army units, and factory 'combat groups' stood ready to clear the Karl-Marx-Platz, East Germany's Tiananmen Square. An article in the local paper by the commander of one of these 'combat groups' said they were prepared to defend socialism 'if need be, with weapon in hand.' But in the event some 70,000 people came out to make their peaceful protest, and this time force was not used to disperse them. . . . It was claimed, by sources close to the Politburo member responsible for internal security, Egon Krenz, that he, being in overall political control of internal security, had taken the brave, Gorbachevian decision not to use force. It was even claimed that he had personally gone to Leipzig to prevent bloodshed.

Subsequent accounts by those actually involved in Leipzig gave a quite different picture. By these accounts, the crucial action was taken by the famous Leipzig conductor, Kurt Masur, together with a well-known cabaret artist, Bernd-Lutz Lange, and a priest, Peter Zimmermann. They managed to persuade three local Party leaders to join them in a dramatic, last-minute appeal for non-violence, which was read in the churches, broadcast over loudspeakers—and relayed to the police by the acting Party chief in Leipzig. This made the difference between triumph and disaster. It was, it seems, only later in the evening that Krenz telephoned to ask what was happening. The moment was, none the less, decisive for Krenz's bid for power. Nine days later he replaced Honecker as Party leader. But in those nine days the revolution had begun.

To say the growth of popular protest was exponential would be an understatement. It was a non-violent explosion. Those extraordinary, peaceful, determined Monday evening demonstrations in Leipzig—always starting with 'peace prayers' in the churches—grew week-by-week, from 70,000 to double that, to 300,000, to perhaps half a million. The whole of East Germany suddenly went into labour, an old world—to recall Marx's image—pregnant with the new. From that time forward the people acted and the Party reacted. 'Freedom!' demanded the Leipzig demonstrators, and Krenz

---

[3]Egon Krenz succeeded Erich Honecker as East Germany's Communist party chief in the fall of 1989 and relinquished the office a few weeks later.

announced a new travel law. 'Free travel!' said the crowds, and Krenz reopened the frontier to Hungary. 'A suggestion for May Day: let the leadership parade past the people,' said a banner, quoted by the writer Christa Wolf in the massive, peaceful demonstration in East Berlin on 4 November. And more leaders stepped down. 'Free elections!' demanded the people, and the Council of Ministers resigned *en masse.* 'We are the people!' they chanted, and the party leadership opened the Wall.

The cup of bitterness was already full to the brim. The years of Wall Sickness, the lies, the stagnation, the Soviet and Hungarian examples, the rigged elections, the police violence—all added their dose. The instant that repression was lifted, the cup flowed over. And then, with amazing speed, the East Germans discovered what the Poles had discovered ten years earlier, during the Pope's visit in 1979. They discovered their solidarity. 'Long live the October Revolution of 1989' proclaimed another banner on the Alexanderplatz. And so it was: the first peaceful revolution in German history. Yet the opening of the Berlin Wall on 9 November, and subsequently of the whole inter-German frontier, changed the terms of the revolution completely. Before 9 November, the issue had been how this state—the German Democratic Republic—should be governed. The people were reclaiming their so-called people's state. They were putting the D for Democratic into the GDR. After 9 November, the issue was whether this state should continue to exist at all.

I witnessed this moment of change at the epicentre of the revolution, in Leipzig, on a bitterly cold Monday evening twelve days after the opening of the Wall. Driving down the 1930s autobahn from Berlin, I listened on the car radio to a discussion with a local leader of the newly formed Social Democratic Party (SDP). What are your basic principles? he was asked. He went on rather vaguely about the lower social strata being able to emancipate themselves, but not oppressing others in their turn, as the communists had. 'So,' said the interviewer, 'you don't want a dictatorship?' 'No, we don't want a dictatorship.' . . .

. . . [I observed] in the vast crowd outside, on and around Karl-Marx-Platz. Placards showed Erich Honecker in prison uniform and behind bars. Speaker after speaker denounced forty years of lies, corruption, privilege and waste. . . .

. . . [S]peakers demanded that the mass youth organization, the so-called Free German Youth, should be dissolved, and that the Party should (as in Hungary) get out of the workplace. Everyone agreed on two immediate central demands: free elections and an end to the Party's *Führungsanspruch*—its 'leadership claim'.

But that was only half the story. The other half was given most eloquently by someone who introduced himself as 'a plain craftsman'. 'Socialism has not delivered what it promised,' he said, and the promised 'new socialism' would not deliver it either. Loud applause. 'We are not laboratory rabbits.' They had waited and laboured long enough. They all knew that a free-market economy works. 'Our compatriots in the Federal Republic are not foreigners.' There should therefore, he said, be a referendum on reunification. At this point a small group started chanting the slogan that was already painted on several banners: '*Deutschland, einig Vaterland!*' 'Germany, united fatherland!' (words from the East German 'national' anthem on account of which the Honecker leadership had ordered that the whole anthem should never be sung, only the music played). The vast crowd quickly took up the chant: '*Deutschland, einig Vaterland!*' they roared, 'DEUTSCHLAND, EINIG VATERLAND!' And I had to pinch myself to make sure that I was not dreaming, that I really was standing on Karl-Marx-Platz, in Leipzig, in the middle of East Germany, while a hundred thousand voices cried, 'Germany, united fatherland!'

. . . The alternative offered by West Germany was just so immediately, so obviously, so overwhelmingly plausible. . . . The frontiers were open. The people had seen West Germany—and it worked.

On the subsequent march around the city's ring boulevard I noticed one elderly man with a home-made hardboard placard on a stick. It carried the slogan of East Germany's October revolution: '*Wir sind das Volk.*' But the *das* was crossed out and replaced by *EIN,* so it now read not 'We are the people' but 'We are one nation'. And '*Wir sind EIN Volk*' increasingly supplanted '*Wir sind das Volk*' in the mouths of the people. . . .

These idealists' reluctance to see East Germany simply disappear into a larger Federal Republic—to 'sell out' as they would put it—was not, however, fully explicable in terms of reason and ideology. Emotion and personal history had as much to do with it. Every one of these men and women had at some point confronted the decision whether to leave for the West, as so many of their friends and colleagues had done—to make, as it were, an individual reunification. They had decided to stay, to go on working inside the country for a better GDR, a better Germany. A close friend of mine, a pastor, actually *returned* to East Germany after the building of the Wall. 'People will need me here,' he said. And they certainly did.

Were they now at once to concede that it had all been in vain? 'I don't want to say these forty years have just been wasted,' observed Bärbel Bohley, an artist and leading figure in the New Forum, 'because in that case I might as well have left twenty years ago.' Already in January 1990 they began to look back to the month from 9 October to 9 November as an irretrievable moment, a brief flowering of civic courage, peaceful maturity and social self-organization that was blighted not by a cold wind from the East, but by the warm, perfumed wind from the West. For it was at once East Germany's chance and its tragedy that, unlike in Poland or Hungary, the boundaries of social self-determination and national self-determination were not the same.

Thomas Omestad
THE VELVET REVOLUTION

After Soviet tanks crushed the Prague Spring in 1968, Czechoslovakia fell victim to a neo-Stalinist regime that made it the most regressive member of the Eastern Bloc for the next twenty years. Even Gorbachev's reforms had remarkably little effect on the rigid Czech leadership. Not all of society was quiescent, however. Charter 77 and the Committee for the Defense of the Unjustly Persecuted (known as VONS), both founded in the late 1970s, stood for the protection of human rights and sought a rapprochement among students, workers, and intellectuals. At the same time, the Catholic Church in Czechoslovakia, while never as influential as its Polish counterpart, began taking a tougher stance toward the brutishness of the government. Nonetheless, it was the example of neighboring countries in 1989 that finally made the difference. As Poles voted out Communists, East Germans headed west in droves, and festive crowds dismantled the Berlin Wall, Czechs and Slovaks looked on with admiration and envy. Their turn to political commitment was sudden but, at the same time, so nonviolent that the transformation here came to be known as the "Velvet Revolution."

The following account appeared in *The New Republic* shortly after demonstrations in Prague drew unprecedentedly huge numbers of people. Author Thomas Omestad was an associate editor of *Foreign Policy* at the time he observed these events and spoke with members of the government and the opposition. In 1997 he joined the staff of *U.S. News & World Report.*

The enormous mass movement that has essentially overthrown Czechoslovak communism rose up with amazing speed. By the last week in November millions of people had participated in demonstrations across the country. Yet as recently as October 28—Czechoslovakia's independence day—dissidents could bring only 10,000 people into the streets. These brave souls had scarcely unfurled their pro-democracy banners before truncheon-wielding police were chasing them through Prague's winding Gothic lanes. Three weeks later throngs of hundreds of thousands of people were routine in Wenceslas Square. In a matter of days they brought down the Communist leadership and dispatched the Party toward permanent oblivion.

The long-suffering dissident community deserves much of the credit for the dramatic turnaround. But news reports have largely overlooked the role played by the students. Hundreds of students from Charles University and other Prague colleges were clubbed by police at a November 17 march marking the 50th anniversary of the Nazi murder of Czech student demonstrators in 1939. The regime's decision to knock heads was a monumental blunder. Milos Jakes, the Communist Party boss, hoped it would frighten the students back into apathy. But the dramatic liberalizations in the Soviet Union, Poland, Hungary, and especially East Germany had primed the Czechoslovak public for rapid change, as had hints of intensifying Soviet pressure on the hard-line Czechoslovak regime to reform. The zeal with which security forces bloodied unarmed students shocked Czechoslovaks more than any other event since Soviet tanks rolled over the Prague Spring reforms 21 years ago. It shattered the passivity that had long frustrated dissident organizers. "This is the start of the finish of this government," one man shouted prophetically during the violence.

The awful parallel between the regime's violence against student demonstrators and that of the Nazis exactly 50 years earlier created an immensely powerful emotional rallying point. The next day young Praguers were mobilizing for a student strike, calling for mass protests and a nationwide work stoppage, and fanning out across the capital with handbills. It was the students who finally cast off the legacy of timidity and fear left by the Prague Spring, and who bridged the considerable gap dividing oppositionists from the public.

The snap founding of Civic Forum, the new umbrella opposition group, just two days after the police beatings signaled clearly that members of the disparate activist community had at last pulled together. They had emerged from a period of soul-searching over strategy with a will to seize the moment and an unsuspected mastery of coalition politics. "Now it isn't a small, foolish group of so-called dissidents," said Civic Forum's leader, Vaclav Havel. "We are at the time of a real beginning of a real opposition movement in this country."

From then on Civic Forum rode a tidal wave of popular discontent. In little more than a week, the democracy movement was transformed from a motley band of dissidents into an organized opposition—and more. "We're no longer the opposition," Michael Horacek, a spokesman, proclaimed during the stunningly successful general strike on November 27. "They [the Communists] are the opposition." In a region where history, seemingly frozen for four decades, now moves with unnatural rapidity, the evolution of the Czechoslovak opposition movement has broken all records. In ten days it achieved what Poland's Solidarity took nine years to extract: a commitment by Communists accustomed to jailing their critics to abandon the Party's monopoly on power.

When the wave of protests hit on November 17, activists were mulling over their past and future. Their principal achievement, as veteran dissident Jiri Dienstbier said, had been preserving the moral will to resist: "We were passing a small candle through the darkness." The movement's major failing had been its inability to spark protest across Czechoslovak society. The massive demonstrations in East Germany seemed to cause only ripples in Czechoslovakia.

As long as the "socialist certainties" of sausage and beer remained in ample supply, the conventional analysis held, the complacent Czechs and Slovaks would not join their East German neighbors in the streets. "In my opinion this society is completely destroyed," Ivan Lamper, an editor of a samizdat political magazine, lamented to me before the first mass rallies. "People want democracy but they don't want to pay for it." Dissidents bemoaned the lack of a central opposition organization and of an alternative political program. And they didn't seem to be closing the gap between the largely Prague-based intelligentsia, which guides the opposition, and the rest of Czechoslovakia's 15 million people. Many of Solidarity's leaders built their legitimacy as representatives through years of close contact with the masses. But the writers, artists, actors, and journalists of Czechoslovakia's opposition functioned mainly as a moral beacon for a demoralized society. As practical politicians, they were a bit inept.

Of course, marginalizing the opposition had been precisely the aim of the government's relentless campaign of harassment, jailings, and surveillance. It usually refused to acknowledge the opposition's existence. When it did, the dissidents were branded as creations of the Western media and human rights groups. Members of the Communist Party who had joined en masse to participate in the Prague Spring reforms had been purged en masse after the 1968 Warsaw Pact invasion. They and other oppositionists who emerged later found themselves stoking coal, cleaning latrines, and the like. Their children encountered mysterious difficulties getting admitted to college. Their telephones and apartments were bugged. They lived under the constant threat of interrogation, searches, and jail. Police were assigned to them like case workers. Fear of such punishments limited the number of Czechoslovaks willing to join up with the intellectuals. Not surprisingly, the independent groups had to concentrate more on mere survival than on developing a political program.

Both the problems and the strengths of the opposition were exemplified by Havel, the country's best-known dissident (see page 415). A slight, soft-spoken playwright of enormous personal courage, Havel spent five years in prison, where he nearly died of illness. His plays have been banned in Czechoslovakia. His prominence as an artist and his persistence against the state made him the symbol of dissent. Yet all along Havel was more a spokesman of conscience than a potential political leader. "I do not intend to take for myself the role of professional politician. I have never had that ambition," he said even as Civic Forum was formed. Some of Havel's fellow dissidents, though not questioning his pre-eminence in the movement, have pushed him to act more boldly. They criticized him sharply for advising the country's young people to avoid a pro-democracy rally in August after the government hinted that it could turn into another Tiananmen Square massacre. "Vaclav Havel is a man of good heart, a humanitarian," Petra Uhl, a prominent and often-jailed dissident, told the *Washington Post* two months later. "The problem is he does not support any concrete political program. He is an intellectual to such a high degree that I don't think he will be able to pursue one."

Through the mid-1980s the sole preserve of open opposition was Charter 77, the renowned human rights manifesto signed by Havel and hundreds of others. The candle was being kept aflame, but just barely. But in the last two years the arrival of a younger generation of students and workers began recharging the movement. Free of their elders' defeatism, they acted out of frustration with the authorities' refusal to accept Gorbachev-era freedoms. They rejected the unwritten social compact by which the Communists filled store shelves in exchange for sullen acceptance of the regime's stifling orthodoxy. The new generation coalesced in more than 30 new groups and began to link up with the older dissidents. A group called the Czech Children, made up of activists in their 20s, joined in demonstrations for political freedoms and environmental protection. The John Lennon Peace

Club grew out of an informal group advocating independent cultural activity and respect for human rights. And the pranksterish Society for a Merrier Present, armed with truncheons made of cucumbers and salami, staged mock police assaults on demonstrators in Prague. Some of the merry policemen later ate their truncheons.

Independent activism spread in other directions. Widely circulated petitions called for the release of jailed dissidents and an open discussion of 1968. Demand grew for samizdat publications. Thousands of Slovaks flocked to Catholic pilgrimages with anti-Communist undertones. Former associates of Alexander Dubček, the ousted father of the Prague Spring's "socialism with a human face," formed Obroda, a self-described "club for socialist restructuring." Dubček himself emerged from his partly self-imposed isolation as a low-level forestry bureaucrat in Bratislava, calling for a Czechoslovak *perestroika* in interviews with foreign newspapers, on Leningrad TV, and on the Voice of America.

Finally, Havel became the publicly recognized leader of the opposition. Intent on making an example of him, the regime staged a harsh show trial in February for his role in prodemocracy demonstrations the previous month. Yet the Communists' vitriolic media campaign against him unwittingly heightened Havel's celebrity status. A covertly made tape recording of a secret speech by Jakes revealed that he felt Havel's jailing had been a tactical error; Jakes suggested instead that police target less prominent dissidents whose incarceration would draw little notice abroad.

From its inception, Civic Forum's role has been—to use Havel's favorite characterization—improvised. The Forum made a set of specific demands that those Communist leaders tied to the Warsaw Pact intervention step down, that an independent investigation of the November 17 police brutality be launched, and that political prisoners be freed. After the first mass protest, Forum representatives opened talks with the more reformist—and opportunistic—prime minister, Ladislav Adamec, securing from him a pledge against further police or army intervention. Havel initially declined to urge people into the streets; that call came from students. Yet one day later he was encouraging a vast crowd in Wenceslas Square to keep up the pressure on the government. Any lingering hesitation to act had been overwhelmed by the revolution from below. The Forum's "improvisation" was taking its cue from the action in the streets, not from the cooler deliberations of the Prague intellectuals.

Yet as the mass demonstrations continued, Civic Forum's organizational skills radically improved. It was increasingly able to channel, if not control, the public outpouring. From its makeshift headquarters in the basement of the Magic Lantern Theater, it organized the later protests and led the general strike. Just as significant, it was able to halt the mass rallies after the strike in order to conduct power-sharing talks in a calmer atmosphere. It won the grudging recognition of the new Communist Party chief, Karel Urbanek, who replaced Jakes on November 25, as a legitimate negotiating partner. And the once-reluctant Havel, who still longs to return to the theater, seemed to find his voice—and to accept his political role—in the week-long national catharsis at Wenceslas Square.

Havel and other opposition leaders originally conceived of Civic Forum as a Czechoslovak version of East Germany's largest opposition group, New Forum. It was to be neither a political party nor an alternative government. Just the same, Civic Forum quickly found itself pushed beyond negotiating the terms of a dialogue with the government to conducting one. Then the Forum abruptly decided to act as a political party, much like Solidarity did in Polish elections earlier this year. Forum leaders announced that they would endorse candidates to run against Communists next year, when Czechoslovakia holds its first free elections since the postwar Communist takeover. Even with the Civic Forum's shortcomings—above all its lack of workers' representatives—no other group was in a position to use the people's power in the streets to wrest concessions from the government. Civic Forum leaders now see their group as a watchdog over the transition to democracy.

The Czechoslovaks' disgust with communism is so pervasive that even the Party soon accepted the need for a transitional coalition government with non-Communists. It had become clear even to the Communists that their monopoly on power was now untenable. The goal of a coalition government, from the Forum's perspective, will be to secure fair, multiparty elections and constitutional guarantees of free speech, a free press, and freedom of association. After next year's elections the Forum may dissolve itself and let traditional political parties do their work.

Some of those parties are already coming into focus. The Socialist Party, long a toady in the Communist-run National Front, switched sides and backed Civic Forum; it could become an electoral force of its own. The Democratic Initiative, an opposition group founded in 1987, is stepping forward as a Western-style liberal party. Non-collectivized farmers are planning to launch a party. And Communist reformers have formed a group called the Democratic Forum, which could conceivably break away from the Communist Party. Other parties will undoubtedly crowd into the field in the coming weeks. . . .

. . . On December 3 [Adamic] announced a new Cabinet, in which only five of 21 posts were transferred to non-Communists and 13 of the ministers had served in the previous Cabinet. The opposition called another mass demonstration and threatened a second general strike unless the Cabinet was recast to reflect the Communists' loss of influence. Another improvisation. Havel and Civic Forum will undoubtedly be making many more of them through this exhilarating season of the Prague Fall.

Martin Sixsmith
MOSCOW COUP

Like Nikita Khrushchev a generation earlier, Mikhail Gorbachev found that his attempts to revitalize Soviet communism provoked opposition at the highest levels of power, including in some cases his own appointees. For several years, Gorbachev successfully maneuvered and fended off attempts to undermine his reforms and sap his political strength. In the summer of 1991 he prepared to sign a treaty that would ease Russia's grip over the other, non-Russian republics that comprised the USSR. Perceiving the document as a capitulation to the increasingly restless national minorities and thus the effective end of the union, Gorbachev's enemies decided to strike. Their attempted coup proved a pathetic failure and actually hastened the dissolution of the multinational state they sought to preserve. It also evoked a powerful, unexpected response among many Russians who chose to stand for democracy, vividly demonstrating the impact of Gorbachev's reforms in the course of just a few years. Gorbachev himself survived the plot to unseat him, but his subsequent efforts at exonerating the Communist party reflected a peculiar lack of political comprehension. Instead, the initiative now passed to Russian President Boris Yeltsin (1930–2007). A one-time Urals party boss, whom Gorbachev had named head of the Moscow party organization and later removed from power, Yeltsin provided dynamic leadership in resisting the coup and thereby positioned himself to lead Russia into its post-Soviet era.

The following description of the first day of the coup—August 19, 1991—comes from Martin Sixsmith, at that time the BBC Moscow correspondent. His account, entitled *Moscow Coup—The Death of the Soviet System,* appeared within weeks of the event.

The first indication that things were badly wrong that Monday morning was the solemn music that Soviet TV was putting out in place of its usual early morning news and chat show. A quick check on the radio revealed all channels broadcasting the same composers—Tchaikovsky and Chopin: the classical harbingers of grave news in the Soviet Union. A growing sense of panic was briefly relieved by a glance through the curtains to the street below: there, people were still going about their business, the usual militiaman was on guard duty outside the front entrance of the flats opposite and cars were heading down the main road into the city centre. But the relief was only momentary. The strains of 'Swan Lake' were unceremoniously interrupted, and a funereal sounding announcer made the proclamation that was to chill the hearts of millions:

> In connection with Mikhail Gorbachov's inability to carry out his duties of President due to reasons of ill health and in accordance with article 127 of the Soviet Constitution, all presidential powers have been transferred to the Vice-President of the USSR, Gennady Yanayev.

For any Russian listening, the situation was already clear: retirement for health reasons was the cynical old formula that had been used for decades to remove public officials unwillingly from their posts. But in case there was any doubt left that a coup was in progress, the announcement went on to spell it out:

> With the aim of overcoming the deep crisis, political, inter-ethnic and civil confrontation, chaos and anarchy which are threatening the life and safety of citizens of the Soviet Union, as well as the sovereignty, integrity, freedom and independence of our fatherland, we the undersigned hereby announce . . . the introduction of a state of emergency in parts of the USSR for a period of six months beginning on 19 August at 4 a.m. Moscow time . . . and the setting up of a State Emergency Committee to run the country and effectively administer the emergency regime.

The list of signatories left little doubt about the nature of the new regime. It was headed by Yanayev, and included all the hardliners from the top Kremlin leadership—Vladimir Kryuchkov, head of the KGB; Valentin Pavlov, the conservative Prime Minister; Boris Pugo, the Interior Minister who controlled the militia and forces of special troops; and Defence Minister, Marshal Dmitri Yazov. These were the men who for months had been expressing growing irritation with the way things were going in the Soviet Union, not overtly criticizing Mikhail Gorbachov, but making plain their belief that reform had gone far enough and that it was time to reintroduce a little law and order. . . .

. . . By mid-day on Monday, one of the first signs of passive resistance to the coup had emerged in the changing voices of the news readers who were forced to declaim the plotters' propaganda. From an emotionless beginning, tones of disgust with the material they were reading slowly began to appear: one woman announcer could hardly disguise her contempt, and her feelings showed more and more clearly in her voice. The plotters were seemingly finding it hard to find supporters of their views in key positions.

Physical resistance was also about to begin on the streets. Reports were coming in of isolated incidents in which civilians had stood in the path of advancing tanks, hurling abuse at the troops or appealing to them to go back to barracks. There was one particularly dramatic incident in which demonstrators clambered onto an armoured personnel carrier and began to drag the driver out of his porthole: the look of terror on the face of the teenaged conscript at the threat of a public beating suggested that some of the troops at least might not be spoiling for a fight. Many of the tank crews had seemed unsure how to respond. Few of them had any idea why they had been ordered onto the streets of Moscow, but nearly all of those we spoke to said they would obey whatever orders they were given.

So far, caution and good sense shown by the tank commanders had averted any injuries to those who stood in their way: when challenged, the tanks simply wheeled around the human obstacles in their path and took another route to their destination. A feeling of impunity began to grow in those who were bold enough to oppose the army. . . .

By Monday afternoon the army was everywhere and the worst fears of supporters of democracy had been realized. The men who claimed to have taken power in the Soviet Union were showing their true face, relying not on the ballot box but on the bullet. Columns of armoured vehicles surrounded strategic buildings in Moscow, meeting resistance from the people, resistance that was still largely token, but which was enough to hint at the violence and bloodshed which more organized opposition seemed certain to provoke.

In mid afternoon a phalanx of the heaviest tanks drew up outside the Russian parliament on the banks of the Moskva river. This was the headquarters of Boris Yeltsin, the Russian President whose outspoken support of radical reform had made him the natural rallying point for resistance to the coup. As soon as the takeover was announced in the early hours of Monday morning, Yeltsin had gathered his trusted aides and taken refuge in the parliament, a soaring white marble building whose nickname of Belyi Dom—the White House—quickly made it a nationally and internationally recognized symbol of democracy. It was here that the fight for the democratic ideal in the Soviet Union was to be fought out over the next two days and nights.

When the tanks arrived, belching acrid fumes and smoke, thundering noisily along the embankment and leaving the deep imprint of their tracks in the tarmac, Yeltsin was inside the building trying to formulate a response to the coup. The parliament was undefended, there were no crowds present and the building was seemingly ripe for the taking. I watched the line of armour draw up at the base of the parliament steps and was convinced they had come to seize the parliament, Boris Yeltsin and all who opposed their masters in the Kremlin.

For twenty minutes the tanks stayed in place, revving their engines and filling the air with a blue haze. But the order to attack did not come, and at the crucial moment it was Yeltsin himself who seized the initiative. Instead of waiting for the troops to come for him, Yeltsin went to the troops. Emerging dramatically from the parliament's main entrance, Yeltsin descended the steps and strode confidently towards the leading tank in the column.

For a moment, all who were present held their breath. Yeltsin was accompanied by his usual bodyguards, but there was no one to save him from a concerted attempt to arrest him, nothing to save him from a sniper's bullet. It seemed then that the one man who could stand in the way of the coup, the one man on whose shoulders the future of Russian democracy had come to rest, was gambling everything on a confrontation he could have avoided. Yeltsin could have stayed safely inside the parliament, kept his head down and waited. But patience was never Yeltsin's strong point and his decision to go for broke was to pay quick dividends.

In a master stroke of public image-making, he heaved his burly frame firmly onto the back of the tank he had selected, and then squarely onto the turret itself. Panting from the effort, he leaned down, shook hands with two startled tank crew who were peering from inside the vehicle, and then rose to his full height. Staring defiantly at the soldiers and militia around him, he declared to all within earshot that the army was with the people, that the troops would not attack the defenders of democracy and that the plotters in the Kremlin were doomed to failure. Right across Russia, said Yeltsin, workers were heeding his appeals for protest strikes and were walking out to show their opposition to the coup.

It was a performance of genius which set the tone for the whole of the resistance campaign in the coming hours and days. But Yeltsin could have felt very little conviction in anything he was saying. There had, presumably, been some secret agreement reached between

Yeltsin's representatives and the tank commanders that he would not be shot or arrested if he came out to speak to them. But there was no record of what passed between Yeltsin and the tank crew in that moment of high drama, there was almost certainly no pledge of loyalty from the army despite Yeltsin's claims, and the next twenty-four hours showed that a large proportion of the armed forces were indeed ready to follow orders issued by the Kremlin, and were not even contemplating switching sides. Yeltsin's appeal for strikes, far from being heeded across the land, had probably gone unheard by the vast majority of workers: all his means of communication, including his access to national radio and newspapers, had been effectively cut off by the coup leaders, and whatever statements he made reached little further than those who could hear the hastily installed public address system outside the Russian parliament.

But, showing himself a man with his ear to the flow of history, Yeltsin on the turret of the tank had seized the genuine mood of the time. Some of the army was indeed wavering in its loyalties, and Yeltsin's intention was to encourage that indecision by suggesting it was more widespread than it really was—the effects were seen later, when a parachute detachment and some tanks did in fact come to help defend the parliament. Similarly, his contention that workers were striking in their thousands was intended to stir up protests against the coup, protests which did eventually begin to materialize.

On the basis of what he knew at the time, though, Yeltsin had no objective grounds for feeling the optimism he professed. It was, it seems, an inspired piece of whistling in the dark; but in the immediate term it did the trick. Shortly after Yeltsin descended from his perch to go back to his parliament under siege, the tank commanders conferred briefly, jumped back on board and the tanks roared off along the embankment leaving the parliament once again in peace.

It is unclear whether the initiative came from the commanders themselves, or whether their original orders had been simply to intimidate Yeltsin and then leave, but the effect on those present was electrifying. Yeltsin had stood up to the tanks and won—a precious psychological victory at a time when the coup looked almost certain to succeed.

The full resonance of the tank episode was confirmed later that day, when the poet Yevgeny Yevtushenko called at the BBC office with a new poem he had written celebrating Yeltsin's appearance. In Russia, poetry is written and read with burning commitment: long-standing restrictions on other means of expression have made it an accepted medium of political struggle and the written word can still fall like a bombshell. Yevtushenko had brought with him his Russian text and a rough English translation with the intention of broadcasting it to the world. For an hour or more we sat over the poem, polishing it and correcting some of his more idiosyncratic uses of English. Entitled 'August 19th', it summed up the feeling that we were living an historic moment and that Yeltsin's courage might just be enough to bring the nation through its torment:

> This August day
> Shall be glorified in songs and ballads.
> Today we are a nation,
> No longer fools, happy to be
> fooled. . . .
> Conscience wakens even in the tanks—
> Yeltsin rises on a turret,
> Freed from ghosts of Kremlin leaders
> past. . . .

Yeltsin's stand at the White House . . . [became] the focal point for all opposition to the junta. The episode with the tanks outside the parliament earlier in the afternoon had revived ominous memories of the previous attempted putsches in Latvia and, in particular, Lithuania, where President Vytautas Landsbergis had taken refuge in his parliament and called for pro-democracy supporters to defend the building with their lives. In Lithuania, the presence of hundreds of civilians outside the parliament had deterred any frontal assault by the tanks, although similar human cordons did not deter a murderous attack to seize the Vilnius television tower, or—later—a similar massacre of unarmed defenders outside the Latvian Council of Ministers building. So when Yeltsin began to appeal for civilians to gather around the White House—his appeals broadcast on his shoestring short-wave radio station, but circulated much more efficiently by Moscow's astoundingly extensive word-of-mouth grapevine—those who responded knew the real and present danger they were exposing themselves to.

The crowds really began to build up from around dusk. Arriving from work, or from colleges and the university, they came first in dribs and drabs, then in larger numbers and finally in their thousands. The emotion of the occasion was all-embracing. These were ordinary men and women, some mere school boys, others gnarled working men, others elderly pensioners or invalids, many of them women toughened by endless hours spent standing in Soviet queues. They were not special; they were not politicians or heroes; they were the people—the *narod*—finally ready to stand up for their rights. They were the living evidence that reform in the Soviet Union had not been in vain: for all its shortcomings, and even if it was now about to be snuffed out, perestroika had created these men and women who were ready to suffer, to fight and—if necessary—to die in defence of what they knew was right.

Prior to 1985 this could not have happened: people then were so cowed and down-trodden that whatever injustices or crimes were inflicted on them by whatever regime was in power, they would have swallowed hard and accepted it. But now the people had seen that life could be different. They knew it would be a long and difficult road before that new life was attained, a life based on human values, with respect for the individual; but they had started on that road and they were determined not to be pushed off it. And, in the end, that was why the thousands who came to the Russian parliament that evening considered that all the discomfort and risks to their personal safety were worth taking. There was a tacit understanding among those present that the political battle-lines had been drawn during the day, the rhetoric and the statements were over, and that it was now down to the people to fight the physical battle on the streets which would really decide the future of the country.

3 The Trauma of Transition from Communism

The collapse of Communist power led to attempts at constructing not only Western-style democracy but also free markets. Socialist regimes throughout the Eastern Bloc had earlier experimented with limited private enterprise, achieving notable success in some cases, e.g., Hungary and East Germany. Now, however, post-Communist governments undertook "shock therapy," the wholesale marketization and privatization of their economic infrastructures, often at the urging of Western academics and consultants. The results, at best, were mixed. In general, the countries of Eastern Europe negotiated the transition more smoothly than post-Soviet Russia, where a Stalinist command economy had been firmly entrenched for well over half a century. In particular, the return of state property to private ownership in Russia turned out to be disappointingly

counterproductive; the chief beneficiaries of the changeover were the same elites that had controlled the levers of power during the Soviet era. In addition, the introduction of a market economy sometimes seemed only to replace socialism's benefits with capitalism's ills. Fixed prices and guaranteed welfare gave way to ruinous inflation and hand-to-mouth subsistence. A new middle class was in the making, but many of its members had amassed their wealth by questionable means, sometimes by criminal methods. In sum, the achievement of economic security, no less than the attainment of participatory democracy, seemed an increasingly remote goal.

At the same time, the years since 1989 have seen the reemergence of serious problems whose origins hark back to historical circumstances that predate the coming of communism. These diffculties often involve long-held religious and national prejudices that are hardly unique to Eastern Europe, but that have weighed heavily on the area nevertheless. Confronting these issues will help to determine the success of this region in achieving the political stability and economic prosperity that its inhabitants seek.

Accounts of Omarska Concentration Camp "EVERY NIGHT THE PRISONERS WERE SEIZED WITH FEAR THAT THIS COULD BE THEIR NIGHT..."

One of the most tragic conflicts of the latter part of the twentieth century occurred in the former Yugoslavia. Successfully administered as a single state until the death of President Tito in 1980, Yugoslavia thereafter began to unravel violently along its major ethnic fault lines. Moreover, ethnic differences were compounded by rival religious affiliations of long standing. Despite many marriages and friendships across ethnic and religious lines, the Serbs, who subscribed to Eastern Orthodoxy, and the Roman Catholic Croats tended to find themselves at odds; and both of these groups tended to stand in opposition to the Muslims, who traced their community's origins to the Ottoman conquests of the late Middle Ages.

Two of Yugoslavia's constituent republics—Slovenia and Croatia—opted to leave the federation and set up their own independent nation-states in 1991. Serbia, the dominant republic from the time of Yugoslavia's establishment at the end of the First World War, sought to realize its territorial ambitions at the expense of neighboring Bosnia-Herzegovina, as it had earlier in the century. Bosnia-Herzegovina was a multiethnic microcosm of Yugoslavia, divided between Serbs, Croats, and Bosniaks (Bosnian Muslims). In fact, the Bosniaks are descended from the Slavs who converted to Islam during the Ottoman era and are therefore ethnically related to the Serbs and Croats—but no less despised by them for that reason. The Serb-dominated Yugoslav state (in effect, Serbia and Montenegro) and the Bosnian Serbs made common cause in 1992 and began seizing large areas of Bosnia, employing "ethnic cleansing"—beatings, rape, plunder, arson, and murder—to drive out the Muslim and Croat populations. Meanwhile, the Croatian government, through its own form of ethnic cleansing, began to evict Serbs from its territory and seize parts of Bosnia populated by a majority of Croats. The Bosniak government, supported by small numbers of Croats or Serbs who still embraced a multiethnic state, formed its own army to protect its population and territory against both Serbs and Croat incursions.

The ruthless civil war claimed some 100,000 lives by 1994 and turned millions into refugees. Only in 1995 did the international community, through NATO, utilize military force to halt Serb aggression. The treaty signed in 1996 reunited Bosnia, if only on paper, and restored peace; however, armed Croat and Serb militias remained and the uneasy Croat-Bosniak alliance forged in the middle of the conflict remained shaky. Yugoslavia has since ceased to exist, and tensions remain quite high. The primary incentive for peace appears to be the potential of EU membership for Serbia—and a reasonable hope for improved economic prospects—in return for continued cooperation in the arrest of war criminals and their delivery to the Hague for adjudication.

One of the sites emblematic of the conflict's wanton brutality was the northern Bosnian mining town of Omarska. Here Bosnian Serb paramilitary authorities established a notorious makeshift prison for prisoners of war and other detainees. Classified as a concentration camp by Human Rights Watch, several thousand Bosnian Croats and Bosniaks were held under appalling conditions, such as a lack of toilets or washing facilities, little water, meager rations, torture, indiscriminate beatings, sexual humiliation, and murder. A number of women were also held there, and were subjected to rape, torture, and death at the whim of the guards. Curiously, international journalists gained rather wide access to the facility during the height of its operations in 1992, but the fact that they were almost always under the watchful eye of guards prevented prisoners from speaking freely and generally permitted journalists to see or hear only that which the Serb paramilitary authorities allowed them. While Omarska was certainly not a death camp on a par with camps in the Nazi-occupied East decades earlier, televised images and written reports revealed conditions that reflected a period Europeans had assumed would never return. Precise death tolls have not yet been ascertained, but some estimates suggest there were as many as 5,000 victims. Several camp guards and camp commander Zelko Mejakic were apprehended years after the war ended and transferred to the International Criminal Tribunal for the Former Yugoslavia (ICTY) in the Hague. Mejakic met with the heaviest sentence: after his conviction on several counts, which included crimes against humanity and war crimes, on May 30, 2008, he was sentenced to twenty-one years' imprisonment.

The following two selections offer different insights into the gruesome conditions in the Omarska camp. The first provides experts from a special UN Commission of Experts to the UN Security Council. The second are representative selections of witness statements from one of the ICTY sessions devoted to prosecution of those charged with crimes at Omarska.

Starting, at the latest, on 27 May 1992, the conditions in Logor Omarska were more than crowded. One former detainee arriving at the camp on that day, recounts that he was squeezed into the room adjacent to the huge garage together with an estimated 400 other prisoners (the group was to prepare lists with the names of those present, with 30 names on each list). He states that the prisoners were packed so close together that their situation resembled that of sardines in a tin. After the doors to the storeroom had been closed, the prisoners had to remain there and in that position for four days, with neither food nor water or any toilet facilities. Everyone had to stand in an upright position all along as there was no space for anyone to lie down. Others estimate that this room may have contained up to 500 detainees at the time. The huge garage may have taken up to 1,000 men at the time. There were also several hundred men cramped in on the first floor of the same building. In addition, hundreds were ordered to stay on the cement floor outdoors—there are said to have been some 700 in early June 1992.

In the canteen building, there was only the garage which held any sizable number of prisoners. It is with reference to this garage that a former prisoner is reported to have informed that he, on 30 May 1992, was stuffed with 130 others [prisoners] into a one-car garage. There were as many as 160 prisoners squeezed into this garage. . . .

Not only was the camp crowded, but the detainees were not to move around freely in the camp either. Whether detained indoors or in the open area outside, they were only to move when specifically permitted to do so—regularly only to receive food and to go to the toilets/the open fields. Under these circumstances, which were aggravated by several other factors as well, sanitation more or less immediately became a problem for the prisoners.

There was far too little water provided for the detainees to drink, and personal hygiene thus naturally came second in the competition for water in the camp. This was mid-summer when the days often were hot. Also, indoors it was hot due to the generally cramped conditions there. The prisoners' clothing was never properly washed, and it became more and more dirtied and ragged by the day. Since most prisoners had only one pair of summer clothes on them when coming to the camp, the clothing also had to serve as bedding such as pillows and blankets. There were no beds or bedding provided for the prisoners in the camp, with the exception that the women were provided with some kind of mattresses, two women sleeping on each. . . .

Twice before the camp for all practical purposes was closed on 6 August 1992, male prisoners had a "shower." In groups of 50, the guards had them disrobe and aimed fire hoses at 10 of them at a time. The high pressure of the water on the prisoners' weakened bodies was painful and not a relief, particularly so as the guards reportedly amused themselves with aiming at the prisoners' wounds and genitals.

There were no sanitary provisions for the prisoners in the camp; some rooms had plastic barrels at times. Reportedly, the Serbian guards frequently beat the prisoners on their way to meals as well as on their way to the toilet—a reason why there were occasions when the prisoners preferred rather to urinate or defecate in their trousers or shoes.

The women in the camp had much better general conditions for personal hygiene, engaged as they were also in cleaning both in the kitchen and the offices (the rooms used for interrogation), etc. But, the relative cleanliness of the female prisoners was possibly more for the advantage of the Serbs abusing them than to themselves under the circumstances. . . .

As the prisoners' hygiene deteriorated, so did the hygiene in the detention locations. This soon became a vicious circle exacerbated as prisoners were maltreated and wounds and illnesses entered the scene. In the White House, it is said, blood, hair, teeth and small pieces of human flesh and bones made the rooms look like a primitive slaughterhouse. . . .

Hair and beards grew long. Soon lice were a problem. Diarrhoea and dysentery quickly became unwelcome frequent, and then later permanent, visitors. Under these circumstances, even minor wounds could represent serious—sometimes lethal—problems because they were easily infected and there were no proper remedies for disinfection available. Like the lice found their breeding ground in open wounds, so did reportedly worms. A variety of illnesses found suitable general conditions to break out, but this does not seem to have plagued the camp inmates to the extent that one could have feared, or which could have become the case, if the camp had been open for a longer period of time.

The combination of unsanitary and depressing conditions, fatigue due also to malnutrition and nutritional deficiencies, physical and mental stress, and maltreatment rapidly weakened the prison population. . . .

When the prisoners first arrived at Logor Omarska, most of them, it is said, did not receive food or water the first four days or so. Later, they were permitted to come out from the buildings and rooms where they normally stayed to obtain daily food rations.

The routine in Logor Omarska allegedly was that when the prisoners were to receive food in the canteen (on the ground floor in the canteen building), they had to run through an L-shaped corridor. The camp guards frequently tossed wax on the floor to make it slippery. There were metallic wardrobe cabinets along the corridor and prisoners fell and hit the cabinets and were beaten by the guards. There were four Serbs in particular who allegedly beat the prisoners. The names of the alleged perpetrators are known but not disclosed for confidentiality or prosecutorial reasons.

To receive their daily food rations, the prisoners normally arrived in groups of 30. They received a piece of bread and a ladle of some soup-like fluid. The groups had to eat their food within two or three minutes. Each piece of bread weighed approximately 800 grams, one piece was normally divided between eight people, sometimes between four. The last prisoners sometimes received no bread at all. The female prisoners (who were charged with distributing the food) sometimes tried to give prisoners in special need a little extra, mainly from their own rations.

Some prisoners were so afraid of being beaten that they disregarded some of their daily rations. The daily food rations were handed out between 9:00 a.m. and 4:00 p.m. Thus, it was often more than 24 hours between times when each person received his rations. Once, a prisoner received some crumbs of bread in a newspaper. He remembers how he tore up the newspaper to get hold of every single of the crumbs. . . .

The male detainees were not given any ordinary work to do, but were called upon to carry maltreated and dead fellow inmates in and out. It was more often than not that the prisoners themselves had to lift corpses up on trucks that would remove the dead, and on occasions when the number of dead was reportedly relatively high, the live workers out of the camps as well. The prisoners who had to follow such transports have allegedly not been heard of again. . . .

Concentration camp inmates were called for interrogation in the offices on the first floor of the canteen building. Interrogations were normally conducted from 8:00 a.m. to 6:00 p.m. The interrogators are generally referred to with the more civilized title of "inspectors". The inspectors arrived at the camp in the morning in a small bus together with clerks assisting with typewriting. Thence, camp guards went around in the camp and collected the unfortunate ones to be interrogated. Camp guards participated in interrogation sessions as well. Sometimes the guards seemed to have started the interrogation sessions elsewhere in the camp before they brought the prisoners to the inspectors. All the time, it is claimed, beating, screaming and moaning could be heard from the interrogation offices. Survivors relate that they were badly maltreated and tortured when interrogated. Beatings with a variety of implements were probably most common, but there are long lists of other methods used as well. The number of prisoners who died during interrogation is not known to anyone other than the Serbs in charge; the number is allegedly not very small. Time and again other prisoners claim that they observed dead bodies taken out from interrogation and left on the ground outside for others to see. Fellow prisoners also noted that a number of prisoners taken for interrogation never returned to their detention room and were later not seen elsewhere either.

During interrogation, some were asked about political activities, a majority perhaps about their access to weapons. In general, the inspector seemed to have asked all kinds of questions—sometimes they questioned the prisoners of things that seemed of no relevance to their case whatsoever. If a prisoner denied any charges made against him or her, the person allegedly was likely to be or continued to be maltreated. Many a time prisoners reportedly agreed to anything held against them just to avoid or reduce the mistreatment, but then the guards and interrogators would find just another excuse to proceed with the mistreatment it seems. . . .

All the women reportedly experienced bad interrogation sessions.

In general, when prisoners were called for interrogation, other prisoners tried to provide them with some clothing which was not all in tatters so that they would have a little protection for the skin. It is stated that it even happened that prisoners—before potential interrogation sessions—smeared themselves with blood from fellow prisoners maltreated already, with the hope that it could give them an easier time. Blood stained clothing served a similar purpose.

Mistreatment and torture were not confined to interrogation sessions. Extreme abuses were reportedly carried out by camp guards at any time, but especially at night. Sometimes the guards seemed to select their victims at random. Sometimes they probably had personal grudges to settle with someone. Sometimes they seemed to act in a kind of follow-up after the day's interrogations, coming back for victims from then. . . .

When prisoners were called out at night—it could, for example, be five to 10 people from the large garage plus some from other rooms—they reportedly more often than not did not come back to their rooms ever.

Every night the prisoners were seized with fear that this could be their night—the night when they would be subjected to maltreatment and possibly, or rather probably, death. The guards allegedly organized sheer orgies in brute force and destruction. Some prisoners were victimized next to or in the bonfire, others in the White House, and some were walked towards the Red House. Some experienced two of these options. It seems that the same prisoners were not taken both to the White House and the Red House.

One former prisoner relates:

"Arriving to Logor Omarska they were ordered up against the wall facing it and with their hands up—they were beaten. All the eight of them were taken to the White House, the second room to the right. The room was approximately 25 square metres and there were some 60 to 70 barely alive prisoners there. It was mainly young people who had surrendered themselves on the Kozara Mountain. Himself he was allowed to settle down next to a person [whose name is not disclosed for confidentiality or prosecutorial reasons], who later was killed in the camp. Of all the other people who were there, it was only one deaf and dumb man and himself who were not killed in the camp. There was one window in the room, and guards outside it. The door was half wood and half glass. Maybe 30 minutes later, it was dead silent in the room, a guard came in screaming that the one who was intended to flee had to come outside. He was ordered outside, where a bonfire was lit. All the guards were drunk. They asked him where he was hiding his weapon. He did not know how Logor Omarska was operated. He said that he had no weapon. They asked him for his name. He was then allowed to return inside. The guards outside the window were poking around like pigs, swearing at him, calling him names. They told him to come to the window and to lean his head out—he could see very little, it was dark. He saw only a knife gleaming in the dark. They asked him if he wanted to buy cigarettes, he answered in the affirmative and was given two packets. He shared one packet and was ordered to shut the window. The next day he saw a horrible—unimaginable and overwhelming—sight outside, they were all his fellow men who had been tormented. [Five men were named by the witness, who stated that two of them were killed in Omarska.]"

Starting from the very beginning of the camp, female prisoners were allegedly raped by the Serbian camp guards. Serbian camp officials, and other Serbs. Rapes were reportedly often combined with beatings and other abuses. Often rapes were committed by several perpetrators one after the other. Sometimes the rapist had an audience, sometimes it was merely fellow perpetrators waiting to take turns. Like the rest of the prison population the women were not as such protected against either ill-treatment or torture.

Two of the youngest women spent most of the time in the White House where they were raped and tortured. Almost all the women were badly tortured when in the camp. Most women were subjected to sexual assault—they were humiliated by being promised privileges and threatened that if they did not obey, they would not survive.

The guards reportedly tried to force one prisoner (whose name is not disclosed for confidentiality or prosecutorial reasons) to rape his fellow prisoner (whose name is also not disclosed for confidentiality or prosecutorial reasons), a young woman. He did not want to. He had angina pectoris. The guards stripped both. The male prisoner begged and screamed, "I cannot, I cannot, she could have been my daughter." The guards beat him, his heart could probably not take it. In any event, he was carried outside where it was raining heavily. The next morning other prisoners saw the male prisoner's dead body laying outside of the White House.

Men were also reportedly sexually abused in the camp. Prisoners were, inter alia, forced to have homosexual intercourse with one another, close relatives—like fathers and sons—among them. Worst of all were numbers of reported castrations carried out by a variety of primitive means. On one occasion, Dusan Tadic allegedly forced one prisoner to bite off the testicles of other prisoners who all died subsequently. In most cases, the guards are said to have performed the castrations themselves. Probably all the victims of castrations died due to severe losses of blood. On one occasion, the guards aimed a fire hose on the victim's wound afterwards. . . .

According to the Gregorian calendar, Saint Peter's Day is on 29 June, but according to the Julian calendar, which is followed by the Serbian Orthodox church, all religious feasts are celebrated 13 days later. Christmas, just to mention one other example, is celebrated on 6 January. On 12 July 1992, Petrovdan (Saint Peter's Day), the Serbian guards reportedly took care to beat every single prisoner on their way to receive the daily food rations. There were 30 prisoners eating at a time. The guards beat them both on their way in and on their way out. The guards reportedly also celebrated this religious feast with other more severe acts of violence, killing more prisoners than they did on an average day and night. . . .

When new prisoners arrived at Logor Omarska, they were normally received with beatings from the very moment they disembarked from the vehicles in which they arrived. Some newcomers died, as they immediately had their heads smashed into a brick wall. Killed upon arrival—they were murdered, but not actually detained in Logor Omarska. . . .

When the camp for most practical purposes had been closed and cleaned with only a limited number of prisoners left to be paraded for international media and aid agencies, journalist Ed Vulliamy described those deemed in good enough condition to be paraded for him as follows:

"Nothing could have prepared us for what we see when we come through the back gates of what was the Omarska iron mine and ore processing works, and are ushered into the canteen area. Across a yard, a group of prisoners who have just emerged from a door in the side of a large rust-coloured metal shed are adjusting their eyes to the sunlight and being ordered into a straight line by the barked commands of a uniformed armed guard. Then, as part of some rigid, well-worn camp drill, they run in single file across the courtyard and into the canteen. Above them in an observation post is the watchful eye, hidden behind reflective sunglasses, of a beefy guard who follows their weary canter with the barrel of his heavy machine gun. There are thirty of them running; their heads newly shaven, their clothes baggy over their skeletal bodies. Some are barely able to move. In the canteen, there are no more barked orders, the men know the drill all right. They line up in obedient and submissive silence and collect their ration: a meager, watery portion of beans augmented with bread crumbs, and stale roll, which they collect as they file along the metal railings. The men are at various stages of human decay and affliction; the bones of their elbows and wrists protrude like pieces of jagged stone from the pencil-thin stalks to which their arms have been reduced. Their skin is putrefied, the complexions of their faces have been corroded. These humans are alive but decomposed, debased, degraded, and utterly subservient, and yet they fix their huge, hollow eyes on us with looks like the blades of knives. There is nothing quite like the sight of the prisoner desperate to talk and to convey some terrible truth that is so near yet so far, but who dares not. Their stares burn, they speak only with their terrified silence, and eyes inflamed with the articulation of stark, undiluted, desolate fear-without-hope.

They sit down at sparse metal tables, and wolf down their meal. It is very obviously the only one of the day; if they ate even twice as much, they would not be so gaunt and withered. The meal takes precisely one minute; the guards signal that time is up, and the men make up another queue by the exit". . . .

In short, all information available about Logor Omarska seems to indicate that it was more than anything else a death camp. The detainees were not there to work or serve a specific purpose. There is no information to sustain a claim that the detainees were in transit to somewhere else. As far as the prisoners were concerned, the interrogations led nowhere out of the camp, and the camp conditions were such that very few, if any, prisoners would have survived long-term detention.

The following interview focuses on the cruel discipline to which prisoners at Omarska were subjected.

A. To the right was the entrance to the school, and to the left was the way to the sports hall, to the gym. That's where we went.
Q. When you went into the gym, did you see any people there that weren't from your group?
A. In the right-hand corner, there was a large group of people. They were sitting down.
Q. And were these Muslims?
A. Yes, because I knew some of them.
Q. And can you describe how many people came into that gym and how that happened?
A. About 2 and a half thousand people, according to my estimate, were pressed together in that gym.
Q. When you say "pressed together," how were you organised?
A. My knees were below my chin. They forced us to. We had to. They said they would shoot if we didn't all press together, so people were fainting. A person would faint and couldn't fall, not to the left, not to the right. They would just continue sitting up unconscious.
Q. How hot was it?
A. It was too hot. And people had no water, so that's why they were fainting.
A. One of the prisoners, probably he felt ill. He got up, and we were told strictly not to get up. And he got up and he said: "What are you afraid of? There are plenty of us. Do not be afraid." Soldiers charged in. They said: "Who said that?" And he said he did. And they told him to get out. He didn't want to get out, and they said they would shoot. They would fire, kill 20, 30 people if he didn't get out. And then he was pushed out by the others so that

they wouldn't be killed, those sitting next to him.

Q. Did you see what happened to this person that got pushed out?

A. Yes. There, right inside the corridor, just outside of the gym, I heard a short burst of fire. He screamed, and he was killed there. . . .

In this conversation the interviewee describes the systematic execution of prisoners at Omarska.

Q. Can you describe the process by which you and other Muslim prisoners were taken out of the gym that day?

A. Inside the gym, to my right-hand side, there was a smaller room. I think it was a kind of locker room or something like that. And that room had another door leading outside. That's where they brought tables. They brought some kind of wooden bars, placed it on the door. And they said we would be leaving one by one, that we shouldn't be pushing and that we shouldn't leave in a disorderly fashion. And that's how the leaving started.

Q. So what did they do with people as they were exiting the gym?

A. The first thing that was done, two of the prisoners were taken out, Nezir Gusic. I knew him because he was a neighbour, and they also brought out another one, Nezir tied the blindfold, and the other one was given water. Everybody had to drink some water. So they would take out 20, 30 people. Then they would put the bar down, and then the lorries would come. And that's how it went. I was in the sixth group. . . .

Q. When you were put in the back of that truck, where did that truck go?

A. I felt that it had gone over some rail tracks, and we got to some kind of a meadow. That's where we stopped, and we were told to line up.

Q. Can you describe for us what happened after that.

A. We got off the lorry, and we were told to line up as quickly as possible. When we did so, I was together with my cousin Hariz, and we held hands. And he said they would kill us. And I said they wouldn't. He didn't even finish speaking when the bursts of fire started.

Q. Can you describe what happened with the burst of fire?

A. The burst of fire killed my cousin. He was shouting, screaming. I fell on the ground. He fell on top of me. That's when screaming and groaning of injured men started.

Q. Were you hurt?

A. No.

Q. What happened after that?

A. Afterwards, they continued to bring more shifts, more groups. They continued to execute those injured people who were screaming. They would be killed off. That's how it proceeded all the way until some people tried to escape. And one was killed, and one managed to escape.

Q. Do you know roughly what time of day it was that your group was executed?

A. I think it was about 1.00 or 2.00. I didn't have a watch, so I can't say accurately what the time was. But I think it was about that time because the sun was high up, well high up. I think it was in the afternoon.

Q. Did the executions continue after dark?

A. Yes.

Q. Do you know roughly how long after dark the executions continued?

A. I had fainted. And when I came round, I took the blindfold off slowly, off my eyes, and I saw some lights, headlights, of vehicles. Because there was a loader and an excavator. They were digging a grave. And there were headlights. They had brought another five groups after that.

Q. Were there any other lights in that field besides the lights of the heavy equipment you saw?

A. No, none. . . .

Q. At any time that night were you able to get a look at how many bodies were in that field around you?

A. It was a meadow full. I didn't count the bodies, but it was—a meadow was full.

Q. Were you—and I don't want to ask you to spend the time to describe this, so if I could just ask you simply, were you able to crawl away from that horrible place and eventually escape to the free territory?

A. I couldn't crawl away. When I got up, I found Hurem who was alive. And I stepped across dead bodies, and there was too much blood that was beginning to congeal. So it was very hard. It was very slippery to walk there.

Q. But you and Hurem were eventually able to escape to the free territory?

A. That's right.

Georgi Arbatov
THE NEGATIVE CONSEQUENCES OF "SHOCK THERAPY" CAPITALISM

Shortly following the collapse of the USSR, President Yeltsin subjected Russia to an icy capitalist bath, believing that only the complete and immediate introduction of private enterprise could free the country's economy from the shackles of Soviet centralized planning. The failure of this attempt led not only to the concentration of enormous wealth in the hands of a relative handful (known as the "oligarchs") but also the impoverishment of a large part of the general population (see next selection). It would remain for Yeltsin's successor Vladimir Putin to try undoing some of the damage.

In the following selection, Russian economist Georgi Arbatov discusses the negative consequences of the "shock therapy program," which was launched in 1992 "to inject laissez-faire capitalism into the Russian economy."

The economic system created by the Soviet Union, and inherited by Russia, was inefficient and wasteful. It was unable to provide proper economic development of the country and a decent standard of living for its citizens. By the time Boris Yeltsin took charge, the problems with the "administrative-command" system were quite obvious and the main subject of political debate.

Different groups of economists prepared possible programs that were openly debated. But the country was taken by surprise by the "Chicago School" program prepared by Yegor Gaidar, and approved in haste by President Yeltsin. On January 2, 1992, Gaidar launched the shock therapy program to inject laissez-faire capitalism immediately into the Russian economy. The West cheered, perhaps for ideological reasons. Influential Western experts . . . all gave their blessings. . . .

The poorly conceived transition program resulted in an unprecedented decline of the national economy. By 1998 Russian GDP was only about one-half its 1990 level, with the crisis spread to virtually all areas of production. Russian industry found itself unable to compete even in its own domestic markets. All of this was accompanied by a sharp reduction in investment and a disintegration of scientific and technological potential. We are now witnessing processes of pauperization and deintellectualization, accompanied by criminalization, as Russia increasingly takes on the appearance of a Third World republic.

The standard of living of most Russians has decreased dramatically. Rampant inflation has eliminated the savings of much of the population, while the increase of salaries and pensions has lagged far behind the price rises. The mortality rate has grown, and the birthrate has plummeted. As a result, Russia has been losing more than one-half million in population each year.

The sharp decline in the standard of living of the overwhelming majority is not only expressed in the obvious fact that diet, health, and elementary conditions of life have become worse for millions of people, but also in the loss of social benefits. The customary summer camp for all children has now become an unusual luxury. Few can still afford to vacation at a resort, be it a most modest one. Such previously expected amenities have become unaffordable because of large increases in railway and airplane ticket prices, making it hardly feasible to visit relatives. People who settled in the Far North or Far Fast have become "hostages" of these distant places. Because of high tariffs on long-distance telephone calls, for many the usual means of communication with relatives and friends has become a rare luxury.

Life has become especially hard for the millions of people who are dependent on pensions, many of whom now live in impoverished conditions. Their savings were practically eliminated by inflation, and the level of pensions is below the minimum necessary, even by the official calculations, for bare survival. Their situation is aggravated by the tremendous increase in the prices of medicines and the lower quality and reduced availability of subsidized health care. In addition, there is a traditionally Russian concern: when you die who will bury you and with what money?

Though the sheer fact of being young makes life look not so hopeless, the situation of Russian youth is also very difficult. Education has deteriorated drastically. Higher education is not free anymore and is unaffordable for many. Even more serious are the problems of unemployment and the financial difficulty that a young family has in getting a house and raising children.

Russians now have less access to culture—books and magazines, museums, libraries, arts, theaters, and music. During the past five years, the overall number of published books fell by 65 percent, circulation of newspapers by 80 percent, and the number of copies of published magazines by over 90 percent. Theater tickets, music concerts, CD, and traditional records have also become unavailable for the majority. The futures of many theatres, music schools, and the large national libraries are in question.

Faced with overwhelming difficulties and misfortunes, ordinary people have become helpless. Government agencies, which in the past cared about them, at least to a minimal degree, disappeared or continued in name only with the decline of the state and its power. The old pseudo trade unions, which represented the state, also disappeared. New ones have just started to be organized. As a result, only spontaneous protests are possible against extreme circumstances such as long overdue payment of salaries.

The way of life for ordinary Russians has deteriorated remarkably. The majority are fully immersed in the day-to-day fight for survival. This is now the major subject that people think and talk about. Friends and colleagues meet each other less frequently and rarely travel. Staying at home is also encouraged by the unprecedented rise in crime, which has made big cities and many of the smaller towns dangerous places . . . Today most people have little hope for improvement. . . .

In a time span of five years, especially during a period of sharp economic decline, it is difficult for a person to prosper in an honest way. There is a practically unanimous belief, to a large degree correct, that the country is being robbed of its wealth. The increasingly obvious growth of crime and corruption have been practically accepted as an inevitable fact of life by the government, which appears to do little to fight back.

Svetlana P. Glinkina, Andre Grigoriev, and Vakhtang Yakobidze
CRIME AND CORRUPTION

The liberalization of the Soviet economy and the breakup of the Soviet Union provided opportunities for government officials and top managers to enrich themselves through illegal activities. Several of these "oligarchs" acquired former state-owned enterprises, from which they reaped huge profits, and gained control of banks "that operate in a pathological fashion." As law enforcement deteriorated, moreover, organized crime became a major force in Russian life.

After Vladimir Putin succeeded Boris Yeltsin as president of Russia, he cracked down on several of the leading oligarchs, whose combination of economic and political influence posed a threat to his own power. Some of the oligarchs fled abroad, while others were jailed. Buoyed by a stabilizing economy and the rising price of oil {Russia's chief export}, Putin oversaw the growth of a sizable middle class and kept inflation in check. Still, despite his centralization of political control and emphasis on order, corruption has remained a fact of life in Russia.

In the selection below, three Russian economists describe the impact of corruption and criminalization on Russian life during the 1990s under Yeltsin.

The Russian economy has been transformed into a highly corrupt and criminalized economic system. Rampant crime and corruption have degraded everyday life, obstructed legitimate business activity, and impaired the functioning of government. The most valuable of state assets have been transferred to a small number of "oligarchs," who compose a politically connected business elite largely oriented toward plunder. Though the proclivity for corruption and illegality predates the economic transition, primary blame resides with the reform strategy. . . .

ORGANIZED CRIME

Taking advantage of weak law enforcement, mafia influences have become prominent in all facets of Russian life. An estimated 200,000 active criminal groups existed in Russia by the mid-1990s, including 5,500 large organizations. In addition to extortion, their activities included burglary, embezzlement, and criminal misappropriation of both public and business funds.

Retail markets in every Russian city are controlled by gangsters who collect a share of the revenues of each vendor. This system is so well established that payments are calculated on the basis of records that the vendor is required to maintain. Gangsters may even agree to defer payments in light of special circumstances, creating, through force of habit, the impression that they are reasonable partners performing a needed security function.

Cities are divided into spheres of influence. For example, rival mafia groups divided the northern city of Arkhangelsk into two parts. It was not possible to start a business in that city without permission from the criminal group in control of the particular locale.

Organized crime has also been active in theft and exportation of fuels and metals. It is estimated that from 1992 to 1994, over 20 percent of the petroleum output and one-third of metals production were smuggled our of the country.

So much of this contraband passed through Estonia that this resource-scarce country became a major exporter of natural resources. At one point, 70 percent of the raw materials shipped from Russia by rail through Lithuania never reached their legal destination, the Russian city of Kaliningrad. Disappearance of trainloads of oil was a daily occurrence. Railway personnel and customs officials conspired in these operations.

Apart from corruption in the primary export industries, nearly every small business or street kiosk had felt the mafia presence by the first year of the transition period. Nevertheless, opportunity for embezzlement from these small businesses could in no way compare with the wealth that could be taken from the state budget. The vast sums of money appropriated by opportunistic Soviet officials attracted the attention of these gangsters, who quickly terrorized them and took over their enterprise. Government information indicates that roughly 70 to 80 percent of banks, as well as state and private companies, make payments to racketeers and corrupt officials. Other data show three-quarters of businessmen routinely make payoffs, and ordinary citizens are also frequently forced to give bribes.

The gangsters did end their terror campaigns against those businessmen who were the most well connected in government. Criminals depended on businessmen to invest their wealth. Businessmen, in turn, made use of gangsters in forcing clientele to honor their obligations. All the while, corrupt officials approved their projects in return for hefty bribes.

Their alliance, of course, soon grew to envelop more than debt collection services. The potential to eliminate unwanted competitors and coerce business partners to soften their terms was a fact that was not lost on the gangsters. Indeed, the large number of murders of businessmen and bankers reflects a general moral breakdown. Due to the availability of former KGB operatives and the fact that law enforcement is lax, the cost of a professional murder in Russia is low.

PRIVATIZATION

The privatization process was key to the transfer of the nation's wealth to a tainted minority. Most enterprises were privatized by the mid-1990s, with employees and managers holding more than 50 percent of all shares of privatized firms. However, employee shares were mostly locked in trusts controlled by management, effectively giving ownership to managers.

The first phase of "official" privatization entitled individual Russians to vouchers that were redeemable for cash or a share of industry. Conversion of vouchers into shares was of little consequence, since dividends were rarely paid and investors had little say in the decision-making process. For those who were able to obtain a large quantity, however, the vouchers were extremely useful. Quick to see the rewards of such a program, criminal and commercial elements soon began to collect vouchers from transients, alcoholics, and gullible citizens who were promised high dividends in television advertisements. With the vast amounts they collected, these groups bought up the most desirable enterprises at giveaway prices. Often the enterprises were quickly shut down as the new owners made gains by simply selling off real estate. . . .

Corrupt privatization aggravated Russia's financial woes, as the state disposed of valuable assets at extremely low prices. Uralmash, the giant machine-building plant in Sverdlovsk, and the Cheliabinsk Metallurgical Combine went for around $4 million each. The Kovrovsky Mechanical Factory, which supplied the Russian military with firearms, sold for under $3 million. Telephone companies were sold for $100 per line compared to about $650 in North America. The power company United Energy Systems was sold for $200 million, whereas a company with similar kilowatt production would be worth $50 billion in the United States. . . .

THE OLIGARCHS

A young, unscrupulous economic elite known as the "oligarchs" now controls much of the Russian economy, including the nation's natural wealth. They also control banks that operate in a pathological fashion, industries that owe billions in unpaid taxes, and media empires. Through their use of money and media to sway elections, as well as by provision of bribes and sinecures, they have influenced all branches and levels of government. While they certainly have influence on government rules, their primary mode of operation is to circumvent them. Overseeing the tainted transfer of government assets and the corrupt allocation of government funds, the oligarchs have been integral to the creation of Russian-style kleptocracy. . . .

From the outset, the oligarchs have been reluctant to invest to modernize production. Little has been accomplished in the way of upgrading the plants, oil companies, banks, and steamship lines that they acquired so cheaply. . . .

In addition to bribery, the oligarchs have employed blackmail in order to influence government appointments. . . .

The oligarchs not only used state funds for their own ends by utilizing and often embezzling money through their own banks, but, as it became clear after the crisis of August 1998, these leaders of Russian business also cheated a great number of their compatriots who entrusted their savings to the banks. . . .

The oligarchs hardly qualify as the Russian version of the "robber barons" who helped to industrialize the United States. Instead of creating and building new industries, they have shunted the wealth of Russia abroad. Rather than transform their profits into domestic investment, they have expatriated them. Illegal capital flight has also helped them shield their gains from taxation, undermining the capacity of government to finance itself adequately.

CONCLUSION

Corruption and criminalization in Russia have created a corrosive economic environment. Productive economic activity is inhibited while the siphoning off of the nation's resources continues. Potential investors are fearful that criminals and corrupt officials will impose unforeseen costs and even expropriate their investments. Forced or enticed to join forces with criminal structures, managers are not inclined toward company strategies that are optimal for the long run. A plundering oligarchic elite, with strong influence over the media and politicians, has had a noxious influence on government. . . .

Russian reality—not only the lack of rule of law but also weak economic policy—may well continue to provide opportunities for the parasitic existence of criminal structures. In the final analysis, the future of any country is jeopardized by swindling of the state and criminal interference with market competition. So long as such activity is not only possible, but acceptable, Russia's prospects will be dim.

Anna Politkovskaya
CHECHNYA: *A DIRTY WAR*

While the multinational character of the Soviet Union proved to be Mikhail Gorbachev's Achilles' heel, the breakup of the USSR into its constituent republics in 1991 did not solve the problem. Russia, the largest and most prominent of the Soviet successor states, was itself a multinational entity pockmarked with enclaves of non-Russians. Especially irksome to the Russian leadership was Chechnya, a small region in the Caucasus. For more than two centuries, the

Muslim Chechens had fought every attempt by Moscow to assert its control. In 1944, Stalin charged the Chechens with treason and deported them to Central Asia, resulting in the death of a quarter of the population. Khrushchev allowed them to return to their homeland in 1957, but this only created conflict with the people who, in the Chechens' absence, had taken over their homes and property. Finally, in November 1991, with the Soviet Union on the brink of collapse, Dzhokhar Dudaev, the leader of the Chechen-Ingush autonomous republic, declared Chechnya independent. Under his inept rule, Chechnya became a hotbed of outlaw activity that threatened neighboring regions.

Late in 1994, President Yeltsin, ignoring the Russian parliament, ordered an invasion of Chechnya to prevent separatist sentiments from spreading to other parts of Russia and to protect the oil pipeline running through the region from the Caspian fields. The disastrous campaign that ensued was characterized by countless atrocities, guerrilla warfare, a death toll numbering in the tens of thousands, and the physical devastation of the country, including its capital Grozny. The mounting cost of the war caused Yeltsin to make a tenuous peace with the Chechens and withdraw Russian forces in 1996. Meanwhile, within Chechnya itself, anarchy continued to reign; the kidnapping of Russians and other foreigners became a common occurrence, as did raids onto Russian soil. Chechnya's newly elected president Aslan Maskhadov, a moderate who favored maintaining ties with Russia, found himself locked in contention with radical forces that sought to create a fundamentalist Islamic state out of several territories in the region. In August 1999 radical Chechens invaded neighboring Dagestan. The following month a series of mysterious bombings destroyed several apartment buildings in Moscow and other cities; Russians concluded that the Chechens had brought the war to them. With popular opinion on his side, Premier Vladimir Putin ordered a new invasion of the country in October. If anything, the second Chechen war proved deadlier than the first. Large-scale fighting concluded by the spring of 2000, and a pro-Moscow Chechen regime was installed. In April 2009 Putin even felt sufficiently confident to withdraw Russian counter-terrorist forces from the region. Sporadic violence continues throughout the North Caucasus, however, and occasionally spills over into Russia itself. In short, a conflict that already has claimed over 100,000 victims continues, with no end in sight.

Anna Politkovskaya (1958–2006), a journalist and human rights activist, was born in New York City of Ukrainian parents and grew up in Moscow. She made her reputation reporting on the war in Chechnya, where she interviewed survivors in hospitals and refugee camps. Her sharp criticism of Russian conduct in the second Chechen war made her a fierce opponent of Vladimir Putin. Such a stance became especially dangerous as the Russian leader was further consolidating his power and cracking down on the independent Russian media. In October 2006 Politkovskaya was shot dead in her apartment building. The murder has never been solved.

The following selection is characteristic of Politkovskaya's poignant reporting on Russia's campaign in Chechnya. She focuses on the toll that the fighting has taken on the natives of the region. The excerpt comes from a collection of her essays entitled *A Dirty War*.

22 January 2001

For the civilian population the tragedy in Novye Aldy was the most terrible incident of the second Chechen war. Yet there has never been a court case or even an investigation. The prosecutor-general's office is doing everything it can to make sure that no one is charged with the war crimes committed there.

Malika Labazanova comes from Novye Aldy on the outskirts of Grozny. She has worked at a bakery all her life and early each and every morning, with no break for holidays or weekends, she journeys into the city centre to work. That is the only joy she now has in life.

Only once has she ever had to stop work for a time and that interval split her life in two—before and after 5 February 2000. For during the taking of Grozny by federal [Russian] forces that winter, Malika stayed at home and witnessed the brutal massacre the soldiers carried out in Novye Aldy on 5 February.

From 6 February onwards Malika herself was laying out the corpses in the basement. It was she who protected them from the hungry dogs and crows, and she who then buried the bodies. After which, she washed down the basement tiles.

That was not the end of the nightmare, however. A tragedy that claimed more than 100 victims was followed by another that drags on to this day. As a result Malika, who had never been involved in any kind of public activity, is today chairwoman of the Aldy committee, set up last autumn by the relatives of the victims. The committee's main goal is to make the authorities reply to one question, and one alone: who was responsible for the terrible death of their loved ones?

OCTOBER 1999 TO FEBRUARY 2000

In September and October 1999, after military operations began and Grozny came under fire, many inhabitants of Novye Aldy left for Ingushetia.[1] Others remained behind and families were separated. The old people and those who looked after them decided to guard their homes from looters of every description, whether the newly arrived federal forces or their fellow citizens.

Those who stayed protected their houses and their village from the Chechen fighters. When the federal forces first moved into Grozny in early December the nearest positions held by Chechen armed groups were only two kilometres away (in the 20th precinct, another district of Grozny). There were no fighters in the village itself. Nevertheless throughout December 1999 and January 2000 Novye Aldy was mercilessly bombed and shelled every day.

People hid in their basements and only once in a while did they come out to draw water from the spring. As a result of these trips, 75 of the basement-dwellers died in two months. They were shot dead, or, lacking medical aid, they died from their wounds. Some were old people who simply could not take the stress, or withstand the hunger and the cold.

On 30 January, as we all know, a special military operation began to lure Chechen fighters out of Grozny—Shamanov's[2] little trick. The Chechen field commanders were deliberately misinformed that, if they were prepared to pay, then the Feds were ready to create a corridor for their organised retreat from the city. The money was handed over, but the fighters soon found they had been led into a minefield. Meanwhile, federal artillery and aviation mercilessly struck at the surrounding villages through which lay the corridor that the General Staff had designated. Novye Aldy took its full share of the punishment.

On 3 February, when it became clear that federal troops were gradually taking over the positions of the Chechen fighters in the 20th precinct, a delegation from Novye Aldy, for the most part old men, set out under a white flag to talk to the commanding officers of the 15th motorized

[1]Ingushetia, located directly west of Chechnya in the North Caucasus, is under Russian control. It became a haven for those fleeing the ravages of the Chechen war.

[2]Vladimir Shamanov (b.1957), a lieutenant general in the Russian army, served in the Chechen campaign and became notorious for his brutal treatment of the Chechen people.

infantry regiment. The soldiers opened fire on the delegation and one of the Russians living in Novye Aldy was killed outright. Nevertheless the old men managed to persuade the soldiers to stop shelling the village and on the afternoon of 4 February it became quiet again in Novye Aldy.

Soon the first checks on people's ID documents and residence permits were carried out. The soldiers thumbed through the passports of those who had now emerged from the basements and said something strange to them: "Get out now. Those coming after us are animals. Their order is to kill." The old men did not believe this, however, and even decided that it was a trick to get them out of their houses so they could be looted.

On 5 February, from early morning, a second "cleansing" operation began in the village. It proved to be an irrational and bloody settling of scores with anyone who got in the way.

THE CLEANSING

Aza Bisultanova is a young schoolteacher. It's hard to understand what she's teaching the children today. How can she give any lessons now? She is still in a state of shock following what happened, though eleven months have passed. On 5 February her 68-year-old father, Akhmet Abulkhanov, died. "If only they'd just shot him . . ." she mutters.

It was Abulkhanov, a respected figure in Novye Aldy, who walked through the village on the morning of that Day of Judgement and persuaded people to leave their basements. It was he who chivvied the doubters: "Why do we need to hide any longer? Things will only get better from now on. If we stay in the basement the soldiers will think we're guilty of something. But we've done nothing wrong." It was Abulkhanov who took the hand of the smiling soldier who entered their courtyard and said. "Thank you, my boy. We were waiting for you. I'm glad to see you come at last."

"Take out your teeth, old man," said the soldier," and bring some money as well, or I'll kill you."

Abulkhanov did not understand and continued to stroke the soldier's hand. But Malika Labazanova, who was standing nearby and would witness the reprisal that followed, quickly took off her earrings, handed over her wedding ring, and explained that the fillings in her teeth were not pure gold but simply plated. They allowed her to go to the neighbours and get some money. Malika came back and held out all that could be found: 300 roubles. The soldier took the notes and roared with laughter: "You call that money . . . ?"

They shot the old man, turning his execution into target practice that took off the top of his head. Next they killed three others. One had been disabled since childhood and tried desperately to make them listen: he was disabled, he had papers to prove it.

For some reason Malika was spared. She was ordered to drag the bodies into the basement and she obeyed. The soldiers decided to burn the cow alive in the barn. And also all of the sheep. The cow was already locked in when one of the young privates suddenly took pity on the beast and tried to help it escape the fire. His senior officer warned him to stop or he would kill him too. The blazing, terrified sheep ran from the fold, their mouths gaping, gasping for air, and dropped dead.

People too were burnt alive. Zina Abdulmejidova, Husein Abdulmejidov, Gula Khaidayev, Kaipa Yusupova, Yelena Kuznetsova and Victor Cheptura were so disfigured that one could no longer tell their age.

The only term for what happened is *hell on earth.*

To begin with, those villagers who by some miracle survived were convinced the soldiers were simply out of their minds. Perhaps insanity had led them to carry out this massacre or perhaps they'd been taking drugs. Someone in his right mind would never permit himself to do such a thing. All subsequent events, however, demonstrated that the motives behind the 5 February events were quite different.

For several weeks, contrary to all their traditions, the families did not bury their dead. They were waiting for staff from the prosecutor's office to take statements, begin an official inquiry, and carry out the necessary investigative procedures. When they could wait no longer, they buried their loved ones. Then they waited for death certificates to be issued. Only a few received them. However, soon the man from the Grozny prosecutor's office who had issued these documents specifying that knife wounds, bullet wounds and so on had been the cause of death was hurriedly transferred somewhere else. All to whom he had given such certificates were called in to the Zavodskoi district administration and ordered to hand them back in exchange for "death certificates on the new forms" (that was the explanation offered). These, it turned out, did not even contain an entry for the cause of death.

JANUARY 2001: ONE YEAR ON

Soon a year will have passed since the atrocity in Novye Aldy, the Khatyn massacre of modern-day Russia.[3] There has been no investigation. During the entire eleven months since it happened, the witnesses have not once been questioned. No one has presumed to create photofit pictures of the criminals, though many of the killers did not hide their faces.

Photofit descriptions, indeed! The majority of the affected families have not even received death certificates. They have almost nothing to present in court, in order to assert their constitutional right to justice.

Today it is quite obvious that the investigation by the Prosecutor-General's office has been successfully halted. Officially the office fobs off any interested parties from Novye Aldy with the assertion that they are monitoring the situation. To everyone else involved they offer the shameless lie that the Chechens, faithful to their customs, refuse to allow the bodies to be exhumed and therefore the investigation is prevented from going ahead.

This lie is logical and understandable if, of course, you look at things from the point of view of those shielding the killers. Hardly any civilians have the chance to check anything since Grozny is almost constantly closed for outside visitors. *Novaya gazeta* [a newspaper critical of governmental policy for which Politkovskaya wrote] has managed to discover a little, however.

The inhabitants of Novye Aldy, it turns out, no matter how terrible they may find it, are begging, pleading and demanding that all the necessary exhumation procedures be completed. They insist that the chief material evidence in this investigation, the bullets that were fired, finally be removed from the bodies and then it will be possible to establish who were the monsters in military uniform that carried out the massacre. The response to all these persistent demands was an outrageous insult. A brigade of forensic experts from the military roared into the village and demanded that people add their signatures to already completed forms stating that the relatives refused to permit exhumation.

The Prosecutor-General's office—which has proved so responsive when the oligarchs are under discussion[4]—begins to wriggle and make excuses in this case. Lower-ranking staff at the office who have had something to do with the Novye Aldy case will agree to "speak out" only if they are given complete anonymity. It is as though they were being asked to reveal the State's most highly guarded nuclear secrets. They say there is pressure from the very highest authority and orders have been given to halt the investigation, codenamed "February 5". Under no circumstances does Putin want to quarrel with the country's leading military figures.

Our sources in the Prosecutor-General's office tell us that if the Novye Aldy nightmare were exhaustively investigated and led to charges against individual officers, then other similar

---

[3]All the inhabitants of the Belorussian village of Khatyn, several hundred people, were massacred or burned alive by German soldiers in 1942.

[4]Since Putin's election as President the two most prominent media magnates in Russia Boris Berezovsky and Vladimir Gusinsky have been pursued by the prosecutor's office on a variety of charges and have both taken refuge abroad.

cases would follow. The staff we talked to also referred to their own fears, since the officers who risk being prosecuted for these atrocities have supposedly been threatening them as well.

That's a little hard to believe, of course. Only time will tell. Meanwhile we must accept the fact that among the majors, colonels and generals that the country is praising, defending and decorating with awards there are also war criminals. Among the heroes are a percentage of unspeakable scum. And we all live together, side by side.

Not long ago, on 23 November, Hasan Musaev was buried in Novye Aldy. On 5 February 2000 this old man had watched as four of his relatives were shot dead. He fell to the ground and a soldier held a gun to his head when he heard a voice say. "You can live. And suffer because we didn't shoot you."

Old Hasan certainly suffered and he died from his third heart attack. Surely no one in Russia feels any relief at that?

CHECHNYA–MOSCOW

EUROPE TODAY

RALLY AGAINST AN INVASION OF IRAQ. On February 15, 2003, a million people demonstrated in London to protest a possible invasion of Iraq by the United States with Britain's military support. Five weeks later President Bush ordered the invasion. *(Tim Smith/Peter Arnold)*

By the end of the first decade of the twenty-first century, Europe found itself in a familiar position: hovering between increased unity and nagging particularism.

A more robust and self-confident Europe began to assert itself more purposefully during this decade. The European Union grew to include twenty-seven member states and a total population of ca. five hundred million, and the Schengen Area (the part of the continent without internal borders) expanded to include two dozen European states fully within its passport-free travel zone, including non-EU members such as Switzerland. The Euro became a currency of great significance in international exchange that has begun to rival and even threatens to supplant the U.S. dollar as the international currency of choice. Movement toward even closer European unity, in the form of the Treaty of Lisbon negotiated in December 2007, held out the promise of the introduction of a European constitution in short order. European states individually, and the European Union as a body, brought a more robust European presence to international diplomacy as both partner and counterweight to the United States. In the latter case, the rise of a new anti-Americanism, born of intense disappointment with the Bush administration's break with an active multilateral approach to U.S. diplomacy, manifested itself strongly in European opinion polls. An assertive and wealthy new Russia, security challenges in Afghanistan, and piracy in the Horn of Africa added to opportunities for Europeans to play a larger role in international affairs.

Economic growth, integration, and the promise of a better life brought new opportunities for many European citizens, but also new challenges. Prosperity and social justice, or at least the potential to achieve them, eluded significant elements of the population, particularly first-generation European-born residents from Africa and the Middle East, a great number of them Muslims. Traditional practices and values stood in marked contrast to mainstream European values, and at the extreme end of the spectrum, mutual intolerance and frustrations fueled Islamic fundamentalists and European rightists alike. Riots born of anger and despair among Muslim youths from North Africa in the Paris suburbs in November 2005 and the angry response of many law-and-order French citizens, Danish cartoons lampooning the prophet Mohammed in *Jyllands-Posten* in September 2005 and the outrage they elicited, and the murder of Dutch filmmaker Theo van Gogh in November 2004 are but a few examples of such tensions. Moreover, indigenous minorities were at the center of mistrust and violence, including the Sami in Finland, the Sinti and Roma in the Czech Republic, and the Hungarians in Slovakia and Romania. In the former Soviet Republic of Georgia, attempts by the Abkhazians and South Ossetians at achieving independence have elicited crackdowns from the government in Tbilisi as well as military intervention from Putin's Russia, leading to the displacement of hundreds of thousands of people. In recent years, moreover, Europe has experienced a resurgence of anti-Semitism, including violence against Jews, attacks on Jewish institutions, and the desecration of Jewish cemeteries.

Much of the luster of Europeans' dynamic economic situation and international engagement appeared significantly challenged by the global economic crisis that began in late 2008. At the time this volume went to press, bank failures and illegal trading schemes hit Europe's economic powerhouses such as Germany, France, and the United Kingdom hard, and shook the economies of countries like Spain, Portugal, Italy, and Greece on the periphery of the giants. Even before the crisis, in June 2008, the Irish electorate's "no" to the Lisbon Treaty marked a setback to the EU forging ahead purposefully on questions of greater unity, including, but not limited to, economic matters. In the near term it will prove a challenge for individual European states and for the EU to engage as ambitiously on international issues as envisioned before the meltdown, but efforts to coordinate a restoration of consumer trust and confidence in markets and the banking system have not flagged.

EU expansion—perhaps to include Turkey—and European responses to terrorism and catastrophe at home and abroad continue to feature prominently in larger debates concerning what it means to be European. Values, lifestyle, and political relevance remain persistent questions that track between regional and national experiences to a broader European experience.

1 European Union: Growing Interdependence

Although Europeans share a common cultural heritage, in the past the diversity of their history and national temperaments burdened them with bloody wars. After two ruinous world wars and the extension of Soviet power, many people recognized the need for some form of European unity. In 1951 France, West Germany, the Netherlands, Belgium, Luxembourg, and Italy formed the European Coal and Steel Community (ECSC) to promote economic cooperation. It soon expanded into the European Economic Community (EEC), or Common Market, a customs union that created a free market among member states. In the 1970s and 1980s, Great Britain, Ireland, and Denmark, followed by Greece, Spain, and Portugal, joined the European Community (EC), which constituted the world's largest trading bloc. In 1991, in the Dutch city of Maastricht, the twelve members of the European Community negotiated the Maastricht Treaty, designed to shape Europe into a unified political and economic union. By 1993 the member states had ratified the treaty, and in recognition of its aims, the European Community transformed itself into the European Union (EU). The EU membership grew to fifteen, with the addition of Austria, Finland, and Sweden in 1995. Some Europeans, particularly in smaller nations, are worried about their country's future in an increasingly integrated Europe: are they surrendering their national identity, along with their sovereignty, to the EU?

Bertie Ahern
"ENLARGEMENT IS ABOUT OPENING MINDS AS WELL AS BORDERS"

In 2004 ten states—Malta, Cyprus, the Czech Republic, Estonia, Latvia, Lithuania, Hungary, Poland, Slovakia, and Slovenia—were added to the European Union, followed in 2007 by Romania and Bulgaria, bringing the total of member countries to twenty-seven. As this book goes to press, three other countries have requested entry—Croatia, the Former Yugoslav Republic of Macedonia, and Turkey. This enlarged membership of predominantly Central European countries represents the reunification of a continent long divided by the iron curtain of communism. The majority of new members are considerably poorer than the West European members; entry into the EU does not in itself bring wealth, and the economic demands of membership are rigorous. Since the EU demands that new members be democracies, its enlargement has contributed to the spread of democracy in former Communist lands. Vaclav Havel, former president of the Czech Republic, sees the essence of enlargement as

> a broadening of the area of commonly shared values. The basic contours of European values—shaped by the troubled intellectual and political history of Europe, and adopted, in part, elsewhere in the world—are, I believe, clear; respect for the individual, his freedom, rights and dignity; . . . the rule of law and equality before the law; protection of minorities; democratic institutions; separation of the powers of the legislative, executive and judiciary; plurality of the political system; inviolability of private ownership; private enterprise and the market economy; and the development of civil society.

In April 2004 Bertie Ahern, prime minister of Ireland and president of the Council of the European Union, delivered a keynote speech in Prague just prior to the enlargement of the European Union. Following are excerpts from Ahern's speech, in which he views the EU as a positive force for Europe's future, for it "is about opening minds as well as borders."

The ten new accession states bring with them new languages and new cultures. They bring with them also a new consciousness of, and fresh approach to, the European Union. Enlargement is about opening minds as well as borders. The new member states will bring a new vision to the European Union. This vision was shaped and determined by unique experience. The contribution that the new member states will bring can only help to make the European Union stronger and broaden its perspective on the world. . . .

The European Union that the Czech Republic and nine other states are about to enter, is a unique endeavour in world history. It was conceived at a time of war and strife. Neighbouring countries in Europe had fought each other to the death over land and resources. The very idea of these countries coming together to work for common goals was inconceivable to many.

And yet a small number of people nurtured a big dream. This dream involved pooling resources and sovereignty in certain areas to try to find a way that was better than war, rivalry and hatred. The result is the European Union that we know today. . . .

The European Union has delivered. It has achieved peace by providing a framework within which war between its members is unthinkable. Over the past fifty years, it has delivered prosperity, enabling economies to grow and people to thrive. It has been a force for democracy and equality, helping members to tackle poverty and exclusion. The old norms of war, invasion, exclusion, discrimination and chauvinism are history. This perhaps is the European Union's greatest achievement.

Proof of the European Union's success is most clearly demonstrated by the voluntary accession of new member states. On the first of May, the Union will have more than four times the number of member states it had at the beginning. The original six member states took a real and considerable risk when they established the European Union. They deserve our gratitude for paving the way and for adopting an inclusive approach to further membership.

In the 1950s, there was a significant group of people who firmly held the view that membership of the European Union represented a "surrender," an "abandonment" or a "dilution" of national sovereignty. Indeed, there are those who hold that view today.

I reject this idea completely. In an age of globalised trade and media, sharing sovereignty in agreed areas does not represent a loss. In fact, it is quite the opposite. It represents a real and tangible gain for states by giving them an influence for which they otherwise could not hope. . . .

Membership of the European Union has in fact enabled Ireland to achieve full sovereignty. Our people are no longer compelled to emigrate to find employment. Our membership of the European Union has enabled us to bring out the full potential of our greatest asset—our people. They are a successful, self-confident and outward-looking people. For me this is a real and concrete expression of increased sovereignty. Our success within the framework provided by the European Union enabled us to do this.

Before we joined the European Union, we were an isolated people on the periphery of Europe. We were in the shadow of our big neighbour, the United Kingdom. But arguing our case at the Council table proved we could punch above our weight. We could hold our own with the most powerful. We learned, in a very real sense, how to stand on our own two feet. We learned that our partners respected us when we made well-founded arguments seeking to protect our interests. We learned what solidarity meant and we came of age as a truly independent state.

As Irish society changed rapidly from being predominantly rural to more urbanised, our people grew in self-confidence. Opportunities were opened up for Irish women whose dignity was copper-fastened by the Union's insistence on equal pay and equal opportunity. Our workers learned the importance of health and safety legislation. Our young people travelled and learned to hold their own amongst their European counterparts.

We have witnessed both our own distinctive language and culture flourish in the context of a wider Europe. Far from being overwhelmed, support for the Irish language has grown considerably. A significant part of our first level education system is now conducted exclusively through the Irish language. The initiative for this came from Irish people who understood the importance of maintaining an indigenous culture within the wider European one. They realise that the European Union is no threat to that cultural identity.

I need hardly remind you of the extent to which our Irish music has touched the hearts of so many European citizens. Before we joined the Union, it was hardly known beyond our island.

So, for Ireland our sense of ourselves as independent and equal has grown within the Union. We do not feel threatened by any notion of big versus small. Our relationship with the United Kingdom has changed beyond recognition. It is now one of genuine partnership in our mutual search for reconciliation on the island of Ireland. I am convinced that the space the European Union provided was critical in allowing that mature relationship to develop.

This is where the real strength of the European Union lies. The spirit of tolerance, the respect for difference, the knowledge that we are all working as equals for all our people is what drives us on. The absolute commitment to finding compromise and providing a sense of ownership for all our people is fundamental to our actions. The idea of winners and losers is not what the Union is about.

As I look back at what thirty-one years of membership has meant for my country, it strikes me that we must never be complacent. Collectively and individually we must stay focused on what needs to be done to ensure that the European Union continues to succeed.

We find ourselves in a new set of circumstances. Twenty years ago, the greatest threat to our national security came from the possibility of a nuclear superpower conflict. Who thought then that the countries behind the iron curtain would shortly begin the process of joining the European Union and rejoining the family of European democracies? Who would have thought then that one of the major security threats facing our people today would be the threat of terrorism from non-state actors?

The European Union must continue to adapt, change and react in a creative way to the new circumstances in which it finds itself. We will have to continue to work for a system of governance appropriate to a complex and changing world. A system that is responsive to the realities which we face. This involves both the adoption of new and effective responses at the European level and the fine-tuning of the European Union itself. . . .

The campaign to elect members to the European Parliament will provide the next opportunity for us to debate European Union issues. The campaign will allow us to articulate the practical advantages of working together within the European Union. These practical advantages range from making our Union safer by sharing information about terrorist threats, to enabling our citizens to travel more freely by providing them, for example, with an EU-wide health card.

The elections to the European Parliament are also a useful and timely reminder of the European Union's democratic foundations.

Democracy is the bedrock on which the European Union is founded and maintained. Membership is itself based on each of the member states being democratic and meeting and maintaining rigid democratic criteria. We cannot be complacent in the face of threats to our democratic systems. We have had a stark reminder of what it means to live without democracy in the Balkans through the 1990s and even up to recent times. The horrendous bombings in Madrid last month brought home to us the devastation possible from a group dedicated to the use of undemocratic means and ends.

Seeking to reengage people with the vital processes that affect their lives will be a key task in the coming years. As politicians, we will have to use every opportunity to reverse the trend towards disengagement from the democratic process.

2 Anti-Americanism in Contemporary Europe

European criticism of American politics, culture, and values has deep roots—as deep, in fact, as European fascination with America's seemingly limitless ability to reinvent itself and its rejection of Old World rules and inhibitions. In fact, both "anti-Americanism" and pro-American sentiments—"Americanism"—have at times been present in the positions taken by one and the same European

observer. Perhaps the most often cited example of the latter is Alexis de Tocqueville's *Democracy in America* (1835). After the United States emerged as a significant economic power by the early twentieth century, and particularly during the 1920s, American cultural goods both attracted and repelled. Criticism was not merely limited to easily identifiable ideological opponents such as Nazi Germany or the Soviet Union; even among liberally minded Europeans, cultural critics decried "crass American materialism" even as Fordist industrial practices, jazz, and the initial incursion of American movies became features of European experience. When the United States emerged as one of two global superpowers after the Second World War, its unmatched economic clout, political and military power, and cultural influence elicited in equal measures glowing admiration and biting criticism. The seeming ubiquity of American cultural goods (Disney and other media products, music, fashion, and American English)—often referred to as "soft power" by social commentators—was no less significant than American "hard power" (military and economic might, political hegemony) when the United States became the world's only superpower during the 1990s. While the events of 9/11 brought tremendous outpourings of sympathy and support from Europeans, by the time the United States exercised its hard power option in the 2003 invasion of Iraq, reservoirs of pro-American sentiment had been significantly tapped out, leaving what opinion polls revealed to be the highest level of anti-American sentiment ever recorded. This negative sentiment cannot be attributed solely to perceptions of George W. Bush's two-term presidency; for as unpopular as many U.S. foreign and military policy decisions were among Europeans, this unpopularity also drew strength from deeper reserves of the long-standing cultural anti-Americanism described above.

Josef Joffe
THE RISE OF ANTI-AMERICANISM

Journalist and academic Josef Joffe is a specialist in international affairs, and in his role as editor-in-chief of the distinguished German weekly *Die Zeit* he has written widely on European-American relations, and other foreign policy topics. In addition to teaching at significant European institutions such as the University of Munich and the University of Salzburg, he received his Ph.D. in government from Harvard and has held research fellow or teaching positions at such American colleges and universities as Dartmouth, Stanford, Harvard, and Princeton. Joffe counts among the most thoughtful of European observers of the United States, and the following selection reveals his insights into the phenomenon of anti-Americanism.

When General Motors announced plans to cut twelve thousand jobs in Germany, *Stern* magazine, with a circulation of one million and a readership four times larger, appeared with a cover replete with some classic symbols of anti-Americanism. It featured a huge cowboy boot with "GM" branded on the sole. The boot, stitched with red, white, and blue colors on its side, was poised to crush hundreds of little people arrayed underneath in the shape of the emblem of Opel, GM's subsidiary in Germany. The cover title read "Ways of the Wild West." . . .

On the most general level, the cover depicted the United States as a profound threat, recalling the oft-quoted diatribe of the French novelist Henry de Montherlant (1896–1972): "I accuse the United States of being in a permanent state of crime against mankind." Another familiar theme is the depiction of the United States as an overwhelming, arrogant power, a victimizer of all these small, and soon to be jobless, people. A third one evokes the ruthless intrusion of the "Other," the outsider, who is about to trample a hallowed way of the good life. A fourth motif is crudeness or violence, as symbolized by the cowboy boot with its fierce-looking spurs; it evokes the quintessential American, who is boorish, brutal, and uncultured. Or to recall a famous quip about America by Talleyrand, "thirty-two religions and only one dish to eat." The whole ensemble sets forth one of the oldest indictments of America: Americans will do anything for a buck; profit is their God, to whom they will sacrifice decency and social justice. As early as 1794, a French visitor to the United States summed up the views of his compatriots as follows: the Americans are "vain, greedy, grasping, and engaged in cheating in all of their business dealings." . . .

Here was an archetype of the long-running story of anti-Americanism. The circumstances were brand-new, but the "reaction-formation" was as old as Heinrich Heine's denunciation of the United States in the early nineteenth century. Though this icon of German literature was as liberal and democratic as any intellectual of his age, he fumed, "Worldly gain is the true religion [of the Americans], and money is their Mammon, their one and only almighty God." The not-so-hidden hand of the market was transmuted into moral degeneracy revolving around inbred greed and false gods. Misery, the image insinuated, was not homemade (Germany's wages are among the highest in the world, and its work rules among the most rigid), but a conspiracy by the "Other," who was previously known as scapegoat. There was no one to blame but the mighty, ruthless stranger. Thus was complexity reduced to demonology, which is a defining feature of anti-Americanism, anti-Semitism, or, indeed, any "anti-ism."

Why is this anti-Americanism, as distinct from "anti-Bushism" or anger against a real object like General Motors? Pure and up-front anti-Americanism today is rare. Montherlant's diatribe against America as such is anti-American, and so was the utterance of the Canadian parliamentarian Carolyn Parrish, when she burst out, "Damn Americans, I hate the bastards." In 1999, two years before the Bush administration took office, the Greek composer Mikis Theodorakis offered another such glimpse: "I hate Americans and everything American." Another example is Peter Zadek, the dean of Germany's stage directors, when he allowed a flash of honesty to illuminate his loathing. "I was never there [but] America deeply disgusts me." And no, he did not mind being called "anti-American," he told a German news magazine. In fact, it was "cowardly that so many today distinguish between the American people and the current American administration, [which] was more or less democratically elected. . . . Hence, you can be against the Americans, just as most of the world was against the Germans in the Second World War. In this sense, I am anti-American." Nonetheless, Germany's most famous theater director was not completely candid. The most monstrous charge was transported by this not-so-subliminal syllogism: Hitler was Germany, Bush is America, and so the Americans of today are like the Nazis of yesterday. "Nazi" is the universal symbol of unprecedented evil; to apply such comparison to contemporary America is to inflict maximal moral damage on it. . . .

In the following section, Joffe offers a discursive definition of anti-Americanism.

. . . America gorges itself on fatty fast food, wallows in tawdry mass entertainment, starves the arts, and prays only to one God, who is Mammon. Instead of subsidizing what is serious and high-minded, as do the Europeans, the United States ruthlessly sacrifices the best of culture to pap and pop—never mind the Metropolitan Opera, MoMA, and the world's most highly touted research universities. Although these schools are much admired, the compliment is routinely followed by "But they are for the rich and well-connected, only." Like all such anti-Americanisms, the myth is promulgated in blissful (or willful) ignorance of the fact that Harvard, Stanford, et al. subsidize 60 percent of their college students with loans and grants, while Ph.D. students normally have both tuition and living expenses paid for by the university. Even though this complaint is routine lore in Germany, German data show that, in spite of open admission and no tuition, 85 percent of all students are middle-class and higher. America's high schools, so another standby goes, breed vast illiteracy and ignorance of the world. Here, too, the facts are more complex. In various comparative studies, as in PISA 2000 and 2003, U.S. high schoolers end up in midfield along with France, but ahead of their contemporaries in Belgium, Spain, Germany, Switzerland, and Italy.

The common theme of these stereotypes is the denigration of America and the elevation of Europe. The motifs are summed up nicely in a piece in *Le Monde* right after the terror attacks of 9/11: "cretinism, Puritanism, barbarian arrogance, unbridled capitalism." America is morally, culturally, and socially inferior to Europe. "The United States," as the British philosopher Bertrand Russell put it as early as 1967, "is a force for suffering, reaction and counter-revolution the world over." It is a society where Europe's finest values—solidarity and community, taste and manners—are ground down by rampant individualism and capitalism. America is Yahoo, whereas Europe is civilization. Europe, in short, is the "Un-America."

So much for stereotypization and denigration. Now to those items that are even more emotionally charged: obsession, demonization, and conspiracy. "Anti-Americanism," the Stanford historian Russell Berman has argued,

> functions like a prejudice, magnifying the power and presence of its presumed opponent, turning it into a ubiquitous threat. The empirical superiority of American military power, for example is transformed by the anti-Americanist imagination into a fantasy of infinite omnipotence: there is no evil in the world that cannot be blamed on American action. . . . Anti-Semites, similarly, have always been able to imagine an ineluctable network of Jewish power. As a paranoid fantasy, anti-Americanism is cut from the same cloth. Instead of facing up to the detailed complexity of reality, it can only see Washington's hands controlling every conflict. . . . Anti-Americanism is not a reasoned response to American policies; it is a hysterical surplus that goes beyond reason. That difference is evident in the constant recycling of anti-American images that have a history that long antedates current policy.

Obsessions are compulsively repeated thoughts and images that allow no room for falsification or alternative explanations. This is why debates on anti-Americanism or any anti-ism turn into spirals without resolution or escape. . . .

Obsessions are not about facts, but about filters. They grant passage only to those facts (or fabrications) that confirm the prejudice. As the Latinate word implies, the judgment comes *before* the evidence, and thus it accepts only what fits, while turning every part into the whole. A telling illustration is the bill of indictment Europeans have leveled a thousand times at the first administration of George W. Bush: the cancellation of the ABM Treaty as well as the refusal to sign on to the Kyoto Climate Protocol, the Land Mine Convention, the Biological Weapons Convention, the Comprehensive Nuclear Test Ban, and the International Criminal Court. Now, all of these choices were open to reasoned attack, and they were so attacked in the United States, as well. What turned the objections into obsessions was the compulsive reiteration at every twist and turn; this is what sprang to mind "on cue." These items were listed not as illustrations of unwanted or misguided policies but as self-evident proofs of maliciousness that required no further examination. Just uttering the indictment was proof of perfidy. Nor was right versus wrong the real issue; the psychological function of this argumentative rosary was to demonstrate the moral superiority of Europe vis-à-vis the Yahoo nation of America.

Another feature of obsession is the tendency to accuse an opponent of one thing and of its opposite. Like the Jews who were simultaneously denounced as capitalist blood suckers and communist subversives, America gets it coming and going. In matters sexual, Americans are both prurient and prudish, a far cry from the wiser ways of Europe. America is both puritanical and self-indulgent, philistine and elitist, sanctimonious and crassly materialist. It is morally derelict when it does not use its awesome force, as against Serbia in the early phase of the Balkan wars, and arrogantly imperialistic when it does, as in the bombing campaign of 1999, let alone during the Afghan and Iraqi campaigns.

Michael Cox
EUROPE'S ENDURING ANTI-AMERICANISM

A specialist on international relations with an interest in U.S. foreign policy, London School of Economics professor Michael Cox has reflected deeply on trans-Atlantic relations. Here he explores European anti-Americanism, particularly the role of reason and prejudice in attitudes toward U.S. policy positions.

VISIONS OF THINGS TO COME

What are the political consequences of the resurgence of anti-American attitudes in Europe? The first is an effect on the tone, not just of public discourse but of political leadership. European politicians increasingly are forced to operate in an environment where anti-American positions are regarded as statements of commonsense wisdom, while statements of support for the US government are subject to prolonged, hostile analysis. There are, as a result, more straightforward political rewards to be reaped from pronouncements, and even off-the-cuff remarks, deriding American positions than from any effort to justify collaboration. This means that, without some realignment of public attitudes, policy in most European states will probably remain tilted over time toward reflexive suspicion of the United States and a predisposition to be critical of US policies whatever they may be.

To be sure, there are leaders from time to time, such as Tony Blair of Britain and Nicolas Sarkozy of France, who are capable of resisting such a trend in the popular sentiment of their nations and are disposed to do so. It would seem foolhardy, however, to predict that a general movement of public feeling in democracies will not tend to dictate a drift in the thinking of elected representatives toward at least compatible positions.

Public anti-Americanism makes it more difficult for European leaders to sustain a pro-American stance, or to support policies that are associated in the public mind with the United States, even if the leaders themselves might by their own instincts be disposed to favor such policies. In short, the political price of visible pro-Americanism has risen substantially, with predictable effects for the number of political actors willing to buy the product. The next US president will have to deal with the consequences.

Second, if domestic political conditions make it more difficult for pro-American politicians, or at least pro-American policy positions, to succeed in Europe, then there will also be an effect on alignment within the broader international community. The world has been accustomed to seeing the United States and leading European nations collaborate closely on the serious issues of international affairs, often to the extent of viewing them as a cohesive Western bloc. It seems unlikely that continuing anti-American sentiment in Europe could produce such an extreme effect as to drive Europe into the arms of any other partner in opposition to America. But it is plausible that the next US administration will have to devote more energy to shoring up support from Europe, which in the past it might have taken for granted.

Third, the drift toward resistance against following the "American course" may be accompanied by another political consequence: a certain forgetfulness regarding the degree to which European and US interests and values still coincide. Much has been written concerning the differences between Europe and the United States—America is a less statist, more individualistic, and more religious society than European nations can claim for themselves. Nevertheless, there are rudimentary principles to which both America and Europe adhere with a steadiness that cannot be found so readily in other places.

WEAKENING THE WEST

Cold war or no, such values—and the interest in trade and access to resources to which they are coupled—still have enemies in the world. For all their disagreements over the war on terror and the invasion of Iraq, Americans and Europeans have far more uniting them with one another than with the proclaimers of Islamist jihad, vicious pseudo-nationalist autocrats such as the late Saddam Hussein, or Stalinist relics like North Korea's Kim Jong-II. Even more acceptable prospective partners such as China or Russia seem on due analysis to be many moons away from having the basis of commonality with either side required to supplant the transatlantic bond.

Their periodic gestures of spectacular lethal nihilism notwithstanding, it still seems highly unlikely that the enemies of the Western social model have the ability to destroy it, though they can certainly visit harm on its citizens. Even so, the throwing of rhetorical stones and the inculcation of a self-conscious "values gap" between the two continents that provide the supporting pillars of the West cannot but weaken the West.

As suggested above, it seems plausible that a more pressingly existential sense of threat to Europe would more likely reinvigorate than destroy the Euro-American partnership. For now, however, in as much as European and American solidarity tends to protect common interests and values, European anti-Americanism (as well as its reciprocal counterpart in American sentiment) threatens to take eyes off the ball when it comes to pursuing what should be both sides' highest priority: the uncompromising defense of their shared way of life. This possibility has to concern the next American president, of whichever party, as much as it offers hope to the enemies of the West.

Fourth, there is a very real risk that anti-Americanism in mainstream political discourse may give comfort to antidemocratic forces within European societies. There will always be in Europe a certain amount of extremism, particularly of the sort characterized by hatred of America and subscription to outlandish conspiracy theories concerning American deeds. We are all by now at least partially familiar, through the analysis of terrorist attacks, successful and foiled, in the United Kingdom and elsewhere, with the processes by which citizens of European nations can be led to draw radical religious and political conclusions as a result of exposure to propaganda blaming the United States for a global "crusade" against Islam.

It would be inaccurate and unfair to hold those who posit more moderate criticisms of the United States responsible for the words and actions of extremists. However, in the same way that the Iraq War provoked an upsurge in terrorist intent—without that statement in any sense suggesting that the former justifies the latter—so it may be justly argued that the culture of intellectual hostility toward US foreign policy which has taken root among the general population of Europe will make fighting the "war on terror" more difficult in the future.

THINKING LIKE ADULTS

Fifth and finally, a sad consequence of the rise of anti-Americanism in Europe may be the entrenchment of an unedifying mental laziness. This is likely to enervate the intellectual content of the European debate about international affairs even as high passions continue to flow. It would doubtless romanticize the process of foreign policy making in democracies to suggest that what emerges is usually the product of dialectics of sweet reason on the part of the general public. Nevertheless, it is to be hoped that, at least on matters of the greatest importance, the public does engage to some degree, and the greater the sophistication and rationality of its analysis the better for the political process.

If, however, European debates continue to feature the kind of reasoning that flows from conclusions to facts and arguments, while assuming the worst concerning agendas associated with America; if crass generalizations about American culture and politics retain their grip over the European public mindset; and if the government of the United States continues to be ascribed a malevolence and omnipotence detached from any balanced reading of the facts; then the result can only be to infantilize and stunt the public discussion of international affairs in Europe, with continuing and unfortunate consequences for transatlantic relations.

Only by eschewing easy intellectual shortcuts that assume generalized good or ill to lie at the root of American policy; only by embracing the reality that the United States is far from all-powerful, and thus far from all-responsible for the world's problems; only by accepting that, despite lacking omnipotence, the United States nevertheless has a shot at achieving at least some important, positive things through the application of its substantial power and is disposed to attempt to do so, even if that may infringe on the claimed prerogatives of others; only in these ways can Europeans who seek to offer critiques of US policy hope to emerge from their analysis with useful, adult conclusions.

It might be noted that Americans themselves would do well to subscribe to similar principles in their judgment of their own nation. Similarly, policy makers in the next administration in Washington would do well to keep their analysis of European political trends clear-headed. Such analysis would offer little support for any hope that the Europeans, even with Bush gone from office, will happily fall in line behind US leadership.

3 Russia: Creeping Autocracy and Burgeoning Nationalism

In August 1991, Boris Yeltsin was the world's hero, standing atop a Soviet tank in Moscow and rallying his fellow Russians to the cause of democracy in the face of an attempted coup by Kremlin hard-liners. Within a few years he had become an international joke, a petty tyrant and physically spent alcoholic whose chances of surviving his term as president seemed questionable. In some respects, Yeltsin, a former Communist apparatchik, embodied the country over

which he ruled. Both underwent an ideological transformation that had begun amidst widespread optimism but now threatened to spin out of control, with devastating consequences for themselves and the world at large. "Shock therapy," the economic policies that all at once established free markets and private property, enriched only those who already controlled the levers of the economy while impoverishing the large majority of the population. Meanwhile, Yeltsin found himself increasingly at odds with the parliament. Faced with deadlock, he ordered army tanks to fire on the legislature and pushed through a constitution that enhanced his own powers. By the end of the 1990s, Russia's major assets (including the media, natural resources, and banks) had been gathered up by a handful of "oligarchs" who formed a clique around the president. Corruption and violent crime became common. Ordinary Russians were often going without their paychecks or pensions. In 1998 the country defaulted on its foreign debt. In short, the dreams of a market economy and political democracy had eluded Russia, which now seemed weaker than ever, a mere shadow of the Soviet superpower whose core it had been.

That Russia would undergo a revival in less than a decade was a development that few would have dared predict toward the end of Yeltsin's term in office. Ironically, it was Yeltsin himself who laid the groundwork for the turnaround when, in 1999, he named as the last of his prime ministers a little known former KGB bureaucrat named Vladimir Putin.

C. J. Chivers
VLADIMIR PUTIN: A NEW TSAR IN THE KREMLIN?

When Vladimir Putin (b. 1952) became Russia's prime minister in August 1999, he struck many people as a fairly colorless and even grim apparatchik in the old Soviet mold. Before long, however, he proved himself a dynamic leader and intrepid political operator who began the restoration of Russian power both at home and abroad. Russia under Putin has diverged considerably from the democratic path that many in the West hoped the country had embarked on following the collapse of the Soviet Union in 1991. Indeed, if anything, he has emerged more clearly as the autocrat that Boris Yeltsin often threatened to become. At the same time, Putin is enormously popular among his countrymen, who are grateful for the economic and national revival he has overseen. In the first decade of the twenty-first century, Putin made Russia a major player in the world arena once again.

Reflecting Putin's global impact, *Time* magazine chose Vladimir Putin late in 2007 as its "Person of the Year." A few months later, in March 2008, Putin, observing the two-term limit stipulated in the Russian constitution, relinquished the reins of power to his elected successor, Dimitri Medvedev, whom he had personally chosen for the job. Medvedev then appointed Putin as his prime minister, giving rise to speculation that Putin would continue to pull the strings from behind the scenes.

Late in 2008 a profile of Putin by C. J. Chivers appeared in *Esquire*. In addition to his years covering Russia for the *New York Times,* Chivers had reported from several of the republics that at one time had made up the former Soviet Union and thus brought to his analysis both a broader and more multilayered perspective. An edited version of his article on Putin appears below.

THE MAN WHO WOULD BE CZAR

Vladimir Putin is a national savior and hero, a man, sober and exceptionally smart, who stepped from shadows to resuscitate a proud country that others had run aground, looted, and left for dead. After eight years as president, a period marked by a surging economy and an unexpectedly victorious war in Chechnya, he surrendered one of the most seductively powerful offices on earth voluntarily and according to Russia's constitution, with Moscow's influence in the world restored and with a large fraction of Russia's citizens better off than they ever had been. He has been a bridge from postcommunist chaos and hardship to national stability, freer markets, individual economic choice, and the possibility of democracy.

Or, he is a cunning, even diabolical strongman atop a scrum of bandit cliques. As a career officer in the KGB, an organization its members never leave, he is fundamentally anti-Western and undemocratic, and comfortable with conflict, crime, and the company of beasts. Moreover, he is nostalgic for empire and covetous of power, and he has surrendered only a title. Instead, he has manipulated Russia's loose political rules and obedient political class to install a puppet successor and transfer the levers to his new post as Russia's premier, where he continues to abuse office and direct the spoils of oil-state excess to his coterie. His talk of public stewardship and personal liberties is farce. The Kremlin has rejected democracy while pretending to embrace it, hardening into a kleptocracy with nuclear weapons and state-controlled television stations purring that all is well.

Depending on the point of view of the commentator (and sometimes the source of the commentator's paycheck), the standard assessments of Putin's nine years in public office reach these rival extremes. What makes them interesting, and makes full and accurate descriptions of Putin elusive, is that both are largely true.

Vladimir Putin is one of the central figures of our times, the man who presided at the Kremlin as the broken remains of a sprawling nation were restored to life, and who used his stature to reorder the Russian-speaking world's relations with the West and become the de facto spokesman of strongmen everywhere. No recent Western leader can claim to have changed a nation and its place in the world so fully. . . .

Is Putin's Russia a retreat to Soviet practices or a capitalist democracy sputtering through early stages of evolution? Putin's signature legacy is not Russia's new wealth and confidence, nor the subjugation of Chechnya, nor the return of an assertive foreign policy, capped by the invasion of Georgia. It is the refinement, if that word could ever be used with this phenomenon, of a more sophisticated and rational police state than the failed USSR. This is no celebration of imaginary virtues; the world of his politics remains ugly and unrepaired. It is meant to pose a question. Putin has reshaped Russian autocracy under another name. To what end?

THE STRONG MAN

From the beginning, the experts' forecasts were wrong. When an exhausted President Boris Yeltsin introduced Putin to the world in the summer of 1999, announcing that Putin was his choice as prime minister (Yeltsin's sixth in less than eighteen months), few expected him to last. It was not just that Putin, then forty-six, was charged with managing a pauper state, a government adrift in disorder, and a population soured by the unmet promises of free markets and democracy. The brewing unrest in Chechnya [see page 452] had drifted beyond separatism and nationalism and become an international Islamic cause. Crime and corruption were pandemic, and a circle of billionaire oligarchs controlled large fractions of the nation's resources and capital, as well as voting blocs in parliament, which was a legislature for sale. . . .

In retrospect, of course, the early assessments were wrong. . . . Putin swiftly displayed his confrontational self. He directed a renewed military campaign in Chechnya, which was foundering under the self-rule separatists had gained after fighting the Russian army to a standstill a few years before. The war had undermined Russia's standing and self-esteem, psychological injuries that Putin seemed to understand viscerally. Vladimir Putin did not just promise to restore Russian rule. He went beyond the typical language of settling unsettled scores. He vowed blood. "We will pursue the terrorists everywhere," he said. "You will forgive me, but if we catch them in the toilet, we will wet them even in the outhouse." Earlier Russian premiers had been rendered inert by the tenacity of the Chechen fighters and the reliable incompetence of Russia's army. (In 1995 Viktor Chernomyrdin had pleaded for the release of hostages with Shamil Basayev, the terrorist, on live television. "I beg you," he had said.) Putin signaled that Russia would not beg. He came from an organization that had used fear to bring a vast nation to heel. Violence for him was a governing tool.

Putin also showed skills as a performer, peppering an understated demeanor with prison-slang coarseness. Hunting terrorists to their toilets? The Russian idiom "to wet" is inmate jargon for soaking a victim in blood. It is a knowing way of saying "to kill" and suggests killing at very close range, as with a knife. Underneath his Italian suits and aura of sobriety, Putin revealed an icy Eastwood deadpan. An ease with crudity simmered beneath what passed for Putin's style. Asked if he worried about Russia's columns inflicting civilian casualties, Putin made clear that he did not, and would not keep company with people who did. "We do not need generals who chew snot," he said.

Such was the mind behind Russia's new war. Russian troops soon leveled much of Grozny, Chechnya's capital, and launched often indiscriminate sweeps through the Chechen countryside. Victims and human-rights organizations assigned much of the blame for the troops' conduct to Putin, whose language seemed to encourage it. Putin was undeterred. He had found a persona. He was not just a stern nationalist who would restore Russian sovereignty. He was the unblinking fighter, untroubled by rules, conscience, or second thought in the pursuit of national order. Russia's losing streak had been long. Putin would be its fist. RUDEST EVER P.M. WINS OVER RUSSIA, another Western newspaper declared. His popularity climbed.

Late in 1999, Yeltsin resigned, making Putin the front-runner in the presidential race. In the spring of 2000, he was elected. His time had begun.

THE BOOM

Eight years on, Russia looks not much like it did then. The value of the Russian stock market has soared. Personal incomes have grown. A society that suffered the forced austerity of communism and economic collapse has entered a carnival of personal spending. Gone are empty shelves, replaced by a rollicking consumer culture that buys what it wants. French perfumes, Austrian chocolates, Japanese electronics, Scandinavian cell phones, Italian handbags, Cuban cigars, Australian wines, and single-malt Scotches—malls have opened offering all of these. Rates of car ownership have multiplied with access to personal credit, and Moscow's roads, cluttered during Yeltsin's time with Zhigulis, are jammed with BMWs and Benzes. Extravagant restaurants cater to the wealthy. Sushi, in the inland reaches of a northern forest, is a minor Russian craze. For people of even modest means, stores stock fresh fruits and vegetables year-round. Yes, *babushkas* [old women] still sell onions on the streets. And yes, rural areas are deeply depressed.

But the expanding Russian wealth has grown beyond the horizon. Visit tourist destinations in Thailand, the Mediterranean, Europe, or the Red Sea and you will hear Russian. Visit a real estate office in any Western capital and you will hear tales of Russian buyers.

Such are the signs of the most tangible freedom associated with Putin's Russia—the freedom to buy whatever you can afford, except, in most cases, power.

No small part of this turnaround resulted from conditions outside Putin's control. Russia's combined oil and natural-gas reserves are the world's largest, and with timber and coal and mineral deposits, these resources positioned Russia to be a global gas pump, lumberyard, and mine long before any of us knew Putin's name. The price explosion of oil enriched Russia with head-spinning speed, creating a huge transfer of global wealth to Slavic hands. Along the way, it transformed parts of dreary Moscow into a northern Vegas and allowed the Kremlin—which not long ago could not afford the fuel in its fighter jets—to pay down foreign debts ahead of schedule. And yet the results cannot be ascribed to sheer chance. It is easy to reduce the arrival of Russian wealth to the indifferent bounty of market forces, but sound macroeconomics and fiscal restraint supported some of the boom. Stephen Kotkin, the professor of Russian history at Princeton, said early this year that if surging oil and gas prices automatically mean that states rich with hydrocarbons will enjoy instant prosperity, ask Nigeria where its boom is.

While Russia's economy roared, Putin was benefiting from another unanticipated success. By 2005, the war in Chechnya had turned. The insurgent bands were either being thinned to pockets or, in many cases, coerced to join a pro-Kremlin government led by Ramzan Kadyrov, the rebel turned Putin loyalist who replaced the chaos of conflict with a local dictatorship. Fighting lingers nearby, in Ingushetia and sometimes Dagestan, but in scale and intensity it is a fraction of the violence of 2004. No one saw this coming. Anyone suggesting four years ago, after the school siege in Beslan, that the war would be reduced to skirmishes in Ingushetia and Dagestan, and that Grozny (think: Mogadishu) would be largely rebuilt in a thousand days, would have been dismissed as a fool. But after the school siege ended in 2004, with more than 330 victims dead and hundreds more injured, Russian counterterrorism was reinvigorated.[1] Two underground Chechen presidents were killed, and Basayev died in a mysterious explosion. On both sides, the war had been a race for the bottom, with horrors trumped by horrors for several years. With Beslan, the separatists had gone too far. Chechnya's Sufi nationalists had once enjoyed a reputation as underdogs. But killing children was not an image-booster; support for them collapsed. . . .

The author then discusses the good fortune that befell Putin: Islamic militants from throughout the Middle East and Central Asia who had been pouring into Chechnya to support its war against Russia suddenly had a new enemy on which to focus—the U.S military presence in Iraq.

Putin, a student of what is wrong with the United States, had loudly opposed the invasion of Iraq. But as the United States bogged down along the Tigris and the Euphrates, the war he had stood against was making his job easier. George Bush limped toward the end of his presidency, facing public unease about his handling of the wars in Afghanistan and Iraq. Vladimir Putin's public-approval ratings exceeded 70 percent. By this year, with memories of terrorism in Moscow streets fading, the Chechen war had slipped from much of the national conversation. Putin was even able to raise the subject himself to divert uncomfortable questions about his personal life. . . .

---

[1]In September 2004 armed terrorists seized a school in the town of Beslan in North Ossetia, an autonomous republic in Russia's North Caucasus. Demanding an end to the Second Chechen War, they took 1,100 people hostage. Eventually Russian forces staged a massive assault on the building. The death toll among the hostages numbered 334, more than half of them children.

AN AGGRESSIVE FOREIGN POLICY

There are many essential moments in Putin's consolidation of power. Most publicly, it began with the arrest of oil oligarch Mikhail Khodorkovsky, an act that propelled his long climb to what he is now. But his handling of Ukraine, at first bungled, proved to be another.

Putin's Ukraine policy had courted disaster. In the elections of 2004, he publicly backed a pro-Russian candidate, Viktor Yanukovich, who had been convicted of robbery but had the support of the sordid political machine built by Leonid Kuchma, the much-hated departing president. Putin jumped in as if the race were a domestic affair. He presided over a Soviet-style military parade in Kiev and committed Russia to an energy deal that pledged to sell natural gas to Ukraine at a deep discount through 2009. Natural gas is the lubricant of the Ukrainian economy. It heats Ukrainian cities and powers electrical plants and factories. Putin's deal—to sell gas for less than a quarter of the market rate through Yanukovich's first presidential term—was a subsidy-for-loyalty exchange, and promised Ukraine's elite ample opportunity for graft. (Reselling subsidized Russian gas at high profits is a common insiders' swindle.)

There was only one problem: Yanukovich was not elected. His rival, Viktor Yushchenko, survived dioxin poisoning and emerged from the hospital as a potent symbol against the enduring nastiness of post-Soviet rule. Kuchma's government falsified an election victory for Yanukovich, but it was not enough. Hundreds of thousands of demonstrators, and then the Ukrainian court, demanded a new vote. Putin was scrambling for credibility.

His retaliation was precise. Russia announced that the gas deal with Ukraine was off, and that Ukraine would have to pay market rates, now more than five times the previous offer. Gazprom, Russia's state gas monopoly, set a deadline for late 2005. The threat's timing was carefully chosen and the irony inescapable. Ukraine faced the prospect of gas shortages in winter. And Putin, the KGB man who had given a Soviet-style energy subsidy to a nation to buy its loyalty, was now lecturing Europe about the need for market rates.

As Yushchenko resisted through the deadline, Russia escalated again, reducing pressure in pipelines feeding Ukraine. Pressure quickly began to fall in Europe, which receives much of its gas on lines that pass through Ukraine. In his anger that Ukraine overturned a falsified election, Putin was cutting off gas to the West. European officials seethed. Could he be such a neophyte? Was he not getting any better advice? Had Putin lost his mind?

With the din rising, Yushchenko capitulated in a deal to buy gas through a mysterious company, Rosukrenergo, at a compromise price. It was an utterly nontransparent arrangement, and raised immediate suspicion that insiders were profiting. After seeming cornered only months before, Putin had won, and been successful in three ways. He had forced Ukraine to accept his terms, he had pulled Yushchenko into an agreement that sullied his government and image as a reformer, and he had shown Europe that he could stand up to it as Yeltsin never did. . . .

THE CRACKDOWN

For all of Putin's domestic success, and in spite of his good luck, Russia remains bedeviled by problems. Social services are poor, and corruption has become total. Russian public services are so wormy with dishonesty and dysfunction that patients bribe doctors for care, parents buy access to schools for their children and grades for their report cards, and the police shake down drivers with a regularity resembling taxation. The court system is a sham, vulnerable to bribery and political instruction. Racial and ethnic violence is widespread, and murders of minorities occur with morbid frequency.

Russia's army, far behind Western levels of professionalism and standards of equipment, is further weakened by high rates of draft dodging, which are elevated by traditions of conscript hazing. Its record of human-rights violations is appalling. Putin has consolidated the Kremlin's control over key economic sectors—oil, gas, pipelines, aircraft and vehicle manufacture, arms dealing, banking, and metals—and the billionaires have been brought under the Kremlin's sway. But there are more oligarchs now than in 2000, suggesting that wealth has not been redistributed in ways Putin had pledged, even as inflation and a real estate bubble have eroded middle-class spending power.

All of these are issues that might motivate a growing middle class to ask questions about its government. So how did Vladimir Putin build so much prestige and muster the strength to assert himself on the world?

The easy answer, the one you've heard, is that he rolled back civil liberties and created a neo-Soviet state, securing his own power by limiting everyone else's. Since 2000, Putin's Kremlin has replaced independent television with lapdog television, stifled political competitors, expelled foreigners and harried nongovernmental organizations that criticize the state, abolished the elections for governors and replaced them with a system in which the Kremlin appoints regional leaders. The effect has been a drought of candor and vibrancy in Russia's public conversation. These days, free speech does not extend much beyond venting online, a single bold radio station, and the work of a few small, rambunctious newspapers.

But the insistence that Russia is returning to Soviet times is a claim resting on omission and exaggeration. This is not the nightmare of Soviet rule, and not just because Russians have access to food and foreign goods. Putin's Russia is a canny autocracy, a system that exerts intensive control over political society but offers pressure-release valves in individual life. In Russia, Internet use is largely unfettered, cellphone ownership is profligate, the pursuit of money is an organizing ideology, and foreign travel is common. Under the old guard, all of these would have been regarded as threats to the state. . . .

The Kremlin's political apparatus routinely falsified elections. It compelled laborers, students, and government employees to vote for its candidates. It doctored voter lists. It used tax inspectors and police to harass opposition members. It manipulated media coverage and released invented vote results. In the daily administration of government affairs, the state perched atop a sprawling machinery of graft that spirited away money from all manner of public works. And the state's penetration of the strategic industries extended the graft throughout the economy. Although checks and balances existed in the law, in practice they had been subverted. The Kremlin controlled the legislature and courts. Law-enforcement agencies—from the tax police to the successors of the KGB—worked at its bidding. No new face could stand against Putin or his men. . . .

Put another way, Putin's autocracy is a cunning blend of ruling ideas from the old Soviet regime with many of the material pleasures of capitalist life, a form of government for strongmen who did their homework. And just as they accept that freer markets are more efficient than planned economies, and that pining for foreign goods is not treason, Putin and his circle understand that Russia's people can say what they wish in their kitchens without endangering the state. This allows for democratic pretenses with centralized rule and insider access to the profits of governing. The Kremlin today does not control everything. It does not try to. Putin's circle exerts control over the profits of the most lucrative industries, and bares its teeth at actual threats to power. Repression is no longer total. It is precise, and its weight is brought down, often publicly, on the few who stand up to the state. . . .

A KINDER, GENTLER POLICE STATE

For years after the Soviet Union's collapse, Russia's liberals and Westerners alike hoped that the freed people and new republics would form law-abiding and democratic states. Putin's rule has labored to prevent that from happening, and the old Soviet world has hardened to its new shape. Across the rolling expanse of steppe, forest, and mountain range formerly under Kremlin rule, every single government unfailingly declares itself democratic. But aside from in the Baltic states, few in the region can speak candidly on television or the radio, or watch a free and independent news broadcast of local origin, or enjoy unmolested public assembly that criticizes the government, or have a fair hearing before an impartial judge in a court where the law is the highest authority, or select leaders from a slate of candidates who have been allowed to campaign openly and without restriction. This is the state of the Russian-speaking world nearly two decades after the wall came down. . . .

TO WHAT END?

Early this year, Putin was challenged by a reporter at a news conference over the continued vote fabrications in Chechnya. There, according to the government's figures for the parliamentary election last year, 99 percent of the voters had cast ballots, and 99 percent of the ballots were for the political party Putin leads. Such election figures have been rivaled only in Kim Jong-il's North Korea, Mao's China, Niyazov's Turkmenistan, and Saddam Hussein's Iraq. They were especially absurd for a vote in Chechnya, a land shaped by cycles of resistance to Russian rule, and that had been brought back to yoke by force. The correspondent wanted to know: Did the president of Russia find these numbers credible?

Putin declined to answer. Instead, he asked a state journalist from Chechnya to answer for him. The young Chechen quickly stood. "These are absolutely realistic figures," he said, grinning obsequiously. And Vladimir Putin watched with a mix of satisfaction and boredom, the face of unchecked power itself.

4 Islam in Europe: Failure of Assimilation and the Threat of Terrorism

In the 1950s and 1960s Western Europe's booming economy created a demand for cheap labor that was met by an influx of millions of Muslims from Turkey, Pakistan, and North Africa, many of them illegals. Like other immigrants, they sought to join relatives, find economic opportunities, or escape from oppressive regimes. As a result, many European countries, including France, Germany, Britain, Belgium, Holland, Sweden, and Spain, now have substantial Muslim populations.

Essentially European countries have tried two approaches to absorbing Muslim immigrants—multiculturalism and assimilation. Practiced in Britain, Holland, and Germany, multiculturalism treats Muslims as members of a separate community with a distinct religious and cultural identity; this approach assumes that the Muslims' way of life could exist side by side with the cultural norms of the host country. Assimilation, the integration model adopted in France, does not grant Muslims a special status but encourages individual Muslims to embrace the nation's culture and values, to think of themselves as proud and loyal French citizens. Both approaches are now perceived as failures, for many Muslims remain profoundly alienated from European society and at odds with its values. European liberal-democracy, which espouses religious freedom, equal rights for

women, separation of church and state, and freedom of expression, conflicts with many facets of Islamic society.

In describing the failure of the multicultural approach, analysts refer to the persistence of tight-knit Muslim ghettos; the terrorist bombings in the London subway on July 7, 2005, by Muslims who were born and educated in Britain; the murder on November 2, 2004, of Dutch filmmaker Theo Van Gogh by an Islamist extremist with Dutch citizenship; the demands of some Muslim groups that they be governed by their own religious law rather than the law of the land; the perpetuation in Europe by some Muslims of cultural mores that sanction polygamy, forced marriages between young girls and much older men, wife-beating, so-called honor killings of "wayward" females, and require women to keep their bodies and faces hidden from view; the high crime rate among Muslims—in Britain Muslims are 2 percent of the population but more than 8 percent of the prison population; and the emergence in European lands of extremist cells that have participated in terrorist acts, including 9/11.

In the fall of 2005, the suburbs of Paris and scores of other French cities were convulsed by two weeks of rioting—nearly 9,000 cars set afire and schools, shops, and churches burned to the ground—by young Muslim males from the bleak housing projects inhabited principally by North African immigrants. That the great majority of rioters were not recent immigrants, but had been born in France, was particularly distressing to officials, for the French government prided itself on creating a uniform French identity that superseded ethnic and religious origins. Whatever the aspirations of the government, many French citizens remain resentful of North African immigrants whom they view as an alien minority that, unlike other immigrants, has failed to integrate into French society. They point to the immigrants' preference for native cultural traditions, the high cost of welfare payments they receive, and the high crime rate among them—Muslims, about 10 percent of the nation, constitute more than 50 percent of France's prison population. Numerous commentators, however, interpreted the riots as a rebellion by a resentful underclass protesting discrimination, segregation, poverty, and a staggering unemployment rate—as much as 40 percent—for young Muslim males.

Faced with what is perceived as a rapidly growing unassimilable Muslim minority that is hostile to Western values, lives in isolated communities, often does not speak the host nation's language, and recruits and finances terrorists, Europe is experiencing a backlash against Muslim immigrants and multiculturalism. An increasing number of Europeans now say that the premise of multiculturalism—assigning equal value to and tolerating Islamic traditions—was a mistake, for several of these traditions undermine democracy and fragment the nation. The sentiments of Jan Wolter, a Dutch judge, are shared by many native Europeans: "We demand a new social contract. We no longer accept that people don't learn our language, we require that they send their daughters to school, and we demand they stop bringing in young brides from the desert and locking them up in third floor apartments." Increasingly, governments are introducing tighter immigration laws and are deporting Muslim radicals. They are also trying to work with moderate Muslims who support integration into European society and value Europe's liberal democratic tradition. However, successful integration, say some commentators, is a two-way street. It is necessary

for European society to address the socioeconomic problems burdening Muslims, overcome racist attitudes toward immigrants, and recognize the fact that numerous Muslims do work and pay taxes, respect the laws of their adopted country, and reject extremism; most important, Muslims must be made to feel that their religion is not being attacked and insulted. For many years to come Europeans will be confronted with—or tormented by—the question of Islam's place in their country.

Walter Laqueur
THE LAST DAYS OF EUROPE

In The *Last Days of Europe: Epitaph for an Old Continent* (2007), Walter Laqueur, a prominent American historian with strong ties to Europe, discusses several threats to Europe's future, one of which is the burgeoning Muslim population. Laqueur raises an important question. In the past, immigrant Jews—and recently Sikhs and Hindus—have thrived in Britain, even when confronted with prejudice. Why is the integration of Muslim immigrants in Western society so fraught with problems? Following is Laqueur's discussion of this issue.

The problem facing West European societies is more often than not the second- and third-generation young immigrants—the very people who it was expected would be well integrated, equal members of these societies but who, on the contrary, revolted against their country of adoption. The reasons usually given are poverty (two-thirds of British Muslims live in low-income households), inadequate housing and overcrowding, ghettoization, unemployment, especially of the young, lack of education, racial prejudice on the part of their non-Muslim neighbors—all of which are said to lead to a lack of social mobility, crime, and general marginalization of the Muslim communities. By implication or directly, it is argued that it is the fault of the state and of society that these and other misfortunes have taken place. However, Muslims who have had successful careers in business or the professions say almost without exception that their ethnic identity did in no way hamper them.

To what extent has ghettoization been enforced by the outside world, and to what degree was it self-imposed? That new immigrants congregate in certain parts of a city is a well-known phenomenon. It can be studied, for instance, in London, where, traditionally, Irish (Camden Town), Jews (East End and later Golders Green), Australians and Poles (near Earls Court and Olympia), blacks (Brixton), Japanese (South Hampstead), and other newcomers settled at first. They were motivated by the wish to be among people who spoke their language and have ethnic food shops, travel agencies, clubs, and other organizations. The Russian immigrants to Berlin in the 1920s congregated in Charlottenburg, while poor Jews from Eastern Europe settled in the eastern part of the city.

A similar process took place as far as the Muslim immigration was concerned, but there was a basic difference: Earlier immigration waves did not receive any help with their housing on the part of the state or the local authorities, whereas in the second half of the twentieth century such assistance was the rule rather than the exception. For this reason there was little incentive to move out from lodgings that, however inadequate or displeasing, were free or inexpensive. When Eastern European Jews first moved to Whitechapel toward the end of the nineteenth century and the beginning of the twentieth, there was no mayor of London who went out of his way to help them. They and other immigrants had to fend for themselves, facing incomparably greater difficulties—for instance, there was no health service or other social assistance—than present-day immigrants. Muslim newcomers apparently like to stick longer with their coreligionists than do other groups of immigrants, and they are encouraged by their preachers to do so. This is true even with regard to India, where there is more ghettoization than in Europe; even middle-class Muslims seem to be reluctant to leave the areas where members of their community live.

The sites around Paris where many of the French Muslim immigrants live and which exploded in November 2005 were uncomfortable and aesthetically displeasing, but they were not slums like London's East End. Yet it was precisely in these quarters that, in the words of a foreign visitor, an antisociety grew up infused with a burning hatred of the other France and deep distrust and alienation. . . . Although they enjoy a far higher standard of living or consumption than they would in the country of their parents, this is no cause for gratitude; on the contrary, it is felt as an insult or a wound, even as they take it for granted as their due. . . .

Housing has been mentioned as perhaps the main reason for the Paris riots of 2005, youth unemployment as another. Unemployment amounts to 30 to 40 percent in France and Germany and not much less in Britain and the Netherlands. As a Berlin head teacher put it, "We are creating an army of long-term unemployed." The rate of dropouts is very high among Turkish youth in Berlin and also in other European countries; it is much higher among boys than among girls. Only 3 percent of Muslim youth make it to college in Germany. Their language skills are low, which is not surprising because Turkish or Arabic is spoken at home, books are not found in many households, and the use of German (or English) is discouraged by the parents, who often do not master the language. Boys are sent to Koran schools but are not encouraged to study other subjects. Girls are often forbidden to go to school beyond the age of sixteen, let alone attend universities, because there they might be exposed to undesirable influences. When a Berlin school decided (after consultation with students and their parents) to insist on the use of the German language only at school, it came under heavy attack by the Turkish media even though most pupils and their parents favored the measure. Some well-meaning local protagonists of multiculturalism joined the protest because they believed that this was tantamount to cultural repression. But can a young generation advance socially and culturally unless they have mastered the language of the land?

Racism and xenophobia have been identified as factors responsible for the underachievement of Muslim youth. But this explanation fails to account for the scholastic success of pupils with an Indian and Far Eastern background, who score higher in most subjects than the average German or British student. Nor does it explain why Muslim girls acquit themselves much better than the boys. Could it be connected with the fact that girls are not allowed to go out in the street unaccompanied, whereas the boys spend most of their time there? Indian pupils in British schools have been doing twice as well as the Pakistanis, and those from the Far East have been outpacing almost everyone else.

There are many explanations, but the idea sometimes voiced that it is all the fault of the state or society is not plausible and will not help remedy the situation. Young people are told day in, day out, that they are victims of society and that it is not really their fault if they fail. As a result of these failures, a youth culture of violence and crime has developed that has little to do with religion. Despite attendance at Koran schools (more in Germany, with higher attendance, than in France and the United Kingdom), these young men are not well versed in their religion. They may go to the mosque on Fridays but will drink and take drugs afterward despite the religious ban. The main influence on these young people is neither the parental home nor the imams but the street gang. The parents have little authority, their way of life does not appeal to the offspring, they are not assertive enough, and they work too hard and earn too little. Old-fashioned Islam is of no great interest to many of them, either; a well-positioned imam in Britain said that "we are losing half of them." Only a few charismatic religious leaders who preach extreme action may have a certain following among young males. To understand the scenes in the schools and streets of Kreuzberg and the *banlieues,* a textbook on juvenile delinquency could be more helpful than the Koran.

School has the least authority; in France and the United Kingdom language is less of an impediment, but in Germany the pupils quite literally often do not understand what the teacher is saying and there is no effort to understand either the teacher or fellow pupils from other countries with different native languages. Many teachers do not succeed in imposing their authority, for if they dare to punish pupils for misbehavior or make any demands on them, they are accused of racism and discrimination. The streetwise pupils are adept at playing the race card.

Muslim youth culture varies to a certain extent from country to country. Common to them is the street sports gear (hooded sweatshirts, sneakers, etc.) and the machismo; their body language expresses aggression. They want respect, though it is not clear how they think such respect has been earned; perhaps it is based on the belief that "this street (quarter) is ours." In France and the United Kingdom hip-hop culture plays a central role; the texts of their songs express strong violence, often sadism. The street gang usually has a territorial base; Turks in Berlin have their own gangs, and the same is true with regard to Arabs and Kurds who arrived later in Germany. Sometimes the street gang is based on a certain village or district in the old country where the (extended) family originated. There has been a great deal of fighting between these territorial gangs; in Britain it has been quite often blacks against Indians (or Pakistanis) or, as in Brussels, Turks against black Africans.

Street gangs linger about aimlessly and often engage in petty crimes. In Britain gangs of Muslim background have largely replaced the Afro-Caribbeans as drug pushers, though the key positions are usually not in their hands. Dealing in stolen goods is another way to earn the money needed for their gear, hashish (heavier drugs are sold but seldom consumed), and other entertainment. Teachers do not dare to interfere, and the local police are reluctant to make arrests, for judges will usually release those who have been arrested, especially if they are underage. Some proceed to more serious forms of crime. This is a theme that the European Muslim communities have been very reluctant to deal with. Crime figures are difficult to obtain, but all experts agree that the percentage of young Muslims in European prisons far exceeds their proportion in the population. This also goes for cases of rape, which in many gangs have become part of the rite of passage, especially in France, and to a lesser degree in the United Kingdom, Scandinavia, and Australia. The victims are by no means always non-Muslim girls or women who "asked for it" through immodest attire and behavior but also sometimes young Muslim women; the *hijab* does not by any means always offer protection. . . .

This rise in European crime cannot, of course, be attributed only to immigration, but there is no doubt that it is one of the main reasons. The head of the London Metropolitan Police made it known that 80 percent of the crime committed on the London Underground was carried out by immigrants from Africa. The head of Berlin's police announced that one out of three young immigrants in that city had a criminal record. Such statistics mentioning ethnic or religious background are forbidden in France, but the high number of young Muslims in French prisons (70 percent of the prison population according to some estimates) is no secret.

How does one account for the great aggressiveness of these gangs, as manifested, for instance, in the French riots of November 2005 but also on many occasions before and after? Their lack of achievement undoubtedly adds to the general discontent. The issue of identity (or lack of it) is frequently mentioned in this context. Many of the young (second) generation do not feel at home in either the parents' homeland or the country in which they live. They feel that they are not accepted in Europe and may curse the host country in all languages, but they would feel even less at home in Turkey or North Africa or on the Indian subcontinent, and they have no wish to return to these homelands. . . .

Sexual repression almost certainly is another factor that is seldom, if ever, discussed within their communities or by outside observers. It could well be that such repression (as Tsvetan Todorov has explained) generates extra aggression, an observation that has also been made by young Muslim women. Young Muslim men cannot freely meet members of the opposite sex from inside their own community; homosexuality is considered an abomination, yet in fact according to many accounts it is frequently practiced—as it has been all through Muslim history. The rejection of the other society manifests itself in many ways, beginning with defacing of walls of buildings and escalating to the torching of cars, as has happened frequently in France. In extreme cases there is an urge to destroy everything at hand and to attack all comers, including the firefighters and first-aid technicians rushing to the ghettos to deal with an emergency.

European Union
ISLAMIST TERRORISM

Many young European Muslims, searching to give their lives a richer meaning and finding Western culture spiritually empty, are returning to their ancestral faith. Those among them who are particularly disaffected—while often seemingly assimilated and educated, even professionals—have been receptive to firebrand imams. Often imported from Arab countries and financed by the Saudi government, these imams despise Western values, demonize Jews, and preach the duty of jihad.* As a result of the preaching of these radical imams and the efforts of militant recruiters who spot likely candidates, terrorist cells have been established in various European cities. The Internet has become a powerful recruiting and networking tool for Al Qaeda, one of whose goals is the Islamization of Europe. Jihadist Web sites, numbering in the thousands, propagate extremism. They feature imams extolling Wahhabism, a puritanical, fundamentalist form of Islam; Islamists providing religious justification for holy war; images of dead Americans killed by "glorious" jihadists; suicide bombers giving their farewell speech; and instructions for making explosive devices.

Analysts fear that the 20 million Muslims residing in Europe, many of them alienated from European culture, poorly integrated into European society, and believing that the West has exploited Muslims and denigrated their faith, are

*Jihad is a complex term whose two essential meanings are: an internal striving by an individual for moral self-improvement, and a collective military struggle to defend Islam against its enemies and to extend Muslim power over other lands so that all people will be subject to God's laws as revealed to Muhammad. Today, when Osama bin Laden and his supporters identify themselves as jihadists or Islamists, moral striving is not their principal concern; for them jihad means the personal duty of every Muslim to wage holy war against God's enemies—those who obstruct the establishment of an Islamic world community in which all the laws ordained by God are strictly enforced. Jihadists view themselves as defenders of the true faith against its enemies and regard terrorism as a legitimate tactic in fulfilment of sacred obligation.

potential recruits for extremist Islamic groups, including Al Qaeda, and that European cities could become targets of fanatical jihadists. Extremist Islamist cells in Europe have engaged in numerous acts of terror. Much of the planning for 9/11 took place in Hamburg, Germany. In 2004, Muslim terrorists of North African origin, who identified with Al Qaeda, blew up four crowded commuter trains in Madrid, Spain, killing 191 and wounding about 2,000. In July 2005, Muslim suicide bombers killed more than 50 people and injured 700 in a terrorist attack on London's transit system. In a second attack two weeks later, the bombs failed to detonate and the suspected suicide bombers were arrested. The following year, British security foiled a terrorist plot to blow up several transatlantic flights departing Heathrow airport that would have killed more people than had perished on 9/11. That the planners and perpetrators of these attacks were not foreign jihadists, but British citizens raised and educated in Britain who were terrorizing their fellow citizens, was viewed by analysts as an ominous sign. German authorities reported that in 2004 some 32,000 Muslims were affiliated with radical Islamist organizations operating on German soil. Frequently these recruits have been radicalized by Arab imams trained in the Middle East, who proclaim that Islam is engaged in a holy war against the West and that martyrdom will redeem Muslim honor and assure victory.

Nor are Western-educated Muslims immune from the lure of jihad. It was a recently radicalized Dutch-born, Dutch-speaking, and Dutch-educated Muslim of Moroccan extraction who cruelly and gleefully ritually butchered Theo Van Gogh for making a film about the suppression of women in Muslim lands. One of the terrorists sentenced to death in Pakistan for the beheading of *Wall Street Journal* reporter Daniel Pearl was born in London and educated at exclusive British schools, including the London School of Economics. Doctors and engineers, in particular, seem drawn to radical Islam; several of these professionals have been involved in terrorist attacks in Britain. These terrorists are filled with moral outrage; they see themselves as idealists striking back at the West, which they perceive as waging a war against Islam in which their fellow Muslims are being humiliated, oppressed, and killed. European jihadists continue to recruit young Muslims to fight in Kashmir, Chechnya, Afghanistan, and Iraq.

Islam is also attracting European Christian converts whose zeal for their new religion can be harnessed for terrorist purposes. At the end of 2001, an alert flight attendant prevented Richard Reid, a recent British convert who discovered Islam while serving a prison sentence, from igniting an explosive device hidden in his shoe that would have blown up the plane in mid-air. In September 2007, German authorities charged a native German and youthful convert to Islam with heading a terrorist cell planning attacks against American targets in Germany that could have killed hundreds of people.

The following document, *EU Terrorism Situation and Trend Report 2007,* issued by the European Union, discusses Islamist terrorist attacks and activities in Europe in recent years.

Along with the failed terrorist attack that took place in Germany, Denmark and the UK each reported one attempted terrorist attack. No further information on prevented or disrupted Islamist terrorist attacks was made available by the Member States' law enforcement authorities.

GERMAN TROLLEY BOMB CASE

On 31 July 2006, two Improvised Explosive Devices (IEDs) packed in two suitcases were placed onboard two regional trains near Cologne in an attempted coordinated attack. The devices failed to detonate. Both so-called 'trolley bombs' were made up of a gas cylinder, an alarm clock, a functioning detonator and three PET bottles filled with petrol. Had the devices detonated, it is estimated that there would have been a significant loss of life in the two trains.

Two Lebanese nationals studying in Germany were subsequently arrested on suspicion of placing the IEDs on the trains.

The suspects were reported to have been motivated by the publication of the Danish cartoons of the Prophet Muhammad in German newspapers; it was also reported that the Internet played a role in preparations. Further, there were reports that the suspects had undergone a swift radicalisation process. The suspects initially intended to carry out the attack during the FIFA World Cup but changed their plans due to the security measures in place.

UK AIRPLANE PLOT

On 10 August 2006, a series of arrests took place in the UK in connection with an alleged suicide bombing plot. The suspects planned to smuggle the component parts of IEDs onto aircrafts and assemble and detonate them on board and in flight. Liquid explosives concealed in plastic soft drink bottles were to be detonated with battery powered detonators aboard trans-Atlantic airliners en route from the UK to the US. If successful, the attack would have caused mass murder of potentially thousands of civilian air travellers. . . .

Eleven suspects were charged in connection with the plot. The suspects were predominantly UK citizens of Pakistani descent. They were reportedly motivated to carry out the attack by the situation in Afghanistan and Iraq, and intended to strike a target that would hit both the UK and the US at the same time. They seem to have undergone a 'rapid radicalisation': in a matter of 'some weeks and months, not years,' they were prepared to kill civilians in a suicide attack.

DANISH 'HOMEGROWN' VOLLSMOSE GROUP

On 5 September 2006, nine individuals were arrested in Vollsmose, a suburb of Odense, Denmark. Seven were remanded in custody on suspicion of preparing a terrorist attack. Allegedly, they procured material and effects for making explosives. According to one account, the explosives were produced using an unknown quantity of ammonium nitrate and Triacetone Triperoxide (TATP) supplemented by metal splinter shrapnel to increase the bombs' destructive power.

The Danish Minister of Justice stated that the group had planned one or several terrorist attacks against undisclosed targets within Denmark. The motivation of the group remains unknown. However, several commentators have pointed to Denmark's military engagement in Iraq and the global row over the cartoons depicting the Prophet Muhammad.

As in the UK case, the members of the Vollsmose group were suspected of being so-called 'homegrown' terrorists. More precisely, they were predominantly young second-generation Muslim immigrants of Middle Eastern origin with Danish citizenship. One member of the group was a Danish convert to Islam.

ARRESTED SUSPECTS

During the period between October 2005 and December 2006, a total of 340 persons were reported as having been arrested on Islamist terrorism related offences. Two hundred and sixty arrests were carried out in 2006.

Less than ten percent of the arrested individuals were suspected of preparation, planning or execution of terrorist attacks. The arrests took place in the Czech Republic, Denmark, France, Germany, Italy, Spain and Sweden.

The vast majority of the arrested individuals were suspected of being members of a terrorist organisation. Other frequent criminal activities were financing of terrorism and facilitation. . . .

The bulk of the arrests took place in France, Spain, Italy and the Netherlands and the majority of those arrested came from Algeria, Morocco and Tunisia. Arrested suspects originating from North Africa were often loosely affiliated with North African terrorist groups, such as the *Salafist Group for Preaching and Combat*. . . .

TERRORIST ACTIVITIES

Propaganda

In October 2006, an Iraqi citizen was arrested in Germany on suspicion of providing support to foreign terrorist groups. He allegedly disseminated audio and video files showing leading personalities of *al-Qaeda* and *al-Qaeda in Mesopotamia*. In addition to this, in 2006 one person was arrested in Denmark for Islamist terrorist propaganda and two in the UK for soliciting murder by publishing inciting statements and running websites inciting murder, urging to fight *jihad* and raising funds, respectively. Law enforcement agencies investigated propaganda offences in Belgium, Denmark, France and Germany. The number of police investigations into this phenomenon seems small compared to the amount of propaganda circulating on the Internet. This is partly explained by the lack of a legal basis for arrests of or investigation against persons using the Internet in this manner. Law enforcement agencies also have difficulties in identifying individuals who spread Islamist terrorist propaganda on the Internet. As an example, in autumn 2005, a suspect arrested in the UK on charges of participating in an alleged bomb plot, turned out to be a key individual that had used the Internet to spread Islamist propaganda.

Financing of Terrorism

Financing of terrorism covers two distinct aspects: financing of terrorist attacks and funding of terrorist networks.

Relatively small sums are necessary to carry out a terrorist attack; estimates for the Madrid bombings in 2004 range from EUR 8,000 to 15,000. Given the small amount of money required, the prevention of terrorist financing appears to some extent unrealistic; hence priority is given to financial investigations into the money trail left by terrorists. . . .

There is little doubt that money for funding Islamist terrorist networks or organisations is gathered in the EU through legal and/or illegal means. In this regard, the fact that almost ten percent of all suspects arrested in the EU during the reporting period were involved in financial and material support to terrorist organisations is significant. These suspects are mostly linked to terrorist organisations, such as the GSPC, the GICM, or *al-Qaeda*.

Financial and logistic support to terrorist organisations is based on funds provided legally or illegally by sympathisers of terrorist groups.

Funding is procured by establishing and managing small companies as sources of legal income, which is then used to support radical groups inside and outside the EU. Another very significant source originates from private donations, and from the misuse of *zakat** payments by Muslims. The funds are mostly collected by charitable organisations or associations and individuals. . . .

There are strong suspicions that *zakat* money collected within the EU is used to fund terrorism. A UK-based charity reportedly remitted a large amount of money declared to be relief funds for earthquake victims to suspects in Pakistan who were involved in the UK airplane plot. Funds collected legally can be transferred worldwide using the banking system without arousing suspicion. . . .

The range of illegal sources for the funding of terrorism appears to cover most criminal activities ranging from vehicle-related crimes to forgery of identity and travel documents or financial crimes, such as the use of false credit cards. . . .

**Zakat* is the third pillar of Islam and refers to spending a fixed portion of one's wealth for the poor or needy.

Recruitment

Six Member States reported investigations into Islamist terrorist recruitment in the EU between October 2005 and December 2006.

In total, 24 individuals were arrested on suspicion of terrorist recruitment.

The individuals reported as having been arrested for recruitment were linked to the Iraqi Sunni organisation *Ansar al-Islam.* This may suggest that they were involved in recruiting volunteers in the EU for the support of the armed struggle against coalition troops in Iraq.

In most instances, the recruitment occurred in schools, spiritual meeting places like mosques, or in prisons. The modus operandi includes the use of propaganda material such as videos, tracts and movies supporting the claim that Muslims must take part in the global *jihad.*

Training

Eight persons were arrested in relation with terrorist training. The charges included plotting to establish a training camp, providing training and receiving training in terrorist techniques. . . .

In general, training in extremist ideology and terrorist techniques takes place overseas, where some of the terrorists receive military and specialist training. Nevertheless, one investigation concerned two training camps that were allegedly established in the South of England. In terrorist training camps, participants are taught a very radical interpretation of Islam and trained in handling explosives, as well as setting up and financing terrorist cells. Trainers usually belong to the militant categories of Islamists, maintaining international contacts with other members or networks.

The camps are mainly located in the Middle or Near East, or in South-East Asia. Training camps in the Sahel region, mostly controlled by *al-Qaeda in the Islamic Maghreb,* seem to acquire increasing importance and are used for the training of several terrorists originating in the Maghreb. Individuals that receive terrorist training remain in contact with both their facilitation networks and support cells. Religious or paramilitary training activities abroad might be an indicator that terrorists are in the early planning phase of an attack.

Facilitation

In 2006, a total of 52 individuals were arrested in seven Member States suspected of a wide range of offences related to facilitation of or support to terrorism. Two thirds of the suspected individuals were arrested in France and Spain.

Eighty-six percent of those arrested for facilitation were men, mainly North African or EU nationals.

In the reports contributed by the Member States, facilitation covers a wide range of support activities: provision of false identity documents, resources and fundraising for terrorist networks engaged in conflict areas. Other supporters of terrorism provide false administrative documents, consultancy services or assistance in marriages of convenience, in particular for illegal immigrants who adhere to Islamist ideologies. Several cells or networks dismantled in Spain and in Italy were found to be supporting North African groups in Europe and facilitating the dispatching of fighters to Iraq. Only a few of the cases reported concern the provision of false documentation for the use by Islamists. However, it should be noted that this offence is often considered a common law crime when no link with Islamist terrorism can be established.

SITUATION OUTSIDE THE EU

The perceived oppression of Islam or the presence of 'foreign' troops in Islamic lands is often invoked as justification for the execution of terrorist acts in several parts of the world, such as Chechnya, Kashmir, Iraq or Afghanistan. The idea that these local struggles are part of a global *jihad,* seen as a worldwide war between Islam and the non-believers, has been actively promoted by Islamist terrorist ideologues and leaders of Islamist terrorist groups, such as *al-Qaeda*. Whereas local insurgency or resistance groups aim at overthrowing or seceding from the affected state's government, the ideology of global *jihad* identifies the Western world, including the EU Member States, as the principle enemy and target. . . .

The report then discusses attacks on Westerners and Western targets in Afghanistan, Egypt, Algeria, Bali, and Jordan.

ISLAMIST TERRORIST PROPAGANDA

For more than a decade, supporters of Islamist terror groups have published written statements, articles by ideological leaders and online magazines on the Internet, exploiting the potential for swift and anonymous communication that this medium offers.

More recently, the use of static websites for the propagation of Islamist terrorist propaganda appears to be in decline: such websites are easily closed down by hackers or law-enforcement agencies. Terrorist groups and their supporters may find online forums that support a radical view of Islam to be a more secure way of disseminating their propaganda material. These forums target a particular audience and offer details of access to files stored on so-called 'free-storage sites.' Files containing, for instance, high-quality full-length films may be obtained from such sites. Since this material is spread over numerous web servers located in different countries, blocking access to all copies of the files becomes virtually impossible.

Arguably, the most professional and most productive propaganda outlet is currently the *al-Sahab Media Production Company. Al-Sahab* mainly produces video files which can take the form of documentaries, interviews, speeches or news programmes. Another characteristic of *al-Sahab's* products is that many of them are accompanied by English subtitles. Where the speaker uses English, Arabic subtitles are added. All known speeches by members of the original *al-Qaeda* leadership released after June 2006 carry the *al-Sahab* logo.

Other Islamist terrorist groups have their own propaganda outlets. Iraqi and Afghan Islamist insurgent groups publish audio and video speeches of their leaders and videos showing attacks on Iraqi and coalition forces under their own labels, such as *al-Furqan Media Production Company* of the *Islamic State of Iraq,* formerly known as *al-Qaeda* in *Mesopotamia,* or the *Voice of Jihad* of the *Taliban* in Afghanistan. It is often the case that these groups attempt to emulate the stylistic features and technical professionalism of *al-Sahab*. . . .

In general, 2006 saw a rise in the frequency of statements and communiqués by Islamist groups, especially *al-Qaeda*. The quality and style of video messages and filmed attacks are more professional and the techniques used are increasingly sophisticated. English, either spoken or in subtitles, is often the language of choice. This may be an indication that propagandists are attempting to reach as wide an audience as possible. The frequency and quality of such propaganda, together with the possibilities for global access, are signs of an ongoing coordinated media offensive by Islamist terrorist groups.

KEY FINDINGS AND TRENDS

- Failed and planned attacks by Islamist terrorist[s] as reported by Member States aimed at indiscriminate mass casualties.
- The London airplane plot and the trolley bomb case in Germany targeted civilians and transportation infrastructure in Member States.

  In both cases, the radicalisation process of the suspects is reported to have been rapid.
- The explosives of choice for Islamist terrorists are IEDs made with home-made explosives. At least two cases involved the use of TATP, a highly volatile explosive requiring a certain degree of expertise.
- The foiled plot in London demonstrates a high level of sophistication in the preparation of an attack and the ability to adapt to the latest security measures, as well as a high degree of creativity in attempting to circumvent them.
- The majority of the arrested suspects were born in Algeria, Morocco and Tunisia and had loose affiliations to North African terrorist groups, such as the GICM and the GSPC.

However, the suspects involved in the foiled airplane plot in London and the Danish Vollsmose group were born or raised in a Member State, including converts, who had been radicalised in Europe.

- The amount of women among those arrested suspected of Islamist terrorism was less than among all terrorism suspects and a large majority were EU citizens. No female suspects were arrested for planning, preparing or executing an attack.
- Islamist terrorist networks are funded from legal and illegal sources depending on the individuals involved. The range of illegal sources for Islamist terrorism funding varied from vehicle-related crimes to forgery of identity and travel documents or financial crimes, such as the use of false credit cards.
- Volunteers are recruited in the EU to support Islamist terrorist activities in Iraq, which has been promoted as the key scene of global *jihad* by Islamist propagandists. It seems likely that, should other regional conflicts, such as those in Somalia and Afghanistan, become 'marketed' as global *jihad,* more volunteers may be recruited in the EU to support them.
- The frequency of video statements by members of the original *al-Qaeda* leadership and other Islamist terrorists has shown a marked increase. The propaganda is of greater sophistication, of high quality and more professional. English is used more often, either in direct speech or in subtitles, allowing potential access to a wider audience than previous Arabic-only publications. These facts may point to a coordinated global media offensive by Islamist terrorists.

5 The New Anti-Semitism: Old Hatreds Revived

In recent years Muslim countries and Europe have experienced a wave of Jew-hatred that has become a cause for alarm. In 2007, the Parliamentary Assembly of the Council of Europe noted: "Far from having been eliminated, anti-Semitism is today on the rise in Europe. It appears in a variety of forms and is becoming relatively commonplace." That same year, Labor MP Denis MacShane, who chaired a committee of British parliamentarians that studies anti-Semitism in Europe, wrote: "Hatred of Jews has reached new heights in Europe and many points south and east of the old continent." And in 2008 a report to Congress prepared by the U.S. State Department stated: "Over much of the past decade, U.S. embassies worldwide have noted an increase in anti-Semitic incidents, such as attacks on Jewish people, property, community institutions, and religious facilities. Other governments, international institutions, and nongovernmental groups have documented similar trends."

Gabriel Schoenfeld
THE RETURN OF ANTI-SEMITISM

The following selection from *The Return of Anti-Semitism* (2004) by Gabriel Schoenfeld describes anti-Semitic attacks in Europe in the first four years of the twenty-first century. In succeeding years anti-Semitic hate crimes persisted, including in 2006 the protracted torture and eventual murder of a young Jew

in a Paris suburb by a predominantly Muslim gang and the stabbing of nine worshippers in a Moscow synagogue by a right-wing extremist. On a positive note, in several lands judicial systems and government leaders are now responding to the resurgence of anti-Semitism, recognizing that this descent into the irrational threatens democratic values.

The outbreak of the second Palestinian uprising in September 2000, the so-called al-Aqsa intifada, triggered a swelling tide of spontaneous and/or semi-organized attacks on Jewish symbols, Jewish institutions, and Jews themselves. In the first weeks alone, more than 250 anti-Semitic incidents occurred in Europe. Though the proximate cause of the violence was the Middle East conflict, it was not directed, as one might suppose, at Israeli visitors, Israeli companies or Israeli diplomatic facilities. Rather, it was aimed at European Jews. It occurred in almost every country on the continent, but it was especially evident in peaceful, democratic, law-abiding Western Europe—a part of the world that for quite some time now has prided itself on the personal safety it affords its inhabitants.

It would require a separate book just to rehearse the entire litany, but even a sampling suffices to convey the scope and intensity of the violence. In England and France, the two countries with the most sizable Jewish populations, six synagogues were burned to the ground in the first weeks of the intifada; another twenty-four were the victims of arson attacks. A number of the attacks were timed to coincide with the High Holy Day of Yom Kippur: in Paris, a sniper fired an M-16 rifle into the city's Great Synagogue while services were going on. Elsewhere, Jews walking to synagogue were struck with stones, and even schoolchildren were harassed by assailants. "Three More Synagogues Attacked in France," was the Associated Press headline in mid-October. In Great Britain, a yeshiva student was stabbed on a bus, synagogues in major cities were vandalized, Torah scrolls destroyed.

Elsewhere it was the same. In Antwerp, Belgium, worshippers were cursed and threatened with violence as they walked to synagogue. In Brussels, an elderly Jewish man was set upon and beaten so badly he required hospitalization. Molotov cocktails were hurled into a Düsseldorf synagogue. In the German city of Weimar, vandals dubbed swastikas and smashed windows at a monument commemorating the Buchenwald concentration camp. More windows were smashed at a synagogue in Berlin. Some 250 people in Essen attacked the local synagogue with stones. In the publication *Anti-Semitism Worldwide*, which records all such incidents, one can read of similar violence in every corner of Europe: Salonika, Florence, Venice, Rome, Madrid, Geneva, Emmen and Oss in the Netherlands, Malmö in Sweden.

As severe as it was, this wave turned out to be merely a prelude. A year later, the September 11 terrorist attack *on America* led to a sharp increase in European violence against Jews. According to the authoritative *Anti-Semitism Worldwide*, anti-Semitic incidents in Great Britain "rose by 150 percent in September and October [2001] over August 2001. The figures for September and October were the second and the third highest monthly totals ever recorded. In France, 44 percent of major violent incidents and attacks for the year 2001 took place in September and October."

And the curve rose still higher when, in late March and April 2002, Israel responded to the ongoing intifada by entering the West Bank in force. That military operation was precipitated by a months-long campaign of Arab terror within Israel whose culminating outrage—the bombing of a hotel ballroom in the central Israeli city of Netanya—had snuffed out the lives of 29 and injured more than 140 as they sat at their seder tables on the first night of Passover. . . .

Another consequence—perhaps predictable by now—of Israel's action to defend itself was an upsurge in anti-Semitic violence *in Europe* unprecedented since the 1930s. From east to west, the list of incidents in April 2002 alone is too long to summarize. In the Ukrainian capital of Kiev, some fifty youths chanting "Kill the kikes" descended on the city's central synagogue on a Saturday evening, broke twenty windows and beat the director of the religious school with stones. In Greece, Jewish cemeteries were vandalized in what the press termed "anti-Jewish acts of revenge," and the Holocaust memorial in Salonika, a city whose fifty thousand Jews had been rounded up and deported to Nazi death camps in 1943, was defaced with Palestinian slogans. In Slovakia, Jewish cemeteries were desecrated in what an official described as the "biggest attack on the Jewish community since the Holocaust."

In the heart of democratic Europe, one particular scene of violent anti-Israel demonstrations was Amsterdam, Holland, where "protesters" hurled rocks and bottles and small roving bands used stones and bicycles to shatter store windows. In neighboring Belgium, five firebombs were tossed into a synagogue in a working-class district of Brussels, and a Jewish bookstore was severely damaged by arsonists; a synagogue in Antwerp was firebombed with Molotov cocktails, while in the same city, a travel agency specializing in trips to Israel was set alight. In Germany, two Orthodox Jews were beaten while walking on Berlin's chic Kurfürstendamm, in the heart of the shopping district. A woman wearing a Star of David necklace was attacked in the subway. Jewish memorials in Berlin were defaced with swastikas. A synagogue was spray-painted with the words, "Six Million Is Not Enough." Anti-Israel demonstrators hurled bricks through windows as they marched.

In England, reported London's *Express*, "race-hate attacks on the Jewish community have soared." In the first ten days of April there were fifteen anti-Semitic incidents, including eight physical assaults. Most of the attacks were on Jews walking alone, set upon and beaten by small roving bands. At least two of the victims required hospitalization.

But it was France, once again, that lay at the epicenter of aggression. Of that country's four major outbreaks of anti-Semitism over the entire post–World War II era, the latest wave, according to one expert analyst, has been "stronger than all the rest." The *New York Times* concurs with this estimate, characterizing the current situation as "the worst spate of anti-Jewish violence" in France in the last half-century.

The first two weeks of April 2002 alone saw "nearly 360 crimes against Jews and Jewish institutions," according to the French interior ministry. Gangs of hooded men descended on Jewish victims and struck them with iron clubs. Buses carrying Jewish schoolchildren were stoned. Cemeteries were desecrated. Synagogues, Jewish schools, student facilities and kosher stores were defaced, battered and firebombed. On April 1, the Or Aviv synagogue in Marseille was burned to the ground, its prayerbooks and Torah scrolls consumed by flames; it was one of five synagogues in France attacked in that period. A kosher butcher store was sprayed with gunfire in Toulouse. Near Lyons, an Orthodox couple was assaulted and beaten on the street. At a soccer field in Bondy, a suburb of Paris, a band of thugs wearing masks and wielding iron bars, heavy steel balls and strips of barbed wired descended upon a teenage Jewish soccer team and set to work beating its members while chanting "death to the Jews." The goalkeeper, a fifteen-year-old boy, ended up in a hospital, requiring a half-dozen stitches on his head. In the heart of Paris's Jewish district, a young Jewish boy was held in captivity for two hours, beaten and humiliated before being released.

This inadequate survey of one brief interval is infinitely expandable, for the passage of time has brought new outrages. In general, the pace of violence rises and falls in conjunction with the intensity of the conflict in the Middle East—a linkage that suggests, correctly, that European Muslims dominate the field in the violence. There have been exceptions: in Germany, France and England, some incidents have been the work of neo-Nazi extremists joined by bands of skinheads, and in the former Soviet bloc, particularly in Ukraine and Russia, soccer hoodlums, neonationalists and neofascists are responsible for a major share of attacks. But elsewhere, and particularly in Western Europe, the identity of the perpetrators has been fairly consistent.

The violence in Belgium, as we learn from arrests made there, has been overwhelmingly the work of Arabs. The stoning of the synagogue in Essen occurred during a demonstration organized by the German-Lebanese Friendship Association. The yeshiva student attacked on a bus in London was stabbed by an Algerian, and it was Arabs who desecrated the synagogues in Great Britain. Almost all of the attacks in France, police records suggest, have been at Muslim hands; according to the French minister of the interior, the perpetrators have generally been "Arab youths from North African countries."

Marvin Perry
MUSLIM DIASPORA, FAR RIGHT, NEW LEFT, AND THE "LONGEST HATRED"

Many Europeans are fearful of Islamic terrorism and of becoming a multicultural society in which alien Muslim ways will undermine traditional European culture. But increasingly they are sharing with the Muslim diaspora a hatred for Zionism and Israel, which is translating into anti-Semitism. In the decades following the Holocaust, overt anti-Semitism appeared to have receded in Western Europe. The outbursts of the far right did not greatly affect the surviving Jews and their descendants, who represented a model of successful integration. But what Labor MP Denis MacShane concludes for Britain also describes much of the Continent: "The most worrying discovery of this inquiry is that anti-Jewish sentiment is entering the mainstream, appearing in everyday conversation of people who consider themselves neither racist nor prejudiced."

The following selection describes the relationship between the Arab/Israel dispute and the recrudescence of anti-Semitism in Europe. Some of the material is drawn from Marvin Perry and Frederick M. Schweitzer, *Anti-Semitism: Myth and Hate from Antiquity to the Present* (New York: Palgrave Macmillan, paperback edition, 2004).

"It is Islamism [extremist Islam] the ideology that has unleashed new twenty-first-century anti-Semitism," observes Labor MP Denis MacShane, "and it is impossible to discuss the problem without dealing with Islamism." The creation of Israel on what is perceived as inviolable Muslim land and the Jewish state's ongoing conflict with the Palestinians have stirred the cauldron of Jew-hatred in the Arab/Muslim world. Now reaching epidemic proportions, anti-Semitism has become a principal theme in Middle Eastern media and a motivation for attacks on Jews by some Muslims living in Europe. As Cardinal Tucci, the director of Vatican Radio, stated in November 2003: "Now in the whole Muslim world, in the media, the radio, television, in schools, a whole system inciting to anti-Semitism exists. It is the worst anti-Semitism that can be imagined after Nazi anti-Semitism, if not its equal."

Contemporary Muslim anti-Semitism borrowed considerably from traditional European anti-Semitism—Christian, nationalist, and Nazi. Like the Nazis, much of the Muslim world perceives Jews as a criminal people that threatens all humanity, blames the Jews for their misfortunes, and holds out the image of a utopian future once Israel is eradicated and the Jews eliminated. As in Nazi Germany, the media in the Arab/Muslim world are often filled with repulsive caricatures of Jews—dark, stooped, sinister, hook-nosed, devil-like creatures—many of them taken from Nazi works. In Arab sermons, classroom school books, and on the Internet, Jews are often referred to as "accursed," "descendants of apes and pigs," "the scum of the human race," "the rats of the world," "bacteria," "vampires," "usurers," and "whoremongers."

No accusation against Jews is too absurd not to be included in the litany of Jewish evil propagated in the Muslim media, and not just by extremists. Hamas holds Jews responsible for the French Revolution, the Russian Revolution, both world wars, and the atomic bombing of Hiroshima and Nagasaki. Osama Bin Laden maintains that Jews, "in accordance with their religion, believe that human beings are their slaves and that those who refuse [to recognize this] should be put to death." Some mainstream Arab media have even revived the medieval canard that Jews are required to murder non-Jewish children in order to obtain their blood for making unleavened bread for Passover. Denying the Holocaust is very common; so too is celebrating Hitler's mass murder of Jews. A columnist for Al-Akhbar, considered a moderate newspaper sponsored by the Egyptian government, gives "thanks to Hitler of blessed memory," but with one reservation: not enough Jews perished. And Dr. Ahmed Abu Halabiyah, rector of advanced studies at the Islamic University of Gaza, is more representative than unique; similar sentiments are frequently voiced in the Arab media and even school textbooks: "The Jews . . . . must be butchered and must be killed. . . . It is forbidden to have mercy in your hearts for the Jews in any place and in any land, make war on them anywhere that you find yourself. Any place that you meet them, kill them." Propagated over the Internet and by radical imams in mosques throughout Europe, this demonization of the Jew—together with scenes of violent conflict between Israelis and Palestinians and Hezbollah frequently depicted on television—has incited some Muslim youth in Europe to acts of intimidation, physical assault, and vandalism against Jews. On a positive note, in a number of European cities, representatives of Muslim and Jewish communities are engaging in interfaith dialogue, and some Muslim intellectuals and organizations have condemned anti-Semitic outbursts.

In addition to the incidents initiated by anti-Semitic Muslims residing in various European lands, analysts have pointed to the ongoing Jew-hatred of the far right, and a rather new phenomenon, a growing anti-Semitism afflicting the left.

As in the past, European anti-Semitism remains a bulwark of the far Right, traditionally hostile to the Enlightenment's legacy of reason, political freedom, and tolerance. Principally extreme nationalists, racists, fascists, and neo-Nazis, they propagate Holocaust denial and Jewish conspiracy theories. For example, Jews invented a "Holocaust hoax" in order to extract compensation from Germany; Jews control the world's media and finances and are conspiring to dominate the planet; Jews are the real power behind the U.S. government; Jews are a threat to the nation.

Particularly in Eastern Europe and the Russian Federation, where hatred of Jews has a long history, extreme nationalist groups employ the terminology and myths of nineteenth- and early twentieth-century Christian and xenophobic racist anti-Semitism to defame Jews, and urge the destruction of Israel. In Russia, Belarus, Romania, and other lands, ultranationalist groups reissue and sell classic anti-Semitic literature, and their newspapers and periodicals feature anti-Jewish diatribes. In the Ukraine, the Interregional Academy of Personal Management (MAUP), a private institution with an enrollment of perhaps 50,000 at its various campuses and with considerable funding from sympathizers abroad, incorporates anti-Semitism in its curriculum, organizes anti-Semitic conferences, and publishes and sells literature that perpetuate anti-Jewish myths. David Duke, former Grand Wizard of the Ku Klux Klan, a white supremacist and propagator of the myth of a Jewish plot for world domination, teaches a course on international relations and was awarded a Ph.D. for a dissertation on Zionism. In a statement expressing solidarity with Iranian president Mahmoud Ahmadinejad's call for Israel's destruction, MAUP's president declared: "We'd like to remind that the Living God Jesus Christ said to the Jews two thousand years ago: 'Your father is a devil!'" He called Israel "the most threat to modern civilization." In 2006, an article in one of its leading publications affirmed the noxious libel that Jews murdered Christian children to obtain their blood for the Passover matzoh. (The Ukrainian government is trying to make it difficult for the school to engage in these anti-Semitic activities.)

During the Nazi era and for decades before, the Left—liberals, socialists, trade unionists, and intellectuals, including many academics—had been the strongest defenders of Jews against their detractors and oppressors. But now the distinguishing feature of the "new anti-Semitism" is its adoption by the Left who employ anti-Semitic language and imagery to express their support for the Palestinians and to delegitimize Israel. Analysts who have investigated this issue point out that the New Left's demonization of Israel as a criminal state and singling it out for vilification among all the states in the world (some of them with dreadful human rights records) transcends legitimate criticism of Israeli policies, which Israelis themselves engage in. In other words, these activities cross the line into anti-Semitism. So too does equating Zionism with Nazism and accusing the Israeli government of using Nazi-like methods in a campaign of genocide or ethnic cleansing against the Palestinian people. Also anti-Semitic is participation in rallies and programs where the Star of David is twisted into a swastika and demonstrators shout "Death to Israel." Or publishing cartoons with Israeli leaders or soldiers dressed in SS uniforms.

Viewing themselves as strongly anti-racist, anti-imperialist, and defenders of oppressed non-Westerners, New Left intellectuals frequently denounce Israel and Zionism as a racist, colonizing, and militaristic force that has to be overcome. New Left anti-Zionists see the Palestinians, including the organizations that sponsor suicide bombers, as victims—the role once assigned to Jews—and freedom fighters; and the Jews, who have lost their victim status, are now castigated as brutal oppressors, today's Nazis. When New Left intellectuals draw parallels between the Jewish state and the Third Reich, they intend to say that Israelis—and by extension Jews everywhere, the vast majority of whom support Israel—are morally equivalent to Nazis, the Jews' worst oppressors. Bernard Harrison, a non-Jewish British analytic philosopher explores the meaning of this parallelism:

> . . . Nazism, and its symbol the swastika, have become universally recognizable stereotypes of evil. Hence, to assert of any group or movement that it is indistinguishable from the Nazis or from Nazism is precisely to stigmatize it *as evil*, with the conceptually licensed implication that there is, literally, *nothing* to be said in its favor; that it is irredeemably bad . . . that the only desirable thing is that . . . it should be brought to an end, expunged from the face of the world. . . . That the Jews are an inherently irredeemably evil race is, after all, the central proposition of political anti-Semitism. To attach the label "Nazi" to Israel, or to couple the Star of David with the swastika. . . . is to defame Israel by association with the most powerful symbol of evil. . . . Moreover, the use of the Star of David in this context, a Jewish rather than a specifically Israeli symbol, makes it easy to extend the identification with absolute evil from Israel to the Jewish people in general.

To the New Left, the very idea of the Jews recreating a state in their ancient homeland is anathema, a hateful legacy of European nationalism, racism, and imperialism. They view Israel as illegitimate and welcome its disappearance as a boon to humanity. Often the Left's thinking is infused with hatred of America, which they demonize as wickedly imperialist, capitalist, and a selfish promoter of globalization; thus in demeaning Israel, they are also attacking the United States, Israel's staunch ally. It has been suggested that the New Left's effort to depict Israelis as brutal racist murderers as bad as the Nazis relieves Europeans of any remaining guilt they might have for the Holocaust in which people from every German-occupied European land assisted the Nazis in rounding up Jews for deportation to death camps and benefited from the seizure of Jewish property.

In their sympathy with the Palestinian cause and disdain for Israel, many journalists and intellectuals have presented an egregiously one-sided account of the conflict, which, often, could only be labeled as anti-Semitic. Reportage in the British press of the Israeli invasion into the West Bank city of Jenin revealingly illustrates this last point. After suffering numerous suicide bombings that killed and maimed hundreds of its citizens, including many children, in the spring of 2002 the Israeli army moved into Jenin in order to break up the terrorist cells. On April 15, a prominent columnist for the *Evening Standard* described the Israeli incursion as a "massacre and a cover-up of genocide." *The Times* of London's correspondent reported from Jenin in ominous tones: "Rarely in more than a decade of war reporting from Bosnia, Chechnya, Sierra Leone, Kosovo, have I seen such deliberate destruction, such disrespect for human life." From Jenin the Jerusalem correspondent for the *London Independent* sent this dispatch: "A monstrous war crime that Israel has tried to cover up for a fortnight has finally been exposed." He then spoke of "killing fields [a naked allusion to the genocidal killings in Cambodia by the Pol Pot regime]" and the "ghastly reek of rotting human bodies everywhere." Some editorial writers and columnists in the British press compared the Israeli government to al-Qaeda and the Taliban. After separate investigations by the Palestine Authority, the Israeli government, and the United Nations, the tale of mass murder was dismissed; it turns out that the number of Palestinian dead was between 46 and 56, most of them combatants in militia uniforms in the vicious house-to-house fighting that also took the lives of 23 Israelis. (Fewer Palestinian noncombatants perished than did the 28 Jews attending a Passover seder in Netanya who were murdered by a suicide bomber.) Had the Israelis relied on artillery and air bombardments, the number of Palestinians killed would have been significantly higher and Israeli casualties fewer. But seeking to avoid civilian casualties, Israel opted to flush out the terrorists by sending its soldiers into Jenin's sniper-infested streets and alleys and booby-trapped houses. Surely some powerful negative images of Israel and Jews—grounded in medieval and modern myths and stereotypes—prompted British reporters to thrash the Jewish state.

That same desire to defame Israel and Jews infected academics, who mutilate language in their rush to vilify. Tom Paulin, a prominent poet and Oxford academic, called the Israeli army the "Zionist SS"; the Portuguese Nobel laureate José Saramago compared Israeli actions in the West Bank with Auschwitz; and British professor Mona Baker spoke of the events "as some kind of Holocaust." And in an e-mail, professor Michael Sinnott, Baker's colleague at the University of Manchester, wrote: "With the recent crop of atrocities the Zionist state is now fully living down to Zionism's historical and cultural origins as the mirror image of Nazism."* In April 2005

---

*Comparisons with Nazism and the Holocaust are not only mean-spirited but also historically absurd. In the second intifada lasting from 2000 to 2007, some 4,200 Palestinians died, more than half of them armed combatants. Casualties for Palestinian civilians would have been considerably lower had militants not fired their rockets from and sought safety in residential areas. Over a two-year period, some 1.1 million Jews perished at Auschwitz, most of them in gas chambers. Millions more were murdered in other death camps or were slaughtered by special murder squads operating on conquered Russian territory. On September 29 and 30, 1941, alone, the Germans killed more than 33,000 Jews at Babi Yar in Ukraine, one of many massacres carried out by these squads. Unfortunately, these insidious comparisons are not without effect. In a poll conducted in 2004 by the German University of Bielefeld, 51 percent of the respondents concurred with the following statement: "What the state of Israel does today to the Palestinians, is in principle not different from what the Nazis did in the Third Reich to the Jews."

the British Association of University Teachers boycotted two Israeli universities, Haifa and Bar-Ilan, supposedly for "repressing" academic freedom; its executive designated Israel a "colonial apartheid state, more insidious than South Africa," and called for "removal of this regime."

The Arab-Israeli struggle, observes British commentator Melanie Phillips, "has unleashed an apparently unstoppable torrent of lies, distortions, libels, abandonment of objectivity and the substitution of malice and hatred for truth, all of which pours relentlessly out of the British and European media and establishment. And this morphs seamlessly into a public animosity against 'the Jews.'" And the roots of this animosity are deep and strong, notes Pilar Roha, a member of the Spanish parliament:

> Europe committed the worst crime: the industrial extermination of a people and a culture; and in spite of everything it did not succeed in vaccinating itself against its old hate. Europe liberated itself from most of its Jews but not from anti-Semitism. This explains its pro-Palestinian hysteria, its ferociously anti-Semitic left, its macabre banalization of the Holocaust.

Jew-hatred and the irrational myths associated with it that undermine rational thinking and incite barbaric violence, transcend a purely Jewish concern. They threaten the core values of Western civilization, as Nazism so painfully demonstrated.

6 In Defense of European Values

Like the period between the world wars, the years leading up to the new millennium represented an appropriate time to reassess the legacy of Europe. By the late twentieth century, its status might have appeared diminished. Europe's global hegemony was dealt an irreparable blow by the Second World War. Subsequent attempts by the peoples of the Third World at securing liberation sometimes elicited a shockingly brutal response from their mother countries. And even though the Common Market and later the European Union helped raise the standard of living on the Continent to unprecedented heights and rendered it an economic dynamo, some observers felt that Europe had lost its soul, opting for creature comforts over the culture and ideals that made it great.

Nevertheless, the traditional values that have underlain and inspired European achievements in the modern age—and that represent Europe's legacy to America—continue to find their advocates. At times they have extolled European civilization in the face of critics inclined to belittle its significance. Others call for Europe to embrace its historic roots. To all such commentators, Europe in the twenty-first century remains vital and enduring.

Jacques Ellul
THE BETRAYAL OF THE WEST

Jacques Ellul (1912–1994), a French sociologist with a pronounced moralist bent, is known for his study of the impact of technology and bureaucracy on the modern world. Ellul wrote *The Betrayal of the West* (1978), excerpts from which

follow, to defend Western civilization from its many detractors. His ideas remain pertinent more than thirty years after the book's appearance.

I am not criticizing or rejecting other civilizations and societies; I have deep admiration for the institutions of the Bantu and other peoples (the Chinese among them) and for the inventions and poetry and architecture of the Arabs. I do not claim at all that the West is superior. In fact, I think it absurd to lay claim to superiority of any kind in these matters. What criterion would you apply? What scale of values would you use? I would add that the greatest fault of the West since the seventeenth century has been precisely its belief in its own unqualified superiority in all areas.

The thing, then, that I am protesting against is the silly attitude of western intellectuals in hating their own world and then illogically exalting all other civilizations. Ask yourself this question: If the Chinese have done away with binding the feet of women, and if the Moroccans, Turks, and Algerians have begun to liberate their women, whence did the impulse to these moves come from? From the West, and nowhere else! Who invented the "rights of man"? The same holds for the elimination of exploitation. Where did the move to socialism originate? In Europe, and in Europe alone. The Chinese, like the Algerians, are inspired by western thinking as they move toward socialism. Marx was not Chinese, nor was Robespierre an Arab. How easily the intellectuals forget this! The whole of the modern world, for better or for worse, is following a western model; no one imposed it on others, they have adopted it themselves, and enthusiastically.

I shall not wax lyrical about the greatness and benefactions of the West. Above all, I shall not offer a defense of the material goods Europe brought to the colonies. We've heard that kind of defense too often: "We built roads, hospitals, schools, and dams; we dug the oil wells. . . ." And the reason I shall say nothing of this invasion by the technological society is that I think it to be the West's greatest crime, as I have said at length elsewhere. The worst thing of all is that we exported our rationalist approach to things, our "science," our conception of the state, our bureaucracy, our nationalist ideology. It is this, far more surely than anything else, that has destroyed the other cultures of the world and shunted the history of the entire world onto a single track.

But is that all we can say of the West? No, the essential, central, undeniable fact is that the West was the first civilization in history to focus attention on the individual and on freedom. Nothing can rob us of the praise due us for that. We have been guilty of denials and betrayals (of these we shall be saying something more), we have committed crimes, but we have also caused the whole of mankind to take a gigantic step forward and to leave its childhood behind.

This is a point we must be quite clear on. If the world is everywhere rising up and accusing the West, if movements of liberation are everywhere under way, what accounts for this? Its sole source is the proclamation of freedom that the West has broadcast to the world. The West, and the West alone, is responsible for the movement that has led to the desire for freedom and to the accusations now turned back upon the West.

Today men point the finger of outrage at slavery and torture. Where did that kind of indignation originate? What civilization or culture cried out that slavery was unacceptable and torture scandalous? Not Islam, or Buddhism, or Confucius, or Zen, or the religions and moral codes of Africa and India! The West alone has defended the inalienable rights of the human person, the dignity of the individual, the man who is alone with everyone against him. But the West did not practice what it preached? The extent of the West's fidelity is indeed debatable: the whole European world has certainly not lived up to its own ideal all the time, but to say that it has never lived up to it would be completely false.

In any case, that is not the point. The point is that the West originated values and goals that spread throughout the world (partly through conquest) and inspired man to demand his freedom, to take his stand in the face of society and affirm his value as an individual. I shall not be presumptuous enough to try to "define" the freedom of the individual. . . .

. . . The West gave expression to what man—every man—was seeking. The West turned the whole human project into a conscious, deliberate business. It set the goal and called it freedom, or, at later date, individual freedom. It gave direction to all the forces that were working in obscure ways, and brought to light the value that gave history its meaning. Thereby, man became man.

The West attempted to apply in a conscious, methodical way the implications of freedom. The Jews were the first to make freedom the key to history and to the whole created order. From the very beginning their God was the God who liberates; his great deeds flowed from a will to give freedom to his people and thereby to all mankind. This God himself, moreover, was understood to be sovereignly free (freedom here was often confused with arbitrariness or with omnipotence). This was something radically new, a discovery with explosive possibilities. The God who was utterly free had nothing in common with the gods of eastern and western religions; he was different precisely because of his autonomy.

The next step in the same movement saw the Greeks affirming both intellectual and political liberty. They consciously formulated the rules for a genuinely free kind of thinking, the conditions for human freedom, and the forms a free society could take. Other peoples were already living in cities, but none of them had fought so zealously for the freedom of the city in relation to other cities, and for the freedom of the citizen within the city.

The Romans took the third step by inventing civil and institutional liberty and making political freedom the key to their entire politics. Even the conquests of the Romans were truly an unhypocritical expression of their intention of freeing peoples who were subject to dictatorships and tyrannies the Romans judged degrading. It is in the light of that basic thrust that we must continue to read Roman history. Economic motives undoubtedly also played a role, but a secondary one; to make economic causes the sole norm for interpreting history is in the proper sense superficial and inadequate. You cannot write history on the basis of your suspicions! If you do, you only project your own fantasies.

I am well aware, of course, that in each concrete case there was darkness as well as light, that liberty led to wars and conquests, that it rested on a base of slavery. I am not concerned here, however, with the excellence or defects of the concrete forms freedom took; I am simply trying to say (as others have before me) that at the beginning of western history we find the awareness, the explanation, the proclamation of freedom as the meaning and goal of history.

No one has ever set his sights as intensely on freedom as did the Jews and Greeks and Romans, the peoples who represented the entire West and furthered its progress. In so doing, they gave expression to what the whole of mankind was confusedly seeking. In the process we can see a progressive approach to the ever more concrete: from the Jews to the Greeks, and from the Greeks to the Romans there is no growth in consciousness, but there is the ongoing search for more concrete answers to the question of how freedom can be brought from the realm of ideas and incarnated in institutions, behavior, thinking, and so on.

Today the whole world has become the heir of the West, and we Westerners now have a twofold heritage: we are heirs to the evil the West has done to the rest of the world, but at the same time we are heirs to our forefathers' consciousness of freedom and to the goals of freedom they set for themselves. Other peoples, too, are heirs to the evil that has been inflicted on them, but now they have also inherited the consciousness of and desire for freedom. Everything they do today and everything they seek is an expression of what the western world has taught them. . . .

. . . Everything used to be so organized that wealth and poverty were stable states, determined (for example) by the traditional, accepted hierarchy, and that this arrangement was regarded as due to destiny or an unchangeable divine will. The West did two things: it destroyed the hierarchic structures and it did away with the idea of destiny. It thus showed the poor that their state was not something inevitable. This is something Marx is often credited with having done, but only because people are ignorant [of history]. It was Christianity that did away with the idea of destiny and fate. . . .

Once Christianity had destroyed the idea of destiny or fate, the poor realized that they were poor, and they realized that their condition was not inevitable. Then the social organisms that had made it possible to gloss over this fact were challenged and undermined from within.

Against all this background we can see why the whole idea of revolution is a western idea. Before the development of western thought, and apart from it, no revolution ever took place. Without the individual and freedom and the contradictory extremes to which freedom leads, a society cannot engender a revolution. Nowhere in the world—and I speak as one with a knowledge of history—has there ever been a revolution, not even in China, until the western message penetrated that part of the world. Present-day revolutions, whether in China or among the American Indians, are the direct, immediate, unmistakable fruit of the western genius. The entire world has been pupil to the West that it now rejects. . . .

. . . I wish only to remind the reader that the West has given the world a certain number of values, movements, and orientations that no one else has provided. No one else has done quite what the West has done. I wish also to remind the reader that the whole world is living, and living almost exclusively, by these values, ideas, and stimuli. There is nothing original about the "new" thing that is coming into existence in China or Latin America or Africa: it is all the fruit and direct consequence of what the West has given the world.

In the fifties it was fashionable to say that "the third world is now entering upon the stage of history." The point was not, of course, to deny that Africa or Japan had a history. What the cliché was saying, and rightly saying, was that these peoples were now participating in the creative freedom of history and the dialectic of the historical process. Another way of putting it is that the West had now set the whole world in motion. It had released a tidal wave that would perhaps eventually drown it. There had been great changes in the past and vast migrations of peoples; there had been planless quests for power and the building of gigantic empires that collapsed overnight. The West represented something entirely new because it set the world in movement in every area and at every level; it represented, that is, a coherent approach to reality. Everything—ideas, armies, the state, philosophy, rational methods, and social organization—conspired in the global change the West had initiated.

It is not for me to judge whether all this was a good thing or bad. I simply observe that the entire initiative came from the West, that everything began there. I simply observe that the peoples of the world had abided in relative ignorance and [religious] repose until the encounter with the West set them on their journey.

Please, then, don't deafen us with talk about the greatness of Chinese or Japanese civilization. These civilizations existed indeed, but in a larval or embryonic state; they were approximations, essays. They always related to only one sector of the human or social totality and tended to be static and immobile. Because the West was motivated by the ideal of freedom and had discovered the individual, it alone launched society in its entirety on its present course.

Again, don't misunderstand me. I am not saying that European science was superior to Chinese science, nor European armies to Japanese armies; I am not saying that the Christian religion was superior to Buddhism or Confucianism; I am not saying that the French or English political system was superior to that of the Han dynasty. I am saying only that the West discovered what no one else had discovered; freedom and the individual, and that this discovery later set everything else in motion. Even the most solidly established religions could not help changing under the influence. . . .

It was not economic power or sudden technological advances that made the West what it is. These played a role, no doubt, but a negligible one in comparison with the great change—the discovery of freedom and the individual—that represents the goal and desire implicit in the history of all civilizations. That is why, in speaking of the West, I unhesitatingly single out freedom from the whole range of values. After all, we find justice, equality, and peace everywhere. Every civilization that has attained a certain level has claimed to be a civilization of justice or peace. But which of them has ever spoken of the individual? Which of them has been reflectively conscious of freedom as a value?

The decisive role of the West's discovery of freedom and the individual is beyond question, but the discovery has brought with it . . . tragic consequences. First, the very works of the West now pass judgment on it. For, having proclaimed freedom and the individual, the West played false in dealing with other peoples. It subjected, conquered, and exploited them, even while it went on talking about freedom. It made the other peoples conscious of their enslavement by intensifying that enslavement and calling it freedom. It destroyed the social structures of tribes and clans, turned men into isolated atoms, and shaped them into a worldwide proletariat, and all the time kept on talking of the great dignity of the individual: his autonomy, his power to decide for himself, his capacity for choice, his complex and many-sided reality. . . .

. . . Reason makes it possible for the individual to master impulse, to choose the ways in which he will exercise his freedom, to calculate the chances for success and the manner in which a particular action will impinge upon the group, to understand human relations, and to communicate. Communication is the highest expression of freedom, but it has little meaning unless there is a content which, in the last analysis, is supplied by reason. . . . Here precisely we have the magnificent discovery made by the West: that the individual's whole life can be, and even is, the subtle, infinitely delicate interplay of reason and freedom.

This interplay achieved its highest form in both the Renaissance and classical literature since the Enlightenment. No other culture made this discovery. We of the West have the most rounded and self-conscious type of man. For, the development of reason necessarily implied reason's critique of its own being and action as well as a critique of both liberty and reason, through a return of reason upon itself and a continuous reflection which gave rise to new possibilities for the use of freedom as controlled by new developments of reason. . . .

Let me return to my main argument. It was the West that established the splendid interplay of freedom, reason, self-control, and coherent behavior. It thus produced a type of human being that is unique in history: true western man. (I repeat: the type belongs neither to nature nor to the animal world; it is a deliberate construct achieved through effort.) I am bound to say that I regard this type as superior to anything I have seen or known elsewhere. A value judgment, a personal and subjective preference? Of course. But I am not ready on that account to turn my back on the construction and on the victory and affirmation it represents. Why? Because the issue is freedom itself, and because I see no other satisfactory model that can replace what the West has produced.

Joseph Cardinal Ratzinger (Pope Benedict XVI) "EUROPE'S CRISIS OF CULTURE"

In April 2005 one of the most momentous pontificates in the history of the Catholic Church came to an end with the death of John Paul II (1920–2005). His successor was Cardinal Joseph Ratzinger, who took as his papal name Benedict XVI. In 1981 John Paul had named Cardinal Ratzinger prefect of the Congregation for the Doctrine of the Faith, formerly known as the Holy Office. In that post, which he occupied for two dozen years, the German-born, scholarly Ratzinger vigorously reaffirmed traditional Catholic theology and enunciated the Church's official position on topical issues such as birth control and homosexuality. Ratzinger seemed the perfect complement to the doctrinally conservative Polish pontiff. Indeed liberal Catholics feared that he would wield papal power with an oppressively orthodox hand. If, however, the first few years of Benedict's pontificate have included some doctrinaire statements and controversial diplomatic gestures, they have also witnessed displays of theological flexibility and personal warmth, winning him supporters around the globe.

On the day before John Paul's death, Cardinal Ratzinger delivered a lecture at the convent of Saint Scholastica in Subiaco, Italy. The address, entitled "Europe's Crisis of Culture," was occasioned by the drafting of a constitution for the European Union that pointedly neglected to make any mention of Christianity. Ratzinger eloquently called on Europeans to acknowledge the religious foundations of their civilization.

We are living in a period of great dangers and of great opportunities both for man and for the world, a period that also imposes a great responsibility on us all. During the past century, the possibilities available to man for dominion over matter have grown in a manner we may truly call unimaginable. But the fact that he has power over the world has also meant that man's destructive power has reached dimensions that can sometimes make us shudder. Here, one thinks spontaneously of the threat of terrorism, this new war without national borders and without lines of battle. . . . Less visible, but not for that reason less disturbing, are the possibilities of self-manipulation that man has acquired. He has investigated the farthest recesses of his being, he has deciphered the components of the human being, and now he is able, so to speak, to "construct" man on his own. . . . To this we must add the great problems of our planet: the inequality in the distribution of the goods of the earth, increasing poverty, the depletion and exploitation of the earth and of its resources, famine, the illnesses that threaten all the world, the clash of cultures. All this demonstrates that the growth of our possibilities is not matched by an equal development of our moral energy. Moral strength has not grown in tandem with the development of science; on the contrary, it has diminished, because the technological mentality confines morality to the subjective sphere. Our need, however, is for a public morality, a morality capable of responding to the threats that impose such a burden on the existence of us all. . . .

It is indeed true that a new moralism exists today. Its key words are justice, peace, and the conservation of creation, and these are words that recall essential moral values, of which we genuinely stand in need. But this moralism remains vague and almost inevitably remains confined to the sphere of party politics, where it is primarily a claim addressed to others, rather than a personal duty in our own daily life. . . . The political moralism we have experienced, and still witness today, is far from opening the path to a real regeneration: instead, it blocks the way. Consequently, the same is true of a Christianity and a theology that reduce the core of the message of Jesus, that is, the "kingdom of God," to the "values of the kingdom," identifying these values with the great slogans of political moralism while at the same time proclaiming that these slogans are the synthesis of the religions. In this way, they forget God, although it is precisely he who is both the subject and the cause of the kingdom. All that remains in the place of God are the big words (and values) that are open to any kind of abuse.

This brief look at the situation of the world leads us to reflect on the situation of Christianity today and, hence, on the foundations on which Europe rests. We can say that while Europe once was the Christian continent, it was also the birthplace of that new scientific rationality which has given us both enormous possibilities and enormous menaces. . . .

In the wake of this form of rationality, Europe has developed a culture that, in a manner hitherto unknown to mankind, excludes God from public awareness. His existence may be denied altogether or considered unprovable and uncertain and, hence, as something belonging to the sphere of subjective choices. In either case, God is irrelevant to public life. This is a purely functional rationality that has shaken the moral consciousness in a way completely unknown to the cultures that existed previously, since it maintains that only that which can be demonstrated experimentally is "rational." . . . If, then, it is true to say that Christianity has found its most efficacious form in Europe, it is also true to say that a culture has developed in Europe that is the most radical contradiction not only of Christianity, but of all the religious and moral traditions of humanity. . . .

Let us look more closely at this antagonism between the two cultures that have both left their mark on Europe. In the debate about the preamble to the European Constitution, this antagonism has come to light in two controversies: the question of the reference to God in the Constitution and the question of mentioning the Christian roots of Europe. We are told that we need not be alarmed, since article 52 of the Constitution guarantees the institutional rights of the churches. But this in fact means that in the life of Europe, the churches are assigned their place on the level of day-to-day political compromises; but the message they proclaim is not allowed to make any impact on the level of the foundations on which Europe rests. Only superficial reasons are given in the public debate for this clear refusal, and it is clear that such justifications conceal the true motivation instead of disclosing it. The claim that a mention of the Christian roots of Europe would wound the feelings of the many non-Christians who live in this continent is not particularly convincing, since this basically involves a historical fact that no one can seriously deny. . . . The same applies to the reference to God: it is not the mention of God that offends those who belong to other religions; rather, it is the attempt to construct the human community in a manner that absolutely excludes God.

The motivations of this double refusal are deeper than one might suspect from the reasons we actually hear. They presuppose the idea that only the radical culture born of the Enlightenment, which has attained its full development in our own age, can be constitutive of European identity. Alongside this culture, various religious cultures with their respective rights can coexist, on condition (and to the degree) that they respect the criteria of the Enlightenment culture and subordinate themselves to it. This Enlightenment culture is substantially defined by the rights to liberty. Its starting point is that liberty is a fundamental value and the criterion of everything else. . . . The concept of discrimination is constantly enlarged, and this means that the prohibition of discrimination can be transformed more and more into a limitation on the freedom of opinion and on religious liberty. Very soon, it will no longer be possible to affirm that homosexuality (as the Catholic Church teaches) constitutes an objective disordering in the structure of human existence, and the fact that the Church is convinced that she does not have the right to confer priestly ordination on women is already seen by some as irreconcilable with the spirit of the European Constitution. . . . A confused ideology of liberty leads to a dogmatism that is proving ever more hostile to real liberty. . . . Since [Enlightenment culture] is the culture of a reason that has finally achieved complete self-awareness, it naturally boasts of its claimed universality and imagines that it is complete in itself, without needing any other cultural factors to complement it. . . .

But at this point, we must ask whether this Enlightenment-laicist culture is truly the culture—finally revealed in all its universality—of a reason that is common to all men, a culture that must be accepted everywhere, even if it is rooted in a soil that is historically and culturally diverse. And one must ask whether this culture is truly complete in itself, so that it does not need any roots outside itself.

In the next section of his address, Ratzinger notes that the philosophies of the Enlightenment are distinguished by their positivist (or anti-metaphysical) character, "so that ultimately there is no place for God in them." Based in this way on a self-limitation of reason that typifies the modern West, they cannot be considered valid throughout the world. They also are incomplete, having abandoned their historical (i.e., Christian) roots.

Does this amount to a simple rejection of the Enlightenment and modernity? Certainly not! From the very beginning, Christianity has understood itself to be the religion of the *Logos,* to be a religion in keeping with reason. When it identified its forerunners, these were primarily, not in the other religions, but in that philosophical enlightenment which cleared the road from the various traditions that cluttered it in order to turn to the search for truth and to turn toward the good, toward the one God who is above all gods. As a religion of the persecuted, and as a universal religion that was wider than any one state or people, it denied the government the right to consider religion as part of the order of the state, thus stating the principle of the liberty of faith. It has always defined men—all men without distinction—as creatures of God, made in his image, proclaiming the principle that they are equal in dignity, though of course within the given limits of societal order. In this sense, the Enlightenment has a Christian origin, and it is not by chance that it was born specifically and exclusively within the sphere of the Christian faith, in places where Christianity, contrary to its own nature, had unfortunately become mere tradition and the religion of the state. . . . In its Constitution on the Church in the Modern World, the Second Vatican Council restated this profound harmony between Christianity and the Enlightenment, seeking to achieve a genuine reconciliation between the Church and modernity, which is the great patrimony of which both parties must take care.

This means that both parties must reflect on their own selves and be ready to accept correction. Christianity must always remember that it is the religion of the *Logos.* Christianity is faith in the *Creator Spiritus,* from whom comes everything that is real. Precisely this ought to give Christianity its philosophical power today, since the problem is whether the world comes from an irrational source, so that reason would be nothing but a "by-product" (perhaps even a harmful by-product) of the development of the world, or whether the world comes from reason, so that its criterion and its goal is reason. The Christian faith opts for this second thesis and has good arguments to back it up, even from a purely philosophical point of view, despite the fact that so many people today consider the first thesis the only "rational" and modern view. A reason that has its origin in the irrational and is itself ultimately irrational does not offer a solution to our problems. Only that creative reason which has manifested itself as love in the crucified God can truly show us what life is. . . .

In the age of the Enlightenment, the attempt was made to understand and define the essential norms of morality by saying that these would be valid *etsi Deus non daretur,* even if God did not exist. In the situation of confessional antagonism and in the crisis that threatened the image of God, they tried to keep the essential moral values outside the controversies and to identify an evidential quality in these values that would make them independent of the many divisions and uncertainties of the various philosophies and religious confessions. The intention was to guarantee the bases of life in society and, in more general terms, the bases of humanity. At that time, this seemed possible, since the great fundamental convictions created by Christianity were largely resistant to attack and seemed undeniable. But that is no longer the case. The search for this kind of reassuring certainty, something that could go unchallenged despite all the disagreements, has not succeeded. . . . [T]he attempt, carried to extremes, to shape human affairs to the total exclusion of God leads us more and more to the brink of the abyss, toward the utter annihilation of man. We must therefore reverse the axiom of the Enlightenment and say: Even the one who does not succeed in finding the path to accepting the existence of God ought nevertheless to try to live and to direct his life *veluti si Deus daretur,* as if God did indeed exist. . . . This does not impose limitations on anyone's freedom; it gives support to all our human affairs and supplies a criterion of which human life stands sorely in need.

Our greatest need in the present historical moment is people who make God credible in this world by means of the enlightened faith they live. The negative testimony of Christians who spoke of God but lived in a manner contrary to him has obscured the image of God and has opened the doors to disbelief.

We need men who keep their eyes fixed on God, learning from him what true humanity means.

We need men whose intellect is enlightened by the light of God, men whose hearts are opened by God, so that their intellect can speak to the intellect of others and their hearts can open the hearts of others. It is only by means of men who have been touched by God that God can return to be with mankind.

CREDITS

Chapter 1

p. 5: L. T. Hobhouse, *Liberalism*.

p. 6: From Herbert Spencer, *The Man versus the State* (London: William & Norgate, 1884), pp. 28, 33, 34, 38, 39, 41, 107.

p. 9: From John Stuart Mill, *The Subjection of Women* (London: Longmans, Green, 1869), pp. 1, 8, 24–28, 91–92, 95–97, 185–186.

p. 11: Jane Marcus, ed., *Suffrage and the Pankhursts*.

p. 14: The Goncourt Brothers, "On Female Inferiority," from Robert Baldick (editor and translator), *Pages from the Goncourt Journal*. Copyright © 1984. Reprinted by permission of Oxford University Press.

p. 15: Almroth E. Wright, *The Unexpurgated Case Against Woman Suffrage* (London: Constable, 1913).

p. 18: Excerpts from Houston Stewart Chamberlain, *The Importance of Race*, Vol. I, pp. 269, 271, 276–277, 283–284, 286–287, 542; Vol. II, pp. 228–229.

p. 20: From *Conquest and Kultur*, compiled by Wallace Notestein and Elmer E. Stoll (Washington, D.C.: Committee on Public Administration, 1918), pp. 90–91.

p. 21: From *Cecil Rhodes* by John Flint. Copyright © 1974 by John Flint. Reprinted by permission of Little, Brown and Company (Inc.).

p. 22: From Joseph Chamberlain, *Foreign and Colonial Speeches* (London: G. Routledge and Sons, 1897), pp. 102, 131–133, 202, 244–246.

p. 24: From Karl Pearson, *National Life from the Standpoint of Science* (London: Adam and Charles Black, 1905), pp. 21, 23–27, 36–37, 44, 46–47, 60–61, 64.

p. 27: "The Semitic Versus the Teutonic Race" by Hermann Ahlwardt from *Rehearsal for Destruction: A Study of Political Anti-Semitism in Imperial Germany* by Paul W. Massing. Copyright © 1949 by The American Jewish Committee. Copyright renewed © 1977 by The American Jewish Committee. Reprinted by permission of HarperCollins Publishers, Inc.

p. 29: From Édouard Drumont, *La France Juive. Essai d'Histoire Contemporaine,* Vol. 1, 50th ed., orig. pub. in 1886, trans. Theodore H. Von Laue (Paris: C. Marpon & E. Flammarion, n.d.), from the Introduction and Chapter 1.

p. 31: Theodor Herzl, *The Jewish State: An Attempt at a Modern Solution of the Jewish Question* (New York: American Zionist Emergency Council, 1946). Reprinted by permission of the American Zionist Movement.

p. 33: From *The Will to Power* by Friedrich Nietzsche, edited by R. J. Hollingdale, translated by Walter Kaufmann. Copyright © 1967 by Walter Kaufman. Used by permission of Random House, Inc.

Twilight of the Idols: Or, How to Philosophize with a Hammer; The Anti-Christ, by Friedrich Nietzsche, translated by R. J. Hollingdale (Penguin Classics, 1968). Copyright © R. J. Hollingdale, 1968. Reproduced by permission of Penguin Books, Ltd.

p. 37: From *Civilization and Its Discontents* by Sigmund Freud, translated by James Strachey. Copyright © 1961 by James Strachey, renewed 1989 by Alix Strachey. Used by permission of W. W. Norton & Company, Inc. and by arrangement with Paterson Marsh Ltd., London.

From *The Standard Edition of the Complete Psychological Works of Sigmund Freud* translated and edited by James Strachey, published by The Hogarth Press. Reprinted by permission of The Random House Group Ltd. and by arrangement with Paterson Marsh Ltd., London.

Chapter 2

p. 42: From Heinrich von Treitschke, *Politics,* ed. by Hans Kohn (New York: Harcourt, Brace & World, Inc., 1963).

p. 43: From Friedrich von Bernhardi, *Germany and the Next War,* Allen H. Fowles, trans. (New York: Longmans, Green, and Company, 1914), pp. 18, 21–24.

p. 44: Henri Massis and Alfred de Tarde, "The Young People of Today," from John Boyer and Jan Goldstein, eds., *Twentieth-Century Europe* (Chicago: University of Chicago Press, 1987), pp. 16–17, 22–23, 26–27. Reprinted by permission of The University of Chicago Press.

p. 46: Trans. Marvin Perry from M. Boghitchevitch, *Le Procès de Salonique, Jiun 1917,* ed. Andrè Delpeuch (Paris, 1927), pp. 41–42, 45–48.

p. 47: Reprinted from Great Britain, Foreign Office, *Collected Diplomatic Documents Relating to the Outbreak of the*

European War (London: His Majesty's Stationery Office, 1915), The Austro-Hungarian Red Book, Document No. 6, pp. 450–452.

p. 49: Roland Doregelès, "After Fifth Years," in George A. Panichas, ed., *Promise of Greatness* (New York: John Day, 1968), pp. 13–15.

p. 50: From *The World of Yesterday* by Stefan Zweig, translated by Helmut Ripperger, translation copyright © 1943 by the Viking Press, Inc. Used by permission of Viking Penguin, a division of Penguin Group (USA) Inc.

p. 52: Philipp Scheidemann, "The Hour We Yearned For," from Michell, James Edward, trans., *The Making of New Germany: The Memoirs of Philipp Scheidemann.* Reproduced by permission of Hodder & Stoughton Ltd.

p. 53: Bertrand Russell, "Average Men and Women were Delighted at the Prospect of War," From *The Autobiography of Bertrand Russell*, Vol. 2, by Bertrand Russell, © 1951, 1956, The Bertrand Russell Peace Foundation. Reproduced by permission of Taylor & Francis Books UK.

p. 54: *Riech,* "8 August 1914," as reproduced in Frank Alfred Golder, *Documents of Russian History,* 1914–1917 (New York: The Century Company, 1927), pp. 31–32.

p. 55: From *All Quiet on the Western Front* by Erich Maria Remarque. "Im Westen Nichts Neues," copyright © 1928 by Ullstein A. G.; Copyright renewed 1956 by Erich Maria Remarque. "All Quiet on the Western Front," copyright © 1929, 1930 by Little, Brown and Company; Copyright renewed © 1957, 1958 by Erich Maria Remarque. Reproduced by permission of the Estate of the Late Paulette Goddard Remarque.

p. 57: Siegfried Sassoon, "Base Details," from *Collected Poems*, 1986. Copyright © Siegfried Sassoon by kind permission of George Sassoon.

"Base Details," from *Collected Poems of Siegfried Sassoon* by Siegfried Sassoon, copyright © 1918, 1920 by E. P. Dutton. Copyright © 1936, 1946, 1947, 1948 by Siegfried Sassoon. Used by permission of Viking Penguin, a division of Penguin Group (USA) Inc.

p. 58: From *Poems* by Wilfred Owen (London: Chatto and Windus, Ltd., 1920, 1963), p. 32.

p. 59: Naomi Loughnan, "Munition Work," in *Women War Workers,* ed. Gilbert Stone (London: George Harrap & Company, 1917), pp. 25, 28–33, 35–38, 40–41.

p. 61: Marilyn Shervin-Coetzee and Frans Coetzee, eds., *World War I and European Society—A Sourcebook.* Copyright © 1995 by D. C. Heath and Company. Used with permission of Cengage Learning.

p. 62: *Current History: A Monthly Magazine of the New York Times* 4 (May 1916), pp. 365–367.

p. 66: *Century of Genocide: Critical Essays and Eyewitness Accounts* by Totten. Copyright © 2006 by Taylor & Francis Group LLC—Books. Reproduced with permission of Taylor & Francis Group LLC—Books in the format Textbook via Copyright Clearance Center.

p. 70: From *The Public Papers of Woodrow Wilson: War and Peace, Part III* (New York: Harper, 1927), I, pp. 50–51, 159–161, 182–183, 199, 326, 363–364, 398–399.

p. 72: From Georges Clemenceau, *The Grandeur and Misery of Victory.* Copyright © 1930 Random House, Inc.

p. 75: From *A History of the Peace Conference of Paris*, ed. H. W. V. Temperley, Vol. II (London: Oxford University Press, 1920), pp. 256–259, 266–268.

p. 77: Excerpts from *Variety* by Paul Valéry, translated by Malcolm Cowley, copyright © 1927 by Harcourt Brace & Company and renewed 1954 by Malcolm Cowley. Reprinted by permission of the publisher.

p. 78: From *All Quiet on the Western Front* by Erich Maria Remarque. "Im Westen Nichts Neues," copyright © 1928 by Ullstein A. G.; Copyright renewed 1956 by Erich Maria Remarque. "All Quiet on the Western Front," copyright © 1929, 1930 by Little, Brown and Company; Copyright renewed © 1957, 1958 by Erich Maria Remarque. Reproduced by permission of the Estate of the Late Paulette Goddard Remarque.

p. 79: "Brutalization of the Individual," from Ernst von Salomon, *Die Geachteten* (Berlin: Ernst Rowohlt Verlag, 1931), pp. 28–30, 34–35. Translated by Theodor H. Von Laue. Copyright © 1931 Ernst Rowohlt Verlag. Reprinted by permission of Sanford J. Greenberger Associates, Inc.

p. 81: From *Sigmund Freud: Collected Works,* Volume 4, by Sigmund Freud. Authorized translation under the supervision of Joan Riviere. Published by Basic Books, Inc., by arrangement with The Hogarth Press Ltd. and The Institute of Psycho-Analysis, London.

Chapter 3

p. 86: Sergei Witte, "A Report for Tsar Nicholas II," from *Journal of Modern History,* XXVI (March 1954), pp. 66, 68–69, 73. Reprinted by permission of the publisher, The University of Chicago Press.

p. 88: From M. I. Pokzovskaya, "The Woman Factory Worker in Russia—II," trans. Sonia Lethes, *Jus Suffragii,* 8, February 1, 1914, pp. 68–69.

p. 89: Semyonova Tian-Shanskaia, Olga, *Village Life in Late Tsarist Russia,* ed. by David L. Ransel, translated by David L. Ransel with Michael Levine. Copyright © 1993. Reprinted by permission of the publisher, Indiana University Press.

p. 92: *Imperial Russia, A Source Book, 1700–1917,* Fourth Edition. Basil Dmytryshyn, ed. (Academic International Press, Gulf Breeze, Fla.)

p. 94: *Polnoe Sobranie Zakonov Ruukoi Imperii . . . (Complete Collection of the Laws of the Russian Empire),* 3rd series, vol. 25, part 1 (St. Petersburg, 1906), no. 26,803, pp. 754–755.

p. 96: Army Intelligence Report for 2–13 October 1917 [original held in the Hoover Institution, Stanford University, under the title Belevsky Papers, No. 7]. Reprinted in *The Bolshevik Revolution 1917–1918—Documents and Materials,* James Bunyn and H. H. Fisher, eds. (Stanford: Stanford University Press, 1934), pp. 24–26.

p. 97: A. L. Popov, *Oktiabrskii perevorot: fakty i dokumenty [The October Upheaval: Facts and Documents]* (Petrograd, 1918), pp. 81–83. Reprinted in *The Bolshevik Revolution 1917–1918—Documents and Materials,* James Bunyan and H. H. Fisher, eds. (Stanford: Stanford University Press, 1934), pp. 31–33.

p. 99: V. I. Lenin, *Collected Works,* Vol. 5, pp. 369–370, 373, 375, 400, 464–466. Copyright © 1964 by Progress Publishers, Moscow, Russia. Reprinted by permission.

p. 101: Reprinted by permission from N. N. Sukhanov, *The Russian Revolution, 1917,* ed. and trans. by Joel Carmichael (1955), pp. 584–585.

p. 103: V. I. Lenin, *Collected Works,* Vol. 26, pp. 234–235. Copyright © 1964 by Progress Publishers, Moscow, Russia. Reprinted by permission.

p. 104: Alexis Babine, "Excerpts," in a *Russian Civil War Diary*, Donald Raleigh, Ed., pp. 93–95, 99–100, 105, 110–114, 117–120. Copyright © 1988, Duke University Press. All rights reserved. Used by permission of the publisher.

p. 109: Excerpts from Peter N. Wrangel, *Always With Honour*, with a foreword by Herbert Hoover (New York: Robert Speller & Sons, 1957), pp. 331–333, 337, 348 are reprinted with permission of Robert Speller & Sons, Publishers, Inc.

p. 112: From Alexander Berkman, "The Kronstadt Rebellion," from *Russian Revolution Series,* No. 3 (Berlin: printed for Der Syndikalist, 1922), pp. 26–28.

p. 114: Joseph Stalin, "The Hard Line," from Joseph Stalin, *Leninism: Selected Writings,* pp. 199–200. Reprinted by permission of International Publishers Co.

p. 115: Joseph Stalin, "Liquidation of the Kulaks," from Joseph Stalin, *Leninism: Selected Writings,* pp. 160–163. Reprinted by permission of International Publishers Co.

p. 117: From *The Education of a True Believer* by Lev Kopelev and Translated by Gary Kern. English translation copyright © 1980 by Harper & Row, Publishers, Inc. Reprinted by permission of HarperCollins Publishers.

p. 119: From *Execution by Hunger: The Hidden Holocaust* by Miron Dolot. Copyright © 1985 by Miron Dolot. Reprinted by permission of W. W. Norton & Company, Inc.

p. 123: Reprinted with the permission of Simon & Schuster from *Stalin*, edited by T. H. Rigby.

p. 124: Excerpt from "Part Two, Chapter II," from *A Precocious Autobiography* by Yevgeny Yevtushenko, translated by Andrew R. MacAndrew, copyright © 1963 by E. P. Dutton, renewed © 1991 by Penguin USA. Copyright © 1963, renewed © 1991 by Yevgeny Yevtushenko. Used by permission of Dutton, a division of Penguin Group (USA) Inc.

p. 126: From *The Anti-Stalin Campaign and International Communism,* by Nikita Krushchev. Copyright © 1956 Columbia University Press. Reprinted with permission of the publisher.

p. 128: From Lev Razgon, *True Stories,* trans. from the Russian by John Crowfoot (Ann Arbor, MI: Ardis, 1997), pp. 25–27, 29–30, 158–59, 161–62, 170–72, 191–93. Reprinted by permission.

p. 133: Arthur Koeslter, *Darkness at Noon*, translated by Daphne Hardy (New York: Bantam Books, 1970), pp. 125–132. Reprinted by permission of SLL/Sterling Lord Literistic, Inc. Copyright © 1941 by Arthur Koestler.

Chapter 4

p. 138: Reprinted with permission of the Carnegie Endowment for International Peace.

p. 141: Klara Zetkin, Rosa Luxemburg, Karl Liebknect, and Franz Mehring, *Spartacist Manifesto,* as it appeared in the *New York Times,* January 24, 1919, p. 3.

p. 143: *Current History* XII: 1 (April 1920), pp. 1–2, 4–6.

p. 144: Excerpts from *Der Fuehrer* by Konrad Heiden. Copyright © 1944 by Konrad Heiden, © renewed 1971 by Bernhard E. Bartels, Executor of the Estate of Konrad Heiden. Reprinted by permission of Houghton Mifflin Harcourt Publishing Company. All rights reserved.

p. 145: Trans. and adapted by Theodore H. Von Laue from Friedrich Georg Jünger, *The Rise of the New Nationalism* (Leipzig, 1925), pp. 5–65 passim.

p. 148: From Max Cohen, *I Was One of the Unemployed* (London: Victor Gollancz), pp. 158–160, 162–165.

p. 151: From Heinrich Hauser, "With Germany's Unemployed," *Living Age,* Vol. 344, No. 4398 (March 1933), pp. 27–31, 34–38; trans. from *Die Tat.*

p. 154: Excerpts from *Mein Kampf* by Adolf Hitler, translated by T. H. Von Laue.

p. 159: Kurt G. W. Ludecke, *I Knew Hitler—The Story of a Nazi Who Escaped the Blood Purge.* Copyright © 1937 Kurt G. W. Ludecke. Copyright renewed © 1965.

p. 160: Thomas Mann, "An Appeal to Reason," from *Order of the Day* by Thomas Mann, translated by H. T. Lowe-Porter. Copyright © 1942 by Alfred A. Knopf, Inc. Reprinted by permission of the publisher.

p. 161: Ernst Rudolf Huber, *Verfassungsrecht des grossdeutschen Reiches* (Hamburg: Hanseatische Verlagsanstalt, 1939), pp. 143–45, 194, 207–08, 230; reprinted in Raymond E. Murphy et al., *National Socialism: Basic Principles, Their Application by the Nazi Party's Foreign Organization, and the Use of Germans Abroad for Nazi Aims* (Washington, D.C.: Government Printing Office, 1943), pp. 34, 36–38.

p. 162: From *Nazi Culture,* ed. George L. Mosse (New York: Grosset & Dunlap, 1966), pp. 206–207. Reprinted by permission.

p. 164: From *Hereditary and Racial Biology for Students* by Jakob Graf.

p. 165: From *The Goebbels Diaries: 1942–1943* by Goebbels. Copyright © 1948 by The Fireside Press, Inc. Used by permission of Doubleday, a division of Random House, Inc.

p. 165: *From What I Saw: Reports from Berlin 1920–1933,* by Joseph Roth, translated by Michael Hofman. Copyright © 1996 by Verlag Kiepenheuer & Witsch Koln and Verlag de Lange Amsterdam. English translation copyright © 2003 by Michael Hofman. Used by permission of W. W. Norton & Company, Inc.

p. 168: Excerpt from Hertha Nathorff, Wolfgang Benz, ed., *Das Tagebuch der Hertha Nathorff.* Berlin, New York, Aufzeichnungen 1933 bis 1945. Copyright © 1987. Reprinted by permission of Oldenbourg Wissenschaftsverlag GmbH.

p. 170: Marta Appel, "Memoirs of a German Jewish Woman," from Marta Appel, *Memoirs.* Undated manuscript, excerpted in *Jewish Life in Germany—Memoirs from Three Centuries,* ed. by Monkia Richarz (Bloomington: Indiana University Press, 1991), pp. 351–356.

p. 173: From United States Chief Counsel for the Prosecution of Axis Criminality, *Nazi Conspiracy and Aggression* (U.S. Printing Office, 1946), Vol. 7, pp. 1037–1041.

p. 175: Fred Thomas, *To Tilt at Windmills.* Copyright © 1996. Reprinted by permission of the publisher, Michigan State University Press.

p. 177: Excerpts from *Dialogue with Death* by Arthur Koestler, translated by Trevor and Phyllis Blewitt (New York, The Macmillan Company, 1966), pp. 162–166, 169–170. Reprinted by permission of SLL/Sterling Lord Literistic, Inc. Copyright © 1966 by Arthur Koestler.

p. 180: Richard N. Coudenhove-Kalergi, *Pan-Europe* (New York: Alfred A. Knopf, 1926).

p. 183: Reprinted from Johan Huizinga, *In the Shadow of Tomorrow.*

p. 185: "I Was Ripe to Be Converted," by Arthur Koestler from *The God That Failed,* edited by Richard Crossman. Copyright © 1949 by Richard Crossman, renewed © 1977 by Anne Crossman. Richard Wright material, copyright © 1944 by Richard Wright. Reprinted by permission of HarperCollins Publishers, Inc.

p. 188: Nicolas Berdyaev, *The Fate of Man in the Modern World.* Copyright © 1961. Reprinted by permission of The University of Michigan Press.

Chapter 5

p. 193: *Documents on British Foreign Policy 1919–1939,* 2nd series, Vol. V (1933), E. L. Woodward and Rohan Butler, eds. (London: Her Majesty's Stationery Office, 1956), pp. 47–51, 53–55.

p. 194: *Peace and War—United States Foreign Policy 1931–1941* (Washington, D.C.: Government Printing Office, 1942), pp. 13–14, 21–22.

p. 196: *Peace and War—United States Foreign Policy 1931–1941* (Washington, D.C.: Government Printing Office, 1942), pp. 15–16.

p. 197: As appeared in the *Times* (London), 3 October 1935, p. 12. Thomas G. Masaryk, *The New Europe (The*

Slave Standpoint), edited by W. Preston Warren and William B. Weist (Lewisburg, PA: Bucknell University Press, 1972), pp. 55–59, 63–67, 69, 163, 189–90. Reprinted by permission.

p. 198: As appeared in the *Times* (London), 1 July 1936, p. 16.

p. 200: Reprinted from William L. Shirer, *Berlin Diary*. Copyright © 1995. Reprinted with permission.

p. 203: From *The World Of Yesterday* by Stefan Zweig, translated by Helmut Ripperger, translation copyright © 1943 by the Viking Press, Inc. Used by permission of Viking Penguin, a division of Penguin Group (USA) Inc.

p. 205: From Neville Chamberlain, *In Search of Peace,* pp. 173–175, 214–215, 217. Reprinted by permission of Century Hutchinson Ltd.

p. 207: From *Parliamentary Debates, House of Commons* (His Majesty's Stationery Office, 1938), Vol. 339, 12th vol. of session 1937–1938, pp. 361–369, 373.

p. 209: *Documents on British Foreign Policy, 1919–1939,* 2nd series, Vol. VII (1939), pp. 258–260.

p. 212: From *Panzer Leader* by Heinz Guderian, translated by Constantine Fitzgibbon, copyright © 1952 by Heinz Guderian. Used by permission of Dutton, a division of Penguin Group (USA) Inc.

p. 214: Hans Habe, *A Thousand Shall Fall* (New York: Harcourt Brace and Company, 1941).

p. 217: Winston Churchill, "Blood, Toil, Tears and Sweat," from T*he War Speeches of the Rt. Ho. Winston S. Churchill*, ed. Charles Eade. Reproduced with permission of Curtis Brown Ltd. on behalf of the Estate of Sir Winston S. Churchill. Copyright the Estate of Sir Winston S. Churchill.

p. 219: From *Hitler's Army: Soldiers, Nazis, and War in the Third Reich* by Omer Bartov. Copyright © 1992 by Oxford University Press, Inc. Used by permission of Oxford University Press, Inc.

p. 222: William Hoffman, "Diary of a German Soldier," pp. 248–254, from *The Battle for Stalingrad* by Vasili Chuikov, translated by Harold Silver. Copyright © 1964 by Henry Holt and Company, LLC. Reprinted by permission of Henry Holt and Company, LLC.

p. 226: Anton Kuzmich Dragan, "A Soviet Veteran Recalls," from *The Battle for Stalingrad* by Vasili Chuikov, translated by Harold Silver. Copyright © 1964 by Henry Holt and Company, LLC. Reprinted by permission of Henry Holt and Company, LLC.

p. 228: From *Nazi Conspiracy and Aggression* (Washington, D.C.: United States Government Printing Office, 1946), V, 696–699, Document PS 2992.

p. 230: From *Nazi Conspiracy and Aggression* (Washington, D.C.: United States Government Printing Office, 1946), Vol. VI, pp. 788–789.

p. 231: Y. Pfeffer, "Concentration Camp Life and Death," from Yehuda Bauer, *History of the Holocaust*, pp. 211–213. Copyright © 1982 by Yehuda Bauer. All rights reserved. Reprinted by permission of Franklin Watts, an imprint of Scholastic Library Publishing, Inc., 90 Sherman Turnpike, Danbury, CT 06816.

p. 234: Albert Camus, "I Am Fighting You Because Your Logic is as Criminal As Your Heart," from *Resistence, Rebellion, and Death* by Albert Camus, translated by Justin O'Brien, translation copyright © 1960, copyright renewed 1988 by Alfred A. Knopf, a division of Random House, Inc. Used by permission of Alfred A. Knopf, a division of Random House, Inc.

p. 236: Inge Scholl, excerpts from pp. 78–88, 91 from *The White Rose: Munich 1942–43,* copyright © 1983 by Inge Aicher-Scholl, Wesleyan University Press by permission of University Press of New England.

p. 239: Reprinted with permission from Marek Edelman, *The Ghetto Fights* (London: Bookmarks, 1990; copyright Mark Edelman), pp. 75–77, 79–85.

p. 243: Tadeusz Bor-Komorowski, *The Secret Army.* Copyright © 1984. Reprinted by permission of The Battery Press.

p. 247: From *Omaha Beachhead*, U.S. Government Printing Office.

p. 249: Reprinted from *The Day of the Americans* by Nerin E. Gun. Copyright © 1966.

p. 252: Reprinted with permission from Alexander McKee, *Dresden 1945: The Devil's Tinderbox.* Copyright © 1982.

p. 256: *Final Entries 1945: The Diaries of Joseph Goebbels*, by Joseph Goebbels, edited by Hugh Trevor-Roper, translated by Richard Barry, copyright © 1978 by Martin Secker & Warberg Ltd and G. P. Putnam's Sons. Orig. German copyright © 1977 by Hoffman und Campe Verlag. Used by permission of G. P. Putnam's Sons, a division of Penguin Group (USA) Inc.

Extract by H. R. Trevor-Roper from *The Diaries of Joseph Goebbels* (© 1978 H. R. Trevor-Roper) is reproduced by permission of PFD (www.pfd.co.uk) on behalf of The Literary Estate of Sir H. R. Trevor-Roper.

p. 258: Reprinted with permission from Louis Hagen, *Follow My Leader*. Copyright © 1951.

p. 261: Alfred-Maurice de Zayas, *A Terrible Revenge.* Copyright © Alfred-Maurice de Zayas. Reprinted with permission of St. Martin's Press, Incorporated.

p. 264: *Nazi Conspiracy and Aggression,* Vol. VI (Washington: United States Government Printing Office, 1946), pp. 260–263.

Chapter 6

p. 269: Excerpts from *European Witness*, by Stephen Spender, pp. 14–17. Originally published in 1946 by Hamish Hamilton.

p. 270: Theodore H. White, "Germany: Spring in the Ruins," from *Fire in the Ashes* (Toronto: George J. McLeod Ltd., 1953), pp. 134–136.

p. 272: Reprinted from *The New Republic* (April 1, 1946), Vol. 114, No. 13, pp. 436–438.

p. 275: Bruno Foa, "Europe in Ruins," from *Foreign Policy Reports,* Volume XXI, No. 7, June 15, 1945.

p. 277: From George C. Marshall, *Foreign Relations of the United States, 1947: The British Commonwealth and Europe,* vol. 3 (Washington, D.C.: United States Government Printing Office, 1972), pp. 237– 239.

p. 280: Reprinted from Ernst Cassirer, *The Myth of the State.* Copyright © 1946 Yale University Press. Reprinted by permission of the publisher.

p. 283: Reprinted by permission of University Press of America *from Main Currents in Modern Political Thought.* Copyright © 1984.

p. 285: Excerpts from *Existentialism* by Jean-Paul Sartre, translated by Bernard Frechtman. Copyright © 1947 Philosophical Library, New York.

p. 289: From the book *Memoirs* by Konrad Adenauer. Copyright © 1966 by Henry Regnery Co. All rights reserved.

p. 291: Reprinted by permission of the publisher from *The German Catastrophe: Reflections and Recollections* by Friedrich Meinecke, translated by Sidney B. Fay, Cambridge, Mass.: Harvard University Press, Copyright © 1950 by the President and Fellows of Harvard College.

p. 294: From *The Burden of Guilt* by Hannah Vogt, translated by Herbert Strauss. Translation copyright © 1964 by Oxford University Press, Inc. Used by permission of Oxford University Press, Inc. Table, "Relative Power of the Offices of Governor," adapted from Thad L. Beyle, in Harold A. Hovey and Kendra A. Hovey, *State Fact Finder 1997: Rankings Across America* (Washington, DC: Congressional Quarterly, Inc., 1197), Table D–11.

p. 296: Theodore H. White, "Germany: Spring in the Ruins," as appeared in Theodore H. White, *Fire in the Ashes*. Reprinted with permission.

p. 300: *The Iron Curtain Speech.* Reproduced with permission of Curtis Brown, Ltd., London, on behalf of the Estate of Sir Winston S. Churchill. Copyright Winston S. Churchill.

p. 301: Translation copyright © 1957 by *The Current Digest of the Soviet Press,* published weekly at Columbus, Ohio. Reprinted by permission of the Digest. p. 318: Reprinted by permission of *Foreign Affairs,* Vol. 26, No. 2. Copyright © 1947 by the Council on Foreign Relations, Inc.

p. 303: From Paul-Henri Spaak, *Why Nato?* (Harmondsworth-Baltimore: Penguin Books, 1959), pp. 16–21.

p. 305: German Propaganda Archive, http://www.calvin.edu/academic/cas/gpa/wall.htm.

Chapter 7

p. 312: Excerpt from G. E. R. Gedye, "Prague: I Saw It Happen Twice—An Eyewitness Account of the Communist Coup," *Commentary*, Vol. 4 (April 1948), pp. 292, 293–296. Reprinted from *Commentary,* April 1948, by permission; all rights reserved.

p. 316: From the book *Child of the Revolution,* by Wolfgang Leonhard. Copyright © 1958 Regnery Publishing. All rights reserved.

p. 319: Reprinted with the permission of Simon & Schuster, Inc., from *International Relations Among Communists,* edited by Robert H. McNeal. Copyright © 1967 by Prentice-Hall, Inc., renewed 1995 by Jacqueline F. McNeal.

p. 321: From *Let History Be the Judge: The Origins and Consequences of Stalinism,* edited and translated by George Shriver. Copyright © 1989 Columbia University Press. Reprinted with the permission of the publisher.

p. 325: Reprinted from Heda Marglius Kovaly, *Under a Cruel Star: A Life in Prague, 1941–1968*. Copyright © 1986. Reprinted with permission.

p. 330: Reprinted with the permission of Scribner, a Division of Simon & Schuster, Inc., from *Memoirs* by Joseph Cardinal Mindszenty. Copyright © 1974 by Macmillan Publishing Company, Inc. All rights reserved.

Reprinted with the permission of George Weidenfeld and Nicolson, Ltd., an imprint of The Orion Publishing Group, London from *Memoirs* by Jozsef Cardinal

Mindszenty, translated by Richard and Clara Winston. Copyright ©1974 by Macmillan Publishing Company.

p. 333: Czesław Miłosz, *The Captive Mind*, trans. from the Polish by Jane Zielonko (New Yark: Vintage, 1981), pp. 191, 192, 193, 194, 195, 196, 197, 200–201, 205, 206, 212–213, 214, 215, 216–217, 218–220, 221.

p. 338: Excerpts from *The New Class* by Milovan Djilas, copyright © 1957 by Harcourt, Inc., and renewed 1985 by Milovan Djilas, reprinted by permission of Houghton Mifflin Harcourt Publishing Company. This material may not be reproduced in any form or by any means without the prior written permission of the publisher.

p. 341: From the book, *No More Comrades*, by Andor Heller. Copyright © 1957 Regnery Publishing. All rights reserved.

p. 344: Excerpts from *Czechoslovakia 1968* by Philip Windsor and Adam Roberts, published by Chatto & Windus. Reprinted by permission of The Random House Group Ltd.

p. 347: Pages 219–220 from *The Promise of Solidarity: Inside the Polish Worker's Struggle, 1980–1982*, Jean-Yves Potel. Copyright © 1982 Praeger Publishers. Reproduced with permission of ABC-CLIO, LLC.

Chapter 8

p. 352: From *The Second Sex* by Simone de Beauvoir, translated by. H. M. Parshley. Copyright © 1952 and renewed © 1980 by Alfred A. Knopf, a division of Random House, Inc. Used by permission.

p. 356: *The French Student Revolt: The Leaders Speak* by Daniel Cohn-Bendit. Edited by Herve Bourges. Originally appeared in French as *La Révolte étudiante*, copyright © 1968 by Editions de Seuil. Used by permission of Georges Borchardt, Inc., on behalf of Editions de Seuil.

p. 360: Excerpts from Joschka Fischer, *Der Umbau der Industriegesellschaft: Pladoyer wider die herrschende Umweltluge* (Frankfurt/M: Eichborn Verlag, 1989), pp. 77–79, 82, 84–85, 88–89 (Translation by Matthew P. Berg). Copyright © Eichborn GmbH & Co Verlag KG, Frankfurt am Main, 1989.

p. 364: Ludwig Erhard: Deutsche Wirtschaftspolitik Econ Verlag Düsseldorf und München.

p. 367: Excerpts as submitted from *The Downing Street Years* by Margaret Thatcher. Copyright © 1993 by Margaret Thatcher. Reprinted by permission of HarperCollins Publishers, Inc.

p. 369: Reprinted by permission of Fourth Estate LTD from New Britain: *My Vision of a Young Country* by Tony Blair. Copyright © 1996 by The Office of Tony Blair.

p. 373: Excerpts from Jean-Marie Le Pen, *Les Francais d'abord* (n.p.: Carrere-Michel Lafon, 1984). Translated by Marvin N. Richards III. Reprinted by permission.

p. 376: Multi-Culturalism and Love of One's Country, reprinted from *The Freedom I Mean*, by Jörg Haider, published in the USA by Swan Books, Pine Plains, New York 12567, pp. 30–38.

p. 381: From *Fuhrer Ex: Memories of a Former Neo-Nazi* by Ingo Hasselbach. Copyright © 1996 by Ingo Hasselbach. Reprinted by permission of Random House, Inc.

p. 387: This speech was originally presented by Enoch Powell in Birmingham, England on April 20, 1968. It can be found in Tom Stacey, *Immigration and Enoch Powell* (London: Tom Stacey Ltd., 1970), pp. 84–88, 91–93.

p. 390: Reprinted by permission of the Center for Migration Studies.

p. 393: Reprinted by permission of Contemporary Review Co., Ltd.

p. 397: Article, "African Immigrants in France: The Controversy over Female Circumcision," from *Women's International Network News*, Spring 1998, vol. 24 #2, p. 46.

p. 399: From *Remembrance, Sorrow, and Reconciliation: Speeches and Declarations in Connection with the 40th Anniversary of the End of the Second World War in Europe*, pp. 59–63. Issued by the Press and Information Office of the Government of the Federal Republic of Germany.

p. 400: Elie Wiesel, "Reflections of a Survivor," pp. 191–202. From *The Kingdom of Memory: Reminiscences* by Elie Wiesel. Copyright © 1990 by Elirion Associates, Inc. Used by permission of Georges Borchardt, Inc., on behalf of Elie Wiesel.

p. 403: "We Remember: A Reflection on the 'Shoah,'" published on March 16, 1998 by the Holy See's Commission for Religious Relations with the Jews. Reprinted with permission.

Chapter 9

p. 411: Excerpts from pp. 17–24, 28–29, 31–32, 75–79 from *Perestroika* by Mikhail Gorbachev. Copyright © 1987 by Mikhail Gorbachev. Reprinted by permission of HarperCollins Publishers.

p. 415: From *Open Letters: Selected Writings 1965–1990* by Václav Havel, translated by Paul Wilson, translation copyright © 1985, 1988, 1991 by Paul Wilson. Reprinted by permission of Alfred A. Knopf, a division of Random House, Inc.

p. 419: Konrad H. Jarausch and Volker Gransow, eds., *Uniting Germany: Documents and Debates, 1944–1993* (Providence, RI/Oxford: Berghahn Books, 1994). Reprinted with permission.

p. 421: Alfred Erich Senn, *Lithuania Awakening*. Copyright © 1999 The Regents of the University of California. Reprinted with permission. (pp. 116–119, 122–124, 127–129.) Reprinted by permission of the author.

p. 424: From *The Magic Lantern* by Timothy Garton Ash. Copyright © 1990 by Timothy Garton Ash. Used by permission of Random House, Inc.

p. 429: Thomas Omestad, "Ten-Day Wonder," *The New Republic,* 201:25 (25 December 1989). Reprinted by permission of The New Republic.

p. 433: Copyright © 1991 Martin Sixsmith, *Moscow Coup—The Death of the Soviet System.* Reprinted by permission of A M Heath & Co. Ltd. on behalf of Martin Sixsmith.

p. 438: United Nations—Security Council, S/1994/674/Add.2 (Vol. I), 28 December 1994; *Final Report of the United Nations Commission of Experts Established Pursuant to Security Council Resolution 780* (1992) "The Prijedor Report," Annex V, http://www.ess.uwe.ac.uk/comexpert/ ANX/V.htm.

International Criminal Tribunal for the Former Yugoslavia, Monday, 21 July 2003, http://www.un.org/icty/transe60/03072IIT.htm.

p. 446: Excerpts from Pomer and Klein, Editors, *The New Russia: Transition Gone Awry*. Copyright © 2001 by the Board of Trustees of the Leland Stanford Jr. University. All rights reserved. Used with the permission of Stanford University Press, www.sup.org.

p. 448: From Lawrence R. Klein and Marshall Pomer, eds., *The New Russia: Transition Gone Awry.* Copyright © 2001 by the Board of Trustees of the Leland Stanford, Jr., University. With the permission of Stanford University Press, www.sup.org.

p. 450: Reprinted from Anna Politkovskaya, A Dirty War: A Russian Reporter in Chechnya, trans. and ed. by John Crowfoot. Copyright © 2001. Reprinted with permission.

Chapter 10

p. 459: From http://www.eu2004.ie/templates/news.asp?sNavlocator+66&list_id+588, speech given April 22, 2004.

p. 462: From *Uberpower: The Imperial Temptation of America* by Josef Joffe. Copyright © 2006 by Josef Joffe. Used by permission of W. W. Norton & Company, Inc.

p. 465: Michael Cox, "Europe's Enduring Anti-Americanism." Reprinted with permission from *Current History* magazine Vol. 107, Nr. 709 (May, 2008). © 2009 Current History, Inc.

p. 468: "Power: The Vladimir Putin Story," by C. J. Chivers, March 9, 2009, *Esquire*. Copyright © 2009 by C. J. Chivers. Reprinted by permission of The Stuart Krichevsky Literary Agency, Inc.

p. 476: From *The Last Days of Europe* by Walter Laqueur. Copyright © 2007 by the author and reprinted by permission of Thomas Dunne Books, an imprint of St. Martin's Press, LLC.

p. 479: *EU Terrorism Situation and Trend Report 2007* (The Hague: Europol, 2007), pp. 18–26.

p. 485: Reprinted from Gabriel Schoenfeld, *The Return of Anti-Semitism*. Copyright © 2004. Reprinted with permission.

p. 488: Excerpts from Marvin Perry and Frederick Schweitzer, *Antisemitism: Myth and Hate from Antiquity to the Present* (2002; pb, 2005). Reproduced with permission of Palgrave Macmillan.

p. 492: Jacques Ellul, *The Betrayal of the West*, trans. Matthew J. O'Connell (New York: Continuum Publishing Company, 1978), pp. 16–21, 23–24, 28–30, 44–45. Reprinted by permission of the publisher.

p. 497: Joseph Cardinal Ratzinger (Pope Benedict XVI), *Christianity and the Crisis of Cultures,* trans. by Brian McNeil (San Francisco: Ignatius Press, 2005), pp. 25–38, 47–52.

CPSIA information can be obtained
at www.ICGtesting.com
Printed in the USA
FFHW010604020119
50042761-54827FF

9 781424 069675